CRAIG ANDERTON'S
REVISED & UPDATED

# Home Recording for Musicians

**Get the most out of today's recording technology, and make professional-quality recordings in your own home. Written with both amateur and professional in mind, this fully illustrated, definitive overview covers mics, mixing, hard disk recording, analog and digital tape, computers for the studio, maintenance, consoles, sequencing, mastering, signal processors, and much more.**

**Foreword by George Martin.**

**Amsco Publications**
New York/London/Sydney

Cover photograph by Randall Wallace
Project editor: Peter Pickow
Interior design and layout: Don Giller



Order No. AM 931370
US International Standard Book Number: 0.8256.1500.3
UK International Standard Book Number: 0.7119.5138.1

Exclusive Distributors:
**Music Sales Corporation**
257 Park Avenue South, New York, NY 10010 USA
**Music Sales Limited**
8/9 Frith Street, London W1V 5TZ England
**Music Sales Pty. Limited**
120 Rothschild Street, Rosebery, Sydney, NSW 2018, Australia

Printed in the United States of America by
Vicks Lithograph and Printing Corporation

# Foreword

When I was a child, tape recording did not exist and the recording industry was still in the "biplane-open-cockpit-fly-by-the-seat-of-your-pants" stage. Starting in the record business in my early twenties, I could count the number of real record producers on my fingers. Today, I believe that every third person I meet is either a record producer or trying to become one.

It is a fascinating and rewarding hobby as well as being an absorbing career and this book is going to give real commonsense guidance to those who want to try it for themselves. Don't be put off by the absurd complications of modern recording techniques. Like the biplane that has turned into a supersonic jet, the controls now look impossibly formidable, but it is still a delightful bird to fly, and the most important thing is the 'feel' you give it.

Musical imagination and awareness of sound are the real keys and the sophisticated hardware and technical wizardry of the professional studio are merely tools. I still believe that some of my best recordings were made directly in mono; even *Sgt. Pepper,* complicated though it was, blossomed very well within the limitations of four-track.

So enjoy yourselves, dabble in sound, paint your pictures, turn on your mind and gently float downstream. . . .

George Martin
Beatles Producer

# Preface to the First Edition

There are many books on recording written by engineers for engineers; this one is written by a musician for musicians. The object is to demystify the art of making a good recording, and to gather as much information as possible—on as many aspects of recording as possible—in one place.

There is so much that can be written about sound recording, from technical to musical considerations, that part of the problem in writing a book like this is figuring what to leave out. So, I've tried to emphasize practical knowledge that translates directly into making better a better recording. But if you want to pursue any subject further, there are texts that get into whatever interests you in the most minute detail imaginable. Like music, recording is a subject with infinite potential: you can always learn more, you can always improve, and there are always new advances in the state of the art that promise even greater things to come.

This book is not like a novel, where you read it once and know the story line. It is more like a reference, where you can come back to certain sections and gain new insights into the material presented. For example, read the chapter on mixing before you do any actual mixing to get an idea of what you are in for; then, read it again after you have mixed for a while and you will be able to extract new ideas. Reread the section on basic concepts from time to time; although you can intellectually understand the concepts of noise and distortion, they will make more sense after you have come face to face with the reality of trying to minimize these problems.

Make no mistake: There will be times when you will be hopelessly frustrated, when nothing seems to go right, and when the noise level on your master sounds like Niagara Falls. But luckily, these times will be in the minority. What's more, they'll be balanced by those times when everything goes right, the instrument sings, your music soars, and chills run up and down your spine.

Best of all, you'll have captured it on your recorder.

# Preface to the Second Edition

When the first edition of this book came out in 1977, recording was a very different world. Musicians were just getting into four-track recorders, DAT was a gleam in some engineer's eye, and there wasn't even a chapter on synchronization because its uses were extremely limited. Analog tape was the only real choice in recording technology, and if you wanted a budget mixer, your best bet was to build it yourself.

Analog tape is still with us, but anyone who now wants to get into project or home recording faces a good news/bad news situation. The bad news first: there is a bewildering array of competing recording technologies (analog tape, digital tape, hard disk recording, MIDI sequencing, etc.) as well as signal processors, mixers, and accessories. Computers have now become a part of the studio, and they have their own advantages and disadvantages. You can now send parts to a studio via phone lines or satellites, or dial up a telecommunications service and download samples. All of this takes time to learn and use, and to complicate matters further, you can just about see a piece of gear's value depreciate before your very eyes. Technology moves rapidly, and you have to be fast on your feet to stay ahead.

The good news is that all of this magic costs less than ever, is vastly more reliable, and delivers an exceptional amount of bang for the buck. It is now possible to make CD-quality recordings in a corner of your house for what it used to cost to buy a hissy, slow four-track analog tape machine. Technology has leveled the playing field to where the musician's main limitation is compositional and playing ability, not the quality of gear. These days, pretty much whatever you imagine can be turned into reality.

The biggest problem in revising this book was including the vast amounts of information that recording now encompasses, yet retaining the generalist, entry-level ambiance of the first edition. I've opted for giving overviews of the various aspects of recording with what I hope is enough detail to explain all the relevant concepts, but not so much as to be intimidating. If you need more information on a specific topic, you can always check out individual books on particular subjects.

Best of all, we're still dealing with a field that, comparatively speaking, is in its infancy. There are many techniques yet to be discovered, and new types of music to be made. My hope is that this book will help you, in some way, to realize your dreams and express yourself through the arts of music and recording—and perhaps inspire you to take things to a level that no one has ever reached before. Good luck!

## A Note about the First Few Chapters

Many musicians are self-taught, and have such instinctive feelings for music that they can create beautiful music without knowing any music theory, such as how to sight-read. But the funny thing is, many of these people at some point wish they had learned a little theory; because when you want to write out a song for other people to play, you're really at a loss if you can't read and write music. The rule seems to be that if you're dealing with other people in the same field, you have to know the language.

In the first few sections of this book, we have to pay some dues by learning some of the technical end of recording. Luckily, these aren't heavy dues; they can be paid with a little time and concentration. The most important requirement is not to have any mental blocks about learning this technical information. So many people lack confidence, and when presented with something new they tend to buckle and say, "I can't possibly do that." Yet, when engineers sit around and talk about decibels, equalization, and signal-to-noise ratios, they will see a good musician and say, "I could never do that." The secret is that you can really do anything you want—just be patient and persistent.

I come from a musical, not an engineering background, and I must admit there were times when I really had a hard time relating to certain electrical concepts. But once you get past the initial shock of dealing with numbers and quantities and strange words, concepts magically fall into place. So if, as you read the book, you find yourself confused, don't get discouraged. You don't have to understand everything instantly. If you read over the first few sections and everything makes sense except the part on, say, decibels, don't worry about it. Just put it out of your mind temporarily and forge ahead. As you gain more practical experience, as you read further in the book and start doing your own sessions, concepts that were abstract and foreign will become real and necessary, and will make more sense. It's like trying to learn to do anything from reading a book—the knowledge only becomes cemented with practical experience. Here is one hint: if something doesn't make sense, read it over out loud. Involving both the eyes and ears seems to help retention.

I must admit I never liked school and being forced to learn things I didn't really care about, but here the situation is different. We're looking to use recorders and studios to increase our pleasure and maybe even make us better people. This is the kind of learning that should be fun, because the results of the knowledge will be sweeter sounds, more professional tapes, and a happier musician. Also, if you know the language, you can talk to other people who know more than you do, and you can learn a lot.

Please remember that this is a handbook: hold it in one hand and run your studio with the other. Use them as a pair. If there's something you don't understand, just bull your way through and it will make sense somewhere down the road. Also remember that I generally like to put the hardest stuff first (not only is it harder for a lot of you to understand, it's the hardest part for me to write!) so that it's out of the way and we can then proceed to getting real sounds. So, let's explore the world of sound, and the language that technical people use to define the characteristics of sound.

## Important Note: Book Support

This book, as well as some of the author's other Amsco books, is supported through the America Online site "Craig Anderton's Sound, Studio, and Stage" (keywords: SSS or ANDERTON). Additional materials and audio samples that illustrate recording techniques mentioned in the book are posted there. Any typos or corrections will also be uploaded to this site. To subscribe to AOL and obtain a disk entitling you to ten free hours, call 1-800-466-5463.

# Contents

# Chapter 1
# The Very Basics

Sound is easy to take for granted, but in the studio we have to think about sound from a somewhat technical standpoint in order to record it, work with it, and listen to it. So, let's discuss some of sound's basic characteristics.

## The Nature of Sound

You've probably heard the term "sound waves"; that's just what they are. Like ocean waves, sound waves moving through the air have crests and troughs (Fig. 1-1). These crests and troughs create differences in air pressure, which we perceive as sound.

These pressure changes can occur at different rates, which leads into the concept of *frequency*. Frequency is the number of waves that occur in a second. We can consider each crest-trough combination as a cycle that repeats itself along the wave; we measure the frequency by noting how many cycles pass by us in a second. This gives us a number, in *cycles per second*. The unit of frequency is called the Hertz (Hz) to commemorate Heinrich Hertz (1857–1894), for his extensive work with wavelength and frequency. So, a wave with three cycles passing by in a single second would be called a 3 cycles per second wave, or simply a 3 Hertz or 3 Hz wave. You will often see the term kHz; it is short for "kiloHertz" and represents 1000 Hz. Thus, 3000 Hz = 3 kHz.

Audio frequencies range from about 20 to 20,000 cycles per second (20 Hz to 20 kHz). These frequency differences give different pitches to the sounds we hear.

With electronic circuits, we can't have air waves moving around inside wires, so electrical waves are a little different: they are waves of increasing and decreasing voltage, with respect to time (Fig. 1-2). As an ocean wave has a greater volume of water at the peak than at the trough, and as a sound or air wave has greater air pressure at the peak and less air pressure at the trough, an electrical wave has greater voltage (or "strength") at the crest, and lower voltage at the trough. The higher the frequency, the more cycles there are in a given amount of time.

These voltage variations must be converted into moving air before we can hear them. This requires a *transducer*, a device that converts one form of energy into another. For example, a loudspeaker can convert voltage variations into changes in air pressure; a microphone can transform air pressure changes into voltage variations. Other transducers include guitar pickups (which convert mechanical energy to electrical energy), and tape recorder heads (which convert magnetic energy into electrical energy).

Now let's discuss how to measure these waves. We already know how to measure the frequency: count the number of cycles that occur in one second. But determining the strength of a varying electrical signal is quite different, and more difficult. It's no problem to measure the voltage with something like a battery, which puts out an electrical signal with a constant voltage. However, our varying signal is another story. At the crest, the signal strength (amplitude) is high; but at the trough, the amplitude is low. So, the measured strength of a varying signal will depend on when you decide to measure that signal. In order to cope with this problem and produce some kind of definitive figure, there are several different ways to measure a signal. We'll go into the two most common ways.

However, first we need to understand the term *volt*. A volt measures electrical activity; the more activity, the more volts. This is sort of like with your car, where the speedometer reads higher as you go faster. We can compare the strength of one signal to another by measuring their voltages. One way to do this is to measure both signals from the top of their peaks to the bottom of their troughs, and call this the *peak-to-peak voltage* (Fig. 1-3). Note that signal X has twice the peak-to-peak voltage of signal Y. However, another way of measuring the strength of a signal is to take a mathematically correct average reading during one cycle, and express the average signal strength. This is known as *RMS voltage*. Actually, the RMS average is not the same as a straight mathematical average, but we don't need to get into too much detail.

I'm sure some people are getting confused at this point. But remember, all we're really talking

Ocean waves (moving water) . . .

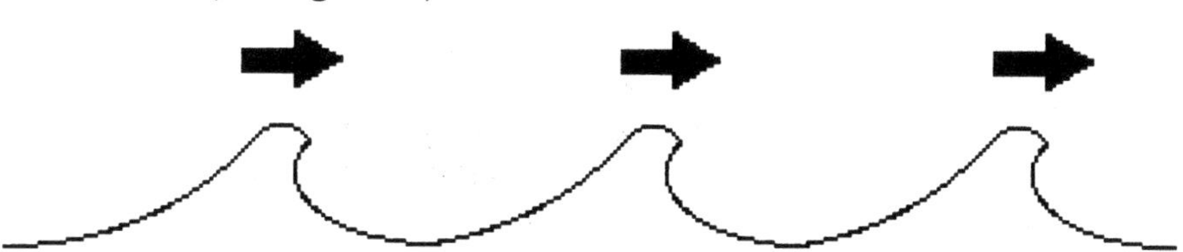

. . . are similar to simple sound waves (moving air)

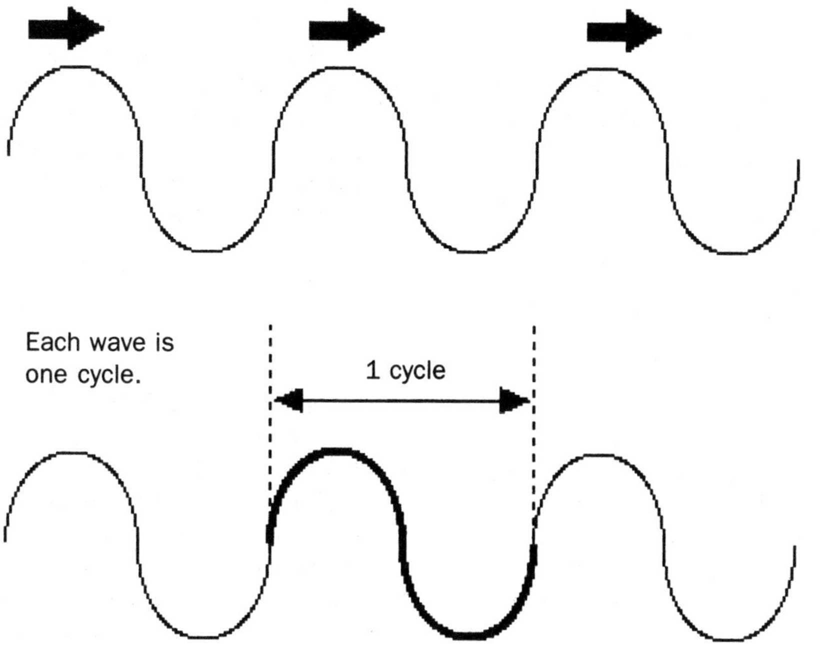


If 20 cycles pass by in one second, then we have a 20-cycles-per-second (or 20 Hz) sound wave.

**Fig. 1-1:** *The nature of sound waves.*

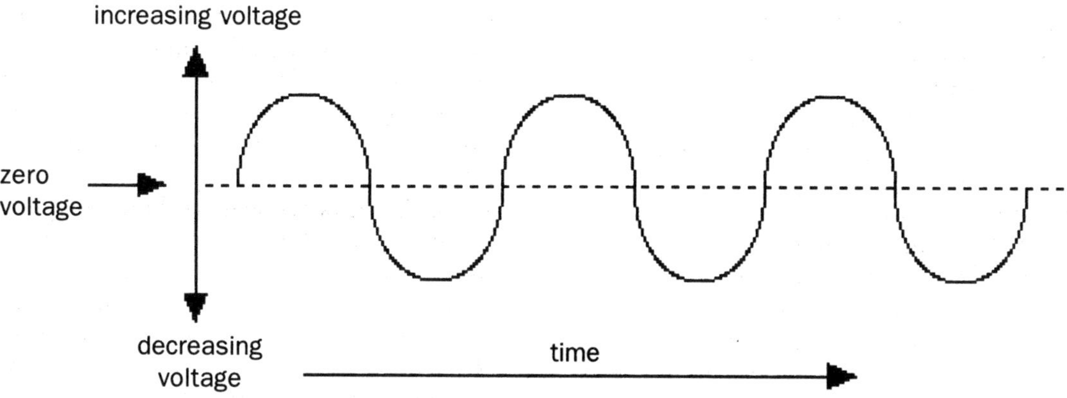


**Fig. 1-2:** *How a wave relates to voltage.*

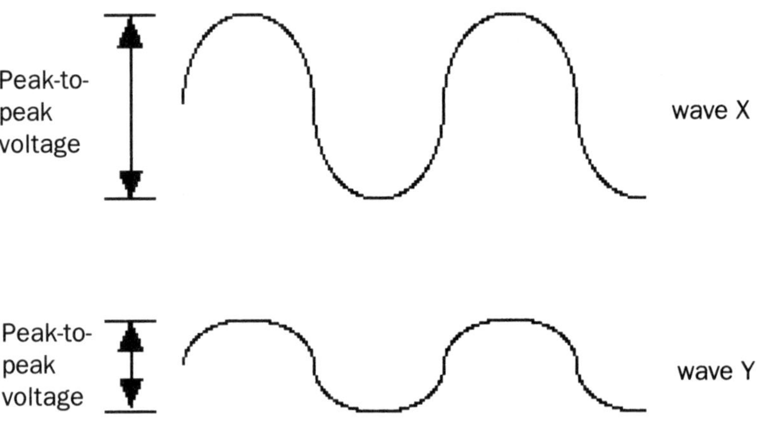


**Fig. 1-3:** *Measuring the peak-to-peak voltage of two different waves.*

about is how to get a handle on these sound waves, so we can say something more definitive than "this one is louder." The more we know, the more precise we can be in defining the relative levels of signals.

Since we do want to compare signals a lot, we need to look at another unit of measurement—the decibel (dB). Even engineers can have a hard time with this one, because it's a unit of measurement that can be applied in many different ways. We're only interested in applying it to signal ratios, though, which simplifies matters.

Simply stated, the decibel expresses the ratio between the strengths of two signals. However, before we can go any further we need to understand a little about how the ear hears.

If you hear a sound and then hear another sound that is twice as powerful as the first, you will not necessarily perceive the second sound as being twice as loud. To hear a constant, *linear* increase in amplitude, the amplitude has to increase *logarithmically* (Fig. 1-4).

As a result, the decibel increases logarithmically to correlate more closely with the ear's characteristics and to avoid using huge, unwieldy numbers. Fig. 1-5 shows a table of how the ratio of peak-to-peak signal voltage relates to the ratio expressed in decibels.

The decibel may seem difficult to use, but once you get the knack of it, the decibel makes it much easier to compare signal strengths. For example, in Fig. 1-3 signal X has twice the peak-to-peak voltage of signal Y. Looking on our voltage ratio versus dB table, we see that this works out to 6 dB (for you mathematical types, Appendix A gives the formula for converting voltage ratios into dB).

Now we see why the dB is so useful. Referring to Fig. 1-6, each pair of signals maintains a 6 dB ratio, even though the actual voltage values of the signals differ. If a signal is 6 dB softer than another signal, we know it is half the peak-to-peak voltage, regardless of the absolute voltage levels involved; only the ratio counts.

Sometimes you don't have a ready reference, such as a signal to which you want to compare other signals. For these cases, you set up an arbitrary reference, then express ratios according to this reference. For example, microphones produce signals that are rated at so many dB below a standardized reference signal they're picking up. Thus, if one microphone produces a signal that is 50 dB below the standard, its output would be rated as –50dB, or about 1/300th of the strength of the standard signal. If a second microphone puts out a signal that is 35

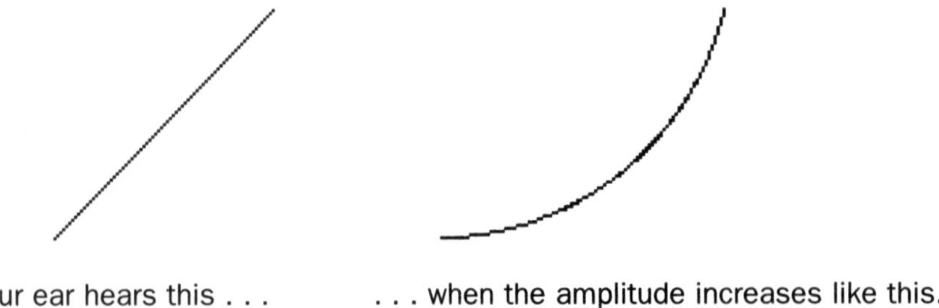


**Fig. 1-4:** *Linear and logarithmic response compared.*

| dB | Approximate peak-to-peak voltage ratio |
|---|---|
| 0 | 1.00 |
| 1 | 1.12 |
| 2 | 1.26 |
| 3 | 1.41 |
| 5 | 1.78 |
| 6 | 2.00 |
| 8 | 2.51 |
| 10 | 3.16 |
| 15 | 5.62 |
| 20 | 10.00 |
| 30 | 31.62 |
| 40 | 100 |
| 60 | 1,000 |
| 80 | 10,000 |
| 100 | 100,000 |

**Fig. 1-5:** *How decibel values relate to peak-to-peak voltage readings.*

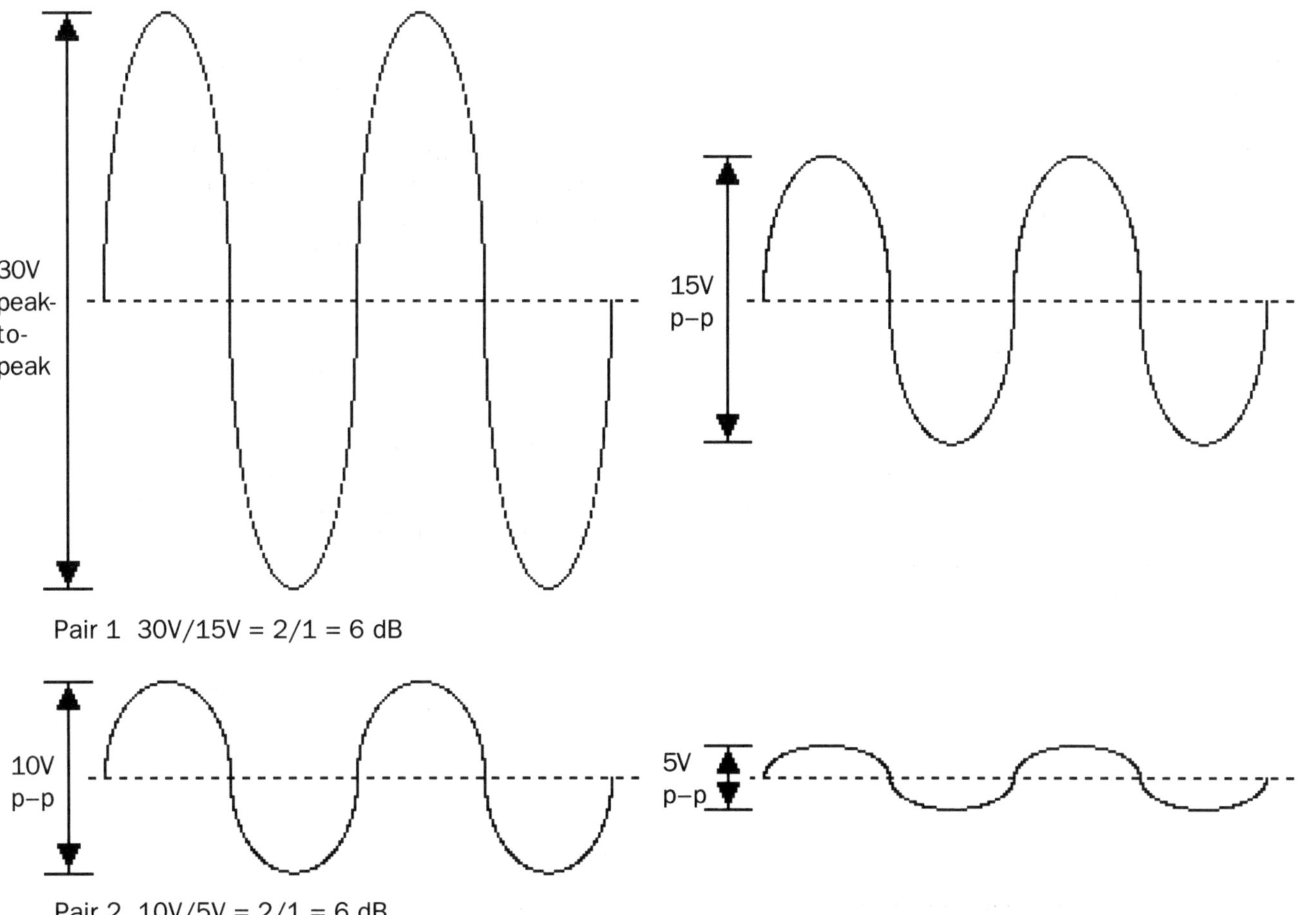


**Fig. 1-6:** *Even though the levels of two pairs of signals differ greatly, each pair has the same ratio, expressed in dB.*

dB weaker than the standard signal (–35dB), then the second microphone's signal strength is about 1/60th the strength of the standard signal. We then know that the second microphone delivers more output. If an electronic device puts out more juice than the standard, the figure would be expressed as + so many dB (*e.g.,* +10dB, +4dB, *etc.*).

## Real World Signals

The simplified waveforms shown above are what comes out of a very simple tone generator, such as the sine-wave oscillators used for test tones. Real-world audio signals look far more complex, and thanks to the miracle of computers, we can display them graphically on a computer screen. Let's look at some examples of typical audio waveforms.

Fig. 1-7 shows four measures of a piece of dance music. Because the sound waves are hundreds and thousands of cycles per second, and since this example is a few seconds long, you can't see individual cycles of the sound but rather the overall amplitude. Notice the kick drum that occurs on each beat; it's the large, loud spike. The snare drum hits on the offbeats, which you should also be able to make out.

Now let's look at a shorter piece of audio. Fig. 1-8 shows how spoken words show up onscreen; you can easily see the spaces between individual words and syllables.

We can "zoom in" even further on this audio, until we can see the individual cycles that make it up. Fig. 1-9 shows a few milliseconds (1 millisecond = 1,000th of a second) of a piece of classical guitar music; note how you can make out an individual cycle in the waveform.

But there's no need to pursue this subject any further for right now. Let's just recap what we have learned so far:

- Sound waves are similar to ocean waves, and can be represented electronically as varying voltages.
- Sound waves or electrical waves have specific frequencies, which are expressed in cycles per second, or Hertz.
- We can measure the amplitude of a sound wave in several ways, two of which are the peak-to-peak method, and the RMS averaging method.
- We can compare the amplitude of one wave to another as a voltage ratio, or we can translate that voltage ratio into decibels, which reflects our hearing response more accurately than the concept of a voltage ratio. In theory, a one decibel change is the smallest change detectable by a human ear at any volume level.

There! That wasn't so bad, although there have been many simplifications along the way. Now let's check out the characteristics of different frequency ranges.

## What Is an Audio Spectrum, Anyway?

We now need to understand two very basic audio concepts that are vital to our understanding of sound and how we record it: the audio frequency spectrum, and flat frequency response.

As any mystic or physicist will tell you, the universe is composed of vibrations—literally. Everything has its own particular resonant frequency and energy level. Some of the vibrations are very slow, others are exceedingly fast. Our ears are designed to pick up very low-frequency vibrations, known as sound waves. In fact, the average ear can pick up these waves from about 20 Hz on up to about 15 kHz, below and above which they have a harder time responding to the vibrations. Even people with exceptionally acute hearing can't hear much sound above 22 kHz.

The range from 20 Hz to 22 kHz, where our various musical instruments hang out, is almost exactly ten octaves. Only electronic instruments can create a full ten-octave response, so the high notes of the instruments we normally encounter seldom extend much beyond 3 to 5 kHz. Above that, we're dealing mostly with overtones and harmonics, finger noise, and other non-tonal sounds.

Note that this audio spectrum of sound is a tiny, tiny part of the overall spectrum of all possible forms of vibration, known as the electromagnetic spectrum. Radio waves are part of this spectrum, but are much higher in frequency than sound waves; light waves are higher still. It's kind of interesting to note that although our ears can hear ten octaves of sound, our eyes can see only one octave of light. But as far as the overall spectrum is concerned, the audio part is sort of the basement of the whole thing, a land of slow and dense vibrations that we perceive as sound, and which we arrange to form music.

Audiophiles and engineers often use the term "flat" frequency response. To understand this concept, let's assume an instrument/amplifier combination that can produce notes of exactly the same volume level, or *amplitude,* from 20 Hz

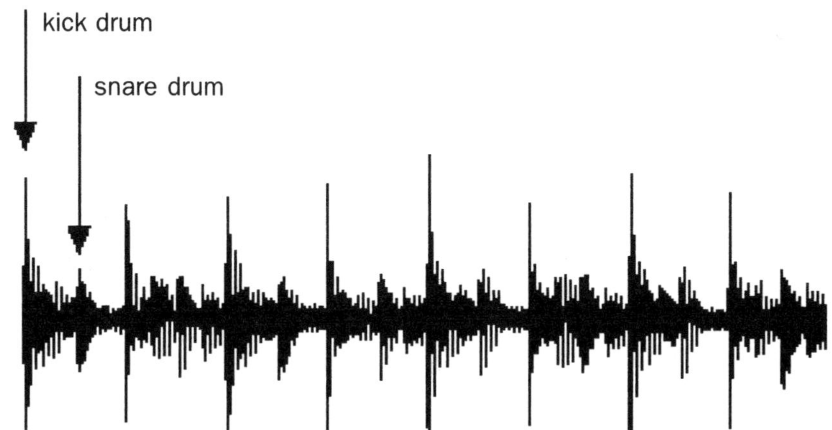


**Fig. 1-7:** *A piece of music, shown as audio on a computer screen.*

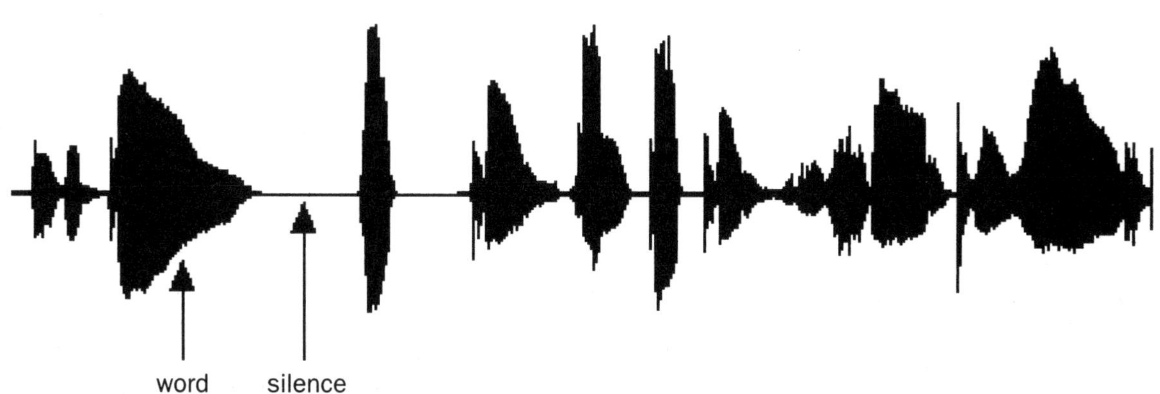


**Fig. 1-8:** *A series of spoken words.*

**Fig. 1-9:** *An example of a real-world waveform from a classical guitar.*

to 20 kHz. If your ear had a flat frequency response, then whether you struck a low note or a high note you would perceive these notes as being exactly the same volume. In this case, the instrument is said to have a *flat frequency response* in terms of our ears, and this is a flat system.

But this perfect system doesn't exist, and our ears aren't perfect either. The biggest problem is that ears do not respond equally to bass as to treble, and, depending on the volume, they respond even less to treble. So even before we've built our first piece of equipment, we've already thrown in a tremendous monkey wrench. Not only does the ear react imperfectly to imperfect instruments, but every person is different: no two sets of ears respond the same way to volume changes. For a further complication, this bass response anomaly of the ears is most pronounced at low listening levels; at very high listening levels, the ears do manage an almost flat response. But as the dynamics of a song change, your ear's response changes along with it.

A partial solution to this problem has been developed over the years. Since no one making a recording knows who will listen to the final product, or at what volume level it will be played back, the recording studio tries for a flat response—from the microphone on up to the amplifier and finally through the speakers—without trying to compensate for problems encountered at the listener's end. Then, listeners can change the frequency response to their particular requirements with tone controls. Thus, if you're listening at a soft volume level, you can boost the bass slightly to compensate for your ears' deficiencies. At higher volume levels, you can leave your system flat. As you get older and the treble response of your ears starts to fade, you can add more treble.

So, the burden of maintaining the integrity of sound lies with the recording engineer, the producer, and the studio itself. If they put out an album that's bass heavy, although it may sound good at low volume, it will sound boomy and muddy at loud listening levels. In theory, if you play back a flat recording over a perfectly flat listening system, it should sound exactly the same as the original—and indeed, it can come very close.

Before we leave the audio spectrum, let's look at its various subdivisions. The audio range is traditionally divided into three broad classifications: bass, midrange, and treble. One possible definition, although there is no general consensus, is that bass extends from about 10 Hz up to 200 Hz or so; midrange covers 200 Hz to about 5 kHz; and 5 kHz on up is the treble region. It's possible to divide these major categories into subcategories, each with these characteristics:

- Lower bass (about 10 Hz to 80 Hz) is the range where you find the lowest musical notes; this is also the area where room resonance, AC power hum, and other low, rumbly entities reside. If you filter out this range, you sense an immediate loss of depth, richness, and power.
- Upper bass (about 80 Hz to 200 Hz) covers the higher end of bass instruments, and the lower range of instruments like guitar. If you were to surgically remove this range from a piece of music almost all of your feeling of power would be lost. You probably wouldn't want to get up and dance, either, since the majority of the rhythm section's energy is located in this region.
- Lower midrange (about 200 Hz to 500 Hz) is where a lot of rhythm and accompaniment happens; rhythm guitar falls mostly into this range.
- Middle midrange (about 500 Hz to 2,500 Hz) is where you find violin solos, the upper parts of guitar and piano solos, and a lot of vocals. Listening to a system with poor response in the lower and middle midrange gives "shallow" music with almost no punch.
- Upper midrange (about 2,500 Hz to 5 kHz). Although there are few actual notes in this range, except the very topmost notes of pianos and a few other instruments, there are many harmonics and overtones. Boosting this part of the spectrum results in a bright sound that's full of presence and "sheen." However, if there is excessive energy in this band, the ear finds it grating after long periods of time. This is called "listener fatigue" and is a problem with inexpensive speaker systems that artificially enhance this portion of the audio spectrum to sound "bright."
- Lower treble (about 5 kHz to 10 kHz) is where the most obvious treble response occurs, and is also where hiss becomes most noticeable, as there are very few other sounds to block it out or mask its effects. Even though, technically, people can hear higher pitches, many times this is considered the limit of response, because there is little energy in much modern music above this range. (In the pre-noise reduction analog era, sometimes a studio would filter out everything over 10 kHz to minimize tape hiss problems.)

- Upper treble (about 10 kHz to 20 kHz) is our final octave, and is the home of very subtle and delicate high frequencies. Hearing good acoustic music over a system with truly fine high-frequency response is an experience, but until the advent of the Compact Disc and other digital audio recording techniques, few budget systems could deliver truly high-quality sound in this region. With the upper treble removed, many people can't really hear any appreciable difference; but with this part intact, and if you have the ears to hear it, there's a beautiful feeling of "liveness" added to the sound.

## Distortion

Probably everyone reading this book can recognize a distorted sound—it has a grittiness and harshness not encountered with an undistorted signal. But since distortion (or rather, the avoidance of it) plays such a large part in music and recording, we should know something about what causes it.

Simply stated, distortion occurs when a system operates beyond its limits. For example, let's look at why a speaker distorts. The movement of a speaker cone produces air waves that we perceive as sound; however, the speaker cone can only travel a certain distance (Fig. 1-10). As long as the speaker reproduces signals within its capabilities, distortion will be minimized. But suppose we put a signal through the speaker that is loud enough to push the cone to its limit of travel, then we double the signal to try to get more output. At this point, the speaker simply cannot go any farther. As a result, it cannot reproduce the signal cleanly; we have gone beyond the limits of linear, acceptable operation, which results in distortion.

Analog tape has limits too, which are the limits of *saturation.* As you try to push more and more signal onto the tape, there is greater and greater magnetization of the tape's magnetic particles. But if you go past a certain point, there will be no more particles left on the tape to magnetize, and therefore the sound will not be cleanly recorded on the tape. Fig. 1-11 shows what this kind of saturation effect "looks" like. Digital technology (see Chapter 3) isn't perfect either, as it has a finite dynamic range. Signals that exceed the maximum available dynamic range often produce a nasty, "splattering" sound.

It's important to recognize distortion, because its presence means that something is being pushed beyond its limits. With a mechanical device like a speaker, you could end up damaging the unit; with tape (and many electronic devices), overloading will not cause physical destruction, but can lead to other, more subtle problems, such as leakage and with analog tape, spillover to other tracks.

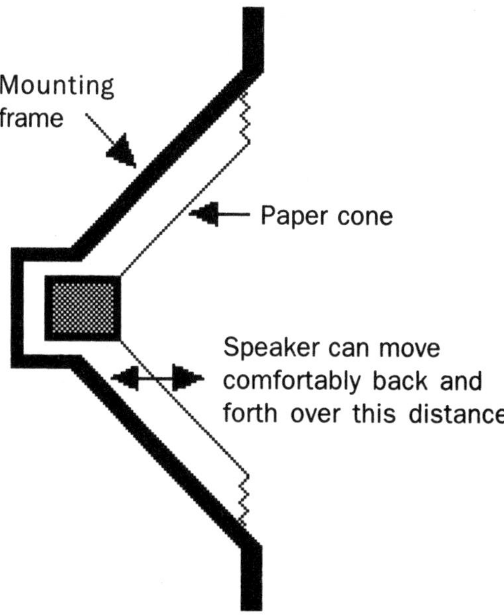


**Fig. 1-10:** *Speaker cones can only move a certain distance, so when you try to push them harder, distortion results.*

When you encounter unintended distortion in a system, trace back through the various stages for a control that may be set improperly, or delivering more output than the next stage can handle; then back off on the control until the grittiness goes away.

## An Overview of the Recording Process

Let's look at the recording studio on a general level, which will make the specific elements easier to understand.

A recording setup is composed of various parts. The first part is you! Someone has to maintain the recorders, turn the knobs, push the buttons, connect the wires, and play the music. You, in turn, will need some tools to do all this.

Tool number one is a multitrack recorder. Currently, there are four common types of multitrack recorders:

- Analog tape recorder
- Digital tape recorder
- Disk (hard disk or optical disk) recorder
- MIDI recorder (sequencer)

We'll cover the characteristics of each type in subsequent chapters, but what they all share is

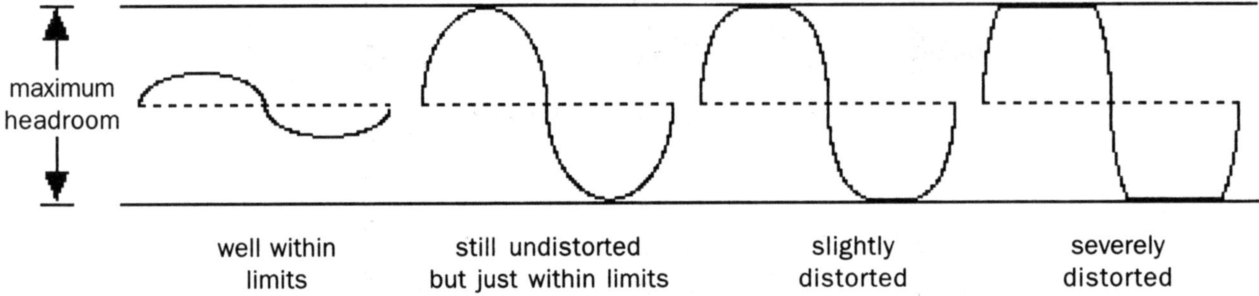


**Fig. 1-11:** *How increasing distortion affects a waveform's shape.*

the ability to partition their particular storage medium into individual *tracks* so that you can make changes to one track only, without disturbing the other ones. With this flexibility, you can play and record an instrument on one track, then go back to the beginning and record another part on a separate track—without changing the first track in any way. Solo performers and composers can build up a tune, one track at a time, by *overdubbing* additional tracks as needed. A track that is laid down against an existing backdrop of one or more tracks is called an *overdub*.

If a take was perfect except for a few bad notes, you can even erase a small portion of a track, and re-record over it. You do this by "punching" the record button where you want to begin recording (called the *punch in* point), and punching it again when you want to stop recording (the *punch out* point). This process is called *punching* (or if you're just getting rid of existing material and not recording new material over it, *spot erasing*).

The next part is the mixing console, which acts as a clearinghouse for all those audio signals and inputs and outputs we encounter while recording. Remember how we said you can record signals on multiple tracks? Well, at some point we're going to want to mix all those signals into a composite mono or stereo signal that we can listen to, presenting the music in a finished form. This leads us to the process of *mixing*, where the various tracks are varied in level, balance, tonal quality, or whatever is necessary to make a pleasing musical product for you to hear on your playback system.

We also need another tape recorder to record the final version of your mixes. This recorder produces what's known as a *master tape,* which contains the mixed and edited versions of musical pieces. A professional studio will have a separate, high quality machine for making master tapes; but for a modest home studio, a decent cassette deck will do. As long as you have your original tracks preserved on the multitrack's storage medium, you can remix at a later date when you become an accomplished mixer, or you can remix into a better machine if you upgrade your studio.

Rounding out the studio requires lots of separate accessories, which depends upon your circumstances. A decent quality microphone, for example, is a necessity for almost all studios, as are any tools required for routine maintenance. You also need microphone stands, extension cords, signal processors (such as reverb), possibly a computer with appropriate software, and so on.

Combining all these elements into an acoustically acceptable environment creates the basis of a studio. However, just as buying a 1928 Steinway doesn't make you a superb pianist, all the equipment in the world won't do you any good unless you have the knowledge, patience, experience, and practice to back it up. You don't gain these overnight—in fact, any good sound engineer will tell you that you never stop learning. There are always new techniques to be tried and new music to record. In any event, strive to run your studio as efficiently, professionally, and pleasantly as possible. When you know what you're doing, it's fun; when you have to fight the equipment, it's work.

## Recording System Basics

The whole point of recording is to "freeze" sound. As a photograph holds an image, a recording must hold sounds in a form that can be played over and over again if need be. When you consider that sounds are caused by moving air, you see the problem we are up against: How do you store a bunch of airwaves, anyway?

Over the years, people have been working on how to translate air waves into electrical impulses and then store these in some kind of permanent medium. Any audio recording system, digital or analog, includes (Fig. 1-12):

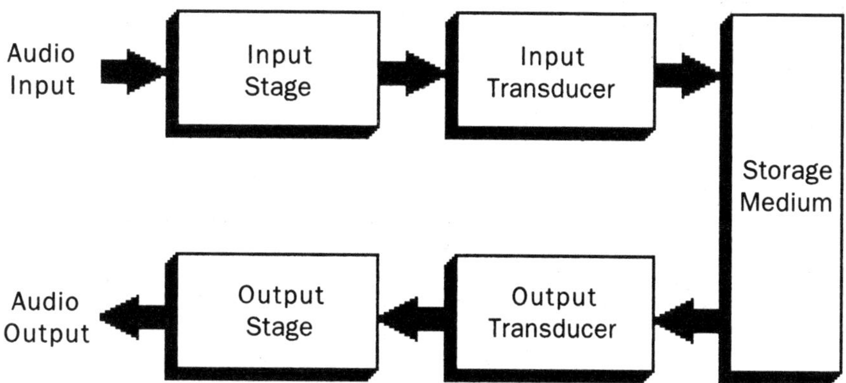


**Fig. 1-12:** *Basic building blocks of an audio recording system.*

- An *input stage* that conditions (amplifies, filters, processes, *etc.*) the real-world signal into something that can drive the . . .
- *Input transducer/converter,* which converts the conditioned signal into a form that can be captured by the . . .
- *Storage medium,* which retains these electrical signals.
- An *output transducer/converter* then pulls signals from the storage medium and sends them to . . .
- An *output stage* that conditions the recovered signal to restore what originally appeared at the input.

Don't forget that there will be other transducers involved in the recording process, such as a mic (an air-waves-to-electricity converter) to generate the audio that feeds the input stage, and a speaker (an electricity-to-air-waves converter) that turns the audio into something we can hear.

Let's look at the various recording processes that let you translate your sonic dreams into reality, and how they adapt these basic elements to a particular technology.

# Chapter 2
# Analog Recording

Analog recording is where recording began, so we'll cover it first. However, much of what we'll discuss also applies to digital tape recording (so don't think you can skip this chapter just because you have some shiny new modular digital multitrack).

Vinyl records (remember those?) work by inscribing a groove whose shape is analogous to an audio waveform into the record's plastic. During playback, the stylus traces this waveform and the phono cartridge sends out voltage variations analogous to the original signal. This low-level signal then passes through an amplifier, which augments the voltage enough to drive a speaker cone back and forth. The result is that the speaker cone follows the waveform motion, thus reproducing the same air pressure variations originally pressed into the vinyl record.

Note that each stage transfers a signal in its own medium (vinyl, wire, air, *etc.*) that is *analogous* to the input signal; hence the term, analog.

## About Transducers

Transducers convert one form of energy to another, such as electrical to mechanical (*e.g.*, a loudspeaker) or mechanical to electrical (*e.g.*, a microphone). Since transducers are crucial to the recording process, let's look at a simple transducer in detail.

### Loudspeaker Basics

Fig. 2-1 shows how a speaker works. Note the three main parts: the permanent magnet, the voice coil (an electromagnet), and the paper cone.

Permanent magnets are bigger versions of the little bar magnets you have probably played with at some point in your life. Magnets can repel or attract each other, depending on their relative positioning (Fig. 2-2). The ability of one magnet to cause another one to move physically forms the basis of the speaker's operation.

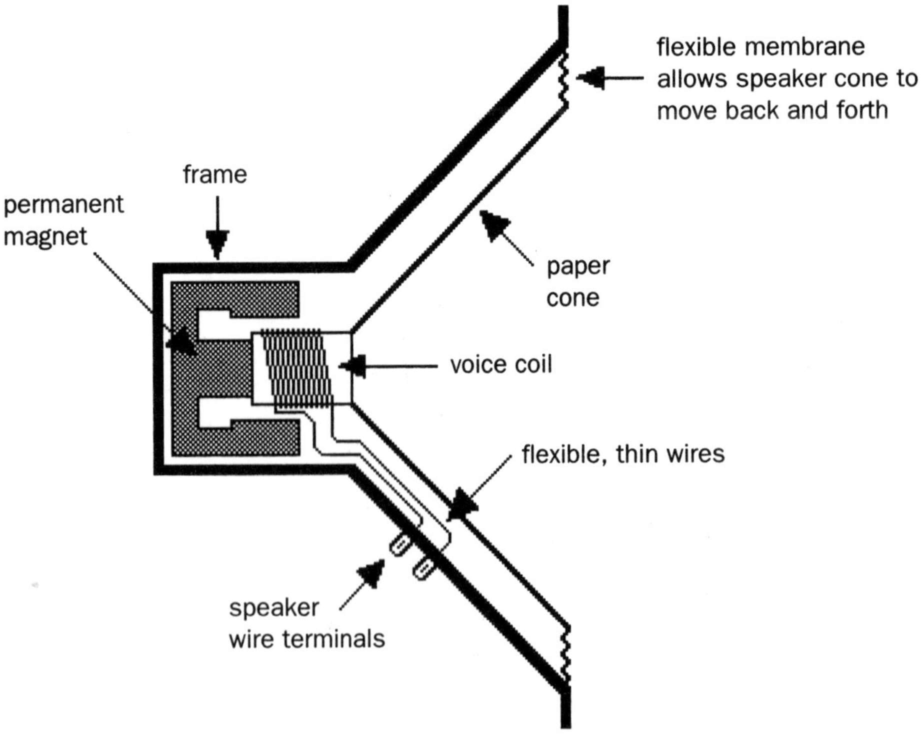


**Fig. 2-1:** *Elements of a loudspeaker*

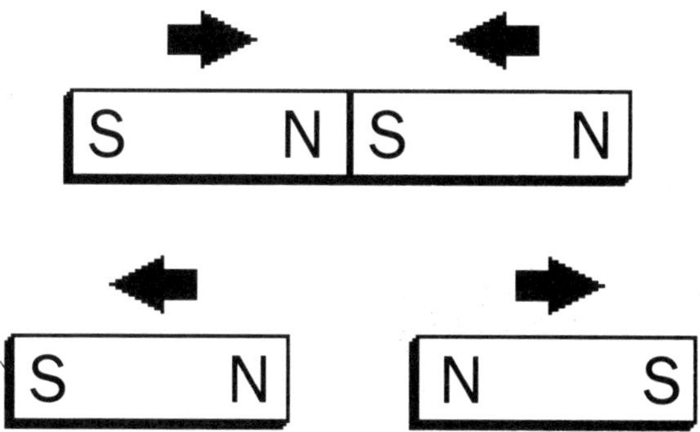


Fig. 2-2: *Opposing poles of bar magnets attract; like poles of bar magnets repel.*

An electromagnet is a coil made of many turns of very fine wire and works similarly to a permanent magnet; but it requires an electrical current passing through it to create a magnetic field. A varying electrical current creates a varying magnetic field.

Now, getting back to the speaker, note that the voice coil attaches to the paper cone, creating an electromagnet positioned within the field of a permanent magnet. Passing a varying electrical current—like the audio signal of a power amp—through the voice coil generates a magnetic field around it, which interacts with the field created by the permanent magnet. Because of the magnetic attraction-repulsion effect, this magnetic interaction translates into speaker cone movement.

As the speaker cone is now moving back and forth at a rate determined by the magnetic field created by an audio signal, then the audio signal controls the speaker cone, and the speaker cone generates air waves that we perceive as sound. To recap, we have managed to convert electrical current into air waves by using a combination of electrical signals and magnetism.

## Microphone Basics

Interestingly, a speaker can also work like a microphone (Fig. 2-3). Air waves striking the speaker cone cause the electromagnet to move within the permanent magnet's magnetic field. As the electromagnet coil cuts across the permanent magnet's magnetic field, the interaction causes a tiny, fluctuating signal—the electrical equivalent of the air waves striking the cone—to be induced into the coil.

This is very much like a guitar pickup, where a vibrating string induces a voltage into an electromagnetic coil. However, when a speaker is used as a microphone, the paper cone is usually too stiff to give very good frequency response; so although microphones work on this principle, they are specifically constructed to receive air waves rather than create them. The minute voltage present at the windings of the microphone's electromagnet duplicates the motion of the air waves striking the microphone's diaphragm; we have managed in this case to turn air waves into a feeble, but measurable and usable, electrical signal.

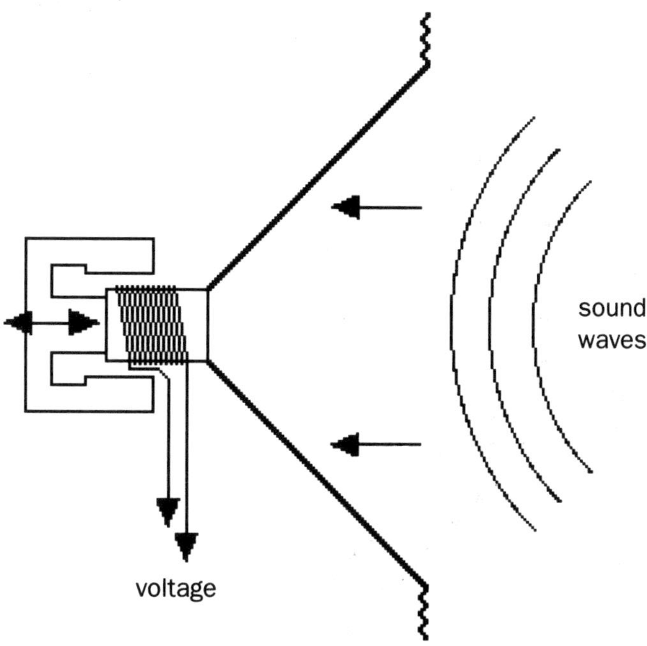


Fig. 2-3: *Sound waves strike the speaker cone, making it move back and forth. This induces a small voltage in the coil, which means we have translated air waves into an electrical signal.*

However, not just any electrical signal can drive a speaker; the signal has to be properly conditioned, usually by giving it enough power to make that cone really move and push the air around. A tiny electrical signal won't drive the speaker at all. The output of your microphone also needs some conditioning, because the signal is so low level that it needs amplification to be usable.

The reason we want to generate an electrical signal is that, as you might suspect, electrical signals are much easier to store than air waves. Now it's time to examine how we store these signals on analog tape.

## The Tale of the Tape

A reel of tape is nothing more than a base material (usually some kind of very thin, space-age plastic), uniformly coated with zillions of tiny magnetic particles (Fig. 2-4).

These particles are like miniature bar magnets, and are only about one micron long; so, you can fit a whole lot of these particles on a piece of tape. Normally, these particles are just kind of floating around in their little molecular world, randomly orienting themselves in a variety of positions and directions, sort of like a crowd of people at a party. During the recording process these particles are lined up in a meaningful way, thus creating a pattern that represents the sound being recorded.

### The Record Head

Taming these particles requires another transducer, the *record head.* Like a speaker, this device feeds electrical signals through the windings of an electromagnet to create a magnetic field. The windings are wrapped around a permanent magnet, although unlike a speaker, the magnet is not free to move. However, this particular magnet is constructed so that there is a small gap at one end. Because the magnetic "circuit" is not complete, a fairly intense magnetic field is generated at the gap; this field fluctuates according to the strength of the electrical impulses, or signal, applied to the record head (Fig. 2-5). As tape goes past the record head, the record head changes the magnetic qualities of the tape's particles, thus leaving a magnetic "imprint" of the sound on the tape.

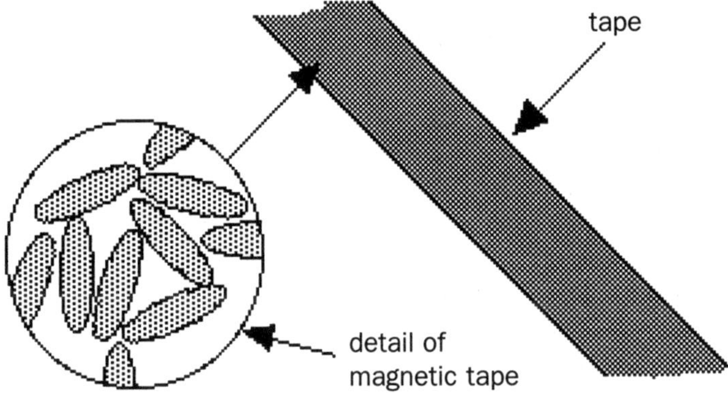


**Fig. 2-4:** *Tape consists of lots of tiny particles attached to a thin plastic backing.*

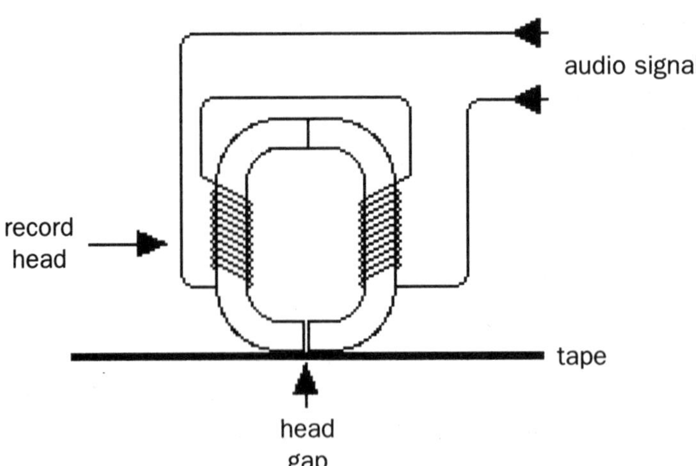


**Fig. 2-5:** *Feeding an electrical signal into the record head's coil generates a varying magnetic field at the head gap. This field leaves its imprint on the particles contained in the magnetic tape.*

## The Playback Head

To hear what we've recorded, we'll apply the same principles—but in reverse—to create a *playback* head. This is similar to a record head but optimized for playback. As the tape moves past this head, the magnetic field pattern imprinted on the tape causes very small voltage changes in the windings of the playback head's electromagnet; once amplified in a suitable way, we have an electrical signal that we can hear through speakers or headphones. So, we've managed to create a near-permanent record, coded in a magnetic language, of what we wanted to record; and we can take that magnetic language and translate it back into something we can listen to and understand.

One fine point: at low frequencies, the response of some playback heads creates a small boost in the frequency response (called a *head bump*), typically somewhere under 100 Hz. Newer heads compensate for this and have a fairly flat response, so this is something that's mostly important with machines made before the mid eighties.

Another point to consider is that in newer machines, the record and playback heads are often one and the same—in other words, the same head that records the signal can also play back the signal. This reduces the cost (one head is cheaper than two), although as record heads and playback heads require slightly different gaps, there's a performance tradeoff. Fortunately, newer models have two actual head gaps within one physical head, which is a definite improvement. In fact, over the years this tradeoff has become less and less noticeable to the point where in newer machines, any performance difference is more or less insignificant.

## The Erase Head

In addition to the record and playback heads, an *erase* head has the job of erasing signals previously recorded on tape. As tape travels through the machine (Fig. 2-6), it goes past this head first to erase any signals so that the tape is fresh and clean for recording. Well, maybe not perfectly fresh and clean; a virgin, unrecorded tape has less noise. However, devices called *bulk erasers* can erase an entire tape in a few seconds to better than new condition (see Chapter 11).

This is a very simple explanation of the workings of a tape machine, and in order to get the point across, we've simplified, and also ignored, some of the complications and limitations. But it's important to understand these basic workings if we're going to get the most out of our equipment.

Now let's turn to some of the components (and eccentricities) of the tape recording process.

# The Tape Transport

There is more to tape recording than electronics; much of the tape recorder is a mechanical system. Whether your machine is a simple cassette deck or a big-bucks digital multitrack recorder, the mechanics of a tape transport are similar, and designed to accomplish the same goal: pull the tape past the machine's various heads in the most uniform, constant way possible. Tape speed is given in inches per second (ips), *i.e.,* how much tape goes past a given point in one second. Typical studio analog tape speeds are 7.5, 15, and 30 ips.

Variations in tape speed show up as *wow* and *flutter.* Wow is a cyclic speed change that is fairly slow; flutter is like a vibrato effect applied to the tape. Neither is desirable, and a lot of engineering effort has gone into making tape transports that move the tape efficiently and smoothly, in order to reduce wow and flutter.

Fig. 2-7 shows a common analog recording system.

A precision motor turns a cylinder called a *capstan,* which revolves at a constant speed. The capstan works in conjunction with a device called a *pinch roller.* When the pinch roller is disengaged from the capstan, the tape is motionless. Pushing the play button forces the pinch roller against the capstan, with the tape pinched

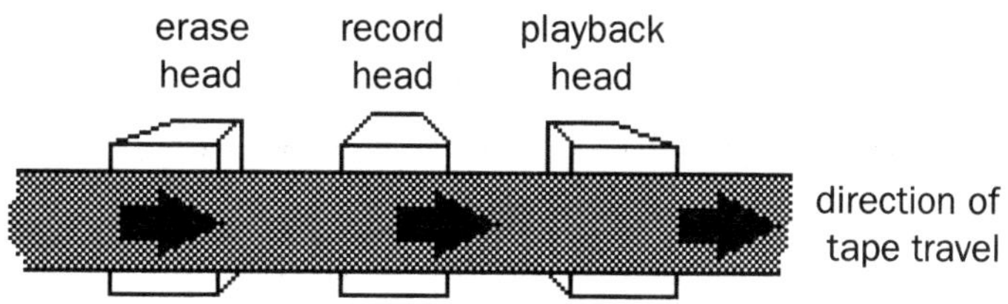


**Fig. 2-7:** *Tape first travels past the erase head, where previously recorded signals can be erased. Then signals are recorded at the record head, and finally pass to the playback head for monitoring. Sometimes the record and playback heads are combined into a single physical unit.*

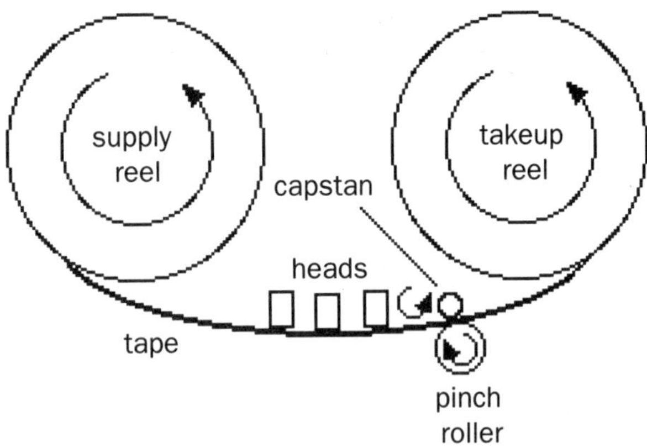


**Fig. 2-7:** *Simplified top view of tape transport in play or record mode.*

in between. As the capstan and pinch roller rotate, they pull the tape through and because the capstan is a constant-speed device, this pulling occurs at a very uniform rate. Speed accuracy within 0.1% is considered adequate for consumer-type analog equipment, with 0.05% accuracy considered excellent. Very few people can detect this amount of variation, except perhaps on long, sustained notes, like those of a piano or organ.

Part of the transport holds the supply reel of tape, and part holds the takeup reel. The reel on the left "supplies" the tape, which is "taken up" by the reel on the right. Applying a slight, counterclockwise "pull" to the takeup reel eliminates any slack as the tape passes through the capstan and pinch roller. Similarly, the supply reel has some clockwise pull to insure a smooth tape flow. This pull, or "back torque," must be slight and precise. Otherwise, the capstan/pinch roller would have to work harder to pull the tape from the supply reel.

Without these compensating tensions on the supply and takeup reels, the tape would not run smoothly, thus creating tape handling problems and speed inaccuracies. The capstan-pinch roller combination controls the actual tape speed, but the takeup and supply reels are an almost equally important part of the process. Note that cassette decks work similarly; the only difference is that the supply and takeup reels are built within the cassette shell itself.

To rapidly fast forward the tape (*e.g.,* to find a later selection), the pinch roller disengages from the capstan, and the takeup reel rotates counterclockwise, pulling the tape at a fast speed. Rewind works in reverse: the supply reel rotates rapidly clockwise to wind the tape back on to the reel (Fig. 2-8).

To prevent tape spillage as the tape shuttles back and forth between fast forward, play, and rewind, the transport also includes electronic logic circuitry to apply braking at the right time, maintain the speed at a constant rate, and so on.

Inexpensive consumer tape recorders, through an intricate collection of pulleys, gears and levers, use one motor to drive the capstan and the supply and takeup reels. Studio decks use three separate motors: one each for the capstan, supply reel, and takeup reel. Not only does this approach eliminate pulleys and belts and gears (which need to be maintained and can be a source of trouble), but it also removes a fair amount of load from the capstan motor, which contributes to better speed reliability.

No matter what kind of analog machine you have, remember that if the pinch roller gets dirty and flaked with minute pieces of tape or dirt, the pinch roller's effective diameter increases, thus throwing off the speed. A dirty capstan will cause the same problem (see Chapter 22 for cleaning instructions).

Several enhancements have appeared over

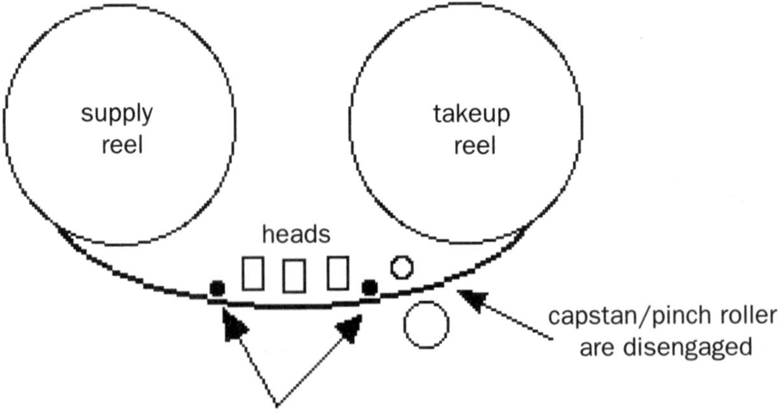


**Fig. 2-8:** *Top view of analog tape transport in fast forward or rewind mode.*

the years to improve transport performance. The *servo-controlled* transport provides extremely stable speed and has the bonus of allowing moderate tape speed changes. Conventional motors lock on to the frequency of AC house current (60 Hz in the USA, 50 Hz in Europe and many other parts of the world), and derive their accuracy from the AC power line frequency, which is typically accurate within 0.01%. It is very difficult to change the speed of these kinds of motors, as it's unlikely that the power companies are going to change the line frequency over to something else just so you can fiddle with your recorder. But a servo-system does not need to lock to the AC frequency and can receive correction information that yields a fairly wide pitch variation—typically, ±3% to ±10%. Better cassette decks, including multitrack types, incorporate servo-controlled motors.

## Connections

All tape recorders have at least two kinds of connectors, or jacks: a set of audio *input* jacks and a set of audio *output* jacks, with at least one of each jack for each channel. The signal you want to record goes into the input jacks; these may be called Rec In, Tape In, Line In, or whatever. Sometimes there will be two different types of input jacks, a Mic In jack and a Line In jack. The Mic In jack goes to a booster amplifier, called a *mic preamp,* which brings the (usually weak) microphone signals up to usable levels. The Line In jack accepts signals that are already at a suitable level, such as the signal from another tape recorder, synthesizers and drum machines, guitar amp preamp outputs, *etc.* It's best to go through the line inputs when possible since that bypasses any noise added by the mic preamp. Also, when feeding the mic inputs you can easily run into impedance or level mismatch problems that give distortion. The playback head connects by way of some electronics to the output jacks, which patch into your playback, or monitoring, system.

You might also find a headphone jack, so that you can monitor the tape directly at the machine. Other jacks may include a jack for a remote control adapter, a spare output, or some other function; but the important ones are the input and output jacks.

## Analog Recording Electronics

You can't just stick a signal into the record head and expect it to come out on tape. Due to the physics of tapes and heads, high-frequency response is harder to achieve than bass response. So, recorders have a built-in high-frequency boost called *pre-emphasis.* Since this can result in an overly bright sound on playback, a complementary *de-emphasis* circuit removes some of the highs (Fig. 2-9). This high-frequency cutting action also attenuates tape hiss, which is most noticeable at high frequencies.

There is also a circuit call a *bias oscillator.* Tape does not have a linear response; at very high and low levels there's distortion. There's not much we can do about distortion caused by overly loud signals other than turn down the input signal, but we can feed a constant signal onto the tape (the *bias* signal) to bring the level up past the point where severe distortion occurs. Any signals we want to record get added to this "background," and are therefore sufficiently high in level not to be plagued by distortion. So that we don't hear the constant background signal, the bias oscillator runs at a supersonic frequency.

If that wasn't clear, don't worry about it; we don't need to know a lot about bias oscillators, except for one aspect: when recording, different

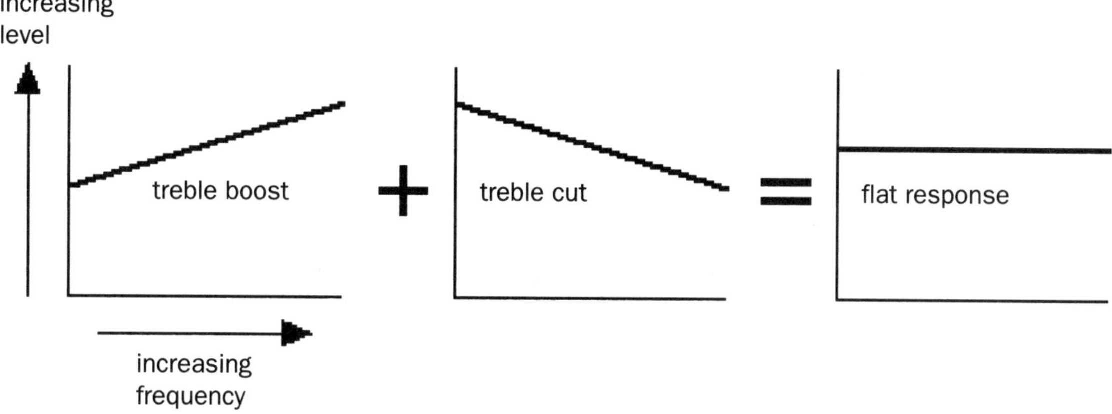


**Fig. 2-9:** *Adding treble emphasis while recording offsets the treble loss that occurs with analog tape; during playback, a complementary de-emphasis circuit restores flat response.*

types of tape require different levels of bias for optimum results (bias isn't used on playback, only during recording). The bias setting influences noise level, frequency response, and distortion. Unfortunately, these all interact, so setting the bias for minimum distortion will not give the best frequency response, while setting the bias for the best frequency response increases distortion. So, the bias setting is a compromise for the best average characteristics.

Most analog recorders have switches, knobs, or trimpots that allow you to change the bias for different kinds of tape, and also tend to include instructions on suggested settings for different brands of tape. Usually the recorder's bias oscillator is calibrated for a particular brand of tape (as stated in the owner's manual), and using that type of tape will give the best results. In fact, for machines that do not include external bias switches or controls, it is almost mandatory that you use the type of tape recommended by the manufacturer.

Incidentally, because cassettes need every possible ounce of performance squeezed out of them, Dolby created a process called Dolby HX. Not to be confused with Dolby noise reduction, this changes the bias at different recording levels to compensate for a cassette's natural lack of high frequency response; a tape with Dolby HX requires no decoding and has a far better-sounding high frequency range that cassettes recorded without Dolby HX.

## The Playback Electronics

There's nothing too exciting here. With more amplification and more frequency shaping, you end up hearing your sounds at the output jack.

## The VU Meter

VU (volume unit) meters are wonderful to look at, as their LEDs light up like a Christmas tree on methedrine. Their intended function is to monitor the signal level being put on the tape, because if you exceed the tape's signal-handling capacity, you generate distortion, which ends up as a "grunching" sound on playback. Most VU meters use multiple LEDs (up to ten or twenty) arranged to give a "bar graph" representation of signal strength, with different colors indicating different signal strengths—green for lower signal levels, yellow for signals approaching overload, and red for signals that reach or exceed the 0 VU (dB) point (Fig. 2-10). Other VU indicators use mechanical analog meters with pointers, or fluorescent displays (as often seen in upper-class cassette decks).

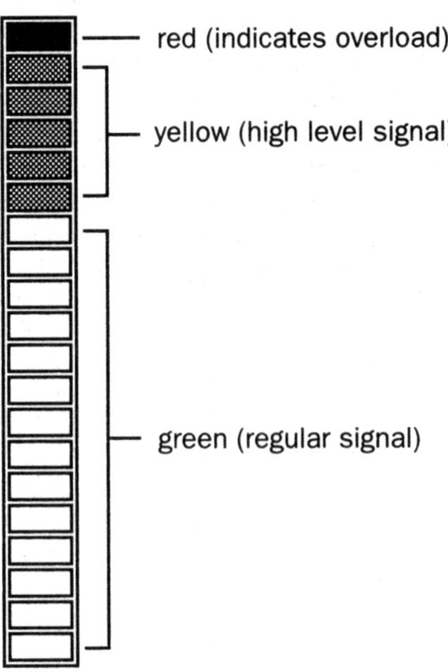


**Fig. 2-10:** *Typical LED VU meter; this one has twenty segments.*

Now, it would be great if all we had to do was look at the meter, and whenever the signal went into the red, we'd know that we had to turn down the level of the signal going to the record head. But meters are not that simple, because in the analog world, not all tapes react the same way. One may saturate and distort easily, yet with another you may be able to keep the pointer in the red most of the time and still obtain a good recording. Mechanical meters are the most difficult to interpret; the pointer has a certain amount of inertia, so while it can react to slowly changing signals adequately, the pointer lags behind sharply percussive sounds. These sounds may be over before the pointer had a chance to start moving, so although the meter didn't show you going into the red, the signal may have been there anyway.

When using mixing consoles, be aware that most meters will be switchable to monitor a variety of sources, such as aux bus outputs, post-fader outputs (useful when mixing), and the like. These functions are explained in Chapter 10 on mixing consoles.

Additionally, consoles don't always have a meter for each input channel—in such cases, a *channel activity LED* is a reasonable substitute. These are located at the input modules and simply show that audio is being received at a particular input. This is a good reality check for when you don't hear something you think you should be hearing, as you at least know the signal is making it to the board. Often these are bicolor LEDs so that red indicates clipping and green indicates activity.

In any event, the main reason for metering is to let you record at the highest level possible short of noticeable distortion. This is important because analog tape tends to have a residual amount of hiss, and nothing will remove it (although noise-reduction equipment can help; see Chapter 13). This hiss is unpleasantly audible and interferes with the music, especially during quiet passages. Although there's not much we can do to lower the hiss, we *can* raise the amount of signal compared to it, so that any hiss appears less noticeable.

From this, it's pretty clear that the more signal we get on the tape, the less noise we'll hear on playback. This concept is expressed as the *signal-to-noise ratio* (Fig. 2-11)—the higher

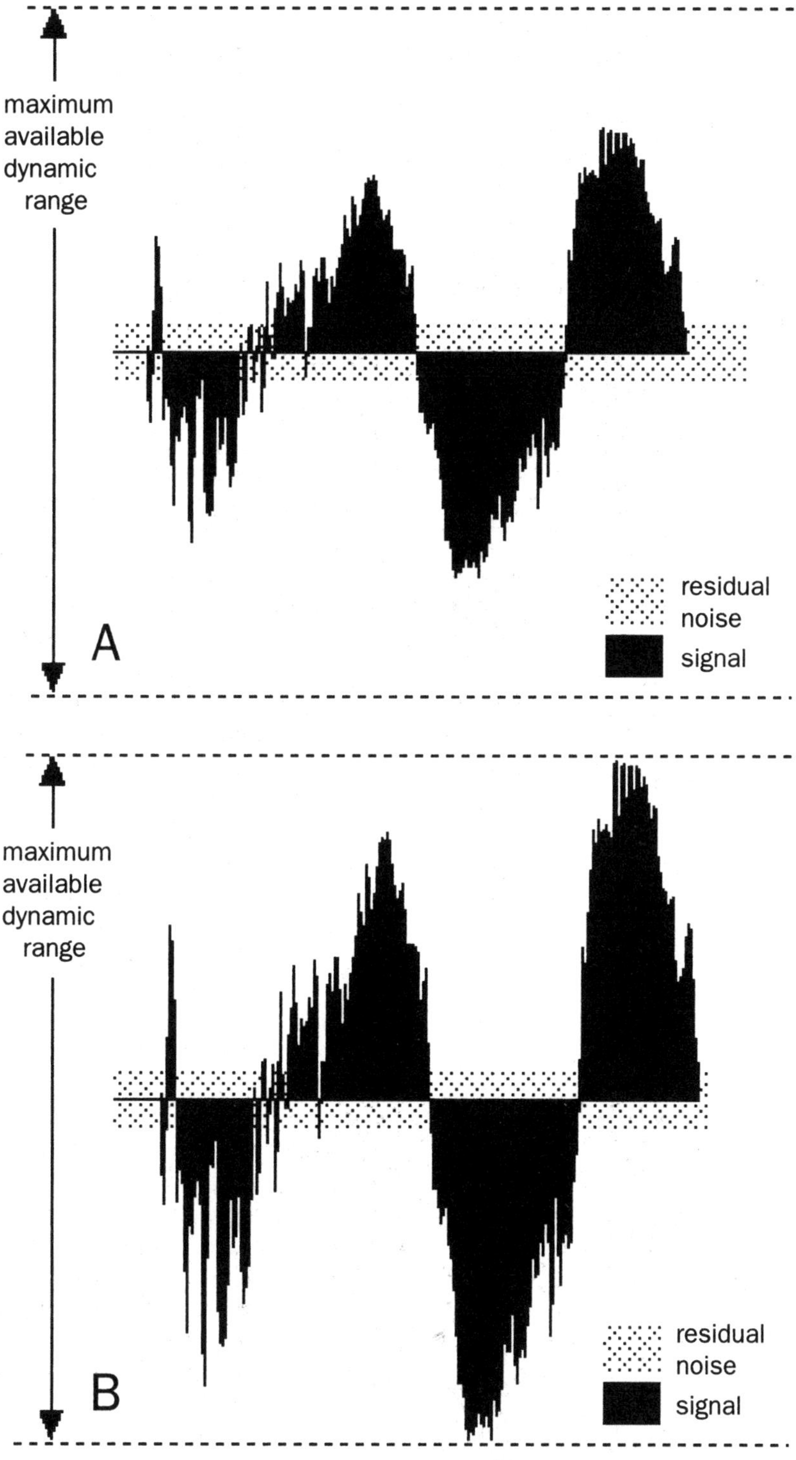


**Fig. 2-11:** *This is a pictorial representation of signal* versus *tape noise. In example A, the signal to noise ratio is lower than in example B. In B we have put more level on the tape, while still remaining within the maximum allowable dynamic range; this higher-level signal masks residual noise better than the under-recorded signal in A.*

the ratio, the quieter the machine. A decent analog tape recorder will have a signal-to-noise ratio of about 1000:1, which at least puts the noise in the background. It may sound like 1000:1 is a lot, but when you consider that your ear is so remarkably sensitive that it can discriminate dynamic changes of 1,000,000,000,000:1 (not a typo!), then it doesn't look so good; but it is adequate. Signal-to-noise is typically expressed in decibels, which we talked about earlier.

## Getting the Signal onto Tape

As mentioned previously, tape is composed of lots of little magnetic particles, attached to a plastic backing. The layer of particles is extremely thin and is measured in microns (1 micron = 1/1,000,000th of a meter). Because the particles are so small, the backing material must be very uniform or the particles will form an uneven surface (Fig. 2-12). An uneven backing prevents the tape from making good contact with the heads, and can cause dropouts where the sound simply disappears for a few milliseconds (or longer, if the tape is of poor quality).

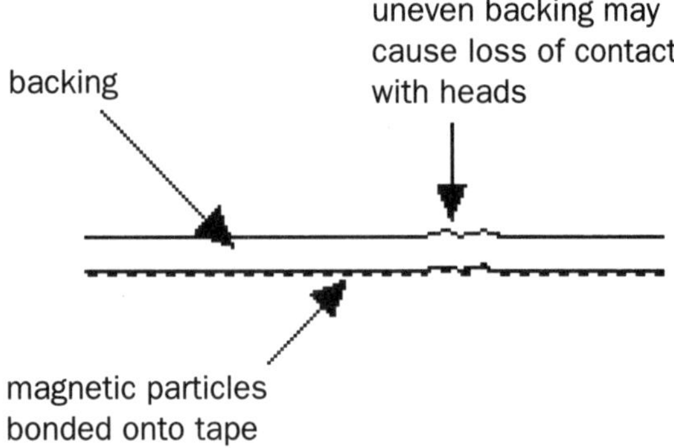


**Fig. 2-12:** *Exaggerated and magnified top view of tape.*

An important tape characteristic is the distribution of the magnetic particles with respect to density and uniformity. Since these particles carry the audio information, you want them to do the best possible job. One way to insure that they do is to pack as many particles on the tape as possible; this increases the potential fidelity, as we can illustrate by an analogy.

If you try to communicate a symbol, like the letter "R," by darkening a series of squares in a grid, the symbol's definition (or fidelity) improves as you increase the number of squares (Fig. 2-13). A similar process happens in recording; the more particles, the better the sound's definition. (This is also a preview of the next chapter, because in digital recording, more bits gives better resolution.)

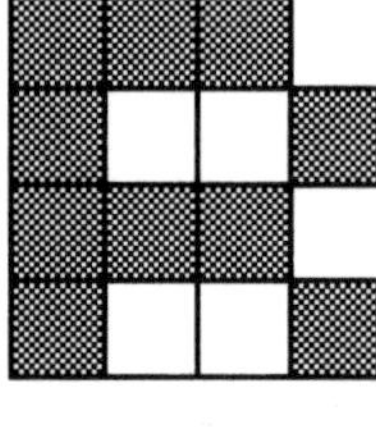

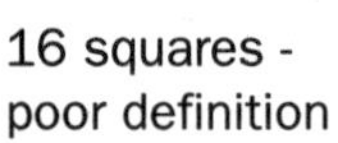


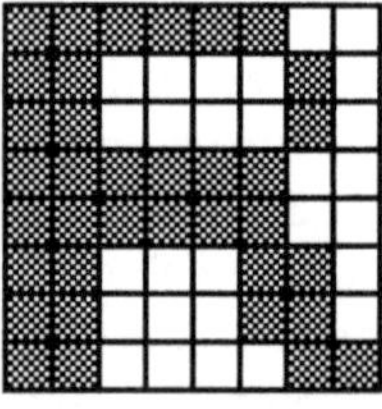


**Fig. 2-13:** *The more squares in a grid, the better the resolution. This is analogous to packing more particles onto tape.*

There is a limit to how many of these particles can be packed on a piece of tape, but we can also increase the number of particles that go past the tape head *in a given period of time* by increasing the tape's speed. For example, suppose a sound lasts exactly one second, and we apply that sound to the record head. If the tape is running at 7.5 ips, then 7.5 inches of tape will go past that record head in one second, and present a certain amount of particles to the head for magnetization. Increasing the speed to 15 ips allows twice as much tape to go past the head in the same amount of time, making twice the amount of particles available for magnetization. This increases the fidelity, and explains why consumer cassette recorders, which only run at 1.875 ips, are so picky about having the best tape possible: you can't increase the speed to improve the performance. (Note, however, that some multitrack cassette decks operate at 3.75 ips for better fidelity.)

Summing up, regarding tape fidelity, the most important factors are:

- The amount of signal level we can put on the tape, to provide the best possible signal-to-noise ratio
- The density of the particles on tape
- The amount of high frequencies we can put on the tape, since that is usually ~~where~~ tape performance falls off the most.

## About Track Width

Along with tape speed, *track width* also affects the potential fidelity. To understand this particular concept a little better, we need to look a little at the tape recorder's evolution.

There are many contradictory stories about just who invented the first recorder and when; however, we do know that the very first machines didn't use tape, but rather wire, and were called wire recorders. When magnetic tape was introduced in Germany, the record head would record signals over the full width of the tape.

This is an example of a full-track, monophonic tape recorder (Fig. 2-14).

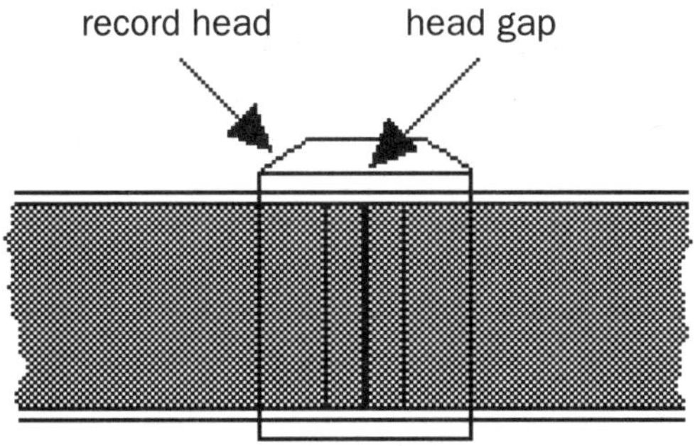


**Fig. 2-14:** *A full-track recorder records over the full width of the track.*

Next, someone got the idea to split the head into two independent, smaller, record heads, and record in stereo; *half-track recording* is when each track occupies half the tape (Fig. 2-15).

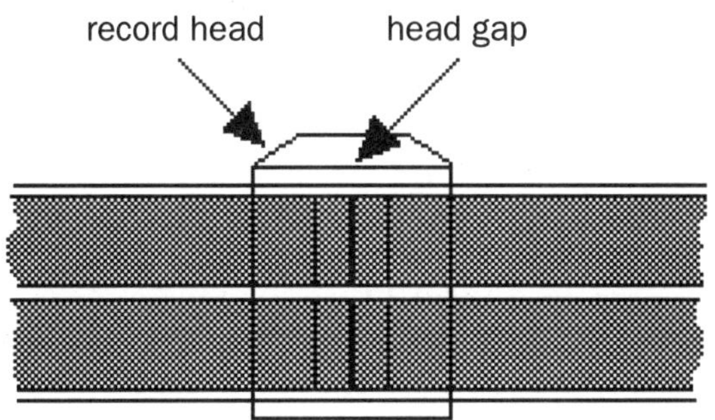


**Fig. 2-15:** *A half-track recorder splits the tape into two halves, and records an independent signal on each track. This allows for recording stereo audio on a single piece of tape.*

However, we paid for this privilege with two tracks of tape hiss as well as two tracks of signal, and we decreased the amount of tape available to each of the two record heads. However, none of these problems was considered serious enough to offset the extra flexibility, so in the 1960s, we progressed to the consumer *quarter-track* reel-to-reel recording format, which became a little more complicated. There were still two record areas in the head, but they were staggered. So, when we put on a tape, we could record two stereo tracks, with each track taking up a quarter of the tape (Fig. 2-16).

Then, we could turn the tape over, and record two more stereo tracks on the remaining half of the tape (Fig. 2-17).

But now we paid another price: we could not make splices in the tape anymore, at least not without interfering with the information going the other way on the tape (Fig. 2-18). In professional applications, where splicing and editing is important, tapes are always recorded in one direction only.

Luckily for us, head technology didn't stop there. Soon, four record heads were put in a line, and now we had four-channel (or *quad* recording), because we could record four separate tracks. This evolved to eight record heads in a line for eight-channel recording, then sixteen for sixteen-track, and so on.

Although in theory we reduced the fidelity somewhat by narrowing the tracks, improve-

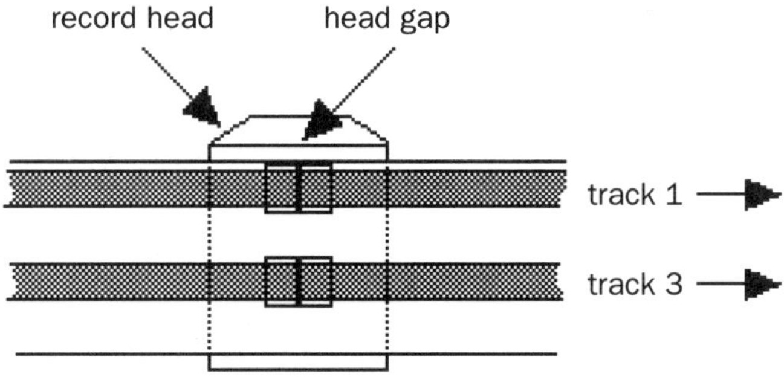


**Fig. 2-16:** *The quarter-track format splits the tape into quarters, and records on two of the quarters (tracks).*

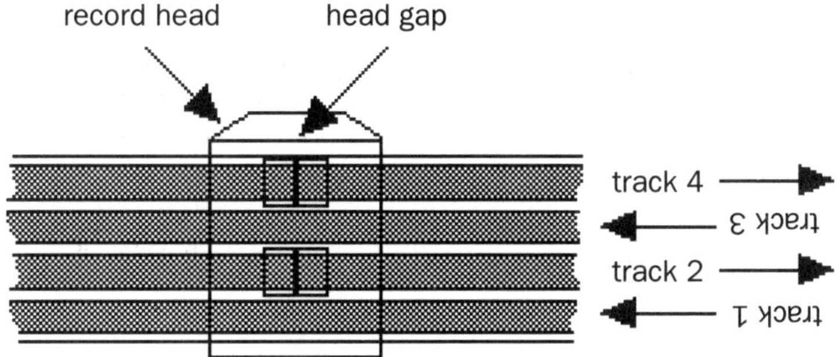


**Fig. 2-17:** *Flip the tape over, and the previously recorded tracks now go in the opposite direction, out of the way of the head gaps, and we can record on the other two quarters of the tape.*

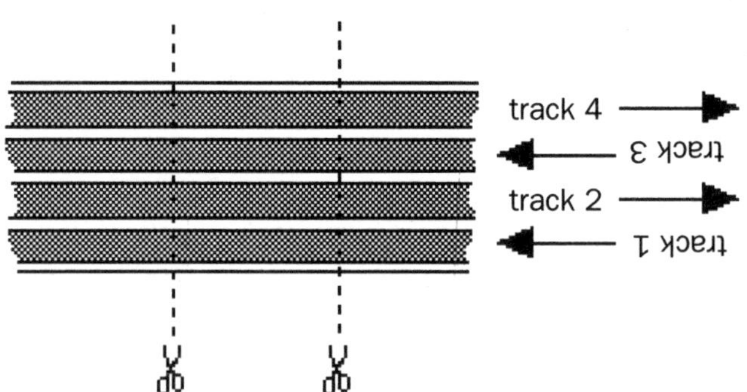


**Fig. 2-18:** *If we splice out a section to remove a sound on tracks 1 and 3, then we also remove part of tracks 2 and 4, whether we want to or not.*

ments in recording electronics, tape formulations, noise reduction, and other whizbang technological events have compensated. But perhaps the most important addition to the recorder, at least from a musician's standpoint, is *synchronized overdubbing* (not to be confused with machine synchronization, as described in Chapter 14).

## Synchronized Overdubbing

When a musician can listen to some previously recorded music and simultaneously add a new part without affecting the other parts, the new part is called an *overdub*. For example, suppose you have a multitrack recorder, and a trio of guitar, bass, and drums. You could record rhythm guitar on track 1, bass on track 2, and drums on track 3. Then the guitarist could overdub a lead part in track 4 while listening to tracks 1, 2, and 3.

This process may not sound complicated, but it is, because overdubbing must be done in synchronization with the basic track. There would be no point in putting a lead guitar solo on a track if it was going to be half a beat late all the way through, and that's the difficulty we face with older tape recorders (newer tape recorders have solved this problem; we'll describe how at the end of this section). Here's why.

As the tape travels past the playback head, we hear the sounds on the tape. But remember that the tape passes by the record head *before* it hits the playback head; if we monitor a sound from the playback head while recording a signal into the record head, it will not go on the tape at the same physical location as the sounds we hear, but rather at the record head (Fig. 2-19). On playback the overdub would come in late—and sound terrible because it would not be synchronized with the original signal.

But luckily, some astute engineering lets you monitor a signal at the record head, so you don't have to wait for the signal to pass the playback head in order to hear it (Fig. 2-20). The traditional name for this technique is Selective Synchronization or *Sel-Sync,* a name originated (and owned) by Ampex. Other companies use other terms, but the net result is the same. When you switch a track into sync mode, it's listening to the record head.

Again, there's somewhat of a compromise since, as pointed out earlier, heads don't like to do double duty. The solution is to optimize the record head for recording only, and just ignore the playback qualities—they really don't matter because, after all, we are simply monitoring the tape for the purposes of synchronizing an overdub. When you want to hear all the tracks in glorious full fidelity, then you monitor off the playback head.

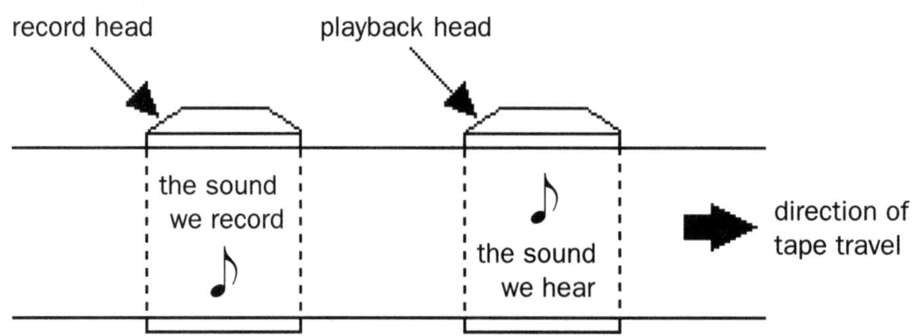


**Fig. 2-19:** *Without synchronization, when we hear a sound at the playback head and record an overdub at the record head, the sounds are separated on the tape. Thus, on playback the original sound plays back before the overdubbed sound.*

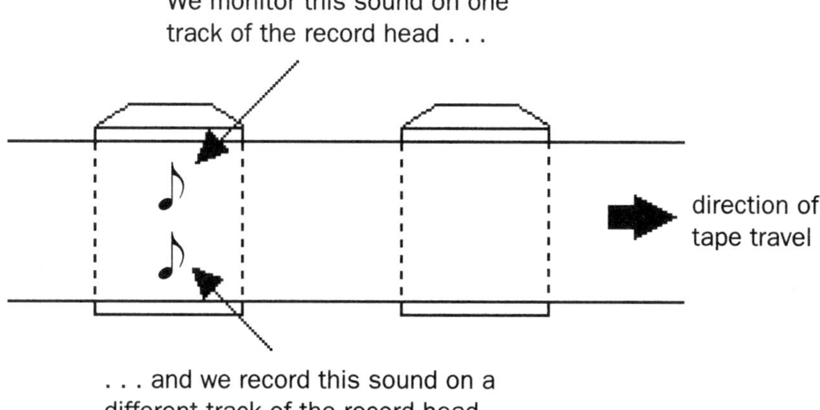


**Fig. 2-20:** *With synchronization, where we monitor from the record head, on playback both sounds hit the playback head at the same time.*

Frankly, though, modern head and electronics technology is such that playing back from the record head can sound just as good as the playback head. Only really old decks have an obvious quality change between the record and playback heads.

Furthermore, these days almost all budget analog multitracks use the same head for recording and playback, thus simplifying matters even further since you don't have to worry about where to monitor. The quality of today's devices is such that there is no audible compromise due to using a single head to do both record and playback functions.

## Tape Recorder Switches

In addition to the sync switch, there will also be an output switch that routes audio to the tape recorder output. The output switch *source* position monitors the signal going into the recorder. In the *tape* position, which works only when the tape is running, you monitor directly from the tape—either by way of the playback head, or from the record head if sync mode is selected. If you monitor the tape position while playing an instrument, the signal from the recorder will appear delayed; nonetheless, by listening directly to the tape it is easy to tell if the recording levels are too high (giving distortion), or if the tape has any imperfections.

## Cassette Multitracks

In an interview with Andy Summers (guitarist for the Police, a band that was very popular in the late seventies and early eighties), he stated that shortly after installing a sixteen-track studio in his home, he ended up selling it all and getting a cassette-based multitrack. Why? Because when translating ideas on to tape, he didn't want to have to fiddle with lots of dials and machines; he just wanted to record something quick-and-dirty on tape before the inspiration left him.

For many musicians the cassette-based multitrack is the perfect introduction into the world of analog recording. These devices are inexpensive to own and maintain, and can produce surprisingly good results. Let's talk a bit about cassette multitrack decks, and why they've remained popular for so many years.

When cassettes were first introduced, they were never intended for high-fidelity applications since one of the rules of analog recording is that the slower the speed and the narrower the tape, the worse the fidelity. The cassette—crawling along at 1.875 ips and using 1/8" wide tape—seemed useless for anything other than dictation and recording messages on phone answering machines. Over a period of about a decade, the quality of cassette tape improved dramatically, tape speed was sometimes doubled to 3.75 ips, noise reduction became a viable way to control tape hiss, and even the transports themselves became far more reliable and accurate.

The cassette format does have some inherent compromises compared to standard reel-to-reel recorders:

- Noise. Cassette recorders are noisier, although noise reduction (Dolby B, Dolby C, Dolby S, and dbx) certainly helps matters. Still, while you can make good quality tapes on a reel-to-reel without noise reduction, a cassette multitrack demands noise reduction. In fact, some models won't let you switch out noise reduction even if you want to.
- Crosstalk. Because the tracks are spaced so closely together, sometimes the sound from one track will "spill over" to another track. In most instances, this is not a serious problem. However, if you're a perfectionist trying to audition one track, hearing other tracks leaking through can be annoying.

- Headroom. Reel-to-reel decks can accept some pretty drastic overloads and still sound acceptable. Cassette multitracks are far less forgiving; distortion and tape saturation occur quite rapidly past a certain point. As a result, recording a signal with wide dynamic range on a cassette multitrack often requires recording at a fairly low volume (thus risking increased noise) to keep signal peaks from saturating the tape.
- High frequency response. Cassettes have difficulty reproducing high frequencies. The highs on a quality reel-to-reel sound cleaner and smoother.
- Compromises in technique. On older models, you may not be able to record on all four tracks at once. Also, you often cannot monitor off the tape itself, so you won't know whether a recording was successful until you actually play it back.

Cassette multitracks also offer several advantages compared to reel-to-reel models. First is size; cassette multitrackers fit into even the most crowded environment. Second is economy of operation. Not only are cassette multitracks less expensive to purchase initially, tape costs are less (even though you must use premium, high-bias cassettes). Maintenance also tends to be less expensive; cassette machines don't require the powerful motors associated with reel-to-reel decks (thus improving reliability), and should the heads wear out, they're generally less expensive to replace than the heads for reel-to-reel machines—a replacement head stack for a pro twenty-four-track costs thousands of dollars!

## About Analog Tape

Stated as simply as possible, buy the best tape possible, consistent with the recommendations of your machine's manufacturer. Tape is the initial basis of your sound quality.

Analog tape comes in different thicknesses; one 7" reel may have 1800 feet of tape, whereas another may have 2400 feet. The difference is that the longer tape is a thinner tape. Although acceptable for consumer situations, thin tapes can cause problems in the studio environment. They are more susceptible to *print-through,* where signals from one layer of wound tape alter signals on an adjoining layer of tape. They are also more fragile, and have a greater tendency to stretch or deform under repeated back and forth tape motion. So, given a choice of two reels of tape occupying the same size reel, take the one with the lowest number of feet unless you *really* need the extra recording time.

Because the quality of analog tape directly affects the overall sound quality, before settling on any specific type, try several available brands and see if any one develops a particularly good relationship with your machine. Once you've found a favorite, then buy it in quantity and save some bucks compared to the single-piece pricing.

The rules for buying cassette tape are similar: use a type designed for music, don't use the extra-long, 120-minute cassettes, and get a tape that's compatible with your recorder. This last point is a little more difficult to deal with than it was with reel-to-reel, as cassette machines are more finicky in their choice of tape.

Avoid house brand and unmarked tapes, and stick to reputable brands. Inferior tape can cause all kinds of problems. Good tape costs money, but the reduced aggravation compensates for the extra cost. Isn't your music worth it?

Here are three more tips about analog tape:

- Always fast forward and rewind a new tape a couple of times before using it; this "unpacks" the tape.
- Leave a minute or two of blank tape at the beginning and end (the ends are the most prone to having quality problems).
- Store all tapes in a cool, dry environment. Heat and humidity increase print-through, and over time, can cause a substantial decrease in sound quality. Making safety copies on a digital deck, either DAT or multitrack, can give you a little extra security.

## The Bottom Line on Analog

Improved tape formulations, multitrack technology, noise reduction units, and super-accurate tape transports have all contributed greatly to the ever-improving quality of analog recorders. These systems are by no means perfect, but many engineers and musicians still prefer the sound of analog technology over digital, not because it necessarily produces better measurable results (although sometimes it can), but because of the way that analog tape "processes" the sound—for example, a little tape saturation can give a very desirable rock drum sound.

Still, analog recording will always have to deal with tape hiss and the deterioration that occurs when copying from one analog medium to another. Digital recording technology, described in the next chapter, solves these and several other problems.

# Chapter 3
# Digital Recording

Although analog recording has served us well for decades, it has limitations such as high frequency saturation, distortion, hiss, wow, and flutter. When you duplicate a master tape using analog techniques (*e.g.,* when making cassettes), other problems will occur due to the flawed nature of the analog transfer process. In fact, every time you copy an analog sound, the sound quality deteriorates.

Digital recording removes some of the variables from the recording and playback process by converting audio into a string of numbers ("encoding" the audio), then processing these numbers—*not the sound itself.* In a bit, we'll see why this improves the sound.

## Digital Recording Theory

Digital recording follows a chain of events similar to analog recording (capture a signal with an input stage, store it, and play it back through an output stage), but uses different technology. It takes advantage of the fact that all sound—no matter how complex—can be represented as an individual waveform whose level varies over time. For example, Fig. 3-1A shows one cycle of a complex string section sound.

A digital system's input stage is an *analog-to-digital converter* (ADC), which "samples" the audio input signal at typically either 44,100 or 48,000 times per second (Fig. 3-1B). Each sample measures the voltage level at the instant the sample occurred, and holds this level until the next sample. Each level corresponds to a particular voltage, so this series of voltage readings—expressed as numbers—represents the waveform.

These numbers are then shuttled onto a storage medium such as digital tape or a *hard disk,* a computer accessory that can store *lots* of numbers (whether they're from an accounting program or are an audio waveform's data). Like tape, hard disks also store signals as magnetic patterns, but on hard circular platters that spin at a very high rate of speed. Also like tape, there's a record/playback head (input transducer and output transducer respectively).

The output stage is a *digital-to-analog*

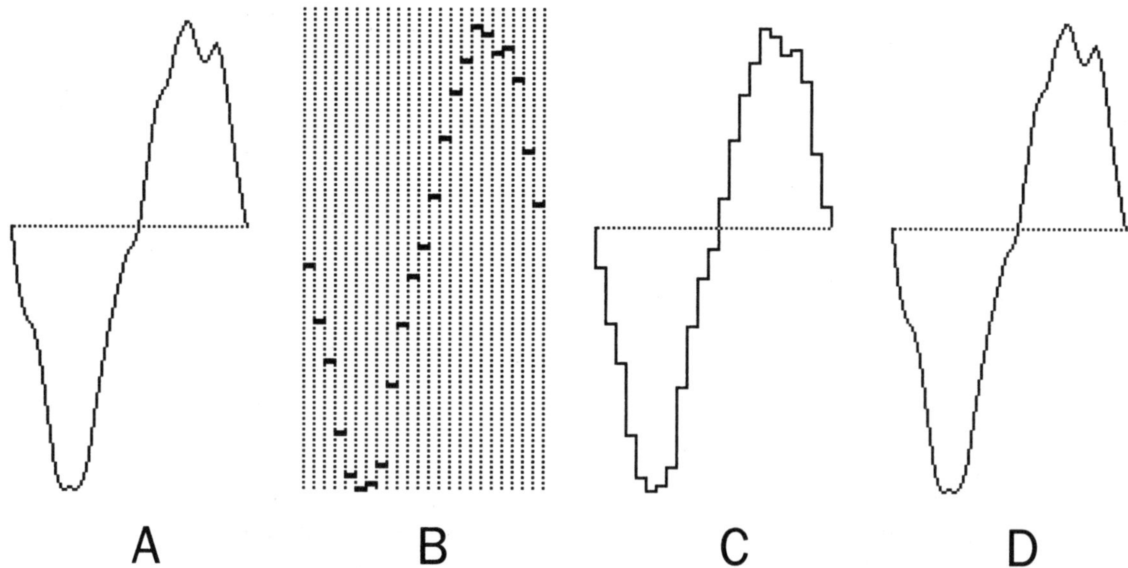


**Fig. 3-1:** *(A) shows the original analog waveform, which is sampled at the rate shown in (B). Each value is stored in some kind of storage medium (tape, computer memory, etc.). On playback, these values are reconstructed to create the waveform shown in (C). This then passes through a smoothing filter to give the final waveform shown in (D).*

*converter (DAC)* that reads the numbers from the hard disk or digital tape and reconstructs an audio waveform (Fig. 1C). Note that because we didn't take an infinite number of samples, but only at a particular rate, that the waveform has a "stairstep" look. A final *lowpass filter* removes high frequencies above the audio range, which smoothes out the stairsteps to more accurately reproduce the original signal.

While converting music into numbers and back into music again may seem like a roundabout way to record, a digitally encoded signal is not subject to deterioration in the same way as an analog signal. Consider the Compact Disc, which stores digital information (data) on a disc. A laser reads this data, and a DAC converts the data back into analog signals. Because of this approach, if a small piece of dust lands on the disc it may not matter—the laser recognizes only numbers, and will tend to ignore extraneous information. Back in the days of vinyl records, the same piece of dust could create a pop since the stylus couldn't differentiate between music and noise.

What is more important, digital audio storage preserves quality during mixdowns, transfers, and duplication. For example, mixing a conventional analog multitrack tape down to an analog two-track tape introduces some sound degradation due to limits of the two-track machine. If you make an analog safety copy from that tape, there's further degradation. Matters get even worse if cassettes are duplicated from the safety copy.

Now suppose we mix down an analog multitrack tape to a two-track DAT (Digital Audio Tape) recorder, which stores sounds as numbers. When it's time to make a safety copy of the DAT to another DAT, the safety tape records *numbers* (not the actual signal). Thus, the copy is a clone of—not just analogous to—the original signal. We can also take the DAT's digital signal and transfer it directly to Compact Disc. No quality is lost during these transfers, not only because we're using numbers, but because digital systems store redundant data and have sophisticated error correction schemes just in case problems occur (such as a tape dropout, where some of the oxide is missing).

With a digital recording playing back through a Compact Disc, the ADC at the beginning of the signal chain has already "freeze dried" the sound, which is not reconstituted until it hits the DAC in the listener's CD player. This is why digital audio sounds so clean: it hasn't been subjected to the petty humiliations endured by an analog signal as it works its way from studio to home stereo speaker.

However, digital audio is not perfect and has different limitations compared to analog technology, such as:

- Sampling rate. The more often we measure a signal's amplitude (the sampling rate), the more accurately this defines the signal. Doubling the sampling rate in Fig. 3-1B would make the waveform in Fig. 3-1C look half as jagged. However, more samples require more memory for storage, and memory isn't cheap. A rate of 44,100 samples per second for CDs and 48,000 for DAT was chosen as a suitable compromise between sound quality and practicality. These values are often expressed as 44.1 kHz and 48 kHz.

  Nor is the reconstruction process perfect. Consider Fig. 3-2, which shows two different waveforms being sampled at the same sampling rate. The original waveforms are the light lines, each sample is taken at the time indicated by the vertical dashed line, and the heavy black line indicates what the waveform looks like after sampling. 3-2A is a reasonably good approximation of the waveform, but 3-2B just happens to have each sample land on a peak of the waveform, so there is no amplitude difference between samples, and the resulting waveform looks nothing at all like the original. Thus, what comes out of the DAC can, in extreme cases, be transformed into an entirely different waveform from what went into the ADC.

  The solution to the above problems is to make sure that enough samples are taken to adequately represent the signal being sampled. One of the basic laws of digital audio is the Nyquist theorem, which states that the sampling frequency should be at least twice as high as the highest frequency being sampled. There is some controversy as to whether the current *de facto* sampling rates of 44.1 and 48 kHz are high enough, but that's a controversy we won't get into here. (As of this writing, DATs are becoming available with 96 kHz sampling rates.)

  *Oversampling* is another technique that improves performance. For example, with two-times (2X) oversampling, the DAC looks at two consecutive samples, calculates the halfway point between them with respect to level, and places an additional sample between the two original samples. This produces a less stairstep-looking output, which allows the use of gentler, less drastic filters.

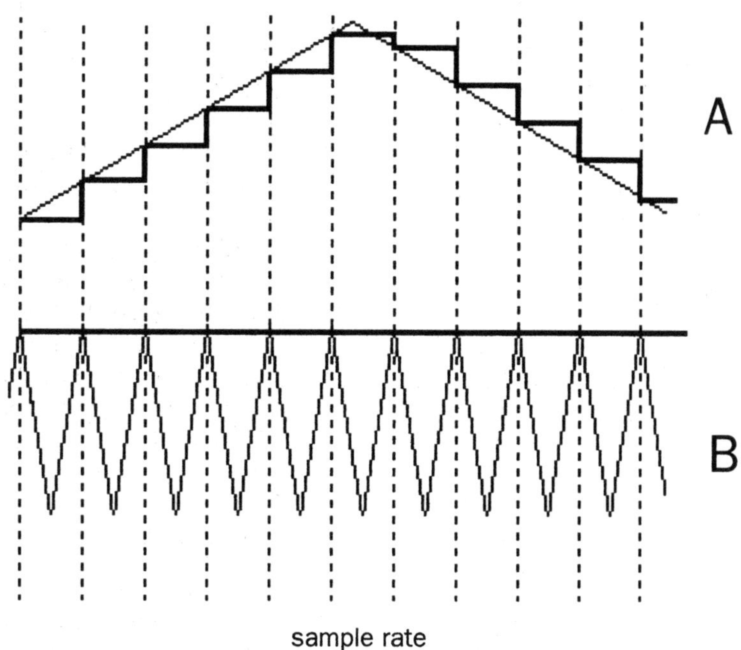


Fig. 3-2

Note that sample rate converters capable of translating between devices having different sample rates are available in hardware- and software-based systems. However, sample rate conversion can cause subtle sonic degradation, so it's prudent in a digital setup to use a consistent sample rate. If you're planning to release your final product on CD, the sample rate of choice is 44.1 kHz.

- Filter coloration. As mentioned earlier, we need a filter after the DAC to convert the stairstep samples into something smooth and continuous. Unfortunately filters can add their own coloration, and some audiophiles feel that the treble response of digital audio systems is adversely affected by this filtering.

- Quantization (resolution). Another sampling problem relates to how accurately the ADC can measure the input voltage. Suppose a digital audio system can resolve levels to 10 mv (1/100th of a volt). With this system, a level of 10 mv would be assigned one number, a level of 20 mv another number, a level of 30 mv yet another number, and so on. Now suppose the computer is trying to sample a 15 mv signal—does it consider this a 10 mv or 20 mv signal? In either case, the sample does not correspond exactly to the original input level, thus producing a quantization error. Interestingly, note that digital audio has more difficulty resolving lower levels (where each quantized level represents a large portion of the overall signal level) than higher levels (where each quantized level represents a small portion of the overall signal level). Thus, unlike analog gear where distortion increases at high amplitudes, digital systems tend to exhibit more distortion at lower levels. (Of course, extremely high level signals can also cause distortion.)

- Dynamic range errors. A computer cannot resolve an infinite number of quantized levels; therefore, the number of levels it can resolve represents the dynamic range of the system. Computers express numbers in terms of binary digits (or "bits"), and the greater the number of bits, the greater the number of voltage levels it can quantize. For example, a 4-bit system can quantize 16 levels, an 8-bit system 256 levels, and a 16-bit system 65,536 levels. Clearly, a 16-bit system offers far greater dynamic range and less quantization error than 4- or 8-bit systems. Incidentally, there's a simple formula to determine dynamic range in dB based on the bits used in a digital audio system: the dynamic range equals approximately six times the number of bits. Thus, a 16-bit system offers around 96 dB of dynamic range.

## The Evolution of Digital Audio Recording

Analog audio takes up a relatively modest bandwidth—20 Hz to 20 kHz. Digital audio has a much higher-bandwidth data stream and cannot be recorded on tape using conventional analog techniques.

As a result, the first digital audio devices to become popular in home and project studios were adapters for video decks, since they can record very high-bandwidth signals (the most popular adapter was Sony's PCM-F1, which had a sampling rate of 44.056 kHz). These adapters took an analog signal and converted it into a high-bandwidth data stream capable of being recorded on standard VCRs. The biggest problem was incompatibility between video decks; inexpensive, consumer-level VHS decks would sometimes mistrack, so Beta decks (Sony's now-obsolete consumer video format) were generally the deck of choice for home applications. (Pros typically used the Sony PCM-1630 adapter, which still remains a standard for CD mastering and is almost invariably used in conjunction with U-Matic, 3/4" pro video decks.)

The reason video decks can handle the higher bandwidth is due to the use of rotating heads. Although the tape moves relatively slowly, a video head spins at a high rate of speed, creating extremely thin diagonal tracks on tape (Fig. 3-3). Because the head spins so fast, it simulates the effect of the tape going by at an extremely high rate of speed. As we mentioned in the previous chapter, the higher the tape speed, the greater the number of particles that can be magnetized, and the higher the frequencies that can be recorded.

In the mid eighties, Digital Audio Tape (DAT) was introduced. This was essentially a miniature VCR optimized for audio recording and based on rotating head technology. Although DAT tape is the same width as a standard analog audio cassette, and moves at only 8.15 mm/second, because of the rotating head design the relative tape speed is a little over three meters (more than nine feet!) per second. DAT established a standard of 16-bit resolution with a 48 kHz sampling rate.

Many digital multitracks are also based on video technology; the first low-cost digital multitrack deck, the Alesis ADAT, used a modified industrial-quality S-VHS video transport with a rotating head created specifically for recording multitrack digital audio, while Tascam's DA-88 was based on Hi-8 video technology. Because the multitracks are modular in the sense that you can stack them to obtain more tracks, they are often referred to as Modular Digital Multitracks, or MDMs (a term coined by our esteemed technical editor).

There are also *stationary head* digital recording systems, as used mainly with early pro-level digital multitracks, because these allow for simpler tape editing than rotating head–based systems. On the consumer level, Philips' ill-fated Digital Compact Cassette format (DCC) also used a stationary head; however, rotating head systems are in the majority.

With hard disk-based digital recording (described in detail later), the transducer is more like a conventional tape head that hovers above a rotating magnetic platter and imprints magnetic information onto the disk.

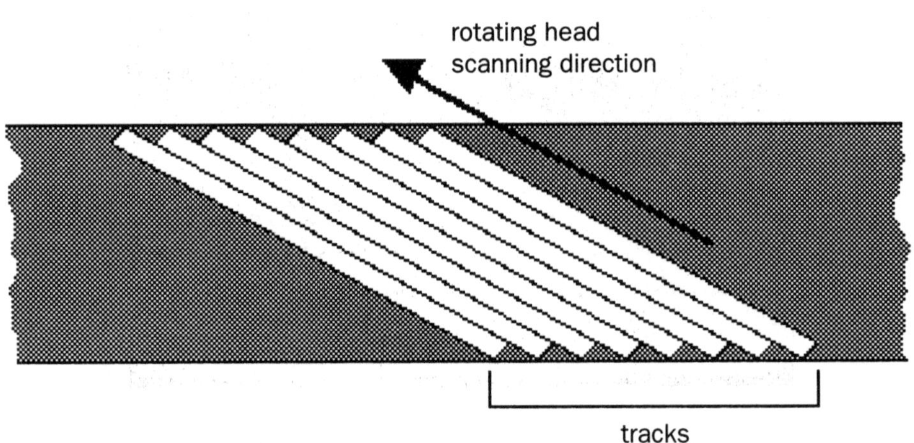


**Fig. 3-3:** *A rotating head records data on tape in a series of extremely thin diagonal tracks. This diagram also makes it clear why you can't just splice a VCR tape with a razor blade; you'd be cutting across a variety of bits and pieces of various tracks.*

## Digital Tape Transports

As mentioned, these resemble video decks. The controls work similarly for both multitracks and DATS.

- Stop. The tape does not move, and the head does not spin.
- Play. Since the head doesn't spin when stopped, if you enter play or record mode, it takes a few seconds to engage the tape and have it contact the head. This is like a VCR, where pressing play after the unit has been stopped does not result in instantaneous playback. However, going into play from the pause mode (described next) results in faster playback.
- Pause. When you don't want to wait, pause mode keeps the head spinning, even when stopped. In this mode, when you press play, playback begins almost immediately. As with video decks, if you leave the deck paused for too long it will automatically stop and disengage the head as a safety measure to prevent excessive tape wear.
- Rewind and Fast Forward. These work like regular recorders: rewind takes you closer to the beginning of the tape, and fast forward goes closer to the end.
- Review and Cue. These modes are similar to rewind and fast forward respectively, but maintain contact between the tape and head so you can hear what's on the tape as it whizzes by. You usually enter these modes by pressing rewind or fast forward while the tape is playing (do *not* press stop first). Cue and review speeds are slower than rewind and fast forward but faster than normal playback; although the monitored sound won't be high fidelity, it's good enough to indicate where you are on the tape. Review and cue cause more tape and head wear than rewind and fast forward because more of the tape is in contact with the head. By the way, if you think your MDM is slow in rewind or fast forward, make sure you're not in review or cue mode instead.
- Record. Depending on the model, you either push this button by itself to enter record, or push record while holding play.

As hard disk recording devices are computer-based, they don't have transports per se, although standard transport functions are emulated in software. These are displayed on-screen and usually configured like regular transport controls (Fig. 3-4). However, some HDR systems also allow for a mechanical interface or remote with various buttons and switches, some of which are configured like a tape transport.

## Making Connections

Since this is not an all-digital world (yet), digital decks usually have a full complement of jacks to interface with the analog world (see the previous chapter for a complete description of the jacks found with tape decks). However, there will often be digital inputs and outputs as well that carry digital data. There are four main types (if you're not familiar with the connector types mentioned, see the end of Chapter 7 on Electricity and Wiring).

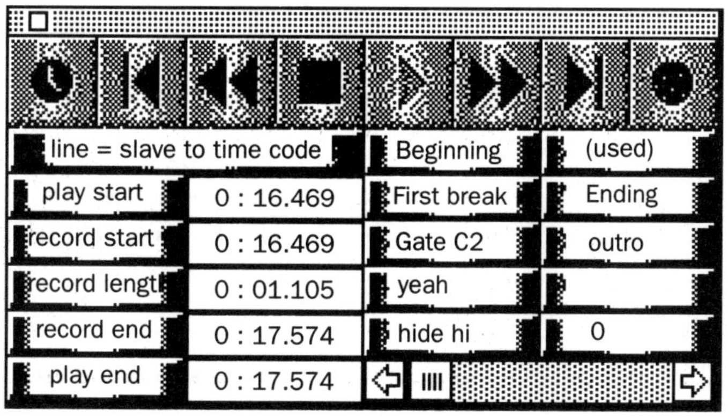

**Fig. 3-4:** *The "transport" controls for a typical computer-based hard disk recording program, Pro Tools by Digidesign; these show up on-screen, as a "window" in the monitor. If you use a mouse to click on the record button (top right corner), the system starts recording. The other buttons with arrows indicate play, rewind, fast forward, etc. The lower part of the transport shows various autolocation points (as described in Chapter 19 on Automation).*

- AES/EBU. This is a professional, two-channel digital audio protocol developed jointly by the Audio Engineering Society and the European Broadcast Union. It is usually carried by XLR (three-pin) connectors or fiber-optic cables.
- S/PDIF (Sony/Philips Digital Interface). This is a consumer-oriented version of the AES/EBU protocol that generally uses RCA phono jacks, although a fiber-optic version of S/PDIF is found on some consumer hi-fi gear.
- MADI. For pro-level multichannel digital decks and mixers, a MADI cable transfers up to fifty-six tracks of digital audio. This is not a commonly used standard for project studio gear.
- Proprietary. Not all decks follow a particular standard (as the old saying goes, "people must like standards . . . there are so many of them"), so they implement a proprietary transfer method. For example, the Alesis ADAT can transfer eight channels of digital audio over a fiber-optic cable; other companies make ADAT-compatible gear that can communicate using the same protocol.

Digital hookups aren't much different from analog ones, with one exception: these signals run at a much higher frequency than standard audio. Fiber-optic cables have no problem with this, but conventional wire cables must be capable of handling high frequencies. In many cases, standard audio cables are not satisfactory. There are also other problems such as clock stability and jitter; we'll get into those later in Chapter 14.

## VU Meters and Digital Audio

Unlike analog recording, going over 0 VU with digital doesn't yield a satisfyingly pleasant grunge, but a nasty, splattering, overloaded sound. As a result, it's very important to pay attention to that 0 VU point. Some digital gear has a "peak hold" option that holds a reading if it exceeds 0 VU. That way, just in case you miss seeing the meter going over 0 VU, you'll know that this level was exceeded.

## Level Matching and Standardization

Combining analog and digital gear can lead to some confusion regarding levels. For example, with an analog mixing board, the 0 VU level is not the maximum level the device can handle; there will be 10 or 20 dB of headroom (maybe even more) to accommodate peaks. However, with digital gear, 0 VU is the maximum level that the device can accommodate. So if you send a test signal into the mixer at 0 VU, then calibrate the digital recorder's input so that the same tone gives a 0 VU reading, any peaks above 0 VU in the mixer will turn into distortion when it goes digital. As a result, DAT and tape machine manufacturers often calibrate the inputs so that a 0 VU analog signal reads –12 or –15 VU on the recorder's meters. This allows for, respectively, 12 or 15 dB of headroom. This reference level has not been standardized at the time of this writing, but should be in the near future.

## Digital Deck Switches

As with analog decks, there will be switches to select between the input or tape output. But you'll find several other switches, such as:

- Sampling rate. Sometimes you'll be able to choose among 44.1, 48, and even some "oddball" sampling rates like 32 kHz (to save memory) and 44.056 (for compatibility with the Sony PCM-F1).
- Digital/analog input. This chooses whether the signal source will be the analog input jacks or the digital inputs (*e.g.*, AES/EBU or S/PDIF connectors).
- AES/EBU or S/PDIF. This selects the type of digital audio transfer protocol.

## About Digital Tape

The tape you use in tape-based systems is crucial. Unlike analog recording, where the quality of the tape directly affects the sound, with digital tape recording the tape is crucial from a mechanical and reliability standpoint.

There are currently two types of tape used in project studio digital multitrack recording, S-VHS for ADAT format machines and Hi-8 for Tascam format. In either case, buy the highest quality, industrial-grade tape you can find. Several manufacturers make tape designed specifically for digital multitracks, although any high-quality tape seems to do the job (sometimes even better).

Concerning DAT, since DAT has become a more or less pro medium, most DAT tapes are now made with pro use in mind and have highly evolved shells and formulations. There are two common types of DAT tape, those designed for audio applications and those designed for computer (data) backup. Either one will work in an audio DAT machine, however, some data tapes exceed the standard one- or two-hour length for conventional audio tapes. While it might seem great to get some extra time, many audio DAT decks are not designed to handle longer tapes, and using these can cause problems. If you do use data tapes, make sure they're the standard one- or two-hour length.

It's always good practice to fast forward and rewind a new tape a couple of times before using it, as this "unpacks" the tape and can prevent sticking. With video cassette-based machines, take up any tape slack before attempting to record (if you're not familiar with this process, any video rental clerk should be able to show you). Slack in the tape can lead to error messages and inconsistent recording.

Leave a minute or two of blank tape at the beginning and end. As with analog tapes, the ends are most prone to having quality problems. Also, never eject a tape where there's audio! Always eject it when the tape is sitting on a blank space.

Store tapes in a cool, dry environment. High heat and humidity can lead to rapid tape deterioration. Since it's so easy to "clone" digital tapes, it's good practice to transfer contents from older tapes to newer tapes every couple of years, retaining the older tapes as backups.

## Hard Disk Recording

Think of hard disk recording (HDR) this way: you can take a Mac or PC, load in a program, and turn it into a recording studio. (Actually, it's not always that simple; you may need to add an extra card or a high-capacity hard disk, but that's still not too much to deal with.) Hard disk recording systems are also available as stand-alone units that are conceptually more like tape recorders than computers. Multitrack computer-based recording can involve a substantial amount of hardware and software, but it continues to become more and more cost-effective—so let's investigate hard disk basics.

Recording into a computer has some significant differences compared to recording onto tape. Did a musician play a perfect solo, but miss one note? Just record that note somewhere else and "paste" it over the mistake. Can't decide whether to keep a take or try for a better one? Unlike tape, with HDR you can do as many takes as you want, and then it's relatively easy to electronically cut and paste the best parts together into the "perfect" part.

Why take a computer-based approach to recording? Analog tape works just fine, and digital tape recording is now affordable. However, because music is converted to numbers sitting in a computer, HDR brings the same precision to recording and editing acoustic instruments as sequencing does to MIDI instruments (as described in the next chapter). HDR is a "word processor" for audio: you can cut, paste, copy, and shift timings of acoustic signals, and often perform digital signal processing (alter dynamic range, tonal quality, *etc.*) as well.

You can also organize discrete bits of audio on the hard drive and play them back in any order by creating a *playlist* of digital audio sound files. For dance music and remixing, the flexibility this offers is exceptional. For example, it's a simple matter to take a four-measure drum pattern and instruct the playlist to play this pattern eight times in a row, then start playing a different pattern.

### Hard Disk Benefits

You might think that only mediocre musicians and engineers would need to edit parts on a note-by-note basis. While HDR can make a passable musician sound much more polished, there are more compelling reasons to check out this new technology.

- Resolve the "feel versus perfection" dilemma. Sometimes spontaneous playing produces the best solos, even though there may be an error or two—over-practicing a part can destroy the feel. With analog tape recording, even the best vocalists tend to cut several solos on different tracks, then bounce the best sections down to a single track. But bouncing degrades fidelity, and it's very difficult to bounce single notes or short phrases. With HDR, you can record multiple solos, then cut and paste them as if you had a precision "electronic splicing block," accurate to the note level. You can also use the playlist approach mentioned earlier.
- Integrate acoustic instruments with MIDI sequencers. Until HDR, using sequencers with acoustic instruments meant synchronizing a tape machine (to record/play back the acoustic instruments) to it. However, some computer-based sequencers can record digital audio data onto hard disk along with MIDI data and even apply some MIDI-style tricks such as quantization (moving notes closer to the beat) and automated mixing.
- Digital signal processing. Got some hum problems? Then apply an ultra-steep notch filter at 60 Hz and get rid of it. Want to add creative echo effects? Copy the part you

want echoed, and paste it wherever you want the echo to occur. Most systems also let you do digital mixing and crossfading. Try that with tape!

- Keep up with the competition. The music business is tough: you're not just competing with the band down the street, since record companies expect you to be on the same level as today's superstars. They have access to the best players, using the best technology. HDR can help level the playing field.

## Hard Disk System Types

There are two main ways to implement a hard disk recording system.

Probably the most cost-effective hard disk recording is based around an existing personal computer. As a bonus, you have a computer around when you're not using it to run hard disk recording programs. Fig. 3-5 shows the typical elements of a hard disk recording system. Note that some computers and stand-alone hard disk recorders integrate all these elements in a single enclosure or system.

You'll generally need a computer with plenty of speed and horsepower. Older computers won't cut it; you'll need at least a Mac II family or PowerMac computer, or 486/Pentium/P6-based PC.

The required hard disk capacity depends on how much audio you need to store. Stereo digital audio requires 10 Megs per minute. So, recording a four-minute stereo part requires around 40 Megs of storage; four mono tracks at the same length would need 80 Megs. Mastering a fifty-minute stereo CD on a hard disk recording system requires at least 500 Megs, and—you guessed it—more storage capacity means more money. Unless you record nothing but jingles and short snippets of sound, a 600 megabyte or larger hard disk is essential.

The hard disk's *access time* (how fast it can read and write data) is also important. Because the data is being shuttled to and from disk in real time, the head has to be able to locate specific portions of the disk very rapidly. Generally, you need a worst-case (not average) access time of 25 milliseconds or less for stereo, and 18 ms or less for multitrack. Faster is better. Fortunately, faster access times and large hard disk capacities go hand-in-hand; for example, a 1 Gigabyte hard drive will have a faster access time than a 100 Meg drive.

As many computers have no way to accept real-world audio (multimedia-oriented computers are generally exceptions), you may need an analog-to-digital converter to get sound into the computer, a digital-to-analog converter to get it back out again, and finally, a plug-in card for the computer that's optimized for processing digitized audio (the computer's existing processor

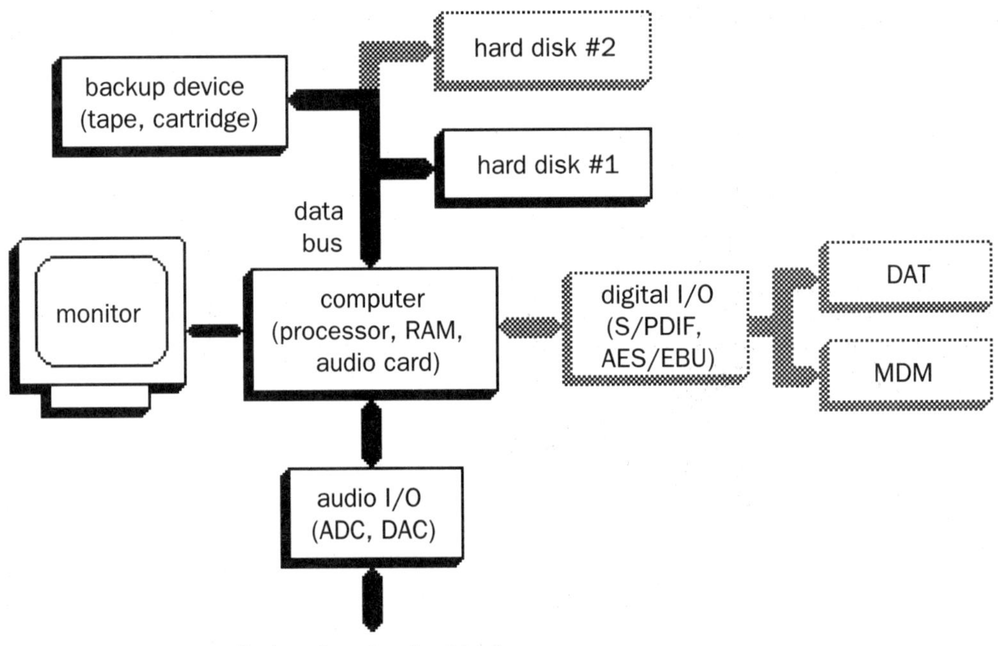


**Fig. 3-5:** *Elements of a typical hard disk recording system. Hard disk #1 is part of the computer; you may also need a second hard disk for additional storage. The backup device saves the hard disk data. These devices connect to the computer over a high-speed data bus such as* SCSI *(Small Computer System Interface). The audio I/O gets audio signals into and out of the computer; this is either an external box, a plug-in card, or part of the computer. The optional digital I/O box lets you feed digital audio signals (S/PDIF, AES/EBU, or a proprietary standard) to compatible devices such as* DAT*, a Modular Digital Multitrack, etc. or the reverse if you want to edit audio on the HDR.*

may not be fast enough). You'll also need lots of RAM—at least 8 Megs, and probably more.

Because hard drives can crash and are easy to fill up, you'll need a backup system. Tape backup devices (optimized for use as computer peripherals) are a popular choice, as are high-capacity *magneto-optical* cartridges. These are similar to hard drives, but write to and read from an optical storage medium. Magneto-optical devices are somewhat slower than hard drives (which is why they are not yet well suited to multitrack digital recording), but are very robust and capable of large capacities. Some systems allow for real-time saving of audio files to DAT machines with digital inputs; to restore a file, you send the DAT's digital outputs back into the HDR. While time-consuming, this approach saves money if you have a DAT. If not, add that to the shopping list.

Finally, you'll need software to turn the computer into a recorder. This is what displays the audio on-screen and lets you manipulate your creation with various processing and audio mutation tools (Fig. 3-6).

If all this seems too daunting, there are alternatives, such as stand-alone, "plug and play" systems that can function without a computer. These are simply hardware boxes that go all the way from two tracks up to twenty-four tracks and higher. They are easier to set up than systems based on personal computers, but are generally not as flexible. They operate in a manner similar to standard multitrack tape recorders, although of course, the spinning reels of tape have been replaced by spinning hard disks (and you never have to thread tape!).

For the budget-minded, several sound cards available for the PC combine an internal synthesizer with the option to record two (and sometimes more) tracks of digital audio. Although the quality is not equal to professional systems, these are excellent for songwriting and are usually adequate for multimedia projects.

## Digital Audio File Formats

Unfortunately, there is no one digital audio file format, although there are popular ones. WAV files, so-called because their file names end with a .WAV suffix, are common on the PC and compatibles. AIFF (Audio Interchange File Format) files are common for Mac pro audio applications. Then again, Digidesign's Sound Designer II has become such a popular program that it has become almost another standard. Sampling keyboards, which also work with digital audio, generally have proprietary formats as well. One notable exception is the SMDI file

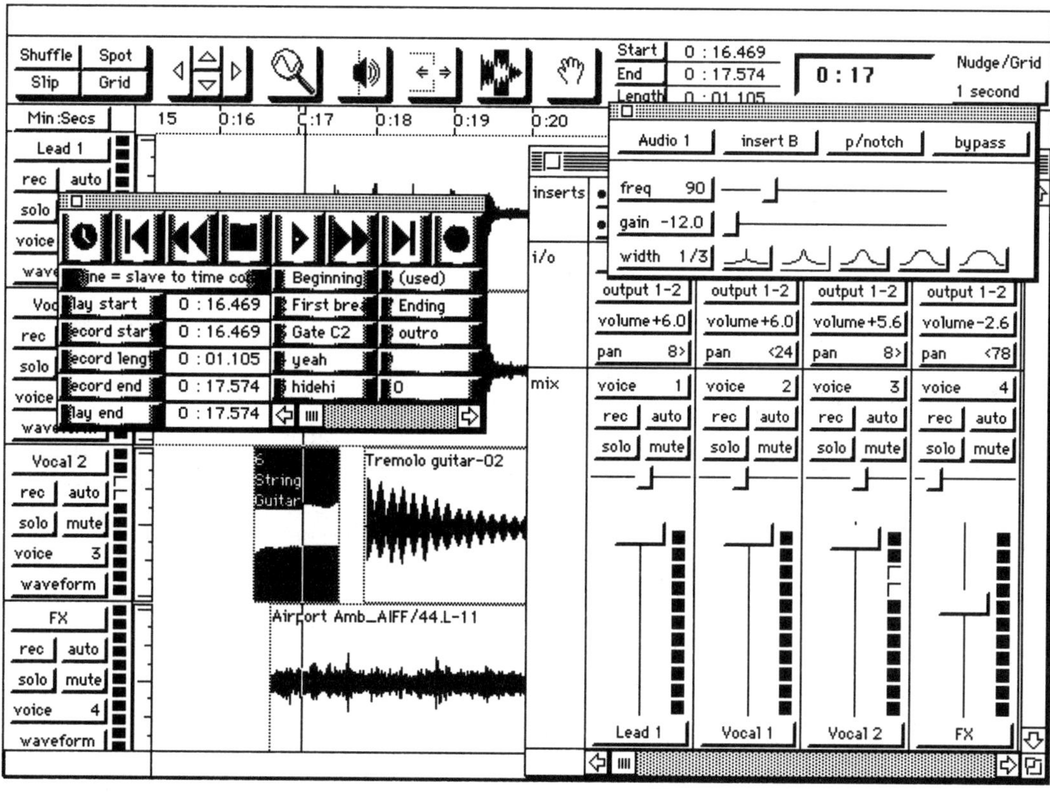


**Fig. 3-6:** *Main screen for Pro Tools. The window in the upper right shows EQ settings; below that is a "virtual mixer" with onscreen meters, faders, and control buttons (solo, mute, record, etc.). The transport is toward the middle and right. To the left of the faders are the actual waveforms that make up the tracks.*

format, which is a variation on MIDI sys ex (see Chapter 4) and specifies a common digital audio file format. More and more samplers are supporting this protocol.

Fortunately, most digital audio programs can import and export various file formats. There are also a number of file translation programs available that can convert just about any format into any other. The best way to get these is to download them from online services such as America Online or CompuServe, where you can get the latest versions.

Note that there are also many sources for pre-existing audio files, such as CDs designed for sampling, and files available online. They can be used in conjunction with your music in various ways, such as importing them into a hard disk recording system or sampler.

## Digital Audio Editing Techniques

Digital audio is a good thing not just for its sonic clarity but because once audio has been converted into digits, you can feed it into your computer and manipulate it until you end up with something completely different. Play it backward (very useful if your hobby is searching for satanic messages in recordings), cut and paste some words from speech (with a little judicious editing, "avoid this movie at all costs, see something else" could become "see this movie at all costs"), transpose a snare drum downward until it becomes an intergalactic cosmic explosion, or . . . well, you get the idea. The following explains some of the common features found in typical digital editing programs.

Digital audio editing programs range from basic, consumer-oriented software to pro versions that have been used to put together everything from hit records to feature films. The examples shown were created with Digidesign's Sound Tools, an older program intended for professional sound designers. Consumer packages will usually have a subset of these features, and some of these will be implemented in a less sophisticated way than shown here. Nonetheless, digital editing commands are surprisingly similar among the various software packages, so you should have little trouble applying this information to whatever program you use.

### Views

It's great to "see" audio, but it takes practice at first to understand how the visual images correspond to audio. For example, with a little experience you can pick out the snare drum in a snippet of rock music because it occurs on a regular basis; with speech, you can recognize spaces that indicate pauses between words, and sharp peaks that indicate consonants.

Since you may do anything from pretty substantial edits (such as cutting out a sentence of talk) to minute changes (such as removing a click), an editing program will offer different "views" of a waveform so you can zoom out and see lots of audio, or zoom in for extreme precision.

Fig. 3-7 shows a couple of seconds of digital audio—a vocal track singing "We can make a miracle." The scale on the left indicates the audio's level (–100% to +100% of the maximum

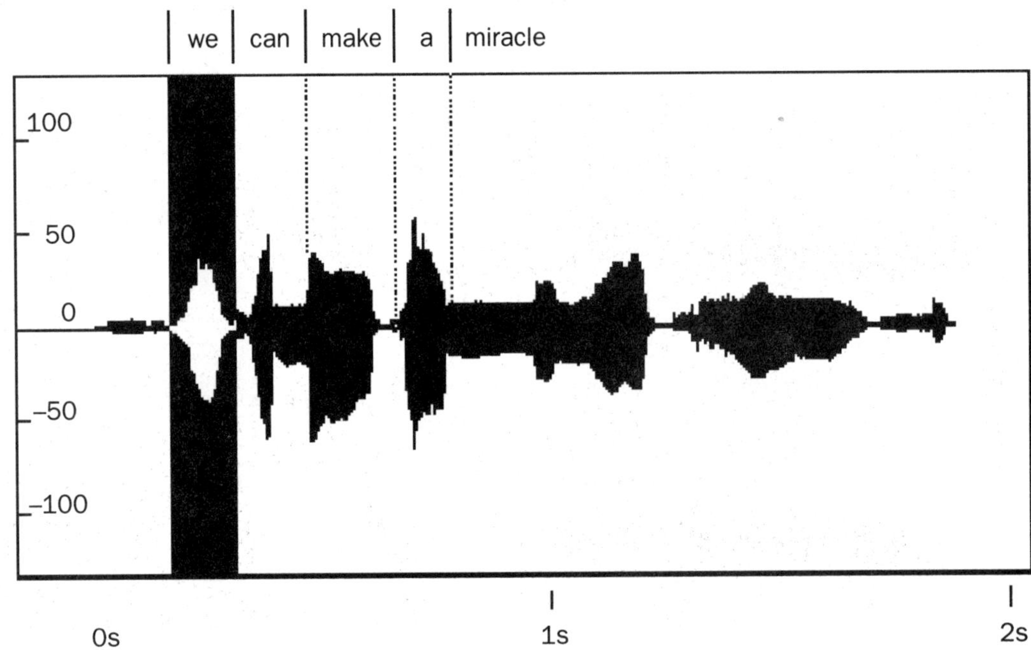


Fig. 3-7: *Digital audio revealed in all its computer geek glory.*

available dynamic range). The scale at bottom indicates the sample's duration in seconds.

Note how the word "we" is highlighted; the next word is "can." The harder, louder "c" sound makes a thin, sharp peak, while the "n" part of the sound is softer and smoother. "Miracle" almost looks like two words. The first part is "mira," there's a brief period of silence, and the last audio blob is the "cle" part. Finally, note the low-level vocal sounds (breathing, lip-smacking, *etc.*) at the beginning and end.

Now let's get a better look at "we can" by zooming in. "We" is still highlighted (Fig. 3-8). You can easily differentiate between the three different sounds that make up "can."

Now we'll zoom in further on "we" (Fig. 3-9). At this point, you can see individual cycles that make up the sound.

We'll zoom in one more level to see more detail in each cycle (Fig. 3-10).

You can generally zoom in or out vertically as well as horizontally so a waveform takes up more or less vertical space on your screen.

## Pencil Pushing

Some programs provide a "virtual pencil" that can draw in new audio waveforms, or modify existing ones. Although you probably wouldn't want to use this to try to create sounds from scratch, the pencil is great for fixing ticks and clicks. For example, the upper part of Fig. 3-

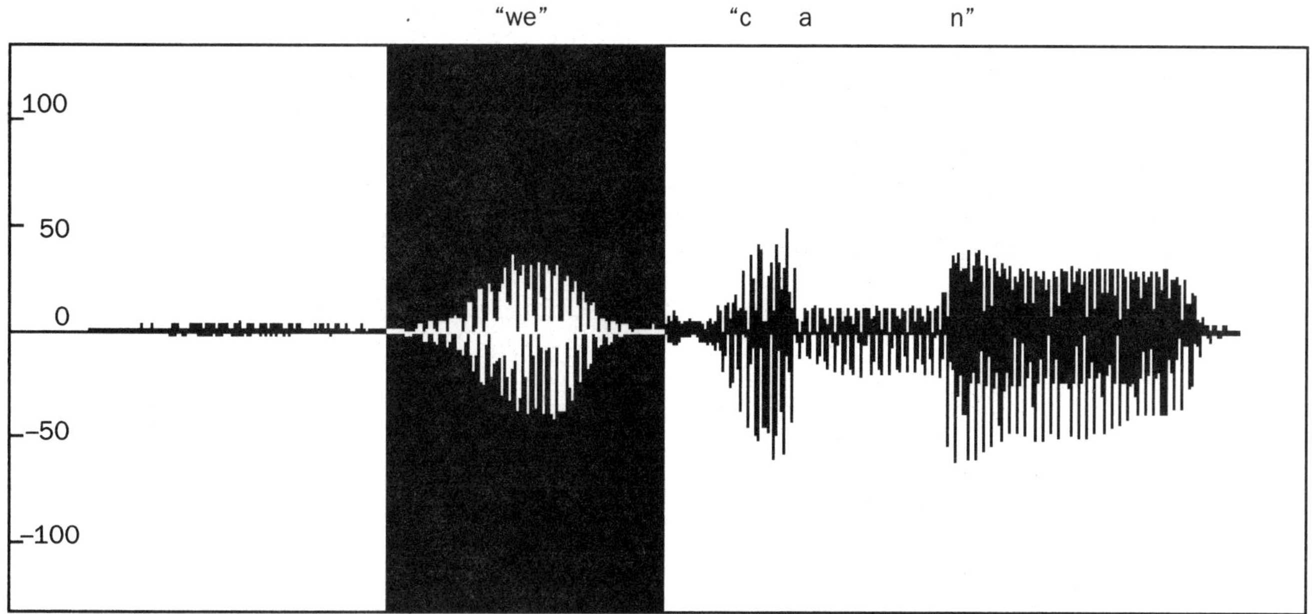


**Fig. 3-8:** *Zooming in provides more detail.*

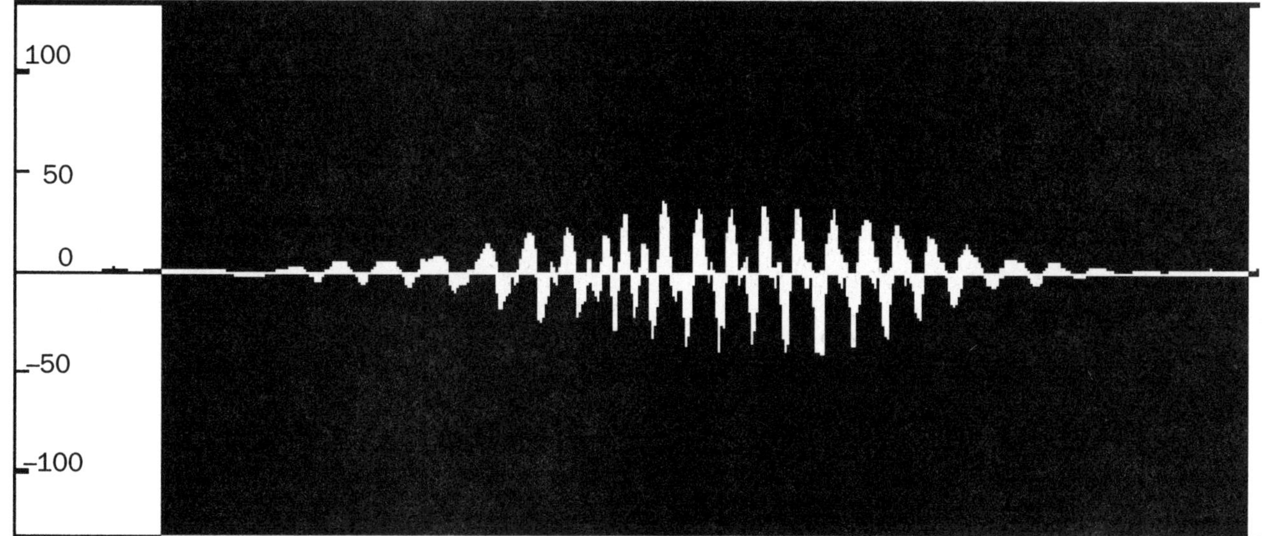


**Fig. 3-9:** *Who's zoomin' who? We're starting to see individual cycles now.*

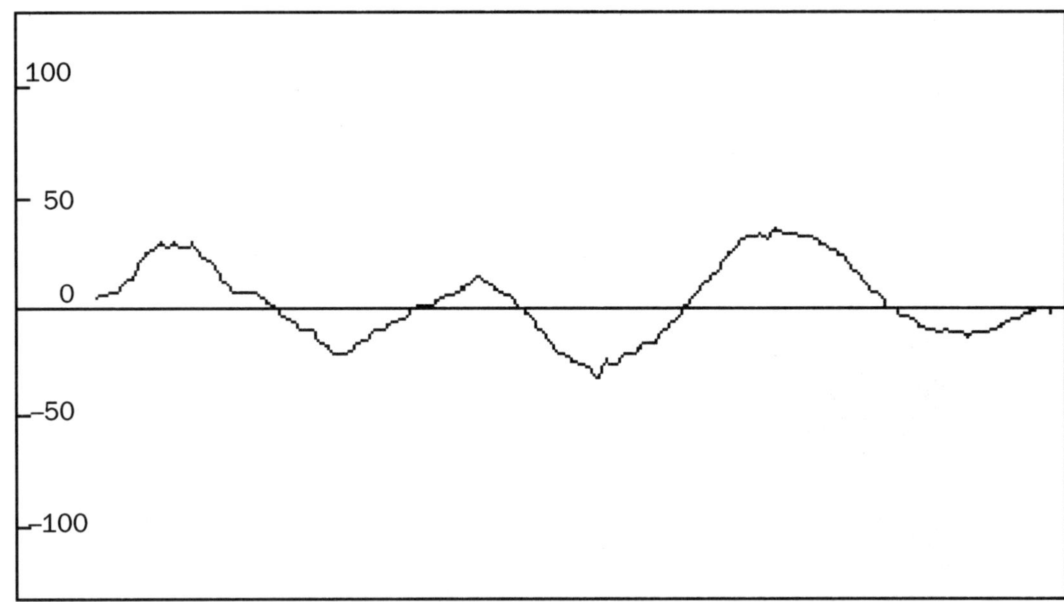


**Fig. 3-10:** *With full zoom in, it's easy to see how the audio amplitude varies.*

11 shows a nasty scratch in a sound taken from a vinyl recording, and a pencil about to draw over it. The lower part shows the same waveform after drawing out the scratch with the pencil. Voilà—no more click! There are also software packages that will do this sort of thing automatically by searching for pops and removing them.

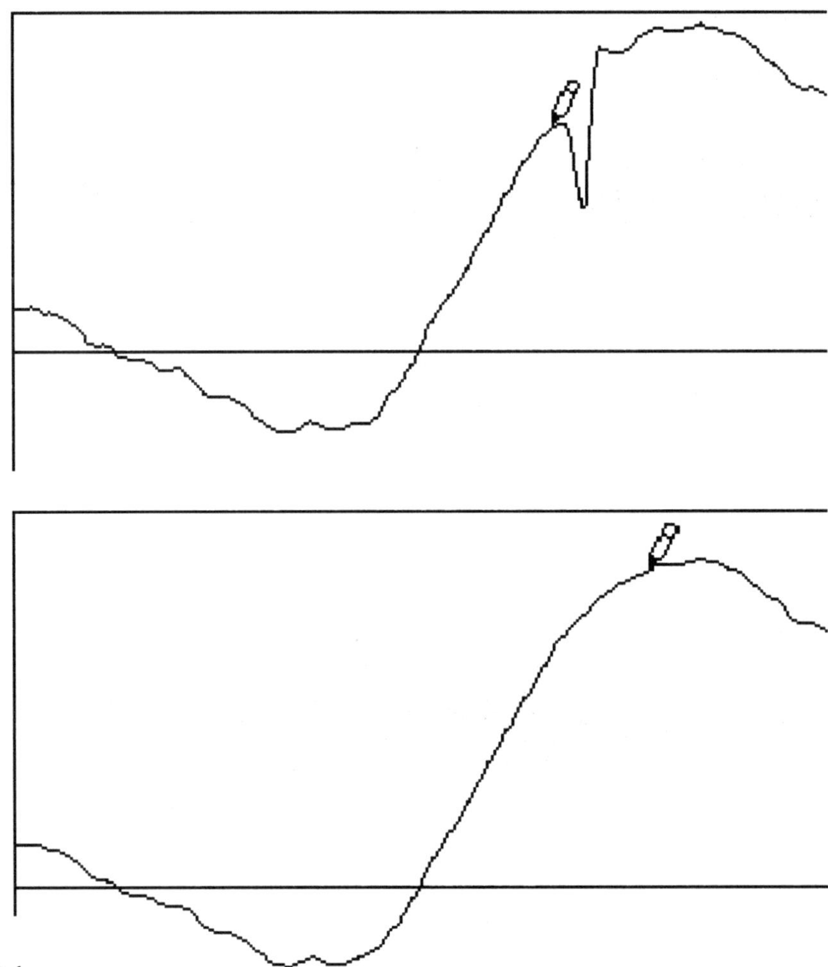

**Fig. 3-11:** *Eliminating a click.*

## Cut, Copy, Paste

Just like a paint program or word processor, you can cut, copy, and paste—but with additional features that are useful when working with audio.

Fig. 3-12A shows the snippet of audio from Fig. 3-7. Suppose we want to eliminate the breath noise at the beginning. No problem—just use the *silence* editing option, which converts everything in the highlighted region to zero level (Fig. 3-12B).

However, "dead air" remains at the sample's beginning. The *cut* command (Fig. 3-12C) removes the highlighted audio; any audio past the cut moves forward to fill up the space.

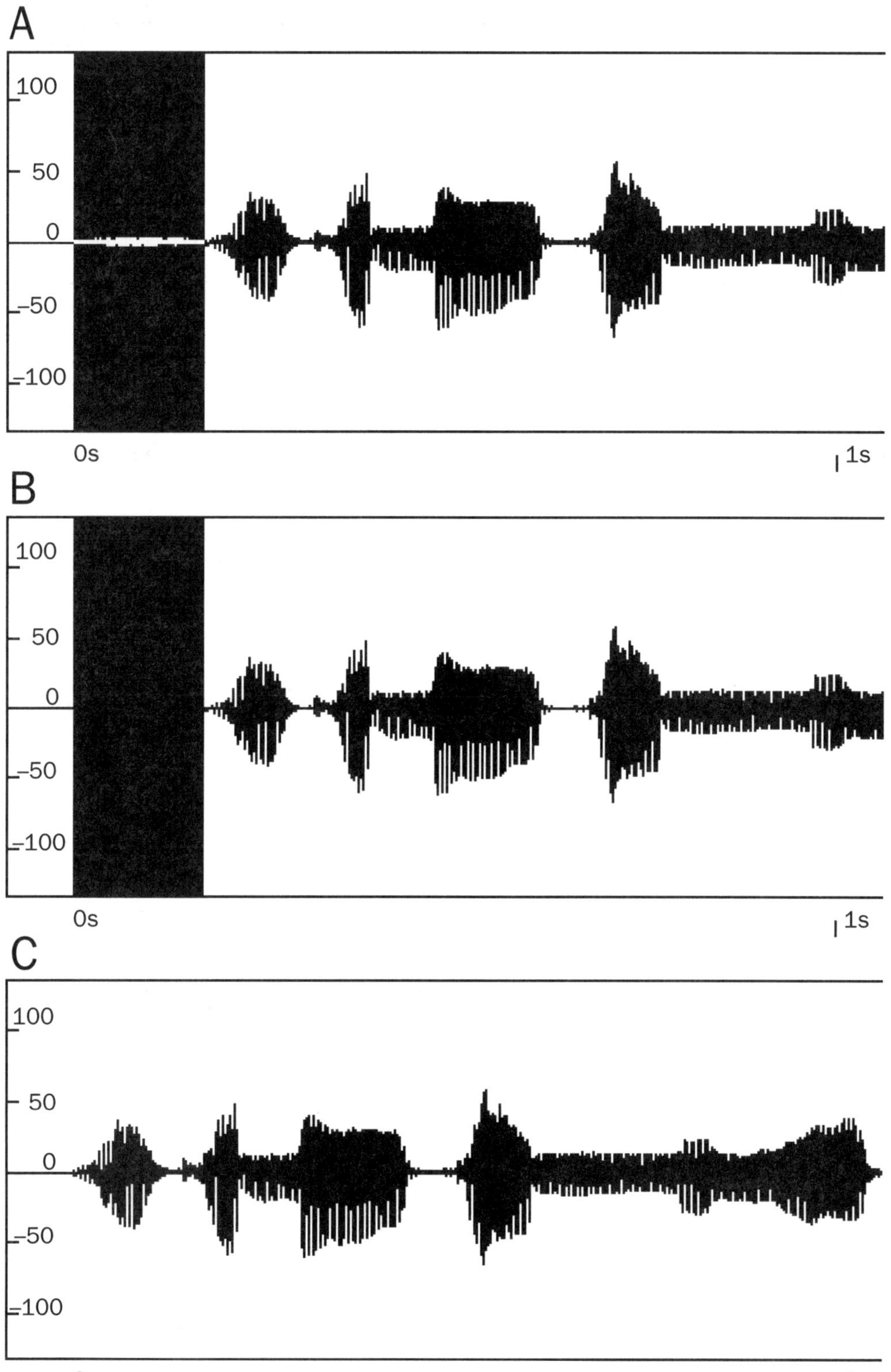


**Fig. 3-12:** *Cutting & clearing.*

*Copy* simply takes the highlighted region and stores it in a "clipboard" (either RAM or hard drive). Suppose in the audio above we want to take the first word and repeat it to create a "stuttering" effect: just copy, then *paste.*

Fig. 3-13A shows the word "we" highlighted. Suppose you want to copy this, then paste it directly at the end of the highlighted region. Fig. 3-13B shows how paste typically works: the region is inserted, and audio past the insertion point moves later to make room for the copied audio. Fig. 3-13C shows what happens if you *replace* what's in 3-13A instead of paste. The rest of the file is not moved; the copy covers over any audio underneath it. Note how the replacement "we" cuts off the "c" of "can."

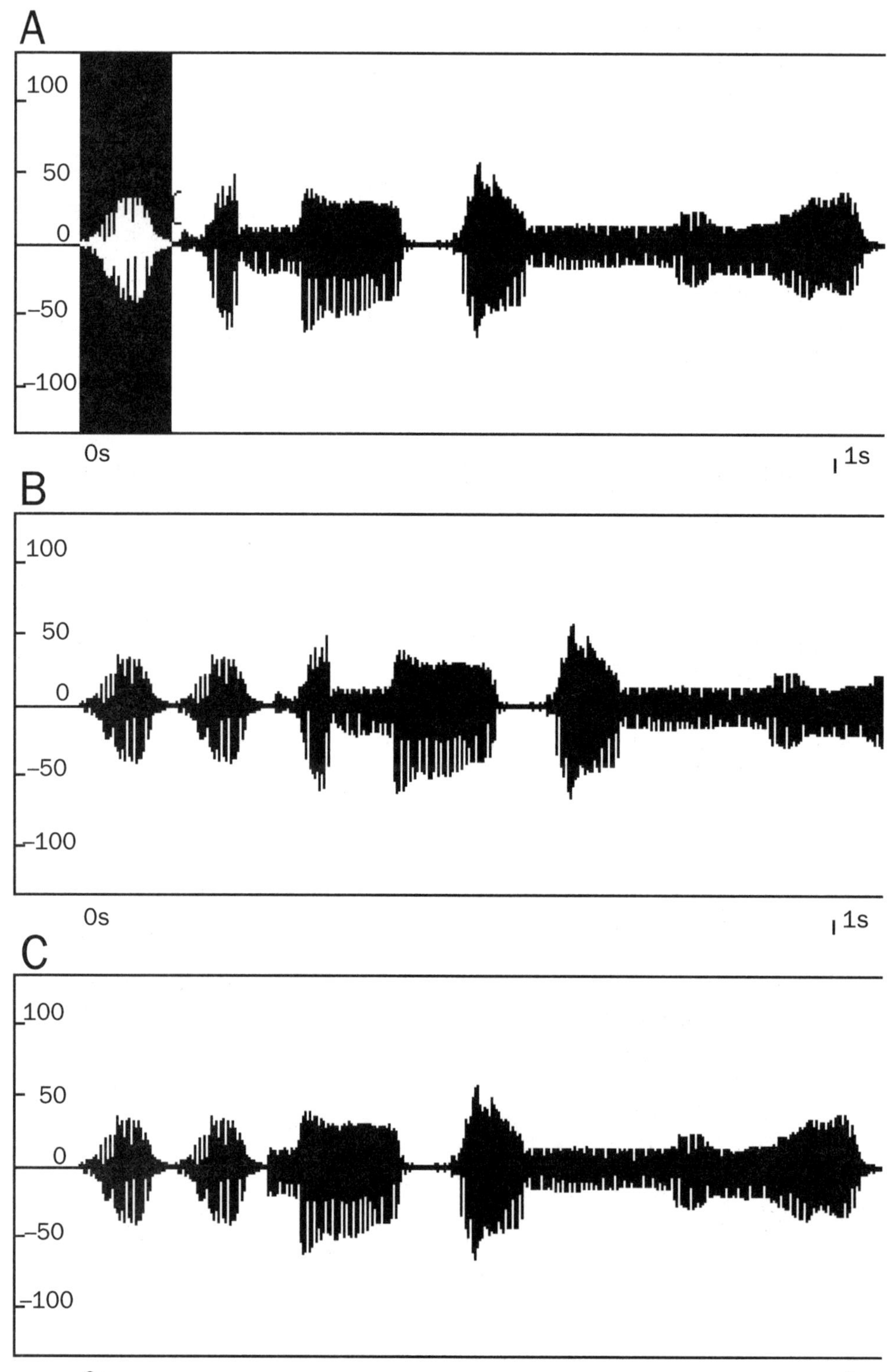


**Fig. 3-13:** *Pasting audio.*

You can use the copy function to do signal processing. Copy the wave and paste it into a second channel to create a stereo file (Fig. 3-14). Pasting the copy slightly late compared to the original audio, as shown, creates an echo effect.

## Destructive versus Nondestructive Editing

When we process the audio, the program can handle this *destructively* or *nondestructively.* With destructive editing, any changes you make permanently alter the sound file. With nondestructive editing, the original file is intact, and any changes are simply "overlaid" on the original file. For example, if 13-3C above was edited destructively, the second "we" cuts off the "c" of can and that's that. With nondestructive editing, the copied audio would be treated like a separate "object." Placing it over the original audio means that it will have precedence over the covered sound; removing this object, or shifting its position elsewhere in the file, reveals the audio underneath.

## Mix

Mix is a close relative of copy and paste, where you copy a piece of audio but instead of pasting it, combine it with another piece of audio to create a composite of the two. Some software automatically checks levels to make sure that adding the two signals together doesn't create so large a signal that distortion results (the simplest solution is to cut each signal by fifty percent before adding them together), but other programs aren't so forgiving.

## Normalization

So far, our waveform has not used the full ±100% dynamic range. The *normalize* or *scale* function raises the level of the digital audio so that the highest peak in a selected region reaches the maximum possible dynamic range. This has two main benefits: all your audio can be referenced to a predictable peak value, and the higher level means less noise as the signal works its way through subsequent mixers, preamps, and power amps.

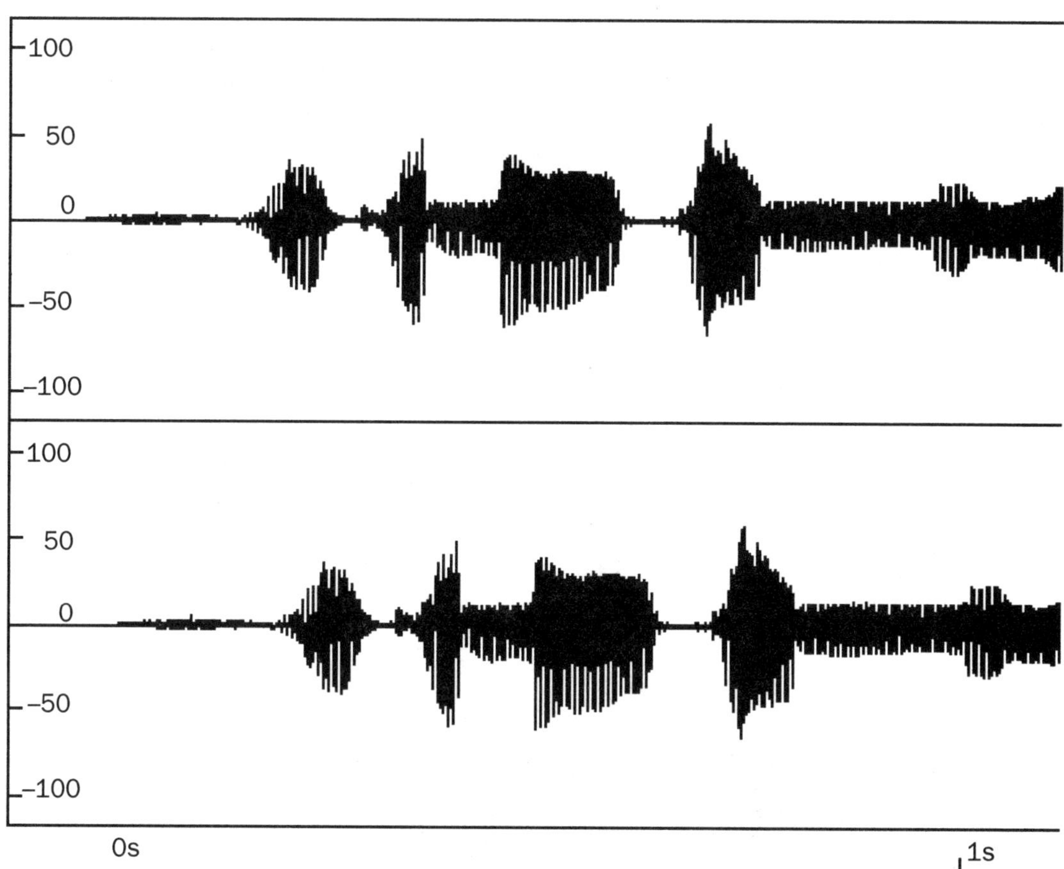


**Fig. 3-14:** *Create echo effects by converting a mono signal into stereo and pasting the copied audio (bottom window) a bit late.*

Fig. 3-15A shows a region about to be normalized; 3-15B shows the normalized version. Note the higher level.

### Fade In and Out

You can apply a fadein or fadeout to a region. In Fig. 3-16, we've taken a piece of digital audio (3-16A) and copied it twice to create a stereo file (3-16B and C). In 3-16B, the signal fades in; in Fig. 3-16C, this signal fades out. If you play the combination back through a stereo system, the sound will seem to pan from one speaker to another—while one audio segment fades out of one speaker the other one fades in, and vice-versa.

### Reverse

Reverse plays audio in reverse order; *i.e.*, it starts playing from the end and moves forward until it reaches the beginning—great for doing alien voices, and totally weirding out the sound of percussive instruments.

Fig. 3-17 shows a stereo signal with the highlighted channel reversed.

### Change Gain

Suppose you think that just one word is a bit too loud or soft. In Fig. 3-18A, note how the highlighted word seems kind of soft compared to what comes before and after. We can fix that: just highlight the word, and increase the gain. Fig. 3-18B shows the original signal after increasing the word's level by fifty percent.

## Digital Signal Processing

Digital signal processing (DSP) applies effects such as compression, expansion, noise gating, and EQ to the selected audio region. Hard disk programs vary greatly in the amount of DSP functions they include, from virtually nothing to complicated effects such as reverb. (Chapter 12 describes signal processing functions in detail.) Following are two examples.

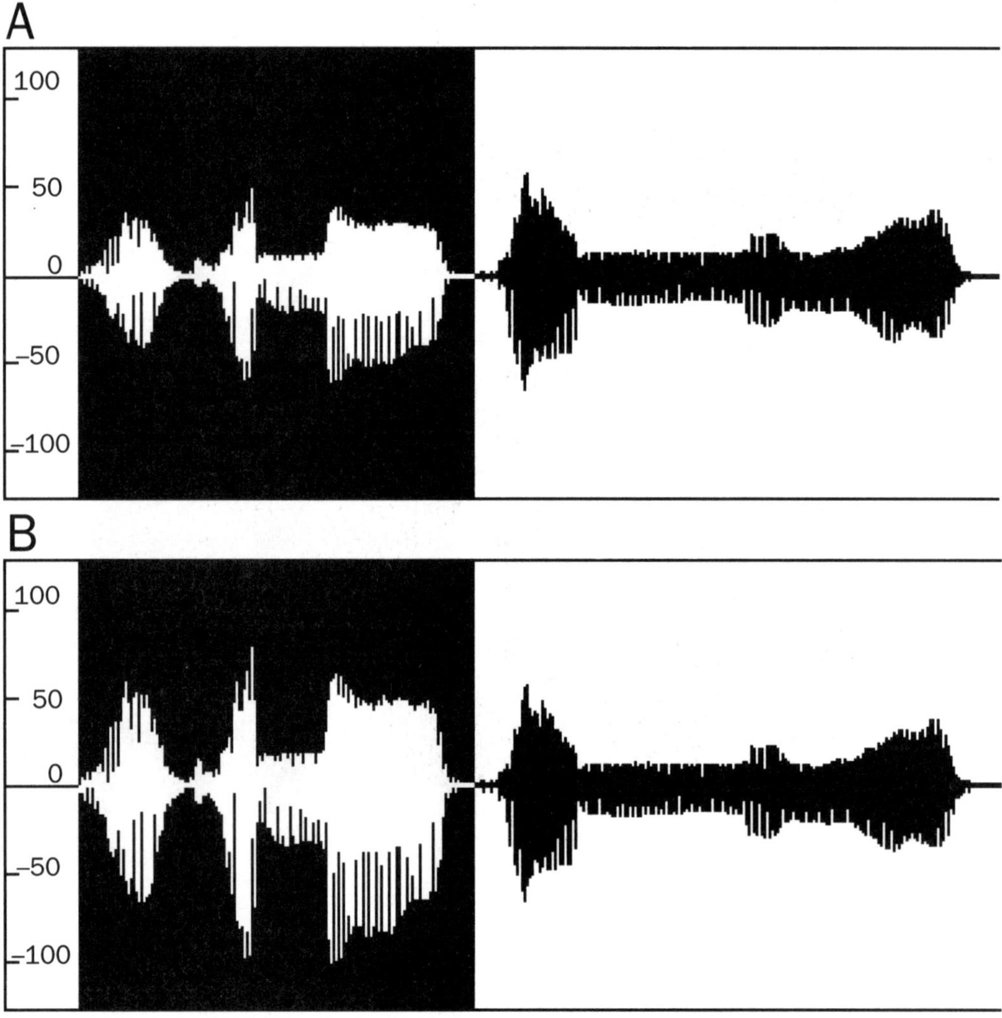


**Fig. 3-15:** *Normalization boosts the peak signal level to the maximum possible.*

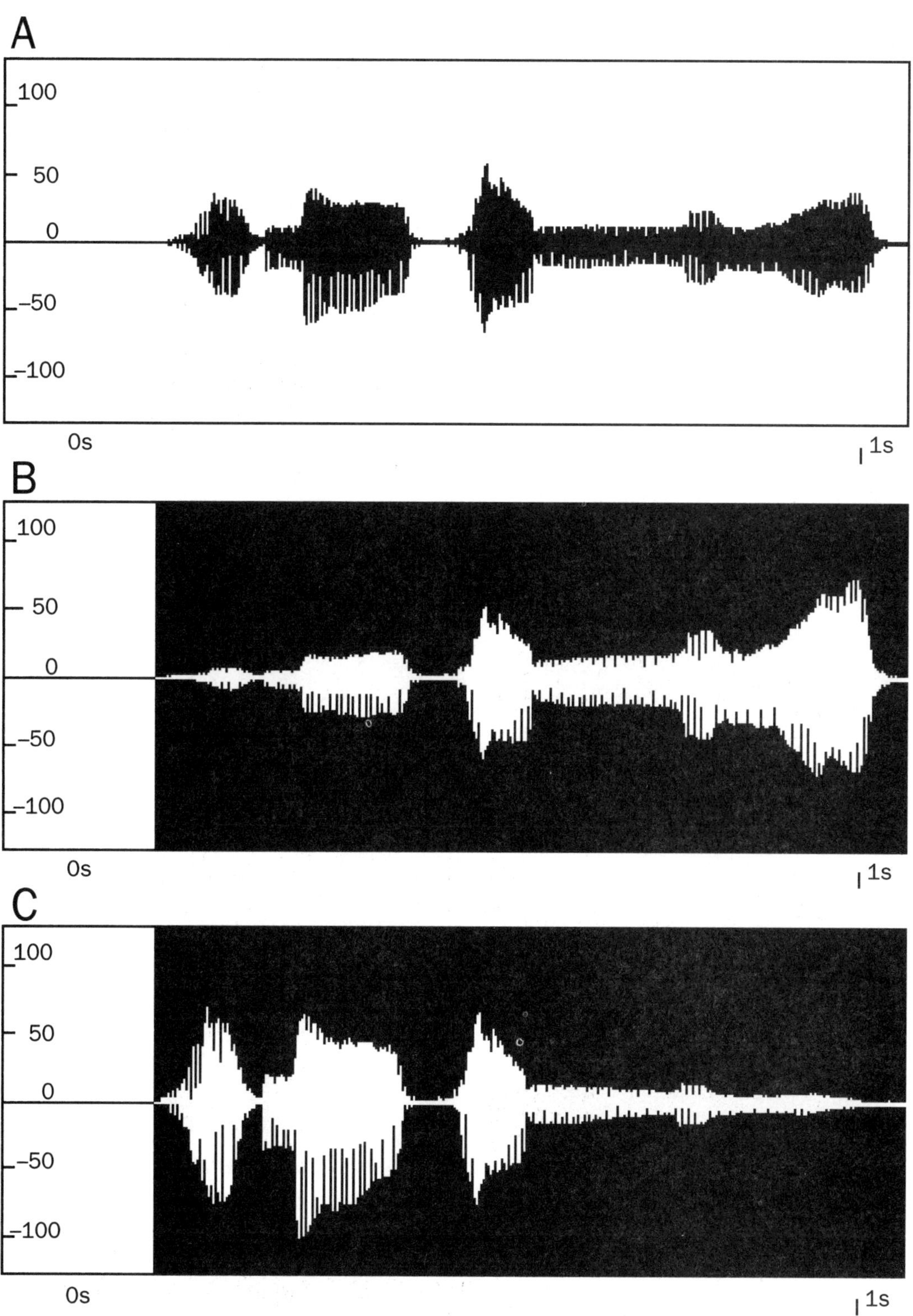


**Fig. 3-16:** *Using fadein and fadeout to create panning effects.*

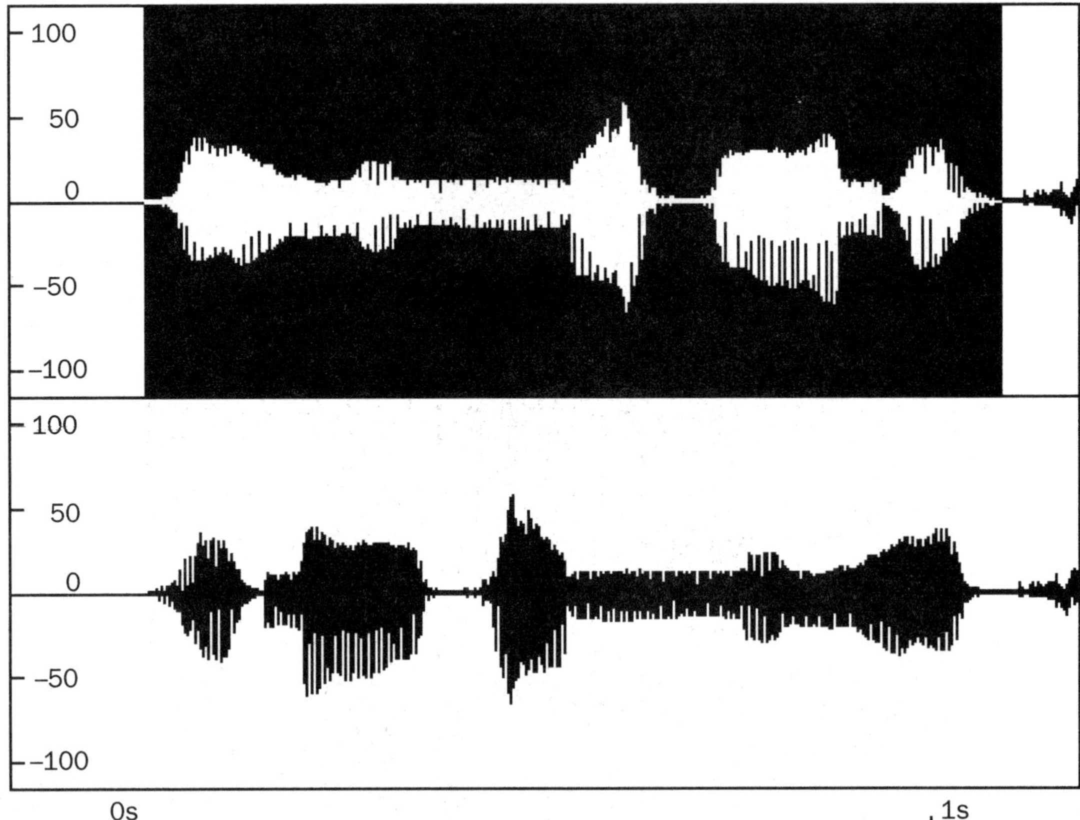


Fig. 3-17: *Shifting into reverse.*

## Transposition & EQ

Transposing (pitch shifting) a sound way up or down can make a radical timbre change, from Darth Vader on the low end to Mickey Mouse on the high end. Fig. 3-19 shows the parameters for a typical pitch shift function.

The tuning reference is there for convenience; the real action occurs with the pitch shift controls, which in this case are set to transpose down five semitones and no cents. *Time correction* adjusts the length of the file to remain the same as it was prior to transposition (normally transposing down lengthens the audio file and transposing up shortens it, which also has its uses). Preview lets you hear the sound without modifying the file; if it's what you want, *process* changes the file permanently.

Equalization alters a signal's tone, and digital technology offers very precise tone-shaping. Fig. 3-20 shows a basic graphic equalizer implemented in software.

The leftmost "slider" alters the overall level (if you boost a lot with the other controls, you'll need to pull the level back to prevent distortion). The middle five controls boost or cut at various frequencies, as shown by the row of numbers along the bottom (125 Hz, 250 Hz, 500 Hz, 1 kHz, and 3 kHz); the numbers directly above indicate the degree of boost or cut. For example, the 3 kHz range is boosted 3 dB. Overall, the bass and upper midrange are boosted, and 500 Hz dropped a little bit.

The channel option determines whether the EQ is to be applied to the left channel, right channel, or both channels.

Various programs have other goodies, such as compression, which restricts the overall dynamic range to give a punchier sound, and noise gating, which shuts off the audio below a certain programmable threshold. This is usually used to squelch hiss by setting the threshold just above the level of the hiss.

## Other Digital Audio Goodies

- *Automated mixing* applies to multitrack hard disk systems, which often include built-in automation to build a mix of the recorded tracks. For more on automation, see Chapter 19.
- *Playlists* let you define particular regions of audio and play back these regions in any order. Example: Suppose you have a hard disk recording of a song and want to try different arrangements of where the solo, verse, and chorus appear. Define each region, then create a playlist that plays back each region in a particular order. Now try another

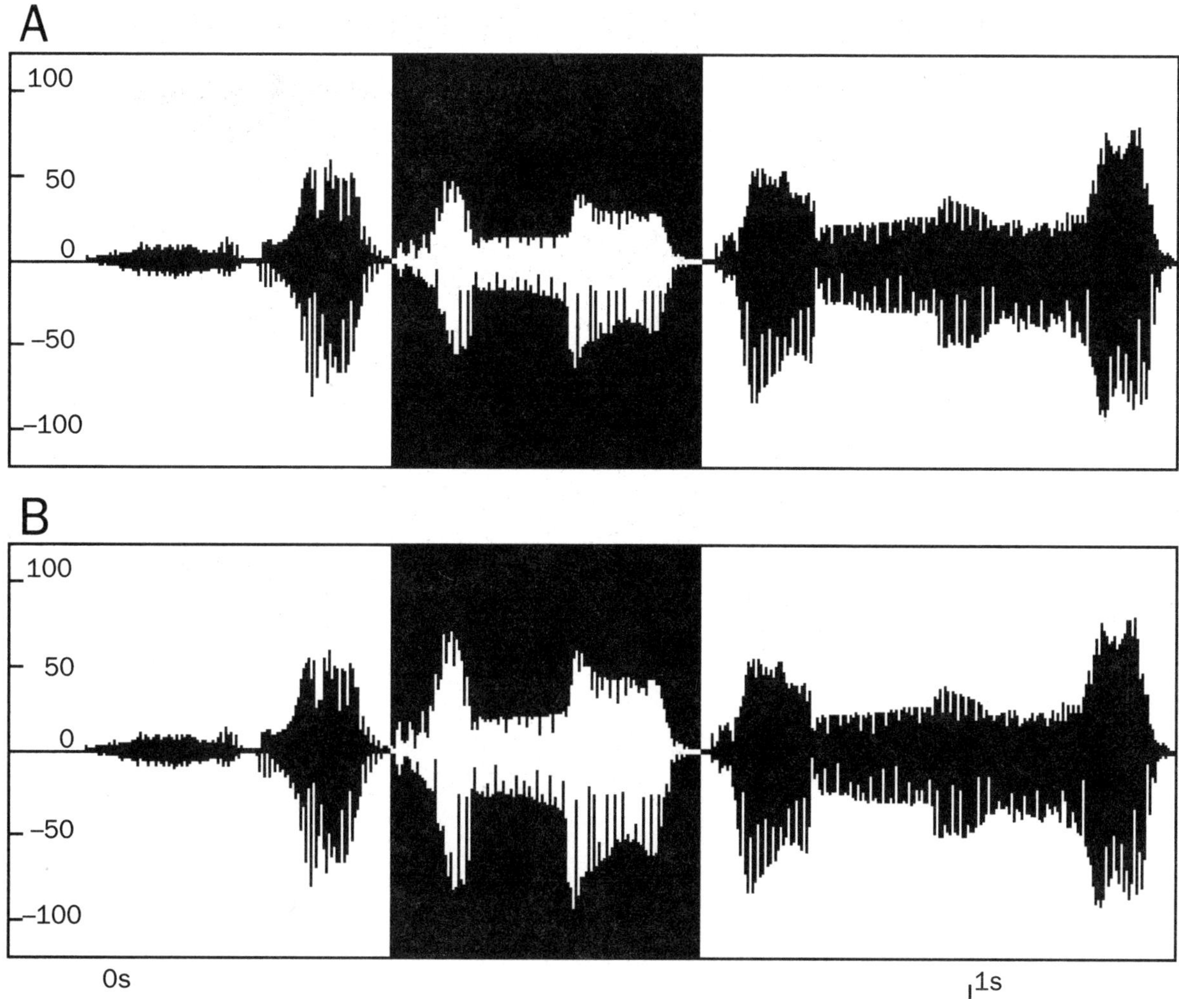


**Fig. 3-18:** *Highlighting and modifying the level of one word.*

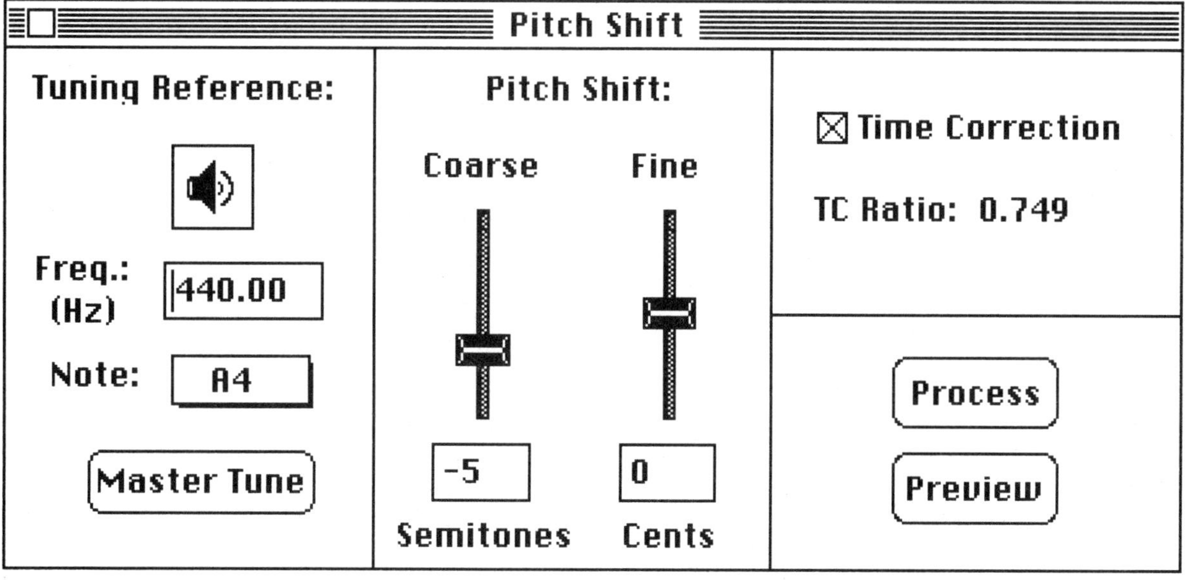


**Fig. 3-19:** *Typical pitch shift options.*

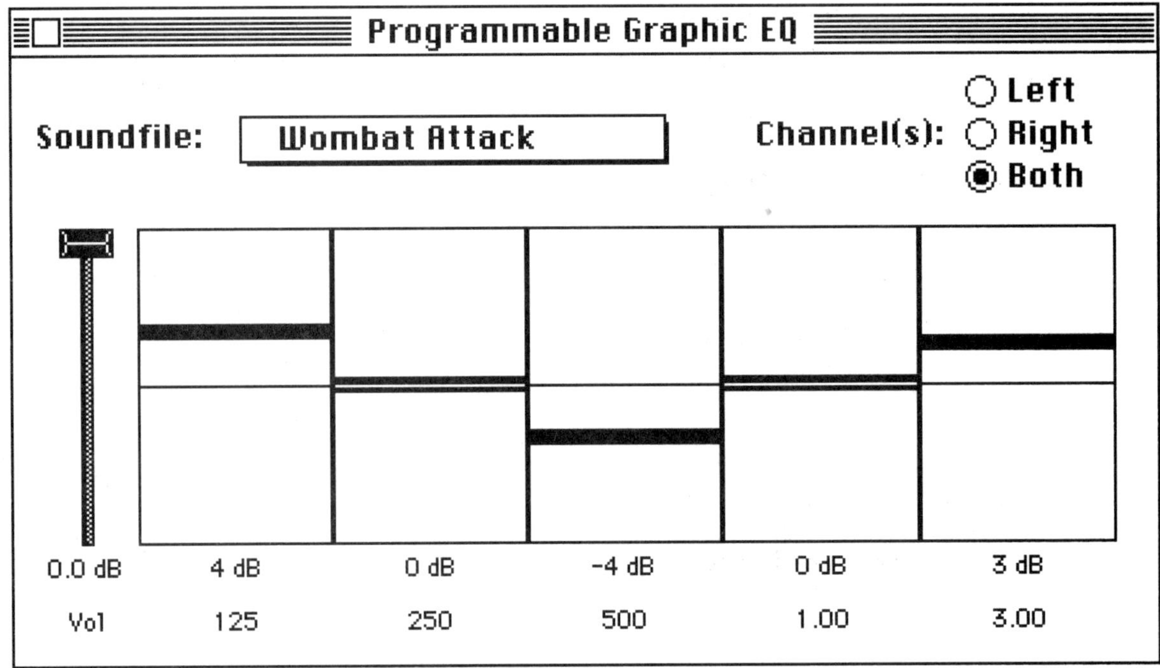


Fig. 3-20: *The graphic equalizer changes an audio file's timbre.*

playlist that uses a different order. Once you decide on the order, you can generally convert the playlist into one contiguous file.

- *Plug-ins* are companion programs that work in conjunction with a main program. Since a single program can't possibly fill the requirements of all users, it will sometimes allow for the option to "plug in" other functions. Example: The current Pro Tools hard disk recording system from Digidesign doesn't include noise reduction or reverb, but plug-ins can add these functions. Other plug-ins can add 3-D sound, guitar-style processing, dynamic range modification, *etc.*
- *Standard MIDI File playback* lets you load a Standard MIDI File into the hard disk recording system so that you can drive MIDI gear along with digital audio. Many times you will not be able to edit these files with the same precision as a MIDI sequencer, but if you need to, don't worry: several top-of-the-line software packages integrate digital audio and MIDI sequencing, and include extensive editing capabilities for both.

## Meet the Learning Curve

Once you have a hard disk system, you still have to make one more investment: time. You're dealing with a new technology and a new way of working, so don't expect to buy a hard disk system one day and be recording sessions the next.

You also need to know a fair amount about computers to get a PC-based hard disk system happening. Do you know what a fragmented hard disk is? If not, you will soon (for the scoop, check out Chapter 22 on maintenance). You had also better learn how to hook up peripherals to your computer, and know what to do if you get error messages about "buffer overflow" and such. Many companies provide good support, but they can only take you so far. You have to do your own hard disk homework.

## Does HDR Obsolete Digital Tape?

Not for now. Digital tape offers inexpensive storage, but very limited editing; HDR offers great editing, but storing all that data can be a bother. However, as mentioned earlier, some hard disk systems include digital I/O to transfer tracks digitally to another medium, such as DAT or MDM (modular digital multitrack). This gives the best of both worlds: you can back up tracks recorded on hard disk to tape, which is a very inexpensive storage medium; or you can take tracks recorded on tape and edit them with total precision in the HDR . . . then bounce them back to tape again. Because all the audio is transferred digitally, it doesn't degrade no matter how many times you copy it.

In any event, the editing power of a hard disk system earns it a place in any modern studio. Once you get the system figured out, and assemble your first perfect vocal by cutting and pasting diverse parts in a matter of minutes, you'll be hooked.

## Living with Digital Recording

If you're used to analog recording, going digital has some ramifications you might not expect. To lessen the culture shock for those who are succumbing to the temptation of translating music into numbers and back again, here are some aspects of life in the digital age.

- With digital tape, you can trust the tape counter because it references to the timing code that the recorder writes to an "invisible" control track (the same track that provides sync information). Readings never slip, so unlike analog decks, you don't have to re-zero the counter occasionally.
- You can forget about modulation noise, audible print-through, noise reduction pumping, wow, flutter, hiss, and scraping reel flanges.
- You may not need to give up a track for SMPTE time code (required for some types of synchronization; see Chapter 19) since this can be derived from the time code already present in the tape machine. Hard disk recorders have SMPTE time code built transparently into the system.
- Some people complain that digital sound lacks warmth. Although I generally like the sound of digital, many people don't realize how much they use analog tape's saturation characteristics until it's not there any more (especially with drum sounds and vocals; guitar parts are often so distorted that you'd never miss a few per cent of THD anyway). Here's are some workarounds for getting a more "analog" sound.

  Find yourself a studio-oriented multieffects with distortion (intentional distortion, that is!), since distortion can sound great on electronic drums. A little bit of overdrive acts as a hard limiter, and "crunches" the drums as it compresses them (you can also apply a little EQ to brighten things up). The sound quality is awesome, and what's really odd is that you *can't tell the drums are being distorted,* even with what seems like a lot of overdrive. But it's better than tape distortion, because you can control it, and you don't saturate the high frequencies. Try a little overdrive on your drum machine sometime—the results may surprise you.

  For vocals, the distortion has to be a lot more subtle. A tube mic preamp with just a hint of distortion seems just about ideal. I'm not a hardcore tube fanatic by any means, but when it comes to vocals, I've seen the light—which is easy with tubes, considering that they glow in the dark.

# Chapter 4
# MIDI Recording

In addition to recording audio, recording can also mean storing data that *represents* music, which brings us to MIDI (Musical Instrument Digital Interface).

Recording engineers who don't have a strong musical background may approach MIDI with some trepidation, but this isn't really justified. In fact, part of MIDI's success is due to enterprising hardware and software engineers who have made MIDI fairly "transparent" to the user; with very few exceptions, it is not necessary to delve into MIDI on a bits and bytes level. (A byte is the basic unit of computer data, and is roughly analogous to a word in spoken language.)

## The Birth of MIDI

Virtually all contemporary electronic instruments—synthesizers, drum machines, and so on—have some type of computer inside. Although it may seem unusual to mix high-tech number-crunching with art, music is a close relative of mathematics. Tempos are given in a certain number of beats per minute, notes are expressed as fractions (quarter notes, eighth notes, sixteenth notes, *etc.*), and the like. Computers are right at home with music thanks to their common mathematical heritage.

In the early eighties, farsighted musical engineers started a cooperative effort to better tap the potential of the computers inside musical instruments, as well as insure inter-manufacturer hardware compatibility. The result of their work was introduced in 1983 as MIDI (Musical Instrument Digital Interface), an internationally recognized specification that expresses musical events (notes played, vibrato, dynamics, tempo, *etc.*) as a common "language" consisting of standardized *digital data.* This data can be understood by MIDI-compatible computers and computer-based musical instruments.

MIDI's main purpose is to allow musical machines to communicate musical data to each other, such as which note is being played, whether a pedal is being moved, and so on. You can think of MIDI as a catchall name for the process of sending control messages from one device (*i.e.,* a keyboard or footswitch) to another device (*i.e.,* synthesizer, mixer, or signal processor) over a MIDI cable that carries these messages.

Conceptually, MIDI is like "sheet music for computers." Before the electronic age, communicating musical ideas required translating musical parameters into special symbols (music notation) to indicate a note's pitch, rhythmic value (duration), dynamics (with crescendo/decrescendo marks), and the like. With MIDI, a computer translates musical parameters into digital data that can convey the type of information shown on sheet music, and much more.

Just one example of a MIDI message that has no equivalent in sheet music is the *program change* command. This message selects different sounds in a synth, presets in a signal processor, "scenes" in a MIDI lighting controller, *etc.*

## MIDI Connections

Virtually every MIDI-equipped device has a *MIDI in* and *MIDI out* jack. It may also have a *MIDI thru* jack, which provides a duplicate of the signal at the MIDI in jack. Thru jacks are not required by the MIDI specification, and will be discussed later.

MIDI data is different from normal audio signals in that MIDI data doesn't make sounds, but rather, consists of digital control signals that represent *what you play* (Fig. 4-1). "Play" doesn't just have to mean notes; you can also "play" a tune's mix using MIDI-compatible volume faders, or "play" timbral changes in a signal processor with a footpedal.

The MIDI out jack transmits MIDI control signals to another MIDI device. Example: Suppose you're playing a keyboard with a MIDI out jack. Data that corresponds to your playing flows out that jack at an extremely rapid rate. Press down a D♯, and a piece of data that stands for "D♯ has been pressed" exits by way of the MIDI out. If the keyboard responds to dynamics, the message will also include dynamics information based on how hard you played the note.

Release the note, and another piece of data goes out that says, "D♯ has been released." If you

4270 McSweeney Road • Mt. Iron, MN 55768 • (218) 262-2480 • Facsimile (218) 263-6392

4270 McSweeney Road • Mt. Iron, MN 55768 • (218) 262-2480 • Facsimile (218) 263-6392

4270 McSweeney Road • Mt. Iron, MN 55768 • (218) 262-2480 • Facsimile (218) 263-6392

4270 McSweeney Road • Mt. Iron, MN 55768 • (218) 262-2480 • Facsimile (218) 263-6392

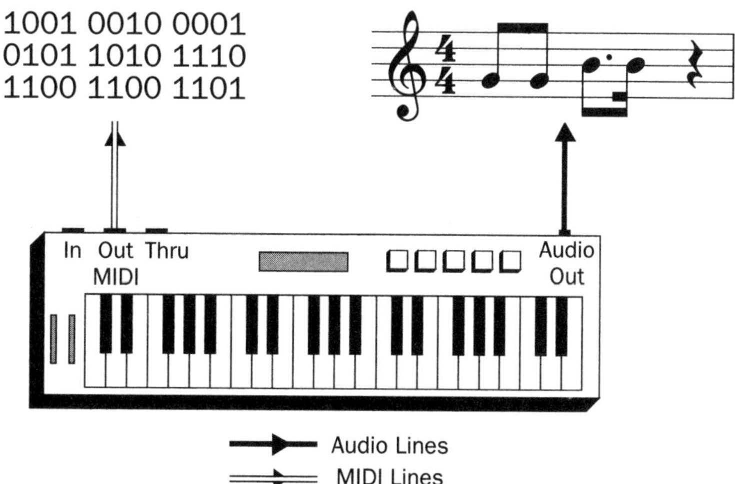


**Fig. 4-1:** *The audio out produces musical sounds that feed an amplifier, which the listener hears. The* MIDI *out produces digital data representing your performance (notes played, modulation, pitch-bending, etc.). Synthesizers,* MIDI*-compatible computers, and other* MIDI *devices can receive and understand this data.*

add pitch bend, vibrato, or other changes, the MIDI out jack transmits corresponding pieces of data for these too.

The MIDI in jack receives MIDI data from another device. This data might tell a synthesizer which notes to play, but MIDI data can also include timing messages to which rhythmically oriented units (such as drum machines and sequencers, as described later) can synchronize. Fig. 4-2 summarizes what the MIDI in, out, and thru jacks do.

MIDI jacks are different from audio jacks not only in the information they carry but also in appearance. MIDI jacks use five-pin DIN connectors (Fig. 4-3), which are different from regular audio jacks to avoid confusion.

In its infancy, MIDI was intended for live performance applications. For example, before MIDI, musicians who wanted to obtain many sound colors when playing live had to use a "stack" of expensive, heavy keyboards. This led to the creation of MIDI master keyboards that

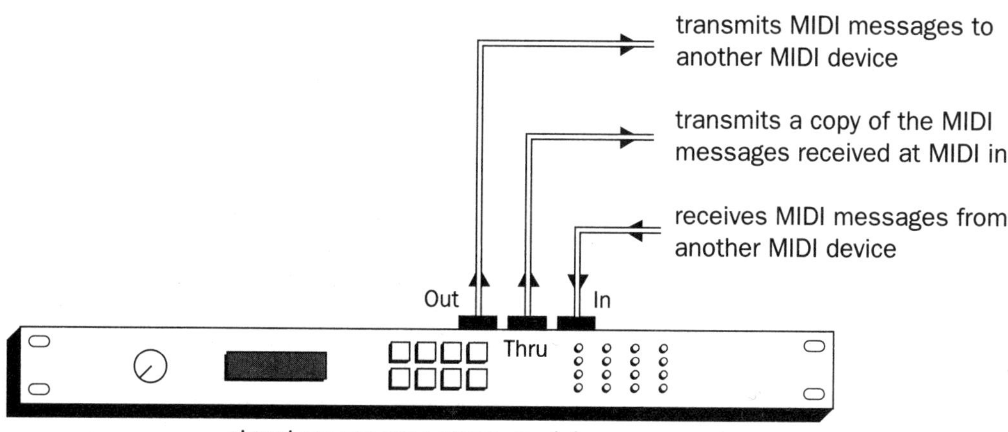


**Fig. 4-2:** *Functions of the three different* MIDI *connectors.*

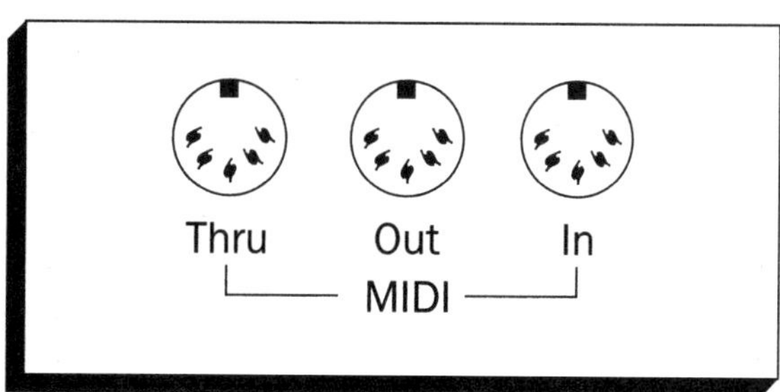


**Fig. 4-3:** *Typical* MIDI *connection panel on a synthesizer or other* MIDI *device.*

simply generate MIDI data but do not necessarily create sound. To complement these, several manufacturers make keyboardless *expander modules* (also called *sound modules* or *tone modules*) that contain only a synthesizer's sound-generating circuitry, thereby saving the cost of adding a keyboard and the packaging necessary to house it. It's assumed that expander modules will be triggered by signals appearing at the MIDI in connector. This approach reduces size, weight, and cost compared to using multiple keyboards (Fig. 4-4).

Separating the sound generating and triggering devices has other implications since anything that creates MIDI signals can drive a tone module or other MIDI device. Drum and guitar controllers are available that change what you play to MIDI data, as are violin-to-MIDI, bass-to-MIDI, voice-to-MIDI, wind-to-MIDI, fader-to-MIDI (for doing automated mixdowns with MIDI-controlled mixers), and a variety of other MIDI-compatible controllers.

Also, MIDI goes way beyond notes; many signal processors, multieffects devices, and mixers respond to other types of MIDI messages. You can therefore automate reverb, mixes, equalization, and so on by way of remote footswitches, hand controls, or even computer-automated setups. There's more on this in Chapter 19 on Automation.

## Channels and Modes

MIDI allows for sixteen "software" channels; data belonging to a specific channel is tagged with an ID number from 1 to 16, so multiple channels of data can be sent down one cable. Transmitters can send data over a particular channel, and receivers can tune in to a specific channel.

There are also MIDI *modes* that determine how a device will respond to channelized data; the following are the most common.

- *Omni* mode accepts data coming in over *any* channel. In other words, regardless of the channel ID, the MIDI device will attempt to act on any incoming data.
- *Poly* mode accepts data over one of the sixteen MIDI channels, and receives only messages intended for that channel. Thus, two MIDI receivers set to receive different channels could be monitoring the same data stream, but be controlled independently of each other.
- *Multitimbral* mode has pretty much replaced the earlier *mono* mode. A multitimbral synthesizer can play several different instrument sounds simultaneously and accept data on several channels at once (mono mode's

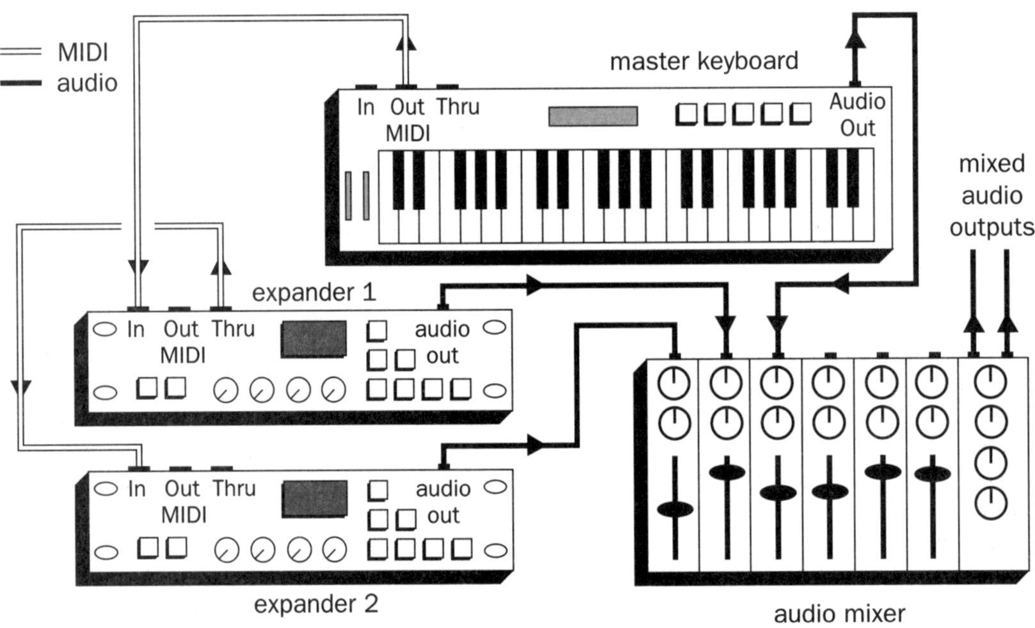


Fig. 4-4: *One master keyboard feeds two expander modules by way of MIDI. A mixer combines the audio outputs from the master keyboard and the two expander modules.*

limitation is that is can produce only one note per channel). Each channel is assigned to a particular instrument. Example: You might assign a multitimbral instrument to play bass on channel 1, piano on channel 2, synth lead on channel 3, and drums on channel 10. Data from these channels, upon entering the device, is routed to the correct sound.

The bottom line: if you have a MIDI transmitter controlling a MIDI receiver, make sure both devices are set to the same channel, or that the receiver is set to omni, so the transmitter and receiver will be able to communicate. In a multitimbral situation, you will need to tell the receiver what you want it to do with the incoming data stream.

## Multiport Interfaces

Sixteen channels seemed like a lot of channels when MIDI was used only for keyboards that cost $5,000 each. However, now with multitimbral synthesizers, automated mixers, and the like, sixteen channels is seldom enough.

One solution is a *multiport interface,* which connects to a computer running compatible software and provides multiple MIDI "cables," each of which can provide sixteen channels. So, an eight-port interface can provide eight MIDI cables for a total of 128 different MIDI channels (1A through 16A, 1B through 16B, 1C through 16C, *etc.*). Sometimes these interfaces can even be cascaded to provide even more cables and MIDI channels.

Why bother with all these channels? After all, it's unlikely you'll play 128 different sounds at once (and if you do, you may need a book on arranging!). However, multiport interfaces let you leave all your instruments set up all the time and minimizes repatching. For example, if you have a multitimbral synth that responds to sixteen channels, you can dedicate one cable to it. That way, even if you only need to use one or two channels, the keyboard is always set up and ready to go, no matter which channels you use.

Multiport interfaces sometimes include "bells and whistles" such as data filters (why record data you don't need to record?), transposition for particular channels, channel muting, *etc.* Some even work in conjunction with compatible software to maintain a file of how your studio is set up and which instruments connect to which cables and channels, so that you can assign instruments by name instead of number (*e.g.,* tell the sequencer to send notes to an "Ensoniq ASR-10" instead of to "channel 5, cable B").

## Recording Using MIDI Sequencers

The MIDI sequencer has made it possible to create an entirely different kind of recording studio for electronically generated music. Here's how it works.

As mentioned before, when you play a MIDI keyboard, digital computer data representing your performance appears at the MIDI out jack. Suppose we can route that data into a computer, and load a program into the computer that instructs it to *remember the timing with which this data appeared at the MIDI in jack.* The computer then acts like a recorder since it stores numbers that represent the notes you played, and the exact timing with which you played those notes (Fig. 4-5).

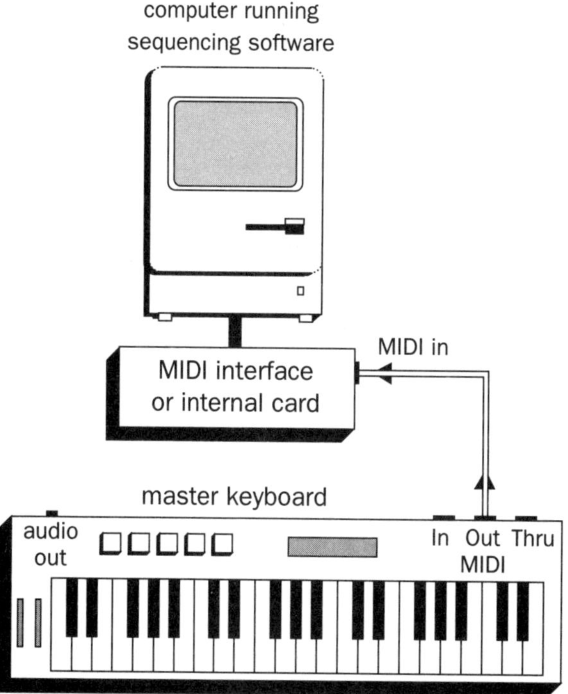


**Fig. 4-5:** *The keyboard sends data to the computer, which "remembers" those keys, buttons, pedals, etc. you moved during your performance.*

If you play a chord, each note gets its own piece of data, which are sent one right after the other. In fact, all MIDI data (notes, pitch bend, amount of vibrato, *etc.*) is transmitted *serially*—one piece of data after another. However, this happens so fast that these numbers appear (for all practical purposes) to occur at the same time as your playing.

To play back the recorded data, we patch the computer's MIDI out jack to the instrument's MIDI in, and data flows from the computer back into the instrument (Fig. 4-6). This is analogous to a player piano, but instead of punching holes in paper, we've "punched" data into the computer. The computer remembers the timing with which we played a series of notes, and then plays back the notes (numbers) from memory. Like a player piano, the keyboard plays the sounds triggered by those numbers—except, of course, the keys don't need to move up and down.

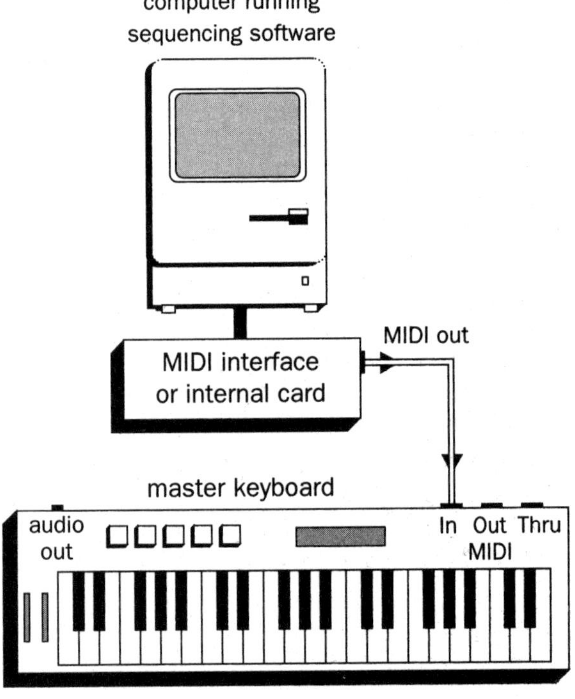


Fig. 4-6: *During playback, the computer sends* MIDI *data back to the* MIDI *device's* MIDI *in; the sound generator, signal processor, mixer, lighting controller, or whatever plays back your performance.*

Virtually all sequencers let you build up multiple tracks, and on playback, send this musical data to multiple MIDI tone generators—thus producing the same effect as if you had multitracked the instruments with a conventional multitrack tape recorder. You may then mix down the outputs of the instruments being sequenced to a conventional two-track recorder.

There are also stand-alone hardware sequencers that are not based on personal computers. They are generally less powerful than computer-based software, but are rugged and excellent to take along on gigs. Furthermore, many keyboard synthesizers and samplers have built-in sequencers that can offer a surprising degree of flexibility and features.

That's a cursory look at the process, but before getting into details, let's consider some of the advantages of MIDI recording with a sequencer over conventional analog tape recording.

- Possibly the best aspect of computer-based sequencing is *editing*. Note duration, loudness, and many other parameters can all be edited easily as MIDI data. This is why having a standardized specification is so important—since all manufacturers agree to the exact meaning of the data, the information coming out of one manufacturer's MIDI out will make perfect sense to the MIDI in of a different manufacturer's gear. There's lots more about this later in the chapter.
- First-generation sound quality. Since MIDI sound generators are driven by a sequencer and can be recorded directly to a master tape, what you hear on your final master is the sound of the MIDI instruments, with no intervening tape processes to degrade their clarity. With samplers, you can even sequence vocal choruses and segments of sound. In a MIDI studio, the multitrack tape recorder is an option, not a necessity.
- No rewind time when working out compositions. Until the final mixdown, everything is stored in computer memory for virtually instant access.
- Dramatically lower maintenance. You don't have to clean a sequencer's heads or oil its motor.
- Instantly change the sound of a track. Would that violin track sound better as a trumpet? Change presets on the instrument being driven from the track and find out; there's no need to rerecord.

And to be fair, let's cover the disadvantages as well.

- MIDI recording by itself cannot capture acoustic instruments unless they're equipped with a MIDI interface; even then, MIDI records only the performance, not the timbre.
- Tape saturation, which many engineers use to "warm up" a sound, is not possible.
- You need a separate synthesizer (or separate instrument in a multitimbral synthesizer) for each sound you want to play back. With conventional multitrack recording, you can overdub the same synth any number of times, but to play back MIDI tracks you need some kind of sound-generating device for every track you record. Obviously, the cost of this approach adds up pretty rapidly, although using one or more multitimbral synths should be able to handle most of your needs. However, even multitimbral machines

have limitations, since they can only play a certain number of notes at a time; this can be a problem in compositions that use lots of sustaining notes.

- With conventional multitrack recording, one signal processor can be used over and over again for different tracks. With MIDI recording, each track to be processed requires its own signal processor.
- Your mixer must be able to accommodate a large number of inputs, as all MIDI-driven audio occurs in real time.

There are ways to minimize some of these disadvantages. To reduce the need for multiple sound-generating devices, you can synchronize the MIDI sequencer to a multitrack tape recorder, and overdub one track at a time into the tape using whatever synthesizer you have. Also, many multitimbral synthesizers have built-in mixing (and even signal processing) which can reduce the number of channels required on your mixer.

## Using Sequencers with Other Recorders

Although MIDI recording does not replace tape or hard disk recording, it is a wonderful supplement. Sequencing can augment the number of tracks by driving MIDI instruments along with tracks recorded on tape or hard disk. By synchronizing the sequencer to a multitrack recorder, the sequencer runs along with the multitrack and can drive MIDI sound generators while the tape or hard disk recorder plays back acoustic instrument parts such as vocals, guitar, drums, *etc.* (For example, if you supplemented a four-track hard disk recorder with sixteen tracks of MIDI instruments, you'd have a twenty-track studio.) As these sequenced tracks are playing in real time, they aren't subject to the problems of being recorded (*i.e.,* noise and distortion with analog decks, expense with digital machines).

For information on how synchronization works, see Chapter 14.

## "Daisy-Chaining" MIDI Thru Connections

As MIDI systems become more complex, a way to distribute data to all the elements in the system—synthesizers, signal processors, automated mixdown modules, *etc.*—becomes important. Since the MIDI thru connector carries the same signal as the one present at the MIDI in, you can "daisy-chain" multiple devices together (Fig. 4-7) if you want one master device to control several other devices simultaneously.

In this example, a sequencer (or similar MIDI generator) is sending program changes to three different signal processors: distortion, delay, and reverb. When the distortion unit changes to a particular sound, the delay and reverb change to complementary sounds. Each signal processor receives the same data from the sequencer, as this data has been passed from one MIDI thru to the next.

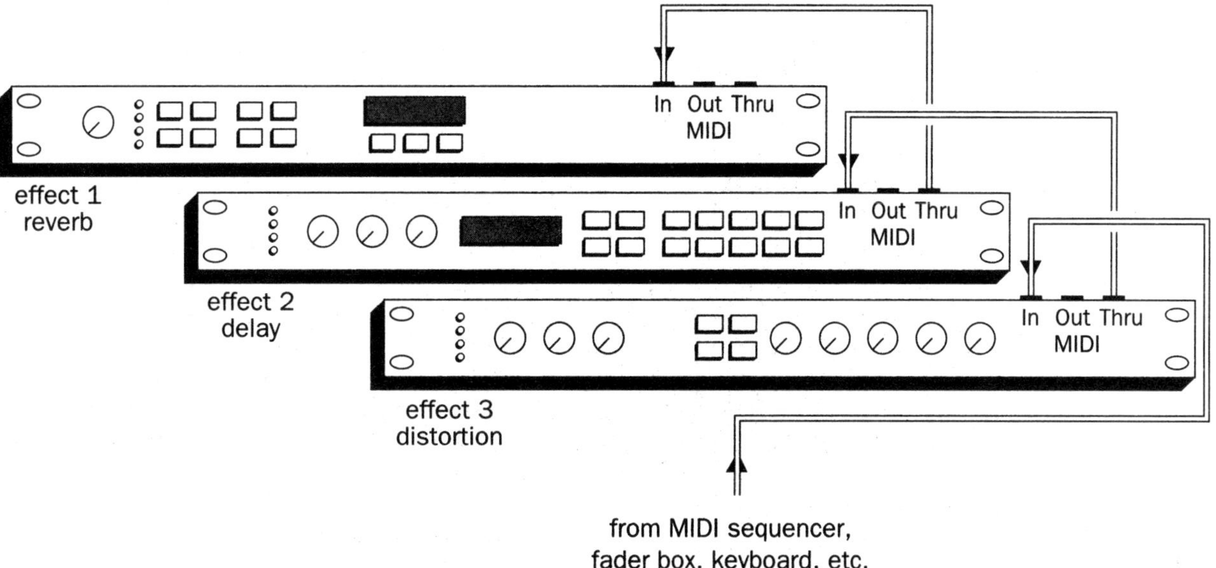


**Fig. 4-7:** *Using MIDI thru connections to drive multiple signal processors from a single MIDI out.*

## Daisy Chain Limitations

To insure accurate data transfer, don't daisy-chain more than four or five MIDI devices. When the MIDI signal passes from the MIDI in to the MIDI thru jack, a slight amount of distortion occurs due to physical limitations of the MIDI interface's components. The more times a signal goes through this circuitry, the greater the amount of distortion. Enough distortion can cause data loss.

Data distortion is sometimes erroneously referred to as "MIDI delay." Actually, the delay caused by going from MIDI in to MIDI thru is only a few microseconds (millionths of a second) and is not audible.

The alternative to excessive daisy-chaining is the MIDI *thru box,* which splits a single MIDI in into several (not just one) independent MIDI thru connections (Fig. 4-8). A MIDI thru box eliminates the need to use multiple Thru jacks on multiple pieces of MIDI gear, thus minimizing MIDI distortion problems.

# The Nuts and Bolts of MIDI Messages

So much for generalities; let's get specific and look at MIDI's vocabulary.

There are two main types of MIDI messages: *Channel* messages and *System* messages. Channel messages are channel-specific and consist of *Voice* and *Mode* messages. System messages, which are not encoded with channel numbers and which all units in a system can receive, consist of *Common, Real Time,* and *Exclusive* messages.

## Voice Messages

The sound-generating elements in synthesizers are called *voices.* Each voice consists of some kind of tone generator, as well as ways to alter the tone generator's timbre and dynamics (*e.g.,* make the sound decay rapidly, like a struck drum, attack slowly like a wind instrument, *etc.*).

Generally each voice can play one note at a time. For example, a six-voice synthesizer allows playing up to six keys (notes) simultaneously. If you press more than six keys, the instrument won't have any voices left to play those notes. Likewise, a sixty-four-voice synth can play up to sixty-four notes at the same time. If you play more than the available number of notes, older notes are "stolen" (which cuts off their sound, even if they're still sustaining) to free up voices that can be assigned to the new notes.

MIDI voice messages describe what notes are being played, their dynamics, and durations. But they can also communicate what sound has been selected, whether any pitch-bending has been added, and if controllers such as *aftertouch* (*i.e.,* pressure applied to a keyboard after the key is down) or *modulation* (usually, but by no means always, vibrato) are being used. A MIDI voice message is stamped with a MIDI channel number, so each channel can carry independent voice messages. These include:

**Note On** Occurs when a note is played by hitting a keyboard's key, striking a MIDI drum pad, *etc.* The allowable range of note numbers extends from 000 (lowest note) to 127 (highest note). Middle C is 60.

**Note Off** Occurs when a note is released. 000 is the lowest note, and 127 the highest note.

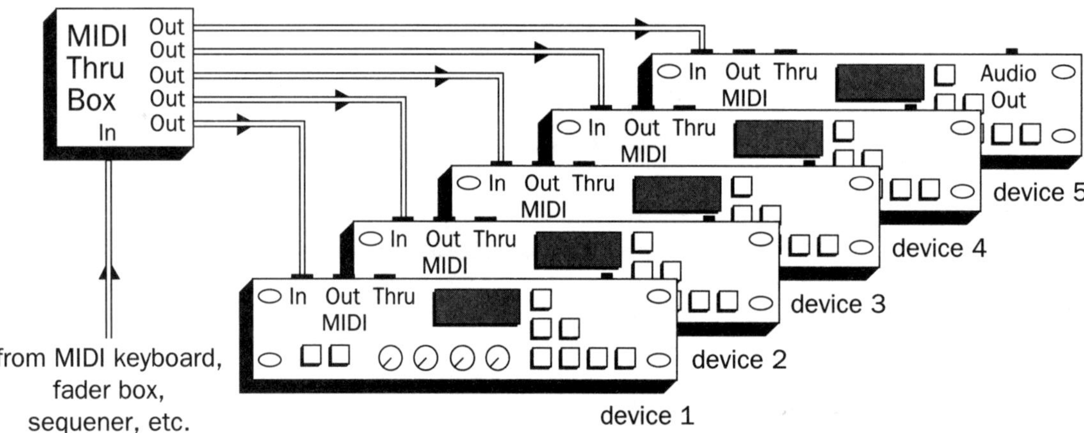


Fig. 4-8: *Using a MIDI thru box to split a single MIDI output into multiple outputs that can feed, for example, expander modules, signal processors, and/or mixers.*

**Velocity** Corresponds to the dynamics of your playing; playing softly gives less velocity, and playing hard gives more velocity. A MIDI keyboard usually derives this value by measuring the time it takes for a key to go from the full up to full down position. It assumes that faster times mean you're hitting the keys harder.

Velocity values range from 001 (minimum velocity) to 127 (maximum velocity). A velocity value of 000 is equivalent to a Note Off.

Some keyboards offer Release Velocity, which measures the time it takes for a key to go from the full down to full up position. However, this feature is rarely implemented.

**Pressure** (also called **Aftertouch**) Indicates how much pressure is being applied to a keyboard after a key is down. Example: On a guitar patch, aftertouch can let you bend pitch when you press down on a key.

There are two kinds of aftertouch: *Mono* (also called *Channel* aftertouch, where the aftertouch data represents an average of all keys being pressed down) and *Polyphonic* or *Key* aftertouch, which sends out individual aftertouch data for each key being pressed down. Aftertouch values range from 000 to 127.

**Program Change** This command lets you call up different programs in a synthesizer, signal processor, or other MIDI device that offers preset programs. For example, if a keyboard's program #1 is a violin sound and #2 is a piano sound, sending program change message #2 selects the piano and sending program change message #1 selects the violin. MIDI allows for 128 Program Change command numbers.

Although Program Change messages are standardized, the way different synthesizer manufacturers number their programs is not. One synthesizer might number 100 programs as 00 through 99, and another as 001 through 100. Some synths number their programs in banks of eight: 1-1 for the first patch, 1-2 for the second, and so on until you hit 1-8 for the eighth program. The ninth program would be 2-1, which stands for Bank 2, first patch. Some musicians make up a reference chart to show what programs are selected on a slave when you call up particular programs on the master.

Many synthesizers also let you *remap* program changes. For example, selecting program 1 on your master controller doesn't have to call up program 1 on a slave sound generator; the message could be remapped at the slave to call up any program number: 2, 56, 127, 362, *etc.*

This is particularly helpful because the original MIDI spec allowed for only 128 different program changes, but modern synthesizers often provide memory for more than 128 programs (synths with 300, 400, or even 500 programs are becoming more common). So, you can set up a map where the 128 program changes generated by a master controller can choose any 128 programs from an available palette of hundreds of programs.

**Bank Select** This represents another way to get around MIDI's 128 program change limit. MIDI Bank Select messages select up to 128 individual banks of 16,384 programs (for a total of over 2,000,000 programs).

**Pitch Bend** A synthesizer's pitch bend wheel (or lever, joystick, footpedal, *etc.*) changes the pitch much like the way a guitarist "bends" a string or whammy bar to change pitch. In addition to being used for bent string effects, slight pitch-bending is characteristic of wind instruments.

**Control Change** Pitch bend is not the only control signal generated by MIDI instruments. Footpedal, modulation wheel, and breath controller (where blowing into a device is converted to MIDI messages—it's great for simulating brass sounds) are just some of the ways to add more expressiveness to your playing. Typically, turning up the modulation wheel will inject vibrato into a signal but it might also change level, open a filter, or control multiple aspects of the sound simultaneously.

MIDI allows for sixty-four continuous controllers (which act like potentiometers since you can choose from many different values) and fifty-eight continuous/switch controllers (these can act like continuous controllers but some are assumed to choose between two possible states, such as on/off). The remaining six controller numbers are dedicated to Mode messages (omni, poly, *etc.*). Some controllers are standardized—for example, modulation wheel is controller 01, and master volume is 07.

Do not confuse controller numbers with channel numbers; each channel can carry its own set of controllers. Example: Channel 1 could be carrying volume (controller 07) messages, while channel 2 carries its own volume messages as well as modulation (controller 01) and footpedal (controller 04) messages.

Each type of controller is stamped in software with a unique controller identification number. Although not all controller numbers have been standardized for specific functions, some of them have been; following are some of the most commonly used controllers.

1 Modulation Wheel
2 Breath Controller
4 Foot Controller
5 Portamento Time
6 Data Slider
7 Main Volume
8 Balance
10 Pan
11 Expression
64 Sustain Pedal
65 Portamento On/Off
96 Data Increment
97 Data Decrement

Controllers tend to generate a lot of data because even seemingly simple processes, such as sweeping a pitch bend wheel, can send out dozens or even hundreds of messages. Many sequencers include "data thinning" algorithms to reduce the amount of data.

## Mode Messages

In addition to the Omni/Poly mode messages mentioned earlier, there are two other important mode messages.

**Local Control On/Off** This message is designed for synthesizers that include both a keyboard controller and internal sound generators. Referring to Fig. 4-9, with Local Control On any controller data goes to the internal sound generators *and* to the MIDI out jack. With Local Control Off, the controller data appears solely at the MIDI out and does not drive the internal sound generators. This feature has several uses; one of the most important lets you play a keyboard with Local Control Off so you can trigger an outboard tone module without triggering the keyboard's internal sound generators.

Another application is turning off Local Control and routing the keyboard's MIDI out through a MIDI data processor such as an arpeggiator or delay, then feeding this processed data back into the synth through the MIDI in. (This is conceptually like the "effects loops" found in guitar amps.)

Many sequencers include a *software MIDI thru* feature, which can interact with the local control setting and can be either off or on. When on, MIDI data at the sequencer's MIDI input passes through to the output. When off, MIDI data at the input does not appear at the output.

If you're using a master MIDI controller that makes no sound and are driving sound generators, then you would leave software thru *on* at the sequencer. This allows the MIDI data you play to be recorded in the sequencer and appear at the output, where it can drive your sound generators. Simple.

Now suppose you're sequencing with a multitimbral keyboard. In this case, you want the sequencer output to drive the keyboard's MIDI in so what you recorded plays back through the keyboard's internal sounds. You also want to trigger the keyboard sounds with what you play, so local control should be on. Finally, you want to feed the sequencer's MIDI in, but not have this data appear at the MIDI out to avoid a MIDI feedback loop. So, software MIDI thru should be off.

To summarize, here are your options (Fig. 4-10).

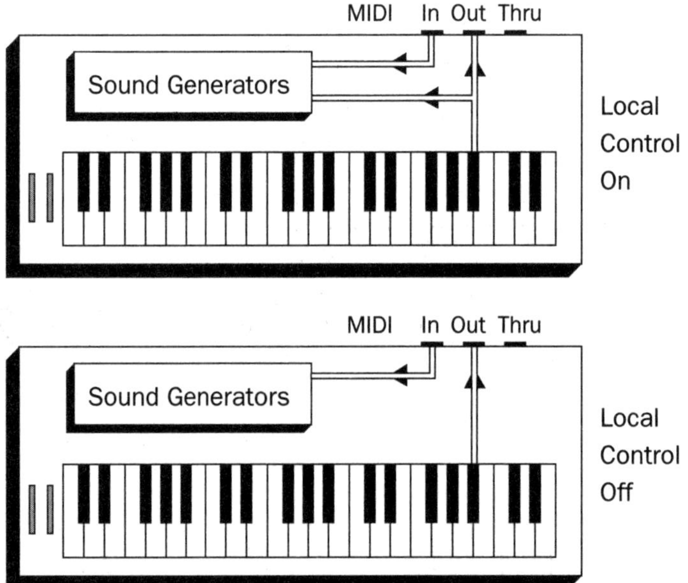


**Fig. 4-9:** *How local control affects a synthesizer's internal sound generators.*

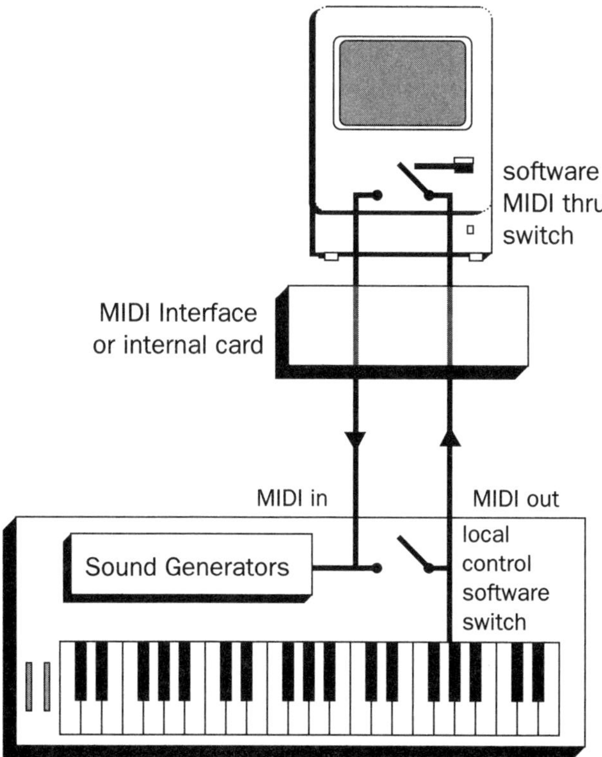


**Fig. 4-10:** *How a keyboard's local control and a sequencer program's software MIDI thru switch interact.*

- Local on, software thru on: Not recommended (potential MIDI feedback loops).
- Local on, software thru off: Recommended mode. The sequencer records data, and you hear what you play on the keys.
- Local off, software thru on: Alternate recommended mode. The keyboard acts like a master controller, but you'll hear what you play only if software thru is on and directing the input signal to a specific channel—the one that feeds the sound you want to hear. Most sequencers let you choose whether MIDI thru echoes data on the incoming channel, or directs this data to a different channel.
- Local off, software thru off: Don't use this. You can play back sounds already recorded into the sequencer, but you will not be able to monitor what you play.

**All Notes Off** This is a "shut up" command—it turns off all notes that currently are on.

## System-Wide Messages

*System Common* messages are not encoded with channel numbers, and are intended for all units in a system. *System Real Time* messages are also intended for all units in a system, but since they control timing and synchronization, may be sent at any time—even sandwiched in the middle of other data.

*System Exclusive* messages start with a manufacturer's ID code and are intended only for equipment made by a specific manufacturer. This allows MIDI to translate nonuniversal data, such as a particular manufacturer's way of encoding synthesizer program information, into something that can be sent down a MIDI cable (as described in more detail later).

## System Common Messages

System Common messages include:

**Song Position Pointer (SPP)** This message keeps track of how many "MIDI beats" (sixteenth notes) have elapsed since the beginning of a piece, up to 16,384 total. Thus, if a sequencer can send Song Position messages and a drum machine can receive them, you could start the sequencer at any point in a song. Before actually starting to play the sequencer would first send out a Song Position Pointer message, which the drum machine would use to autolocate itself to the same point in the song. After sending out the Song Position, the sequencer would then go into play mode and send the drum machine a continue message so that the drums follow along from that point on. For more information, see Chapter 14 on Synchronization.

**Song Select** This message tells devices—such as sequencers and drum machines—which song to play.

**MTC 1/4 Frame Message** MIDI Time Code (MTC) provides MIDI systems with timing messages based on SMPTE Time Code. For more information, see Chapter 14 on Synchronization.

**EOX** This is a "flag" that indicates the end of a System Exclusive transmission.

## System Real Time Messages

Most System messages consist of rhythmically related timing information that synchronizes the units in a MIDI system, including parameters such as delay time or LFO frequency in some MIDI-compatible signal processors (Chapter 12). Timing messages are covered in detail in Chapter 14. There are also two other "utility" messages that are seldom used for recording applications, System Reset (returns gear to its default state) and Active Sensing (turns off "stuck" notes if the device senses a faulty MIDI cable).

## System Exclusive Messages

As each MIDI device has different parameters, there is no standardized way to include device-specific information in the main MIDI spec. (For example, a sys ex message that sets the pitch of a synthesizer's oscillator wouldn't make much sense to a MIDI-controlled reverb unit.) System Exclusive (sys ex) messages provide a way to communicate nonstandard data over MIDI; MIDI gear ignores all sys ex information except those with a matching ID.

System exclusive information often encodes a synthesizer's parameter settings by taking a "snapshot" of all of its values. This data is compatible with *librarian* software programs that run on a personal computer and can store all of a synthesizer's parameters on disk for later recall. This is useful if you fill up a synth's memory banks; you can save the contents with the librarian program, clear the memory, and create a new bank of sounds.

System Exclusive messages are also used with computer-based *editing* programs, which display all of a device's patch parameters on a computer screen for easy editing.

## MIDI Extensions

The MIDI specification is a living document that changes when technology changes, yet doesn't obsolete previously made MIDI gear. One of MIDI's goals, to be open-ended enough for future growth, has been realized. Over the years there have been several significant additions to the MIDI spec of interest to those who do recording, such as:

- **Standard MIDI Files.** A Standard MIDI File follows a particular sequence file format that virtually all computer-based sequencers can generate and read. In other words, we can use Sequencer "A" to create a sequence, save it as a Standard MIDI File, then import this file into Sequencer "B," even if it runs on a different computer platform. Standard MIDI Files have been a boon for those who work with different sequencers on different computers (or who collaborate with people who use different programs), as well as for those who telecommunicate musical files.
- **Sample Dump Standard.** This sends digital audio signals over MIDI (albeit very slowly), and is mostly used with samplers. For example, suppose samplers "Y" and "Z" support the Sample Dump Standard. If you have a superb guitar sample that you sampled on "Y," you can transfer it to sampler "Z" over MIDI.
- **SCSI Musical Data Interchange** (SMDI). This addresses the slow transfer time of standard sample dumps by sending sample data over SCSI (Small Computer System Interface), speeding up transfers between computer and sampler by a factor of 50. For more on SCSI, see Chapter 15.
- **MIDI Time Code.** Intended primarily for audio-for-video applications, MIDI Time Code bridges the gap between MIDI and SMPTE (Society of Motion Picture and Television Engineers), the timing specification used in film and video. This is covered in Chapter 14 (synchronization).
- **MIDI Show Control.** Now you can control theatrics—fireworks, lighting, hydraulics, scene changes, and much more—from MIDI (and who among us hasn't wanted to jump on a footswitch and unleash a pyrotechnics display?).
- **MIDI Machine Control.** MMC allows MIDI to control studio devices such as audio/video tape recorders and hard disk recorders. Applications: Use a sequencer to control punch in and out, do "intelligent" tape motion (*e.g.*, rewind at the end of the second chorus and start playing from the first verse), and/or autolocate to specific points in a song. For more information, see Chapter 19 (Automation).
- **General MIDI.** Although MIDI always seemed like a good way to distribute music by releasing diskettes with MIDI data, in practice there has been no standardization regarding program changes. For example, program 11 might call up a trumpet on one synthesizer and a harpsichord on another. General MIDI specifies a set of program numbers and drum sound note assignments to insure that a sequence played back through any General MIDI-compatible machine will sound more or less the same. General MIDI is optional; some synthesizers can be made into "General MIDI" devices simply by loading patches and drum sounds that follow the General MIDI specification.
- **Tuning.** The subject of alternate tunings (such as just intonation, mean tone, and microtunings with more than twelve steps to the octave) is extremely intriguing, and modern computer technology is making it easier to revive this lost art. The MIDI specification now accommodates a standardized way to create alternate pitch tables for MIDI instruments.

## Sequencer Editing Options

The ease with which you can mutate data is what makes sequencing so valuable to the music-making process. If a note came in a little late, or if you hit the wrong one altogether, change it. Need to play a song in a different key to match a singer's range? Click on the transpose option. Fix the volume on one note if needed, or mix down all your tracks with onscreen faders.

In many cases, you don't have to commit to edits as some programs let you apply edits to playback only, while leaving the original data undisturbed. This takes the pressure off when trying out different effects. Even if an edit does change the data, there's usually an undo button if you change your mind in time. What's more, most sequencers let you edit during playback, which helps keep the creative juices flowing (in the old days, you had to stop, edit, then restart playback to listen).

The options presented by today's sequencers are amazing—if you can imagine something, you can probably get it to spit out of your speakers. Let's investigate those options.

### Windows with a View

A sequencer offers several ways of looking at musical data. Each way is optimized for a particular type of editing operation.

The Song Editor, Overview, or Arrangement window gives an overview of the tune. It's intended for making sweeping, major changes, such as modifying one or more tracks, or even changing everything within a particular region of the song (Fig. 4-11).

Another window, the Track Editor, lets you "zoom in" on the data in a particular track. There are three popular options (Fig. 4-12); most sequencers include all three options, the remainder stick with one or two of the three.

- Piano roll editing. Note data shows up as blocks, which is probably the most "intuitive" way of seeing track data. It's good for making changes quickly. You can shift and move notes manually with an onscreen tool, click with an eraser to erase, *etc.*
- Event list editing. This gives detailed, numerical information on each piece of data—

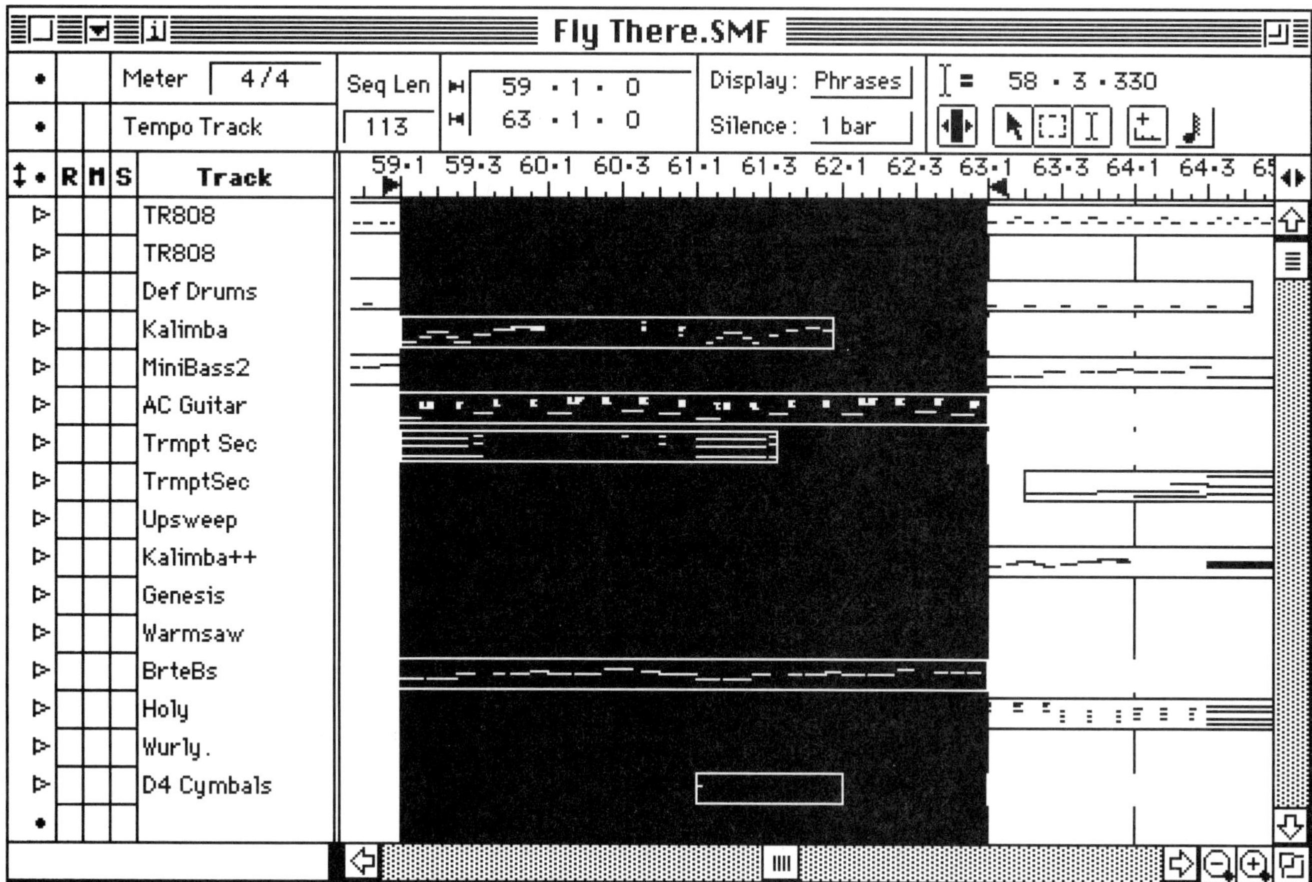


**Fig. 4-11:** *With Opcode's* Vision *sequencing program, clicking and dragging across a four-bar region (in this example, from measure 59 beat 1, to measure 63 beat 1) in the Track Overview window highlights that area. It's now ready to be cut, copied, or otherwise processed.*

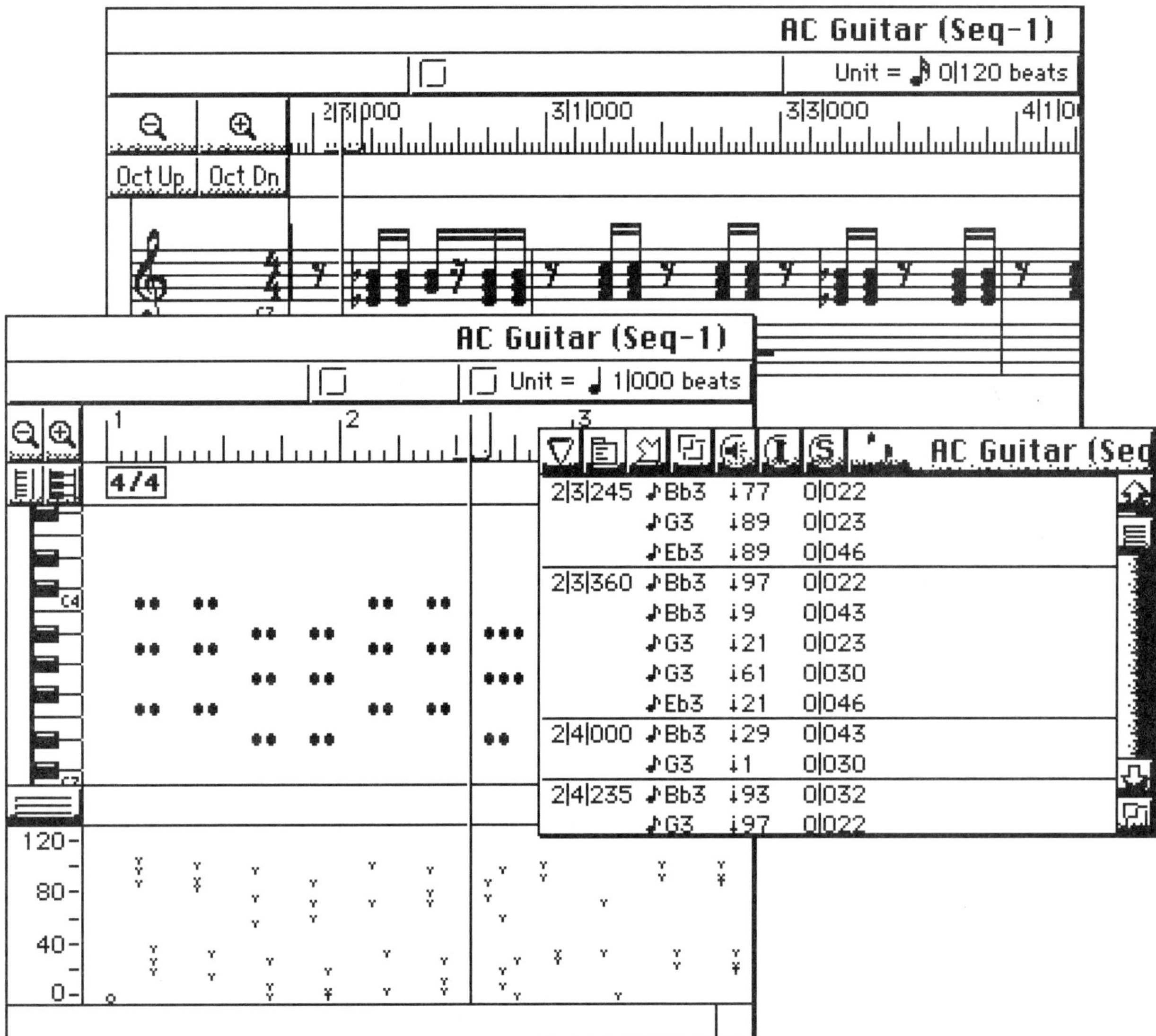


Fig. 4-12: *Like many sequencers,* Performer *offers notation editing (upper window), piano roll editing (lower left window), and event list editing (foreground window). The lower strip chart in the piano roll window shows velocities. The event list shows the note's start point (in measures/beats/clocks), pitch, velocity, and duration in clocks. Note: Clock pulses are also sometimes called "clicks" or "ticks" and represent the smallest rhythmic division available with a sequencer.*

note value, velocity, controllers if present, aftertouch, *etc.* It is the most precise way to edit notes, but lacks the "friendliness" of a graphical interface. It's best for detailed edits, and seeing the characteristics of a passage of notes in one glance. Event lists generally let you view only the data you specify. This is great so you don't have to, for example, wade through hundreds of pitch bend messages looking for note data you want to modify; view only the note data.

- Notation editing. If you were raised on sheet music, you may find this the most comfortable way to work. However, it does not convey as much information about individual notes as the other two methods. For example, if a note starts a little bit early, it will be easier to see that with piano roll or event list editors.

Controller, modulation, aftertouch, and other parameters might be edited in the same window as the notes (often taking the form of one or more "strip charts"; see Fig. 4-13), or in their own window (Fig. 4-14).

## Tracks versus Channels

If there are only sixteen MIDI channels, why do some sequencers offer 64, 256, or even "unlimited" tracks? This isn't just to accommodate multiport interfaces; multiple tracks are handy for creating composite parts where you take the best bits from several different takes. This leads us to . . .

## Cut & Paste

Suppose you record a decent drum part on one track, but think you can record a better one.

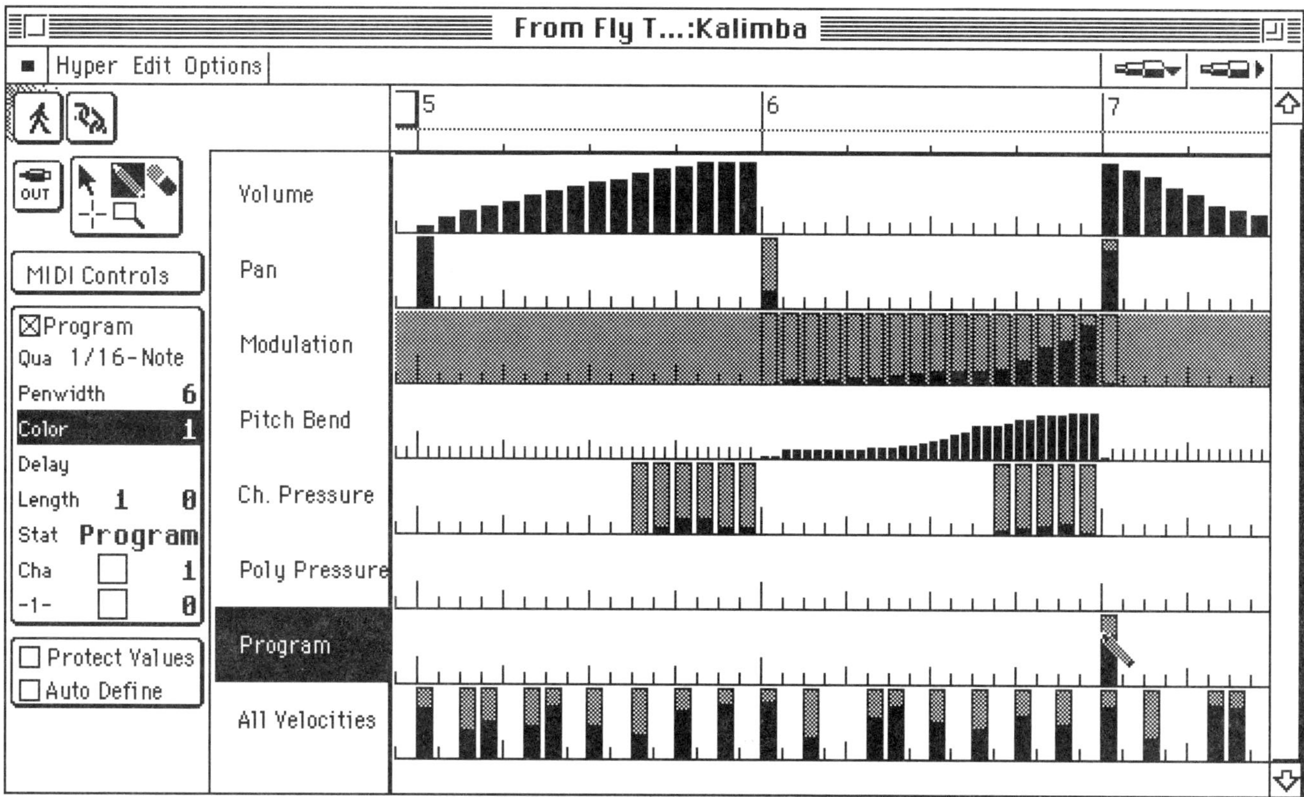


**Fig. 4-13:** *Emagic's* Logic *can show several strips of continuous controllers simultaneously. The strips can have their own background to make them easier to differentiate. In this example, the pencil tool is entering a program change command at the beginning of measure 7.*

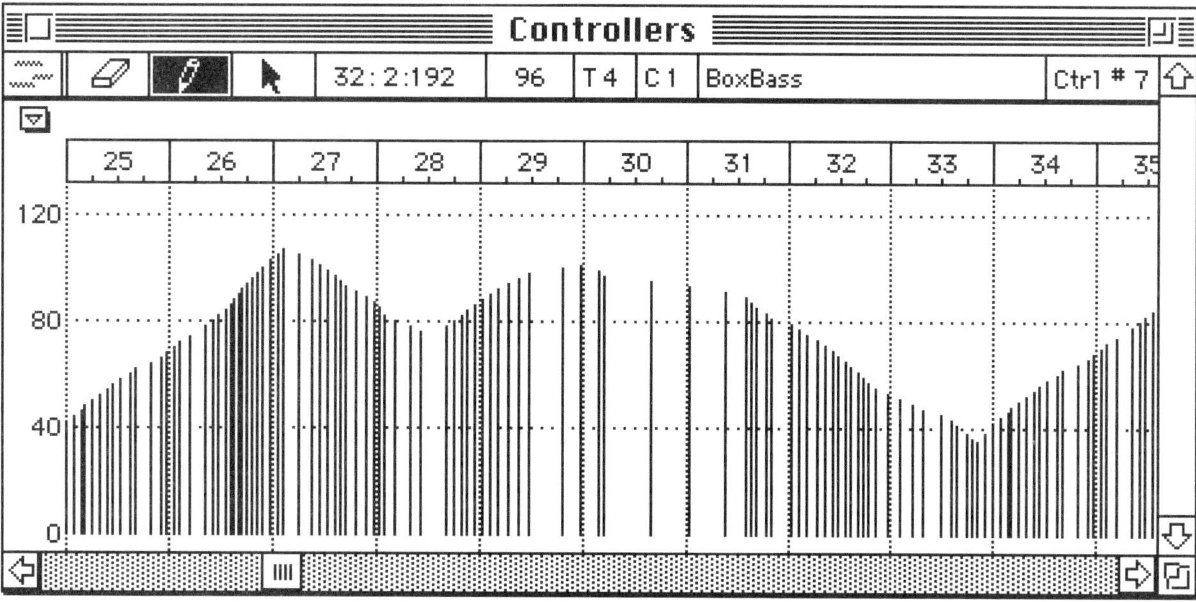


**Fig. 4-14:** *The controllers window from* Pro 6. *It's currently set to controller #7, as shown in the upper right box; therefore, this curve is controlling the main volume for the selected channel (in this case, channel 1, as indicated to the left of the track name box).*

Mute the original track, then play into a new track. You may even decide to *cut* or *copy* the best bits from the two tracks and *paste* them into a third track to create an awesome composite track. These tracks would be assigned to the channel that drives the drums. After creating the composite track, you'll probably want to delete the source tracks to minimize confusion.

## Record Filter

You may not want to record all types of data at all times. For example, some keyboards produce *aftertouch*, which represents how much pressure is applied to a key after it is down (for adding vibrato, increasing volume, *etc.*). However, aftertouch produces a lot of data, and should be used only when necessary. Filtering out aftertouch avoids clogging up a sequence with unneeded data.

To illustrate another application: you decide to overdub pitch bend data to notes that have already been played. Set the record filter to ignore notes, and play the part into a new track. This records only the pitch bend data, which can then merge (mix) with the existing notes.

## Quantization

Quantization lets you specify a rhythmic "grid" (eighth notes, sixteenth notes, *etc.*) to which notes "snap." This is great for cleaning up parts where the rhythm is a little off; quantize the part, and all notes fall right on the desired beat or sub-beat. It's sort of like a spell checker for rhythm.

However, real humans don't play with machinelike precision. To prevent the quantized sound from being too sterile, many sequences allow for setting the quantization *strength* or *percentage*. This shifts the note a certain percentage closer to the ideal (*e.g.*, 50% strength moves a note halfway to the nearest specified rhythmic value). You can keep doing this over and over until you get the right tradeoff between precision and "groove." Fig. 4-15 shows the original passage of notes, the same notes after 50% quantization, then the original notes after being quantized 100%.

There are also various ways to quantize: attack only (retains note length), entire note (may change note length), and "groove" quantize. The latter sets up a rhythmic grid that matches a particular kind of rhythm pattern (*e.g.*, the clave pattern used in salsa, a certain type of shuffle, or a Motown groove). Generally these "push" or "lag" particular notes to give a certain feel.

## Controller Processing

Controllers are some of the coolest signals around because they enable real time, dynamic changes to the sound, which adds expressiveness. Whenever you move a keyboard's mod wheel to add vibrato, or push down on the volume pedal, you're sending out controller data.

We covered controllers earlier in "The Nuts and Bolts of MIDI." There are several editing options that let you tweak controller values (Fig. 4-16).

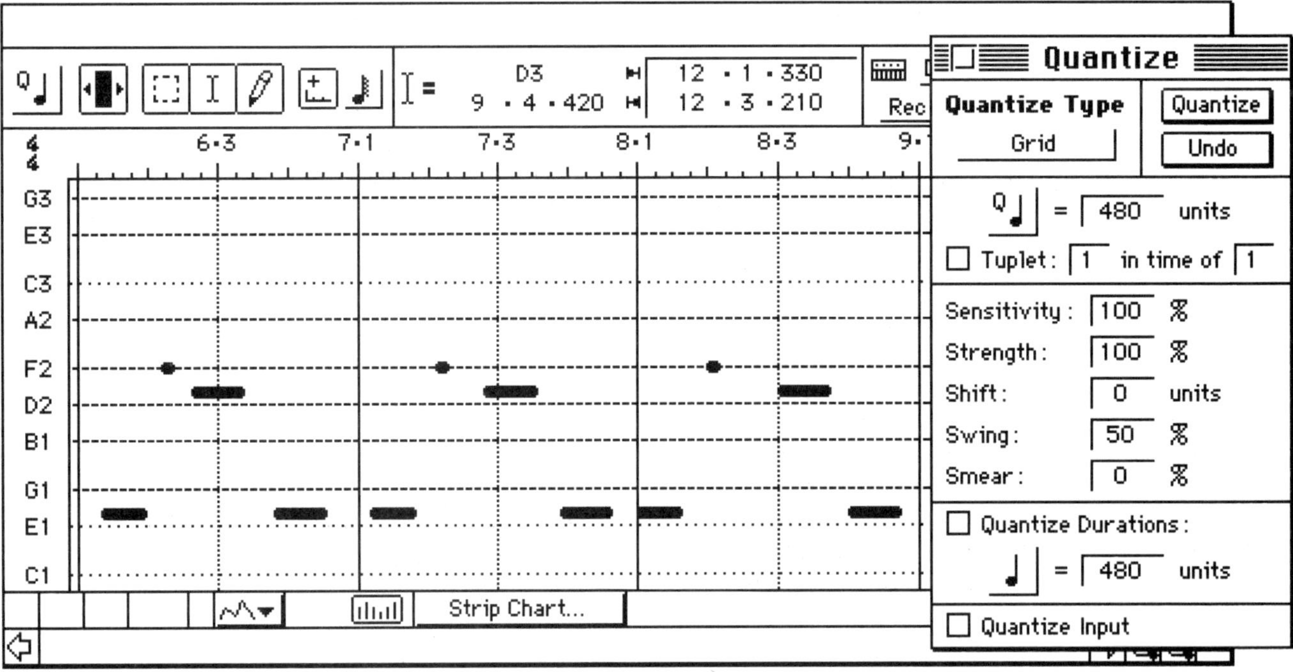


**Fig. 4-15:** Vision's *quantization option in action. Measure 6 shows notes as originally played. Measure 7 shows the same notes quantized with 50% strength to the nearest quarter note. The notes are closer to the beat, but not quite there yet. The notes in measure 8 have been quantized according to the instructions in the Quantize dialog box on the right (100% strength, quarter notes) and are right on the beat.*

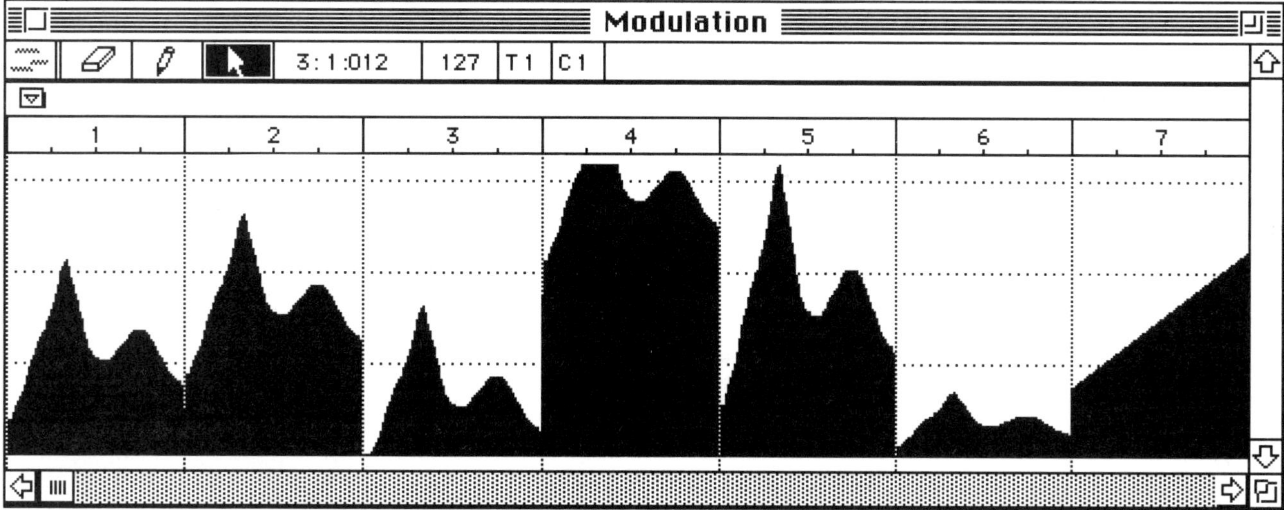


**Fig. 4-16:** *Using* Pro 6's *continuous controller editing options to add, subtract, limit, multiply, divide, and smooth the original data values.*

- Add: This adds a constant to make a wholesale change to the selected controllers (make something louder, softer, faster, *etc.*). Measure 1 in Fig. 4-16 shows the original controller data, measure 2 the original data plus 20, measure 3 subtracts 20 from the original data, and measure 4 shows what happens if you add 70. Note how this last example acts like "limiting" (*i.e.,* the signal cannot exceed a certain amount), because no matter how much you add, a controller value cannot exceed 127.
- Scale: This multiplies or divides by a constant. Measure 5 shows the original signal after multiplying by 150%, and Measure 6 after dividing by 3. Dividing reduces a controller's "dynamic range," because it lowers the difference between high and low values, which gives less radical changes. Multiplying increases the dynamic range, which emphasizes any changes the controller makes. You can always add or subtract a constant to change the overall level of the scaled sound.
- Change smoothly between two values: Select a region of notes, and a starting and ending value; all values in between will change smoothly between those two values. For example, Measure 7 of Fig. 4-16 shows the original data after being edited to change smoothly between 30 and 90. This command is ideal for creating fades and crescendos.
- Change smoothly by percentage: This variation on the above lets you specify the percentage of change instead of an absolute value. For example, you could define a region to change from, for example, 50% of the first value in the region to 75% of the last value in the region.
- Random: Assigns random values to any controller values in the selected region, often with settable limits (*e.g.,* no lower and/or higher than a certain value). This is used mostly for special effects.

## Duration and Legato

Duration changes note length (specified in clicks as well as standard notational symbols), and usually offers the same editing operations as controllers (add, subtract, scale, *etc.*). You can turn a part into instant staccato by cutting duration.

The legato option determines how much the tail of one note overlaps the head of the next. This is useful when cleaning up woodwind, brass, or other single-note lines, as these instruments cannot have two notes overlap. Fig. 4-17 shows a duration dialog box setting that is stretching a note's duration to the next note attack, thus creating a legato effect.

Preventing overlap can also help with voice-stealing if your synthesizer has limited polyphony—why make it play two voices at once if it needs to play only one?

## Logical (Conditional) Editing

Different manufacturers refer to conditional editing by different names (such as logical editing, change filter, selection filter, split notes, *etc.*). But these all have the same basic purpose: set up note criteria (such as pitch range, above or below a particular velocity level, placement within a measure, only notes of less than or more

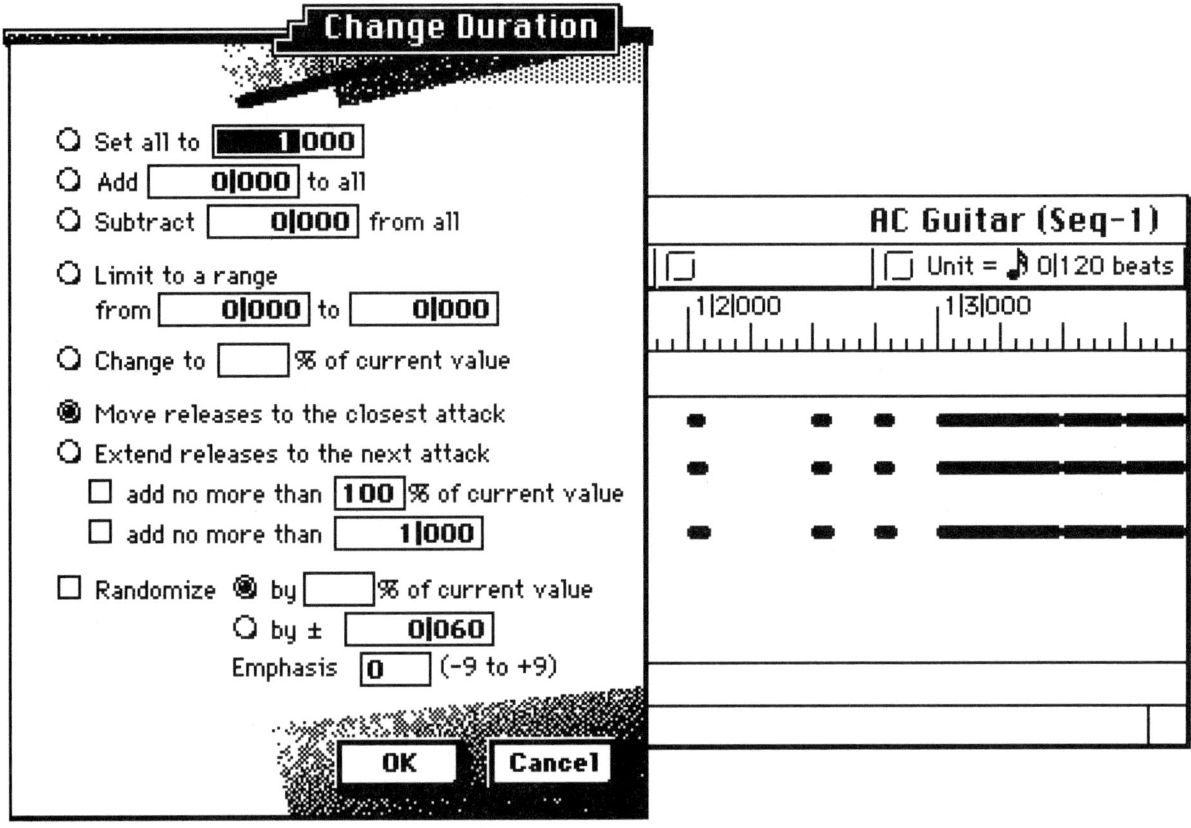


**Fig. 4-17:** Performer's *duration edit window also allows for legato effects. Beat 2 of measure 1 (the leftmost visible beat, with three distinct chords) shows the original note data, which has been edited in beat 3 to "move releases to the closest attack." These notes have been extended right up to the beginning of the next notes.*

than a particular duration, and the like) to which editing operations—cut, transpose, quantize, *etc.*—then apply. Fig. 4-18 shows the logical editor from Cubase, one of the most complicated looking, but powerful, conditional editors.

As an example of logical editing, suppose you want to accent a kick drum part on just the first beat of every measure. Rather than go to each measure, click on the note, then change it, you can simply tell the sequencer to increase velocity on only those notes falling within a certain number of clicks from the first beat of each measure. You could even tell it to accent those notes only if they had, for example, a velocity of 105 or less. If there are several drum sounds on the track, then specify the pitch range that affects only the kick drum.

There's also another form of conditional selection that works with piano roll, event list, and notation windows called *noncontiguous* selection. With noncontiguous selection, it's possible to select several different regions simultaneously, and have them all subject to the same editing operation. With contiguous editing, you can click and drag across only one region of data.

## Tempo Changes

Unlike audio recording, you can change the tempo anytime in the MIDI environment without affecting a sequence's pitch. Sequencing pros know that a sequence isn't really finished until you've tweaked the tempo track—real musicians speed up and slow down, sometimes imperceptibly, to add emotional shading to a song. (Tempo changes are also important for people who do music for commercials, since they often have to "fudge" the tempo so that particular visual actions happen on the beat.)

Want to really set up your song as it goes into the chorus? Drop the tempo just before the chorus for about a measure or so (Fig. 4-19). Want to energize a solo passage? Then up the tempo a shade.

There are several ways to approach tempo editing. One option, tap tempo, lets you create a tempo track by simply tapping a key on the keyboard at whatever rhythm you'd like. Or, you can draw a line to represent tempo, or use some of the same types of commands used for parameters like controllers (add, subtract, and change smoothly are the most common options).

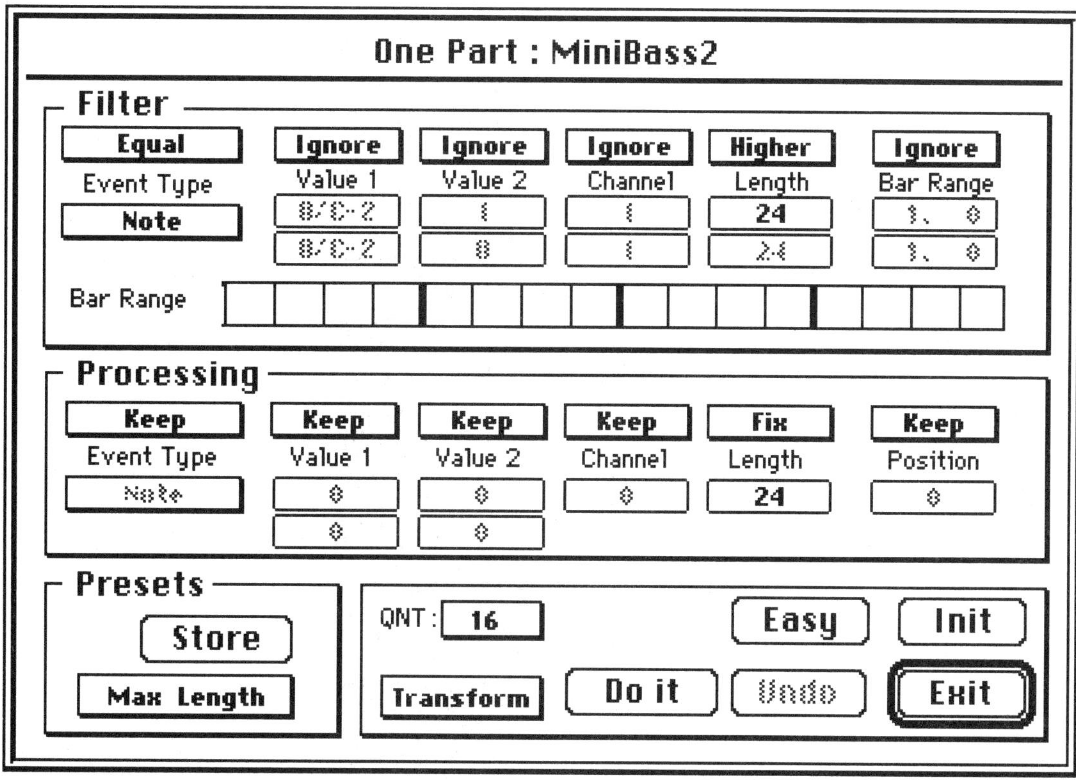


**Fig. 4-18:** Cubase *logical edit screen. In order to create a staccato part, this editor has been set to select (here it's called filter) only notes with a length value higher than 24 ticks. The processing that is applied fixes the length of these notes to 24 ticks. Thus, notes shorter than 24 ticks are unprocessed, whereas those over 24 ticks are fixed at 24 ticks.*

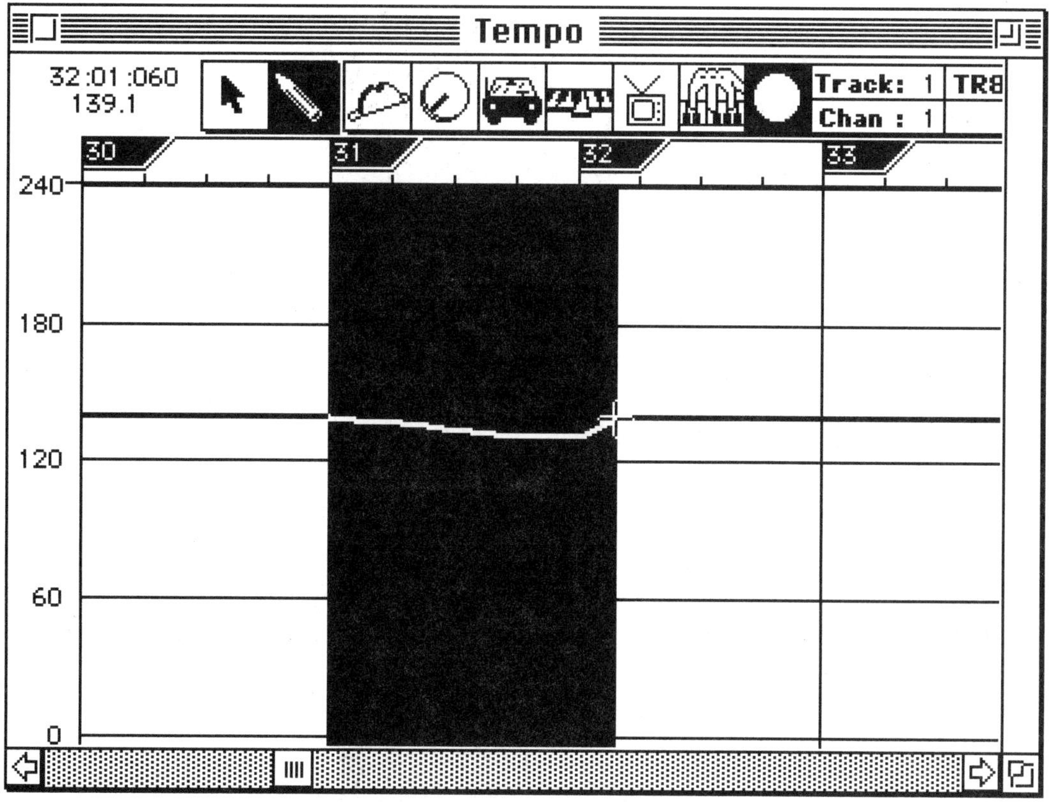


**Fig. 4-19:** Metro *lets you change tempo simply by drawing in a new curve on a graphic editing window. In this example, the tempo dips down a little bit before measure 32, which is where the chorus comes in.*

## Slide Data

Sliding data moves a track forward or backward in time, so it can hit earlier or later than what you played. This has practical uses, such as moving a string part with a long attack time ahead so that it sounds more "on the beat," as well as more groove-oriented techniques. For example, moving a part ahead of the beat gives a more "nervous" feel, while moving the part later sounds more "laid back."

Another trick is to move two harmony lines so that one is slightly ahead of the beat, and the other slightly behind. This helps separate the two and makes each one more distinct.

Usually, the delay amount is measured in ticks (clocks). To translate this to milliseconds, use the formula:

(60,000/tempo)/sequencer resolution = milliseconds per tick

. . . where sequencer resolution is in ticks per quarter note. For example, at 140 beats per minute with a sequencer that has 480 ticks per quarter note resolution, each tick is about 0.9 milliseconds.

## Insert/Delete Measure(s)

Back in the days of tape recorders, you'd rearrange parts of a song by grabbing a razor, then cutting and splicing pieces of tape. Those days are gone, thanks to insert and delete measure commands.

Sometimes this is handled in a dialog box (click at a point in the song, then enter how many measures you want to insert). Other sequencers require you to drag over the region where you want the insert. Assume you want to insert four measures; doing so pushes the rest of the song four measures later, leaving four blank measures in its place (Fig. 4-20).

Cutting measures is usually simpler: just drag across what you want to cut and blast 'em away. Inserting and deleting measures is wonderful for arranging after the fact—you can add space for a solo where none existed, or turn an overindulgent sixteen-bar solo into a tightly edited four-bar version.

## Delete Data

This gets rid of unwanted data from a track. Suppose you forgot to use the record filter, and

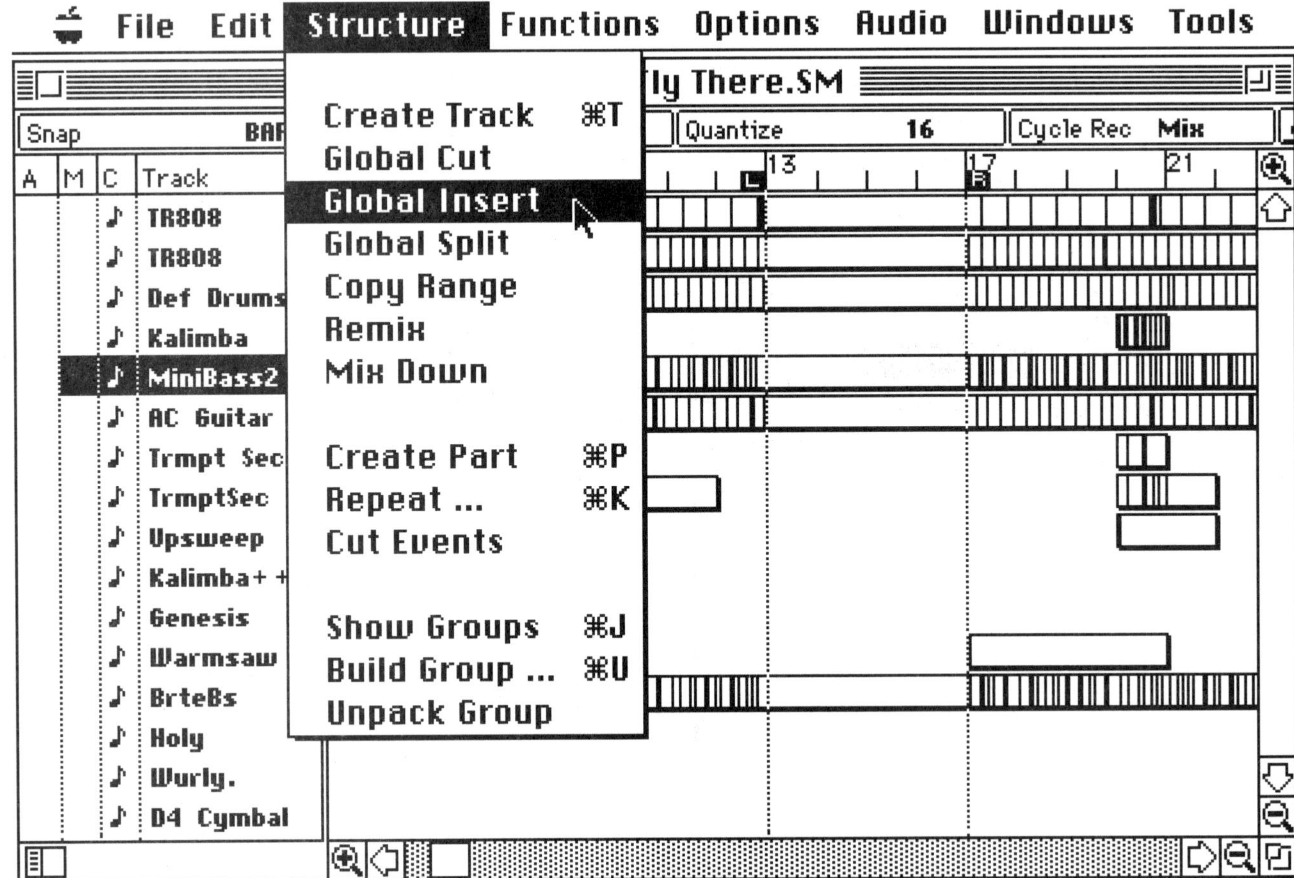


Fig. 4-20: *Inserting four measures in* Cubase's *arrangement window. Markers have been placed at measures 13 and 17. Selecting Global Insert pushes what was in these measures to the right of the R marker, thus leaving four measures empty (from measure 13 to 17).*

ended up recording several hundred kilobytes of aftertouch for patches that aren't even set to respond to it. Imagine trying to get rid of this data one event at a time in an event list editor (truly tedious). With delete or strip data, you can define a region or track and say "remove all aftertouch." The same could be done to notes, controllers, pitch bend, program changes, etc.

You can usually specify the channel where you want the data stripped. This is handy if you happen to import a Type 0 Standard MIDI File, which records all channels in a single track. Strip channel 2 data and paste it to track 2, strip channel 3 data and paste it to track 3, and so on until each channel's worth of data lives in its own track. This makes it much easier to edit and manipulate data.

## Thin data

Most controllers generate huge amounts of unneeded data. As one example, your ear isn't very sensitive to volume variations, so if you're moving a volume pedal, you could probably get by with much less data and obtain the same apparent effect.

Thinning data selectively removes data, either by some kind of fixed algorithm, or according to criteria you specify. Pro 6 has a useful thinning menu (Fig. 4-21): it looks at a piece of data and if the next one changes less than the amount you specify, or occurs closer together than specified, it's deleted. This way, a piece of data has to represent a significant amount of change in order to be kept.

## Humanize

This introduces slight, random changes to the timing, velocity, duration, and possibly other parameters of a track. Its main use is to make quantized tracks sound not quite so machine like, but there's a problem: humans tend to make changes in a conscious way, such as leading or lagging the beat. Random changes seem to occur mostly if the musician has been drinking to excess, so if you want to simulate a drunken musician, the humanize option is the ticket.

But randomize has serious uses as well. If you slightly humanize timing and velocity with drum parts, they'll "breathe" a little bit more.

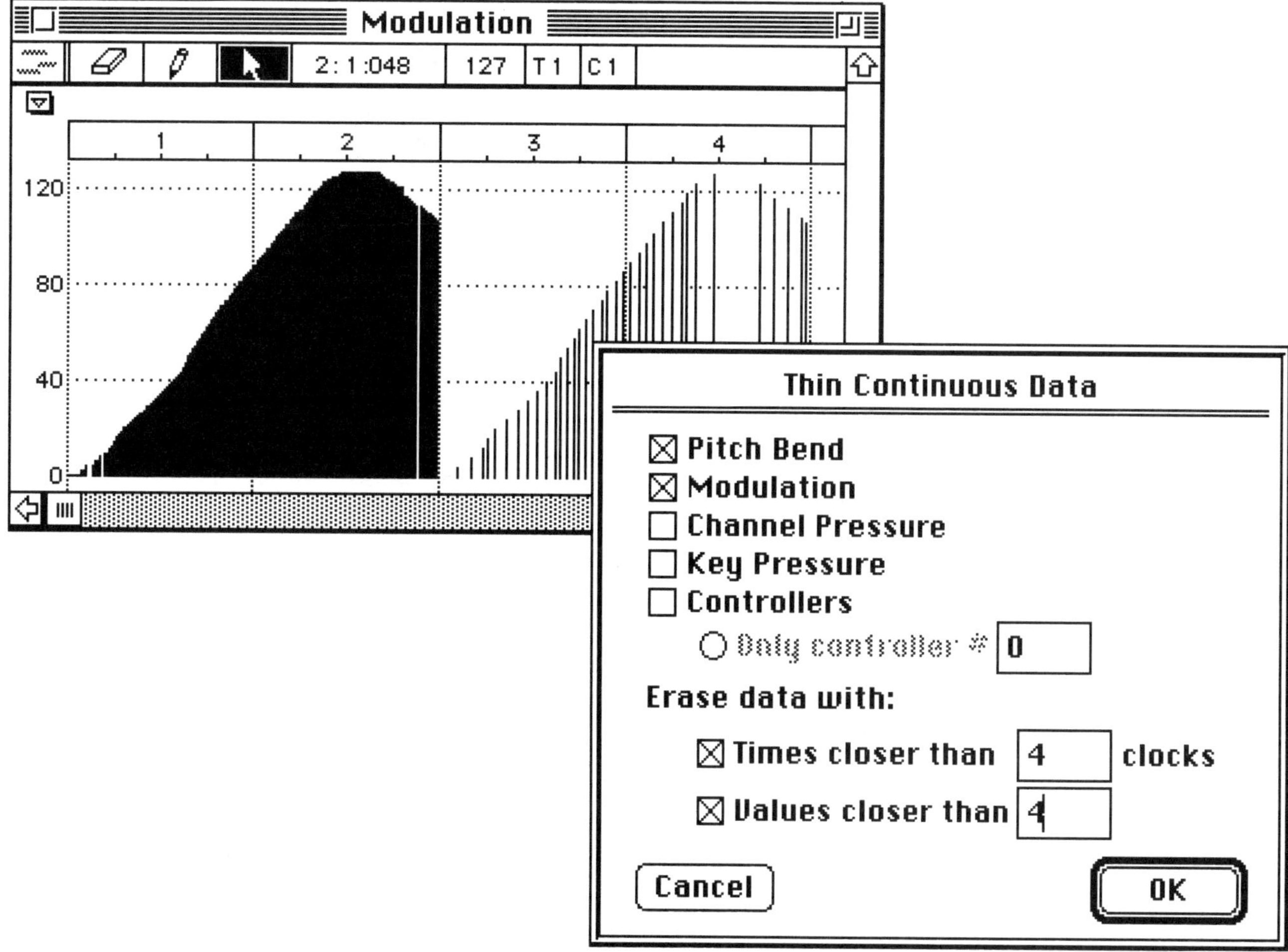


**Fig. 4-21:** Pro 6's *Thin Continuous Data menu is set here to erase data with times closer than 4 clocks (ticks) or values closer than 4. Applying this to the data in measures 1 and 2 creates the svelte data stream in measures 3 and 4.*

Humanizing is also great for flanging effects; copy a track and humanize it, then play the edited copy and the original track into the same instrument. The slight timing changes will provide ultracool flanging effects.

## Transpose

When it was first introduced, one of the MIDI sequencer's most endearing characteristics was its ability to change pitch without changing tempo, which was a major change from the world of tape recording. Need to compensate for a singer's range? No problem. Want to turn your six-string guitar into a soprano? Try this (Fig. 4-22).

Transposition has other, less obvious uses. Take drum machines: in the real world each drum stroke has a slightly different sound, whereas with most drum machines, each stroke sounds exactly the same. There's an easy fix: assign the same sound, but with very slightly different tuning, to two notes. Transpose every other note to the second drum sound, and the drum part will have a lot more variation.

## Chase Controllers

Continuous controllers generate a particular value which remains in effect until the next controller value comes along. This can cause problems if you start playing a sequence from somewhere other than the beginning; here's why.

Suppose you have a part where a series of controller messages causes the volume to fade out after the first verse. At the start of the second verse, there's a volume message that turns everything back on full again, and it stays that way until the end of the song.

Now assume you play through the end of the first verse. As expected, the volume gets turned down. Now you decide to move forward to the

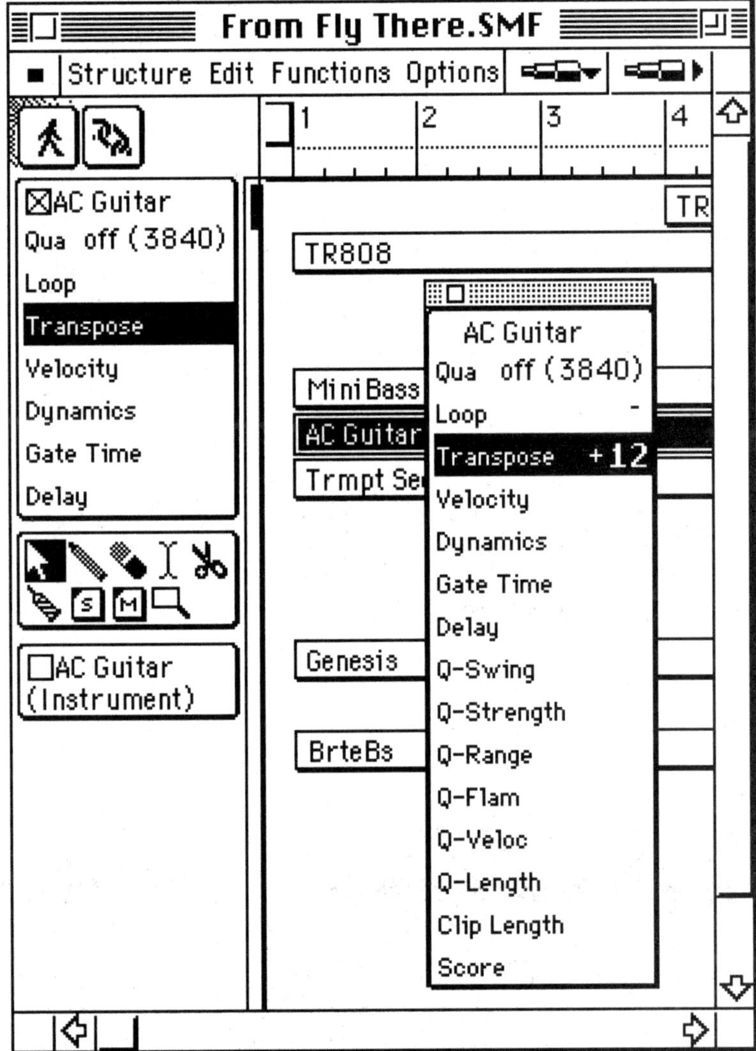


**Fig. 4-22:** Logic *transposing an acoustic guitar track. Simply holding the mouse down on transpose and dragging the mouse up or down transposes notes up or down, respectively. Here, the guitar is being transposed up +12 semitones.*

last part of the sequence. If you bypass that "maximum volume" message at verse 2, the instrument will retain the previous message it received, which was to be at minimum volume (the end of the fadeout). So, the instrument won't make a peep when you land at the end of the sequence.

With controller chasing, whenever you start the sequencer it looks back for the most recent controller, pitch bend, aftertouch, and similar parameters, and sets everything accordingly. The only tradeoff is that sometimes it takes a little time for the sequencer to check back on all the tracks, but it's worth the wait if it saves you the time of troubleshooting your MIDI rig to figure out why one of your instruments isn't making any noise.

## Autolocation and Finding Places

If you need to jump back and forth between two points (for example, making changes to one chorus and comparing it to another chorus), it's helpful to be able to jump from one section of a sequence to another. Different sequencers handle this in different ways; there may be markers that you "tab" between to move from one section of a song to another, or a "hot key" that places you at some defined place (like where you last clicked). Sometimes different keystrokes will take you different places, such as hitting a key once to go to where you last clicked, or hitting a key twice to go back to the beginning of the song.

## Special Record Modes

You can record in the usual way—press record to record, and stop to stop—but sequencers offer far more imaginative ways to do things.

As one example, the precision of sequencers is ideal for setting automated punch-in and punch-out points. This eliminates once and for all the chance of punching in at the wrong place (and if you do, there's always the undo command) since the computer does that work for you.

Looped (cycled) recording is another punching tool (Fig. 4-23). With this, a piece of music you define "loops" over and over again. The new data can either replace previously played data as you go along, or add to what was played previously (sound on sound). Replacing is great for trying out solos—just keep playing until you get something you like, then stop. Sound on sound works well for building up drum parts (play a kick, then overdub the snare, the high-hats, *etc.*).

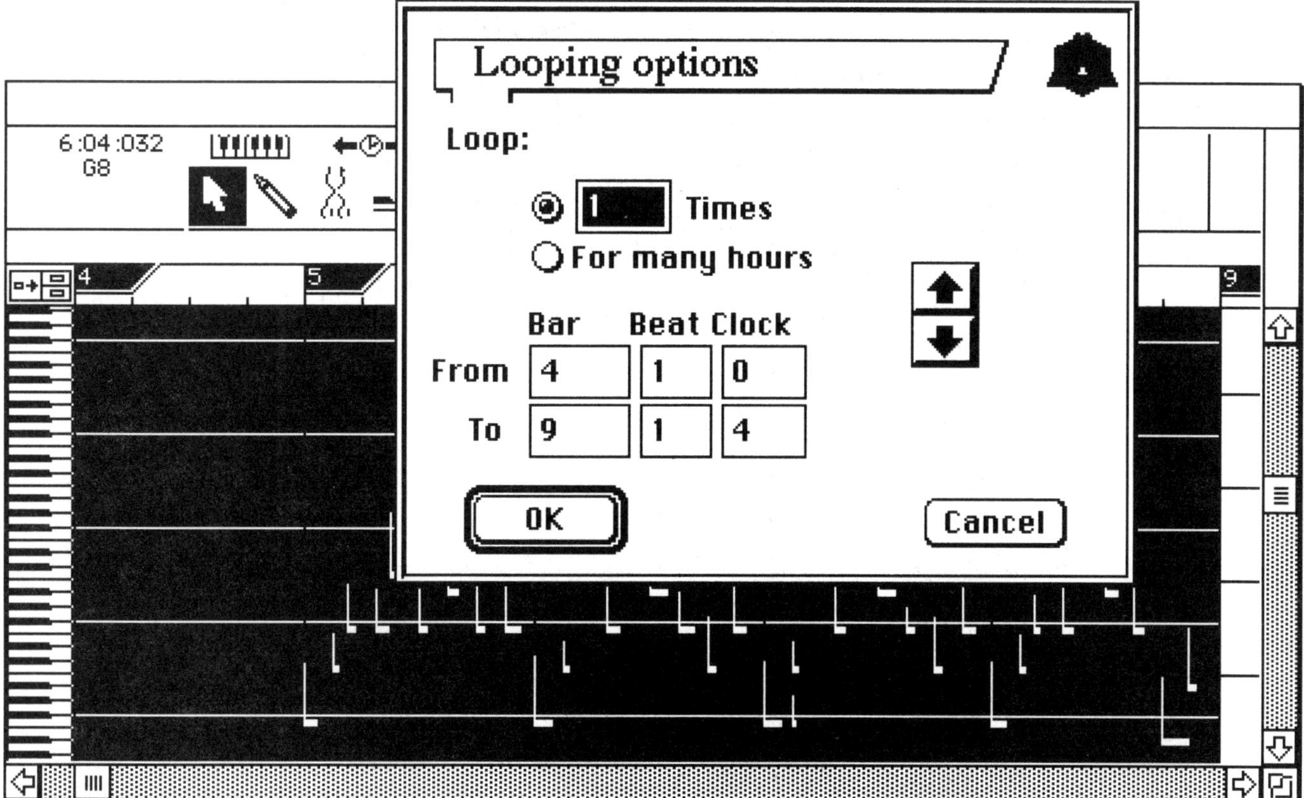


Fig. 4-23: Metro's *loop record lets you determine how many times you're going to loop (right now, 1 is highlighted and ready to be changed). It uses the last selected region as the loop area—in this case, bars 4 to 9.*

Some sequencers will even create a new track for every pass so that new data is easy to differentiate from old data, yet nothing gets erased. This is the best choice for recording *composite* tracks, where you cut and paste together different parts of different tracks to create one mind-bogglingly incredible track with all the best bits.

## MIDI Mixing Sliders

Not only can you sequence with today's sequencer, you can mix as well by using a mouse to move onscreen faders (see Fig. 4-24). On playback, the faders will move in response to the recorded controller changes. Moving faders are even better than blinking lights! What's more, you can usually customize a "console" of faders, each assigned to whatever controller you want, on whatever channel you want.

But would you want to program sixteen onscreen faders with a mouse? Of course not. Companies such as JL Cooper and Peavey make external, hardware boxes with standard long-throw faders that you can link to the onscreen faders you want to control. For example, if one of the onscreen faders is set to channel 1, controller 7, setting one of the external faders to channel 1, controller 7 will move the onscreen slider.

Using sliders to do a mix is a lot easier than using a mouse, but this can produce mucho data if you're not careful. The thin data option mentioned earlier helps.

## Recording Program Changes on a Track

Want to change sounds in the middle of a track (*e.g.*, turn a muted trumpet into a nonmuted version)? You can cut the part you want, paste it to a separate track, and assign it to a separate channel to drive the alternative sound . . . or you could simply insert a program change command in the existing track to switch from one instrument to another.

However, there are some potential problems with inserting program changes. If notes are sustaining, selecting a new program may cut them off abruptly. Also, there may be a slight lag between the time a synthesizer receives a program change, and when it actually flushes out the old data and loads in the new. It's often a good idea to place program changes slightly before the beat to compensate for this.

## Recording Sys Ex

System exclusive messages (sys ex for short) contain nonstandard MIDI data, such as representations of a synthesizer's control settings. If you record sys ex representing a particular patch at the beginning of a track, playing back that track will actually load all the correct parameters into the synth. In this respect, the sequencer acts like a "librarian" as it can store not only compositions, but the data needed to create the required sounds in the instruments you're using.

Sys ex can take up a lot of memory, which means it may not be recorded (or play back) correctly (some sequencers don't even try to record sys ex). For this reason, it's usually better to record the sys ex for an individual patch, not for all the programs in the synthesizer. Also, most record filters default to not recording sys ex, so if a program doesn't seem to record sys ex, check if this is a problem.

Of course, all we've done is cover the basics. Sequencer manuals are often hundreds of pages long, which means there are a lot of features that remain to be discussed. But one of the nice characteristics of sequencers is you can use them on a fairly basic level at first, then move along into exploring more advanced options. One last word of advice: edit *after* you've laid down your tracks. If you edit as you go along, you'll lose the flow.

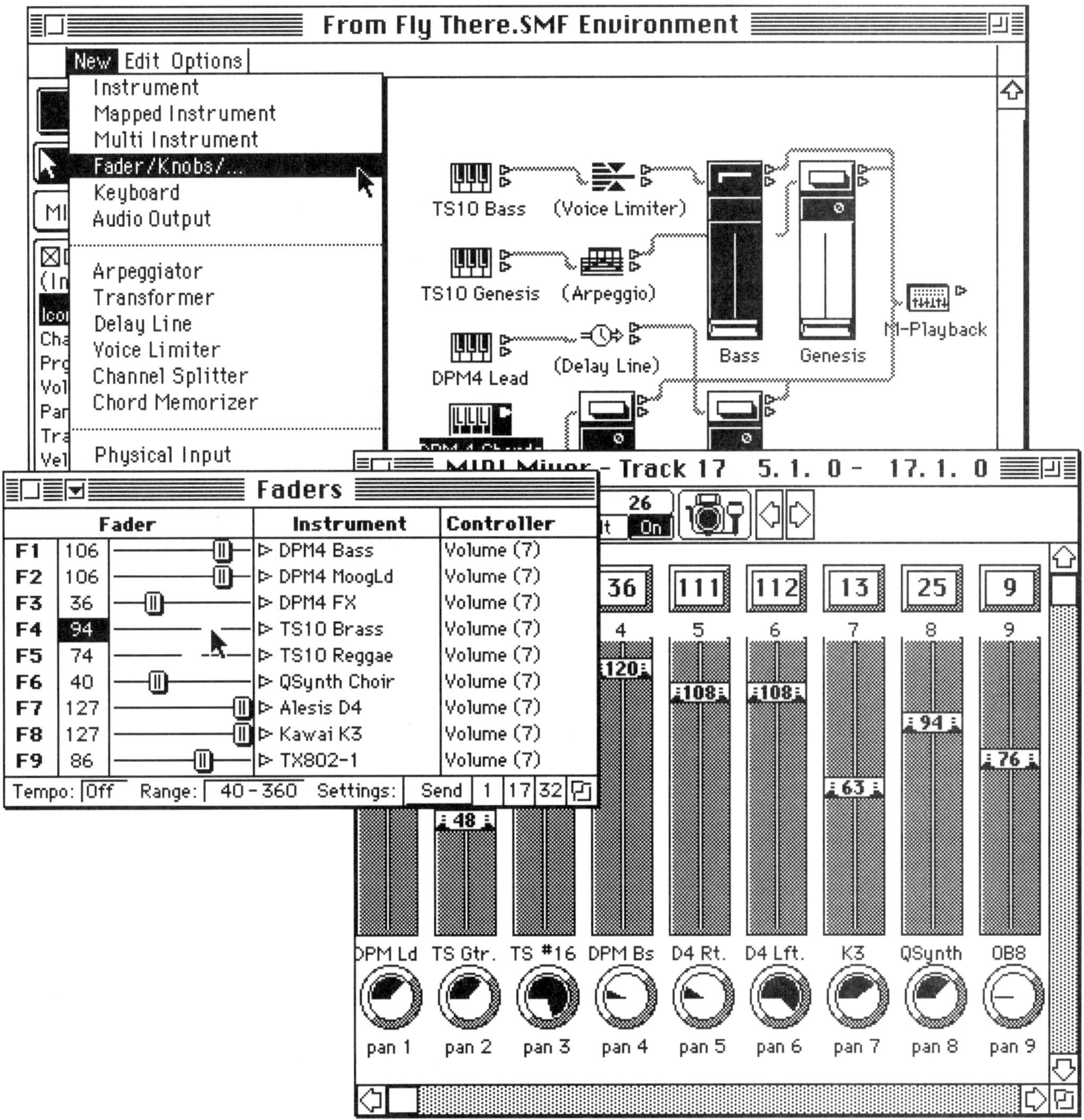


**Fig. 4-24:** *Three different approaches to faders. The top window, from* Logic, *shows not just faders but other processors (arpeggiator, delay line, etc.) you can insert into your "virtual mixer." At this moment, a fader is about to be created on screen. The lower left window shows* Vision's *easily understood fader implementation. The lower right shows a* Cubase *"mixermap," set up for program changes, mixing, and panning.*

# Chapter 5
# Selecting and Purchasing Your Studio Gear

Now it's time to choose and purchase your particular recording medium. Recorders offer a (perhaps bewildering) variety of technologies at multiple price points, so let's look at the pros and cons of what's available. Remember that increased sophistication doesn't necessarily lead to better music; after all, some records that have stood the test of time (such as *Sgt. Peppers' Lonely Hearts Club Band* by the Beatles and *Are You Experienced?* by Jimi Hendrix) were recorded with four-track, analog machines.

## The Cassette Multitrack

Multitrack recorders based on the standard cassette format (Fig. 5-1) are excellent "sketchpads" for getting down ideas and cutting demos. Available in four-, six-, and eight-track configurations, some are even built in a mixer chassis to create a self-contained "portable studio." Advantages include low tape costs, small size, fast operation, cost-effectiveness, and reasonably good fidelity. However, these machines aren't really good enough to produce master-quality tapes (although some would argue that point).

Pros: Inexpensive, easy and quick to operate, low tape costs, low learning curve

Cons: Lowest audio quality of current multitrack technologies, limited recording time, limited to maximum of eight tracks

Bottom line: If you mainly cut demos and don't want to become a rocket scientist, this is probably your best bet.

### What to Look For in a Multitrack Cassette Recorder

Not all models offer all the features listed below; therefore, choosing the right deck will involve deciding exactly what your needs are, then finding the deck that (for your application) makes the right compromises.

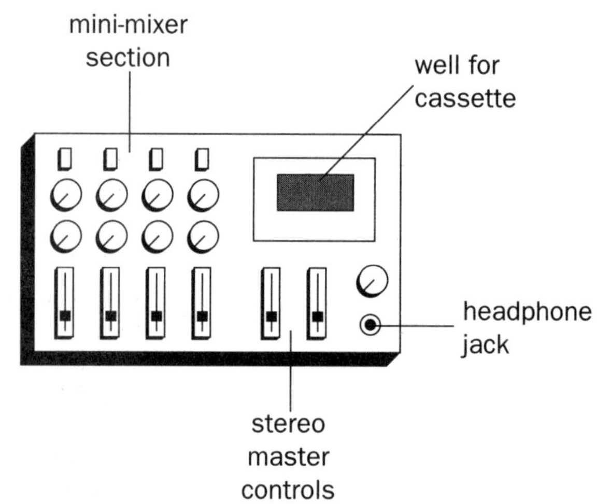


**Fig. 5-1:** *Typical portable, four-track cassette recorder with built-in mixer. These types of machines weigh only a few pounds; rack mount versions, particularly for eight-track models, are also available.*

- Standard cassette compatibility. To improve fidelity, some cassette multitracks run at 3.75 IPS instead of the usual 1.875 IPS. The disadvantage is you can't play back (or record) standard-format cassettes. If you want your multitracker to double as a standard cassette player, select a machine that can run at 1.875 IPS, or both high and low speeds.
- Pitch (speed) control. If you play piano, you will never regret getting a tape recorder with pitch control! A pitch control lets you vary the tape speed (sometimes as much as ±20%) on record and/or playback, thus changing the recorded sound's pitch. If your piano is perfectly in tune with itself but out of tune with a basic track, no problem; change the tuning of the track, not of the piano. By the way, pitch controls are good for much more than touching up your tuning—at extreme settings, you can obtain special effects such as Darth Vader and Munchkin voices, unusual drum sounds, and so on.

- Noise reduction. While all multitrackers have noise reduction, some use Dolby B, some Dolby C, some Dolby S, and some dbx. If you need compatibility with an existing library of Dolby B cassettes, then your deck should include Dolby B; but for absolute minimum noise, it's important that the deck provide Dolby S or dbx as well. To my ears, both noise reduction systems are effective but there are some differences. To hear how noise reduction affects the sound so you can decide which type you like better, try recording trebly bass guitar since this instrument tends to show up noise problems more readily than some other instruments.
- Automatic tape transport functions. Many cassette (and reel to reel) machines include rewind-to-cue (also called return-to-zero) so that when you rewind, the machine will automatically stop at a particular cue point (usually where the index counter says 000). For more information, see Chapter 19 on Automation.

  One problem with most mechanically based autolocation systems is that the index counter readings can "creep" over time with analog gear. For example, the machine might gradually rewind farther and farther toward the beginning of a song each time you initiate the rewind-to-cue function. Therefore, it's a good idea to check the setting on the index counter occasionally and reset it if necessary.
- Headphone output. Headphone outputs are a useful accessory when you need to do quick recordings—simply slap a mic into an input, clamp on the phones, and go. (Incidentally, don't use open air headphones for recording vocals, since there can be enough leakage between the phones and the vocal mic to cause feedback problems. You're better off with headphones that seal completely around the ear, even though these can be less comfortable and more bulky.)
- Mic preamps and tone controls. Some manufacturers make cassette multitrack recorders that are more like mini recording studios (*i.e.,* they include tone controls, faders, panpots, mic preamps, and so on). Other companies assume that you will be using the recorder with an existing mixer, and therefore delete all but the most essential controls in order to reduce cost and size. If you plan to transport your machine a lot, integrating the mixer with the recorder makes life much easier. If you're more interested in recording at home, a stripped-down model might be better since this gives you more choices for the accompanying mixer.
- Simultaneous recording on several tracks. Although most modern cassette multitrackers can record on all tracks simultaneously, others only allow for recording two tracks at a time. For solo artists, being able to record on two tracks is usually good enough since most parts will be overdubbed. However, if you often record "live," then it's important to be able to record on all available tracks at once.
- Bouncing capabilities. Ping-ponging (or "bouncing") is the process of recording several tracks, then mixing them down to a single track to make more tracks available for overdubs. If you use this technique a lot, check for restrictions on ping-ponging. Some older machines will not let you bounce to adjacent tracks (*e.g.,* 1, 2, and 3 to 4) but will let you bounce to nonadjacent tracks (*e.g.,* 1 and 2 into 4).

## Analog Reel-to-Reel Multitrack

These were "king of the hill" for decades, and many top-selling albums have been cut on budget four-, eight-, sixteen-, and twenty-four-track analog multitrack machines (Fig. 5-2). There are both pro studio models that cost five figures as well as project studio versions that use narrower tape and tend toward four figures or less.

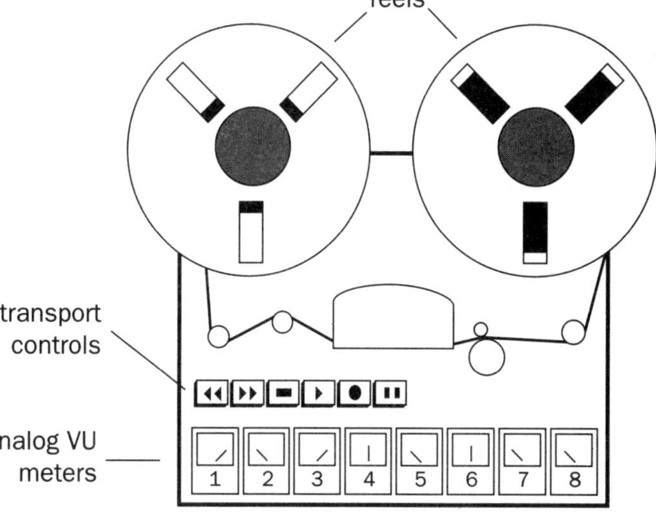


**Fig. 5-2:** *Eight-track analog recorder with analog meters and 10.5" reels.*

Analog multitrack is a proven, mature technology that is capable of good sonic performance if used with noise reduction (Dolby S and

SR are particularly effective). The down side is that unlike digital recorders, you can't bounce tracks or make multiple copies without some sonic degradation.

However, another factor is that many musicians prefer the sound of analog over digital. Also, as inexpensive digital multitracks become more popular (see next), older, secondhand analog decks are showing up at very attractive prices.

Pros: Proven technology, relatively inexpensive, distinctive sound quality

Cons: Higher noise levels than digital, wow and flutter, audio quality deteriorates over time, duplicating creates generation loss

Bottom line: If you don't particularly like the sound of digital, need to do master-quality work without breaking the bank, don't mind getting in at the tail end of an older technology instead of the ground floor of a new technology, and are willing to be a bit of a tech (analog decks need periodic maintenance), this may be your best option.

### What to Look For in a Multitrack Reel-to-Reel Recorder

- Pitch (speed) control. See above, under cassette multitracks.
- Automatic tape transport functions. See above, under cassettes.
- Noise reduction. Not all reel-to-reel decks include noise reduction, though most narrow-format types (*e.g.*, sixteen- and twenty-four-track machines) do. Unlike cassette decks, there is no need to maintain compatibility with a particular standard, as most tapes recorded on a particular multitrack will be played back on that multitrack. However, the other comments about cassette-based systems regarding Dolby and dbx also apply to reel-to-reel types.
- Accessible bias and equalization trim controls. As bias has such an important effect on audio quality, make sure the bias controls are readily accessible so you can optimize the audio quality for different types of tape.
- Spooling or edit mode. Many times when recording, you'll need to get rid of excess tape from a reel or do splicing. In *edit* mode, the tape remains in contact with the head but the supply and takeup reels have no pull, allowing you to manually rock the tape back and forth over the head to find the best splice point. In *spooling* mode, you can go into play mode and simply have the tape spill onto the floor rather than be taken up by the takeup reel. This is handy when you want to assemble a master tape from several reels and need to get rid of excess or damaged tape.

## Budget Digital Multitrack Tape

Eight-track modular digital multitrack (MDM) tape recorders are based on video technology and combine CD-quality sound, no need for noise reduction, the ability to make backups and safeties that are literal clones of the master tape, and usually, easy expandability—all with the same basic ease of use as analog recorders (Fig. 5-3).

Although these are compelling features, digital does have a dark side. Lose a few bits from inferior tape, and you could end up with nasty, unfixable glitches; lose an equal amount of oxide from analog tape, and you may not even notice the difference. Also, digital technology in general is notorious for being subject to change without notice—today's hot product often ends up as tomorrow's doorstop.

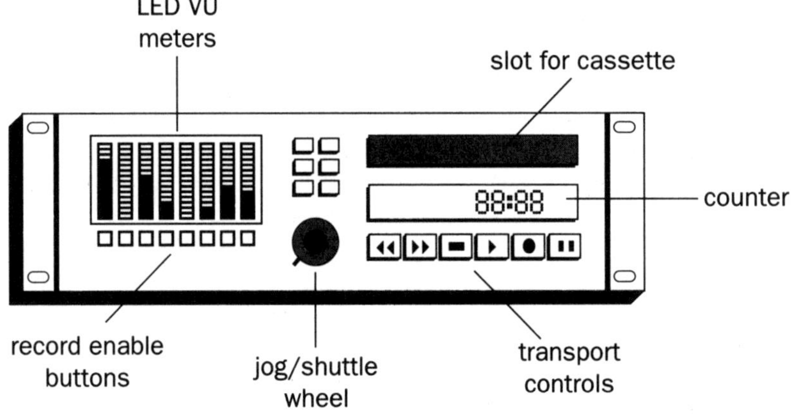


**Fig. 5-3:** *Generic eight-track, rack mount MDM. The S-VHS or Hi-8 cassette feeds into the indicated slot, like a VCR.*

Pros: Superb sound quality, compatibility with users of the same format, easy expansion to more tracks, short learning curve, no tape alignment, relatively maintenance free

Cons: Difficult to edit, relatively expensive, tape dropouts can be fatal instead of just annoying, competing formats (S-VHS tape versus Hi-8) complicate the buying decision

Bottom line: If pristine sound quality and expandability are important, and you don't mind being on the leading edge, digital multitrack tape is extremely appealing.

### What to Look For in an MDM

- Pitch (speed) control. See above, under cassettes.
- Automatic tape transport functions. See above, under cassettes.
- Error correction indicator. This lets you know if there is a problem that requires the intervention of the error correction circuitry. If this indicator lights a lot, the heads are getting dirty or the tape is starting to deteriorate; this means it's time to clean the heads and if that doesn't help, "clone" a copy and work with that instead of the original tape.
- Digital inputs and outputs. This lets you transfer data digitally to other machines (as opposed to going through the analog inputs and outputs), thus preserving sound quality. An increasing number of devices can now interface directly with digital connections (for example, you can feed the digital output of some synthesizers and hard disk recorders directly into an MDM, without having to visit the analog domain).
- Expandability. This doesn't only mean adding more MDMs to create more tracks, but also, the option to add remote control devices, additional interfacing (such as MIDI Machine Control, as described in Chapter 19), and the like.
- Jog/shuttle wheel. While not essential, this lets you move the tape small amounts at a time to make it easier to find a specific location. This is sort of like "rocking the reels" with analog gear.

## Budget Multitrack Hard Disk Recording

The precision offered by hard disk recording isn't cheap, and a hard disk crash can turn your hair prematurely gray. Still, the power, flexibility, and fidelity are intoxicating. Versions are available from two to sixteen tracks, and are usually easily expandable. Some are stand-alone "black boxes" that look pretty much like an MDM or even a cassette-based multitrack, while some are based on personal computer systems such as the PC or Mac.

Pros: Superb sound quality, extremely flexible editing, well suited to audio-for-video applications, may be able to use multitrack digital tape for storage, easy upgrading, stand-alone models are easy to use

Cons: Somewhat expensive (you need a fast, high-capacity hard drive and a way to back up vast amounts of data), computer-based systems require lots of computer savvy, some operations take a while, upgrading can be costly

Bottom line: If you have the bucks, hard disk recording is the most state-of-the-art and flexible audio recording medium.

### What to Look For in a Multitrack Hard Disk Recorder

- Synchronization options. The hard disk recorder should be able to function as a slave or master with respect to MIDI and SMPTE signals.
- Digital inputs and outputs. See above, under Multitrack Digital Recorder.
- Expandability for stand-alone units. Computer-based units are inherently expandable since you can add peripherals to the computer. Stand-alone units have various degrees of expandability, but at the very least, you should be able to add more hard drives for extra storage. Some devices also let you add a computer interface for graphic editing.

## DAT/VHS Hi-Fi Recorder

For capturing a live performance in stereo or mixing down to a two-track master, DAT (Digital Audio Tape recorder; see Fig. 5-4) or a VHS or S-VHS Hi-Fi deck (which use analog frequency modulation techniques that approach, or equal, CD quality) are excellent choices. Their wide dynamic range lets you allocate 10 to 20 extra dB for headroom to accommodate peaks, yet still have wider dynamic range than all but the best analog gear. Get a DAT with digital inputs and outputs; even if you can't use them now, someday you'll be glad you have them. If you go the VCR route, look for models with meters as well as the ability to defeat compression (if used).

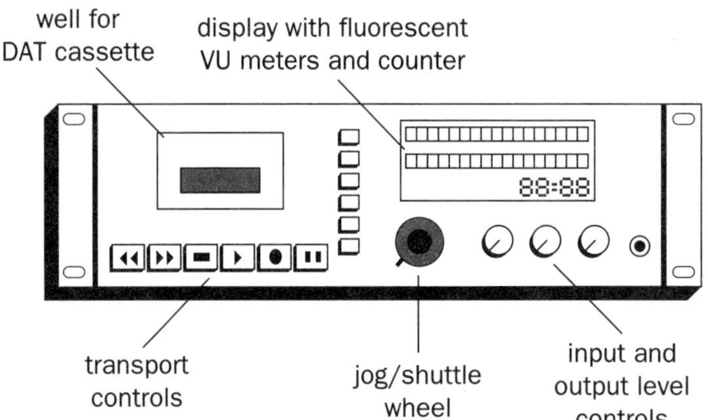


Fig. 5-4: *Rack mount* DAT *recorder. This one has a jog/shuttle wheel, which is found on more high-end gear. Also note the two large, horizontal VU meters.*

Pros: Excellent sound quality, relatively low media cost, ease of use

Cons: No overdubbing, difficult to edit, limited to two tracks, some VCRs can't record audio without feeding in a video signal too

Bottom line: If you're a soloist or a group that plays "live" and doesn't need to do overdubs, DAT produces high-fidelity, stereo master tapes, with VHS Hi-Fi coming in second.

### What to Look For in a DAT Deck

- Pitch (speed) control. See above, under Cassette Multitracks. This is found only on big-bucks machines.
- Off-tape monitoring. Again, found only on high-priced decks; it's the equivalent of having a third head on an analog deck since you can hear what's being recorded on tape.
- Error correction indicator. See above, under Digital Multitracks.
- Digital inputs and outputs. See above, under Digital Multitracks.

## Two-Track Cassette Deck

Although not as good as a DAT, a cassette deck with Dolby S gives very acceptable results for a lot less money. However, a cassette deck for the studio requires different features than if you're using it in the home.

Pros: Decent sound quality, low tape cost, ease of use

Cons: No overdubbing, difficult to edit, limited to two tracks

Bottom line: You can get acceptable quality two-track masters, and after you upgrade to a multitrack, you'll still have this to make copies for your friends.

### What to Look For in a Two-Track Cassette Deck

- Pitch (speed) control. See above, under Cassette Multitracks. This is rare.
- Off-tape monitoring. Having three heads lets you monitor the taped signal, which makes setting levels and bias a piece of cake.
- Dolby HX Pro. This is a circuit that improves treble response by shifting the tape bias according to level. It does not need decoding for playback, so tapes recorded with HX Pro sound good on any deck.
- Avoid models with auto reverse. It's just one more thing to go wrong, which you don't need in the studio.
- Variable bias. Hard to find, but well worth it: by tweaking the bias you can often make inexpensive tapes sound really good.

## MIDI Sequencer

A standard MIDI sequencer, whether computer-based or a stand-alone device (Fig. 5-5), records performance data from MIDI instruments such as keyboards and drum machines. Although most sequencers do not record audio (there are exceptions, see the next category), you can sing or play in real time over a sequencer playing a backing track, and record the results to DAT, for an inexpensive yet high-quality master tape.

Furthermore, many keyboards include multiple instrument sounds and a built-in sequencer. As one instrument can let you sequence an entire backup band, you can produce CD-quality tapes for the cost of a good keyboard, DAT, mic (for vocals), and mixer. If the vocals need beefing up, use a signal processor.

Pros: Low cost, capable of excellent audio quality (depends on quality of sound generators), extensive editing features

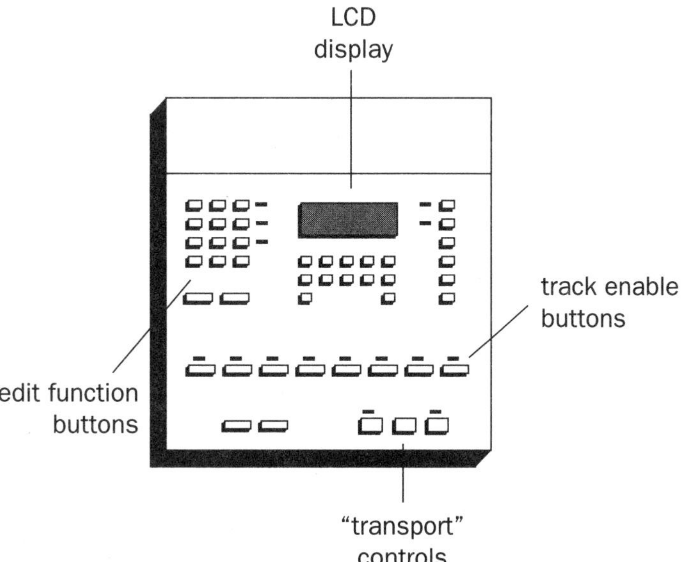


**Fig. 5-5:** *Inexpensive, stand-alone sequencer. One of the main disadvantages compared to a computer-based type is the LCD, which can't show as much information as a computer monitor. However, the dedicated control surface can be quicker to use than a computer's QWERTY keyboard.*

Cons: All sounds have to play back in real time (unlike tape or hard disk recording, where one instrument can do multiple overdubs). This requires more sound generators, mixer inputs, and signal processors.

Bottom line: There are some limitations, but if you're on a tight budget, this approach can create high quality demos.

## What to Look For in a Computer-Based MIDI Sequencer

- Upgradeability. Several sequencers let you upgrade to advanced versions that integrate hard disk recording with MIDI sequencing.
- Notation. Although this function may not be as sophisticated as the ones found in dedicated notation programs, having standard notation available lets you print out quick lead sheets.
- Integration with other programs. For example, some sequencers work with companion editor/librarian programs for synthesizers so you can edit sounds while the sequencer is running (it's much easier to have a context when editing), and also let you assign patches to tracks by name instead of having to specify a MIDI channel and program number. There are also "MIDI operating systems" for some computers, such as OMS (Open MIDI System) for the Mac and Windows. Programs that are compatible with a particular operating system tend to work well together.
- Well-defined keyboard shortcuts. You don't want to have to use a mouse all the time; it's often faster to use the computer's keyboard for various operations.

## Integrated MIDI Sequencer/ Hard Disk Recorder

A few high-ticket computer-based sequencers integrate hard disk recording technology by including provisions for recording two to sixteen tracks of digital audio on hard disk along with the sequence data. The audio can also be edited (cut, paste, copy, *etc.*), and other types of processing—EQ, compression, and the like—may also be available.

If you work with synths and acoustic instruments, this technology is ideal although you have the same downers as hard disk recording: expense, computer savvy required, *etc.* Still, songwriters who use this approach swear by it. Note that some sampling keyboards also include onboard hard disk recording.

Pros and Cons: Essentially the same as hard disk recording. The main disadvantage is a steep learning curve since you have to learn both sequencing and hard disk recording.

Bottom line: If you want the best and can pay for it, and have enough of a tech head that you know what to do when messages like "Warning: Defragment Disk" show up, this is the Rolls Royce of the current recording scene.

### What to Look For in a MIDI Sequencer/Hard Disk Recorder

See the respective sections on MIDI sequencing and hard disk recording.

## MiniDisc and Digital Compact Cassette

These formats were originally launched as a digital alternative to the cassette. Offering two tracks of record and playback (although multitrack MiniDiscs have been demonstrated), DCC and MD both use data compression to store more music in less memory. How much this colors the sound is a matter of debate, but most engineers agree there is a noticeable difference compared to nondata compressed recorders, such as DAT. Although neither format has caught on with consumers, MD may survive.

Pros: Near-CD sound quality, compact, relatively low cost

Cons: No overdubbing, difficult to edit, data compression alters the sound, as of this writing neither has captured the public's interest

Bottom line: If you can't swing the bucks for a pro DAT, your alternatives are one of these: a cassette deck with Dolby S, or a consumer DAT deck on sale.

### What to Look For with DCC and MiniDisc

As of this writing, the selection of both types of units is sufficiently limited that your choice is basically between playback only and playback/record MiniDiscs.

## PC Computer Sound Cards

Many sound cards for the PC include MIDI sequencing, sound generation, and two channels of hard disk recording. While not as sophisticated as the integrated MIDI sequencer/hard disk systems mentioned previously, these products are acceptable for producing multimedia music and decent two-track mastering (although quality varies widely, so be careful).

Pros: Relatively inexpensive, combines digital audio and sequencing

Cons: Can be difficult to get up and running, generally not CD-quality audio

Bottom line: If you have a PC and a tight budget, this is a good entry-level system.

### What to Look For in a PC Sound Card

- Onboard General MIDI sound set for playing back Standard MIDI Files.
- Built-in MIDI interface. Some cards include MIDI in and out.
- Sound quality. Sounds based on high-quality samples are far superior to the old, "two-operator FM synthesis" used in the first generation of sound cards.
- Upgradeable to more than two tracks of recording.
- Built-in mixing functions and signal processing.

## And Now, a Warning . . .

So is the newest, baddest technology also the best? Not necessarily. The object is to make music, and some of today's high-tech gear can be so daunting that it inhibits, rather than encourages, the musical process. When considering your various options, ask yourself "What's easy to use? What's not going to get in the way when I'm feeling creative? With which approach do I feel most comfortable?" These are the specs that never show up in spec sheets, but can be the most important specs by far.

Another warning: don't always trust specs. A well-engineered 12-bit system can be sonically superior to a poorly designed 16-bit system, and 16 bits don't guarantee what we'd like to think of as "CD quality sound."

## Buying the Gear for Your Studio

Once you've decided what gear you need, it's time to convert cash into equipment. You can spend as little or as much as you want, from a $300 ministudio (such as Yamaha's QY series of portable sequencers/sound sources) to a digital studio with a zillion tracks of tape and/or hard disk recording. Don't forget second-hand gear; technology changes so fast that you can pick up what used to be state-of-the-art machines for pennies on the dollar. Even a used three-head, reel-to-reel recorder you pick up at a garage sale for $50 can be your ticket to the world of recording.

When you go to buy any gear, keep the following in mind:

- You are spending lots of your hard-earned money on a product—let them sell you on it, and make sure any salesperson doesn't try to evade any questions you might have.

- Get different opinions, and go to different stores. Call up other stores for quotes. You wouldn't just buy the first car you saw advertised in the paper, and recording gear can cost as much as a car (and sometimes more).
- Attend trade shows and conventions, such as the Audio Engineering Society convention or local music fairs. This is one way to get hands-on experience with lots of different gear, as well as check out demos from various vendors.
- Always assume that you can get a discount. Let's say Store A is selling a Supertaper Model X and hangs a sign over it that says "$1,250" (the list price). However, Store B around the corner sells the same item for $1,000. The only trouble is that a friend of yours bought a deck from Store B and it took six months to get a replacement part—whereas Store A has some in-house technicians who get repairs done in a couple of days. So, you go to Store A and offer them $1,000 for the tape recorder. Let's say the store buys the machine for $800; they'd rather sell it to you for $1,000 and make $200 than give the business to Store B (they also know that it's around the corner). If you don't barter and play a little hard to get, you'll probably pay what the traffic will bear (after all, no salesperson is going to tell you where to get something cheaper); but know what you're talking about. Compare what's available and compare prices. An intelligent, informed, courteous buyer can often get a better deal.
- Be careful of buying mail order. Mail order definitely has its place, but a local store can give better product support, and often has a better liaison with manufacturers should something go wrong. If the price differential isn't too significant, it's a good idea to support your local merchants, and use mail order for products that don't require support (such as buying blank tape in bulk).

# Chapter 6
# Creating the Home Studio Environment

Now that we've covered some home recording gear, we need a studio to house it. Although it's doubtful you'll be able to have all the amenities of a professional studio, there are some ways to cut corners and adapt the studio to fit your specific conditions and budget.

## The Room(s)

A recording studio usually consists of the studio itself, where the musicians actually play, and a control room. If the recording facility is big, there can be several rooms; they're usually given letter designations (Studio A, Studio B, *etc.*). The rooms usually are different sizes, have different characteristics, and can accommodate different numbers of musicians. While this dramatically increases scheduling flexibility, it creates horrendous soundproofing problems. Ambient noise can also be a problem. There's a story of a prominent New York studio that had selected a prime location—which was later discovered to be directly over a subway! They spent a lot trying to dig out from that mistake, but it just goes to show what kind of problems you run into.

Chances are you'll run into different problems. You may have neighbors or other members of the household who might not appreciate hearing a piece of tape go by for the twenty-third time en route to the ultimate mix. Also, chances are that you will have to compromise concerning construction and size (very few houses were built with studio installations in mind). A large, acoustically dead room is the best general-purpose recording area, but you may not be able to afford that luxury.

The required size of your studio depends on what you want to record. Probably the hardest single entity to record is a symphony orchestra—and the average home recordist is going to have a hard time finding a room that could hold one. But a three- or five-piece group is another matter. For that, a much smaller room will do. If you're a solo musician making a demo, then all you really need is some place to stuff the recorder and a mixer. And if you can feed directly into the tape recorder instead of using a mic (*i.e.*, plug an electric guitar or synthesizer directly into the board rather than use a microphone and acoustic guitar), the acoustics are of very little importance, and you'll get the added benefit of a generally "cleaner" sound.

Let's define, and talk about, four common situations (we'll refer to these situations by number throughout the chapter):

No. 1: There are two separate, adjoining rooms for recording

No. 2: There is one room

No. 3: You have a part of a large room (like a corner of the living room)

No. 4: All you have is closet space.

### Separate Control Room and Studio

With situation No. 1, you can have a separate control room and studio, thus achieving the best possible acoustic isolation between the engineer/producer team and the musicians. In this type of situation, some kind of talk back or intercom system is mandatory for communications; also, take into account the extra cable runs required to feed mic signals into the control room, and cue signals out to the musicians.

If you're recording a solo effort and doing your own engineering, you'll probably record directly into the control room's console. In that case, using a separate control room and studio is unnecessary. In pro studios, you'll generally find a thick glass pane (triple-thick with air spaces in between for maximum sound rejection) between the control room and studio so that the engineers can see the performers. This isn't really necessary for a home environment, so you can save yourself a bundle by forgetting about visual contact. About the only time you need contact is if someone in the control room has to cue the performer, but that can also be handled by hooking a little cue light up to a switch.

## dio in Its Own Room

is probably the most com- ou will encounter. The better; a larger size will onant frequency (*i.e.*, the the room's frequency any bass player is familiar es and how they can make a tain notes; it is best to minimize these because they will drive you up the wall when recording. Any room, unless it has been very well built and tuned, acts almost like a random-action tone control, peaking and dipping the frequency response at several fixed points throughout the audio spectrum. If your tapes sound good in your studio but strange everywhere else, your mix may be compensating for room anomalies.

A larger room will also give more reverberation; this can be either an asset or a liability, depending upon what you are recording. However, I feel that if you have limited resources, a studio should be as acoustically dead as possible. You can always add reverberation or echo electronically, but it's very difficult to add deadness. On the other hand, if you have a large room, then you can deaden one end and not the other so you have a choice of recording environments.

When recording, you usually want to obtain as accurate a sound as possible because that gives maximum flexibility during mixing, so generally a dry, natural track works best. Also, if you have to combine the control room and studio into one room, a dead one is arguably the best for mixing.

The ultimate nonreverberent recording area is outdoors, where the reverberation is essentially non-existent because there are no reflective surfaces. If you can set up drums outside, not only will you get no leakage from the other instruments that are located inside, but you will also achieve a very crisp sound. In fact, you'll probably have to add a little reverb in order to get some warmth (and hopefully it won't be a windy day).

To make a room as dead as possible means either tearing down the walls or putting up new ones, renovating the ceiling and floors, and adding sound-absorbent material. Good luck, especially on the part about tearing down the walls if you're a renter! Professional studios have elaborate, double-wall structures with internal air spaces and sound absorbent material, like cloth, foam, *etc.* on the outside surfaces (Fig. 6-1). Having two sets of staggered studs minimizes sound coupling from the inner Sheetrock wall to the outer wall. Ceilings, and sometimes even floors, are treated along the same lines, but chances are that most people reading this book will have to settle for less.

One way to minimize room reflections is to line the walls and ceilings with thick material. You can save money if you go to a carpet remnants and overruns shop, and buy a larger piece of carpet than you need. Then, run the carpet up the walls as far as it will go. Also, install one or

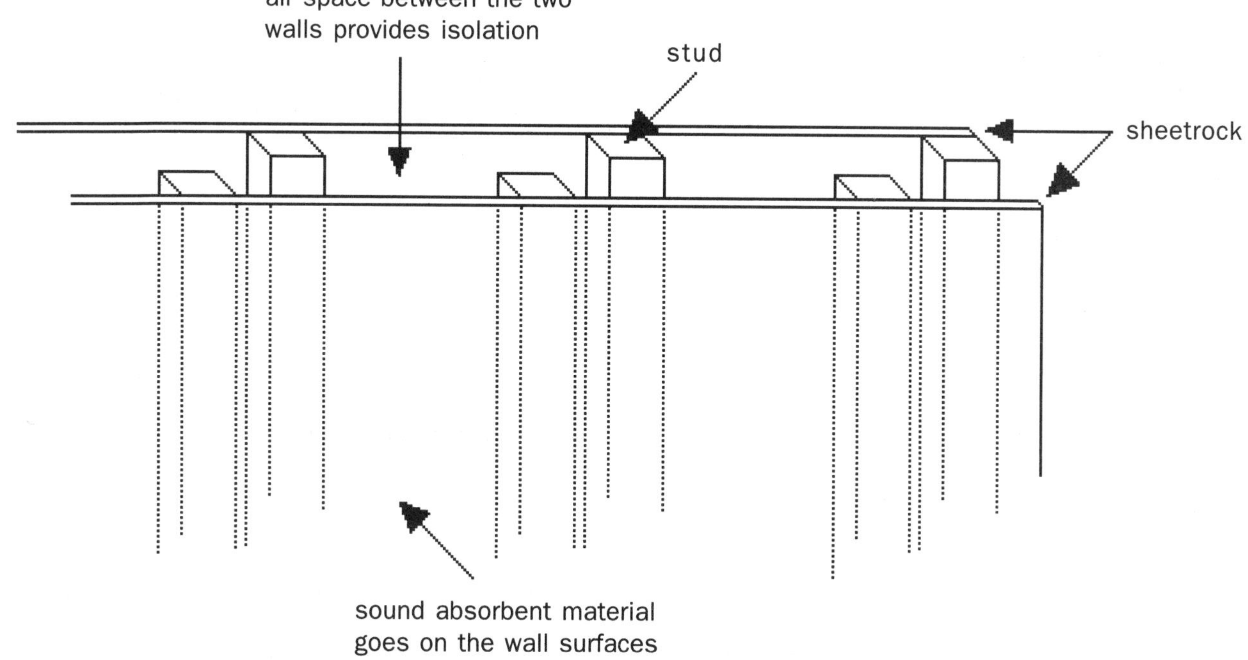


**Fig. 6-1:** *In pro studios, instead of simply having one set of Sheetrock and studs, there are two walls with a sound absorbing air space in between.*

two pads under the carpet. This will help absorb vibration being transmitted through the floor, and provide the side benefit of keeping drums from wandering around as much.

Another way to reduce reflections is to hang a piece of canvas from the ceiling (Fig. 6-2). This isn't too expensive (look under "canvas" in the *Yellow Pages*). Bedspreads hung from the walls are good, and there is always the traditional egg carton. However, note that none of these methods do much to absorb sound; that's the job of proper wall construction, with interior air spaces. Most "deadening" techniques absorb high frequency energy, which can reduce intelligibility, thus causing musicians to "turn it up." Dead rooms work best if you're doing near-field monitoring and want to avoid having room reflections come back at you.

In addition to the general soundproofing and deadening you need, you may also need localized, acoustically isolated, dead zones. In professional recording studios, there are usually two permanent or semi-permanent dead zones: a vocal booth, which is extensively padded and deadened in its own right, and some kind of drum booth. This can be anything from a corner of the room that is heavily padded, to a cage-like structure, or even a separate booth. Professional studios also have structures, called *baffles* or *goboes,* to help create localized acoustics.

Fig. 6-3 shows two simple baffle designs. (A) shows a wooden box that serves as the baffle, with sound absorbing material on both sides. (B) is a somewhat simpler design that uses a wooden frame; canvas or some other thick material is stretched across the back and front, with acoustic fiberglass insulation packed in between. You can combine the two approaches; for example, the box in A could be hollow, or have fiberglass inside. (Of course, be very careful when working with fiberglass; use gloves, and don't inhale any loose fibers.)

Placing baffles between drums and amps, around pianos, or wherever can help minimize leakage (Fig. 6-4). However, there's not much these can do about low frequency energy leakage—just midrange and highs.

We've talked a lot about eliminating leakage, but what makes leakage such a bad thing?

A lot of times during mixdown, you'll edit out some parts of a track. Let's say you want to fade the drums way back on some part, but there's a substantial amount of drum leakage on the bass track. The leaked sound won't have the quality of the original sound recorded from the drums; but as you fade back the drum track, this leakage becomes the dominant drum sound. No good! Also, suppose the bass sounds a little thin so you boost its low end a bit. This simultaneously boosts the bass on the leaked drum, perhaps forcing the bass drum into a prominent position not originally intended. Too much leakage defeats the purpose of having instruments on separate tracks in the first place.

If you don't feel like building baffles for your home studio, there's an easier (though not as effective) substitute: hang bedspreads or heavy cloth from the ceiling as required (Fig. 6-5). Note that you can also pull back a bit on the "curtains" if you want a more live sound. If you elect to use some kind of drapery pull for a semi-permanent installation, make sure that the draw

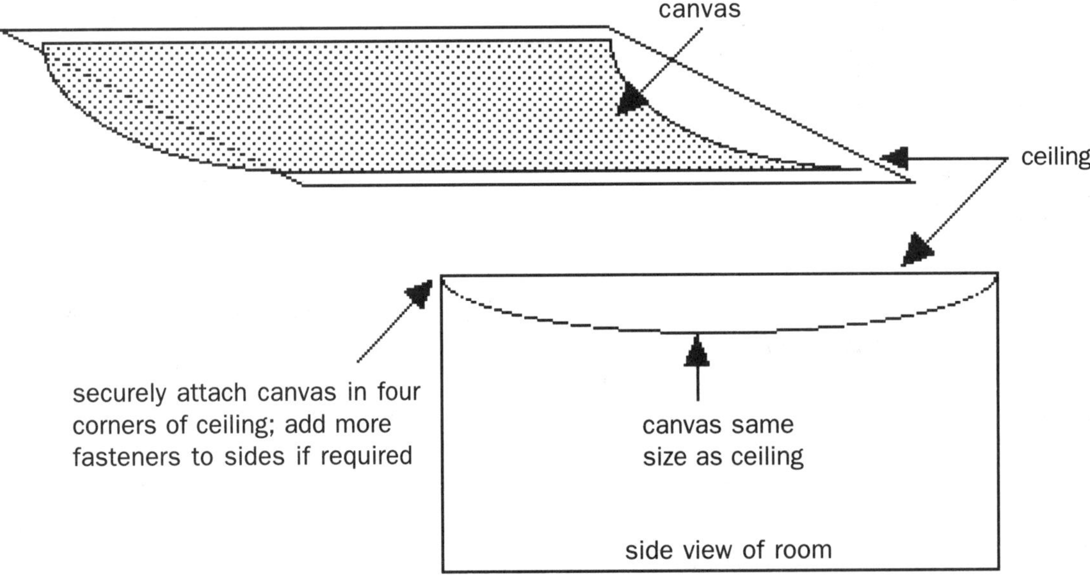


**Fig. 6-2:** *Suspending canvas from the ceiling makes a good sound deadener.*

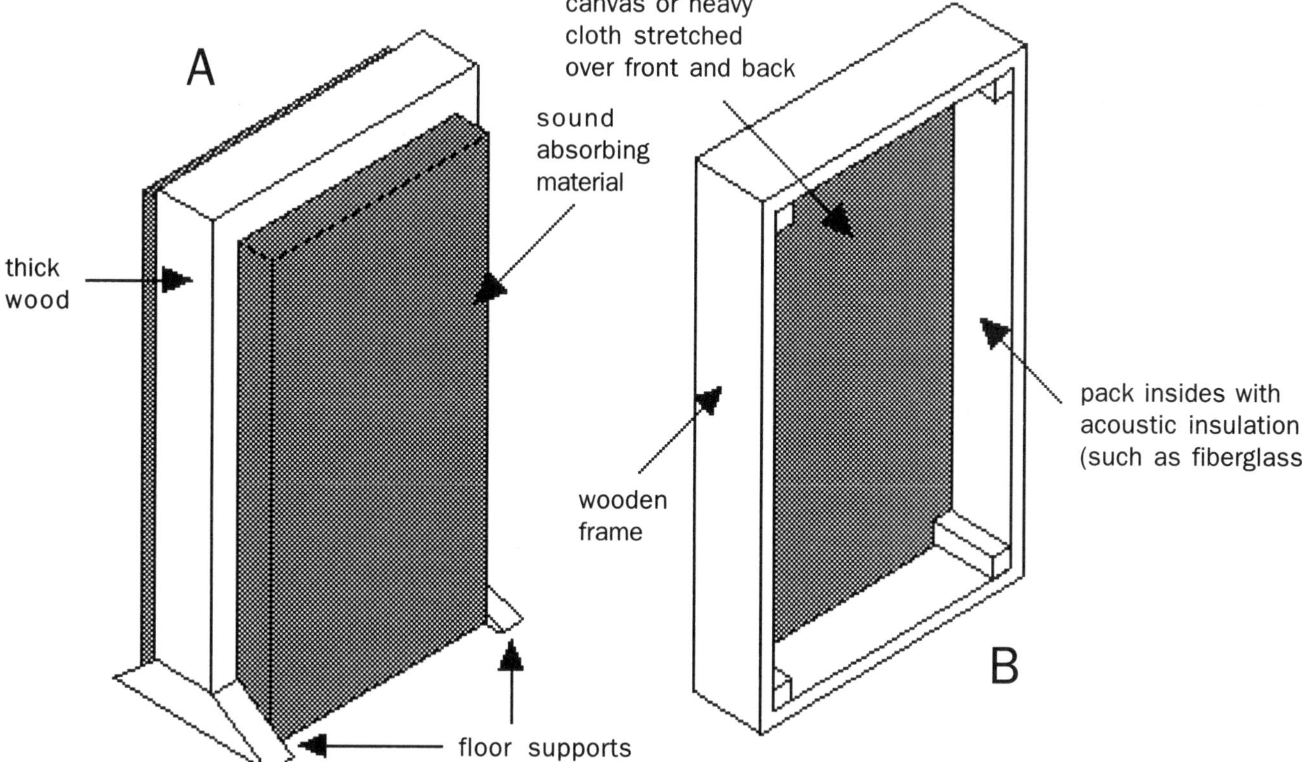


**Fig. 6-3:** *Two different types of baffle construction.*

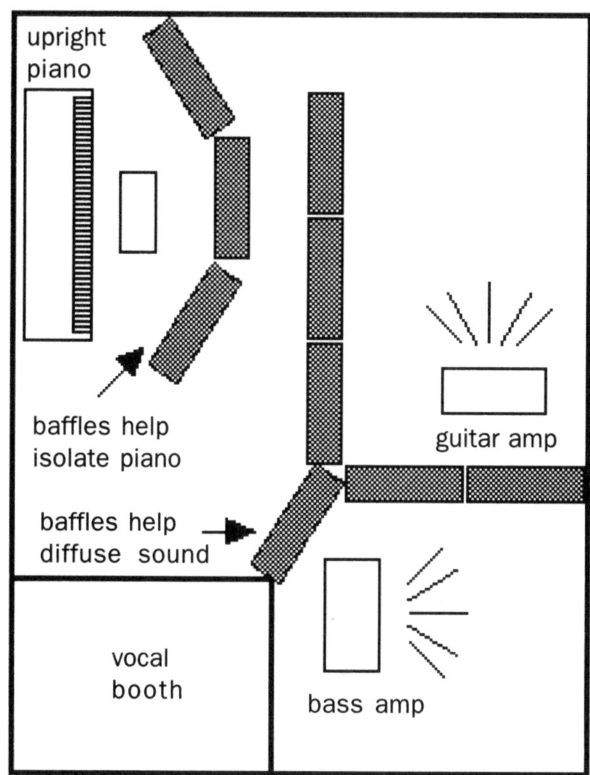


**Fig. 6-4:** *Using baffles to provide acoustic insulation between instruments.*

mechanism doesn't have any little rings or metal buckles that could rattle when subjected to high noise levels.

In addition to room considerations involving sound, you may have to contend with keeping sound away from other people, like neighbors. This is seldom easy with loud music. A solution that relies on changing the fundamental acoustics of a room is bound to be very expensive. Your best bet is to do as much direct-into-the-console recording as possible, record only during legal noisemaking hours (most towns have ordinances that specify no "excessive" noise after a certain hour), and keep all windows and doors closed. You can also monitor on headphones when possible. Other than that, there's not much you can do.

Well, now we've covered ideas on how to optimize situations No. 1 and No. 2 for home recording. But if there isn't an entire room available, we're back to situations No. 3 and No. 4.

## Carving a Studio Out of a Room

If you're in situation No. 3 and your studio is part of the room, there's probably little you can do about the acoustics. For example, if you're set up in a living room, you obviously aren't going to run carpets up over the windows and hang old clothes from the walls unless you have very tolerant friends. One of the tricks mentioned before is applicable, and that's hanging canvas from the ceiling. The canvas also

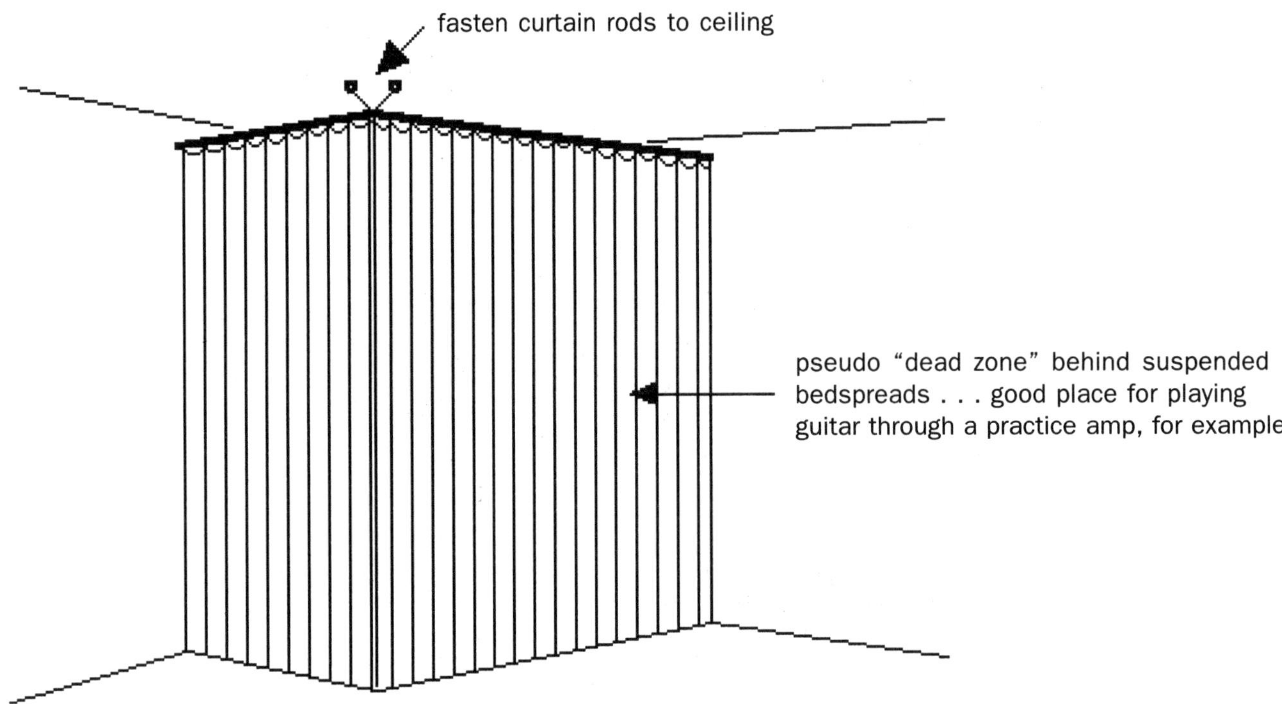


**Fig. 6-5:** *How to create a somewhat acoustically dead area by suspending bedspreads or other heavy cloth from curtain rods.*

helps keep your room warmer in winter since it adds insulation between you and your roof—so it not only improves the sound, it's ecologically correct. Although this may not appear to make too much of a difference while recording, for monitoring and mixing the difference is very clear. Also, putting a drape or two, pillows, padded furniture, *etc.* in the room helps to absorb sound, so that you may end up with a decent acoustical environment in your living room after all.

### The Studio in a Closet

Situation No. 4 is when you just don't have any room at all—but if you have a closet, you have a studio (Fig. 6-6). Here you really have to pretty much relegate yourself to solo-type recordings. However, as closets usually lead out to a room or at least a corridor, you'll probably have a spot where you can sing, play, or whatever. As for shaping your acoustics, good luck! Your best bet is to buy a set of small speakers for near-field monitoring and headphones, and develop a good relationship with them.

### Other Noise Considerations

Some of your soundproofing problems will involve keeping control room noise out of the studio. Hard disks make a lot of noise, and many computers and power amps include cooling fans. If the control room is separate, this may not be a problem. If the studio is in a single room, putting the noise-generating elements in a sound-proof box, like the kind used to deaden the noise from old-style daisywheel printers, can help a lot. Sometimes hard disks and such can fit in a closet, but use caution: there are often limits on the maximum cable length you can run to computer peripherals, and make sure that there's enough ventilation to prevent overheating.

## Studio Layout

Many people fail to recognize the importance of an efficient studio layout. You can't trip over cords or adjust monitor speakers every day; you don't want people banging into recording devices, so they have to be out of the flow of traffic, and so on. An efficiently-laid-out studio can make all the difference between effortless sessions and hard work.

George Petersen, this book's technical editor, recommends setting up your mixer and speakers in the corner of a room (Fig. 6-7). This saves a lot of space, and also gives a close-by work surface on both your immediate right and left. As to other equipment, the general rule is the more often you have to adjust a piece of gear, the closer it should be to your fingertips. Set-and-forget reverbs and power amps can sit on the bottom of racks, but not a multieffects that you use all the time.

Many solo musicians favor a "horseshoe"

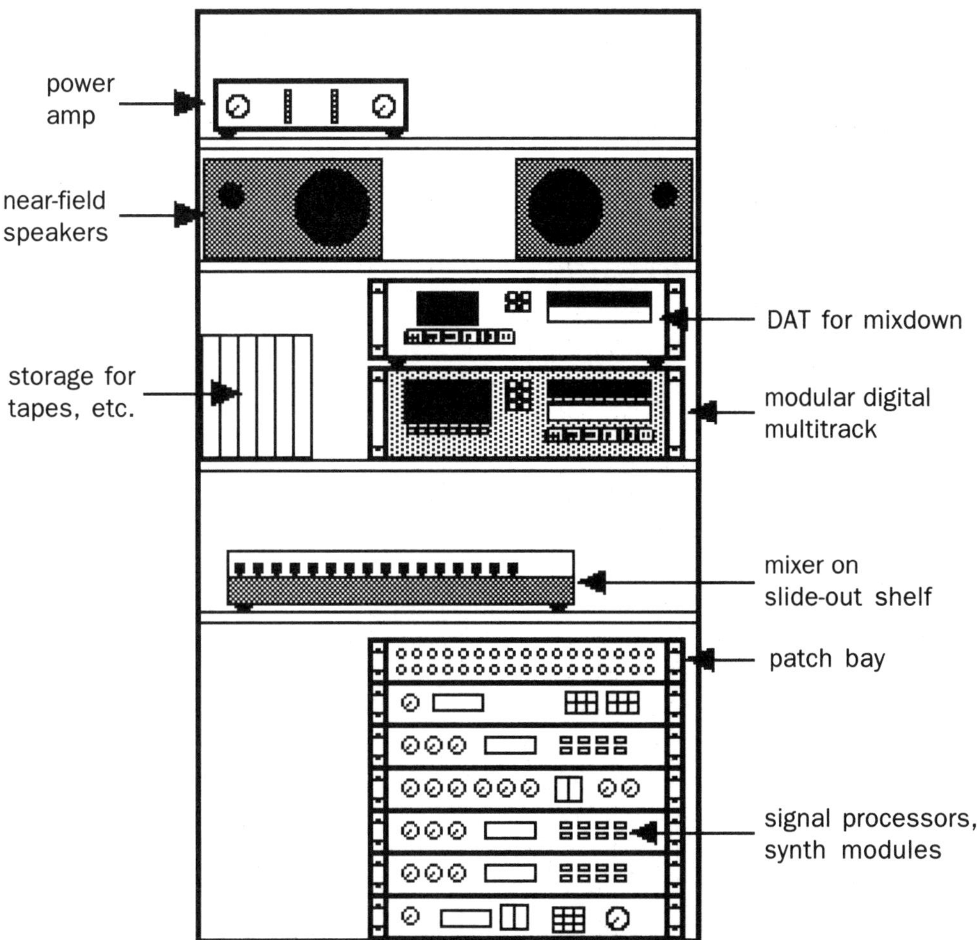


**Fig. 6-6:** *Studio built into a closet. The power amp is far away from the tape decks, so any heat it generates doesn't flow upward into sensitive equipment. The mixer can be on a slide-out shelf, or a rack mount mixer that mounts on the same rack frame as the signal processors and patch bay.*

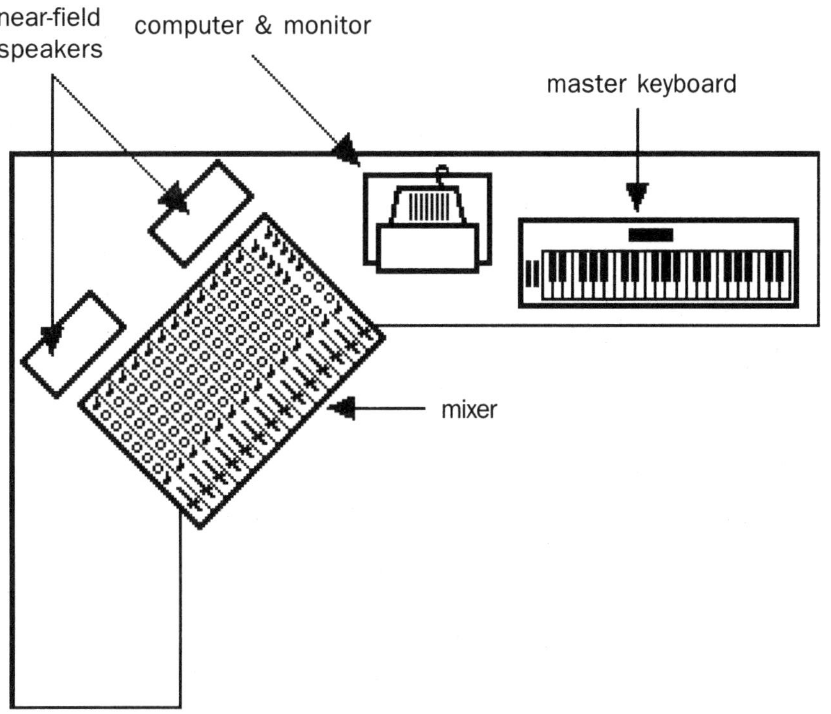


**Fig. 6-7:** *Setting up in the corner of a room provides good space for the mixer and monitors, as well as work surfaces to the right and left of the mixer.*

type of arrangement, where there are a number of surfaces available for keyboards (both piano and computer types), trackballs, alternative controllers such as drum pads, note pads, monitors, and so on. This puts as many devices as possible within arm's reach.

## Furniture Time

There are quite a few tables designed for computer installations that work well for studios. They have room for a computer, QWERTY keyboard, monitor, and so on. Setting up one of these, with a stand for a master keyboard controller and a couple of racks of gear, can make for a compact and efficient setup. Although these types of tables can be expensive, if you're handy with woodworking you can build your own for substantially less.

Several companies offer off-the-shelf rack mount enclosures, but it's not too difficult to build your own. The hardest part is finding and drilling the rack rails, but once they're done, they're easy to mount in a wood frame.

One of the most important expenses is a good chair. You're going to spend a lot of time sitting; get something that's comfortable, can roll around, has adjustable height, and includes decent back support. A good office chair can set you back a few hundred dollars, but your body will thank you.

## One Step of Planning Saves Two of Execution . . .

Because studios are so personal and the rooms they're in vary so much, it's impossible to give universally applicable guidelines. It's a good idea to get some graph paper and do a room layout, or maybe even do some sketches. (If you have any architect friend with a computer program like Virtus, check it out. This lets you create a virtual room and "walk" through it.) Try to imagine what it would be like to work in that environment, and make as many alterations as possible on paper before you commit to the real thing.

# Chapter 7
# Electricity and Wiring

Here's where a lot of potentially good studios turn into noisy, nasty studios. But before we talk about cables, let's discuss the electrical environment in general.

## Electrical Basics

Most homes connect to the power line through two "hot," 117 volt wires and one ground wire (Fig. 7-1). The signals on the hot wires are somewhat out of phase, so connecting a device between the two produces 208 volts (for heavy appliances such as washers). Connecting between either hot line and ground yields 120 volts (or more typically, 115 to 117 volts).

The ground wire usually connects to a stake pounded into the ground, or a metal cold water pipe. (Note that some pipes in newer buildings are nonconductive, which can prevent electrical contact with earth ground. If needed, a licensed electrician can help you install a suitable ground connection.)

Voltage values fluctuate due to changing loads, conditions at the generating station, which country you're in (not everyone uses 120 volts), and so on. However, the AC line frequency (60 Hz in the USA, 50 Hz in Europe) is accurate to at least 0.01%. This precision allows motors, clocks, and other timing-critical devices to synchronize to the AC line frequency.

The AC line can carry a lot of spurious signals and noise, which ride along with the electricity and get into your gear. You've probably noticed how light dimmers and some fluorescent lights can interfere with radios and guitar amps; these can be particularly "dirty," and aren't recommended for the studio. Incandescent lights may be too bright for the relaxed studio atmosphere, but you can always use low wattage bulbs and provide indirect lighting.

It's best if all your equipment uses three-wire plugs. Three-wire AC lines have color-coded wires for ground (green or bare wire), neutral (white), and hot (any color other than white or green, such as black). Current flows into the device through the hot wire, and returns to

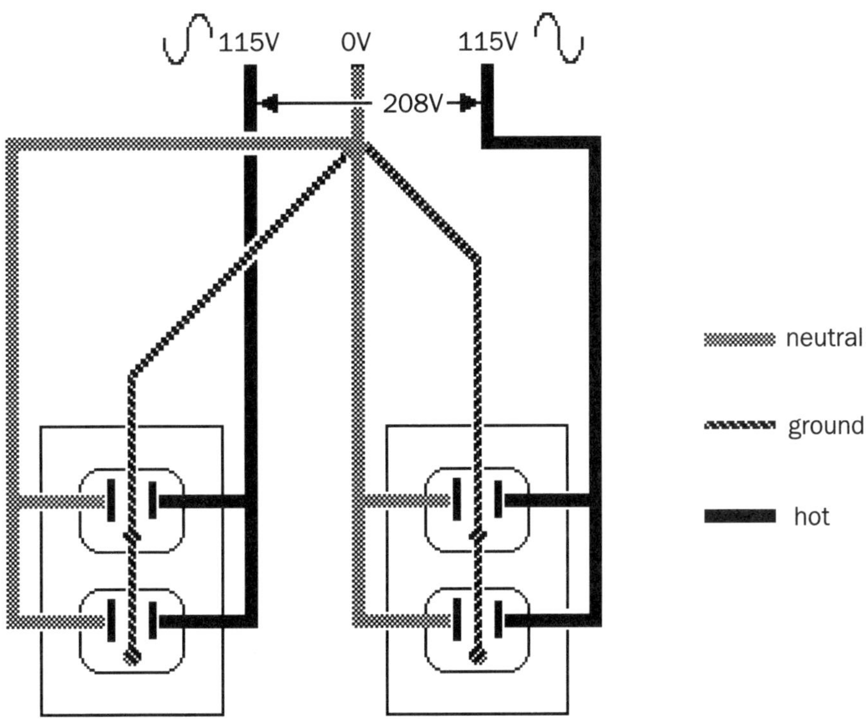


**Fig. 7-1:** *How electricity feeds the typical home.*

ground through the neutral wire. To insure that the device's hot and neutral lines match up with the receptacle's hot and neutral connections, modern outlets are polarized so you can insert the plug only one way (*i.e.,* one plug contact is bigger than the other).

Three-wire outlets add an element of safety since a device's chassis, if plugged into the outlet, connects to the ground line. Grounding the metal enclosure of a piece of electrical equipment is a universally recommended procedure for reducing hum and shock hazard. If some problem develops where there's an internal short to the chassis, then the AC connects to ground and (assuming everything is properly wired) this should blow a fuse or circuit breaker. If grounding a piece of equipment blows a fuse, take the gear in for repairs—it's unsafe.

You can sometimes convert a two-wire outlet into a three-wire outlet by using a two-to-three wire adapter (as sold in hardware stores), and connecting the adapter's ground wire to the metal screw that holds the faceplate to the outlet box. However, not all outlet boxes are grounded, particularly in older buildings; have a licensed electrician check this.

Some equipment with two-prong plugs includes a little binding post labeled "ground" (or, on British equipment, "earth"), suitable for attaching a piece of wire. This is called a *ground wire,* and you can run it to the central ground point on your barrier strip or outlet.

Although the neutral wire should be at ground potential, it will always have a small amount of resistance. According to Ohm's Law, pushing current through a resistance creates a voltage. Since the neutral can't be assumed to be a true, zero voltage ground point, the separate ground line—which carries no current—serves that purpose.

A quality ground connection can minimize AC line noise. Many people don't pay very close attention to ground wires because they don't hear any sound at the time they set up their equipment; but insidious noises can come along the AC line when you least expect them, not necessarily while you're listening for them. Also, the more equipment you use, the greater your chances of experiencing problems.

## Balancing AC Lines

The two main, out of phase "hot" wires share the neutral wire, so if the current drain from one hot lead is a lot higher than the other, a small amount of current may flow through the neutral line. Matching the loads on both lines as evenly as possible results in the neutral line voltage being closer to zero, since any currents that flow tend to be equal and opposite, canceling each other out.

It's generally a good idea to wire all studio outlets to one leg of the AC line, with other, "dirty" noise-generating devices (refrigerators, dimmers, motors, appliances, *etc.*) hooked up to the other leg. This is particularly important with studio gear, which can be sensitive to noise on the AC line.

## Getting Wired

With older houses, pay attention to the wiring. Large diameter wire can not only handle more current, but also results in less voltage drop for long wire runs. Wire diameter is given as a number called the *gauge;* the smaller the number, the larger the diameter. Twelve-gauge wire generally works fine up to 20 amps or so for wire runs less than thirty feet; 8-gauge wire can handle 40 amps for runs of forty feet or less.

The wiring you use should be able to handle any power required with a very large safety factor. This is not just for safety—although that is the primary reason—but to keep the line voltage from pooping out. At one home studio I visited, the line voltage was about 100 volts because the studio's outlet was not being fed with large enough wire to carry the studio's electrical demands. As a result, the electronic instruments played out of tune and had general stability problems, and the tape deck's motor was working under a strain—not to mention the potential fire hazard of an overloaded outlet. If you have a voltmeter and know how to use it, check your line voltage with the studio on full blast. If there is a voltage drop compared to the normal reading, you had best contemplate rewiring, and soon.

Check the wall behind various AC outlets. If you detect any warmth at all, you're drawing too much current for the given gauge of wire. This could be dangerous and indicate the need for rewiring. As always, your best bet is to work with a reputable, licensed electrician.

Also, choose your extension cords carefully. Ones with 14-gauge wire aren't really acceptable for high-current devices (*e.g.,* tape recorders, some computer peripherals, *etc.*). Just remember that no electrical fire ever started because a cord was rated to carry too much current.

Concerning barrier strips, these are ideal for studio applications because they often have an on-off switch (so you can turn off all your gear with a flick of a switch) and sometimes even have a fuse. Again, make sure that you don't overload a strip's current-carrying capacity.

## Safety Devices

The circuit breaker, which interrupts the flow of electricity if it senses a problem, sits between your studio wiring and the main distribution box (breaker box). The current rating should be based on what your wiring can handle; for example, if the wiring is rated at 25 amps, use a 20 amp circuit breaker. This gives a reasonable safety margin and if it opens, will indicate that the current flow is approaching your wiring's capacity.

Ground fault interrupters (GFIs), which are built into individual outlet units or located at the circuit breaker box, are useful if your studio's in a damp location (*e.g.*, a basement). The GFI compares the current flowing through the hot and neutral wires. If there's extra current flow from the hot line to ground (this would happen if, for example, you tossed your synthesizer into the bathtub), the GFI cuts off power. The difference between a GFI and a circuit breaker is that the circuit breaker is designed to protect wiring; the GFI is designed to protect people.

I hope that you'll never need to use a fire extinguisher, but keep one around and make sure it's fully charged. There are different kinds of extinguishers, so get the type that's intended for fighting electrical fires. It's the cheapest insurance you can buy.

## Cleaning the AC Line

There are several devices that help clean up electricity before it gets to your gear. Following are some of the most popular.

### RFI/EMI Filters

The AC line can carry electromagnetic interference (EMI), such as dimmer noise and radio signals. RFI/EMI filters are low pass filters (sometimes using multiple stages to provide greater attenuation) that shunt high frequencies to ground.

### Surge/Spike Suppressors

AC line spikes can be caused by a variety of sources, from nearby lightning strikes to a heavy-duty motor kicking in on the same line. A serious spike can scramble the memory of microprocessor-based gear and in extreme cases, cause physical damage. A spike or surge suppressor deflects transients to ground in one of two ways: *common-mode* types suppress spikes from either the neutral or hot line to ground, while *transverse-mode* types suppress spikes across the neutral and hot lines. Ideally a suppressor should offer both types of protection; some surge suppressors also have RFI/EMI filters built in. There are also specialized spike protectors for phone lines, which can be important if you use a modem, fax, or answering machine—particularly if you live in an area that is subject to electrical storms.

Some suppressors deteriorate after being subjected to surges. If there's been a major surge and you're using an inexpensive surge suppressor, it's a good idea to test whether it still works, and replace it if necessary.

### Isolation Transformers

These do what the name implies—isolate a load from the AC line. The transformer doesn't alter the voltage; one transformer winding plugs into the AC line, and the other winding connects to your gear. This can provide a fairly "clean" source of AC power from a dirty line, and can be less expensive than installing a separate AC line. However, make sure that it is rated at sufficient wattage to power the appropriate gear and provide a reasonable safety margin.

### Line Regulators

These devices, also called *line stabilizers,* maintain a constant output voltage even if the input voltage fluctuates from around 90 to 130 volts. If your electrical environment is subject to brownouts and you use a computer, a line regulator can help prevent losing data from RAM if there's a momentary power dip.

There are two main types of regulating technologies. A *multitap transformer* switches taps to provide a constant voltage, but this switching has to occur in a carefully controlled way to prevent putting small spikes on the line. A *ferro-resonant transformer* is more expensive and has a fast response to voltage fluctuations, but compensates for low-voltage conditions by drawing more power from the AC line rather than stepping up the output voltage. If the power rating of your electrical system is marginal, there may not be enough juice to let the ferro-resonant transformer operate at full efficiency.

### Uninterruptible Power Supply

A UPS contains an internal battery that is constantly being charged. When AC power goes away, the battery goes through an inverter and provides power for a limited amount of time (typically ten minutes, but much longer under light loads). This is usually enough time to shut down a computer system in an orderly way (you certainly don't want a hard disk to lose its power while it's in the process of writing data!). A UPS costs about $1 per watt of protection, but is well worth the investment if your studio has a lot of microprocessor-controlled devices or computers. Look for a unit with a fast detection time (so it knows that the power has gone away), and fast transfer time over to the auxiliary power. The switchover process should take under ten milliseconds.

One caution: select a UPS that generates a sine wave, like what you get from the wall. Cheaper models may generate square waves or clipped sine waves, which are not suitable for sensitive gear.

## If You're Building a Studio . . .

Most of us don't have the resources to build a studio from scratch. But if you do, note that one of your biggest problems will be heating and cooling systems—not just because they often generate noise, but because if they're electrical, they can cause power dips and generally annoy your expensive, high-tech gear. One partial solution is passive heating and cooling systems; a lot of progress has been made in the past few years, and there are simple, inexpensive measures you can take to cut your utilities (as well as help offset the current your studio draws). Most towns have consultants who specialize in passive heating and cooling techniques; any consultation costs can pay for themselves many times over.

## Ground Loops: Problems and Solutions

Using multiple AC-powered devices can create a situation known as a *ground loop*. Under worst-case conditions, ground loops can contribute unexplainable hum, noise, and interference problems to your setup. Eliminating ground loops can be quite difficult; to solve these problems, it's necessary to understand what causes ground loops.

A ground loop is a condition where there is more than one ground path available to an effect. In Fig. 7-2, one path goes from device A to ground via the ground terminal of the three-conductor AC power cord, but A also sees a path to ground through the shielded cable and AC ground of device B. Because ground wires have a small amount of resistance (the electronic equivalent of friction), small amounts of current can flow through ground and generate a voltage along the cable shield. This signal may end up being induced into the hot conductor.

The loop can also act like an antenna into which hum is induced, or can even pick up radio frequencies. Furthermore, many components in a circuit connect to ground. If that ground is "dirty" and contains noise, it might be picked up by the circuit. Ground loops cause the most problems with high-gain circuits, since massive amplification of even a couple of millivolts of noise can give an audible signal.

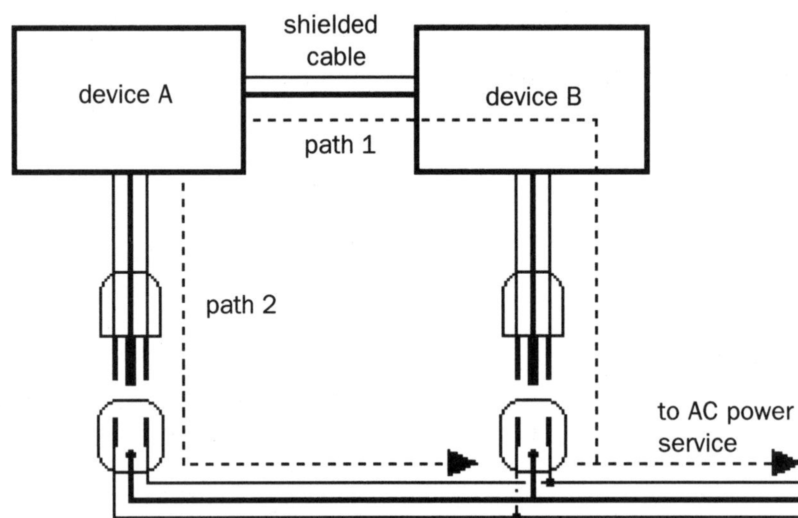


**Fig. 7-2:** *How ground loops form.*

Most ground loop problems can be solved by plugging all equipment into the same grounded AC source, which attaches all ground leads to a single ground point (for example, a barrier strip that feeds an AC outlet through a short cord). Just routing your AC in this way can often be enough to eliminate the spurious noises created by ground loops. However, it is important to make sure that the AC source is not overloaded and is properly rated to handle the gear plugged into it. Note that simply using a ground lifter can also prevent ground loops, but this is *definitely not recommended* since it negates the safety protection afforded by a grounded chassis.

A solution for stubborn ground loop problems in unbalanced line systems is to isolate the piece of gear causing the problem, and break the ground lead (shield) in the audio patch cords between it and any other devices to which it connects. This doesn't mean eliminating the ground line, but just disconnecting it at one end. This way the inner conductor is still protected by a shield connected to ground, yet there's no completed electrical path between the two devices.

If you make your cables, it's worth wiring up a few special ground loop-buster cords. These should be used only to prevent ground loop situations; if used as conventional cords, you'll encounter hum, loss of level, and other problems.

## Outlets and Wire Routing

With a separate control room and studio, each room will probably have a couple of different outlets, possibly on different electrical circuits. This is good, as you can run the control room electronics from one circuit and the studio amps from another. But make sure that whatever circuit you plug into is fused at a master fusebox. I can't emphasize enough the importance of safety in terms of electrical wiring. This isn't meant to make you paranoid, but to emphasize that electricity coming from the wall is not something you can take for granted: it has limits, it has tremendous power, and it can be lethal.

You also want to keep any extension cords as short as possible. This may force you to locate equipment near the part of the studio that happens to have power. So be it; those are the breaks.

If everything is in one room you have to be even more careful, since this generally means that one circuit has to take the full load. Determine the line's current rating, add up the wattages of your various devices, then allow a comfortable safety margin. Rewiring is not particularly difficult, but chances are you will not be able to do it yourself. Local zoning laws establish certain mandatory building codes, and you must conform to those codes or risk possible lawsuits. Let's say some neighbors don't like the noise, and want to stop you from doing sessions—maybe they even have a legitimate gripe. If someone comes to investigate the situation and you have strange noncode wiring draped all over the place, you aren't making things any easier, and you could get into trouble. I hate to bring up stuff like this in a book that's supposed to get you closer to the joys of music, but I would be overly optimistic if I didn't mention potential problems as well as potential delights. This is a complex world; as our toys get more complex, it is our responsibility to use them correctly.

### Routing AC Lines

Keep AC away from sensitive electronic circuits like preamplifiers, reverb units, audio inputs, *etc.;* the current flowing through the line can induce hum into the equipment. Guitar pickups are extremely prone to picking up hum, but by changing the position of the guitar, you can frequently minimize this problem. Also, AC lines will frequently terminate in a transformer inside the equipment being powered. These transformers create stray AC fields, so it's essential that you never set tape and other magnetic media on top of, or nearby, a transformer.

If your studio takes up a corner of a room or a closet, the compact size means less acute wiring problems. Nonetheless, it is just as vital to ground properly, to make sure that the current drain is within acceptable limits, and to pay attention to the other points covered previously.

### Routing Other Cables

We need to run more than AC lines from one place to another. With a separate studio and control room, both mic and cue signal cables need to connect between the studio and the mixing console. Most often, mic cables should use low-impedance, balanced line; this tends to reject hum even with long cable runs (see Chapter 9 on microphones for background on balanced-line systems). If you have several individual shielded cables, you can surround them all by another shield; this produces one big cable. Professional sound people refer to this as a *snake.*

Handling the cue function is another matter. To drive four or five headphones, if each earcup draws half a watt, you still need at least a 5 watt amplifier. Usually an audio power amp connects to the cue bus output. Any output wires run from the control room into the studio; there you'll find a number of little boxes with headphone jacks, usually connected to the main line through some isolating resistors. These are chosen for the headphones in question, and are typically 47Ω power resistors.

## Cables and Patching

The other wiring your studio needs involves cables that interconnect equipment. These can carry anything from low-level microphone signals to high-frequency digital signals. There are five main types of connectors used in the project studio:

- RCA phono jacks (Fig. 7-3). Used in consumer stereo systems as well as some project studio gear. They are also the standard connector for S/PDIF digital connections.
- 1/4" phone jacks (as used with musical instruments such as electric guitar) (Fig. 7-4). These are available in mono and stereo for unbalanced and balanced applications, respectively.
- MIDI (five-pin DIN) connectors (Fig. 7-5). These handle MIDI in, out, and thru connections.
- XLR (Cannon) connectors (Fig. 7-6). These are used primarily for balanced line mic connections and AES/EBU digital audio signals, and are very rugged. Digital audio applications require cable that can handle very high frequency signals.
- Fiber-optic connectors. With more digital audio being handled over fiber-optics, optical connectors are on the rise. These are generally much smaller than audio connectors and look like small plastic cubes.

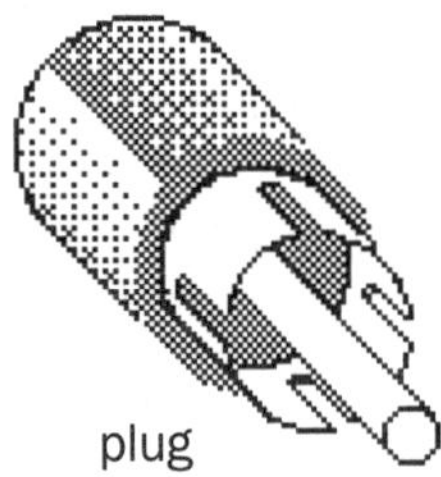


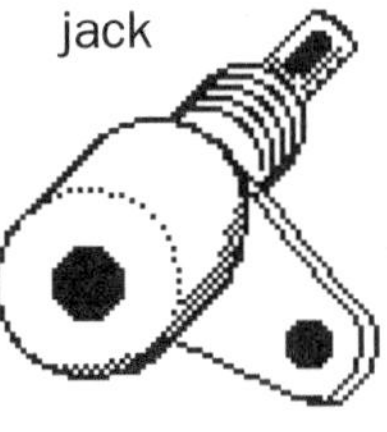


**Fig. 7-3:** *RCA phono plug and jack. The jacks come in several different styles; this jack is designed for chassis mounting. The plug inserts into the front, cylindrical part. The tab sticking off to the right is a ground tab that goes behind the chassis. The hot connector attaches to the lug at the rear of the jack. A hex screw screws over the jack from the back, sandwiching the ground lug between the chassis and nut.*

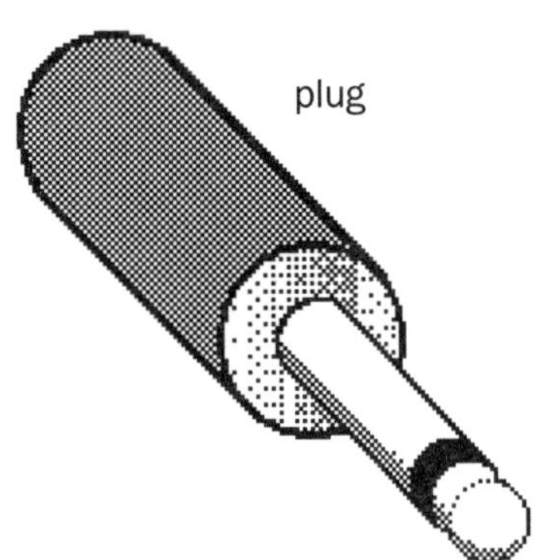


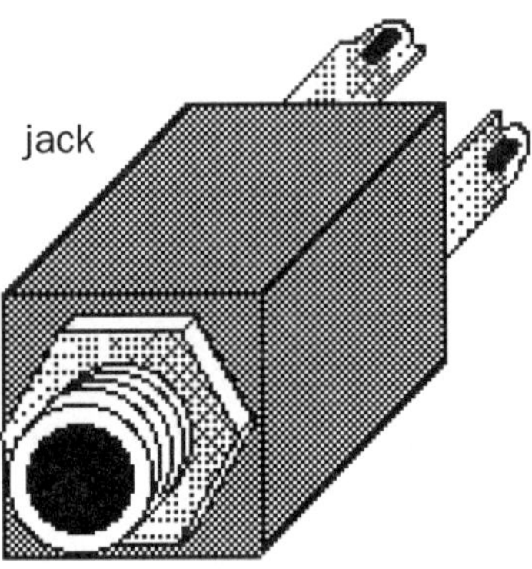


**Fig. 7-4:** *1/4" phone plug and jack. The jack is an enclosed type. The two lugs coming out of the back are for the hot and ground connections.*

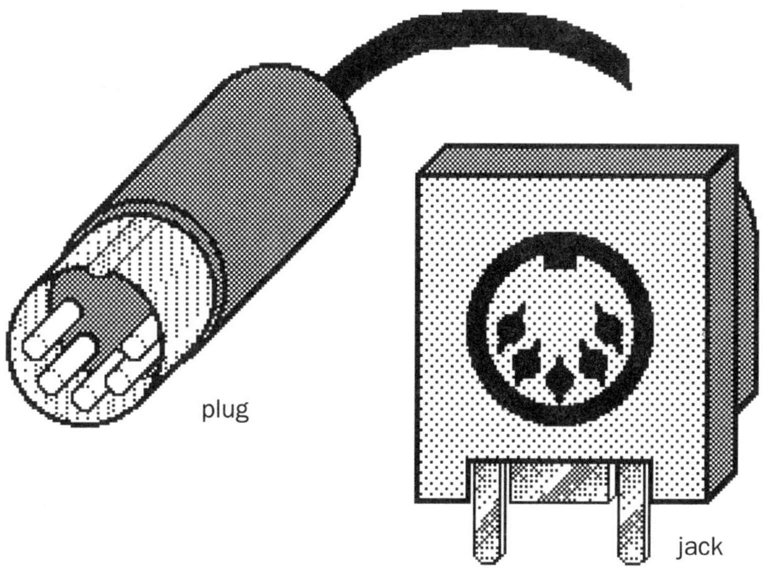


**Fig. 7-5:** *Five-pin* DIN *connectors are used for* MIDI. *This type of jack mounts on a printed circuit board.*

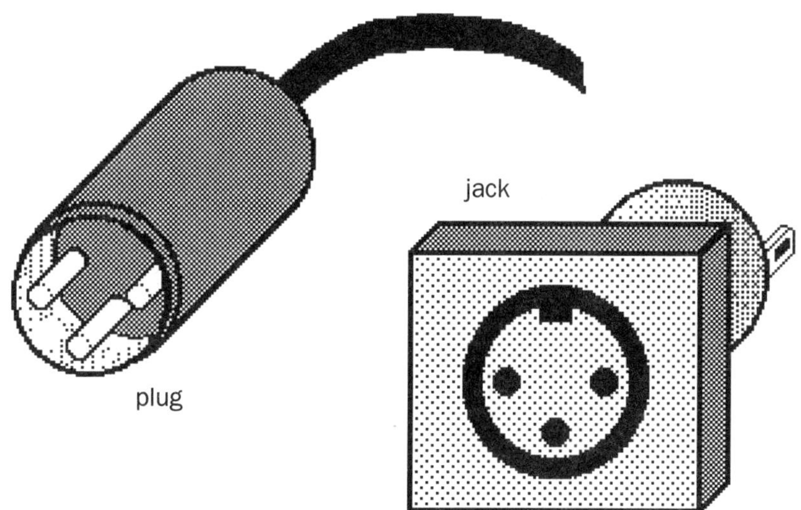


**Fig. 7-6:** *XLR, three-pin connectors.*

# Chapter 8
# Monitoring Speakers

Monitoring is a crucial element of the recording process. You want to hear exactly what's being recorded, as well as have an accurate reference for mixing. For example, if you're mixing on speakers that have poor high-frequency response, then you'll tend to turn up the treble to compensate, giving super-boosted highs on systems with normal high frequency response. This is why monitor systems aim for flat frequency response: your sound will be butchered the least amount possible by other systems, all of which are bound to deviate from a flat response.

Achieving flat response is no easy task. The monitor amplifier is the least of your problems, since all decent high-fidelity power amplifiers have flat response (or very close to it) from at least 20 Hz to 20 kHz. You don't really need more than about 100 watts/channel unless you're driving very inefficient speakers. This should be enough to handle any transients without clipping.

## Monitor Speakers (And Headphones)

There are a variety of monitor speakers available at reasonable prices, although of course you can spend thousands of dollars if you want. As with any speaker purchase, all you really can do is listen to several different types and decide which one sounds best. If possible, audition a speaker with program material that you've heard played over very high-quality speakers so that you can make some kind of comparison. Also remember that all else being equal, a louder speaker will sound better than a softer one—so match levels very carefully when comparing speakers.

As to using headphones for monitoring, sealed-ear types (Fig. 8-1) are fine for cueing and overdubbing; don't use open-air types, as they tend to have a more deceptive bass response. Also, open-air headphones are terrible for vocalists because the sound can leak into the mic, or even cause feedback.

For mixdown, where all sounds are super-critically evaluated, headphones are not enough; you also need speakers. More people listen to music over speakers than through headphones, and a piece of music mixed exclusively on headphones will sound right only when played back through headphones. In addition, headphones are much more sensitive to subtleties. For example, what sounds like a bit too much reverb on headphones can seem nonexistent on speak-

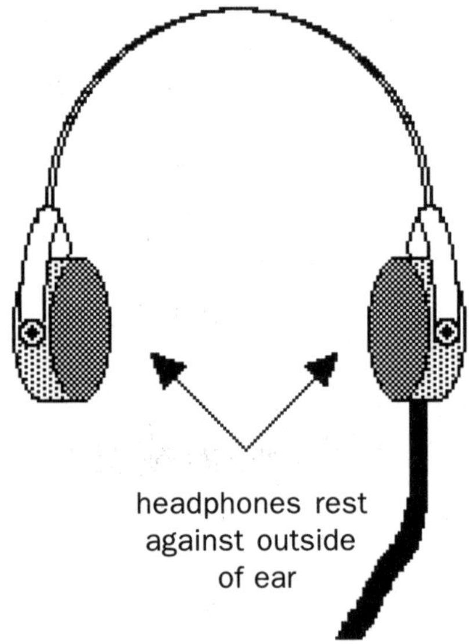


**Fig. 8-1:** *A sealed-ear headphone (left) is more useful for studio applications that open air types (right).*

ers—another reason for choosing speakers for monitor and mixdown work. Still, I use headphones a lot during the preliminary stages of a mix so that I can hear little problems, like clicks or hums; and by sealing out the effects of the room, it's possible to get yet another "reality check" on the sound. Hint: When listening, press the earcups lightly against your head for as good a seal as possible. This will give the maximum amount of bass coupling into your ear. And watch the volume; it's easy to turn the level way up with headphones and not really notice how loud it is.

Generally, the most common approach to monitoring in the project studio is *near-field monitoring*. This simply means you have the speakers positioned only a few feet away from your ear so that you get mostly direct sound and very little reflected sound, on the assumption that this will give the truest reproduction. If you use hi-fi speakers as near-field speakers, unless the manufacturer recommends otherwise, mount them horizontally, not vertically, with the tweeters at the extreme left and right sides and the woofers in the middle (Fig. 8-2). The speakers should also face inward slightly so they have a straight shot to your ears. When mounted this way, the highs (which are directional) have maximum separation, while the low frequencies (which aren't so directional) emanate more from the middle.

It's also important to monitor over a variety of speakers. Your music may be played over a boombox, a set of tinny headphones connected to a personal tape player, or electrostatic audiophile monstrosities that sound godlike and cost thousands of dollars. A good mix is one that sounds great on any of these. Many engineers mix to a "lowest common denominator" speaker under the premise that if a mix sounds good on these, it will sound *spectacular* over quality speakers. Another reality check is to run off a cassette and play a tune in your car stereo. Whatever, the more systems you can monitor your tunes on, the better.

The ultimate reality check is to book an hour of studio time at a world-class studio, then play your final audio mix over their system. Before doing that, though, listen to your audio so many times on your own system—paying particular attention to the overall frequency response—that you know it by heart. Now go into a pro-level studio and listen to the tape. If all is well, the tape should sound exactly as it did back in your studio. If there are differences (*e.g.*, boomy bass, overly "zingy" high end), note what they are.

If there is a consistent difference between what you thought your audio sounded like and what it sounds like on other systems, take this into account next time you record or mix. For example, if your tapes sound bass-heavy on other systems, back off a bit on the bass when working in your own studio. (Since you've already booked the time, you might as well run off a safety copy of your tape on one of the studio's tape or recordable CD machines. In fact, if your tape sounds wrong when played back over a super-accurate system, you might be able to equalize or otherwise alter the copy to produce a dub that's better than the original.)

## Headphones for Cueing

When you buy headphones for musicians to use when overdubbing, don't bother to get really expensive ones, since they tend to have a short life expectancy. They also get kicked around a lot and fall on the floor. Your best bet is to get one particular model of headphone and stick to it. This way, they'll present similar loads to the cue amp (and you may be able to obtain a quantity discount). Different brands may have different impedances and hog more output from the cue amp than others.

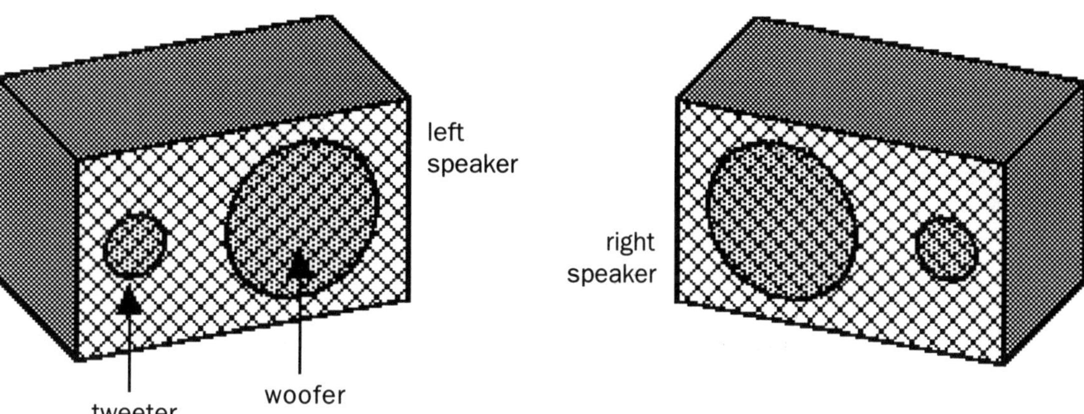


**Fig. 8-2:** *By mounting speakers horizontally and having the tweeters on the outside, you'll experience a wider stereo spread when listening in the near field.*

Headphones with built-in volume controls are handy. They're a drag for hi-fi use because the pots are usually not ultra-high quality, but they sure are a handy feature for cue systems, since no two musicians ever seem to want the same cue level.

## Room Tuning

Ideally, your monitor speaker should be in a totally flat listening room. However, this simply isn't possible; every room exhibits a variety of response anomalies.

To check the room response, a sound level meter is ideal. Budget models are often available for around $50. They consist of a flat response microphone connected to a level meter. You run several different tones through your system, then monitor their levels in the location where you'll be listening to your speakers. Prepare yourself for a shock when you do this; room responses are anything but flat, and drawing a graph of the levels of the various tones will probably look like a picture of the Alps.

If you have some problems with your room (as determined by the above test) and want to improve matters, you might be tempted to flirt with perfection and try to "tune" the room using a multiband room-tuning equalizer. This process involves pumping a pink noise source (which exhibits constant energy per octave) through your loudspeakers, then picking up the signal with a precisely calibrated microphone. The mic output feeds a multiband equalizer, which indicates whether the response for a particular band is high or low compared to the other bands. You then vary the equalizer controls to "tune out" these differences. For example, if the highs seem somewhat anemic, you can boost the equalizer's high frequency bands to compensate.

Concerning hardware, room tuners can be anything from microprocessor-controlled wonder boxes that do all the work for you to relatively simple devices that have "high," "low," or "correct" LEDs for each band (you simply adjust the equalizer controls until only the "correct" LEDs are on). But as you might expect, nothing is perfect and the room tuning process involves certain tradeoffs. Generally, if you use equalization to tune a room you are tuning it for that one place where the calibrated microphone sits. Even if the room seems perfectly tuned, if you move the mic a couple of feet in another direction your response will change.

In my opinion, room tuning must be done carefully. Just like Anderton's First Law of Noise Reduction ("noise reduction works best on signals with very little noise"), room tuning seems to work best with rooms that are already pretty good from an acoustic standpoint. In other words, if you have a bad-sounding room with poor speakers, all a room equalizer will do is give you a highly equalized bad-sounding room with poor speakers. This may represent an improvement, but as noted earlier this improvement may only be apparent to listeners in certain selected areas of the room. On the other hand, if you have an already good-sounding room, adding a few dB of boost or cut here and there can turn a good room into a very good room. Generally, though, you might be better off learning the room acoustics and compensating for any anomalies as you work.

## Getting Rid of Resonances

Make sure there aren't any sympathetic vibrations resonating along with the speakers. For example, after spending months installing a brand new isolation booth and speaker mounting system in my studio, I played some drum tapes to hear how the room sounded. Although the sound was consistent no matter where I stood in the room, it was accompanied by a strange ringing noise. After a few moments of panic, I started zeroing in on the source of the resonance, which (thankfully) had nothing to do with the room. Instead, the metal bottom panel on one of the rack mount cases was vibrating whenever a signal occurred around 300 Hz. I wedged a piece of carpet between the panel and casing to deaden the sound, and all was well.

There's a simple way to find resonances in a room. Use a low distortion sine wave oscillator (a keyboard synthesizer will also do, provided that you close the low-pass filter down as much as is necessary for the output to approximate a sine wave) and plug it into your board. Then, sweep from 20 Hz to 20 kHz at varying volume levels. Listen for any buzzes that indicate loose screws, vibrating surfaces, or similar problems, then do whatever is necessary to fix the problem. If a panel is vibrating, glue some heavy material on it to help inhibit any tendencies toward vibration.

You can also minimize response anomalies with acoustically absorbent tubes placed strategically around a room. These "trap" resonances and produce a flatter frequency response. Knowing which kind to buy and where to put them requires either a lot of trial and error or specialized knowledge. It can be worth a few hundred dollars to hire a professional studio designer as a consultant to help you. Sometimes a few minor acoustical touches in the right place can make a huge difference in a room's acoustics.

# Chapter 9
# Microphones

The microphone has the critical, and difficult, task of turning minute variations in air pressure into electrical signals. As such, it is the first link in the audio "chain," and as the cliché goes, a chain is only as strong as its weakest link. Selecting the proper microphone for a specific task, and placing it to pick up a signal optimally, is a cross between an art and a science; so let's present some microphone basics so that you can match the right type of microphone to the right application.

Keep in mind, though, that microphones are surrounded by mythology as well as by sound waves. Both engineers and performers place a tremendous amount of emphasis on selecting the "right" microphone (mic), but this may be a bit old-fashioned. Recent advances in microphone technology, coupled with large demand and high-volume manufacturing techniques, have minimized the differences between microphones and have brought prices down to a reasonable level. Additionally, equalization can help reduce the differences between various models of mics.

Microphones have different physical constructions, different sound pickup patterns, and even different ways of connecting into your mixer. This last difference is probably the hardest for many musicians to understand as it involves the concept of impedance (abbreviated Z), so let's get that out of the way first.

## Impedance

You have undoubtedly heard of high-impedance and low-impedance systems. You may have also heard that they are incompatible. In other words, if a mixer has inputs designed to accept a high-impedance device, it cannot accept a low-impedance mic without some modifications. Also, the opposite holds true, although there are some (very few) instances where you can violate this rule.

Most stage setups that involve electric guitars and pianos, guitar amplifiers, and the like, are high-impedance systems, and we'll cover these first.

*Input impedance* is the amount of resistance a signal will encounter on its way into, or out of, an electronic device or amplifying stage. For example, your stage amplifier has an input impedance (Fig. 9-1). This is just like having a resistance across the input to ground, even if there isn't an actual physical resistor in that part of the circuit. This "pseudo-resistance" shunts part of the signal away to ground, thus diminishing the signal's power.

The *output impedance* is like having a resistance in series with the output of your amplifier, which also acts to diminish the signal strength (Fig. 9-2 relates this to an instrument amp). The input impedance acts like a shunt

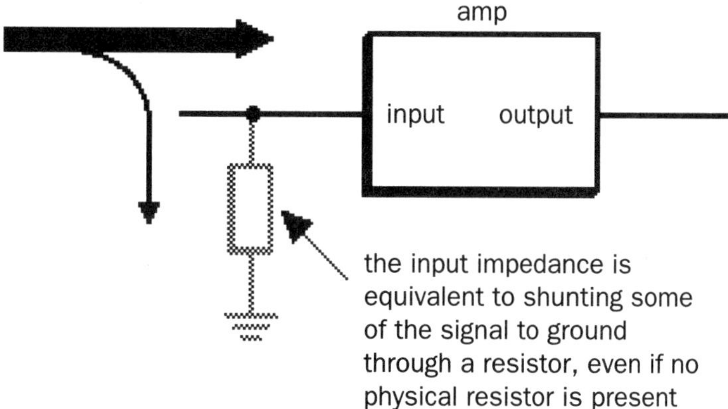


**Fig. 9-1:** *Most of the input signal goes to the amp, but some shunts to ground. The less resistance there is to ground, the more signal gets shunted to ground.*

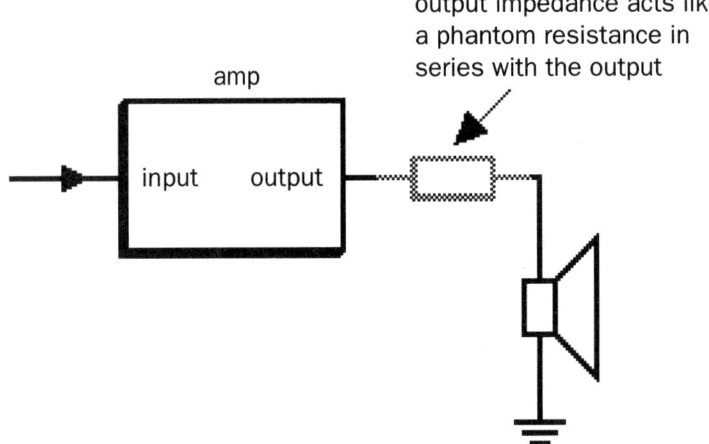


**Fig. 9-2:** *The grayed-out resistor represents an amplifier's output impedance.*

across the input, while the output impedance acts like a resistance between the amp output and the speaker.

Microphones also have an output impedance. The unit of impedance is the ohm (abbreviated Ω), and a lower number means a lower impedance. Thus, a 50Ω microphone would be a low-impedance device, and a 10,000Ω microphone would be a high-impedance output device. Most guitar pickups are of the high-Z variety.

Remembering what we said about an output impedance being in series with a signal, then we can see, from an electrical point of view, how a microphone would look (Fig. 9-3).

**Fig. 9-3:** *Microphones come in both low and high output impedance varieties. Some offer a switchable output impedance.*

Now, let's see what happens if you take a high-Z microphone and connect it to an amp with a low-Z input (Fig. 9-4).

You are no longer getting all of the signal from the microphone, but are picking up the signal at the junction of two resistances; namely, at the output impedance of the mic and at the input impedance of the amp. Now, put that thought on hold for a second as we look at a volume control.

A volume control is also called a *voltage divider* because, as you move the knob, you're actually tapping off a point along a piece of resistive material (Fig. 9-5).

If you connect that volume control between a signal source (guitar, mic, synthesizer, tape out, *etc.*) and an input (*e.g.*, mixer, amp) according to Fig. 9-6, you essentially turn down the volume by progressively adding more resistance between the source and the amp, while simultaneously shunting more and more of the signal to ground through the volume control's other leg. Turning it up does the exact opposite: less signal shunts to ground, and more is allowed into the amplifier. Thus, for maximum energy transfer, we want as high a resistance as possible between the signal and ground, and the lowest possible resistance between the signal and the amp it is feeding.

Now let's relate this back to impedance. As shown in Fig. 9-4, the combined output and

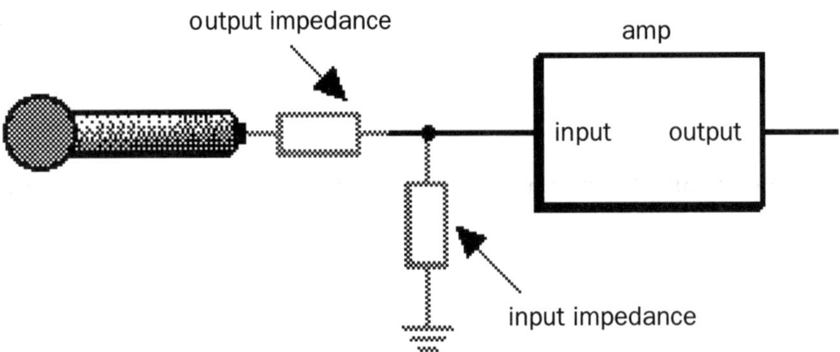


**Fig. 9-4:** *The combination of input and output impedance forms the electrical equivalent of a volume control.*

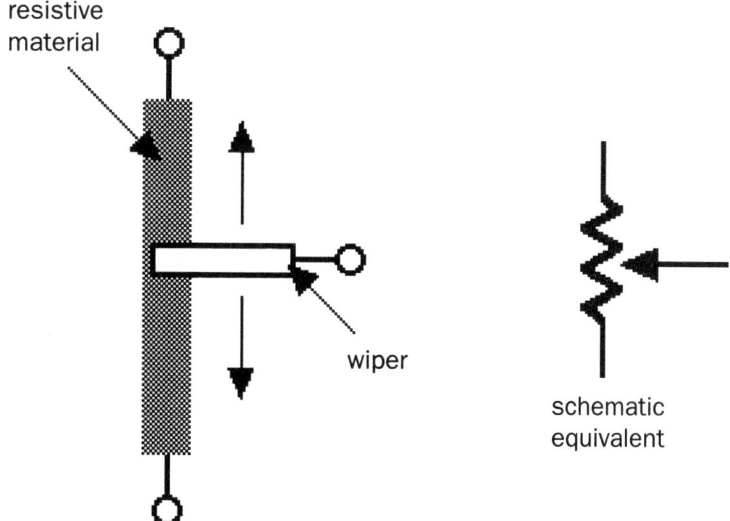


**Fig. 9-5:** *A typical volume control consists of a resistive element and a wiper that slides across the element. As the wiper moves closer to one end of the element (less resistance between wiper and end), it's simultaneously moving farther away from the other end (which creates more resistance between the wiper and the other end).*

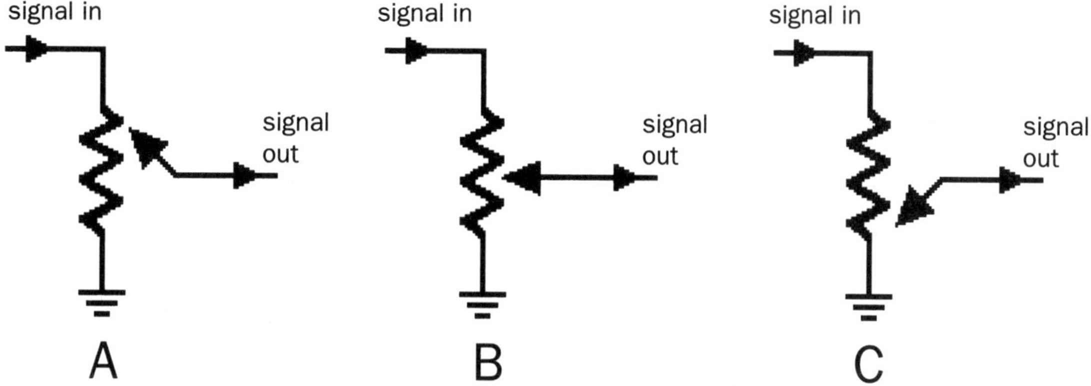


**Fig. 9-6:** *In (A), there is little resistance between the signal input and output. Also, there is very little of the signal shunted to ground. In (B), with the volume control up halfway, there is some resistance between the input and output; additionally, the resistance that shunts the signal to ground is getting smaller, which shunts more signal to ground. In (C), no signal gets through: the resistance between input and output is very large, and the signal gets shunted to ground anyway.*

input impedances form a sort of involuntary volume control. Thus, if an output impedance is many times greater than the input impedance, a lot of power will shunt to ground. On the other hand, if the input impedance is much higher than the output impedance, very little of the signal will be lost.

Before going any further let's clarify one point. Many people are under the misconception that impedances must be matched—*i.e.,* a 10,000Ω output impedance should feed a 10,000Ω input impedance. This is not necessarily so. I don't want to get too involved with this; let's just say that, for minimum signal loss in an audio system, in most cases an input impedance should be approximately ten times greater than the output impedance feeding it. There are exceptions (aren't there always?) but this rule generally holds. Thus, a 10,000Ω microphone would like to feed at least a 100,000Ω input Z; sometimes with guitar pickups and other coil-based devices, a 1,000,000Ω input impedance is required to keep loading of the signal to an absolute minimum.

Are you still with me? Let's sum up. A microphone with a high-Z output, like 5,000Ω to 10,000Ω, must "see" an input Z of at least 50,000Ω to 100,000Ω to transfer the maximum amount of signal to the next stage. A low-impedance device, on the other hand, can feed a much lower input impedance; a 50Ω output Z mic, for example, can feed a 600Ω line and still fit our "input Z should be at least ten times output Z" requirement.

But we aren't finished yet, because a few more problems creep in. High-Z inputs are much more sensitive to noise and hum. As less and less of the signal is shunted toward ground by the input impedance, the input cable can act like a long, floating antenna that picks up a lot of garbage as it winds its way across a stage or studio. Additionally, the cables tying the various units together have problems: as the output Z of a device goes up, requiring that it feed a higher input impedance, the cable starts acting like a tone control and shunts away high frequencies (treble) to ground. This is because the cable acts like a giant capacitor, but let's not open that can of worms. Instead, we'll jump immediately to the solution for the problem: a low-impedance, balanced-line system.

The high-Z system we were talking about earlier had two wires, just like musical instrument cables. One wire is the ground line, which can also be called common, earth, shield, or DC return; the other is the signal line, which is often referred to as the "hot" line. The hot line carries the signal, and the ground acts as a voltage reference. This is called an *unbalanced* system, and uses two-wire 1/4" phone jacks and plugs (Fig. 9-7).

A *balanced* system adds another signal line (called the "cold" or "neutral" line) to the "hot" signal-line-plus-ground combination in an unbalanced system. The basic principle here is that the two hot leads carry signals that are identical, but 180 degrees out of phase (Fig. 9-8); thus, as a signal increases in voltage along one line, its mirror image on the other line decreases.

This type of signal has to feed a special type of input, found in transformers and certain types of amplifiers, called a *differential input* that responds to the difference between these out-of-phase signals. The differential input is a somewhat unusual beast, but it comes in very handy here because it rejects signals that are in phase, such as hum and noise. Let's look further into why this happens.

The simplest way to explain the concept of a differential input is by analogy (Fig. 9-9). The balanced signals arriving from the previous stage feed the input, and are "differenced" to produce a final, unbalanced output (we'll explain why we need to get back to the unbalanced form

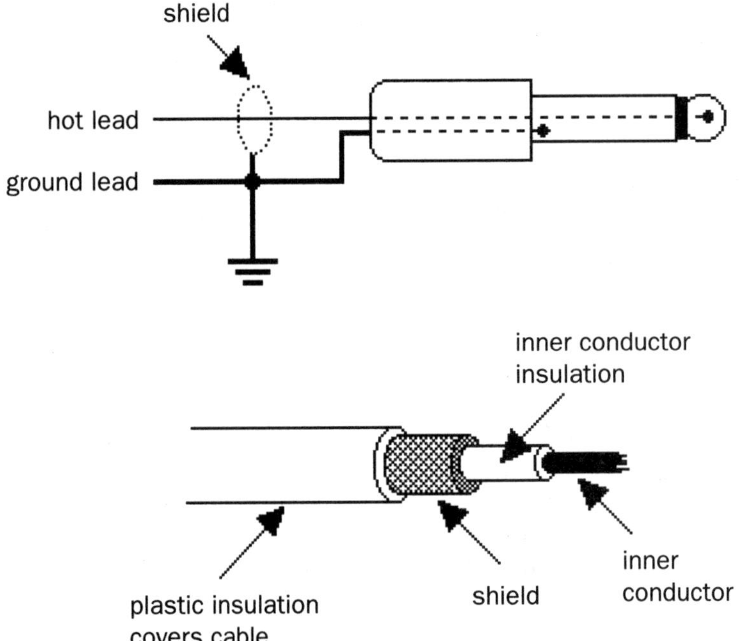


**Fig. 9-7:** *The inner, "hot" conductor is surrounded by a grounded shield that fences hum and interference (although shielding is not 100 percent effective).*

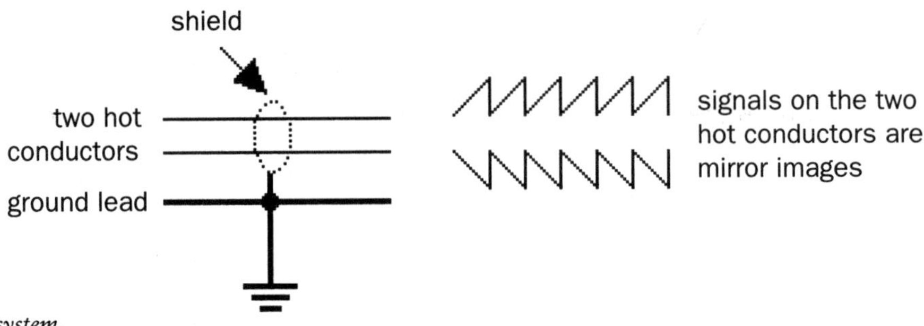


**Fig. 9-8:** *Balanced line system.*

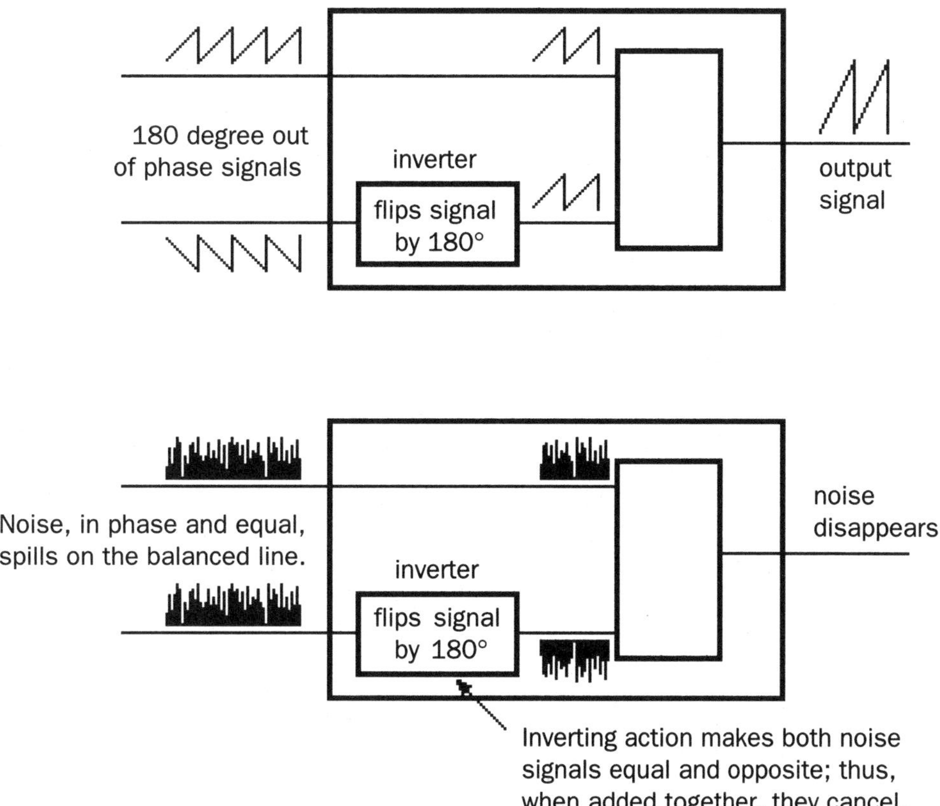


**Fig. 9-9:** *Conceptual equivalent of a differential amp.*

shortly). Fine, but the real strength of this approach is that signals that are in phase are canceled. If you think back to the beginning of this book, you'll remember that when you have two sound waves meeting so that the crest of one is at the trough of the other, then the net result is no wave at all.

Luckily, the kinds of noise and garbage that get into a mic line are not produced by a nice, controlled, balanced output. Instead, the signal spills over both signal lines equally. Since the differential input responds only to the differences between the two signal lines, when you have the same signal present on both lines, then there isn't any difference, and the differential input ignores them. Some differential amplifiers can reduce these interfering signals (technically called *common-mode* signals) over 30,000 times—that is, an interfering signal as strong as the desired signal at the amp input can be reduced so that it appears to be only 1/30,000th as strong at the differential amp output. That's about 90 dB worth of rejection—a most useful trick.

This provides a way to run really long cables without having them act as antennas, and we're beginning to see the end of all this orgy of theory. We now have a nice, low-Z mic, say with a 50Ω output Z, feeding a 600Ω line, which terminates in a differential input that rejects any of the common-mode noise picked up along the way. As an added bonus, if you're feeding a circuit with a transistor input, you can also keep the noise level lower (by keeping the input Z down) than you could with a higher-Z, more sensitive input. An input impedance of about 10,000Ω for a transistor amplifier produces the least amount of noise, and this is why many mixers have a 10,000Ω input impedance if they are the high-Z input type.

Now it's time to return to why we want to convert back to a high-Z signal, and then the puzzle will be nearly solved. As you can see, using a balanced-line system requires all these differential inputs and (sometimes) transformers. High-Z systems use only two lines, are easier to deal with, and are less expensive. Additionally, once you get inside the console, your cable runs are much shorter and less prone to pick up interference; also, the signal levels are line-level rather than mic-level, and don't need the sheltered environment that those weak mic-level signals require. So, the usual procedure is to use a low-Z mic, feed a balanced transmission line with that weak signal to the mixer, and then convert that balanced signal back to a two-line, far stronger, unbalanced signal for further processing.

In many cases, the conversion back to high-Z

uses matching transformers. These are wonderful little devices that can match a three-wire, balanced system at one end, and a two-wire, unbalanced system at the other. You can use this type of transformer either way—so if you have a high-Z instrument output and a low-Z board, hook the instrument into the high-Z end and the mixer into the low-Z end and you're ready to go.

Sometimes these transformers are wired into a device called a *direct box,* which allows you to plug the instrument directly into a mixing console without going through a microphone. Conversely, if you have a high-Z input mixer but a low-Z mic, then you plug the mic into the low-Z end of the transformer and the mixer input into the high-Z end. Simple? Mixers featuring low-Z inputs almost always have a matching transformer or active differential amplifier stage built inside the console. If you have a mixer with high-Z inputs, you can buy audio matching transformers and connect them to the inputs (though at $15 to $100 each, they are not cheap).

Transformers, however, are not perfect devices. They can pick up hum and introduce a small amount of distortion and coloration. Sometimes, active circuits (like preamps and circuits that require power supplies) perform the conversion instead. The only trouble is that they aren't perfect either, since they add noise because lots of gain is required. On the other hand, they can be less expensive for home setups.

Golden ear types have pitched battles over which is better to use, transformers or active circuitry, but it all comes down to a matter of taste. Some people swear that transformers help "warm up" the sound of digital gear, but that active circuitry is best when you want minimum coloration. Use your ears, and you be the judge.

Whew! We're almost done, but we need to look at one more aspect of this whole mess—the actual connectors themselves (for illustrations, see the end of Chapter 7). The two-wire, unbalanced system almost universally uses 1/4" phone jacks and plugs. Three-wire systems present a choice: you can use 1/4" *stereo* phone plugs and jacks, as they have the required capacity for handling two signal lines as well as ground; or you can use XLR connectors, which are more rugged. Also, because the ground pin is brought out separately, you can separate the signal ground line from the shield itself, which can be very handy in some circumstances.

In low-Z systems, the microphone will terminate in a male XLR connector, which then mates with a female XLR on the line. An unfortunate problem is that the three pins of the XLR connector are not always wired in the same way; either pin 2 or pin 3 can be the hot signal (although pin 2 hot is the internationally accepted standard), with the other two being the other signal line and ground. As a result, it never hurts to have a couple of adapters around to convert from one pin wiring to another. You may be tempted to figure out the wiring scheme by probing around the pins with a continuity tester like a multimeter—don't do it, as it could damage the mic element.

## The Different Types of Microphones

Four basic types of microphones are used in recording: dynamic, condenser, ribbon, and PZM. Each operates on a different principle, but they all have similarities. In each case, air waves hitting a sensitive diaphragm inside the body of the mic are translated into electrical energy.

Although these different types of mics used to sound extremely different, recent advances have increased the versatility and usefulness of all types. There are still differences, but they tend to be more subtle. Proper tone shaping through equalization (see the section on consoles) can also minimize differences between different types of microphones. Older dynamic mics, for instance, used to have very poor high-frequency response; lighter diaphragms have solved that problem.

### Dynamic Microphones

We talked briefly about the dynamic mic in the beginning of the book. Fig. 9-10 shows its physical construction. As the coil of a dynamic mic moves through a magnetic field, the action of cutting across this field induces a voltage into the coil, which we can then amplify and use.

This is a very rugged mic—the kind you'd want to take on tour. It has few complications, and requires no power supply. If you drop it, the thing will probably still keep on working. One disadvantage of this mic is a lack of response at both extremes of the audio spectrum; a dynamic microphone that does a really super job in the high-frequency range can be expensive. Another disadvantage is low output, but this is something all mics have in common.

A final problem is poor *transient response* (the ability to respond rapidly to a rapidly changing signal). A mic with poor transient response gives a less crisp, less precise sound.

Dynamic mics resist overload well (remember, microphones are physical systems and can be driven to the point of distortion, where they

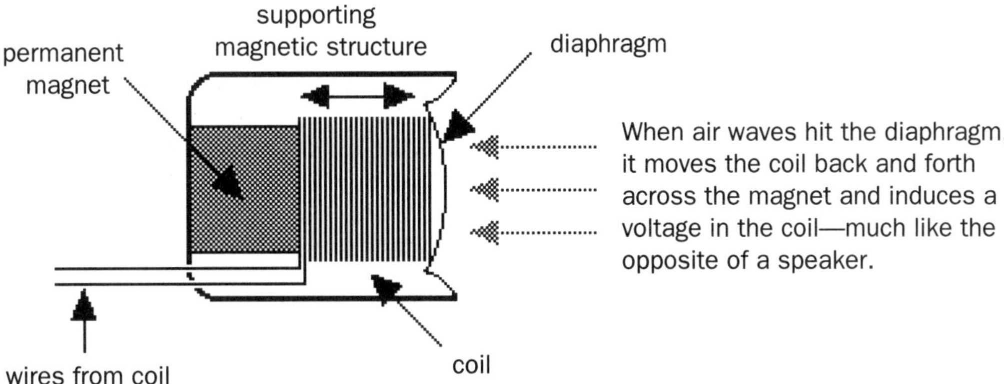


**Fig. 9-10:** *How the dynamic mic works.*

just don't respond in a nice, predictable fashion anymore). Dynamic mics can handle powerful signals well, and are frequently used for kick drums, guitar amps, and "screamer" vocalists.

## Condenser/Electret Microphones

The condenser microphone (Fig. 9-11) is based on the construction of a capacitor, and takes advantage of the fact that capacitance changes will show up as voltage changes if the capacitor is *biased* (permanently connected to a constant voltage).

Compared to a dynamic, condenser mics offer superior high-frequency and transient response. Many condensers exhibit a peak in the high frequencies, giving a larger-than-life sound that is very shimmering and crisp (however, to get a more natural sound you may have to add some high-frequency rolloff in the 10 to 20 kHz region).

Condenser mics have always been good, but inconvenient, as they required a separate power supply and some heavy-duty preamplification in order to be usable. Now, new condenser materials have resulted in a modern version of the condenser mic, called the electret microphone, which doesn't require any weird, high-voltage supplies, like the old condenser types did. In fact, a good electret microphone can be quite affordable.

As to disadvantages, condenser mics put out so little power by themselves that they need the help of a preamp stage, which of course adds a finite amount of noise and distortion. (Incidentally, some people greatly prefer the sound of condenser mics with tube preamps, because of the particular coloration a tube can add.) Additionally, the preamp needs power, so an electret microphone will usually have a battery that needs to be replaced from time to time, or require the use of phantom power (a voltage that is generally run through the mic cable; for more information, see the next chapter on mixers). Standard condenser mics are nice but not really applicable to home recording. Condenser electret types cost less, require less external circuitry, and are easier to use.

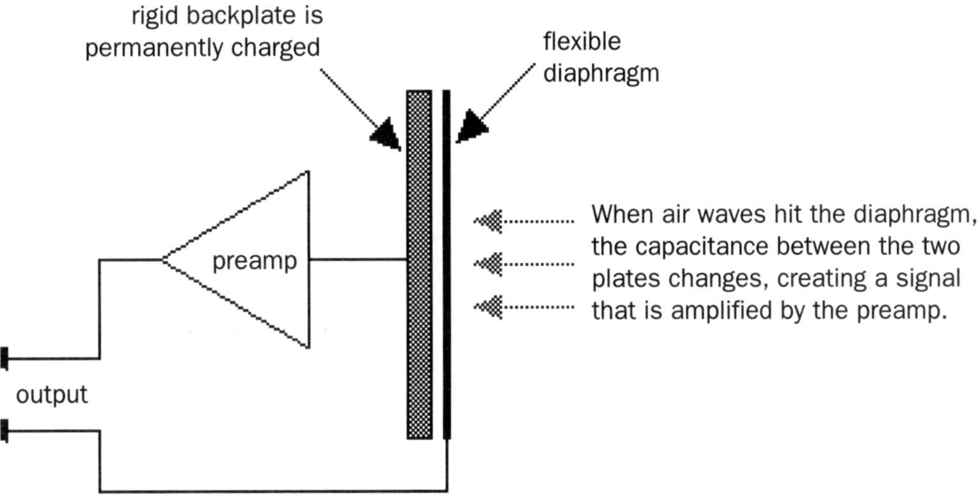


**Fig. 9-11:** *Condenser/electret mic.*

But now we have another problem: the condenser/electret can't take as strong a signal as the dynamic mic—it overloads. With a dynamic mic, you need worry about overloading only the microphone element itself. With an electret or condenser, you can overload the preamp too, and electronic circuits have a lower dynamic range than real-life instruments. Studios generally favor condenser mics for acoustic guitar, some drums (like snare, where crispness is important), and certain vocalists. However, voices vary widely, so some sound better with electrets, some with dynamics, and some with ribbon mics.

## Ribbon Microphones

The ribbon type (Fig. 9-12) uses a thin metal ribbon that moves when air waves hit it. I've only experienced these in the studio, because I can't afford one for my own use—even the reasonable ones are fairly expensive. In general, these mics are mechanically fragile (although newer models are more rugged than the old classics), but paradoxically, they resist high-temperature and high humidity environments that can cripple electret and dynamic mics.

They have the best transient response of the lot, but again paradoxically, suffer from a little bit of ringing after responding to a sharp transient. The audible effect of this is a slight additional resonance to the sound, which gives a subtly warm feel to acoustic instruments and voices. Although not as much in demand as it was many years ago—mainly due to improvements in other mic types—the ribbon mic nonetheless has a well-defined place in the recording world, and are often favored for recording brass instruments.

## PZM Microphones

I've used these (also called pressure zone mics) for vocals and sampling acoustic instruments. It's possible to buy fairly inexpensive PZM mics, so it doesn't cost much to add one of these to your arsenal for special occasions. Overall, though, the electret and dynamic microphones are going to the be the workhorses in your studio.

The PZM (Pressure-Zone Mic) microphone mounts a condenser mic in a special package above a square, metal plate. This helps overcome the common microphone placement problem of phase cancellation; normally when you set up a mic on a podium, the same sound can hit the microphone at slightly different times—specifically, the direct sound hits before the reflected sound. This can lead to partial or total cancellation at certain frequencies, thus creating a thin sound. With a PZM, the mic faces down toward the plate through a small gap. With this design, reflected waves occur at essentially the same time as the direct wave. Many engineers stick PZMs under a piano's cover to supplement traditional mics pointed at the soundboard.

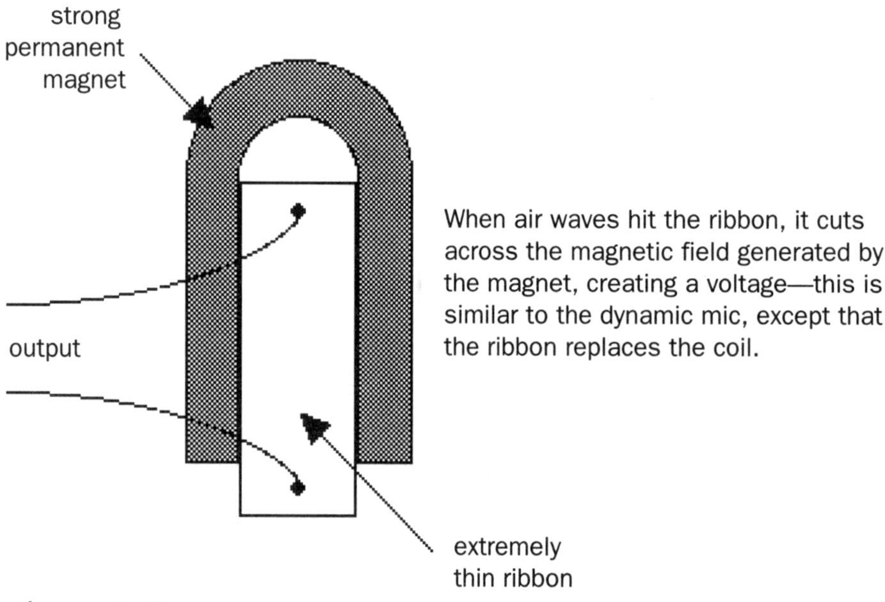


**Fig. 9-12:** *Ribbon microphone construction.*

## Microphone Directionality

Different mics have different pickup patterns: some are *omnidirectional,* meaning they pick up sound from all directions—front, rear, side, whatever. Some (mostly ribbon types) are *bidirectional,* so they pick up sound from the front and back, but not from the sides. Others are called *cardioid,* or unidirectional, because they have a heart-shaped pickup pattern that tends to pick up sound from one direction only (Fig. 9-13).

Before we go any further, note that directionality is not absolute; in fact, response patterns don't mean all that much. Low frequencies are less directional than high frequencies, so even your omnidirectional mic may be "omni" only for certain frequencies and more "uni" at other ones.

Directionality is most important for PA or sound reinforcement work, because in these cases it's easy to pick up signals that could cause feedback. In the studio, directionality can help increase separation without using extra baffles or acoustical isolation. However, keep in mind that most mics use internal acoustic pathways to derive these responses, and are not necessarily that precise. The point is to believe your ears, not the spec, when the two conflict.

One tip: blocking the acoustical ports (usually slots) along the rear of a mic's capsule assembly (a small bit of duct tape on the outside of the mic body will do), you can temporarily convert a cardioid mic to omni. It's not perfect, but when you need an omni mic in a pinch, this does the trick.

## Recording with Microphones

This is one of the most controversial aspects of recording. Everybody has their own favorite mic to record specific instruments, their own particular ideas of where to position microphones for best pickup, the correct number of mics to use with a drum set, and so on.

No one knows all the answers, and that certainly includes me. However, I have found out something important: if you know what you like, you can experiment around until you find the perfect sound for your purposes. Our main rule of recording—"If it sounds good, use it"—transcends any other rules. Here are some thought about how to use microphones, but first we'll have to look at some of their peculiarities and characteristics so we can use them to maximum advantage.

### The Proximity Effect

No, this isn't a science-fiction movie; it's a phenomenon that occurs with all mics, but is most pronounced with dynamic cardioid types. It means that as you get closer to the mic, the apparent bass response goes up. Singers proficient in mic technique use this to advantage: on soft, intimate parts, they'll sing softly, holding the mic close to the mouth, to exaggerate the bass and give a warmer sound. Then during louder parts, they'll hold the microphone farther back and sing louder to compensate for the extra distance. Classical guitars can also take advantage of the proximity effect to get a warmer recorded sound. In any event, you should be

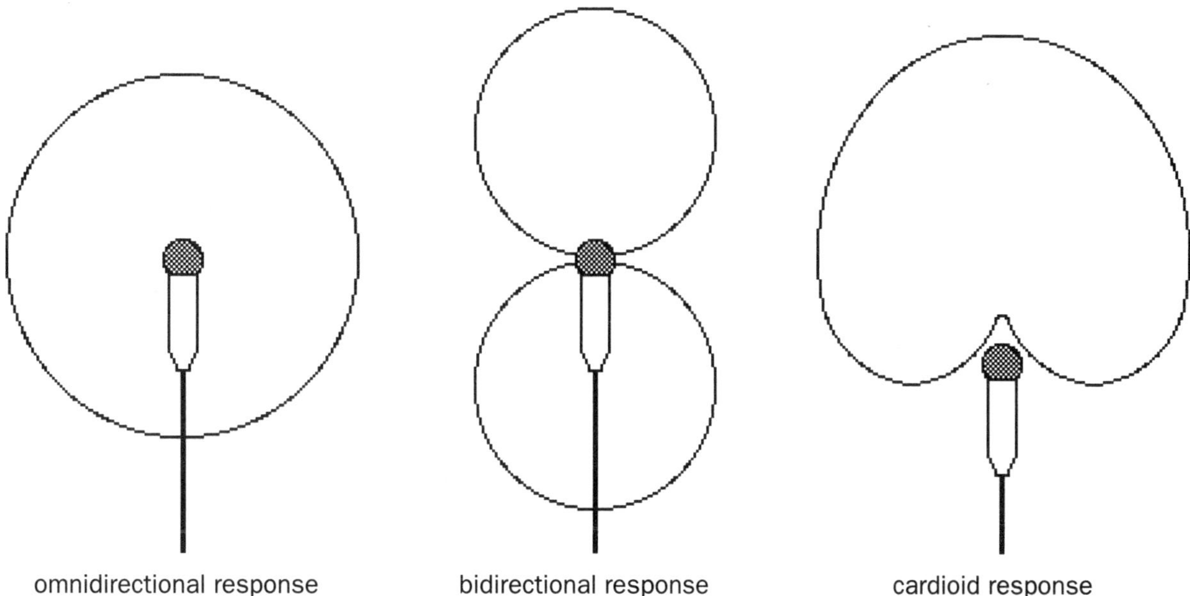


**Fig. 9-13:** *Different microphone directionality patterns.*

aware of this and either use it to your advantage or compensate for it.

## The Inverse Square Law

This is a fancy way of saying that the farther you get away from a mic, the more the sound drops off. However, the sound does not fall off uniformly as the sound source moves away; rather, the mic's ability to pick up sound decreases dramatically when the sound source moves only a few inches away (Fig. 9-14).

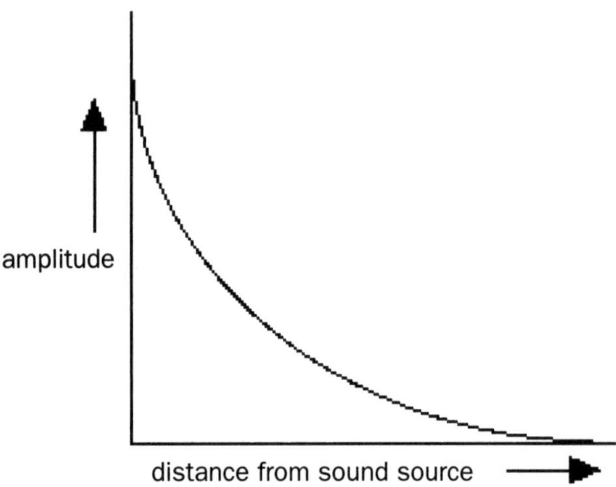


**Fig. 9-14:** *How the inverse square law affects mic output.*

This can be a serious problem with vocalists who aren't really good with mic technique and who wander around the vicinity of the mic, alternately swallowing it and then backing away, without changing their volume to compensate. The electronic solution is to add compression, but it's better if you can explain to the artist that one can achieve a consistent signal only by recognizing the demands of the inverse square law and the proximity effect. After you explain this, just tell the singer to quit moving around during vocal takes.

## Popping and Wind Noises

Microphones are sensitive to sounds that linguists call *plosives* (b, p, and the like). These produce nasty pops and thumps in the output. Also, wind noise can create interference. To cope with this problem, you can buy a little foam cover that slips over the head of the mic and attenuates these sounds, as well as keeps breath moisture from the mic. The foam must be acoustically transparent to high frequencies, which rules out regular styrofoam—use the acoustic foam designed for the job.

Another option is one of the many clip-on nylon screen filters on the market, which are not only effective, but can be adjusted to keep the vocalist a few inches away from the mic. Again, the performer can help reduce vocal popping with proper mic techniques, such as singing off-center into the mic during sections containing these problem sounds.

## Phasing Problems

Earlier in the chapter, we covered how two signals arriving at the same place 180 degrees out of phase could cancel each other out, unless they happened to be feeding a differential input. Signals arriving in phase can also *add* to each other; and if signals are neither totally in phase nor totally out of phase, other responses will occur. So when you're using two mics, you can run into phasing problems if one mic is picking up the crest of a signal while another is picking up the trough (situations are rarely this clean cut, though; we're simplifying for the sake of illustration). Actually, the phase changes will be different at different frequencies, so that some bass notes might be reinforced while some of the treble cancels, or then again, the opposite could be true. So, although each mic might sound all right when monitored by itself, when it is combined with others, the sound can be considerably altered.

The bottom line: if you're using two mics to record an instrument like a piano, check to hear what they sound like together as well as separately. Phase problems are particularly acute if you feed one mic into the right channel and one into the left channel of a stereo system to obtain a stereo spread, then play the recording back over a mono system; the inherent phase changes could cause cancellations and weaken the sound.

These difficulties are compounded when miking drums, since several mics must then be used to get an acceptable sound from the set. The phase relationships in such a case can be horribly complex. Again, your only real option is to monitor, listen, check, and compare, until the sound is correct. If you are dealing with a stereo spread, also check the mono combination from time to time. Some mixing consoles have phase switches that can change the phase of a microphone from the console rather than by placement. If combining the mics in mono temporarily and flipping the phase switch solves the problem of cancellation, great. But it should be emphasized that by simply flipping the mic's phasing 180 degrees, you will not necessarily solve your problems, and you may introduce some new ones. Oh well.

## Mounting Microphones

You should have mic stands, booms, and the like to mount mics; a goose-neck extension helps for close miking, where you stick the mic right up next to your sound source (*e.g.*, close to the soundhole of a guitar). If you are some distance away from the sound source—say, in a live recording situation—you have a couple of options: you can place the microphone on the floor, but have it lying on top of lots of foam and stuff so that it doesn't pick up floor vibrations and rumble. Also, you can try hanging the mic from the ceiling. This will produce the same general results, and may even be better because you won't have people stomping on the ceiling (if your mic is on the floor and there are people dancing then you'll probably pick up the thumps).

## Using Your Mic's Little Switches

Sometimes mics have extra little built-in features. One of my favorites is a low-frequency rolloff switch. This basically reduces response from below about 100 Hz, and is very useful with voice recording, as it can delete many of the pops and breath sounds without forcing you to resort to the wind screen devices that we mentioned earlier. Also, some voices tend to sound almost murky if they're too bassy, and in this case the low-frequency rolloff comes in handy. For musical uses, where you want full frequency response, you can take the rolloff out by putting the switch back in its flat position.

Another switch that you'll find, but only on electret and condenser mics, is an on-off switch for the battery. Use it! Even though the current drain is small, continuous extended use is what drains a battery. And whatever you do, don't use those cheap carbon-zinc batteries; if they leak, and corrode the inside of a microphone, you've just lost a substantial investment by trying to save a few cents on batteries. Use the better alkaline types.

## Microphone Tips

- Vocals. Although there are several recommended best ways to use a mic (such as holding it away, holding it close, singing across it, singing above it, or singing into it), every person's voice requires a different technique because every voice is different. For many voices, only a condenser mic will do; for others, a dynamic gives the right sound.

  For my vocals I often use a dynamic mic. It's rugged, so that I can use it in as many situations and on as many different instruments as possible, and it doesn't have built-in electronics that add noise. My particular model also has a low-frequency cut switch that minimizes popping, and can clean up the sound of some instruments. By singing close to the mic (to take advantage of the proximity effect) and rolling off some bass to avoid sounding too boomy, I can obtain just the right balance—even though in theory these two actions could cancel each other out. But the point is that no one would necessarily have recommended that for me; and to someone who doesn't need a little extra fullness, it would probably sound inappropriate. If you are recording a vocalist, emphasize the necessity of keeping the volume level constant. It's amazing how few singers are aware of good mic technique—they could learn a lot from the engineers who earn their living by properly applying it.

- Acoustic instruments. Most signals from the "real world" of acoustic instruments are very subtle in character and hard to capture with a microphone. As an additional complication, the dynamic range of an acoustic instrument is huge—even for digital systems—so that you can easily go from a signal that can't get over system noise to one that distorts. Intelligent mic placement and sympathetic playing are both equally important in solving this problem. Some players just don't understand dynamic range, and don't realize that playing in the studio is different from playing live.

  Some instruments are harder to mic than others. Saxophones aren't too difficult: you surely know where the sound comes out, although just sticking a mic in front of the bell results in missing some of the instrument's resonant properties. But then consider something like an acoustic guitar, where the soundhole is covered by your picking hand and the whole body resonates to produce a sound. In this case, there are several options, and a good one to consider is the *acoustic transducer* (also called a *contact mic*). These work with acoustic instruments by picking up the vibrations of the body and turning them into electrical signals. A popular example is the piezo transducer placed in the bridges of acoustic guitars.

  However, it is almost mandatory to use some

kind of equalization. Transducers tend to accentuate peaks and deficiencies in the instrument's response, and an equalizer can smooth these out. Again, the typical transducer signal output is weak and requires some kind of preamp to become usable, and of course the preamp adds noise (but you can't have everything).

A better, but more complex, approach is to use the transducer in conjunction with one or more mics. During one classical guitar session, I used a contact mic to pick up the basic notes and qualities of the guitar, with suitable equalization to take out a dreadful midrange peak. A condenser microphone was pointed at the strings near the guitarist's left hand, equalized with a little high-end sheen to accent the brightness of sound, and a dynamic microphone was pointed towards the end, and to the rear of the guitar, adding a deep kind of resonant, warm sound to the guitar's basic character. These were mixed together in stereo, with the transducer in the center of the spread, the bassier mic on the left, and the trebly mic on the right, mixed fairly low. The sound was really nice, but there were probably a hundred other equally valid ways of miking that guitar. Keep in mind, though, that there is a point of diminishing return in the number of mics you use: you become vulnerable to phase mismatch and other uglies with more mics. But as we've noted, you can't have everything.

- Drums. Drums are a real challenge. First, they're loud, and if you want to pick up one drum without picking up the rest of the kit, you'll have to figure out how to eliminate massive amounts of leakage. Second, the dynamic range is huge, and covers a very wide range of frequencies—from deep bass drum, to cymbals whose energy can extend beyond 20 kHz. In professional studios, drums are frequently isolated in as dead an area as possible, and this does help give a good drum sound. For rough-sounding drums, you can record in any room; but if you want maximum flexibility, the acoustics are very important.

  One common trick is to set up drums in a corner, because the configuration of the walls tends to boost the bass and add to the feeling of power. Although most drum miking is close miking, you will also probably want to add some overhead mics for an overall sound. For a while it was in vogue to just cover a drum set with mics, but then the interaction problems mentioned earlier became obvious; it seems that the best approach is to use the least number of mics consistent with a good sound. This means a minimum of separate mics for bass drum, high-hat/snare, and overhead (such as above the toms, slightly in front of the bass drum, or above the drummer's seat). It also helps to have another mic or two specifically for tom-toms. Have a good time experimenting!

# Chapter 10
# The Mixer

If the multitrack recorder is the heart of a studio and the rooms comprise the body, then the mixer (also called the console, board, or in England, the desk) is the brain. It combines signals, routes them to appropriate places along the signal path, provides headphone monitoring signals, generates playback outputs, and even converts signals (*e.g.*, amplifies a low-level mic signal to line level). In short, it's the audio traffic director.

A traditional, big analog mixer is a wonderfully imposing piece of equipment, filled with little lights, zillions of controls, meters, cryptic calibrations, and bright colors; it resembles the cockpit of a 747. We now have digital mixers that don't look quite so imposing, but that's deceptive—most of the controls appear on a computer screen instead of a box with lots of knobs. Still, there are a ton of parameters you need to adjust.

Any kind of mixer has a right to appear intimidating, as it demands practice and study from anyone who wants to master it. But luckily, whether analog or digital, a mixer is not a large, monolithic batch of circuitry. It includes many identical modules so that once you've learned how one module works, you know how ninety-nine percent of the board works.

Furthermore, digital control has made mixers easier to use. If you've ever worked on a conventional board and didn't have enough hands to move all the desired controls, a computer can memorize your mixing moves and play them back the same way each time. This chapter covers traditional mixer functions only; Chapter 19 describes digital control and automation.

Since mixers scare a lot of people, we'll start simply and work our way up to a professional-type setup. We can't describe all the various types in detail—virtually every mixer has its own quirks, features, and applications. Some are designed for sound reinforcement or PA work, but also work with multitracks. Some are designed for minimum cost, some for maximum flexibility, and so on. The important point here is to understand how the various components that make up a mixer operate. Then, no matter what variation you encounter, it will make sense.

By the way, don't put too much faith in mixer specs. For example, a mic preamp will add noise; but do you measure noise with all the mic preamp levels set to maximum, or with the preamp gain turned all the way down? The latter specs out better, but it doesn't tell you too much about real-world performance. And some elements are extremely subjective. Equalizers that sound "plastic" on acoustic sessions may sound great for dance music, and engineering fanatics can differentiate subtle tonal differences between different mic preamps and even individual mic transformers (although many times individual devices aren't really better or worse, just different).

Because a mixer has so many variables, before committing to a particular model you really need to work with it for a while to get a feel for the sound and performance. The following explains various mixer features and technologies so that you can decide what kind of mixer will be best for your studio. For example, if you record mostly synthesizers and drum machines with multiple outputs, having more inputs will be more important than having lots of mic preamps.

## A Simple Mixer That Becomes Complex

A mixer's primary function is to combine multiple input signals into a lesser number of output signals, while adjusting the relative balance, stereo position, and tonal quality of the various inputs. For example, a mixer can take eight multitrack recorder outputs, blend them into two outputs (left and right), and send these to a stereo DAT mastering deck.

To illustrate basic mixing principles, here's a simple example: a two-input, one-output mixer. Suppose you have two monophonic keyboards on stage—an electric piano and a synthesizer. By feeding these into the mixer, you can adjust the volume level of one relative to that of the other. That way, if you're playing a right-hand part on the synthesizer and a left-hand part on the piano, you can balance their volumes exactly, so that neither instrument dominates. Instead, they form a unified, blended sound.

Fig. 10-1 shows this type of arrangement: the mixer has two inputs, which accept the instrument outputs. These go through two volume controls that regulate the balance, then the combined signals feed to a common output *bus,* which goes to your amplifier. You can think of the input signal path as a vertical, downward flow into the mixer, and the bus (output signal path) as a horizontal flow from left to right out of the mixer. At the input/output line junction, you'll find a control to set the level. Usually this is a linear motion (slider) control called a *fader.*

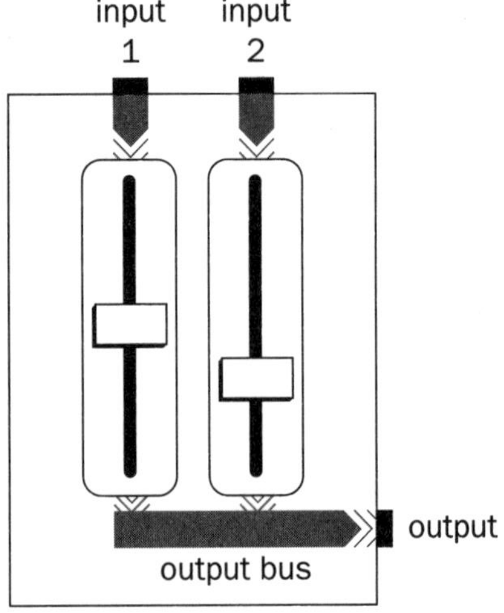


**Fig. 10-1:** *Simple two-input, one-output mixer.*

Typical mixers have anywhere from eight to dozens of inputs, which often handle both low-level (microphone) and high-level (instrument) signals. A mixer has three main applications during the recording process:

- Blend several instruments together to feed a mono or stereo input (Fig. 10-2).
- Premix tracks within the multitrack recorder to free up more tracks (Fig. 10-3).
- Play back all tracks and combine them in the proper balance (Fig. 10-4).

## Getting on the Bus

For most applications you'll want a stereo mixer so you can have a different mix going into the left and right channels. This requires adding another output bus, and introduces the concept of the *panpot* (short for panoramic potentiometer, but no one ever calls them that). This is a control that can sweep a signal between two buses with a single knob (Fig. 10-5).

Typically, the two buses involved are right and left, so that shifting the signal between these two channels places the signal at different points in the stereo spread (Fig. 10-6)—pan left, and the signal comes out of the left speaker; pan right and it comes out of the right speaker. Set the panpot to center, and the audio appears to come out of the center of the stereo field, because sound emanates equally from both speakers.

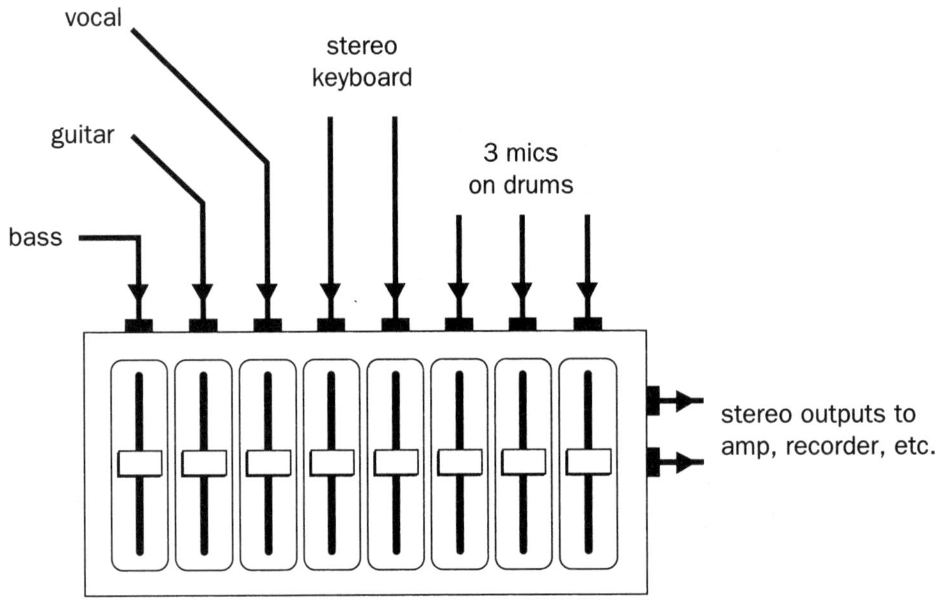


**Fig. 10-2:** *An eight-in, two-out mixer mixing a band.*

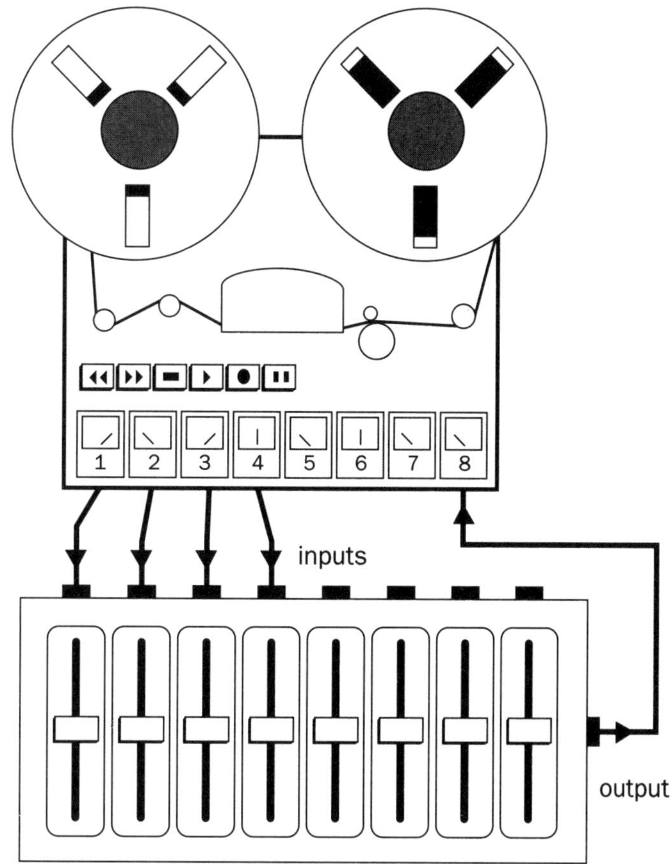


**Fig. 10-3:** *Tracks 1 through 4 are being mixed into track 8.*

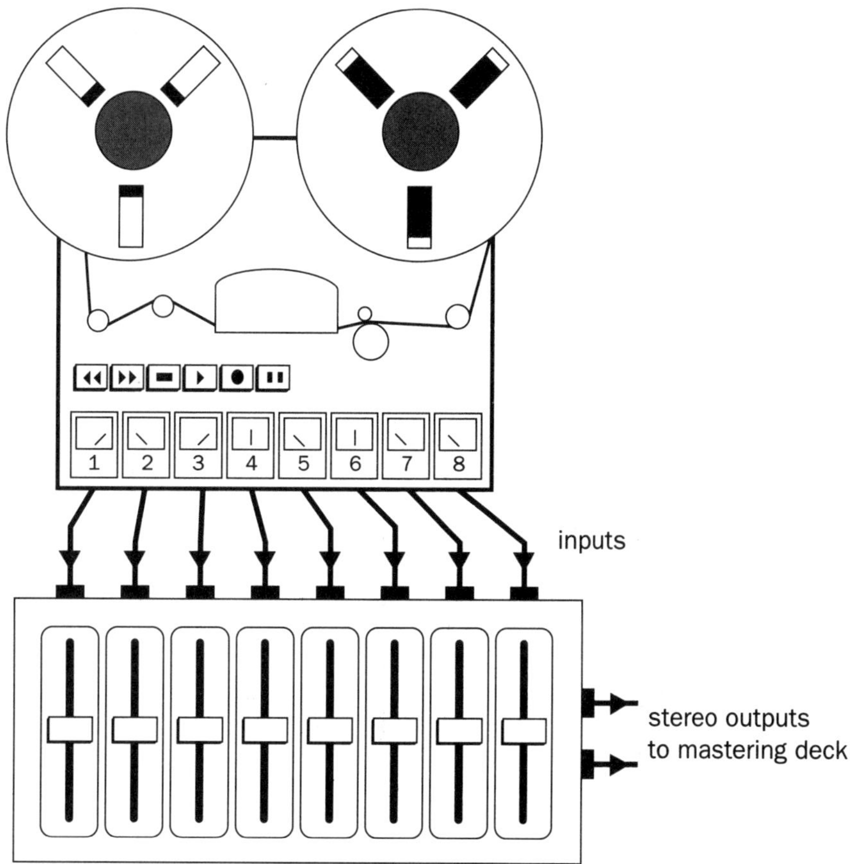


**Fig. 10-4:** *Mixing down eight tape tracks to stereo outputs.*

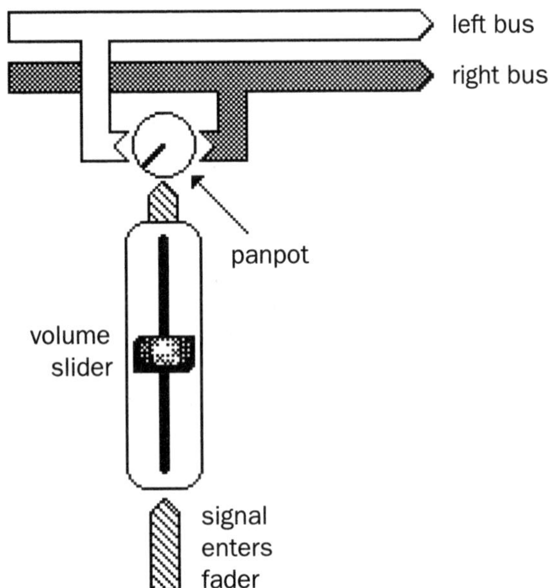


**Fig. 10-5:** *A panpot sweeps a signal between two buses.*

Adjusting the level control and panpot together lets you adjust the signal to any desired level, and sit anywhere in the stereo field. In quad, you can pan a signal from front to back as well as from right to left. This is done either with a joystick that moves in two directions, or with two knobs.

Only the simplest mixers have only two output buses. Most have several buses (eight-bus studios are common in project studios) and let you set up different mixes on these different buses. This opens up many options. For example, you don't have to use two output buses to set up a stereo mix. You could just as easily connect the "right" output to a monaural PA system, and the "left" output to a cue or monitor system. One mix would be what the audience hears through the PA, with the other mix set up for the musician's monitor system. If you need more vocals in the monitor than in the PA, adjust the mix accordingly.

In general, mixers are characterized by the number of inputs and outputs. For example, an "eight in, two out" mixer has eight input channels that let you plug in up to eight signal sources and two output buses. A "twenty-four in, eight out" mixer has twenty-four input channels and eight output channels. Sometimes these are abbreviated as 8:2 and 24:8, or 8×2 and 24×8, respectively.

Some mixers also let you mix the output buses down to a smaller number of additional output buses, as indicated by a third number (*e.g.*, a 16:8:4 mixer would have sixteen inputs and eight output buses; those eight buses mix down further into four buses).

As to why you need multiple output buses, some bands use quad mixdown for live performance, which necessitates four separate output buses, one for each channel. And you might need a separate monitor bus for a hired string section so they can have their own monitor mix. Now we're up to six output buses. But you can see that even though we've dramatically increased the number of functions and knobs, we're still dealing with the same basic principles as before. And, we can extend the inputs as well as outputs; you'll typically see eight, twelve, sixteen, twenty, twenty-four, and even seventy-two inputs.

As using a control for every possible function could get unwieldy, there are a variety of ways to eliminate some knobs and replace them with switches. For example, rather than having a fader at the intersection of each input line and output bus, we could have stereo fader and a switch that selects between output buses 1 and 2, 3 and 4, 5 and 6, or 7 and 8.

It's important to have separate mixes on separate buses because different destinations require different mixes. A singer listening to the cue bus through headphones might want the melodic instruments loudest so that they serve as a pitch reference, while those monitoring in the

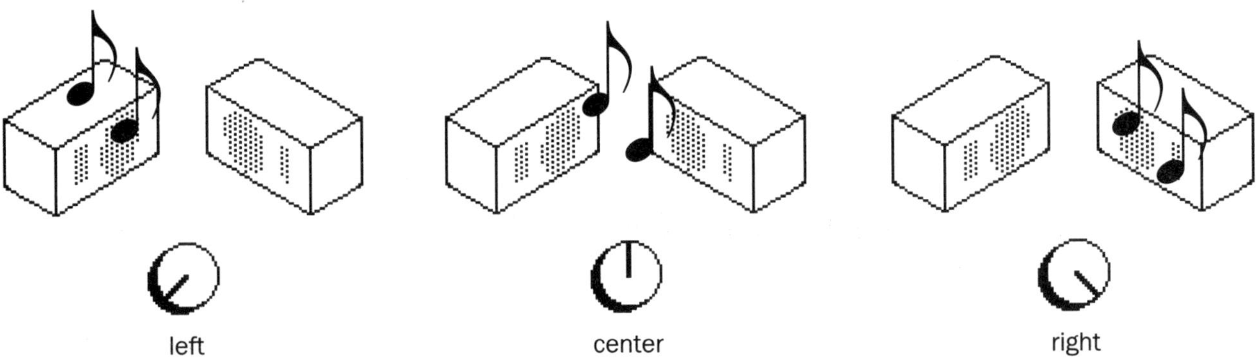


**Fig. 10-6:** *How panning changes a sound's position in the stereo field.*

control room might want the voice louder to concentrate on the performance and make sure there aren't any glitches.

There may even be additional buses called *subgroups* that provide a master volume control for several individual channels. For example, suppose you're mixing a choir with each group of voices assigned to its own channel, and you get a perfect balance among the various voices. Later in the song, you decide to increase the choir's volume as a whole. If you move each fader individually, you'll probably upset the balance. But if these channels feed a subgroup bus, the subgroup master control can raise and lower the level of the entire group simultaneously. This technique is also applicable to drums, brass sections, rhythm sections, *etc.*

If you want to record multiple tracks in real time to a multitrack recorder (which happens a lot in live concert recording), multiple buses are extremely useful since you can send each instrument to its own bus, then feed these to the multitrack. However, it is not necessary to dedicate one output bus for each track of the multitrack recorder. It's often better to bypass the bus electronics to obtain a cleaner sound. You do this by patching an instrument from the mixer's input module directly to the recorder via a *direct-to-multitrack* or *direct-to-tape* output, as described later.

## Using Auxiliary (Aux) Buses with Effects

The way that the output buses are used and accessed creates some of the major differences between boards. Another important output bus function is adding effects like reverberation to the sound of one or more instruments.

Consider a simple eight-in, four-out mixer that feeds a PA system. We can use the extra bus to add reverb by patching the second pair of outputs into the reverb input. Then, take the reverb outputs and feed them back into a set of spare inputs, such as channels 7 and 8 (by the way, now you see why it's good to have more inputs than you think you need; you'll often find yourself plugging into "spare" inputs).

We can now send a portion of any signal to the reverb unit (Fig. 10-7). If we turn up the controls feeding the reverb system for inputs 1, 4, and 5, then we'll add reverb to those channels.

As the reverb output goes to inputs 7 and 8, turning the fader down on these channels removes any reverb, while turning them up increases the reverb effect (note how the panpots for these channels are panned left and right to give the maximum possible reverb spread). These controls serve as the master reverb controls, whereas the aux bus level controls set the amount of reverb for the individual channels.

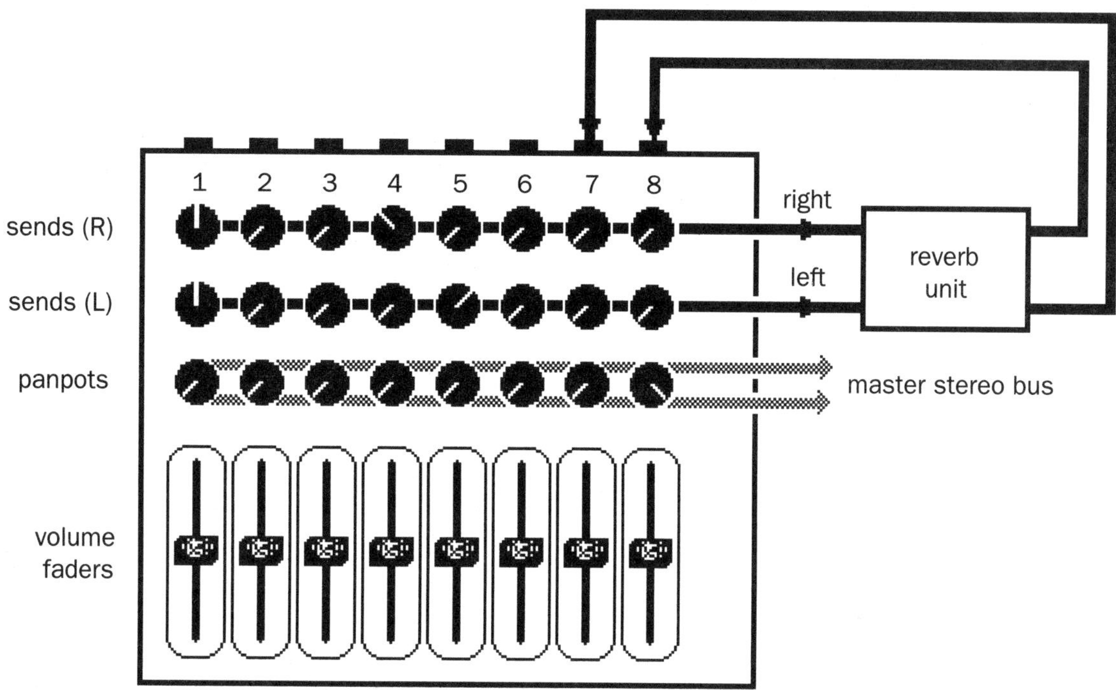


**Fig. 10-7:** *Setting up auxiliary buses with effects. Note that input 1 feeds both the left and right channels equally, input 4 feeds only the right reverb bus, and input 5 feeds only the left input bus. Remember, because each bus is independent of the others, we can have separate reverb and master mixes.*

The individual faders are called *effects send* controls, because they send signals to the reverb (or whatever effect you're using). The master control is called the *effects return,* since the effects sound returns through the control.

Again, we can get as complex as we want. With a typical budget mixer, you might have two effects buses, which you'd generally assign to the left and right channels. This allows for stereo effects, like having an instrument coming through the right channel with the processed signal appearing in the left channel. (A particularly effective trick with two vocal parts is to put the parts in opposite channels, with the reverb signals reversed so that the right vocal has reverb coming out of the left channel, and vice-versa.)

It seems that just as there are never enough inputs, there are never enough output buses. A studio mixer will commonly have eight, sixteen, twenty-four or even more output buses. In addition, these buses are basically interchangeable; if you only need one cue bus, you can press another cue bus into service as an extra effects bus. Conversely, if you don't need quad and are only mixing down in stereo, that frees two more buses for other applications.

Finally, each auxiliary bus should have its own master level control so that you don't have to go back and re-tweak all the individual send controls to make an overall change of the signal going to the bus; a mute control is also helpful.

The bottom line is that, although mixers are optimized for particular applications, the way you patch them into your studio can change the configuration dramatically. However, while it's not difficult to push patch cords around, it's considerably more difficult to recognize how to utilize this hardware to maximum advantage. That comes with experience, and explains why creative engineers are worth a lot of money to the record business: They can operate the same mixer as other engineers, yet have the imagination to apply it in different ways.

To recap, we now know that a mixer has a variable number of inputs (the more the better—systems have a way of expanding and gobbling up inputs), a variable number of output buses (again, the more the better—within limits), and possibly some subgroup buses as well. But there are still lots of knobs left over that we need to explain, so let's look at the input module.

## Input Modules: The Mixer's Signal Conditioners

Each mixer channel has its own input module, which connects the mixer input and the fader. This module's placement allows processing or routing a signal (changing tone, level, effects bus assignments, *etc.*) before sending it to the output bus. This module may be a single unit, or a collection of submodules. Different channels may have different input modules.

In any event, as the signal works its way from input to fader, it's going to encounter several signal processing and routing options; Fig. 10-8 shows the controls found on a typical input module. It is the choice and implementation of the options that makes one board radically different from another. Let's look at those options for a fairly sophisticated input module; remember that we're talking about a representative example, so don't expect to find a mixer that has identical features.

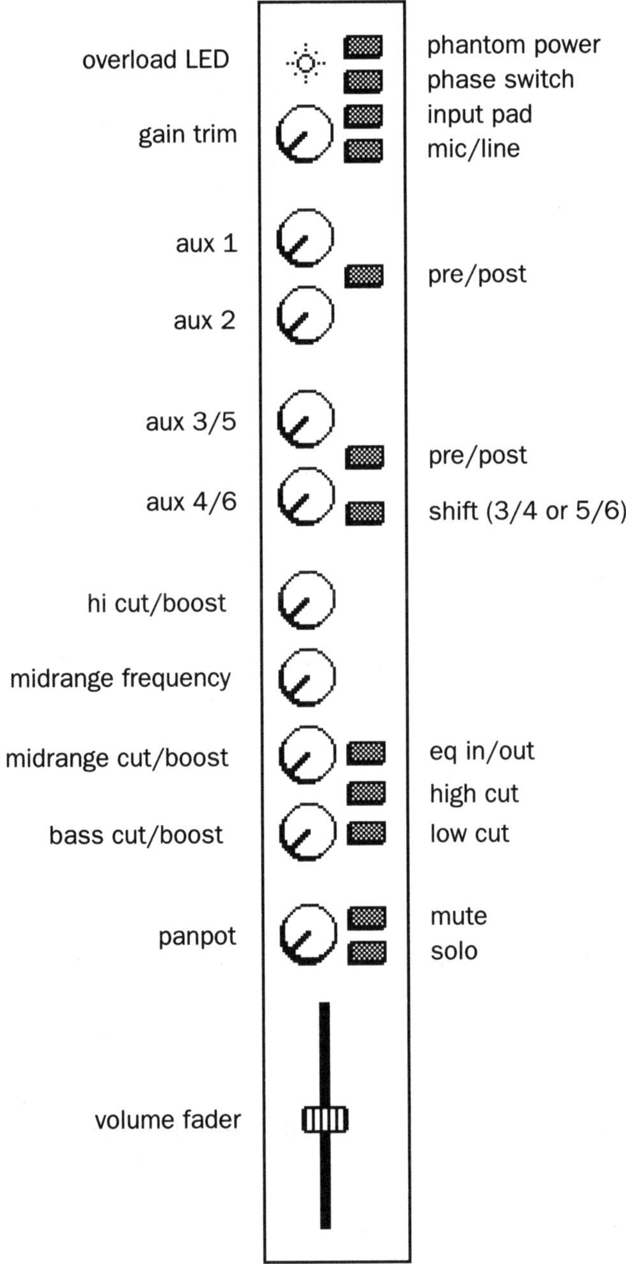


**Fig. 10-8:** *A typical input module for a mid priced mixer.*

## Input Connectors

Unfortunately, there is no standard audio jack. Low-end mixers often use RCA phono jacks, midrange mixers offer 1/4" unbalanced phone jacks, and pro mixers include XLR-style balanced line connectors. But this is not etched in stone; some budget mixers include a few XLR inputs for interfacing mics, or accept balanced 1/4" plugs. (For more information on balanced and unbalanced line systems, see Chapter 9 on microphones.)

XLR inputs (with associated mic preamps, as described later) are important if you plan to do a lot of acoustic instrument recording. Most quality mics generate balanced outputs and terminate in XLR connectors. However, if you plan to record electronic and electrical instruments directly into the mixer (called *direct injection*), you'll mostly need 1/4" unbalanced phone jacks. This is why many mid-level mixers compromise on having all inputs with 1/4" jacks, but some with additional XLRs.

Many mixers now include stereo inputs to accommodate synths, drum machines, guitars, effects, and other devices with stereo outputs. Generally both channels run independently through the same module but share the same channel fader and controls (*e.g.*, if you change the preamp level, it affects both inputs). However, it's also possible to send two mono signals through a stereo input, which lets you double the number of inputs for mono devices. Again, though, these end up sharing controls so they are not totally independent. The panning control may turn into a balance control with stereo or dual mono inputs, but act as a standard panpot with a single mono input. Some mixers with stereo inputs also include a stereo image (width) control that can narrow the stereo image all the way down to mono.

## Input Select Switch

The input select switch is a way to save money without affecting functionality too much. Smaller mixers frequently include a switch that selects between mic, line, or multitrack track output. When recording, you'd select input signals; when mixing or overdubbing, monitor the multitrack outputs.

Pro-level mixers often include comprehensive routing options, such as pushbuttons that send the preamplified and equalized input module signal to an individual track of the multitrack recorder (this is one implementation of the direct-to-tape, or direct-to-multitrack, option that bypasses a large portion of the mixer's electronics), or subgroup options that send the input signal directly to a subgroup bus or the multitrack. While these features save time, those with budget mixers can often accomplish the same results by simply moving some patch cords around.

## Polarity Switch

This is also called a *phase* switch, although polarity switch is technically correct. A polarity switch is particularly useful with mixers having XLR inputs. We already covered phase changes in Chapter 9 on microphones, but for now let's just say that balanced lines are sometimes wired incorrectly, so that the "hot" lead is actually the "cold" and vice-versa. Suppose you're recording a guitar with two mics, and one cable is wired so that its polarity is reversed with respect to the other cable. A positive-going signal on one line will show up as a negative-going signal on the other, which leads to cancellation and a "thin" sound. A polarity switch reverses the polarity so that the signals add together instead of canceling. Choose whichever polarity switch setting gives the fullest, most accurate sound when listening to the two (or more) signals in mono.

## Microphone Preamp

In addition to relatively high-level signals, called *line-level* signals, there are also *microphone-level* signals. These are much weaker, and need to be amplified before they are strong enough to be used by the mixer.

Not all mic signal levels are the same—some are high-impedance, unbalanced signals; some are low-impedance, balanced-line signals. High-impedance signals are very common in the musical world (*e.g.*, guitar pickups and amps). The professional audio world still revolves around the balanced-line system due to its superior noise and hum canceling characteristics (we covered this in greater detail in Chapter 9). There are two main ways to convert mic-level, balanced line signals into higher level signals of the proper impedance; each has its own advantages and disadvantages.

*Mic transformers* are passive devices that create no noise and have a natural tendency to reject electrical "hash" (such as dimmer noise), although they are more prone to pick up hum if they're close to a hum-generating device like a power transformer. A transformer may add some degree of coloration (inexpensive devices are particularly prone to this), but interestingly, many people prefer the sound of mic transformers because they add "warmth" to the sound.

*Active circuits* tend to be sonically transparent, but do add hiss and have more potential for distortion than transformers. A good active circuit also tends to be less expensive than a good transformer.

Still, even transformers need to be followed by amplification—which brings us to the microphone preamp. The preamp may have either variable gain (the ratio of increase of output over input) or switch-selected gain in discrete steps, to accommodate microphones with different level outputs. As preamps often need to interface with both balanced and unbalanced signals, you'll find jacks for both a high-impedance input and a low-impedance, balanced input.

Because mic preamps often involve high gain, they add noise. There are two ways to measure mic input noise. The standard signal-to-noise spec compares the maximum output level with the amount of residual noise. Lower-cost mic preamps typically have S/N ratios of around –70 to –80 dB, while high-ticket versions start at –90 dB and can go up to –100 dB or more.

An EIN (Equivalent Input Noise) rating measures the system's output noise and gain; subtracting the gain from the output noise leaves the amount of input noise. An EIN spec of –125 dB with a 150Ω input impedance is excellent. A less negative number (*e.g.*, –110 dB) indicates more noise. Shorting the input to ground during the measurement process can give a better figure, but is not representative of the way mixers work in the real world.

Other mic preamp features include:

- Overload or clipping indicator. This flashes if the preamp is distorting (or on the verge of distorting).
- Low cut filter. This is a very sharp filter with a cutoff frequency around 40 to 80 Hz. Reducing this low frequency energy tends to minimize mic "popping," room rumble, hum, and excessive low end with some instruments.
- High cut filter. This complements the lowpass filter and cuts off sharply at around 10 kHz to reduce sibilance and hiss.
- Input attenuator. Mic preamps usually have a fixed, high-gain stage to amplify the microphone, followed by a volume control. While this type of design gives good noise performance, a very strong signal can drive the high-gain preamp into distortion. An input attenuator adds an attenuation pad (volume-loss network) between the microphone and preamp; this prevents overload problems that can occur when miking very loud singers, amplifiers, and other loud sounds.
- Phantom power switch. Some condenser mics require an external power supply to charge their plates. To eliminate the need for a power supply at each mic, phantom power couples the required voltage (typically +48 volts DC) into the mic cable, which feeds the mic. Not all mics need phantom power, so this switch lets you turn the option on or off. Incidentally, some direct boxes also run from phantom power.

What all this means is that we can feed just about any signal into the preamp, and, by selecting the right combination of input and gain, can make any signal look like any other signal in terms of level; now we're ready for more processing.

## Insert Jacks

Insert jacks allow easy patching of external devices (*e.g.*, signal processors) into the mixer. For input modules, insert jacks are usually post-input module but pre-fader (Fig. 10-9). They may be pre- or post-EQ. Insert jacks are also

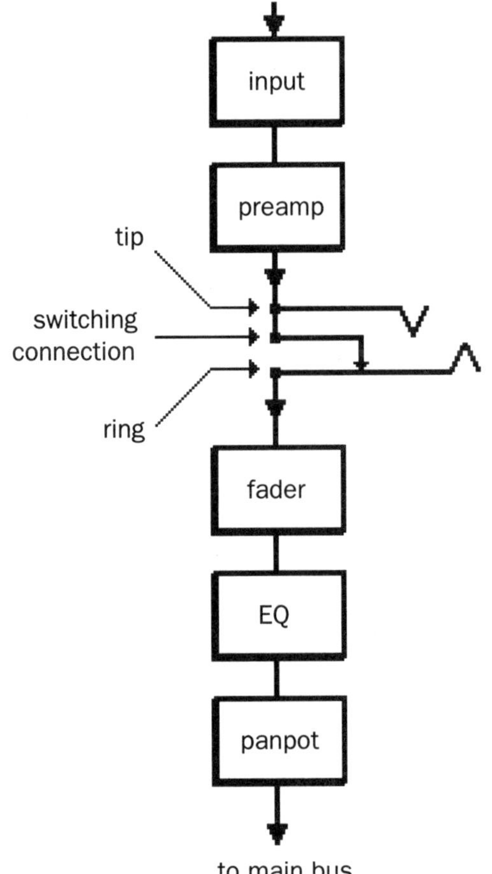


**Fig. 10-9:** *Inserts are generally stereo jacks, wired into the input module as shown. The tip connection can "send" the signal to another device, and the ring connection "receives" the signal and re-inserts it into the mixer signal path. The jack will include a switching action so that when no plug is inserted, the send and receive connect, and the input signal flows through to the mixer.*

frequently available for the main bus and various auxiliary buses so you can process an entire bus with a particular signal processor. EQ, limiting, and "exciter" devices commonly insert into this signal path.

Because this is a switched stereo jack, there are several options on how to plug into it.

- If you push a mono cord in halfway so it contacts only the ring, then the input module signal goes to the cord *and* continues to the mixer. This is because the ring/tip connection isn't broken until you plug the cord in all the way. The send could go to a tape recorder input, or to a signal processor that returns to a second channel so the signal processor can have independent panning, effects, and/or level settings compared to the main signal in channel 1 (Fig. 10-10).
- Pushing a mono cord in all the way creates a direct out. The input module signal goes to the cord, but does not continue through to the mixer since the jack's switching action interrupts the flow between the ring and tip connections.
- Plugging in a special "stereo-to-dual-mono" adapter cord provides individual plugs for the send and return connections (Fig. 10-11). These typically plug into a signal processor, such as a compressor/limiter or EQ, which processes the signal before sending it on to the rest of the mixer.

Caution: Some equipment wires the insert jacks as tip = receive and ring = send. If you plug a stereo-to-dual-mono adapter into an insert jack and the processor doesn't work, reversing the tip and ring plugs might solve the problem.

## Direct-to-Tape or Multitrack Jacks

These send the signal from a mixer input directly to a multitrack recorder input, which bypasses the mixer electronics for the highest possible fidelity.

# Equalization

An equalizer lets you make precise tonal adjustments to a signal; think of it as a fancy, flexible tone control. The term "equalizer" comes from the concept of using this device to even out, or *equalize,* overall frequency response, making it flat. This is an important application with transducers such as microphones, guitar pickups, and contact mics since these devices seldom have a flat frequency response.

However, nowadays equalization (EQ for short) is also used as an effect, to create (for example) a super bass sound and shimmering highs in a normally uninteresting signal. If fact, even if all transducers had a flat frequency response, I suspect people would still use EQ because one instrument processed through ten different equalization settings can sound like ten different instruments. In this case we're concerned with creating a sound in its own right, not trying to faithfully reproduce a previously existing sound.

Equalization can be used while recording, while mixing down, or both. While mixing, instruments sometimes occupy the same general part of the audio spectrum and "mask" each other. EQ is often the best way to keep instruments separated since you can shift the emphasis from one part of the spectrum to another so that they don't interfere.

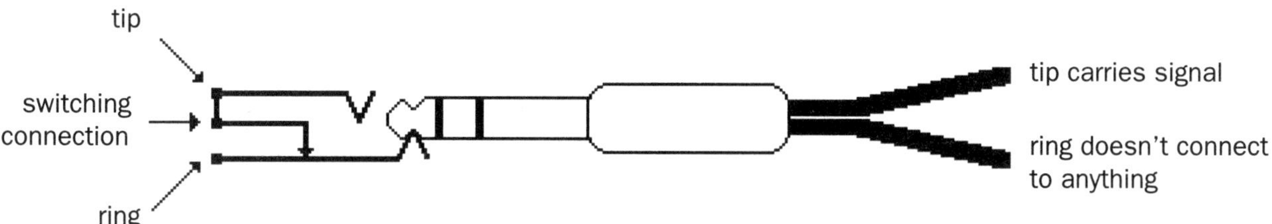


**Fig. 10-10:** *Adding a send by plugging in part way.*

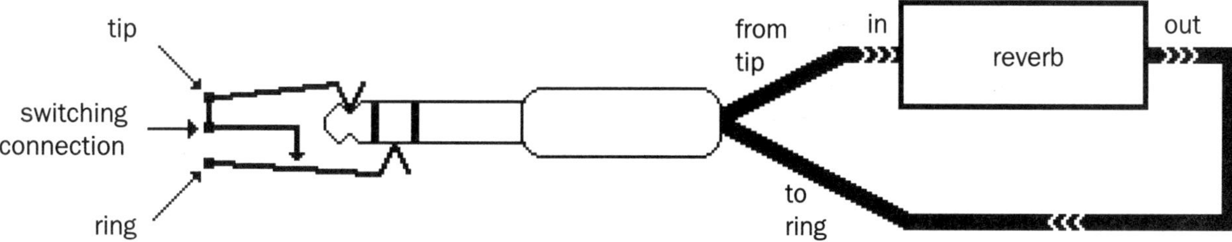


**Fig. 10-11:** *Using the insert jack to insert an effects device.*

Here are some examples of equalizer applications:

- If a vocal is thin and brittle, boost the bass somewhat and roll off the highs a bit.
- If the vocals interfere with the rhythm guitar (since both instruments can cover a similar part of the midrange), cutting the guitar's midrange makes more room for the vocals.
- For an instrument that's "boomy" and lacks crispness, increase the treble and pull back on the bass.
- Suppose you have a dual lead guitar part, overdubbed by the same musician using the same guitar. To make the sound of the guitars "bigger," you can boost the treble slightly on one and the bass slightly on the other. The net effect of this is a slightly larger-than-life sound.

Equalization is to recording as spices are to food; if used properly, the results are delicious. If abused, the overall effect is unpalatable. Unusually large amounts of boost added with EQ can exceed the mixer or multitrack recorder's dynamic range and produce distortion. This is true of both analog and digital equalization.

Equalizers can be very simple or very complex, but they all have one electrical characteristic in common: they use filter circuits that isolate some desired portion of the sound. This allows cutting or boosting the desired signal, while leaving all the other portions intact. In fact, the perfect equalizer would be able to create any kind of boost or cut, anywhere in the audio spectrum while adding no noise, distortion, phase shift, or other coloration.

## Passive Equalizers

The simplest type of equalizer found on audio equipment is called a passive equalizer (or passive filter). In this case, there are no amplifying circuits; rather, various electronic components (resistors, capacitors, and inductors) are arranged to form a frequency-selective circuit. However, these types of passive filters can only remove parts of a signal; they can't boost or provide gain.

A good example of a passive filter (of the treble cut variety) is the tone control found on the majority of electric guitars. Turning the control counterclockwise cuts out treble, which appears to make the bass more prominent. Passive circuits can also be designed to cut bass, give a midrange "boost" (by cutting bass and treble), or a midrange cut. Many of the tone control circuits in tube amps are based on passive designs.

Despite the low cost and lack of flexibility, these simple passive filters can help reduce hiss by removing unwanted high frequencies, and reduce rumble or hum by removing low frequencies. A midrange boost can add presence to signals; a midrange cut can give a flat sort of "dryness." But, using passive circuits produces an unavoidable amount of loss unless you either precede them with a preamp, or follow them with a postamp, to boost the signal.

The advantage of passive circuitry is that the filter itself introduces no noise. Unfortunately, you usually need an amplifier to make up for the loss, and the amplifier adds noise. Also, the type of response obtainable with a passive circuit is fairly inflexible; you can achieve more drastic filtering effects only at the expense of much greater loss through the circuit.

## Active Equalizer Types

Because of the limitations of passive equalization, most equalizers are built around *active* filter circuits, which use frequency-selective components in conjunction with a low-noise amplifier. With this type of circuitry, the amplifier can not only boost, but isolate the filter components that provide the "tuning" so that they are not loaded down by subsequent stages.

Before going any further, we should talk a bit about filter characteristics. Fig. 10-12 shows an ideal low-pass response. This circuit rolls off the high frequencies, at a rate specified in decibels per octave. In a typical curve, each octave rolls off the high frequencies by a factor of two (the frequency ratio of an octave is 2:1), which equates to a 6 dB per octave rolloff. The point at which the rolloff begins is called the *cutoff* or *corner* frequency.

Fig. 10-13 shows a high-pass curve, which cuts off low frequencies at a rate of 6 dB per octave. Again, the cutoff frequency is where this action begins.

Fig. 10-14 shows a bandpass filter's response, which amplifies a specific range or band of the audio spectrum. The boosting occurs at the *center* or *resonant* frequency; the degree of boost is specified in decibels. We could have a 3 dB boost, a 6 dB boost, a 10 dB boost, or whatever, within the limits of the circuitry. The range of frequencies boosted, coupled with the amount of gain, determines the resonance or sharpness of the peak. The response curve in (b) clearly has higher resonance than the curve on the left (a).

The inverse of the bandpass filter is the *notch*

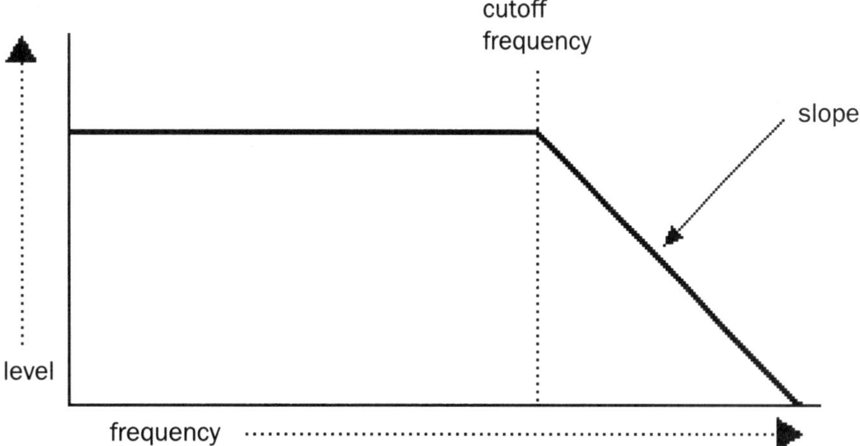


**Fig. 10-12:** *Lowpass filter response.*

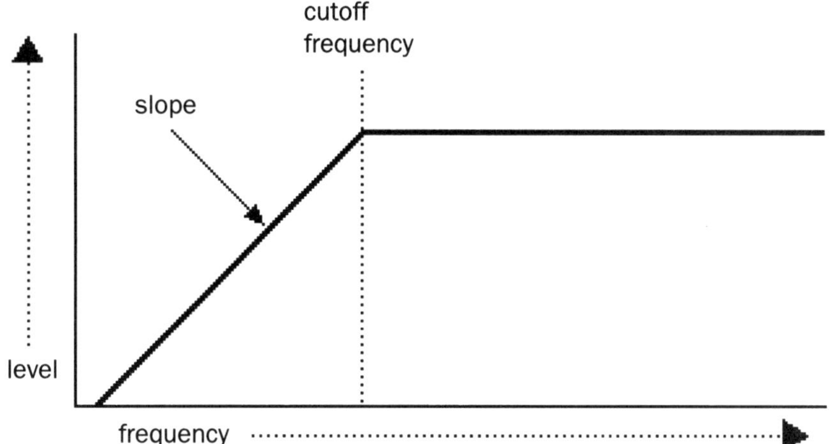


**Fig. 10-13:** *Highpass filter response.*

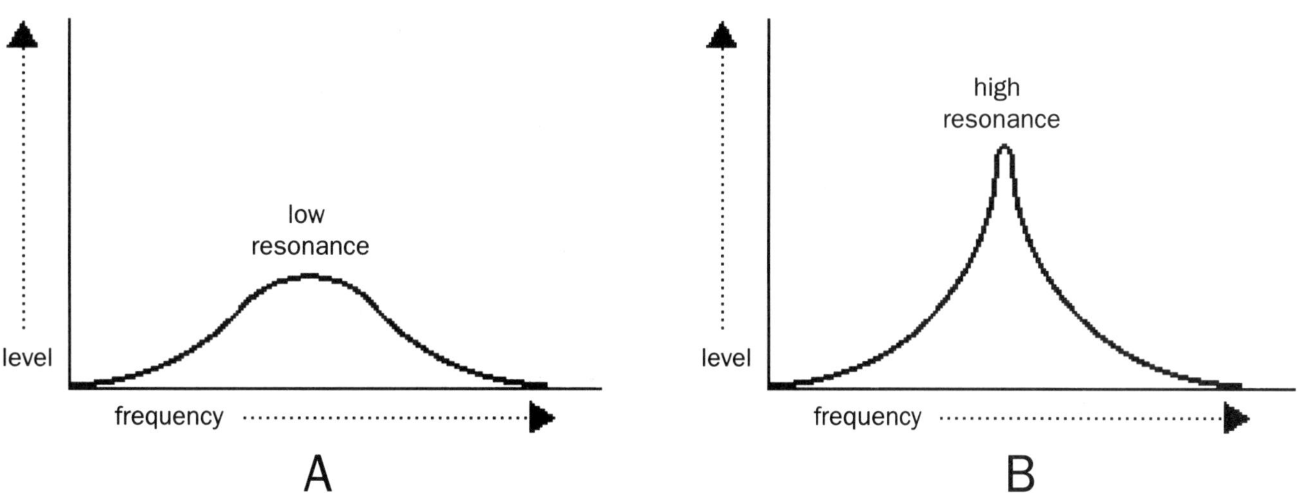


**Fig. 10-14:** *Bandpass filter response, with two different resonance characteristics.*

filter (Fig. 10-15), which puts a dip in the response, and is very handy for taking out one specific "problem" frequency (such as 60 Hz, where hum can occur). Increasing the resonance increases the depth and sharpness of the notch.

## Real World Equalizer Types

The simplest type of active equalizer is the *shelving* equalizer, which is similar to the type found in a typical hi-fi amplifier. This equalizer can shape response in four different ways: boost the treble, cut the treble, boost the bass, or cut the bass. Additionally, the bass and treble controls can be adjusted independently. Fig. 10-16 shows this type of equalizer's response; note that the corner frequency is not selectable. Common corner frequencies are 100 Hz for bass and 10 kHz for treble.

The next step up in complexity is to add a midrange control, which can boost or cut a given number of decibels (typically 12 to 18 dB) at a (hopefully) user-settable frequency. A stepped switch generally selects the resonant frequency, and a potentiometer gives the desired amount of boost or cut. The resonant frequencies are usually spaced an octave or so apart.

Note that lower-end mixers often don't let you select a midrange frequency, but are fixed (1 kHz is a popular choice). However, if you boost the midrange on several channels they'll all boost at the same frequency. This builds up energy at one specific frequency band and tends to make the sound unnaturally "peaky."

The next step would be to add an adjustable midrange position. But we can change over to the *parametric* equalizer, and get even more flexible frequency responses.

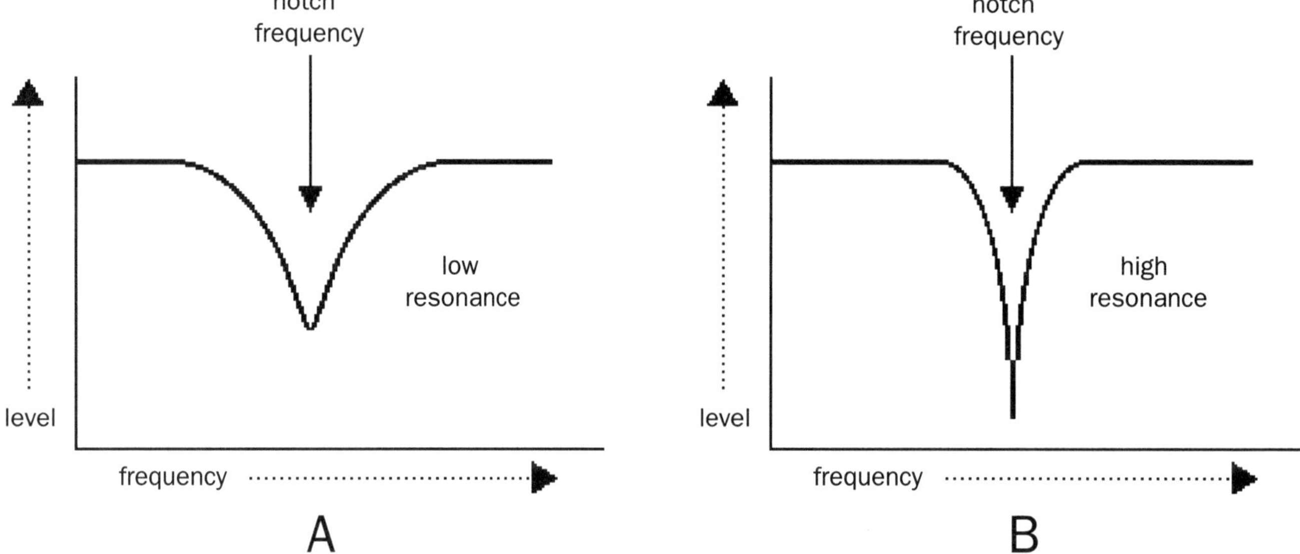


**Fig. 10-15:** *Typical notch filter responses.*

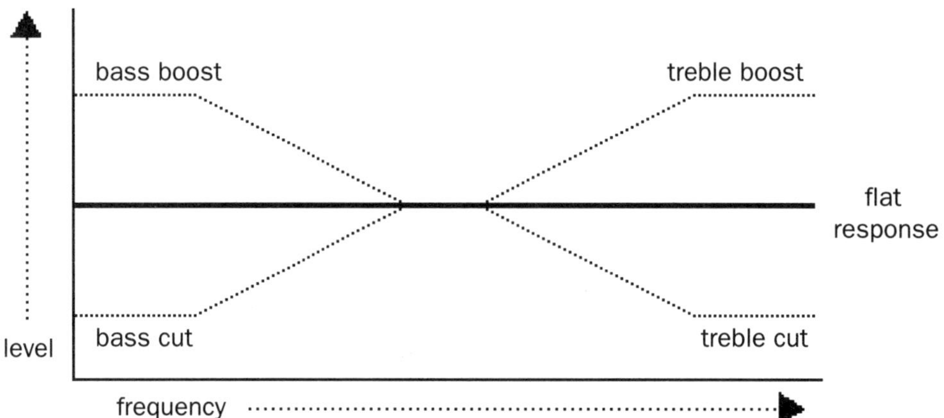


**Fig. 10-16:** *Shelving equalizer response.*

## The Parametric Equalizer

The parametric equalizer spaces several full-function, active filters (usually three or four) throughout the audio spectrum; each of these filters may be optimized for a specific frequency band (*e.g.*, low, midrange, or high). Controls include boost/cut, resonant frequency, and bandwidth (the range of frequencies boosted). Bandwidth is similar to resonance; Fig. 10-17 shows both the response of a typical parametric equalizer and the concept of bandwidth.

Some boards have *quasiparametric* EQ. This resembles a standard parametric, but lacks the bandwidth control.

Since parametric EQs are very versatile, it's easy to get unnatural-sounding effects if you don't exercise some degree of restraint. Never use EQ just because it's there—add only what's necessary to give the desired sound.

## The Graphic Equalizer

The *graphic equalizer* uses multiple bandpass filters to split the audio spectrum up into a number of bands, with an individual boost/cut control for each band. The term graphic equalizer refers to the fact that hardware graphic EQs use linear slide pots for the boost/cut controls, so looking at the position of the knobs gives a "graphic" indication of frequency response (Fig. 10-18). Some graphic equalizers that are built into multieffects still show a "curve" on the LCD to maintain this tradition.

The more bands a graphic EQ offers, the more precise the adjustments you can make. A five-band graphic, for example, is good for general sound-shaping; twelve or more bands let you boost or cut specific frequency ranges with much more accuracy. Top-of-the-line graphics provide a band every third of an octave.

Mixing consoles seldom include graphic equalizers. However, mixers designed for PA use often have a master stereo graphic equalizer to equalize the final stereo output. This is handy for compensating for general room response variations.

## Cutting versus Boosting

Many musicians use EQ primarily to boost a signal, but it's often better to cut than to boost. For example, suppose you wanted to boost the midrange. You could add a midrange boost, but you could also cut the highs and lows, which would also accentuate the midrange.

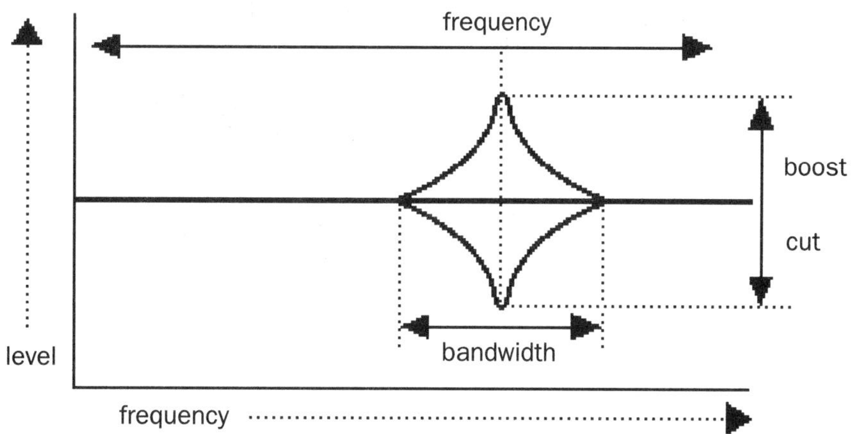


**Fig. 10-17:** *Graphic representation of parametric equalizer parameters.*

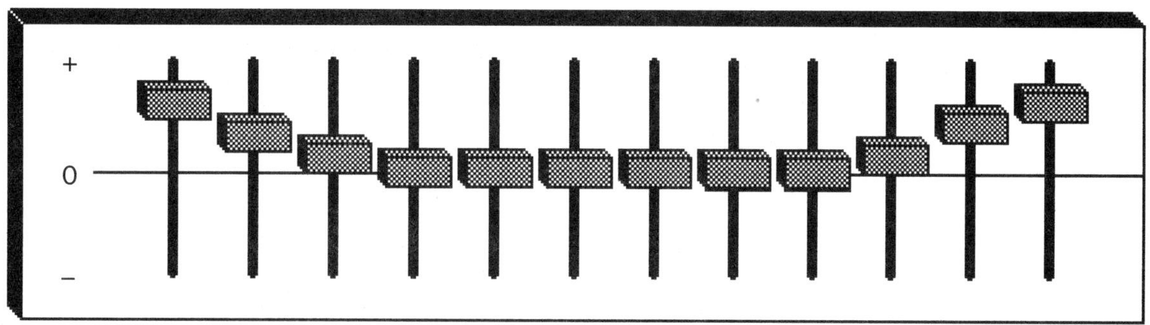


**Fig. 10-18:** *The sliders on a graphic equalizer give a "graphic" representation of the frequency response. In this example, the low and high ends are boosted.*

For example, let's say the vocals in your mix have an undesirable nasal sound. Before you go boosting everything else in a mix to compensate for a tonal flaw, try this trick: Start by boosting the midrange EQ to make the nasal sound as bad as possible, which should be something like +6 dB at 1400 Hz. Once you've figured out where the problem lies, then set the gain control for cut—rather than boost—and adjust to taste.

Boosting a signal adds gain, which could exceed the equalizer's maximum dynamic range and lead to clipping. But a more insidious problem occurs if you're using a mixer with several channels of equalization. Boost one channel, and it will sound louder than others, which means you might be tempted to add some boost to the other channels too. All this added gain might start to exceed the overall headroom of the mixer itself because each channel is now hotter than before. Even though there may not be obvious clipping distortion, there could be enough peak clipping to give a muddier, less distinct sound.

## EQ: Making the Right Judgment Calls

It may seem like we've gone overboard on this subject, but the altering of tonal quality is vital to the modern recording process. A good engineer can hear remarkably small sonic changes, but even people with untrained ears can perceive differences between sounds—although they may not be able to identify the exact nature of those differences.

For example, suppose there's a situation where a bass guitar and kick drum sort of "mush" together on mixdown, causing a lack of differentiation between the two sound sources. An engineer might feel the appropriate remedy is to roll off a little bit of deep bass from the kick drum and accentuate the lower midrange very slightly to give the sound more punch, while rolling off some upper midrange and high frequencies from the bass to give a sound that's more muted and laid back in the overall mix. An untrained listener might compare the equalized and unequalized versions and call the equalized version "less muddy" or something similar; the engineer goes a step further and knows the technical translation—where to do the boosting or cutting, and how much to use.

Of course, this isn't a universal situation: If the bass part was sort of choppy and trebly, with a funk type of feel, then making it bassier and further back in the track could destroy the part's character. In a case like this, it might be better to soften the kick drum to acquire a proper balance and leave the bass as it is, or maybe even boost the midrange on the bass a bit for more punch. In any event, different situations require vastly different control settings, which is why equalizers have enjoyed such a high degree of refinement.

EQ also lets you change a sound's character—for example, turn a brash rock piano sound into something more classical. This type of application requires relatively gentle EQ, possibly at several different frequencies; a graphic equalizer works well. Parametric EQs may not have enough bands to affect all the desired sections of the audio spectrum.

Musicians often summarize an instrument's character with various terms, both positive and negative, depending on whether the sound is "too much" or "just right." Table 1 below is a *very* subjective interpretation of which frequencies correspond to these terms.

For example, to increase warmth, apply a gentle boost (3 dB or so) somewhere in the 200 to 500 Hz range. On the other hand, if you consider a sound muddy, try cutting the response in the same region.

Generally, the larger and more expensive the mixer, the more sophisticated the EQ. A typical high-end board will have a couple of bands of parametric EQ with bass and treble shelving controls, or three or four individual bands of parametric EQ. However, not all parametrics have the same sonic "character"—this is one area where subtle tonal differences can really influence the overall sound.

In many ways, I prefer a board with simple EQ because that means fewer bucks, and the money that's saved can go into a batch of different outboard EQs. A parametric EQ, no matter

| Range | Positive Correlation | Negative Correlation |
|---|---|---|
| 20 Hz–200 Hz | Bottom, depth | Boomy |
| 200 Hz–500 Hz | Warmth, dark | Muddy |
| 500 Hz–1.5 kHz | Definition | Honk or nasal |
| 1.5 kHz–4 kHz | Articulation, "snap," presence | Strident |
| 4 kHz–10 kHz | Bright, higher range of presence | Screechy, thin |
| 10 kHz–20 kHz | Sheen, transparency | Thin |

**Table 1**

how versatile, is not always the perfect tool for the job; you might prefer to use a graphic EQ, or a multieffects set to some sort of EQ patch.

Finally, note that equalizers generally have a bypass switch, so you can compare the equalized and unequalized sound (for an interesting experiment, set the EQ for flat response, then see if switching between the straight and "equalized" sound exhibits any audible difference). However, the bypass feature also comes in handy when using EQ as an effect: a guitar can be churning along doing a rhythm part, and then you can cut in the equalizer to modify the sound when it switches to lead. Switch on the beat, though, so that any glitches or clicks are masked by the music.

## Bus Access Control

As noted earlier, mixers have several buses, and how these are handled is where boards exhibit some of their greatest differences. Buses may be *normalled,* or *prepatched* into specific locations. For example, to send a signal to a reverb bus, you simply turn up a control (reverb send) that mixes the signal into the reverb input.

With other boards, bus outputs and other strategic board locations may be brought out to a patch bay. In a case like this, the board is set up in a general way, and is tailored to specific applications through appropriate patching. Some boards combine the two approaches: connections are usually normalled together unless you insert a plug, which breaks the normalled connection and allows you to insert patch cords (Fig. 10-19). Just for kicks, this is shown with balanced lines.

In 10-19A, the output connects to the input through the normalled jack connections. In 10-19B, we take another output signal, but the output still normals to the corresponding input. This is handy when splitting an output to two different inputs. In 10-19C, inserting the jack feeds the input, but breaks the connection from the output. A typical use for this: suppose you're recording an acoustic guitar, and the mixer output goes to the tape recorder. You decide to avoid going through the mixer and use a high quality, tube mic preamp instead. Take the tube mic preamp out, and feed it into the tape input via the patch bay to disconnect the normalled connection from the mixer.

### Bus Access—Patch Bay Style

With systems using a patch bay (this includes many large mixers), you can patch different output buses into different destinations, and patch the multitrack recorder inputs and outputs into the board (Fig. 10-20). For example, while recording, you may patch one bus into a cue system, another bus into a separate cue system, and run another bus as an effects bus, with two buses dedicated to stereo control-room monitoring. Then, for mixdown, when you don't need cueing buses anymore, you can patch those bus outputs into the reverb system. With a patch bay, the various points are (hopefully) clearly labeled, and if you understand what you're trying to do with your signal (*e.g.,* trying to get it to a recorder, or to the mixing board), then you can patch accordingly.

### Bus Access—Normalized

In a normalled patch arrangement, you select routing options with switches and controls, not patch cords. Every board has its own way of mixing signals in with buses. You will often find:

- Bus select switches. Each input has a row of pushbuttons, which connect the input signal to the selected bus(es). Frequently, these have a mechanical locking action so that more than one button can be pushed down at a time, and there will be a level control to regulate the amount of signal sent to the bus.
- Panpots. Since stereo requires two buses (one left, one right), and sending a signal to both channels makes it seem to come out of the center, sometimes the panpot will pan between two specific buses (for example, all odd-numbered and all even-numbered buses).
- Auxiliary send control. Earlier, we talked about adding a reverb send control, and having a return control to mix the reverb output back into the system so that we can hear it. Sometimes, you'll see a single send control for each channel, but some mixers have stereo buses that may require a couple of controls to send the signal to either, or both, the right and left reverb buses.
- Cue control. Sometimes you'll find this control on the input module itself; sometimes it's off to one side to avoid cluttering up the board. In any event, it sends some of the input module signal to the cue bus, which proceeds, through the cue amp, to the musician's headphones. Frequently, you'll find two or more cue controls per input to accommodate multiple cue buses.
- Direct-to-multitrack or tape switch. While this doesn't actually put a signal on a bus, it

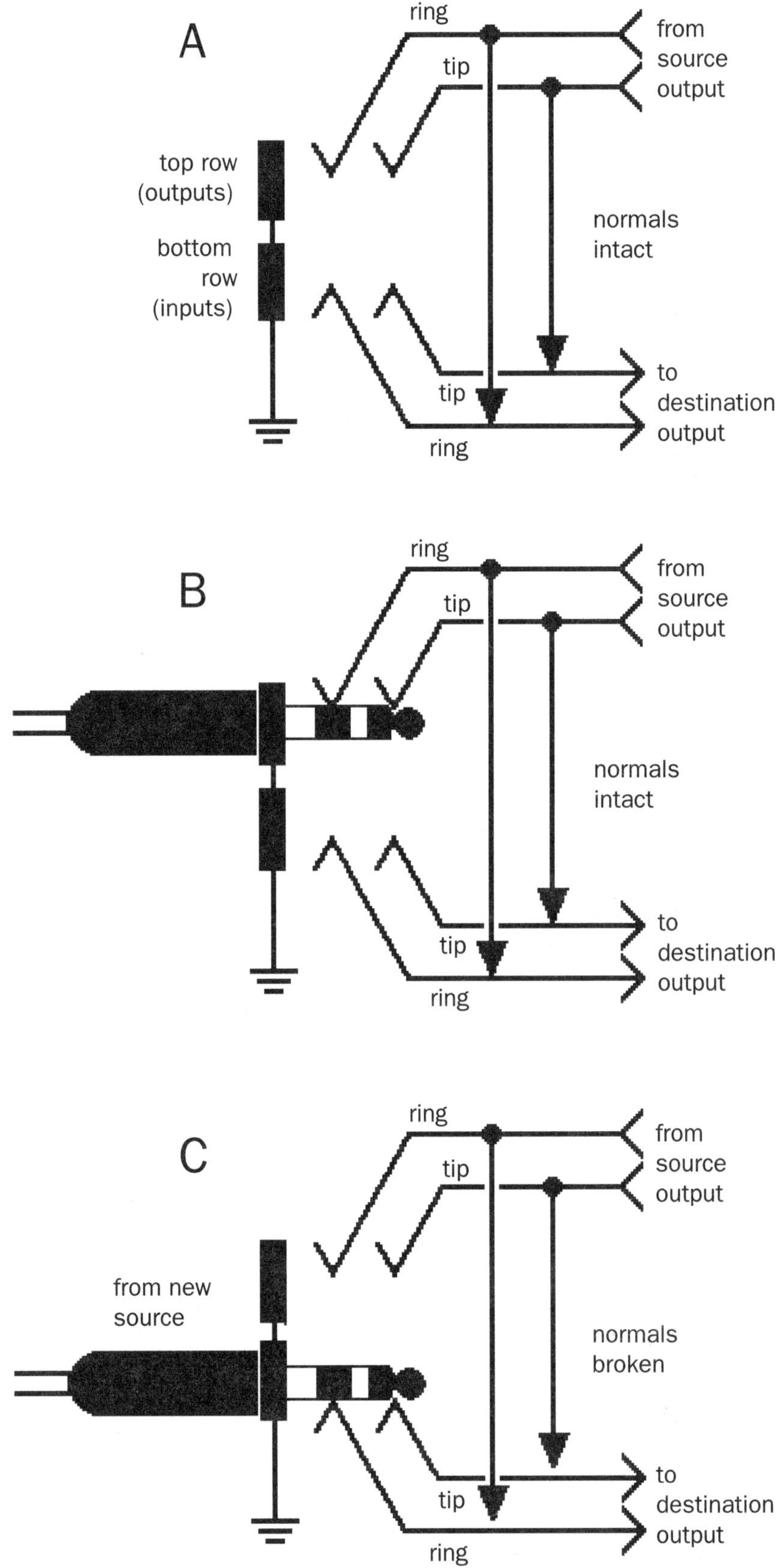


**Fig. 10-19:** *How normalled bus jacks work.*

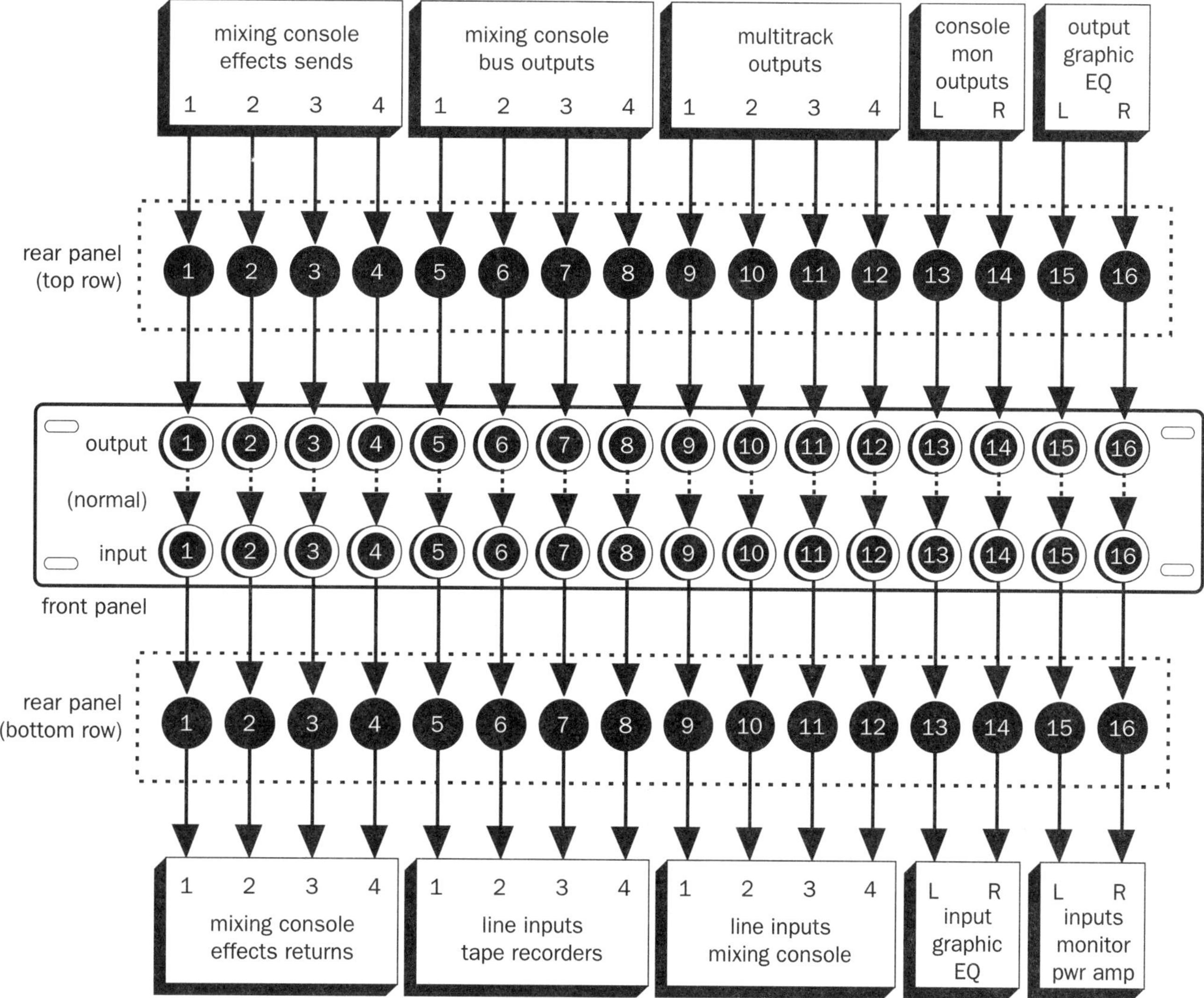


**Fig. 10-20:** *Normalized bus access via patch bay. The various units at the top feed into jacks on the rear of the patch bay; these parallel the top row of front panel jacks. The equipment to which these connections are normalled also feed into jacks on the rear of the patch bay, which are paralleled with the bottom row of front panel jacks.*

does send the input module signal directly to an equivalent multitrack recorder channel. For example, channel 3 would go to track 3 of an eight-track recorder; channel 7 would go directly to track 7, and so on.

Auxiliary sends often have an associated pre/post-fader switch, which determines whether the input module signal comes from before or after the fader. With the post-fader setting, turning down the fader also turns down the signal going to the bus. Otherwise, the level going to the auxiliary bus remains constant, regardless of the fader setting (even if it's all the way off).

For a real-world aux bus implementation, look at Fig. 10-8. There are two mono aux buses, 1 and 2. These are further modified by a pre/post switch. Two more mono buses are labeled 3/5 and 4/6. These have their own pre-post switch, and also work with a "shift" switch. In the 3/4 position, these two mono buses feed output buses 3 and 4. In the 5/6 position, they feed output buses 5 and 6.

## Monitor Mix Controls

You can use just about any bus for monitoring, but having a dedicated set of monitor controls simplifies matters. *Inline* monitoring means that a single control can switch between monitoring a bus output or multitrack output. For example, you could switch the input channel 3 monitor control to either bus out 3 or multitrack out 3. The monitor section may also include a panpot, and the option to switch the monitor mix to the main stereo bus.

## Master Output Controls

These provide an overall level adjustment for the master stereo bus. In other words, when you want to fade out a tune, these are the controls to use.

If the master outputs are turned up too high, distortion may result. Generally, a mixer will have a certain amount of headroom (*e.g.*, 10 to 25 dB) above 0 VU, so peaks can go over 0 VU and not cause distortion. However, this can cause confusion with digital gear, such as when you're mixing down to a DAT or other digital recorder. A level of 0 VU on a DAT is an absolute limit; there's no headroom past that point. Therefore, many DATs set their "0 VU" point at –12 to –15 dB, which means that if you put a 0 VU tone through your console, it will register as much lower on the DAT. The remedy is simple: turn up the DAT's input control, and monitor its VU meter to make sure the maximum level signals don't exceed 0 VU.

## Split versus Inline Configurations

For yet another variation on a theme, there's the *split* configuration, which physically separates ("splits") its controls into three basic sections: input, output and monitor. Because the sections are separated, they are easy to locate and difficult to confuse with each other. Generally, the number of inputs is greater than the number of outputs (which typically go to tape tracks). Split configuration mixers minimize repatching and make sessions go faster, but are costlier than traditional designs. Another disadvantage is that as the number of tape tracks in your studio grows, your console doesn't grow with them. Furthermore, once the console size (outputs) grows to match your tape tracks, it becomes tougher to physically reach the board's controls. thirty-two input channels plus twenty-four outputs plus a monitor section requires the arm length of a giant.

The in-line console solves the problem of reaching because the monitor, input and output functions are all located on one channel's input strip. Because you need to learn more functions per input channel, this does create a slightly more difficult learning curve. However, once you've learned one channel, you've learned them all. And, of course, purchasing a thirty-two-input board allows you to match it with thirty-two tape tracks, because, by design, the in-line board will bring you thirty-two outputs and monitor controls. All master controls such as effects sends, studio talkback, monitor levels and aux functions generally remain separate on both design types.

## Digital Control, Automation, and Recall

More and more analog mixers use digital control to store preset control settings (*e.g.*, a particular combination of control settings for the verse, chorus, solo, *etc.*) as well as remember dynamically varying mixing "moves," like sliding a fader up and down. Digital control can be built into the mixer, or available as an add-on. For more information, see Chapter 19 on automation.

## Other Features

There are many other controls and options that are not necessarily universal, but should be considered when you're shopping for a mixer. Here are some of the most common features.

- Preview (or solo) push-button. Pushing a button associated with a particular input mutes all other input modules so that you hear only what's going through the soloed input module. Pushing two solo buttons monitors two inputs, and so on. These are very handy for balancing tracks relative to one another, and for making delicate equalization changes in one track that would normally be overwhelmed by the other tracks. Because the preview button often hits the signal path before the fader does, even with the fader down you can still preview on most boards.
- Mute switch. If there's no preview button, you probably have a mute switch, which automatically cuts out (or mutes) its associated channel. Again, you can mute more than one channel by simply activating more buttons. Mute switches are wonderful for keeping noisy signals—such as a buzzing guitar amp—out of the mix until right before the instrument begins to play.
- Meters. Older mixers generally use mechanical meters, with pointers that swing across a calibrated scale. These show average signal levels, so loud transients (such as a tambourine hit) may not even move the pointer, misleading you into thinking the levels are lower than they really are. Often these meters are supplemented with peak LEDs that flash when peaks exceed a certain level,

such as +5 VU. Newer mixers use multistep LED VU meters, which can indicate peaks and often use different colors to differentiate between ranges of levels (green for normal, yellow for close to overload, and red for "hey—watch out!"). The meters may be able to monitor a variety of sources, such as inputs, aux bus outputs, master outputs, *etc.*

- Some inputs also have "activity" LEDs. These simply light up if there's a signal present (which can save a lot of head-scratching if you have a level control turned down accidentally and aren't sure that signals are reaching the mixer).
- Rumble filter. This is usually a simple low-cut filter that rolls off frequencies below about 100 Hz. It's useful for getting rid of microphone pops, hum, room rumble, air conditioning drone, and seismic activity.
- Talkback module. These are also separate from the input module area, and connect a microphone under the engineer's control to an audio or cue bus (or both). With this microphone, the engineer can cue musicians, identify takes on the tape or hard drive, and so forth.
- Test tone generator. Popular test tone frequencies are 400 Hz, 1000 Hz, and a high frequency tone somewhere between 7 kHz and 10 kHz (helpful in setting bias and EQ controls for analog gear).
- Control room section. This section or module includes convenience features for the control room, such as letting you switch between different pairs of speakers, compare mono and stereo to check for possible phase cancellation problems, choose between a couple of different two-track decks when mixing down, and the like.
- Long-throw faders. Pro boards usually have 100 mm faders because longer fader travel makes it easier to create subtle mixing "moves."
- Modular versus fixed construction. Modular mixers have removable input modules that can be replaced with different types of modules. For example, if you need a lot of aux buses you might want to replace an input module with an auxiliary send module. Note that large modular mixers usually offer a choice of frame sizes; larger frame sizes accommodate more modules and allow for easy expansion.
- Stereo effects returns. Most current signal processors are stereo, so every time you return the outputs to the mixer, you use up two inputs. Dedicated inputs for stereo effects don't have the "bells and whistles" of standard inputs, but let you save the main inputs for other signals. Effects return inputs can also be used as auxiliary inputs in a pinch—this is great for MIDI studios, which typically generate lots of output signals.

## About Distributed Mixing

MIDI-oriented studios never seem to have enough mixer inputs due to the real-time nature of MIDI sequencing. Your option is to get a mixer with a huge number of inputs, do lots of repatching, or use mono sound sources instead of stereo. But even if you do have lots of inputs, your problems aren't over: long cables are necessary to connect the instrument outputs to your mixer, and you've paid for lots of mic preamps you don't need (also, as many synths can have their levels set via MIDI messages, you may not need automation or even long-throw faders).

A more economical alternative is to distribute the mixing chores over several smaller "satellite" submixers—for example, one for effects returns, one for MIDI keyboard outputs, and one for electronic percussion. This is like the ultimate split console—the console is split into different boxes, not just different sections of the same mixer. The submixed outputs then feed your main mixer, into which tracks from the multitrack feed as well. The submixers don't need the extensive EQ or mic preamps of standard mixers, which saves you lots of money, and you don't have to deal with the patching hassles that happen when you don't have enough inputs.

### Real World Example

Distributed mixing is also a good way to add tracks to an existing setup. You can add something like a line mixer (we'll call it split A) with something like a sixteen-track mixer (split B).

The trick is getting the A and B splits to "talk" to each other. Fig. 10-21 shows a setup that worked for me with dual MDMs, lots of virtual tracks, and acoustic and electric instruments.

Consider a typical recording scenario using this setup. We'll assume you're sequencing various MIDI instruments for the rhythm track, overdubbing several acoustic and electric instruments on two digital eight-track recorders, and mixing down to DAT.

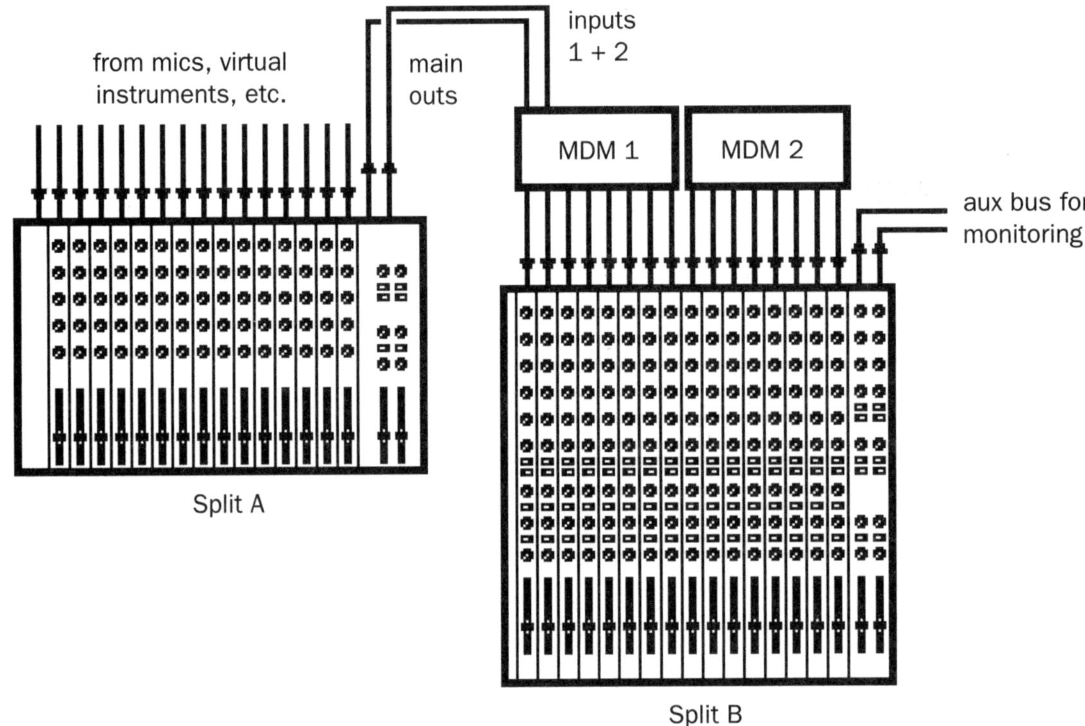


**Fig. 10-21:** *"Distributed mixing" setup using a conventional mixer for one split and a line mixer for the other split.*

The MIDI instrument outputs feed into Split A, and go through the master outs to inputs 1 and 2 of recorder #1. It's often a good idea to record a premix of the MIDI instruments into tracks 1 and 2 so that you have them on tape as a reference as you overdub the other instruments. This way you don't have to deal with the computer and sequencer during overdubbing. Monitor the inputs to tracks 1 and 2 via a Split B aux bus patched into a monitoring system.

When it's time to record the overdubs, play back recorder #1 tracks 1 and 2 (which contain the premix of the MIDI instruments) over the monitor or aux bus. Meanwhile, feed the instruments being overdubbed into Split A. Because of the way my MDMs are set up, if you plug into inputs 1 and 2, input 1 is also normalled to tracks 3, 5, and 7, while 2 is normalled to 4, 6, and 8. Therefore, you need not do any repatching to change tracks as you overdub; just hit the record enable switches for the desired tracks as needed, and you're ready to record. Monitor the tracks through Split B's monitor or aux bus.

After filling up recorder #1 with tracks, you have two options if you want to record more tracks. Either repatch Split A's main outs to inputs 1 and 2 on recorder #2, or simply switch tapes between recorder #1 and #2 if you don't want to be bothered with repatching. In the latter case you'd monitor the premix on tracks 9 and 10, and the existing overdubs on tracks 11 through 16. Meanwhile, monitor the new instruments as you did the previous instruments—send them into Split A, record-enable tracks on the recorder as needed, and monitor via Split B's aux bus.

As to effects, I generally leave them patched into another aux bus in Split B, and bring them into Split B's effects returns. These effects get used for the overall mix. If I need effects on specific instruments, they patch into Split A.

## Mixdown Time

During mixdown, the virtual tracks exit via Split A's main outs and go to recorder tracks 1 and 2, then pass through to the mixer. I also run the recorder in record mode for tracks 1 and 2 to replace the rough premix with the new premix. I do this so that if I need to remix at a later date, or do alternate mixes (vocals down, vocals up, *etc.*) I may not have to re-create the premix of virtual instruments since it's already captured on tape. Meanwhile, the acoustic and electric instruments recorded in the remaining recorder tracks feed Split B, whose outputs in turn go to DAT or other mastering deck.

If you have two spare recorder tracks (*e.g.*, 15 and 16), you can do one more trick: mix down all the tracks to those tracks instead of DAT. That way, you can simulate "automated mixing"; if you make a mistake as you mix, simply rewind and set the levels as desired.

When you reach the point where you want the levels to change, punch in. The seamless punching and tight inter-machine sync of today's MDMs make this possible.

## Pushing the Envelope . . .

To take things even further, try multiple splits—for example, another submixer for drums whose outputs feed into recorder tracks 3 and 4, or another submixer for bringing lots of effects returns back into Split B. By keeping these splits separate, you have many of the advantages of a traditional split console, without the cost penalty of having to buy a huge console all at once; you can add inputs as needed. Meanwhile, Split B provides your output section, so you're covered for feeding bunches of tape tracks simultaneously (just because we're assuming the recorder uses a normalized input scheme to feed a stereo bus into two inputs at a time doesn't mean you're locked into this approach).

# Chapter 11
# Studio Accessories

Now that we have the basics under control, let's look at accessories.

Store accessories so that they're instantly accessible, yet out of the immediate way. Shelves are usually the best solution, with a few boxes to hold items like percussion toys, session logbooks, patch cords, and extra cables. Don't keep microphones, or for that matter anything else of value, on the floor—they will get stepped on somewhere along the line. Remember to store magnetic media away from moisture, temperature excesses, and electrical devices.

Following are some of the most useful recording accessories. The chapter on maintenance describes accessories used for maintenance.

- AC line/grounding monitor. Are you really, really sure that every single AC outlet is properly wired and grounded? If not, a monitor (such as the Radio Shack #22-101) will tell you at a glance if all is well. It's inexpensive and is essential for the gigging musician.
- Accurate musical instrument tuner. This isn't just for tuning instruments, especially if you use analog gear. Record about twenty seconds of A 440 Hz at the head of a tape. If you need to take that tape to another studio where the recorder runs at a slightly different speed, you can feed the reference tone into the tuner and adjust the recorder's variable speed control until the tuner reads A 440. This will insure that the tape runs at the same speed as which it was originally recorded. A tone is also a good reference when working with variable speed; if you want to varispeed up a half tone, just adjust the speed until the tuner reads As. Note: Make sure your tuner can generate tones as well as well as read them.
- Adapters. You can never have enough adapters—1/4" phone to phono, female phone to female phone, XLR to stereo phone balanced, XLR to mono phone unbalanced, mini to phono, and so on.
- Adhesive labels. Have a good selection around for labeling cords, identifying reels of tape, and writing the date on a battery when it goes into service (this provides data that will help you determine if it's about due for a change).
- Antistatic treatment. Treat your rugs with an appropriate antistatic chemical. If you build up a significant static charge and touch a piece of microprocessor-based gear, you might scramble its brains or even worse, damage it.
- Bulk eraser. This will wipe every single bit of audio from a tape, thus making blank tape "blanker" than it was when new. Versions are available for analog tape as well as VCR-type cassettes.
- Contact cleaner. For scratchy controls or switches, pick up some contact cleaner from your local electronics emporium (make sure it's labeled as "safe for plastics"). Use the supplied nozzle to spray the cleaner into the body of the offending part, then work the switch or pot back and forth. Unless the control is severely damaged this will cure the scratchiness.
- CD player. This has two main uses. One is to play reference CDs so you can compare your mixes with CDs that have true sonic excellence, such as those engineered by Roger Nichols or other industry heavyweights. As you A–B between your tune and the CD, you can hear if what you've mixed is too bass-heavy or bass-light, *etc.* Also, many samples and rhythmic loops are available on CD that provide excellent "raw materials" for tunes.
- Low impedance balanced to high impedance unbalanced matching transformer(s). While many professional facilities use balanced low impedance devices, many smaller studios use more economical high impedance unbalanced gear. A matching transformer can interface the occasional balanced low impedance device (such as certain microphones) to high impedance lines and inputs.

- Direct box. A direct box solves the reverse of the above problem, namely, interfacing a high impedance unbalanced device to a low impedance balanced or unbalanced setup.
- Equipment covers. Dust can be harmful to equipment, so cover your equipment with a nonporous cover material. Plastic covers have pros and cons; they'll keep out fluids like spilled coffee, but can generate static electricity.
- Flashlight. If you have to rummage around behind a rackful of gear and do some repatching, a flashlight is usually the tool of choice.
- Fuses. Make sure you have a couple of spare fuses on hand for every piece of equipment. I usually tape a couple to the underside of a device's case so that if a fuse needs to be replaced, one is ready to go.
- Mic stands. Have at least one upright and one boom stand (Fig. 11-1). The boom is useful for miking instruments like acoustic guitar, while the upright type is good for vocalists. Gooseneck extensions are inexpensive and versatile. And while you're shopping, pick up a couple of spare mic clips.
- "No smoking" sign. Smoking isn't good for your equipment, particularly if it uses disk drives. Compared to the extremely narrow gap between the disk and read/write head of the disk drive, smoke particles are the size of boulders. If you must smoke, at least keep it out of the control room.
- Punch in/punch out footswitch. To free up your hands (guitarists take note), many recorders allow you to plug in an accessory footswitch for punch in and punch out. In a pinch, the sustain pedal switch that comes with most synths can double as a footswitch.
- Remotes. Being able to control your gear from your fingertips is a vast improvement over shuttling your hands (and sometimes your body) back and forth between different pieces of equipment.
- Soldering iron. You never know when you're going to have to do a repair. If you don't know how to use a soldering iron, learn! It's an invaluable skill.
- Stopwatch. Yes, the one on your little Casio do-all wonder watch will work; but one with a remote start/stop switch and big, easily readable digits might be worth the investment. You can time songs when mixing, and cue performers to come in at particular times if they're not too familiar with the music. When assembling a final tape, timings are also useful. Suppose you want to record some of your material on forty-five-minute cassettes, with twenty-two and one half minutes on each side; the timings enable you to combine the songs in a suitable order.
- Take sheets. Draw up a take sheet, photocopy or print up a bunch, and make sure that every reel of tape is completely documented. A studio logbook is also useful when you're trying to recall how you got a particular sound on a particular tape.

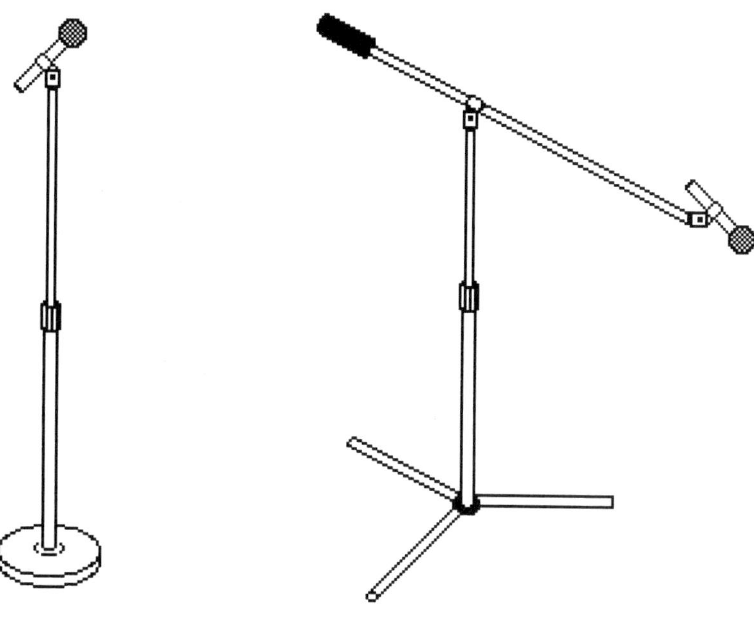


**Fig. 11-1:** *Two different types of mic stands.*

- Test tone oscillator. A variable-frequency test-tone oscillator will let you check an audio device's frequency response at a number of different points. One application is to check whether a "head bump" (a low frequency boost) occurs on an analog deck recorder; you can then set a parametric equalizer to notch out this response anomaly. Fixed frequency test oscillators will allow you to do basic alignment, but you will not be able to check the frequency response at as many different points.
- Voltmeter. Whether you want to check battery strength, cable continuity, or see whether the AC line voltage is undergoing a brownout, a voltmeter is ideal.
- Volume pedal. There will be times when you need three hands during mixing. A volume pedal will let you fade a track in or out with your foot, thus leaving your hands free to do other things.

## Analog Recording Accessories

Analog recording requires a particular set of accessories that digital gear doesn't need. These include:

- Splicing block (see Fig. 21-1 in Chapter 21). You also need splicing tape (don't use regular adhesive tape!) and single-edged razor blades. Be sure to demagnetize the blades before using them; otherwise you might induce a pop on the tape when you cut it.
- High intensity light. Shine a bright light on your splicing block as you work. Caution: Don't buy a light that uses a transformer, as you don't want transformers too close to the tape or heads. I use incandescent lamps with small 40W, 117V bulbs.
- Rubber gloves. When splicing, finger grease and tape do not get along; putting on some gloves prevents problems.
- Cassette splicer. Even if you have to make only one cassette splice per year, get a splicer designed specifically for cassettes.
- Test tape. If you don't have a test tape, you're going to have to pay someone else to keep your analog recorder properly aligned. Test tapes are expensive, but worth it if you want to keep your gear in good shape. Incidentally, once your recorder is aligned according to the test tape, you can make your own backup test tape by simply recording tones from a variable oscillator to the 0 VU standard as previously calibrated by the test tape. Keep the master test tape stored safely away, and use the copy for calibration. Periodically compare the two in order to catch any deterioration of the copy.
- Empty plastic reels. If you're mixing to an analog deck and do lots of short demo tapes and jingles, you can never have enough empty plastic reels around. It's silly (and uneconomical) to send a client a couple of sixty-second spots on a 10 1/2" metal reel.

Accessories can really make life easier for you (and your clients). And there's no better feeling than averting disaster on a project because you were prepared and had the necessary fuse sitting around, or could locate some ancient tape in seconds because of your thorough approach to documentation.

# Chapter 12
# Signal Processors

No studio is complete without some external accessories and special effects. We've already covered equalization in Chapter 10 on mixers, since most mixers include EQ.

Signal processors can patch into the signal path in many different places, such as the insert jacks mentioned in Chapter 10. They can also patch between recorder outputs and mixer inputs, or mixer outputs and subsequent devices (such as mixdown decks).

Although covering all possible signal processors is beyond the scope of this book (for that, see *Multieffects for Musicians*, published by Amsco Publications), the following are the most commonly used and necessary processors used in project and home studios.

## Compressor/Limiters

Any kind of recorder, analog or digital, has a limited dynamic range. However, the real world is not too accommodating—sudden peaks can cause distortion, and low-level signals can get lost in the noise floor. Therefore, sometimes it's necessary to restrict a signal's dynamic range, either out of necessity or as an effect. Compression is all about restricting dynamic range in a predictable, (hopefully) transparent way.

For vocals, the simplest form of compression/limiting is free, distortionless, and never breaks down: good mic technique. Check out any recent k. d. lang concert video; she evens out her vocals simply by how far she holds the mic from her mouth, and maneuvers it almost the way a slide trombone player moves a slide. An electronic compressor emulates the same action, but electronically. If a loud signal comes along, a detector recognizes this and turns down the gain. If the output signal gets softer, the detector turns up the gain. This results in a relatively constant output.

Incidentally, the classic definition is that a limiter "flattens" all peaks above a certain level, but leaves lower-level sounds intact, while a compressor can lower peaks *and* raise "valleys" of the sound. However, newer devices combine elements of both, and are often called compressor/limiters.

Compression was originally invented to shoehorn the dynamics of live music (which can exceed 100 dB) into the restricted dynamic range of radio and TV broadcasts (around 40 dB to 50 dB), vinyl (50 dB to 60 dB), and tape (40 dB to 105 dB, depending on type, speed, and noise reduction used). As shown in Fig. 12-1, this process lowers only the peaks of signals while leaving lower levels unchanged, then boosts the overall level to bring the signal peaks back up to maximum. (Bringing up the level also brings up any noise as well, but that's life.)

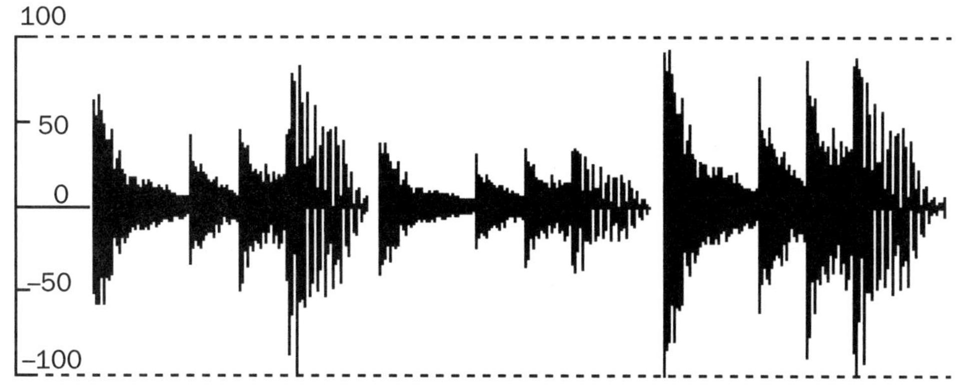


**Fig. 12-1:** *The left-hand section shows a piece of audio. The middle section shows the same audio after compression; the right-hand section shows the same audio after compression and turning up the output control. Note how softer parts of the first section have much higher levels in the third section, yet the peak values are the same.*

Even though media such as the CD have a decent dynamic range, people are accustomed to a compressed sound. Compression has been standard practice to help soft signals overcome the ambient noise in typical listening environments; furthermore, analog tape has an inherent, natural compression that engineers have used (consciously or not) for nearly half a century.

There are other reasons for compression. With digital encoding, higher levels have less distortion than lower levels—the opposite of analog technology. So, when recording into digital systems (tape or hard disk), compression can shift most of the signal to a higher overall average level to maximize resolution.

Compression can create greater apparent loudness (commercials on TV sound so much louder than the programs because they are compressed without mercy). Given a choice between two roughly equivalent signal sources, people will often prefer the louder one; radio stations will compress the signal not just for bandwidth reasons, but to make the signal fly out of the speakers. And of course, compression can smooth out a sound—from increasing guitar or piano sustain to compensating for a singer's poor mic technique.

## Compressor Basics

Compression is often misapplied because of the way we hear. Our ear/brain combination can differentiate between very fine pitch changes, but not amplitude. So, there is a tendency to overcompress until you can "hear the effect," giving an unnatural sound. Until you've trained your ears to recognize subtle amounts of compression, keep an eye on the meters. You may be surprised to find that even with 6 dB of compression, you don't hear much apparent difference—but bypass the effect, and you'll hear a change.

Compressors, whether software- or hardware-based, have these general controls:

*Threshold* sets the level at which compression begins. Above this level, the output increases at a lesser rate than the corresponding input change. Bottom line: With lower thresholds, more of the signal gets compressed.

*Ratio* defines how much the output signal changes for a given input signal change. For example, with 2:1 compression, a 2 dB increase at the input yields a 1 dB increase at the output. With 4:1 compression, a 16 dB increase at the input gives a 4 dB increase at the output. With "infinite" compression, the output remains constant no matter how much you pump up the input. Bottom line: Higher ratios increase the effect of the compression. Fig. 12-2 shows how input, output, ratio, and threshold relate.

*Attack* determines how long it takes for the compression to start once it senses an input level change. Bottom line: Longer attack times let more of a signal's natural dynamics through, but those signals are not being compressed. In the days of analog recording, the tape would absorb any overload caused by sudden transients. In digiland, those transients clip as soon as they exceed 0 VU. In some cases, this doesn't produce

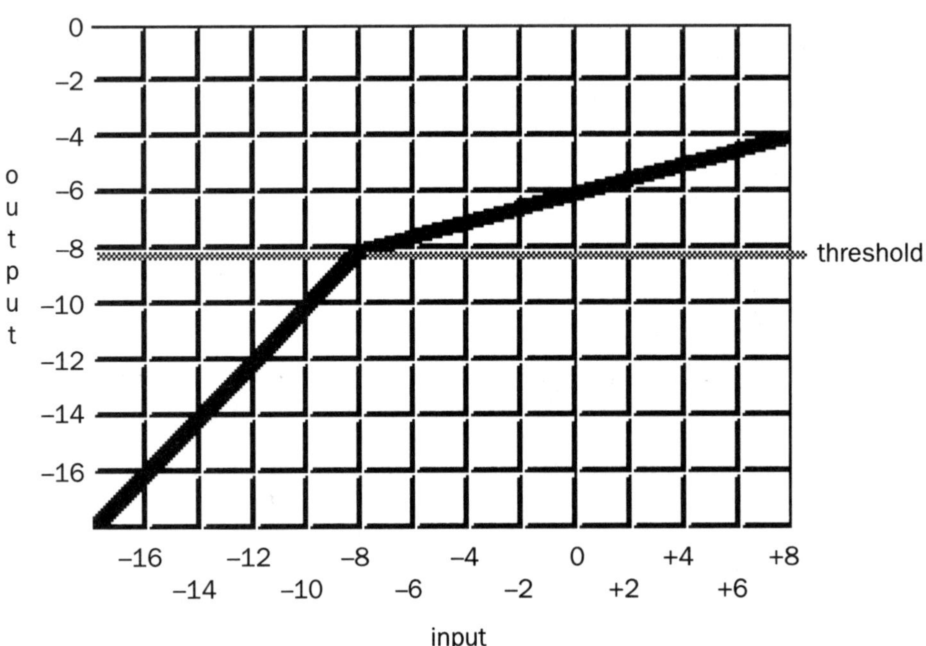


**Fig. 12-2:** *The threshold is set at –8. If the input increases by 8 dB (e.g., from –8 to 0), the output only increases by 2 dB (from –8 to –6). This means the compression ratio is 4:1.*

any significant audible degradation (that sound you hear is thousands of mastering engineers recoiling in horror). If there is distortion, lower the overall level with the . . .

*Output control.* Since we're squashing peaks, we're actually reducing the overall peak level. Increasing the output compensates for the volume drop. Bottom line: Turn this control up until the peak levels of the compressed signal match the peak levels of the bypassed signal.

*Decay* sets the time required for the compressor to give up its death grip on the signal once the input passes below the threshold. Bottom line: Short settings are great for special effects, like those psychedelic sixties drum sounds where hitting the cymbal would create a giant sucking sound on the whole kit. Longer settings work well with program material, since the level changes are more gradual and produce a less noticeable effect.

The *hard knee/soft knee* option controls how rapidly the compression kicks in. With soft knee, when the input exceeds the threshold, the compression ratio is less at first, then increases up to the specified ratio as the input increases. With hard knee, as soon as the input signal crosses the threshold, it's subject to the full amount of compression. Bottom line: use hard when you want to clamp levels down tight (*e.g.*, prevent clipping in a power amp), and soft when you want a gentler compression effect.

*Side chain* jacks are available on many hardware compressors. These let you insert filters in the compressor's feedback loop to restrict compression to a specific frequency range. For example, if you insert a high pass filter, only high frequencies are compressed—perfect for de-essing vocals.

*Peak/average response* affects how the detector reacts to sounds. With *peak* response, the detector monitors the instantaneous signal level. Therefore, as soon as it sees a peak—like a hard-hit snare—the compression/limiting action is immediate (subject to the attack time control setting). *Average* response monitors the average signal level over a short time period, and applies this signal to the gain control element.

The *link* switch in stereo compressors switches the mode of operation from dual mono to stereo. Linking the two channels together allows changes in one channel to affect the other channel, necessary to preserve the stereo image.

Fig. 12-3 shows the compression module from the Antares Voice Processor, a software plug-in for Sound Tools running on the Mac. This is a typical setting used for vocals. There was close to –6 dB of gain reduction at the moment this screen shot was taken, as shown by the Gain Redux meter. There are the expected threshold, ratio, attack, release, knee amount, and output controls; this module also includes a noise gate section (see Chapter 13) with its own threshold and ratio controls.

## Compressor Types: Thumbnail Descriptions

Compressors now come in both hardware varieties (usually a rack mount design) and as software "plug-ins" to existing digital audio-based programs. Following is a description of various compressor types, along with some common models.

- **Old faithful.** Whether rack-mount or software-based, typical features include two channels with gain reduction amount meters (yes! lots of blinking lights!) that show how much your signal is being compressed.
- **Multiband compressors.** These divide the audio spectrum into multiple bands, with each one compressed individually. This allows for a less "effected" sound (for example, low frequencies don't end up compressing high frequencies), and some models let you compress only the frequency ranges that need to be compressed.
- **Octal compressors.** Now that every man, woman, and child on the face of the earth has an eight-track digital recorder, accessories were sure to follow. Octal compressors house eight compressors in a single rack mount space. These help reduce the possibility of overload for signals going into your recorder, as well as bring back some of the tape compression effects associated with analog tape compression (minus the distortion). These units are overkill if you're overdubbing tracks one or two at a time (just get a good stereo compressor), but for live recording, they can literally save a session.
- **Vintage & Specialty Compressors.** Some swear that only the compressor in an SSL console will do the job. Others find the ultimate squeeze to be a big bucks tube compressor, like the Demeter or Groove Tubes models. And some can't live without their Dan Armstrong Orange Squeezer, held by many to be the finest guitar sustainer ever made. Fact is, all compressors have a distinctive sound, and what might work for one sound source might not work for another.

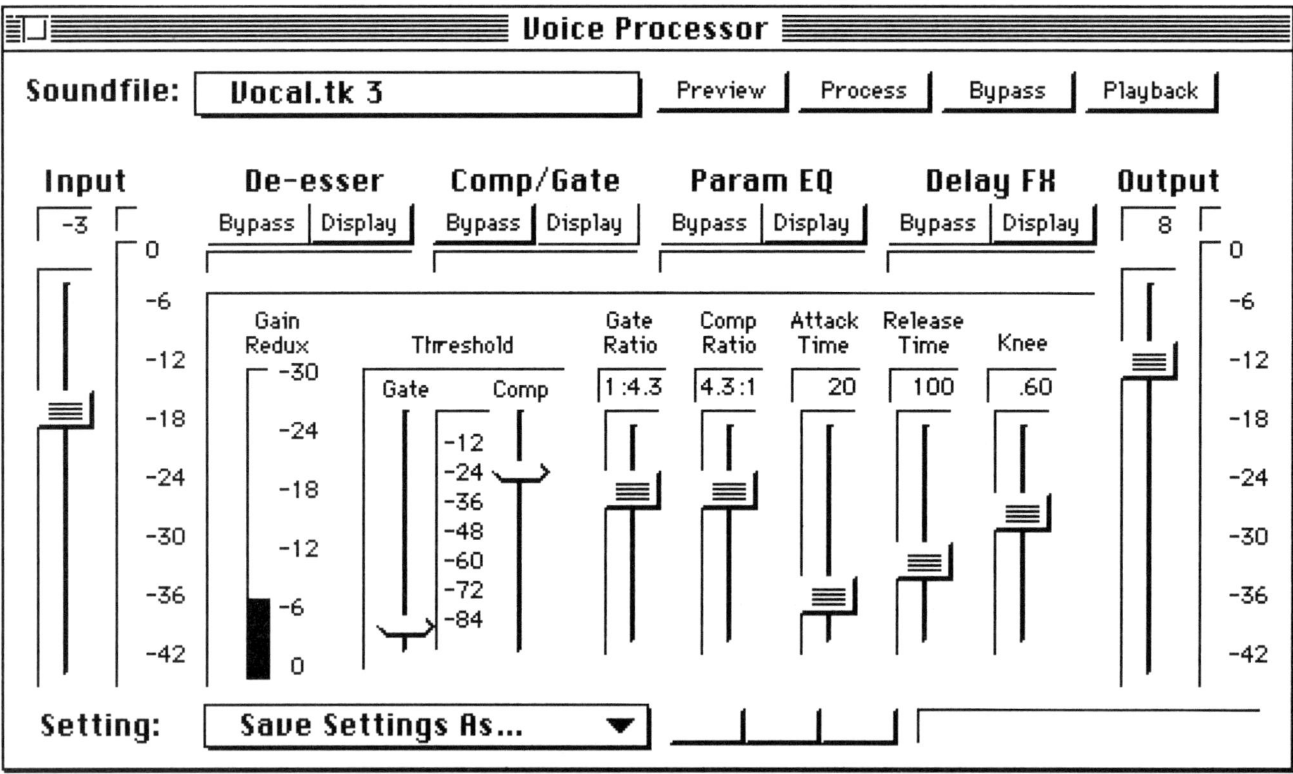


Fig. 12-3: *The compressor module from the Antares Voice Processor.*

## Setup and Avoiding Mistakes

Here's a suggested way for vocalists to set up a compressor whose output feeds a mixer or tape recorder.

1. Bypass the compressor and observe how high the peaks of your singing go on the mixer or recorder meters, then take the compressor out of bypass.

2. Set the ratio control to 4:1.

3. Set the attack time to 5 ms, peak/average response to peak, and release time to 150 ms.

4. Set the threshold control until the compressor's meter shows about 4 to 8 dB of gain reduction.

5. Adjust the output until the peaks of the compressed hit the same level on the mixer or tape recorder meters as the peaks of the bypassed signal.

The compressed/limited sound should be punchier than the bypassed version, even though they have the same peak level. If the sound is too compressed, raise the threshold (and lower the output to compensate), lower the ratio, and/or increase the attack time and decrease the decay time. Do the opposite if the signal doesn't seem compressed enough.

The best way to find what works for you is to experiment. Don't overcompress—in fact, avoid using compression as a fix for bad mic technique or dead strings on a guitar. I wouldn't go as far as those who disdain all kinds of compression, but it is an effect that needs to be used subtly to do its best. Just remember to switch between the processed and straight sounds often so you have a "reality check"—you want to make sure any effects you add *enhance* the sound!

Finally, if you use compression on the stereo two-track, here's a tip to avoid getting an overly squeezed sound: mix in some of the straight, noncompressed signal. This helps restore a bit of the dynamics yet you still have the thick, compressed sound taking up most of the available dynamic range.

## Reverberation and Gated Reverberation

For thousands of years, music was heard exclusively in an acoustical environment. Recording direct (*i.e.,* plugging an instrument directly into the mixer console) forfeits this sense of acoustical space. A reverb unit helps put this space back in again by simulating the sound of playing in a large room.

A room's acoustical characteristics create a characteristic "ambiance." The audience hears not only the sound that comes directly from an instrument or amplifier, but myriad sound waves reflecting and re-reflecting off the room's walls, ceiling, and floor. As a result, what the audience hears is a composite of the original audio signal, the first reflections from various surfaces, and the delayed reflections. Eventually these sound waves lose their energy and become inaudible.

What's in the room also affects the sound. A thickly carpeted room will easily absorb reflected waves, while a room with extremely hard surfaces will tend to keep the sounds bouncing around. Also, high frequencies are more prone to absorption than lower frequencies.

The best reverb is a large, acoustically treated room, but few of us can borrow the local cathedral or auditorium as our own personal reverb units. Most studios use digital reverbs, which lack the spaciousness and transparency of acoustic reverb, but are compact, convenient, and capable of simulating anything from a tiled bathroom to the Taj Mahal.

Many budget reverbs do not have true stereo inputs (even if there are two inputs, they are often mixed together). However, these devices generally do synthesize a stereo field electronically and have stereo outputs. If you have a limited number of effects bus sends, most of the time you'll get good results if you feed only one reverb input (consult the manual to see if feeding one input is preferred over the other) and bring the outputs back as stereo returns. With a stereo effects send, this technique lets you feed two reverb units at once—use the right send for one unit, and the left send for the other.

Digital reverb can also create spaces that don't exist in nature, such as *gated reverb.* This does the equivalent of adding a noise gate (see Chapter 13) to the end of the reverb, allowing for an abrupt cutoff of the reverb tail. This effect is often used with drums.

## Typical Reverb Unit Parameters

Fig. 12-4 graphically illustrates reverb parameters.

*Type* determines the kind of reverb to be simulated: room, hall, plate (a bright, clean type of older reverb unit used in recording studios), spring (the classic "twangy" reverb sound used in guitar amps), etc.

*Room size* determines the apparent volume of the room (this parameter is sometimes calibrated in cubic feet or meters). Changing this parameter will often change other parameters, such as low and/or high frequency decay.

*Early reflections predelay* sets the amount of time before the first group of reflections begins, and is usually less than 100 ms (20 to 50 ms are typical values). A longer predelay setting gives the feeling of a larger acoustical space.

*Reverb predelay* controls the amount of time before the room reverb sound begins. As with early reflections predelay, this is usually 100 ms or less. Note that reverbs sometimes do not

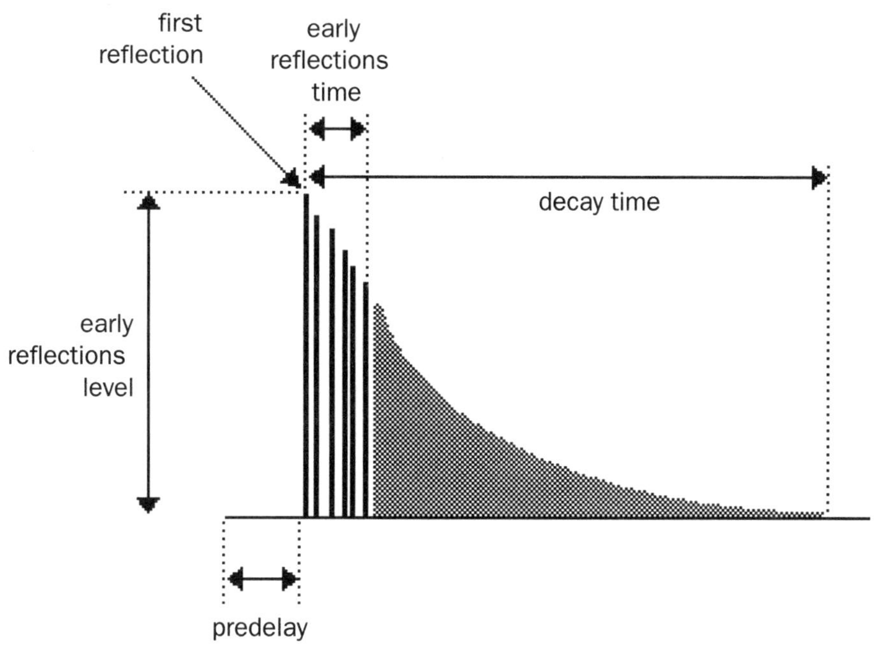


**Fig. 12-4:** *Common reverb parameters.*

include separate predelay settings for early reflections and reverb, but a combined setting.

*Early reflections level.* Early reflections are closely spaced discrete echoes, as opposed to the later "wash" of sound that constitutes the tail of the reverb. This parameter determines the level of these discrete echoes.

*Early reflections shape* imparts an envelope to the early reflections. The envelope may attack instantly then decay slowly, build up over time then decay, take a long time to attack then decay abruptly, etc.

*Early reflections diffusion* is a "smoothness/ thickness" parameter. Increasing diffusion packs the early reflections closer together, giving a thicker sound. Decreasing diffusion spreads the early reflections farther apart.

*Decay time* sets how long it takes for the reverb tail to decay to the point of inaudibility. Note that there may be separate decay times for higher and lower frequencies (and possibly midrange as well), so you can more precisely tailor the room characteristics.

*Crossover frequency* applies only to units with separate decay times for high and low frequencies. This parameter determines the "dividing line" between the highs and lows. For example, setting the crossover frequency to 1 kHz means that frequencies below 1 kHz will be subject to the low frequency decay time, while frequencies above 1 kHz will be subject to the high frequency decay time. Really fancy reverbs may have separate high, mid, and low frequency crossover frequencies. Each of these may have a level control too.

*High frequency rolloff.* In a natural reverberant space, high frequencies tend to dissipate more rapidly than lows. High frequency rolloff helps simulate this effect.

*Mix, balance,* or *blend.* This determines the mix between the reverberated (wet) and unprocessed (dry) signals. This is sometimes referred to as the "wet/dry" mix.

*Reverb density* or *spread* determines the space between the first reflection and subsequent reflections. With lower density settings, the first reflection is audible as a separate event, followed by the remaining reflections. Higher density settings move the remaining reflections closer to the first reflection, so that the first reflection joins the overall "wash" of reverb.

*Reverb diffusion* is similar to early reflections diffusion, but affects the room reverb sound. Some simpler reverbs combine diffusion for the early reflections and the overall reverb into a single parameter.

*Gated reverb* parameters vary considerably from manufacturer to manufacturer; some multieffects even include gated reverb as a separate effect. Typical parameters are gate *threshold* (how much of the reverb tail is cut off), gate *shape* (even *reverse* or *backwards reverbs* are possible, where the tail increases to a certain level instead of fading out), and others. It's best to consult the manual for more information on these types of effects since they vary so much among different units.

Note: There is some disagreement among manufacturers as to the exact definition of "diffusion" and "density," so your reverb may function somewhat differently than described above.

## Time Delay: Flanging, Chorus, Echo

A variety of effects are based on time delay. These include flanging, echo, chorusing, tapped delay, and even esoteric functions like stereo generation from a mono signal, or "psychoacoustic" panning (*i.e.,* you're not panning the signal conventionally with level changes, but it sounds like it).

Some multieffects include dedicated effects for each function; others simply include a general purpose time delay effect that is flexible enough to provide these different options. In any event, all time delay-based effects have many common parameters.

### Understanding Time Delay

Fig. 12-5 shows the block diagram for a typical mono time delay effect. In addition to delaying the signal being processed, there will also be a parameter to mix the unprocessed and delayed signals, and usually, the option to feed some of the delayed signal back to the input (called *regeneration, recirculation,* or *feedback*). With echo, listening to the delayed output without any regeneration produces a single echo. Adding regeneration means that when the echo appears at the output, it also feeds back to the input. Once this regenerated signal passes through the time-delaying circuitry, it creates a second echo; continuing to feed back more of the output produces more echoes.

*Modulation,* a regular (or sometimes random) varying of the delay time over a particular range, is another key element of time delay-based

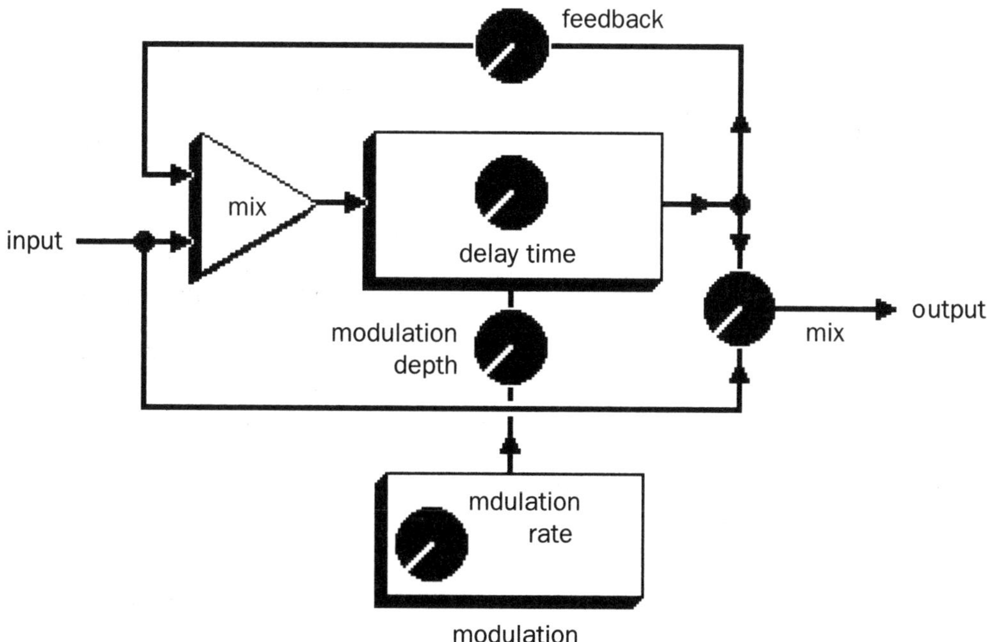


Fig. 12-5: *Block diagram of a mono delay line effect. In a digital effects unit this is all implemented in software, but the functions emulate traditional analog delay line hardware. A stereo delay will include an additional set of controls for the second channel.*

effects. These variations produce an animated kind of sound as the delay time sweeps back and forth between a maximum and minimum value. Modulation parameters include modulation *speed* or *rate* (how fast the variations occur) and *depth* or *intensity* (the spread between the minimum and maximum delay times).

Tapped delays offer several delay lines, each with adjustable delay time and feedback (Fig. 12-6). Some provide individual modulation for the different taps. This makes a more complex sound than simple stereo or mono delay lines.

## The Time-Shift Spectrum

Different amounts of time delay give different effects. While there is no standard definition of the time-shift spectrum, here are some guidelines as to what sounds are associated with various delay times. These delays are so short that they're given in milliseconds (1/1000 of a second, abbreviated ms).

- **0 to 15 ms delays.** Mixing a signal delayed by 0 to 15 ms with an equal amount of nondelayed signal produces *flanging*, a

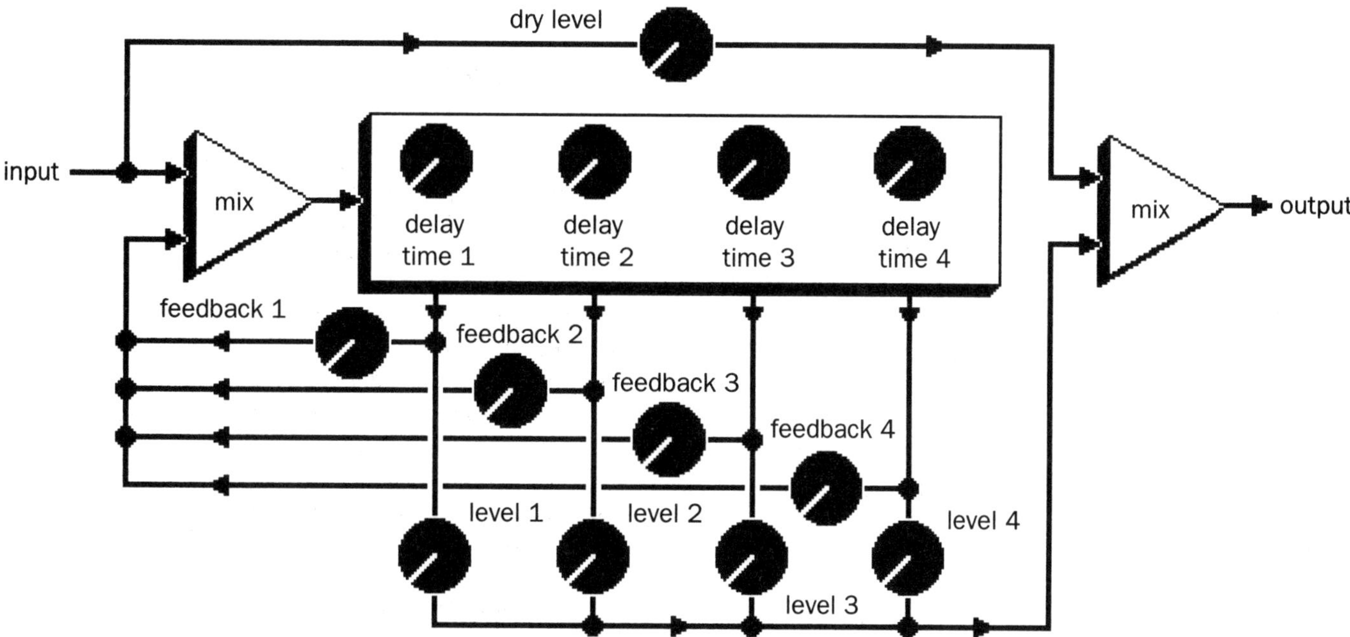


Fig. 12-6: *A tapped mono delay line with four taps. Each tap has adjustable delay time, feedback, and output control.*

dramatic special effect that imparts a "jet airplane"–like sound to the signal going through the flanger.

- **10 to 25 ms delays.** Mixing a signal delayed by 10 to 25 ms with a nondelayed signal produces a *chorus* effect. This creates a full, animated sound that resembles the sound of two instruments playing at once. Modulating (varying) the delayed signal's delay time adds "motion."
- **25 to 50 ms delays.** This starts crossing over into the echo range, where you can perceive that the delayed signal is occurring later in time with respect to the nondelayed signal (with flanging and chorusing effects, it's difficult to tell that an actual delay is taking place because the delay time is so short). Delays of 30 to 80 ms yield what is popularly called "slapback" echo, a very tight echo sound.
- **50 ms and up.** This is the range covered by most echo units. Longer delays (say, over 250 ms) give a spacey, emotional sound, while shorter delays give more of a doubling effect, or the effect associated with playing an instrument in a small room with hard surfaces.

## Typical Time Delay Parameters

*Initial delay* sets the amount of delay time. With echo, this is the time interval between the straight sound and the appearance of the first echo. With flanging and chorusing, modulation occurs around this initial time delay. Stereo devices usually provide independent delay times for the left and right channels.

Some multieffects let you synchronize the delay time to MIDI clocks (see Chapter 4 for more information on MIDI). Providing that MIDI clock messages set the song's tempo, this feature locks the multieffects' delay time to the tempo. Another option is a "tap" function, where hitting a switch or button twice sets the delay time interval (in other words, this is the time between the first and second taps).

*Balance, mix,* or *blend.* Since you rarely want to hear the sound of the delayed signal by itself, this parameter adjusts the balance between the unprocessed and delayed signals. With flanging, you generally set this control for an equal blend of unprocessed and delayed signals; chorusing typically uses more unprocessed than delayed sound. With slapback echo, the delayed sound will tend to be mixed further back. With longer echoes, the amount of delayed sound will depend on how "murky" a sound you want: increasing the amount of delayed sound gives a swimming-in-echo effect, while adding in only a little delayed sound provides more of an ambiance effect.

*Feedback, recirculation,* or *regeneration.* This parameter determines how much of the output feeds back into the input. With echo, minimum feedback gives a single echo; increasing this parameter increases the number of echoes.

With flanging, introducing feedback increases the effect's sharpness, much like increasing the resonance control on a filter. The effect with chorusing is similar. However, dedicated chorus effects may not include a feedback parameter because adding feedback makes the sound more "unnatural."

*Feedback phase.* This parameter is most relevant to flanging but can also be useful with chorusing. With in-phase (positive) feedback, the flanged sound is metallic and "zingy" since it accentuates positive harmonics. Out-of-phase (negative) feedback emphasizes odd harmonics, which produces a hollower, "whooshing" sound. With longer delays, out-of-phase feedback can sometimes interact with your straight signal in such a way that it weakens the straight signal sound.

There are several ways to implement this function. One option is a phase "switch" parameter that selects positive or negative phase. Another is to calibrate the feedback parameter in positive or negative numbers (*e.g.,* 0 to +100 varies the amount of positive feedback from minimum to maximum, while 0 to –100 similarly varies the amount of negative feedback).

*Feedback tone controls.* Some musicians prefer the sound of tape echo instead of digital echo, probably because tape's inferior high frequency means that as each echo recirculates through the delay line, it loses more and more of its high frequency edge. As a result, the early echoes never "step on" the straight sound or on newer echoes. With a digital delay, echoes become progressively softer in terms of level, but their frequency response doesn't necessarily change. Psychoacoustically, this sounds unnatural since in a traditional acoustic space, echoes indeed lose higher frequencies faster than lower frequencies. So, many digital delay effects include a parameter to restrict the feedback path's high frequency bandwidth.

*Sweep range, modulation amount,* or *depth* determines how much the modulation section (also called LFO, or sweep) varies the delay time. For example, a delay with a 2:1 sweep range could sweep over a two-to-one time interval (*e.g.*, 5 ms to 10 ms, or 100 ms to 200 ms). Practically speaking, a wide sweep range is most important for dramatic flanging effects—chorus and echo don't need much sweep range to be effective. With longer delays, adding a little bit of modulation can give choruslike sounds, but too much modulation will cause detuning effects.

With chorusing, the main use for depth is to strike the correct balance between detuning and chorusing; too little depth gives a weak chorusing sound, whereas too much depth sounds out-of-tune.

*Modulation type.* Fig. 12-7 shows the most popular forms of modulation.

- *Triangle wave* varies the delay time smoothly from a maximum to minimum value in a cyclical manner, and is most often used with flanging and chorusing.
- *Sine wave* sounds very similar to the triangle wave but can be a little bit "smoother."
- *Square wave* switches cyclically between two delay times.
- *Logarithmic* is particularly useful with flanging. It stays for a longer time at the top end of the sweep, then dips down rapidly into the lower range.
- *Exponential* is another flanging-oriented waveform that stays for a proportionately longer amount of time at the lower end of the sweep range, then sweeps up rapidly to the peak.
- *Random* changes delay time values at random.
- *Smoothed random* is like random, but rounds off the edges.
- *Envelope follower* is not a periodic waveform, but causes the delay time to vary in response to the dynamics of the instrument's signal. The delay time variations always relate rhythmically to your playing, rather than being controlled by a modulation source (such as the triangle wave) which is seldom in sync with the song's tempo. Envelope followers are less common than the types of modulation mentioned above, but can work very well with flanging and chorusing effects.

*Modulation rate* sets the modulation frequency. Typical rates are 0.1 Hz (one cycle every ten seconds) to 20 Hz. With flanging and chorusing, modulation causes the original pitch to go flat to a point of maximum flatness, return to the original pitch, go sharp to a point of maximum sharpness, then come back to the original pitch and start the cycle all over again. A slower rate produces a slow, gradual detuning that gives a majestic, rolling chorusing or flanging sound. Faster rates produce a more "bubbly" effect.

Note that the rate parameter interacts with the depth parameter because the total amount of pitch change depends not just on the amount of pitch change, but also on the rate. For example, combining full depth with a fast rate setting can sound out-of-tune, whereas the same amount of depth coupled with a slow rate sounds just fine.

*Hold* or *"freeze."* Sometimes this is a separate function, but some delays let you capture (sample) a sound in the delay's memory and repeat that captured section of sound indefinitely. If you're into electronic sounds and special effects, hold is definitely a useful option. You can usually adjust the pitch, record trigger threshold, sample start and end point, and looping on/off.

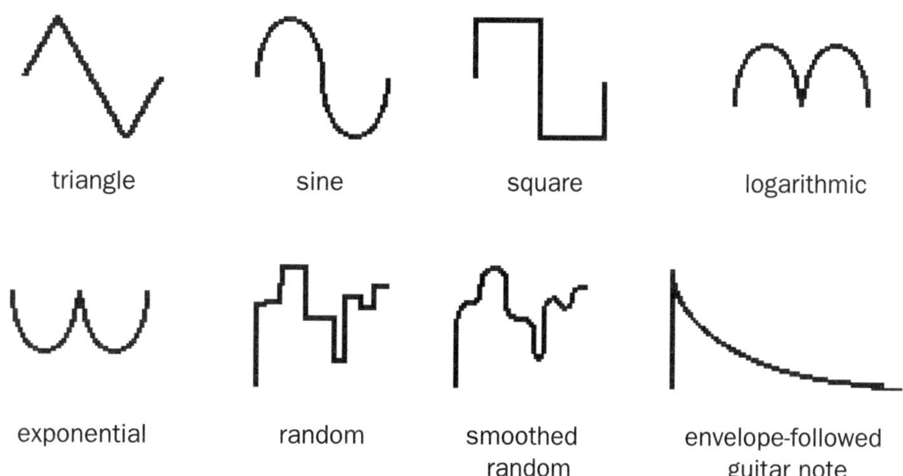


**Fig. 12-7:** *The most common types of modulation signals.*

With loop on (Fig. 12-8), once the sound reaches the loop end point it jumps back to the loop start point and continues playing *ad infinitum.* With loop off (also called *one-shot* mode), the sampled sound simply plays through from beginning to end.

Long freeze times can create solid-state tape loop effects. Shorter loops are good for special effects and generating unusual tones, but tend to be not as musically useful (in a conventional sense) as longer loops.

## Time Delay Tips

Time delay-based functions can give a rich repertoire of sounds. Here are some applications that are particularly useful in the studio, with suggested parameter values to get you started.

- **Vibrato.** Set a short initial delay (5 ms or so), listen to the delayed sound *only,* and modulate the delay with a triangle or sine wave at a 5 to 14 Hz rate. The greater the amount of modulation, the deeper the vibrato effect.
- **Rotating speaker simulation.** For best results, set the initial delay in the 5 to 15 ms range, add modulation sparingly, set the blend control for slightly less delayed sound than unprocessed sound, and don't use any recirculation. The rotating speaker simulation works best at faster modulation speeds.
- **Tone control (comb filter).** Mixing an unprocessed signal with the same signal passing through a short, fixed (unmodulated) delay produces a filtering effect that changes the signal's tone. This type of filter is called a "comb filter" since plotting its frequency response looks somewhat like a comb—there are lots of peaks and valleys. Suggested control settings are an initial delay of 0 to 10 ms, minimum feedback, no modulation, and an equal blend of processed and straight sound (this produces the sharpest peaks). Increase the amount of feedback to increase the depth of the filter peaks and dips; this creates a more "resonant" sound. For a variation on this timbre, change the feedback phase from positive to negative to reverse the positions of the frequency response peaks and valleys.
- **Automatic Double Tracking (ADT).** This simulates the effect of playing a part then overdubbing a second part to give a thicker sound. Set the initial delay for a short echo (around 30 to 40 ms). Adding a very small amount of modulation (preferably random) alters the delay time to better simulate true double tracking, where small timing inconsistencies keep each track from being identical. While the effect is similar to chorusing, chorusing is more closely related to flanging, while ADT is more closely related to echo.

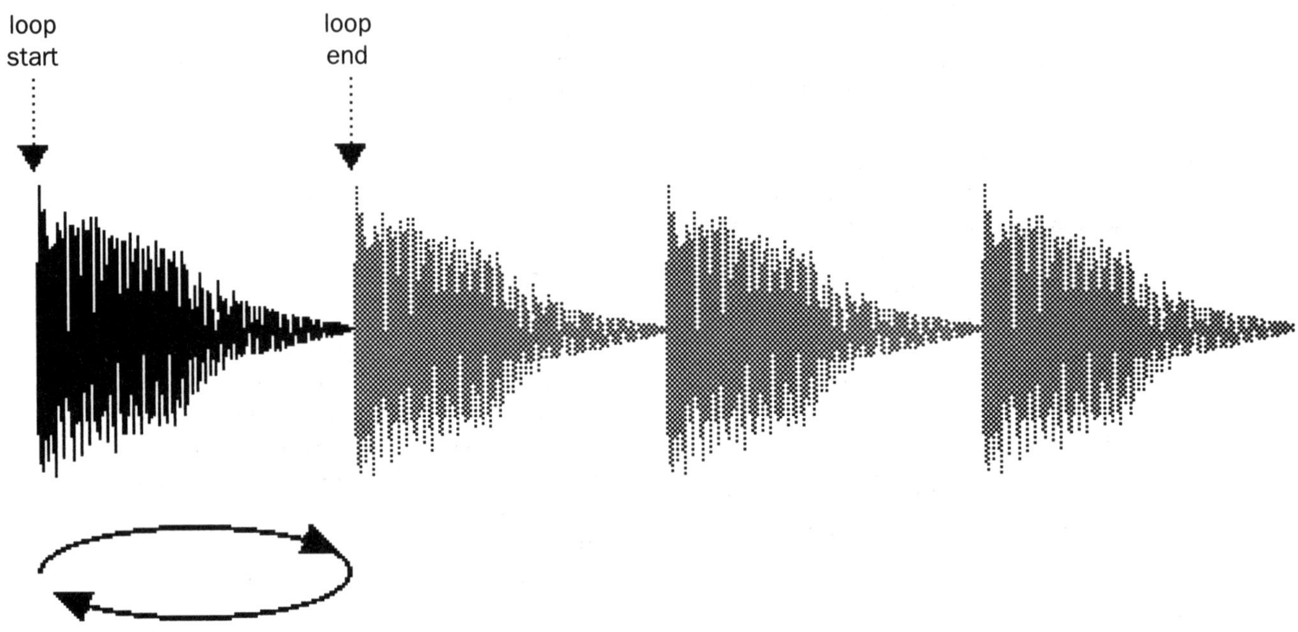


**Fig. 12-8:** *In one-shot mode, only the portion of the sound shown in black would play. With loop on, this portion would repeat over and over again, as represented by the additional sounds shown in gray.*

- **Fifties-style slapback echo.** In the early days of recording, echo effects were provided by tape recorders rather than by the digital wonder boxes we know today. Feeding a signal into the tape recorder input, going into record, rolling tape, and monitoring the signal coming from the playback head produced a typical delay of around 70 ms. Select a delay program, and set the delay time to 70 ms to recreate the vintage echo sound; add feedback to taste (use positive feedback) and minimum modulation.
- **Mono to pseudo-stereo conversion.** With stereo chorus (and flanging), set the chorus depth to maximum and rate to minimum. This creates a stereo spread without the motion that would result from having a higher modulation rate.

You can also use delay to create stereo from mono. Referring to Fig. 12-9, the basic idea is to split the track output into a mixer, with the straight signal panned to the left channel and the right channel split going through a delay line set for *delayed sound only* (no dry sound). Note, however, that if the delay line is set for a short delay, cancellations may occur between the two channels when played back in mono; and if the delay is set somewhat longer, combining the tracks in mono can produce a disconcerting slapback echo effect. For best results, select a delay in the 10 to 20 ms range that sounds good whether the tracks are panned left and right for stereo, or panned center for mono.

## Relating Echo Times to Song Tempos

Setting the echo repeat time to equal a particular rhythmic value, such as an eighth or quarter note, "synchronizes" the echo time to the tempo (synchronizing to MIDI clocks does this automatically, but only a few multieffects incorporate this feature). Here's a simple formula that translates beats per minute (tempo) into milliseconds per beat (echo time; remember that there are 60,000 milliseconds in one minute):

60,000/tempo = time (in ms)

For example, if a tune's tempo is 120 beats per minute, then the number of milliseconds per beat is:

60,000/120 = 500 ms

So, setting the echo for 500 ms gives an echo every beat. Repeatedly dividing the delay time by two (*e.g.*, 250 ms, 125 ms, 62 ms, and 31 ms) gives progressively tighter echoes that remain in sync with the tempo. Similarly, multiplying by two gives longer echo intervals. (By the way, multieffects calibrations may vary somewhat, so treat the displayed value as a close approximation. It might be necessary to tweak the delay time a bit to have it sync up perfectly with your music.)

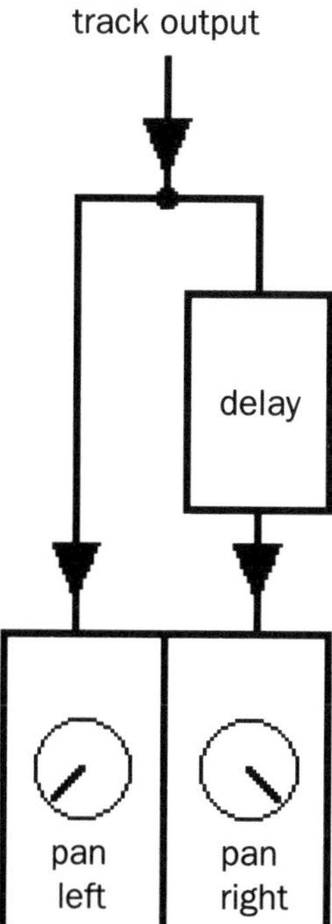


**Fig. 12-9:** *Using a delay line to widen the stereo image. Set a short delay (10 to 20 ms) and use delayed signal only.*

Stereo echo allows for even more options, such as polyrhythmic effects and panned echoes that add a real spaciousness to the sound. Try setting one channel as described above, then adjust the other channel's echo time to some triplet value—say, sixty-six or thirty-three percent of the first channel's delay time. This sounds so great you have to hear it to believe it.

## Speaker Emulator

In many home studios, it's often not practical to mic a huge, loud stack of amps (at least not without neighbors calling the police). Much of a guitar amp's characteristic sound depends on how the speaker and cabinet shape frequency response; a speaker emulator provides the equalization needed to approximate a guitar amp and cabinet.

There are two ways to do this:

- Electronic frequency-shaping. This uses either analog or digital filters to create different response curves typical of guitar amps and cabinets.

- Artificial loading. This presents a load to a guitar amp that "looks" like a speaker, but simply soaks up the amp's power instead of producing noise. This allows you to turn your amp way up and get the sound that only happens with an amp cranked at full volume. These devices may also include equalization to simulate the response of a speaker cabinet.

## Multieffects Devices

Instead of devoting all of a box's processing power to simulating something like a great reverb, we can divide that processing power up among several individual effects. For example, a typical multieffects will let you do compression, equalization, delay, reverb, and more, often simultaneously.

You can think of multieffects as the Swiss Army knife of audio: what's cool about it is not the quality of individual effects, but that it puts so many effects in such a compact package. The tradeoff for this versatility is usually a compromise in overall sound quality. However, this is all relative—today's multieffects often provide sound quality that surpasses older, dedicated devices that cost much more when they were introduced.

Great strides have been made recently in improving signal processor quality. For example, even though a signal processor might be able to do a bunch of effects at once, several manufacturers give you the option of pouring all the device's power into one great effect (such as a "killer" reverb) if desired.

## Exciters

"Exciters" (as made by companies such as Aphex and BBE) are generally used during mixdown to add clarity and detail to a mix. The effect is similar to boosting the treble, but without the stridency you'd normally get with equalization. Exciters can also give an airy, transparent sound to a mix and improve the stereo imaging and separation. The effect should be used sparingly, just like adding a tiny bit of spice to bring out the flavor of fine foods.

Some love 'em and some hate 'em—but one thing's for sure, a lot of people overuse them. Our ears have a tendency to get used to loud sounds (otherwise, how could anyone live in New York?), so if you crank up the exciter to get more sizzle and sheen, your ears will rapidly acclimate, which makes you increase the amount of exciter, which you then get used to so you turn it up further, and so on. Eventually, the song sounds tinny, strident, and well, just plain bad (at this point, the unenlightened engineer pronounces that the exciter in question is "a piece of garbage" without realizing the major problem is pilot error).

I like exciters, but only when I add them at the very end—after everything is EQed, reverberated, level set, etc. Excitation shouldn't even be the frosting on the cake, but the powdered sugar that goes on the frosting. And don't have unrealistic expectations; even under the best of circumstances, proper use of an exciter will only add about another five percent of coolness to the tune—but that five percent can be significant.

I've used many of these devices, from low-end treble enhancers to expensive devices that combine limiting and EQ and almost let you "pull out" individual parts of a mix and put them under the audio equivalent of a magnifying glass. Exciters are one of reasons "pro" recordings have a shiny, defined high end with good stereo imaging; prices on these processors are now low enough that you can take advantage of this effect as well.

## Noise Gates as Effects

Although the gate in a noise gate (described in Chapter 13) usually triggers according to the input signal, many noise gates have a separate "key input" (also called external trigger) that can trigger the gate instead of the input. This can really tighten up parts; for example, Fig. 12-10 shows a sustained bass note being gated by a kick drum pattern. You can hear the bass at the output only when the kick drum level exceeds the gate threshold, which imparts a strongly rhythmic quality to the bass.

## MIDI and Signal Processors

Almost all modern signal processors include MIDI (Musical Instrument Digital Interface) connections. Most effects respond to only two kinds of MIDI messages: *program changes* (which call up different effects programs) and *continuous controller* messages (which alter individual parameters, such as equalization boost, reverb decay, compression ratio, *etc.* in real time). This allows you to automate effects along with a mix. For more information, see Chapter 19 on Automation.

## Are Effects "Gimmicks"?

Trends come and go, so every now and then it becomes trendy to look down on signal processing and other "effects." Yet baroque com-

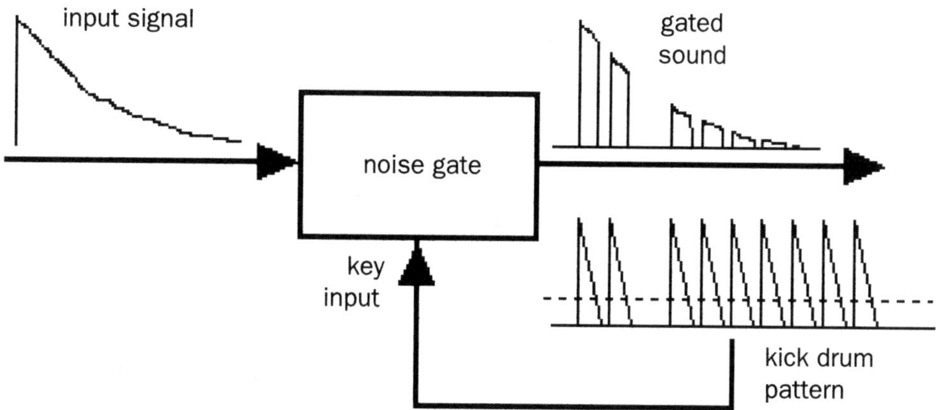


**Fig. 12-10:** *Noise gates can work as special effects, thanks to the key input.*

posers used phase shifters, extensive reverberation, and effects in their compositions. Sound incredible? Well, listen to a pipe organ in a cathedral sometime. The various standing waves and resonating pipes create an effect like hundreds of phase shifters, with the body of the building giving excellent and lush reverb characteristics. And different organ voicings resemble synthesizer presets.

So, don't just treat the studio as a static reproducer of reality, or your sounds may be static, too. The studio is a processor of reality; use the studio and work with it as an extension of your music, not as a barrier to it. If something hasn't been done before, go ahead and try it—Bach might very well have used sequencers had they been available. The effects that may be passé years from now are still waiting to be discovered. You might as well contribute to, and share in, those discoveries.

# Chapter 13
# Noise Reduction Techniques

Noise reduction not only helped the cassette make the transition from dictation to music, it allowed budget analog multitrack recording to have acceptable noise specs. Remember, adding another track of program material adds more noise, so with a sixteen- or twenty-four-track recorder, the noise contribution is substantial. And now, with digital gear putting all signals "under the microscope," we need signal sources that are as quiet as possible.

## Analog Recording and Noise Reduction

Let's see how noise creeps into an analog system. Fig. 13-1 shows a high-level signal, with the tape's residual noise level (or hiss) shown in half-tone. With a high-amplitude signal, the noise is small enough so that the signal swamps it, and we can't perceive the noise. But with a low-level signal, on playback the noise represents a significant part of the signal, which makes it much more obvious.

In the early days of recording, recording engineers used to "ride the gain" to improve the signal-to-noise ratio. Turning up the signal level going on tape during low-level passages helps keep it above the noise level, and turning down during loud signals prevents distortion . . . most of the time, at least. Riding gain requires an alert engineer who knows every nuance of a piece (it also reduces the overall dynamic range, but you can't have everything).

You could use a compressor/limiter to prevent strong peaks from overloading the tape and help raise signals above the noise, but adding even relatively conservative amounts of compression during recording does interfere with the music's dynamics.

Enter the expander, a complementary device that can "undo" the effects of compression on playback by making the soft passages soft again, and restoring the loud musical peaks we previously had to turn down to prevent tape saturation. When the expander senses a lower signal level coming from the tape, it turns itself down to approximate the original dynamics. When it senses a high level signal, it turns itself up to increase the signal level further and restore the dynamic range peaks. Although this sounds like it might really mess the signal around, in practice

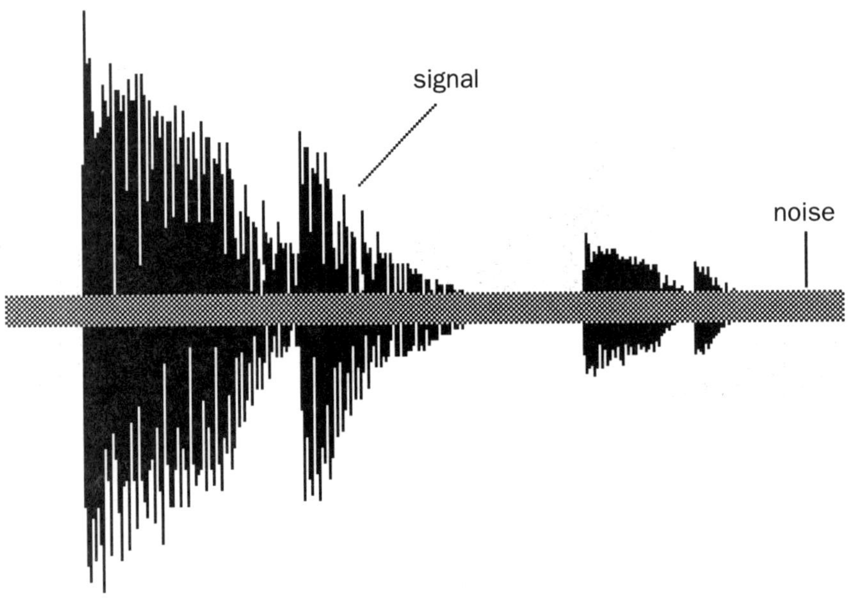


**Fig. 13-1:** *Noise is far more noticeable with low-amplitude signals than high-amplitude signals.*

compression/expansion (also called "companion") works very well and forms the basis of most modern day analog noise reduction systems.

Expansion also has a very desirable side effect: it cuts down substantially on the noise (Fig. 13-2). Expanding a low-level passage by a particular amount attenuates the tape hiss it picked up along the way by the same amount. So, we've managed to restore the music's original dynamic range, but ditched the hiss—pretty slick. Note, however, that the compressor and expander must be exactly complementary to each other, or errors will creep into the system (you don't want the expander to mistrack and create a signal that's louder or softer than the original).

There is a catch: as a piece of music must first be modified through precise compression (*encoding* the signal), and then be equivalently expanded (decoded), we cannot improve non-encoded tapes that happen to have noise; we can only reduce the noise on tapes that have been encoded using the noise-reduction system of our choice.

There are also *single-ended* noise reduction systems, such as National Semiconductor's DNR and RSP Technologies' Hush system. While not as common as the double-ended systems used for recording, they can nonetheless help salvage old tape tracks, reduce the hiss from noisy effects, and so on. These are particularly useful for cleaning up analog tracks before recording them digitally.

Now, let's look in detail at various ways of reducing noise.

## Manual Noise Reduction

Many noise reduction techniques do not require commercial devices. Keep your signal sources as clean as possible; for example, suppose you're recording an electric guitar through a hissy amp. Feed the guitar directly into the board through a direct box or preamp to eliminate the amp hiss. If the amp is required to get a certain sound, then try gain-riding and turn down the level when the guitarist isn't playing. But if you want to turn the fader on and off between individual notes, then you have to have a very high degree of skill—or you can use a noise gate.

## The Noise Gate

A *noise gate* consists of a mutable amplifier and appropriate trigger circuitry. The amplifier is like a normal amplifier, except that it may be easily muted so that it gives no gain. Thus, the amp has two possible states: full on (gate open) and full off (gate closed). This trigger circuit has an input that connects up to the signal you are processing, and is level-sensitive. If the signal appearing at its input exceeds a certain user-settable reference level (threshold), the trigger tells the gate to open. If the signal drops below the threshold, the trigger tells the gate to close. Setting the threshold just above the noise level insures that the noise will be muted when no signal is present (Fig. 13-3).

The noise gate takes advantage of the way the ear perceives sound. If a strong sound is

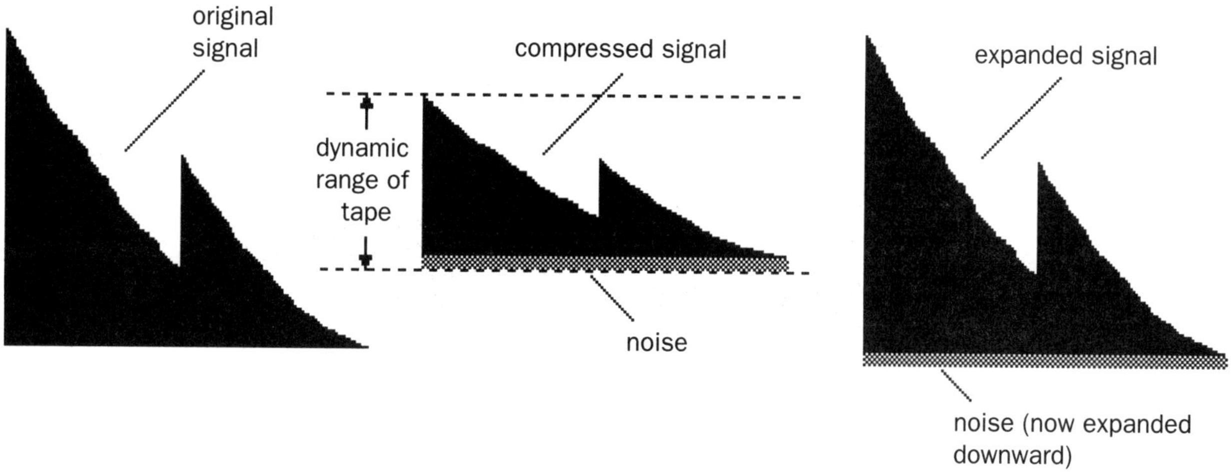


**Fig. 13-2:** *The original signal is compressed to fit within analog tape's limited dynamic range, but it also picks up some noise. On playback, expanding by an amount equal and opposite to the amount of compression restores the signal's original dynamic range, and pushes the hiss downward.*

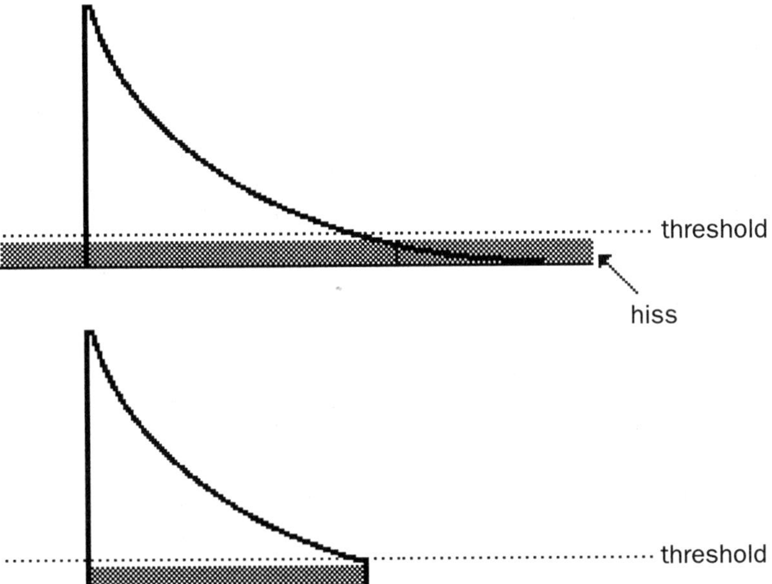


**Fig. 13-3:** *How a noise gate removes noise. The upper diagram shows the signal before gating. In the lower diagram, note that although we've masked the noise while the signal is present, the decay cuts off more abruptly than normal.*

masking a weak sound, we tend not to hear the weak sound. Although a noise gate doesn't attenuate the noise like a double-ended noise-reduction system, we have nonetheless masked a weak sound with a strong sound, so we perceive a lot less total noise coming out of the noise gate. Noise gates are also useful for getting rid of leakage.

Noise gates work best on signals that don't need to be cleaned up too much. If the noise is really severe, eliminating lots of noise also means nuking substantial portions of the signal. Another problem occurs with sounds that have long decay times. For example, a guitar's signal level can become erratic towards the end of its decay, and start criss-crossing back and forth across the threshold. This gives a "chattering" effect.

There have been several improvements to the basic noise gate to minimize these and other problems. Some noise gates include adjustable attenuation in case the contrast between the gate on and gate off conditions is too severe. With less attenuation, the gate doesn't shut down all the way so that some of the signal can still pass through.

A function called *hysteresis* affects the way the threshold works. With no hysteresis, the gate opens and closes at the same threshold. Increasing hysteresis widens the difference between the gate on and gate off levels so that a signal turns on at a slightly higher level than the threshold, and turns off at a slightly lower level than the threshold. This helps minimize accidental retriggering.

Many noise gates include a *decay time* option. This prevents the gate from closing down abruptly; instead, when the signal goes under the threshold, a certain amount of time elapses over which the noise gate fades out (Fig. 13-4).

Noise gates work best on single-instrument tracks, rather than with complex material involving lots of instruments; with so many signals going above and below the threshold, you can get some highly choppy effects. Noise gates are also very effective with vocals, since vocal lines seldom sustain throughout a song. During instrumental passages, intros, and the like, a noise gate shuts off the microphone and tape noise. This requires a singer who understands the gating process and who doesn't do some-

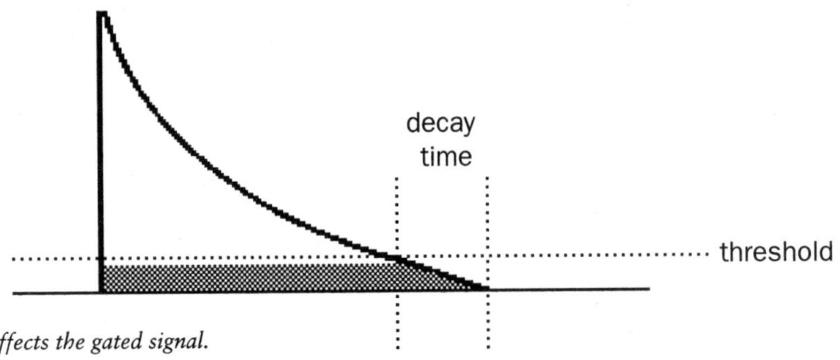


**Fig. 13-4:** *How decay time affects the gated signal.*

thing like breathe at an improper moment, thus causing the gate to open and let the breath through.

One of the best times to use noise gates is when premixing tracks. If, for example, the instrument on track 2 begins two measures after track 1, and track 3 begins four measures after track 1, during those moments when there is no signal the noise gates can shut the tracks off and prevent any noise contribution. When the tracks do come in, the noise gates can be left in or switched out. Also, as premixing implies that you'll be recording more overdubs, these overdubs and subsequent processing (such as reverb) can mask some of the noise gate's choppiness.

Noise gates by themselves are no panacea; skillful engineering, combined with noise gates, gives the best results.

## Noise Reduction Through Equalization

Eliminating a signal's high frequencies, where tape hiss is most obvious and objectionable, helps curb hiss. This technique works best with an instrument such as bass, which has little high-frequency content—removing all the treble from a cymbal would sound terrible. Cutting back on high frequencies isn't always a solution, but there's no reason to give a signal more frequency response than needed. This principle applies at low frequencies, too; if a lead guitar solo has some hum, rolling off the bass will take little away from the solo (it may even help it to cut through and sound a bit brighter), but the hum will be reduced.

## Commercial Noise Reduction Systems

The Dolby company offers five different noise reduction systems, Dolby A (the original, for professional applications), Dolby B (for consumer applications), Dolby C (for semi-pro and higher-end consumer applications), Dolby SR (top-of-the-line pro noise reduction), and Dolby S (the consumer version of SR).

Dolby B, the simplest of the bunch, uses compansion only on the higher frequencies where hiss is most apparent. While recording, high-level signals pass unmodified through the Dolby encoder, as high level signals tend to mask tape hiss. However, low-level signals have their high frequencies boosted by about 10 dB, starting at about 5 kHz. During playback, strong signals pass unchanged through the Dolby decoder, but the encoder reduces the high frequencies of low-level signals to compensate for the high frequency boost that occurred while recording. This returns the audio to its original state, and in the process, reduces high-frequency tape hiss picked up during recording.

Dolby A splits the audio spectrum into four bands, and compands (compresses/expands) each band individually. The reason for choosing four bands is to eliminate not just hiss, but other types of objectionable noise such as hum and rumble (which typically occur below 80 Hz or so), and crosstalk (generally most noticeable in the 80 Hz to 3 kHz range). Dolby A also includes two high-frequency bands for hiss control. The overall system improves the signal-to-noise ratio by about 10 dB across the entire audio range, unlike Dolby B which reduces noise only in the higher part of the spectrum.

Dolby C has fallen out of favor since Dolby S appeared, which is based on Dolby's most advanced noise reduction system, Dolby SR. The latter allows analog gear to exceed most digital technology with respect to noise and dynamic range. Its method of operation is similar to Dolby A, but far more advanced. A cassette system with Dolby S is extremely quiet.

As the Dolby system operates only on low-level signals, any mistracking between the record and playback modes is hardly noticeable (a small percentage of error on an already soft signal is hard to detect but with a high-level signal, even a small error can sound quite obvious).

## The dbx System

This is a straight compression-expansion system, along with some pre-emphasis and de-emphasis. In many ways, dbx noise reduction is the ultimate in automated gain riding during record and complementary expansion during playback.

During record, the dbx encoder compresses signals by a 2:1 ratio so that for every 2 dB increase at the input, the output increases only 1 dB. Therefore, a signal with 80 dB of dynamic range (which most analog recorders cannot handle) gets squeezed into 40 dB of dynamic range (which even a cassette can handle). On playback, this compressed signal gets expanded by a circuit that increases the gain when the input signal increases, and decreases the gain when the signal level decreases. As long as the compressor and expander are exactly complementary, the output signal will duplicate the input signal except that it will not have picked up any noise during the recording process.

Since dbx works on the overall signal, noise

problems other than hiss (hum, modulation noise, *etc.*) are also controlled. The use of pre-emphasis/de-emphasis helps reduce hiss and also contributes to a more natural sound.

## Does Noise Reduction Interfere with the Sound?

Any time you pass a signal through an electronic circuit, it's going to be altered. It just so happens that noise also goes away when altered according to the wishes of a noise reduction unit, so if you want to get rid of noise, you are going to have to mess with the signal.

A carefully set up and aligned noise reduction system should be virtually undetectable, but electronic circuits are never perfect, so any mistracking—no matter now minuscule—is going to be noticed; after all, an engineer's livelihood depends upon being able to hear infinitesimal changes of sound.

The main complaint about the Dolby system is that it splits the audio spectrum into several bands, so it is conceivable that an instrument's fundamental could be processed differently from the harmonics. Also, Dolby must be carefully calibrated before use. But the bottom line is simple: if you object to tape hiss, and if you want to avoid hiss build-up while overdubbing, then you must use some form of noise reduction. And although you can nitpick them, they are really quite sophisticated, and have advanced the quality of sound tremendously.

## Digital Recording and Noise Reduction

Digital recorders have inherently less hiss than analog recorders, which generally eliminates the need for noise reduction. However, there are still many elements that contribute just as much noise to a digital system as they do to an analog system, such as consoles, guitar amps, effects, mic preamps, *etc.* It's important to be aware of these potential noise sources and do all you can to keep them from getting recorded. Here are some tips on how to find and minimize each noise contribution.

First, listen using headphones—you'll hear much more detail. Then, start from your mastering deck and work "upstream." Turn down all the volume sliders; any noise you hear is the residual mixer noise. Now work your way back toward each signal source. Turn up individual faders, enable/bypass EQ, vary the mic preamp gain, *etc.* to help isolate the main noise sources.

Here's how to reduce some noise problems you might encounter.

### Mixers

- Use proper gain staging. The relationship between channel and master faders is crucial in keeping noise to a minimum. This is because the master control is typically post-summing amp (an active stage that contributes noise), while the channel faders are pre-summing amp (Figs. 13-5A and B). The goal is to keep the master level down to minimize summing amp noise, while turning the input faders up as much as possible short of distortion. Here's why.

  We'll assume the mixer has a gain of two. In Fig. 13-5A, channel fader (B) reduces audio (A) to half its level. Meanwhile, the mixer generates some noise (C). The gain of two brings the signal back to its original level, which now includes the mixer noise (D).

  In 13-5B, the channel fader is up full, so the audio (B) hitting the mixer is at full strength. However, since the mixer adds a gain of two, we cut the master volume in half to return the signal to its original level (D). Cutting the output in half also turns down the noise coming out of the mixer by half. So, the signal-to-noise ratio in Fig. 13-5B is twice that of Fig. 13-5A.

  Note: With many mixers, in solo mode the level meters indicate how close you are to exceeding the available headroom. It's good to check this periodically.

- Keep any unused level control turned down, including effects returns, even if there is no signal feeding the input. Also check for "gotchas"—for example, if a switch lets you send a subgroup to the master and the subgroup level controls are up, they will contribute hiss.
- If your system can switch between –10 and +4 dB, use +4 dB. The extra level improves the signal-to-noise ratio enough to make a difference, assuming your gear is +4 compatible.
- Sometimes the effects used for "mastering" (*i.e.,* they patch between the mixer out and master deck input) include single-ended noise reduction. Examples: The Dolby 740 (multi-band low-level compressor) and RSP Technologies Reanimator (compressor/limiter) can not only provide their respective effects, but reduce noise.

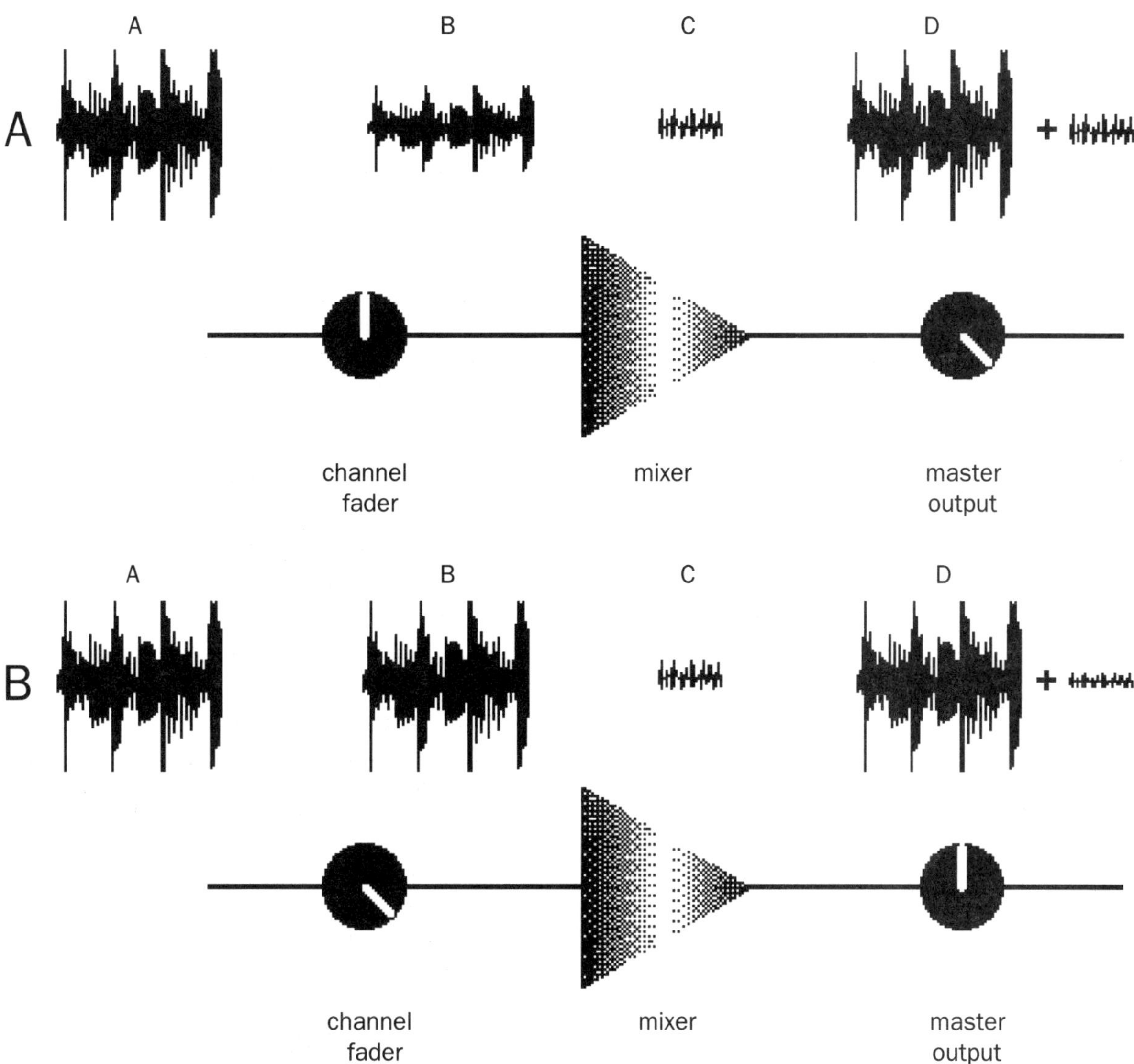


**Fig. 13-5:** *How proper mixer gain staging reduces noise.*

## Guitars

- Tube preamps and emulators are often far quieter than miking a tube amp. But if you're also adding some amp sound in the background, be careful: Positioning the mic more than a couple of feet from the amp could create phase cancellations because the miked sound will be delayed compared to the direct sound. It's easy to move the audio with a hard disk system so that the two signals lock together. With an MDM, either delay the direct sound by a few milliseconds, or better yet, set a track offset (if available) to advance the miked track by a few milliseconds to bring it into line with the direct track.
- Transformers, computers, hard drives, *etc.* can leak interference into pickups. While the guitarist can angle away from sources of noise, even the slightest movement could allow noise to re-enter. Turn off computers, synths, and other digital gear (unless needed) while recording.

## Synthesizers

- Turn the master volume slider up full. This usually varies the level going *into* the output stage, so the output noise remains constant regardless of the level going into it. If this setting causes distortion, decrease levels elsewhere in the synth (see the next tip). Note that varying MIDI controller 7 to control master volume may or may not exhibit the same problem.
- Proper gain staging is important. Like mixers, a synth has several program parameters that affect level—DCA or oscillator output, an overall level for the patch, levels for various "links" in a multitimbral "perfor-

mance," and so on. Keep levels as high as possible (short of distortion), especially toward the beginning of the signal chain.

- Use onboard effects sparingly. External effects can be better and quieter.

## Signal Processors

- Check what's coming out of your effects returns; reverbs are notorious for dumping noise into the master output bus. Also determine whether the effects unit has internal noise gating. Sometimes adjusting the threshold up a little from the factory setting is all that's needed.
- For devices such as reverb that "chatter" with normal noise gating, single-ended noise reduction systems (*e.g.*, RSP Hush) are the answer. (These can also reduce the output noise of the mixer itself, and tame hissy guitar amps.)
- Using an old analog noise reduction unit with your effects will work only if the output signal has the same amplitude envelope as the input signal (the *level* can be different, but the *shape* has to be the same). This pretty much limits companion-style noise reduction to processing delay lines.
- Hit the inputs with as much signal level as possible, but be careful. Some effects monitor the level coming into the unit, so if the preset adds a lot of gain and overloads the internal circuitry, this won't show up on the meters, yet the sound will be distorted. If your processor can monitor the output headroom rather than the input, this tells you more.

## Using Hard Disk Editing

If you're *really* picky, use a hard disk recording system (or bounce tracks over to one) and apply a noise reduction "plug-in" program. You can also do noise reduction manually by applying a variety of edits including silence, fades, and EQ to minimize noise, as described in Chapter 3. It's time-consuming, but hard disk editing can do absolute wonders for hissy tracks.

# Chapter 14
# Understanding Synchronization

Musical synchronization has not changed much since the days when people first began beating on logs. In fact, it's easier to understand all these mysterious little SMPTE/MIDI/synchronizing boxes if you realize that deep down, they're just trying to emulate human behavior.

With human players, one person (typically a drummer) keeps time and the other players follow that person for their timing cues. The players constantly monitor the drummer, and if the tempo speeds up or slows down a little bit, adjust their speed to compensate.

Electronic synchronization works similarly: you appoint one device as a master timekeeper, and have all other devices respond to the timing data generated by the master rather than follow their own internal timing. This chapter covers the many possible ways to synchronize, from early clock-pulse based systems on up to SMPTE.

## Synchronization Applications

Synchronization has several important functions in the project studio:

- Synchronize multitrack recorders together (whether analog or digital tape, hard disk, MIDI sequencing, or some combination) to create more tracks. For example, you can sync two eight-track modular digital multitracks together for sixteen tracks. When you press the transport controls on one machine, the other one follows right along. You can also synchronize a MIDI sequencer to tape or hard disk and record MIDI data in the sequencer along with audio data in the hard disk or tape recorder.
- Synchronize an automated mixdown system and/or signal processing system to a multitrack recorder to automate your mixing moves.
- Interdevice MIDI communication. For example, sync a drum machine to a sequencer that is itself synchronized to tape or hard disk.
- Synchronizing two or more dissimilar devices together to create a "multimedia" setup (*e.g.,* synchronizing an audio recorder to a video recorder to create a soundtrack that matches with the video, or a sequencer and audio recorder synched to a video recorder).
- Digital audio synchronization. In many situations, digital audio signals need to be synchronized to a master clock to prevent "jitter" that can degrade sound quality.

## Synchronization Basics

Suppose you have two rhythmically oriented devices, such as a sequencer and drum machine, and want them to play together (*i.e.,* when the sequencer starts playing, the drum machine starts at the same time; and if the sequencer plays through a certain number of measures, the drum machine will have played through the same number of measures). You could set both units to the same tempo and press their play buttons at the same time, but this doesn't insure sync. It is unlikely you'd push both play buttons at *exactly* the same time, and if the tempo of one of the units drifts by even a tiny amount, the two units will drift out of sync.

However, many digital devices are so stable that these days, if they do start at the same time, they will at least appear to remain in sync because the amount of drift is so small. I've "free-synched" a digital multitrack recorder to a video recorder and at the end of twenty minutes, there was only a few milliseconds of drift. I've also free-synched a MIDI sequencer to a digital audio recorder with similar results. Although with sufficient patience you can coax this kind of "nonsynchronization" to work, a more consistent answer to all these problems is synchronization.

We'll start off by covering pre-MIDI synchronization systems, then MIDI sync, then SMPTE synchronization (the standard used in most modern studios).

## Audio Sync Signals

A very basic synchronization method involves sending a stream of evenly spaced pulses (sort of like a high-speed metronome click) from one unit to another. Each clock is a pulse of energy, like the "tick" or "tock" of a clock, except that a clock pulse swings back and forth between a maximum and minimum voltage. This is a very unambiguous type of signal; it's either full on or full off.

Suppose the master unit—say, a drum machine—generates a timing pulse every thirty-second note as it plays. If we set up the slave (perhaps a sequencer) so that each timing pulse it receives advances the sequence one thirty-second note, the drum machine and sequencer will play together. Just start them at the same time, and they'll remain synchronized, as the sequencer follows the drum's synchronization pulses.

Clock rates for this type of gear are usually specified in pulses per quarter note (PPQN for short). In the above example, since there are eight thirty-second notes in a quarter note, the clock rate is eight PPQN. However, this limits us to thirty-second note resolution, since there would be no way to step through the sequence at a finer resolution, such as sixty-fourth notes. Therefore, many manufacturers have agreed on a timing standard of twenty-four PPQN, which gives sixty-fourth note triplet resolution. As one example, MIDI timing messages (described later) are emitted twenty-four times per quarter note. (However, it is possible to obtain higher resolutions within MIDI's twenty-four PPQN protocol, as described later.)

One problem with pulse-based systems is that one pulse looks just like any other pulse from an electrical standpoint. So, if you start a master drum machine and halfway through the song put a slave sequencer into play mode, the sequencer will interpret the first pulse received as the start of the song. (This assumes that the slave is set to follow an external clock.) If you put the sequencer into play mode three-quarters of the way through the song, it will *still* interpret the first pulse received as the start of the song. Therefore, to insure proper sync, you would press play on the slave unit first. Because it would be set to receive an external clock, it would just sit there until you pressed play on the master drum machine, whereupon the drum machine would send out its first pulse, the sequencer would recognize it as the first pulse of the song, and the two would start playing away. As the drum machine generated more pulses, the sequencer would keep counting right along and maintain proper synchronization.

Stopping is simple: just tell the master to stop. It will stop generating pulses, and the sequencer will no longer advance if it doesn't receive any more pulses.

The simplest (and least reliable) method of audio sync-to-tape involves recording audio sync pulses on tape, and on playback, feeding the taped sync signal back into a device's external clock jack. The taped sync track provides the system's master clock. If acoustic tracks are recorded in sync with this track (by playing along with a drum machine or sequencer that uses the sync track as a master clock), then the acoustic tracks and electronic tracks will be in sync with each other.

It's not easy to make simple audio tape synchronization work reliably. If any tape dropouts occur, some pulses may be lost. Once those pulses are lost, it is usually not possible to regain synchronization past the last pulse.

## MIDI Sync

The MIDI specification includes extensive synchronization capabilities that are much more sophisticated than audio sync. MIDI synchronization occurs through digital timing messages that are exchanged between pieces of equipment over the MIDI cable.

### Start, Stop, and Continue

Synchronization messages are examples of System Common data, so called because this type of data affects the entire system (all instruments on all channels), not just individual instruments on individual channels. There are three main MIDI timing messages:

- *Start* tells the slave when the master has started so that the two units can start together. Start always causes a device to start at the very beginning.
- *Stop* tells the slave when the master has stopped so that the two units can stop together.
- *Continue* tells the slave to resume playing from where it was last stopped so that the two units can continue together from that point.

The master MIDI clock emits twenty-four MIDI clock messages every quarter note. When a slave receives one of these clock messages, it advances its internal clock 1/24th of a quarter note. In MIDI, clock messages have priority over all other messages to insure accurate timekeeping. Many devices further subdivide this clock rate internally so that events may be recorded with greater resolution—up to every 1/480th of a quarter note (or even more) for some sequencers.

## Song Position Pointer Messages

MIDI Song Position Pointer messages (SPP messages for short) keep track of how many sixteenth notes have elapsed since the beginning of a tune (up to 16,384 total). An SPP message is usually issued just prior to a continue command, which provides autolocation. For example, suppose a sequencer provides the master clock, and a drum machine is the slave. If you start the sequencer somewhere in the middle of a song (*e.g.*, 324 sixteenth notes into the song), as soon as you start the sequencer, the following events happen:

1. The sequencer issues an SPP message that tells the drum machine, "Hey, we're 324 sixteenth notes into the song!"

2. The drum machine then finds the spot in its song that's 324 sixteenth notes from the beginning.

3. The sequencer pauses long enough for the drum machine to autolocate, then sends a continue message.

4. Both units start at the same point.

## Song Select Messages

This doesn't really relate to synchronization, but MIDI allows for sending a Song Select message that tells the various devices (drum machine, sequencer, *etc.*) which song is about to be played from a possible 128 songs.

## MIDI Synchronization in Action

Synching MIDI gear to tape (or hard disk) is the equivalent of two multitrack recorders operating in tandem. This eliminates the need to record drum machine or sequenced synthesizer parts, because you can use the master clock (or "sync track") coming from the master multitrack to trigger the drum machine and/or sequencer in real time. Thus, the audio outputs of the drum machine or sequenced synthesizers are virtually equivalent to the tape track outputs: they sound just like a tape track, play along with the other tape tracks, and feed into your mixing console just like a tape track. In fact, the outputs from the electronic instruments are often called "virtual tracks" because they are "virtually" the same as the tape tracks (Fig. 14-1).

Using this type of approach offers many advantages compared to simply recording everything on tape. If your MIDI gear responds to MIDI volume controller messages, you can record that data in your sequencer, and use it to control levels during playback. This is the equivalent of instant automated mixdown for your MIDI gear, and with nothing to degrade performance (for more information, see Chapter 19 on Automation).

If the keyboard is a "workstation" type, which includes an onboard sequencer that responds to SPP, you can sync it to the same timing signals as the main sequencer. You can therefore record your keyboard parts into the keyboard, and free up your main sequencer to record lots of other tracks. And since the keyboard operates independently of the main sequencer (timing data is not sent over any specific channel, but is "globally" received), this strategy also circumvents MIDI's sixteen-channel limitation, as the main sequencer can still send out signals on sixteen different MIDI channels. You could also synchronize a drum machine to this setup and gain even more tracks.

Sequencers are also useful for controlling automated mixing and signal processing. The sequencer could be the usual "stand-alone" type, or it could be part of an automated mixdown system, and run concurrently with other MIDI sequencers if desired.

Not having to record sequenced synthesizer parts on tape economizes on tape or hard disk tracks. Many home studios use a digital or analog multitrack to handle acoustic instruments, and virtual tracks to expand the total number of tracks.

Hard disk systems, because they are computer-based, can often add some useful twists. For example, a MIDI sequencer might be built into the program, so it then becomes unnecessary to sync an external device. The hard disk system might also generate SMPTE Time Code, as discussed later, to provide synchronization signals.

# Advanced Tape Synchronization

In the constant quest for more reliable musical synchronization methods, three main methods have evolved: Song Pointer, SMPTE-to-MIDI conversion, and MIDI Time Code. In today's studio, SMPTE generally provides the system master clock, while MIDI acts as an intelligent interface between various pieces of equipment.

Because the sync track is crucial, it must be consistent. A tape dropout, or crosstalk from an adjacent track, could cause problems. With analog gear, it's traditional to record the sync

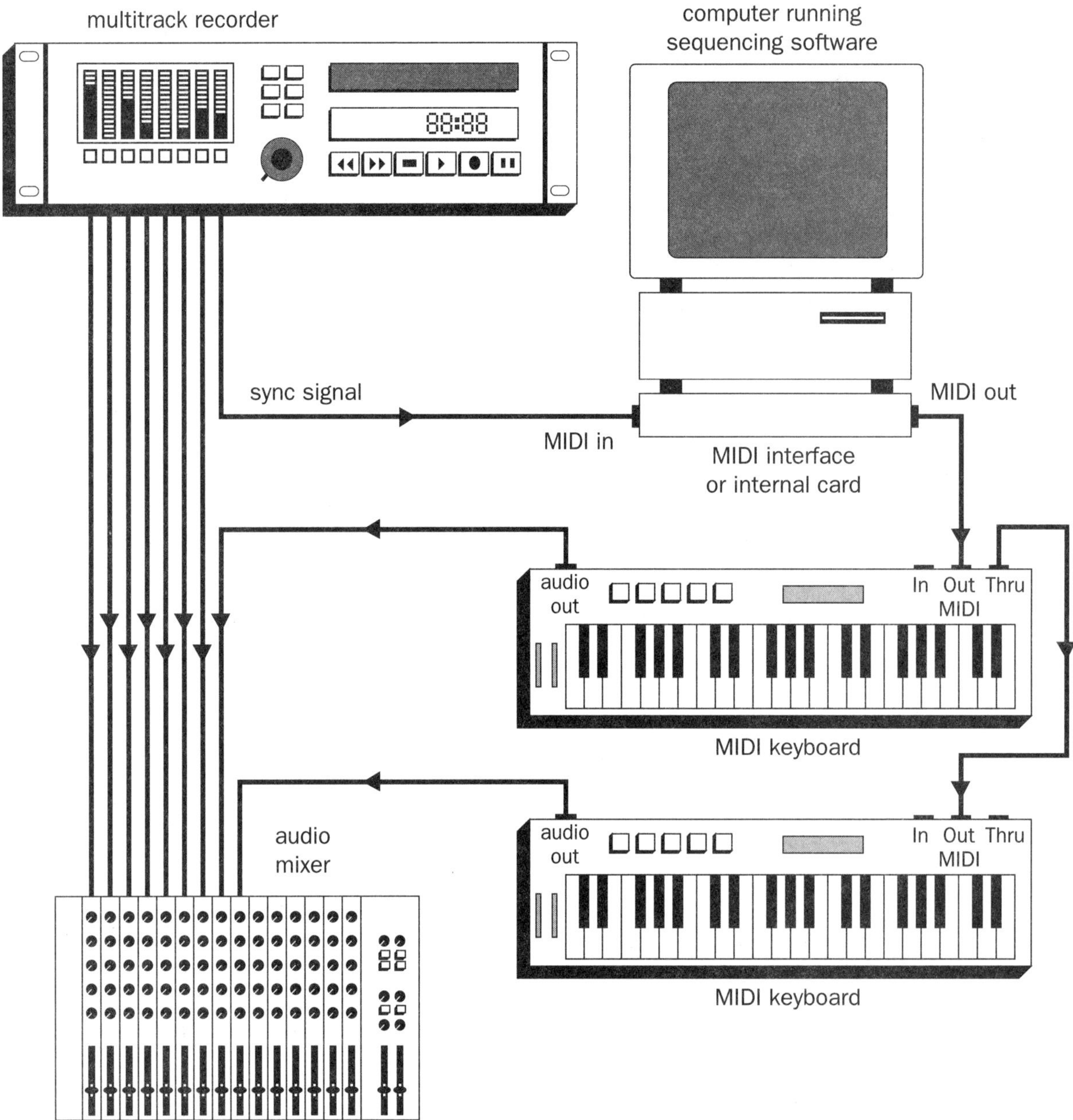


**Fig. 14-1:** *Typical virtual tracks setup. The multitrack digital tape recorder provides a sync signal to which the sequencer synchronizes. The sequencer in turn drives two* MIDI *keyboards in time with the tape, whose outputs feed a conventional audio mixer along with the multitrack's audio outputs to give more tracks. With this setup, you don't really need to think about starting and stopping the sequencer; as you start and stop the tape, the sync converter produces the appropriate commands to start and stop the sequencer.*

track on an outside tape track (*i.e.*, the highest- or lowest-numbered track). That way, there will only be one adjacent track to contribute crosstalk. This also reduces the chance that the sync track, which is often recorded at a reasonable level (*e.g.*, –10 to –6 VU), will bleed into audio tracks. With digital recording, this is not an issue.

## Song Pointer Tape Sync

It would be great to simply record SPP messages on a tape track and use these to provide sync, but MIDI sync signals cannot be recorded directly on tape because they run at 31.25 kHz—a higher frequency than multitracks can handle. However, there are hardware boxes (such as those made by the JL Cooper company) that translate SPP data and clock pulses into audio tones (called FSK, or Frequency-Shift Keying) that can be recorded on tape. As you play back a sequence, the SPP data gets recorded on tape as an audio sync signal. On playback, these audio tones are decoded back into SPP messages; therefore the tape serves as a master MIDI clock that issues SPP messages.

The big advantage over recording regular audio sync on tape is that SPP identifies the precise tape location, expressed as the number of sixteenth notes that have elapsed since a composition began. One limitation, though, is that once the SPP data is recorded on tape, the tempo is fixed and cannot be altered. However, you can initially record a sync track whose tempo varies.

## SMPTE-to-MIDI Conversion

SMPTE stands for Society of Motion Picture and Television Engineers, the professional organization that devised a time code system (based on a protocol developed by NASA for logging data from space probes) for synchronizing audio to film and video. A *SMPTE Time Code generator* generates "timing markers" that are recorded on one track of tape at regular intervals, thus serving as a super-accurate index counter. Hard disk recording systems, since they run off an internal clock, often generate SMPTE timing messages without requiring external hardware or a dedicated sync track. Sync control units for digital tape machines, such as the Alesis BRC, can also provide the same function.

Each SMPTE marker specifies the elapsed time in hours, minutes, seconds, and frames. The exact duration of a frame varies for different applications. For film work, there are twenty-four frames per second (*i.e.,* each frame equals 1/24th of a second). For black and white video, the rate is thirty frames per second in the U.S. and twenty-five frames per second in Europe. For USA-standard NTSC color, the rate is 29.97 frames per second (for reasons far too complicated to go into here). Most of the time, if you live in the U.S. you will work with thirty or twenty-four frames per second for audio work; in Europe, twenty-five or twenty-four frames per second.

Furthermore, each frame is further divided into eighty subframes, with each subframe being a little less than half a millisecond long. A typical time code location might be 00:10:08:20:(76), which you would read as 00 hours, 10 minutes, 8 seconds, 20 frames, and 76 subframes. SMPTE also provides "user bits" for including custom pieces of data in the time code, but most of the time you'll be dealing with just hours, minutes, seconds, and frames.

*A SMPTE Time Code reader* reads the SMPTE markers from tape for synchronization purposes. Like SPP, this is a major improvement over the simple audio tape sync system, since all pulses don't look the same; each SMPTE marker is unique. This is considered an "intelligent" sync system since it knows where it is on the tape.

However, we do have one problem. SMPTE Time Code is based on *absolute* time in hours, minutes, second, and frames. Musical rhythm, on the other hand, is based on measures and beats, which relate to *relative* time. For example, with $\frac{4}{4}$ music at 40 beats per minute, each measure lasts six seconds; with $\frac{4}{4}$ music at 120 beats per minute, each measure lasts two seconds. Therefore, we need a way to convert absolute time (as represented by SMPTE) into "musical time," which brings us to the SMPTE-to-MIDI converter. This type of box reads SMPTE, then translates SMPTE times into MIDI SPP data.

Advanced SMPTE-to-MIDI boxes accommodate tempo changes by letting you define a "beat map" or "tempo map," where every time you enter or tap a beat, it is related to SMPTE Time Code (*e.g.,* at 0 hours, 2 minutes, and 12 frames, increase the tempo by two beats per minute). On playback, the SMPTE Time Code serves as a consistent reference point for the beat map. With audio sync (whether pulse- or SPP-based), once you lay down a sync track you are locked to that tempo. With SMPTE, you can always create a different beat map if you want to change tempos. Many jingle and film scorers also use the beat map feature to "fudge" the tempo a bit in spots so that particular visual cues (*e.g.,* cereal pours out of a box, Godzilla eats Tokyo, *etc.*) land exactly on the beat. In other words, if the cue lags a bit behind the beat, the tempo will subtly speed up for a couple of measures prior to the cue. This moves the beat where the cue is supposed to hit closer to the cue point.

SMPTE Time Code is a reliable, and increasingly universal, method of synchronization. Its big advantage is that it allows for autolocating MIDI devices to tape; start the tape anywhere, and the SMPTE-to-MIDI converter will read the SMPTE time, translate that to an SPP message, send a Continue command, and *voilà*—your MIDI gear is synchronized perfectly to tape. What's more, should the tape become slightly damaged in one or two places so that SMPTE data is lost, most SMPTE boxes will "guess" where the markers would have been until the real markers appear again. In contrast to Song Pointer tape sync, SMPTE is a standard. SPP boxes have their own proprietary way of translating SPP messages into audio tones, so you usually have to use the same device for recording and playback.

Many computer interfaces have SMPTE-to-MIDI conversion built in, which simplifies matters. Feed the SMPTE sync track audio signal into the interface's SMPTE audio input, and SPP messages magically flow out the interface's MIDI out jack. SMPTE is the synchronization system of choice in the film and video industries. As a result, SMPTE sync is commonplace in major studios, and is now a mainstay even in budget studios.

## MIDI Time Code (MTC)

This part of the MIDI specification allows SMPTE times to be communicated directly over MIDI, thus allowing MIDI devices to respond to absolute times if necessary. An example will help get the point across of why this is desirable.

Suppose you're scoring a commercial, and also providing some sampled sound effects to be played back from a sampler. You sync your sequencer to the video, and start creating the background music. Then as you see where specific effects are to take place—a sexy kiss, car crash, crowd applause, *etc.*—you play the corresponding keys on the sampler that trigger those sound effects, and record those keypresses into the sequencer. Perfect—on playback, the tune is in sync with the video, and all the effects are triggered in just the right places.

Then the producer comes in next day, and thinks you've done a great job—but wants the song tempo sped up by five percent. So you speed up the sequence tempo, but now the rate at which the sound effects occur speeds up too, to the point where they no longer match the film. The problem is simple: the sound effects relate to absolute time—in other words, the door should slam at perhaps 12 seconds and 11 frames into the film, regardless of what the music is doing. The music itself relates to relative time.

With a MIDI Time Code–equipped sampler, you could create an *event list* of SMPTE Time Code cues, and trigger the samples via MIDI Time Code at specific times. Problem solved; you can change the sequencer tempo, yet the MIDI Time Code values remain constant, since they relate directly back to SMPTE. Therefore, the samples will be triggered at the specified times regardless of what happens with the sequencer.

In addition to specifying how SMPTE times should appear over MIDI, MIDI Time Code provides a standardized way of exchanging event lists between pieces of gear.

## Machine-to-Machine Sync with SMPTE

Before MIDI sequencers and hard disk recorders became commonplace, SMPTE's main audio use was to synchronize two tape recorders together by way of an expensive *chase-locking synchronizer,* so called because the synchronizer causes the slave to "chase" the master and "lock" to the master's time code. Both the master and the slave must have SMPTE Time Code recorded on one track; when the tape is rolling, this data feeds into the synchronizer. The synchronizer reads the time code from the two machines and compares them. If the slave is running a little slow or fast compared to the master, the synchronizer sends an appropriate correction signal to the slave so that the two machines maintain sync.

Today's modular digital multitracks build in chase-locking synchronization to allow for hassle-free machine-to-machine sync. Normally, you don't even have to adjust any parameters; send one machine's sync out to another machine's sync in, and you're set. You can even "daisy-chain" multiple machines together (Fig. 14-2).

Machine-to-machine sync has several applications. In addition to locking multitrack machines together to obtain more tracks (*e.g.,* three eight-track recorders slaved together give twenty-four tracks total), a popular analog recording application is to create "slave reels" in order to avoid playing a master tape too many times. Once the rhythm tracks are recorded on the master machine, these tracks can be premixed to one or two tracks on the slave machine. Overdubs are then added to the reel on the slave machine. Once overdubs are complete, sync the slave and master machines together, then transfer the overdubbed parts to the master reel.

A final SMPTE application involves "pyramiding." Suppose you have an eight-track analog deck at home, but need more than eight tracks to complete a project. Here's what you'd do:

1. Record SMPTE on one track of the eight-track, then fill up the other tracks with parts.

2. Book some time at a twenty-four-track studio and transfer the eight tracks, including SMPTE, over to the twenty-four track. It's best practice to regenerate the SMPTE Time Code so the twenty-four track has fresh code. You do this by using a SMPTE generator for the sync signal, and recording its output on the target deck.

3. Sync the twenty-four track and eight-track together, and make a premix from the twenty-four to one track of the eight-track.

4. Go home, and load up the remaining six tracks on your eight-track.

5. Book some more time, sync the twenty-four-track and eight-track machines together, transfer the new overdubs, and so on until all twenty-four tracks are filled up.

This can save a lot of money; the time required to transfer the parts is minimal, so the only significant studio cost is for mixdown time.

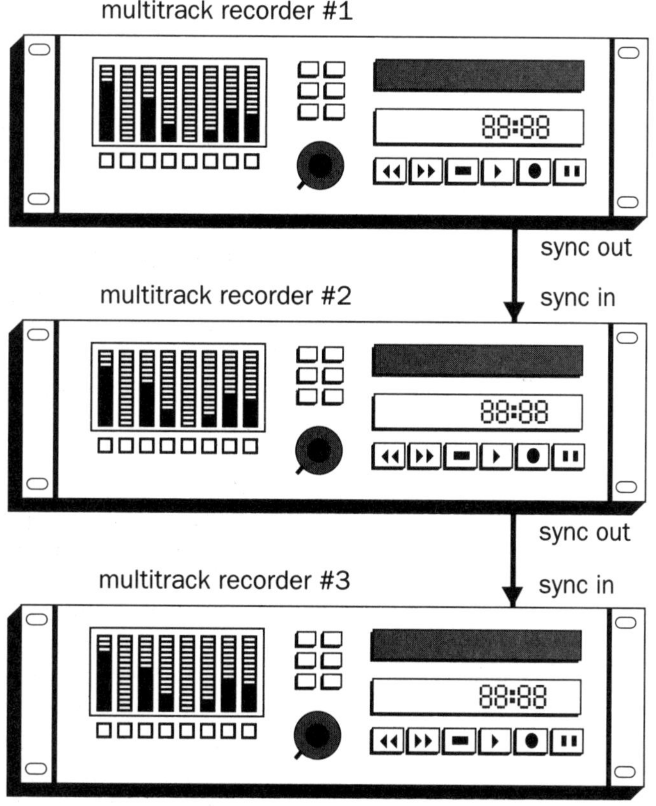


**Fig. 14-2:** *How to "daisy chain" several modular digital multitracks together so that they operate as one unified machine.*

## Timing "Slop"

Unfortunately, sync is not perfect and sometimes you may hear some sloppiness in the tempo. This can happen with any kind of machine-to-machine sync, including sequencer-to-recorder sync. Slop can be caused by several different problems; following is a list of these, as well as possible solutions.

- Keyboard is slow to respond to MIDI. Solution: Do not operate in a multitimbral mode if possible, as this usually degrades response time.
- Computer itself is slow. Solutions: Turn off all extraneous extensions that could be asking the computer for attention, such as screen savers, background fax receivers, *etc.* Add an accelerator board. Run in black and white instead of color.
- Sequencer does a poor job of decoding SMPTE. Solution: Use SPP messages instead for synchronization.

## Digital Audio Clock Sync

Digital signals, such as those carried by AES/EBU lines, are clocked at a particular rate; the transmitter and receiver must synchronize to this rate. In general, the transmitter provides the sync signal to which the receiver synchronizes. For example, in the Pro Tools hard disk recording program, there is a menu selection for hardware that specifies whether the system will respond to its own internal clock or an external digital clock. When sending data from Pro Tools, this should be set on internal. When Pro Tools is receiving data (*e.g.*, from a DAT machine), then it is set to digital so it can receive the external digital clock.

Sometimes you'll hear little ticks and pops if you monitor the audio during a transfer process. Generally, these are caused by slight timing anomalies between the two signals that disappear when you play back the transferred signal by itself. If you hear massive clicks, distorted sound, or pitch variations, odds are the receiver is not synchronizing properly to the transmitter.

## Feedback Loops

It is also possible to get digital feedback loops. Suppose you have a two-track, computer-based hard disk editing system hooked up to DAT by way of AES/EBU cables (Fig. 14-3). The hard disk provides the clock to which the DAT syncs, but the DAT itself provides a clock signal at its output. The hard disk sees this at its input and tries to sync to it. Uh-oh, feedback loop. This manifests itself not as a howl, but instead creates audio confusion that sounds somewhat like a shortwave receiver having a very bad nightmare.

The simplest solution is to disconnect the line that's not being used. For example, if you're trying to get data from the hard disk system to DAT, disconnect the line going from the DAT AES/EBU out to the hard disk in.

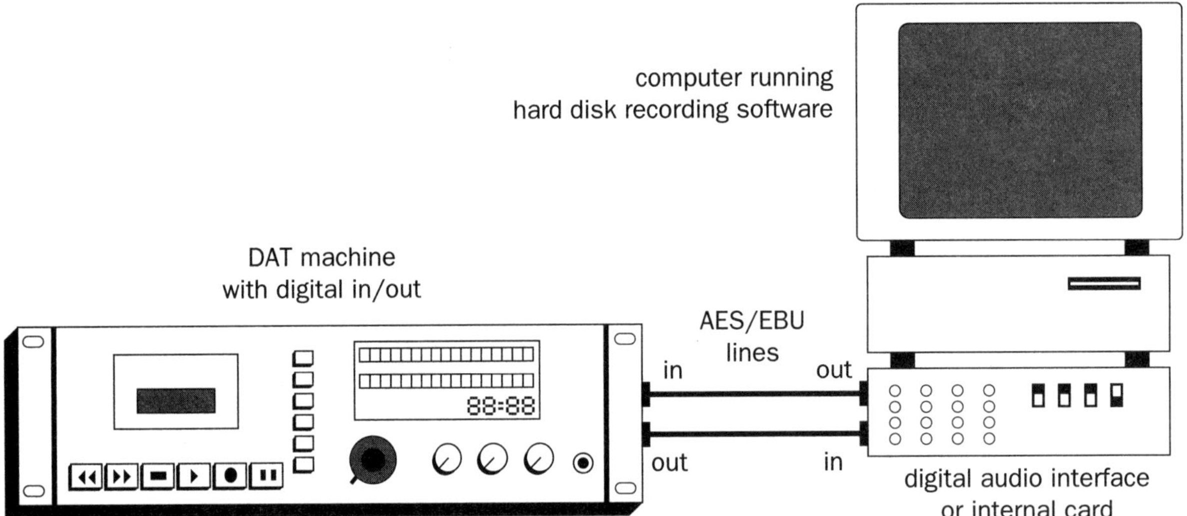


**Fig. 14-3:** *Hooking up a digital two-track editing system to a* DAT *using AES/EBU lines. In more consumer-oriented gear, the transfer protocol might be S/PDIF instead of AES/EBU.*

# Chapter 15
# Computers and the Studio

The computer has revolutionized the studio. Whether concealed within an instrument like a programmable polyphonic synthesizer, or as the center of a complete music system, computers have made it easier to play, record, and compose music. This chapter discusses some music/studio-related computer concepts, as well as practical tips on getting along with computers.

## Computer Basics

Those who study the sociological impact of computers talk about "computer literacy"—the idea that computers do not operate like machines from the industrial age, and that only those who are "literate" in computers can obtain maximum benefits from them. While this may be somewhat of an overstatement (after all, companies strive to develop computers that do not require specialized knowledge), computers do require a different mindset from what we're used to with traditional recording gear. Let's examine some of those differences.

### Hardware versus Software

Hardware refers to a machine. A piece of hardware (like a guitar) is said to be *dedicated*—namely, it performs a specific set of functions, and to change those functions would require changing the hardware. A computer, on the other hand, is a general purpose piece of hardware whose operating characteristics are defined by the software that controls it.

For an analogy, consider the player piano, which is a piece of hardware. It is more or less useless as a player piano until you insert a piano roll, which you can think of as the "software" that defines what the piano will play. Stick in a piano roll of "Tiger Rag," and the player piano becomes a "Tiger Rag" generator. Stick in a piano roll of "What's Love Got to Do with It," and it becomes a "What's Love Got to Do with It" generator.

In one sense, this instrument is free from obsolescence because as new songs become available they may be transcribed in punched paper form, allowing a player piano created decades ago to play a song that hit the Top 40 last week. (This is the same reasoning computer companies use to claim that software-driven devices will "never become obsolete.") Of course, this assumes that some company will continue to make compatible piano rolls. . . .

A computer plays with numbers, and these numbers can stand for anything—the alphabet, musical notes, Klingons in a space shoot 'em up game, whatever. The software defines how the computer will process these numbers. Thus, if new functions are needed (*e.g.*, the ability to take a series of notes and play them in reverse or transpose them), you simply edit the software so that the machine manipulates these numbers (or notes) as desired.

Software also helps forestall obsolescence because the same software that tells the computer what to do with its data also tells the computer how to communicate with the outside world. For example, after MIDI Machine Control became popular (see Chapter 19), several manufacturers offered new software that allowed a device to respond to MMC commands.

### Peripherals

Peripherals are devices that attach to the computer—MIDI interfaces, video monitors, printers, modems, external memory devices, *etc.*—that supplement the main computer and perform specific tasks.

### Understanding Memory

In the player piano example, the piano does not remember which notes to play: that information is stored on the paper rolls, in the form of holes cut in the paper. Computer memory is conceptually similar, except you have semiconductor chips instead of paper, and instead of cutting holes, you store data electrically in these chips.

There are two main types of memory used in a computer, *volatile* memory (also known as random access memory or RAM, where data is retained as long as the machine is on), and *nonvolatile* memory (also known as read-only memory or ROM, where data is stored permanently). A use of nonvolatile memory is holding the software that tells a recorder how to respond to transport switch presses, as this software fulfills the same function every time you use the recorder. On the other hand, RAM might hold a series of autolocation points. These are parameters that need to be memorized, but only temporarily.

There are occasions where even though some data might not be permanent, you want to save it for later use (such as the data for synthesizer patches you've edited). This requires battery-backup RAM, which trickles enough current into the memory to retain any stored data, but doesn't draw much power. Most computer-based devices offer some kind of data backup option (anything from an internal disk drive to the ability to translate parameters into MIDI data that can be stored by a MIDI device) so you can save multiple copies of data.

### About Interfaces

An *interface* is the hardware/software go-between between your computer and the outside world. Because computers are general-purpose devices, the interfaces included with most computers communicate with common peripherals like printers, terminals, modems, *etc.* (although some computers do include a MIDI interface as standard equipment). A MIDI interface is required because MIDI does not use the same kind of signals associated with printers or terminals, so the MIDI interface translates MIDI messages into a form your computer can understand (and similarly translates computer messages into MIDI). The interface may be an external hardware box or a plug-in card.

### Function Keys

Software can instruct the computer to think of a switch as having one function under one set of conditions, but a different function under a different set of conditions. So, with many computer-based devices, one pushbutton can perform multiple functions by pressing a *function* key. This is like using a typewriter and pressing the "shift" button, which transforms all the lower case letter keys into upper case letter keys.

For example, if you're editing punch points with a multitrack recorder's remote control, then a numeric keypad would provide punch point locations. If you're in a mode where you want to recall a particular song, then the numeric keypad would provide song number information. This saves hardware (often the most expensive part of a product), since one switch can do double duty.

### Sequenced Instructions

Sometimes buttons must be pressed in a specific order. For example, you may need to press and hold down one pushbutton, and while holding down this button, tap another button momentarily to complete the function. This might seem confusing at first, but it becomes second nature after a while.

### The Concept of "Entering"

Instructing a computer to do something is often a two-step process, where you first give it an instruction, then *enter* that instruction into the computer's memory. This two-step process is necessary because if you type in one instruction, and then another, the computer might interpret this combination as one big instruction. Entering alerts the computer to the fact that the instruction is complete. Once entered, you may move along to the next instruction.

### Power and Other Considerations

Computers can be sensitive, and it is a credit to manufacturers that they make computer-based machines that are reliable enough to take on the road and use in unfriendly environments. Still, if you have power dropouts, brownouts, or improper AC voltage, problems can result. Sometimes adding a line filter or voltage stabilizer (available at computer stores) will give an extra measure of reliability (see Chapter 7 for more information on AC power line protection).

Remember that computers generate heat, so do not block any ventilation holes, or expose a computer-based instrument to heat sources (putting a computerized device in direct sunlight is not a good idea). Dust and dirt can also cause problems with the tight traces found on circuit boards; don't blow smoke toward microprocessor-controlled gear. See Chapter 22 for other tips on computer preventive maintenance.

## Computer Applications

A computer has five main applications in the studio:

- Sequencing/notation (see Chapter 4 on MIDI recording).
- Synth storage/patch editing. This type of software provides a "virtual front panel" for instruments that have a less-than-wonderful

user interface. All, or most, of the device parameters are editable on-screen and can be saved to memory.

- Hard disk recording (see Chapter 3 on digital recording).
- Visual sample editing. This lets you process sampled sound and digital audio in several ways: cut/copy/paste audio, alter equalization, loop repetitive segments, mix samples, and so on.
- Business (client lists, keeping track of the potfuls of money from your triple platinum album, *etc.*).

Hobbyists and songwriters may not really need a computer; a good keyboard workstation will have an onboard sequencer and include a disk drive for mass storage of programs. (And however inconvenient, you can always edit from the front panel.) Use tape recorders instead of hard disk recording, and for business, use paper and pencil.

However, if you've contemplated buying a computer or upgrading your current model, putting a studio together may be all the incentive you need to finally make the move. But which machine?

The computer business is always in flux. Currently, IBM's PC architecture dominates the hardware, and Microsoft's Windows the software. Apple's Macintosh hardware and software is the main competitor, but has a far smaller market share. The Amiga and Atari computers, which were once major players for music and recording, have moved on to a special form of computer heaven reserved for gear produced by companies with great products but deficient marketing.

Both the PC and Mac are capable music and recording machines. In fact, in many ways they are equivalent, as much music software was developed on the Macintosh and ported over to the PC once it started to achieve market dominance. However, Mac enthusiasts still claim—with much justification—that the Mac system is easier to learn, configure, and use.

The computer you choose may depend on what other applications you want to run along with music and/or recording. The Macintosh reigns for desktop publishing and graphics, whereas the PC has an abundance of business and scientific programs available. So if you're a musician moonlighting as a graphic artist, the Mac might be the way to go. If you're an engineer who dabbles with music as a hobby, then the PC is probably the computer of choice.

## Computer Peripherals

Whichever type of computer you get, your quest for computerization doesn't stop there. You will also need several accessories.

### Mass Storage

For digital recording, you need a really high-capacity storage device—at approximately 40 Megabytes (Megs) per minute for eight tracks of audio, 250 Megs can record a little over a five-minute tune; 600 Megs buys you enough stereo recording time for a typical CD (if you want to maintain a backup file, double these figures).

Floppy disks are out of the question; although current floppies hold 1.4 megabytes of data and are easy to use, they are too slow to capture digital audio, and can't store more than a few seconds of quality sound. A hard disk is much more suitable, but it needs to be fast (the more tracks you want to record, the faster the drive needs to be), and it must also be able to maintain continuous throughput. Some hard drives stop periodically to thermally recalibrate themselves, which usually messes up the digital audio recording process. If you plan to use a particular hard disk recording system, check with the manufacturer for a suggested list of hard drives.

Hard drives are also available in removable cartridge versions of varying capacities (but overall, they have smaller capacities than fixed hard disks). This makes it easy to add more storage; just pop out the old cartridge and insert a new one. That's a costly approach, and they don't tend to be quite as fast as fixed hard disks.

Magneto-optical drives are cartridge-based, and have large memory capacities (*e.g.*, 1.3 gigabyte versions are popular). They're usually not fast enough for multitrack digital audio applications (some are, though), but they're great for backup and when you need removeable cartridges.

No matter what you store your data on, you'll need some sort of backup (unless you like to live *very* dangerously). Although removeable hard drives or magneto-optical drives are one option, tape backup can store gigabytes of data on inexpensive, DAT-like data cassettes. This requires a tape backup drive, which is relatively inexpensive.

The recordable CD (called CD-R) is a wonderful backup medium for archiving files. Currently, you can only write on a CD once (although multisession CD recorders let you record over part of the disk, then later on, continue recording on unused parts of the disk). Many

CD recorders let you create one-off audio CDs as well as CD-ROMs that hold computer files. As prices come down, CDs will probably become the archive medium of choice.

However, if you're tight for cash, a modular digital multitrack (MDM) recorder with digital inputs/outputs can often back up digital audio files. This is because digital audio files can usually be transmitted via the AES/EBU digital interface, and received at an MDM's AES/EBU input. Put the MDM into record, and presto—inexpensive digital audio backup.

A more unusual, but potentially helpful, form of backup uses telecommunications. Some telecommunications networks allow each user a certain amount of free storage each month. If you're working on something whose loss would be catastrophic, save it to the network into your workspace (assuming the file isn't too large). This works well as insurance for works in progress, and is great for work done on the road.

## MIDI Interface

Only a few computers have been produced with built-in MIDI ports; for most computers, MIDI is not yet part of their native language. This requires adding a *MIDI interface,* which usually hooks into the serial port (or sometimes ports). An interface can be a simple box with a single MIDI in and MIDI out, or a complex, microprocessor-controlled rack-mount device that can provide multiple "cables" of MIDI outputs (each cable allows for sixteen channels, so an interface with eight cables can provide 128 MIDI channels) and functions such as routing, MIDI filtering, transposition, and SMPTE sync (generate and receive). With the PC, MIDI interfaces are often built into sound cards that install in the PC, however they generally require a special cable.

The more complex the interface, the more important it is to make sure that any software you have can communicate with the interface. Sophisticated interfaces are usually made by companies that make sequencers, so not surprisingly, their sequencers seem to work best with their interfaces. But they will often have emulation modes to accommodate other interfaces as well. Sequencers made by manufacturers who don't make interfaces will usually be able to talk to anything (why limit your market?).

## Digital Audio Boards

A growing number of computers have audio inputs along with audio outputs; if not, you'll need to add a digital audio interface that includes analog-to-digital and digital-to-analog conversion. As with MIDI interfaces, these can be simple boards (the tradeoff is usually lower fidelity for lower cost) or complicated interfaces with metering, XLR inputs and outputs, AES/EBU and S/PDIF outputs, and so on.

As with MIDI interfaces, whatever software you use needs to be able to access the particular card you're using.

## CD-ROMs

If you need access to large sound libraries, a CD-ROM drive can be indispensable. Many companies offer sound effects and samples on CD-ROM that you can copy over to your computer.

CD-ROMs are available in several formats. Some have Mac-compatible AIFF (Audio Interchange File Format) files, while others cater to the PC and its .WAV file format; some CDs are *cross-platform* and work on either the Mac or PC. These files can be used directly by the computer, or brought into sample editors, tweaked to your specific needs, then sent out digitally to a sampler, hard disk recorder, or modular digital multitrack.

Some samplers are also compatible with CD-ROM drives. These often read a proprietary CD-ROM format that is not AIFF or .WAV compatible.

Finally, there are many audio sample CDs that play back over conventional CD players. If your CD player has digital outputs, great; these are usually S/PDIF, and can connect to a digital audio card for direct digital transfer from CD to computer. However, most CD-ROM drives can also play audio CDs with a suitable CD audio access program, and other programs exist that let you "grab" audio from the CD and transfer it over to the computer.

The bottom line: If you need quick access to a lot of sounds, a CD-ROM may be more of a necessity in your studio than a luxury.

## Modems

Why are we talking about modems, which hook your computer up to the phone lines, in a book about recording? Because not only is it possible to exchange MIDI and digital audio files via modem, but there are several telecommunications services that offer forums and files relating to MIDI and music. Get as fast a modem as possible; it should be able to handle at least 14.4 kilobaud (a baud is a unit of data transfer), and 28.8 kbaud modems are becoming the preferred standard. In Europe, most users are going directly to 28.8 from slower speeds, and bypassing 14.4 altogether.

## MIDI Operating Systems

Because the computer has to communicate with MIDI peripherals, traditionally different programs have used different *drivers* that translate MIDI data into something the computer's serial or parallel ports can understand. This led to a sort of "tower of Babel" situation where some programs could communicate with some interfaces, but not with others. Although there have been many attempts at creating a standardized MIDI operating system, most of these have been built around a specific manufacturer's "suite" of products, and other manufacturers were reluctant to support another company's protocol.

Fortunately, Opcode Systems devised a standard MIDI operating system (OMS, for Open MIDI System) for both the Mac and PC which is being incorporated into QuickTime (for the Mac) and Windows 95 (for the PC). This relieves software manufacturers of having to re-invent the wheel each time they want to access the serial ports; they can simply say "use the OMS drivers to get the data where I want it." Most software programs are already OMS-compatible, and thanks to the computer industry embracing this standard, virtually all should be soon.

## SCSI and the Studio

The tools of today's studio, such as hard disk recording, MIDI sequencers that also sequence digital audio, and programs that transfer samples between computers and samplers, make extreme demands on the host computer.

Although computers continue to get faster, the main speed bottleneck often doesn't occur within the computer, but in communicating to the outside world. Moving data rapidly is crucial to today's studios because digitized audio files take up huge amounts of memory. Not only that, but hard disk recording has to happen in near-real-time, so speed is of the essence.

A high-speed, computer/peripheral data transfer protocol called SCSI (Small Computer System Interface, commonly pronounced "skuzzy") appeared in the mid eighties. Its initial application was to move data between computers and hard disks, optical disks, and CD-ROMs. Shortly thereafter, SCSI started showing up in recording and musical equipment such as samplers.

MIDI's speed is not sufficient for digital audio; it can send a maximum of 31,250 bits per second. SCSI is a parallel interface that handles eight bits at a time instead of one, and can move up to around twelve *million* bits per second. Even so, the 8-bit wide limitation means that it's easy to run out of horsepower in multitrack digital audio applications. This is being addressed by new versions of SCSI and related protocols.

The SCSI bus can also be fussy because of its high speed. Only eight devices, each with its own unique ID number, can connect to the bus (most SCSI devices let you specify a particular ID number, but some cannot be changed from a default ID). Adding more than eight devices requires the use of complicated switching boxes; having more than one device set to the same ID is taboo.

SCSI cables, which should be as short as possible, go in a daisy-chain from the first device in the chain (usually the computer) to other peripherals, to the last device in the chain. Devices at each end of the chain—but not those in the middle—should be *terminated.* Termination provides the proper impedances and line characteristics, but having more than two terminators in the system can damage the SCSI chip by drawing excessive current. Many SCSI devices come with internally installed terminators that can be removed, while other devices let you switch termination on or off. In some cases, termination cannot be easily removed.

In general, SCSI peripherals are turned on first (starting with devices that take a while to become operational, such as hard disks that need to spin up), then the computer. However, there are exceptions to this rule; some keyboard instruments look at the bus to see if SCSI devices are present, and need to be turned on last.

The availability of a SCSI port doesn't guarantee compatibility with all SCSI devices. Some keyboards can communicate with hard disks and optical drives, but not with sample editing programs unless those programs have software *driver routines* that communicate with the keyboards. And sometimes, SCSI devices are just plain finicky; turning on devices in different orders, or changing ID numbers, can sometimes solve otherwise mysterious problems.

## Backing Up Is Hard (but Necessary) to Do

A wise person once told me digital's dirty little secret: "Digital data is not real until it exists in at least two places." Once a computer enters your studio, you'll become dependent on not only it, but the data it holds. Losing this data, whether it's a digital audio file or client list, can be devastating. So, we can't really look at computers without looking at how to back up data.

The same technologies described above for recording digital audio (hard drive, magneto-optical drive, CD recorder, tape backup) apply to backing up computer and digital audio files. However, you usually cannot use MDMs to back up computer files.

## Incremental Backup Programs

Several computer programs can back up a hard disk or other mass storage device incrementally (*i.e.,* after creating the first backup, subsequent backups save only the changes that occurred since the previous backup). You can save data to floppies (if you're a masochist or own stock in a floppy disk company), another hard drive, removable cartridge drive (hard drive or magneto-optical), tape drive, *etc.*

With some programs, the backup disk(s) contain a directory of files that must be updated after backing up. If you back up to two or more removable cartridge-based hard drives, try using a floppy for the first disk of a backup set. This will usually contain the directory, and it's easier to mount and unmount a floppy to update the directory than wait for a cartridge to spin down and spin up to speed.

Every now and then I back up my hard disk to a second mass storage device the old-fashioned way—copying or dragging files over manually. If any problems happen during the incremental backup process (which can happen), you're left with a corrupted backup disk in some proprietary format; you usually cannot recover individual files. Having the other set of conventional backups provides a last resort.

## Data Compression

There are several utilities that compress data on-the-fly, as you're working on it. I don't recommend these. Other data compression programs work "after the fact" and compress a file for storage, or for sending over the phone lines. Programs such as StuffIt (for the Mac) are reliable and can save a fair amount of space.

Also note that saving a sequencer file as a Standard MIDI File can also compress data, typically by thirty to forty percent. However, you will lose data not specified in MIDI, such as interface "cable" assignments and "notepad" notes.

## Backing Up MIDI Data

Many MIDI devices can save their data in the form of System Exclusive messages (for more information, see Chapter 4 on MIDI). There are several ways to store sys ex data.

- **Dedicated devices.** These are boxes (typically rack mount) whose sole purpose in life is to store sys ex data to standard disks.
- **Keyboards/samplers.** Several keyboards and samplers let you load sys ex data into memory, then save it to the unit's internal disk drive. However, keyboards usually have some storage limitations, such as not being able to handle real large files. Also, most disk formats are incompatible—you can't take sys ex data stored on the disk drive in one manufacturer's keyboard and play it back from a different brand of keyboard.
- **Computer software.** Many sequencer programs let you store sys ex messages as part of a sequence. Also, universal "librarian" software can store sys ex messages from a variety of gear.

The basic procedure for backing up sys ex is pretty simple: hook the MIDI out of the device whose data is to be saved to the sys ex storage device's MIDI in, set up the storage device to receive MIDI data, and send a sys ex data dump from the device whose data you want to save. If the MIDI data ends up getting stored in a buffer, you then save the received data to disk or some other nonvolatile storage medium.

## In Case of Disaster . . .

No one likes to contemplate the possibility that everything you own (including your data) could be wiped out in seconds from a fire or other disaster, but see about arranging a "data exchange" program with a friend or two where you'll look after some of their data if they'll look after yours. Swap some cartridges, and you'll have more peace of mind. Another option is a safe deposit box, although if it's important to get at the data in case of your death (sorry to remind you, but we're all headed there eventually!), bear in mind that sometimes safe deposit boxes are sealed and require legal maneuvering to be opened.

People often ask how often they should back up. The answer is simple: *back up whenever you've done something you don't want to lose.* I always keep a "temporary" backup floppy around so that if the time isn't right to go through the incremental process, I can at least save to something until I do the official backup shuffle. And above all, be kind to your data. Remember that removable cartridges, floppies, backup tapes, and even magneto-optical cartridges are fragile. Treat them with much care.

# Chapter 16
# Studio Construction Set: Which Gear Is Right for You?

With today's variety of gear, it's getting harder and harder to choose the components for a home or project studio. Wrong decisions can be costly, whereas getting the right equipment from the beginning gives your studio a firm foundation.

But how do you know what's the right gear? The answer depends on how you plan to use your studio: a rock musician has different needs from someone who does instrumental dance music, or those who work with audio-for-video. So, let's look at which equipment works best for particular musical needs, as exemplified by five typical types of users. You can modify these starting points as appropriate for your own situation.

## The Cast of Characters

Here are five categories of home and project studio users:

- Rock musician ("rocker" for short) with traditional instrumentation of drums, guitar, bass, vocals, and keyboards. Jazz, classical, "real time" rap, and world beat (reggae, Afropop, *etc.*) musicians have similar needs.
- Pop music producer ("producer") who does lots of one-person MIDI tracks, with the occasional vocal or instrumental track. This also applies to those who do most kinds of dance music. Electronically oriented instrumental artists fall under this category as well.
- Hobbyists who mainly create music for their own enjoyment. This person may do solo recording or work with a few friends, using MIDI-based or traditional instruments. Rockers on a tight budget fall into this category as well.
- Songwriter who uses the studio mostly to work out songs and do arranging. Producers and musicians on a budget may fit in this category as well.
- Audio-for-video ("A/V"). This musician tends to work with soundtracks, commercials, industrial videos, and the like.

Now let's consider each component in a typical studio to see what works best for the above applications.

## The Recorder

*Rocker:* The extensive use of acoustic and electric instruments makes it difficult to take advantage of virtual MIDI tracks. An eight-track tape (analog or digital) or hard disk recorder is a minimum, but for more "pro-level" productions, sixteen tracks allow for recording more instruments and make stereo recording of individual instruments a more realistic option.

At the high end, a 2" analog twenty-four-track remains the *de facto* standard (although stacking together three modular digital multitracks is an increasingly popular alternative). If you expect to do release-quality tapes, or record and mix in various first-class recording studios, this is your best—albeit most expensive—choice.

*Producer or Songwriter:* By relying on virtual MIDI tracks, an eight-track multitrack is usually sufficient. However, if you plan to use lots of acoustic or electric instruments (for example, if you work with jazz musicians), then sixteen tracks may be worth the extra investment.

Those who are mostly interested in doing demos that won't be released commercially might consider some of the cassette-based, eight-track rack mount or standalone "ministudio" type devices. These offer surprisingly good sound quality, fast operation (you don't need to spend lots of time winding tape), and low operating costs (cassettes are an inexpensive recording medium). If you buy one with an integrated mixer, then you save even more.

*Upscale Hobbyist or Downscale Songwriter:* The type of setup described above works here, but those with more modest needs can get by with a four-track cassette multitrack, inexpensive software if they have a PC (for two-track recording and MIDI sequencing), or a used four-track reel-to-reel machine. Through judicious track bouncing, it is possible to have up to ten tracks without sacrificing too much quality; combining tape with virtual MIDI tracks expands the number of sounds that can play back in real time.

Hobbyists and Songwriters may not even need a multitrack tape recorder at all if they deal exclusively with MIDI tracks and one or two acoustic tracks (*e.g.*, vocal or guitar). A MIDI sequencer can record all the note data necessary to drive various sound generators. Mix their outputs along with an acoustic sound played into your final two-track master, and you have a master tape. For example, you can get very high-quality results by recording several MIDI instruments on a sequencer, then singing along with them as you record into a two-track DAT (Digital Audio Tape recorder).

*A/V:* Here the ability to synchronize to video is crucial. The easiest way to do this is with MIDI sequencing. However, if you need to add acoustic tracks, then you have two options: a hard disk recording system (which allows for both easy synchronization and pinpoint editing), or a synchronizable eight- or sixteen-track tape recorder. The ability to synchronize to SMPTE Time Code does not come cheap; however, some analog machines can be retrofitted for sync at a reasonable cost, and synchronizers are available for MDMs.

*Comments:* In any of these applications, hard disk recording systems open up many additional possibilities.

One workaround for those with limited budgets is to use a two-track hard disk system with tape. Synching a hard disk system to tape lets you "capture" acoustic instruments into the hard disk system, edit them on computer, then bounce them over to tape for inexpensive, nonvolatile storage. If you're using a small hard disk, you can then erase the hard disk, record more tracks, and bounce these over to tape.

## Mastering Deck

Eventually, you'll want to mix what you've recorded into a form that can be listened to repeatedly, as well as transported to other studios. This is where the two-track mastering deck comes in.

For all types except A/V, there are three main choices for mixdown decks. Here are the advantages and disadvantages of each.

*DAT (Digital Audio Tape) Recorder.* Offering high fidelity, small size, and reasonable cost considering the level of performance, DAT machines are the current standard mixdown format, and will probably remain so until recordable CDs drop further in price. However, there are both consumer and professional models available; avoid the consumer types, because they often include only a 48 kHz sampling rate and not 44.1 kHz (the same rate used for CDs), and generally do not have digital inputs and outputs. Making a CD from a DAT tape recorded at 48 kHz requires a format conversion, or taking the signal from the DAT's analog outputs.

Consumer machines also include SCMS (Serial Copy Management System), an utterly silly attempt to prevent piracy of recordings. This allows you to make one copy of source material, but no more. So, you could end up in a situation where you record several mixes on various DAT tapes, but when you want to record them again to a master tape, you can't.

Incidentally, hard disk recording systems such as Sound Tools usually let you dump DAT digital audio over to the hard disk system for editing. This means you can crossfade between songs, use DSP functions such as digital limiting and EQ, and do other digital magic to tweak your master to perfection. The main disadvantage of DAT is that not everyone has one, so you'll probably need a cassette deck as well to run off copies for friends.

Duplicating a DAT tape digitally requires a second DAT machine unless you have a hard disk recording system with digital I/O. With this, you can bounce the DAT tape to the hard disk, then bounce the hard disk data over to a blank DAT tape.

*Cassette deck:* Although convenient and inexpensive, cassette deck fidelity pales next to DAT. However, for hobbyists and songwriters, a cassette mix may be all you need. In any event, the cassette has become such a universal way to exchange tunes that every studio usually has one around somewhere. One tip: record your mixes with noise reduction off. Yes, it will sound noisier, but that's better than what happens if someone plays back the tape using different noise reduction, or the same noise reduction type with improper calibration (everyone's deck is always properly calibrated, right?).

*Analog reel-to-reel two-track:* This was the standard for decades, but is being supplanted by DAT. Unlike DAT, it offers easy editing—just get out a razor blade, splicing block, and some spare empty reels to rearrange your recorded bits into the desired running sequence. The specs are not as good as DAT, but are far superior to cassettes. For pro studios, some engineers prefer a two-track reel to reel tape processed through Dolby SR noise reduction. The specs rival (and in some cases surpass) digital, you can "crunch" the tape to add some distortion-induced warmth, and splicing is possible.

*Recordable CD:* As of this writing, recordable CDs are not erasable so they are more limited for mixdown than tape. However, it is common to supply mastering houses (the people who actually transform your master into something that can be mass produced) with CDs rather than DATS.

A/V people will generally end up mixing their sounds down to the audio tracks on a video tape, or to a format that can be synchronized to videotape. For the latter, a SMPTE-synchronizable DAT is pricey but well worth it.

*Comments:* You can often find used two-track decks (probably sold by someone who just purchased a DAT!) at reasonable prices. Those on a really tight budget can sometimes dispense with a mastering deck altogether by mixing down to two tracks of a multitrack machine. For example, if you have an eight-track, you could record on tracks 1 through 6 then mix them down into tracks 7 and 8. The main disadvantage of this approach is that whenever you want to run off a copy of the mix, you have to play the master tape.

## The Mixing Console

Mixers come in two main flavors: traditional mixers that include multiple mic preamps, per-channel equalization, effects sends and returns, *etc.*, and stripped-down line mixers that cost less but include a limited number of mic preamps and fewer amenities.

Rockers will need a traditional mixer for recording acoustic/electric sounds. This implies multiple mic preamps, all available simultaneously. Equalization is also important as you don't want to rely on lots of outboard equalizers, and altering mic placement can only do so much to change the overall sound.

Producer, hobbyist, songwriter, and A/V musicians can often get by with a simple line mixer since MIDI instruments don't need multiple mic preamps. Furthermore, many MIDI devices offer onboard equalization and effects, which means a mixer doesn't need sophisticated EQ or zillions of effects sends. If you need mic preamps or options such as parametric equalization, simply add outboard rack mount devices.

Musicians who use Portastudio-style devices with built-in mixers can, of course, simply use that mixer and do not need an outboard unit.

A "distributed mixing" approach (see Chapter 10) works well for studios that combine acoustic and MIDI sounds. This method combines a smaller, traditional mixer to handle acoustic signals and tape returns with line mixers for the MIDI instruments. The line mixers provide submixes for the MIDI instruments as well as effects sends, and these feed the main mixer. Because many MIDI sound generators include onboard panning, effects, automated level control, and equalization, they can send a preprocessed stereo image that goes directly to the main mixer.

*Comments:* The number of channels you need depends on your applications, but plan on more than you think you need. As a rule of thumb, figure on a minimum of twice the number of multitrack tracks for non-MIDIfied studios or studios that use traditional mixing, and at least triple that number in studios that don't use distributed mixing but have several MIDI instruments.

Mixers are easy to outgrow, which is why adding line mixers at a later date can be a cost-effective way to expand a setup.

## Sequencers

*Rocker:* Although it may seem that rockers (and others who don't rely on MIDI instruments) don't need sequencers, a sequencer can be synched to tape during mixdown to provide automated mixing and signal processing, or change presets on a guitar multieffects to prevent having to overdub tracks with two different sounds. Of course, a sequencer can also provide MIDI instrumentation to augment drum sounds, add keyboard parts, *etc.*

For relatively simple sequencing applications, the latest, greatest sequencing software and computer aren't necessary—a simple stand-alone device will do the job. However, you will probably need a SMPTE-to-MIDI Song Pointer or SMPTE-to-MIDI Time Code adapter to sync the sequencer to tape, because few stand-alone units can sync directly to SMPTE.

*Producer or Songwriter:* Since this application usually involves a lot of MIDI gear, a sophisticated sequencing setup is important. The preferred approach is a computer running dedicated sequencing software, since the graphic interface and easy editing capabilities can streamline the sequencing process compared to hardware sequencers. Stand-alone sequencers work well if you have good musical technique and can treat the sequencer more like a tape recorder; however, those who need to edit will find the limited editing capabilities frustrating.

Programs that combine hard disk recording and sequencing are often ideal for producers and songwriters with sufficient disposable income. Integrating digital audio and MIDI sequencing can simplify the compositional process by eliminating the need to move back and forth between tape or hard disk and sequencing environments (MIDI Machine Control can integrate a sequencer and multitrack, but of course without the editing capabilities of hard disk recording).

*Hobbyist:* An entry-level sequencing program for personal computers, or budget stand-alone unit, will usually do the job. However, there is another option. As described later, many keyboard "workstations" include an onboard sequencer. This can not only drive onboard sounds but often external equipment including signal processing and automated mixdown gear. A setup consisting of a multitrack cassette-style recorder and workstation synchronized to tape can give a lot of flexibility for comparatively low cost.

*A/V:* The requirements are very similar to producers and songwriters, but SMPTE sync is essential. Choose a sequencer that can reference events to SMPTE times as well as the usual bars, beats, and measures; being able to assemble cue lists to trigger events according to SMPTE times is also helpful.

## Sound Generators

*Rocker:* Assuming the band has a keyboard player, that person will probably provide the appropriate sound generators. In the studio, though, you may also want a sampler with reasonable memory capacity to do tricks like fly in vocal sounds, or repair tracks by bouncing a track to the sampler, editing it, then bouncing the edited track back to tape.

*Producer:* Here an arsenal of synthesizers comes in handy—a multitimbral synthesizer with a lot of onboard programs for quick selection of various sounds, a sampler for occasional no-compromise sounds (8 Megabyte pianos and the like), and a drum module for percussion. A master MIDI controller—keyboard, guitar, wind, *etc.*—is also needed. To further extend the sonic palette, consider picking up some used synths as secondary sound generators. They won't be that expensive, and can add extra textures.

*Songwriters:* Those with sophisticated setups, or who want to make relatively complete demos, can use the same setup as producers. With limited budgets, a multitimbral rack mount synthesizer coupled with a sequencer is a good bet. Synths with onboard RAM expansion are particularly useful because they can be customized for various types of music by loading in samples. If you have the extra cash, consider adding a sampler to extend your options.

*Hobbyist:* A keyboard workstation synth is an excellent choice because not only does it provide sounds, it offers sequencing and often, signal processing. It therefore represents the best overall value. However, if you already have a computer and sequencer, consider some second-hand synth modules—last year's state-of-the-art can be this year's bargain.

*A/V:* The needs are similar to producers, but often, sampling becomes more important because most samplers are supported with sound effects disks. Given a choice between having only synths and only samplers, an A/V person might very well choose samplers.

## Computers

*Rocker:* A computer may not be necessary. If it is, an IBM clone, lower-end Mac, or similar inexpensive computer should handle all sequencing needs.

*Producer:* Because of the time spent working with MIDI instruments, a powerful computer with a big-screen monitor becomes important—and essential if you plan to do any work with digital audio. You will need a high-end, fast machine—especially since many current programs do not promise to provide all features, or run at optimum efficiency, with older computers.

*Songwriter or Hobbyist:* For doing demos, an inexpensive IBM clone or Mac is probably your best choice. As with producers, though, if computer-based hard disk recording is in your future, you'll need a top-of-the-line machine.

*A/V:* A powerful computer is necessary not just to handle SMPTE and sequencing, but the sample editing software that lets you get the most out of your sampler.

## Signal Processors

*Rocker:* A quality reverb unit is essential, as is a good compressor/limiter for smoothing out the dynamic range of miked sounds. Equalizers are less important since they will already be built into the mixing console. A good multieffects can come in handy to add special effects such as chorusing, doubling, distortion, *etc.*

*Producer and Songwriter:* With several MIDI instruments and a line mixer-based setup, outboard equalizers become important. A good multistage parametric, where individual stages can be used individually to process multiple tracks, is recommended as is a graphic equalizer for overall sound shaping. Although a compressor/limiter may not be as useful as for rockers, it can still help a lot when mastering to two-track to give a final mix a bit more "radio-readiness," as well as process vocals or other acoustic instruments you want to record. Naturally, a good reverb is always desirable.

*Hobbyist:* A workstation will often have built-in effects which, while generally not useable on other sound sources, may take care of your needs if the workstation provides most of your sound sources.

*A/V:* More is better if you know how to use it—reverb, compression, equalization—but add a multieffects to the list of essentials. Those designed for guitar can be particularly useful in creating unusual sound effects.

*Comments:* There are several MIDI-controllable automated mixdown accessories. These can help create more professional mixes, as you only have to get a mixing move right once—the sequencer remembers it. A workstation's onboard sequencer will generally handle this application, but a computer-based sequencer with graphic editing will make the task easier.

Although some people think multieffects with distortion apply only to guitar, light distortion applied to electronic drums can provide "hard limiting" effects that provide more punch and level but don't sound distorted. And the right touch of distortion on an organ track can transform a mellow church organ setting into a screaming freight train.

## Accessories

Accessories can be purchased as needed. But if you plan on doing any recording of acoustic sources, you'll need a high quality condenser mic (for vocals and "delicate" acoustic instruments) and a dynamic mic for kick drums, guitar amp stacks, and other heavy-duty sounds. For "warm" synth and vocal sounds, a tube preamp really does make a difference compared to solid-state types.

The most important accessory, though, is a sense of adventure. You have your own studio—no one's looking at the clock or making you do anything you don't want to do, so take a few chances and see what happens!

# Chapter 17
# Preparing for the Session

## Setting Up

With a little planning before a session, the recording process proceeds smoothly, without interruptions or frustrating/embarrassing breakdowns. It's helpful to do the following while setting up for a session:

### Clean Your Machine

This is key with analog decks, but digital machines need cleaning too (see Chapter 22, maintenance). Do maintenance right after a session so you'll be ready for the next session. Sometimes it's also a good idea to "zero" your controls so there aren't any surprises—turn off any record switches, set output switches to "source," choose the correct speed, *etc.*

Hard disk recording systems need maintenance too. Defragment the disk periodically (see Chapter 22) to keep all the pieces of a file together, erase unused pieces of audio from the disk, and implement a cohesive backup scheme. The rule about backups is simple: whenever you have something you don't want to lose, back it up. Always back up your hard disk at the end of a session, but if you're paranoid about losing some great piece of music, back up during a break in the recording.

### Warm Up Your Machines

Although this isn't essential (especially if the muse is impatient!), letting your system idle for fifteen minutes or so lets everything get up to temperature and up to spec. It certainly can't hurt, and you can spend that time getting the rest of your act together (labeling tapes, formatting disks, and the like). Some people recommend letting MDMs warm up before formatting tapes.

### Thread Reel-to-Reel Tape

With analog reel-to-reel machines, select, leader, and thread your tape. First, though, it's a good idea to splice some paper leader tape to the head of the magnetic tape (for info on splicing, see Chapter 21). With paper leader, you can use a felt-tip pen—sparingly—to write on the leader and identify the tape (Fig. 17-1). Also, when rewinding back to the beginning of the tape, you can hit the stop button as soon as the leader tape appears before the tape has a chance to unravel; without the leader tape it's very easy to rewind the tape off the takeup reel, necessitating the hassle of rethreading. Finally, a paper leader tape keeps the end of the magnetic tape from getting ratty. Plastic leader tape is also available, but the paper type is less prone to static build-up.

Threading tape on to a reel is never fun. Make sure that the tape it lies evenly around the hub of the reel (Fig. 17-2); any bumps will affect the smoothness of the tape's travel. If you have to stop in the middle of a session and you're in the middle of a reel, it's all right to leave the tape on the machine overnight or for a few days, but cover the recorder with a plastic or other nonporous dust cover (which you should do anyway).

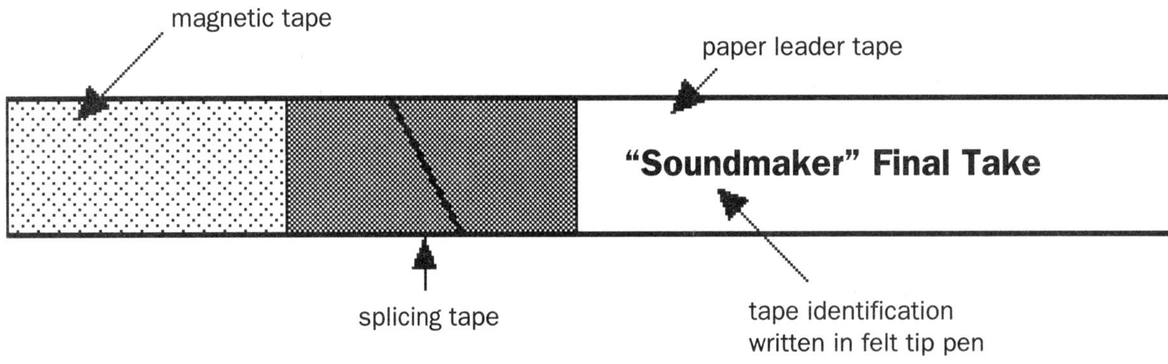


**Fig. 17-1:** *With paper leader tape, you can identify the tape that follows.*

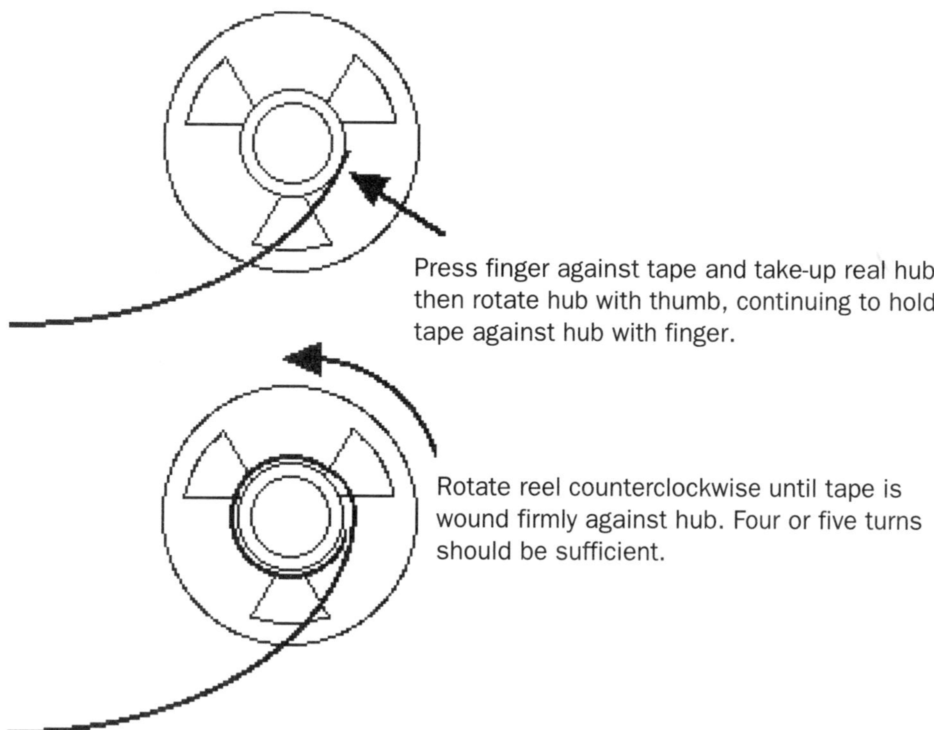


**Fig. 17-2:** *Threading tape on a reel.*

With digital tape, have plenty of formatted tapes around in case you get inspired. With hard disk recording, make sure there is enough disk space to hold the material you want to record. If not, you may need to back up, then erase, some older files to make room for the new ones.

In any case, before you start to record on any medium, listen to parts of it and see if there is any prerecorded material. Nine times out of ten there won't be, but you'll be grateful that you checked if there ever is.

## Routing Wires

Now you have to get AC to all those musicians and headphones. It's important that the wires are not underfoot and are out of danger's way; be especially wary of damp cellar floors, which can be lethal. There is nothing more frustrating than having someone blow a take (or a fuse) by walking on a wire or tripping over it.

Fig. 17-3 shows a typical layout for a jazz quintet consisting of electric guitar, electric bass, piano, drums, and sax, including mic and headphone cords.

## Setting Up Baffles and Getting the Equipment Ready

When recording a group of musicians, consider leakage. Should someone be recorded in another room, for example, or will baffles be sufficient? If you are simply overdubbing, leakage isn't an issue, but basic tracks can sometimes sound really terrible because of excessive leakage (there are exceptions—for example, drum sounds picked up through a heavily equalized channel can work to your advantage). Yet people frequently need eye contact for cues, players like to hear a song's vocals as they play, and equipment may not fit in a way that allows an optimum arrangement.

It helps to have the vocalist do a reference vocal through the cue system only, so that the musicians can hear vocals through the phones, but they don't get picked up by the mics recording the group. Afterward, the final vocals may be overdubbed without leakage problems. Sometimes it's easier to overdub an instrument like acoustic piano instead of trying to isolate it from other instruments through baffling. If you're short for tracks, perhaps you could mix in another overdub so that you record, for example, harmony vocals or an acoustic guitar part at the same time as the piano.

## Zeroing Levels with Analog Tape

Although your tape machine may have input level and output level controls, these are almost always superseded by the mixer controls. As a result, the multitrack level controls are adjusted

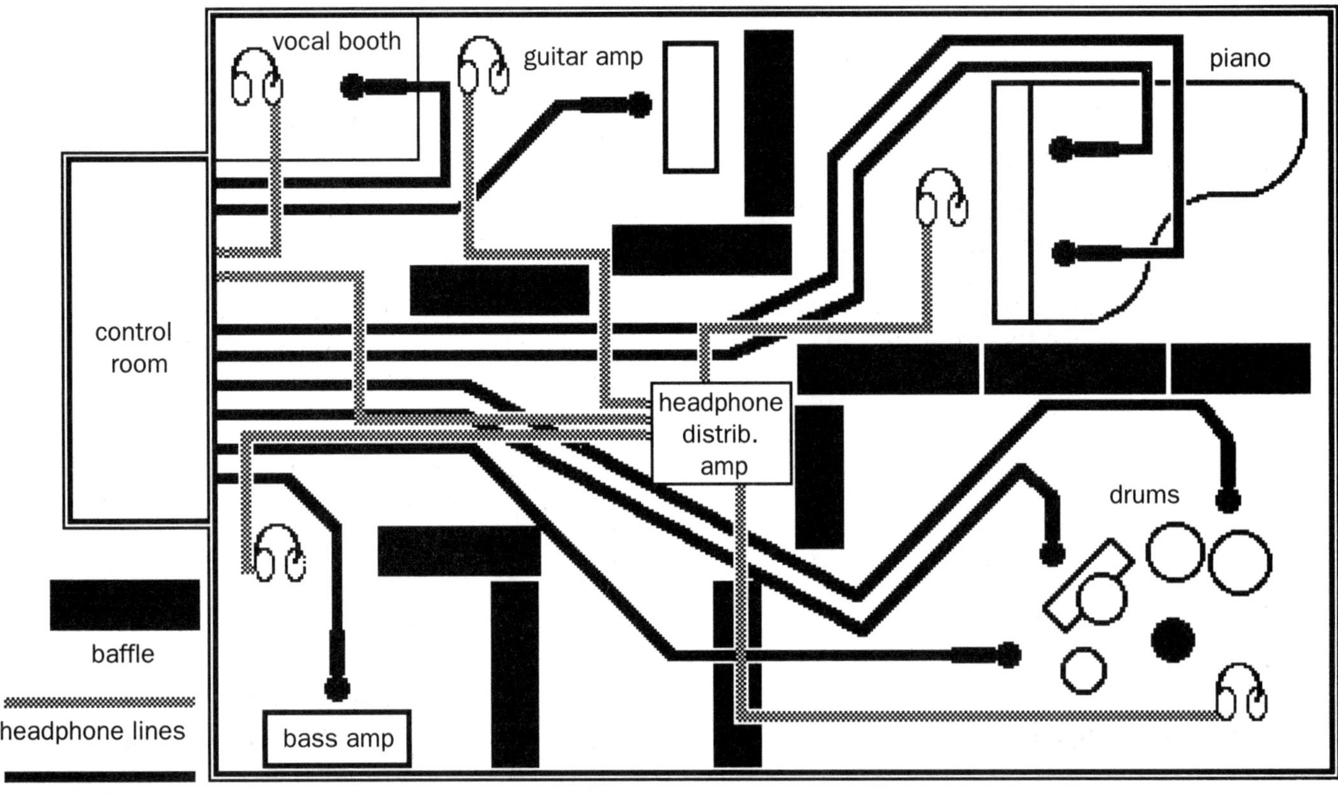


**Fig. 17-3:** *Baffles provide acoustical isolation between instruments; the headphone distribution amp provides audio to the headphones during overdubs.*

to a specific point of reference so that all channels behave the same way with regard to level matching. Professional studios adjust to very accurate test tapes or tones; we don't always need that much accuracy. Here's one approach to zeroing with analog tape.

1. Feed a constant tone into the first multitrack input. If you don't have some kind of electronic oscillator to use as a standard, invent your own (*e.g.,* place a microphone in front of a speaker that's tuned between FM stations). This produces a source of "white noise," which is a very consistent sort of signal. Something like an organ or synthesizer (without tremolo or gadgets) will also work.

2. Turn the input control about three-fourths of the way up, and set the input selector to source. Adjust the input control until the meter for channel 1 reads 0 VU.

3. Thread some of the tape onto the analog tape recorder, at the speed you're going to use. Turn on the record switch for channel 1, then push play and record simultaneously so that you're recording the test tone.

4. Switch the output selector to tape to monitor directly from the tape, and adjust the output level control until the meter reads 0 VU (the same as the input level reading). Then stop the tape, rewind back to the beginning, and run the same procedure on the other recorder channels. Note that if there's an extreme imbalance between levels (such as having to turn up a particular output control much more than another to get a 0 VU reading), you may have problems with the record or playback head, such as excessive wear due to a skewed tape path.

## Zeroing Levels with Digital Recording

One of the beauties of digital tape and hard disk recording is that setting levels is easy—as long as you don't go over 0 VU, you're okay. But you do want to make sure that your mixer is matched to the hard disk audio interface.

1. Feed a test tone into your mixer and adjust the level controls to their nominal optimum setting (this will usually be about eighty percent of the fader's full travel; refer to your mixer's manual for details).

2. Adjust the test tone volume so that the mixer output meter reads 0 VU.

3. Trim the hard disk audio interface or digital tape input levels so that this signal reads around

–12 at each input. This allows up to 12 dB of headroom for signals that exceed the mixer's nominal 0 VU point.

### Check Over Your Mixer

Before starting a session, make sure that everything is returned to normal—turn down sends, switch out preamps and EQ, and the like. Nothing's worse than wondering why you're getting distortion, when the problem is simply having an input preamp turned up. While you're checking things over, look for any LEDs that aren't working, or other symptoms of trouble.

Now the equipment is set up and ready to record. But now you have to make a choice between recording the signal(s) in question via microphone, or by plugging directly into the mixing console. We already covered recording techniques for mics in Chapter 9 on microphones, so let's look at recording direct.

## Recording Direct

This is the easiest way to get a signal into a tape recorder, but it works only with electric instruments. You feed the output from an electric guitar, electric piano, organ, drum machine, *etc.*, and simply plug it into a tape recorder or mixer line input. However, some instruments may have insufficient level to drive the input; or they may be loaded down by the tape recorder input and give a dull sound. A mic or instrument preamp solves this problem.

Many guitarists, because they use preamps to overload their amplifiers and obtain a distorted effect, associate a preamp with distortion. However, a preamp by itself, unless overdriven, should be a clean device that adds no significant coloration of its own. Generally, a preamp with a gain of 20 dB will take almost any electric instrument up to 0 VU at your tape recorder input. Preamps are available commercially, at varying price points and with varying degrees of complexity—from an inexpensive level booster to an audiophile-quality, tube-based effects device.

You can also go direct into the mixing console, which probably has an internal preamp. However, the input impedance may be low enough to load down your instrument. A direct box, as described in Chapter 11 on accessories, can provide a suitable interface between a low-output instrument like a guitar and a low impedance input.

Recording directly from the instrument has a disadvantage: if the amplifier is part of your "sound," then going direct as described previously cuts out that part of the sound. However, you can still record direct by adding a tap from the amplifier's speaker (Fig. 17-4). You can then feed this line into the mixer.

### Resolving the "Going Direct versus Miking an Amplifier" Controversy

Small practice amps are a good alternative to loud amps. Practice amps are usually about a foot square, and can be made to sound just as distorted and raunchy as bigger amps, but at far lower volume levels. Although they may not produce enough sound for live playing, in the studio this doesn't matter. Stick the mic up close to the speaker and, in the control room, you won't know whether the amp is one foot high or twenty feet high. Small amps can also help your cause if you are trying to record hard rock in a residential neighborhood.

## Setting Levels

With digital recording, just make sure the signal doesn't exceed 0 VU, otherwise nasty splattering will result (the manufacturer may

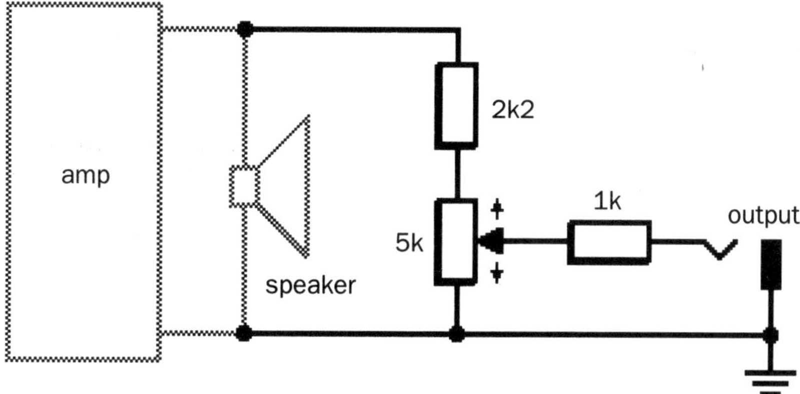


**Fig. 17-4:** *Going direct from a guitar amp by tapping off the speaker. The 5 k potentiometer controls volume.*

have built in a bit more headroom, but don't count on it). However, analog recording is a whole other matter, since you have to learn a tape's "character"—how much signal it can take before it distorts, noise characteristics, how the hiss level changes when you record a signal, and so on.

To do this, find a consistent live music source (someone practicing guitar or piano into your tape recorder for a half hour or so is ideal). Put on your headphones so you can hear every little sound on the tape and block out the sound of whoever is practicing.

Send your test sound source into channel 1, and switch the meter for that channel into the source position. With analog meters, turn up the level until the meter indicates a signal that seldom, if ever, pins. Avoid pinning (when the meter pointer swings all the way to the right-hand retaining pin on the meter face) to prevent damaging the meter. With LED meters, set the level for a nominal +3 VU.

Now, run the tape in record mode, switch the output selector to tape, and listen to the sound coming from the tape. You should notice a delay compared to the sound source as soon as you start running the tape—it's bothersome, but try to tune it out and concentrate on the tape sound.

After you've tuned into what's going on, decrease the input level and notice how the noise seems to increase. Occasionally switch into the source position to monitor the signal going into the recorder. Then, turn up the input—very slowly—until you start getting audible distortion, and note how the quality of the sound changes from clean to progressively "gritty." Also, with very loud low-frequency signals (*e.g.*, bass and kick drum), you'll hear a swishing sound (like white noise) along with your signal. This is called *modulation noise,* and can be minimized with certain types of noise reduction.

Another excellent source to help you get a feel for levels is a drum machine, which covers a very broad range. The kick drum is particularly good for hearing how the tape reacts to low frequencies; cymbals are good for checking out high-frequency saturation characteristics (many people still prefer analog tape over digital because they can use tape saturation as an effect).

However, if you do overload the tape, it's likely that some sound will spill over into adjacent channels and cause *crosstalk;* furthermore, the extra level may change the magnetic fields imprinted on adjacent portions of tape when the tape is wound on its reel (called *print-through*). Also, the modulation noise can become pretty nasty. Nonetheless, tape saturation is a useful effect—it's similar to what happens when a tube preamp distorts.

An additional problem is that tape recorders are very sensitive to high-frequency overload, due to the internal pre-emphasis and to some of the new noise-reduction systems. Be very careful when setting levels with any instrument that has significant high-frequency energy.

By doing all these exercises, you hopefully have some idea of how the meter readings correlate with tape sounds. Here's another exercise that doesn't really relate to setting levels, but it's still instructive.

With the tape recorder in record mode, and with headphones on, listen to the tape output from one of the channels with its associated input control turned all the way down. Turn the output all the way up so that you are hearing only the noise that the machine-plus-tape combination produces. At this high amplification, dropouts on the tape will cause little sounds like corn popping; the familiar tape hiss becomes a wonderland of constantly changing white noise. You'll probably pick up a faint bit of hum, too.

Listen to the tape's character; for comparison listen to a cheap tape (if you have any around—it's better if you don't, actually). With cheap tape, the clicks will sound like explosions and the tape hiss will sound "gritty" and inconsistent. You will probably also notice that the head contact, or the tape quality, is not quite as good on the outermost tracks of a piece of tape; compare these to the inner tracks. Listen to your recorder through the audio equivalent of a microscope and you'll learn many interesting things, and probably feel a little closer to it.

## Logbooks

Keep track of what's going on as you record—which instruments are on which tracks, and the timings and tape counter numbers for introductions, solos, and so forth. This is not as much of a problem with sequencers, which not only allow for unambiguous track names and labels, but often include a "notepad" option that stores written notes along with the sequencer file. With a personal computer-based hard disk recording system, it's worth getting a simple word processor to take notes. This can live in the same folder as the digital audio files.

Also take notes on how you obtained certain sounds. When you're busy working on a session, your memory isn't putting much effort into remembering the specifics. If you want to remix a tune six months later, you'll be very happy to have some notes.

## Tuning and Identifying

When you start recording, don't just begin immediately with the music; here are some ideas on what to put on tape as a "header."

- Test tone. Begin each selection on the tape with around twenty seconds of an A 440 or other standard musical tone. By recording at a level that gives 0 VU on the output meter of an analog machine (use a lower reference, such as –12, with digital gear), you have a reference level for subsequent dubs if required, or if you end up playing the tape on a different machine. If you transfer to analog, having a test tone with a known pitch will allow you to use the variable-speed control to compensate for any machine-to-machine speed inconsistencies. Speaking of tuning, record hard-to-tune instruments (pianos, harps), or instruments whose tuning can't be changed easily (vibes, electric pianos), and then have singers and stringed instrument players use notes from them to determine pitch. In a case like this, it's helpful to have a tuning standard that can vary a slight and predictable amount to compensate for slightly off-pitch instruments.
- Identification tone (slate). The term slating comes from movie production—you know, that whole take 1, take 2, type of thing. It's not a bad idea if, after the test tone, you speak the title of the selection and the take number.

Having a header on sequences can also be useful for storing such data as:

- System exclusive data. If you use a particular program on a particular track, record the program's sys ex data in the track. On playback, the sequencer will reload the data into the sound generator.
- Program change. Use this to select the desired program from the sound generator being driven by the track.
- Controllers. Use controller 7 to set the starting level for the track. You might also want to include a default value of 0 for pitch bend, modulation, *etc.* so that these all have a known starting point.

Another advantage to including a header is that many sequencers exhibit somewhat unstable timing when they start up. Starting the music on the second measure avoids this problem.

## The Click Track

Sometimes while recording it's necessary to have a rhythmic reference such as a *click track,* which consists of rhythmic pulses generated by something like a metronome or drum machine. In pro studios, where tracks may be laid down to follow scheduling demands rather than musical considerations, the click track can be very helpful—you could record bass, guitar, pianos, horns, and singers against the click reference, and *then* put on the drums. MIDI sequencers usually have a click option built in, so if the sequencer is synched to tape, you always have a click reference available.

Rhythm units also make good click tracks. When using one of these, I usually also set up a microphone, and cue the beginnings and endings of solos, remind myself of arrangements, speak words of encouragement during difficult overdubs, and so on. It can be very handy to have a narrative track that sort of conducts you along the musical trail.

One caution: a click track tends to have an unvarying tempo, which is not the way the real world works. Good drummers subtly speed up and slow down to help a track "breathe." If at all possible, orchestrate the click track tempo—*e.g.,* increase the speed a bit during a hot solo, then pull back a bit for the soulful chorus.

# Chapter 18
# Recording Techniques

We now have all this knowledge about the equipment, it's time to apply it; this chapter is a collection of applications for various types of recording, presented in no particular order.

To begin, the basic rule of recording is that anything goes if it sounds good to you. There are no rights and wrongs, no "proper" microphones, and no rule books. Engineers will disagree strongly over extremely basic points; one might say that the choice of a microphone is crucial, another will maintain that it doesn't matter if you follow it up with a good equalizer. All of this is very much a matter of taste, since *all that matters is the ultimate emotional impact of the piece of music.* Keep this in mind if you start getting overwhelmed by technology.

This translates into more work, because if you're working solo, you have to learn about the equipment as well as the art. In a professional studio, all the musician has to think about is making the music—the engineer figures out the equipment, and the producer arranges and gives direction to the music. If you're going to perform all these functions at once, you have to become proficient at them. Although it takes years of practice to become an expert, you can enjoy your work almost immediately with studio machines.

You'll probably never be completely satisfied with any tape you create; while you're making it, you will learn something new that you can't apply unless you start all over again. Although sometimes it's a good idea to scrap something that's not working out in order to work in new ideas, often it's better to simply save your new pieces of knowledge for a future tape. Don't look back, look ahead. Like music, recording itself is also a fine art. The keys are the same that make someone a good musician: practice, experimentation, and a desire to learn from others as well as from yourself.

## Cheapo Cheapo Techniques: The $30 Cassette Recorder

The lowly portable cassette recorder is where a lot of people, including myself, have started. They won't turn out super tapes; the fidelity is limited, the wow and flutter are pretty terrible, and the noise is—well, they're noisy. But these machines are cheap and plentiful. If you decide at the last minute that you want to record your band in concert, you can always put a portable cassette machine in front of the PA speaker and hope for the best. Even if the overall fidelity is pretty bad, if there's a solo in there that cooks, it will come through. Was the second song in the set really too slow? Did the transition between the third and the fourth songs sound smooth? With a tape recording you have a reality check, even if it is lo-fi.

You can also use the cassette machine (or a small dictation recorder) as a notebook for song ideas. Inexpensive models often have compressors that bring everything up to a constant recording level, so that even if you play a solid body guitar without an amp, you'll still hear something. Don't overestimate what one of these machines can do, but don't underestimate it either. Here are some additional points that will improve your chances of getting something bearable:

- Use really good tape. You can always erase it and use it with a better machine later; a cheapo tape may self-destruct.
- Keep the machine clean, especially the heads and tape transport path.
- Use an AC adapter. As batteries wear down, the speed sometimes changes. Recording with low batteries and playing back with fresh batteries may give a sped-up effect because the tape will play back faster than it was recorded. AC adapters keep the speed more constant, but make sure that you always have a set of fresh batteries inside the recorder in case you forget an extension cord.
- Always use an external microphone. Even an inexpensive model will be better than the internal mics that pick up motor noise as well as sound waves. Keep the cord short to avoid picking up hum. If you can use a really good mic, you will hear the difference—even

with inexpensive cassette machines. Many recorders have an auxiliary input jack (called Aux In or Line In) that can accept an output from another tape recorder or a simple mixer. When you feed into this input you will be able to bypass the machine's (usually noisy) mic preamp.

- Though they are portable, don't knock these machines around too much, as the heads can go out of alignment, yielding inferior quality recordings.
- You can also use an inexpensive machine to save wear and tear on a multitrack. Most wear occurs when you're learning a new part, because you have to repeatedly go over specific sections of that tape. So, record a premix of the tracks on to your cheapo cassette deck, then play that tape over and over again as a practice tape. As soon as you feel that you're getting close to coming up with the perfect part, switch over to the multitrack and start overdubbing.

## Better Live Recordings

If you plan to do live recording, a little cassette machine isn't good enough yet it may be impractical to lug a multitrack around. There are several possible compromises.

- "Pro" cassette machines designed for field recording. While battery-operated and not much bigger than a cheap machine, several refinements put these ahead of your average cassette deck. They will have more rugged and precise motors to control wow and flutter, an integral AC adapter, some external microphones of an acceptable quality level, and noise reduction. Stereo recordings are possible as well as mono, and the noise levels will be lower. All the other comments made about optimizing recordings are also applicable to this breed of machine.
- DAT machines are excellent for live recording. They have a wide enough dynamic range that you can afford to set levels 10 or so dB lower than you would with an analog machine to accommodate the occasional peak, and still have dynamic range to spare. Portable DATs are unobtrusive and inexpensive, and you can record up to two hours' worth of material on a single tape. Get a direct feed from the PA, and the results may be good enough for your contractual-obligation live album.
- Analog reel-to-reel (R-T-R) machines work, but they are heavier, larger, have less overall recording time (unless you use large reels and record at slow speeds), and it's a drag to thread tape in a dark club. As a result, many people who wouldn't carry around an R-T-R recorder can easily deal with carrying around a cassette or DAT machine. Make the recording process as easy as possible on yourself, or you'll lose interest; for this reason, I recommend DAT or cassettes when you want to tape performances or rehearsals.

So now you have a tape machine, you're at a small club, and you want to record some music. If you are recording solely for educational value (such as listening to a rehearsal), you don't have to be too careful. Ask the sound person for a direct output from the mixer, but if that's not possible, stick the mic in front of the PA and let the internal compressor do the rest. If the system overloads, put it farther away from the sound source.

Much has been written and conjectured about live mic placement, and it is true that every situation is different; but the similarities between them make it possible to take advantage of the knowledge you've gained in previous recordings. One rule is to have a couple of foam pads with you. If you just put the microphone on top of a table, you will hear every little floor vibration, and every time anybody taps a finger against the table, you'll have a resonant "thump." Cradling the microphone in a foam pad (Fig. 18-1) helps isolate the mic from shocks and noise.

It is even better to hang the microphone if you can. But this requires a longer microphone

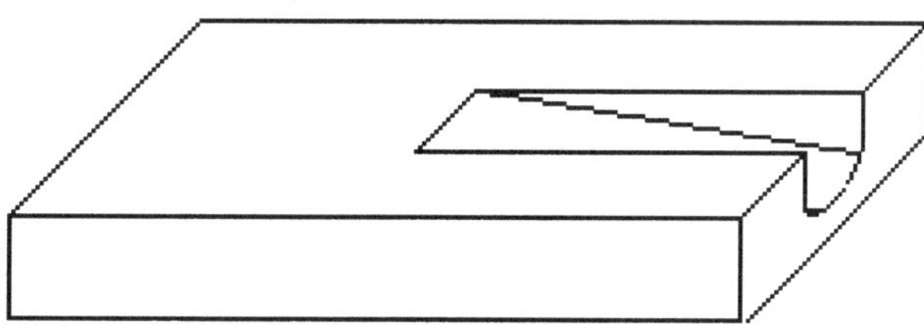

**Fig. 18-1:** *Cut a sloping groove in a foam block to keep the mic from moving around. The capsule end of the mic would point toward the left in this illustration, and the barrel end would fit in the groove.*

cable, so a balanced line system is recommended (as discussed earlier in Chapter 9 on microphones), and don't forget to bring an extension cord for the mic. Fig. 18-2 shows two ways to hang a mic. The "pointing at" works well for groups, but don't overlook the overhead position. Many times this will give good results on instruments such as drums. Again, experimentation is the key to good results.

A stereo recorder gives some extra latitude. In addition to making stereo recordings, you can also consider that you're recording two separate mono tracks, and place the microphones accordingly (*e.g.*, one mic in front of a PA to pick up vocals and some background, another to go overhead on the drums). When you play back in mono, you can vary the levels of the two channels for the best balance.

Making live tapes that sound good is an art, because you frequently have to work against crowd noise, rotten acoustics, difficult-to-mic stage setups, and other problems. But, as in the case of a musical instrument, practice helps make successful tapes. As long as each tape is an improvement over the previous one, you're doing all right. And if there isn't an improvement, you've just learned something not to do, which is sometimes more valuable than knowing what to do.

## How to Generate Overdubs without a Multitrack Recorder

Eight-track digital multitrack tape and hard disk recorders are still beyond many people's budgets. Fortunately, if you're willing to trade off convenience for expense there are some more wallet-friendly alternatives for digital multitracking.

We'll cover two ways to get great-sounding demos: one primarily for synth/drum machine-based music, and the other for more acoustically or electrically oriented material.

The miracle worker in both cases is the DAT (Digital Audio Tape) recorder. However, there are alternatives; anything with good recording characteristics will do the job, such as VCRs with hi-fi tracks, better-quality cassette recorders, or decent analog two-head machines. (Possibly MiniDisc recorders will work too, but the jury's still out.)

### The Workstation/DAT Connection

Today's keyboard workstations often integrate realistic instrument sounds, a sequencer, onboard effects, and internal voice panning—in short, everything needed to create a complete

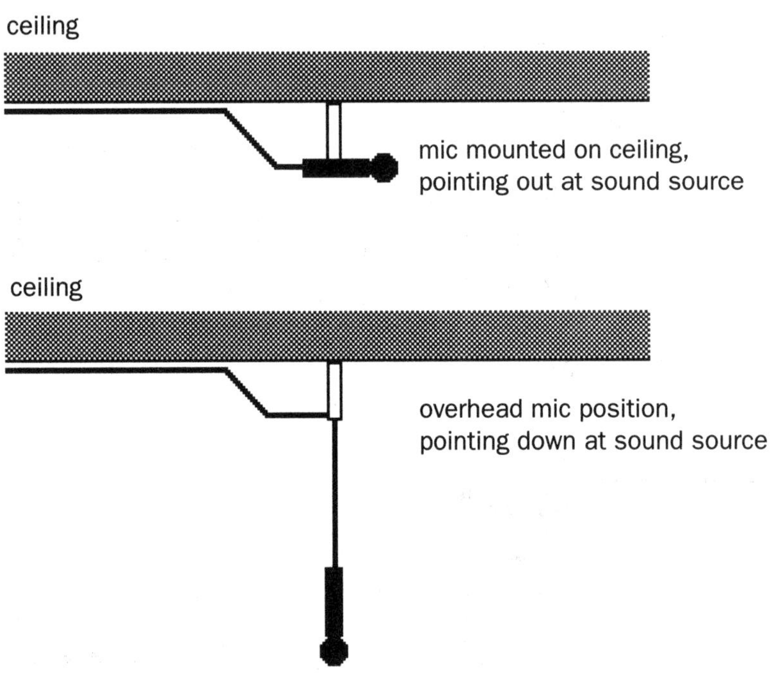


**Fig. 18-2:** *Two ways to hang a mic for live recording. Neither is optimum (the first method picks up stray reflections from the ceiling, causing phase problems; the second can seldom point straight at the source) but either one can be an improvement over simply pointing the mic at the stage.*

composition, except for vocals or acoustic instruments. Use a mixer to combine the workstation output with acoustic sources (Fig. 18-3), and record the result into DAT for a master tape of exceptionally high quality. Since the instrument tracks are sequenced, you can sing (and/or play) over a consistent background until you get the take you want.

Incidentally, I've seen some solo live acts that used a keyboard synth for backing and did vocals and leads over that. If you record the mixer output on DAT, you could end up with some excellent demos.

If you can't afford a mixer, some tape recorders have a feature called mic/line mixing, which provides two separate sets of inputs—one for mic-level, and one for line-level signals. A recorder with mic/line mixing will have separate level controls for each set of inputs; the manufacturer's reason for including this feature is to let you add voice-overs to tapes as you record them.

## Bouncing Your Way to Digital Multitracking

Before affordable multitrack recording, musicians would often build up tracks by *bouncing*—recording into one machine, then sending that output along with additional live sounds into a second machine. This process could be repeated several times to build up more tracks, but unfortunately, with analog tape more bouncing meant more tape hiss, noise reduction coloration, and distortion. Therefore, once budget multitracks arrived, bouncing became a lost art (except for those with four-track studios).

Digital's superior audio characteristics make bouncing viable again; here's a typical application. Record, for example, a rock group's backing tracks into DAT machine A (Fig. 18-4).

Next mix A's output, along with perhaps lead guitar and vocals, into DAT machine B (Fig. 18-5).

You can now take the tape out of B, load it

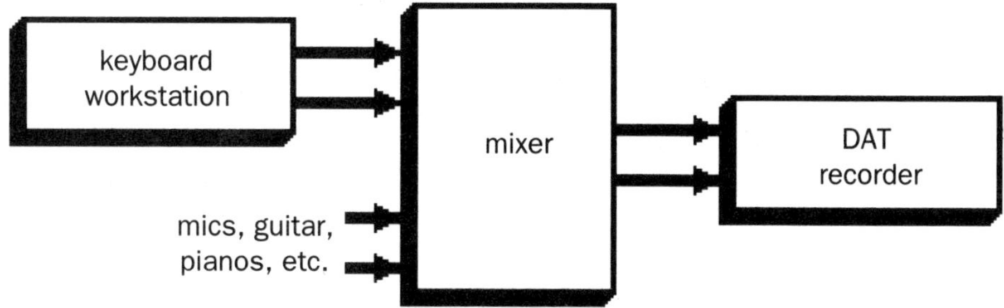


**Fig. 18-3:** *Making a master tape by recording a synthesized backup band along with real-time instruments into a* DAT.

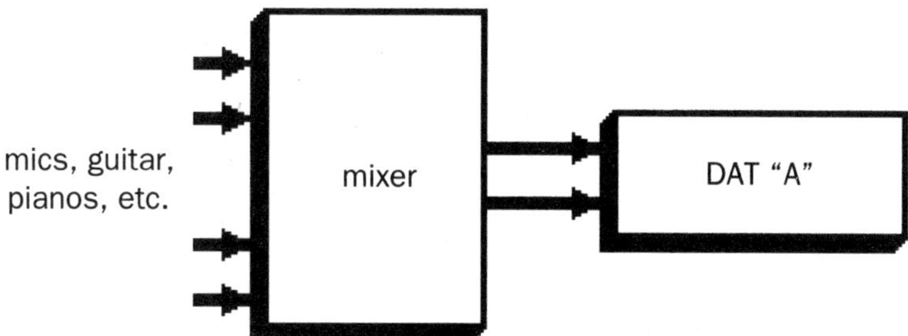


**Fig. 18-4:** DAT *A ends up containing the rhythm tracks.*

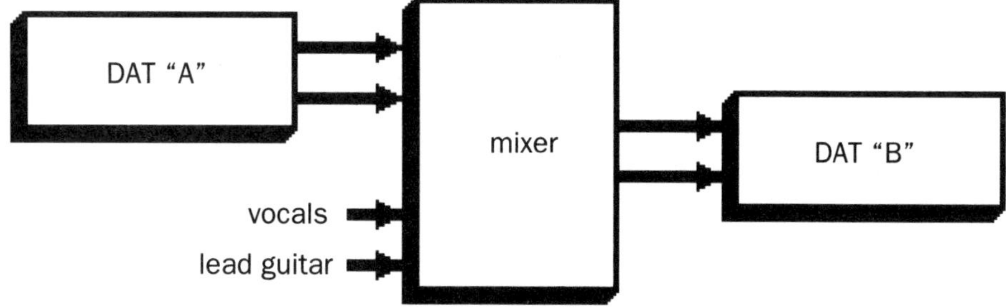


**Fig. 18-5:** DAT *B combines the parts from* DAT *A with new parts played along with* DAT *A in real time.*

into A, put a fresh tape in B, and use the procedure shown in Fig. 18-5 to add more tracks. The tape in B now becomes your master tape.

The biggest limitation is that you must premix parts as you go along; unlike multitrack recording, you can't separate parts once they've been committed to tape. However, if you'd like some insurance, save each premix. If you decide you blew it somewhere along the line, go back to the last properly premixed version so that all you'll need to redo are subsequent overdubs.

The other limitation is that each bounce picks up another overlay of mixer noise. Fortunately, most mixers are pretty quiet these days, and you'll be able to do multiple bounces without objectionable noise.

Incidentally, since you've managed to get two DATs in the same place at the same time, don't forget to back up your master tape on the other DAT machine. After all, DATs do contain digital data and need to be backed up, just like computer disks.

Machines with mic/line mixing are ideal for what we just discussed; if DAT machine B in our previous example had this feature, we could record an instrumental track on DAT A, then play that back into DAT B's line inputs while singing into the mic inputs.

## Squeezing More Tracks out of Multitrack Recorders

Whether you have a four-track cassette deck, eight-track modular digital multitrack, or even a twenty-four-track hard disk recording system, at some point you're going to want more tracks than the machine can deliver. There are many ways to get more tracks out of a machine than you might think; here are some tips.

### Premixing

We can use a variation of the premixing (bouncing) techniques described above within a single recorder. For example, with an eight-track digital recorder, you could record six tracks of rhythm section, then mix them down to tracks 7 and 8. You can now record new material in tracks 1 through 6. Because of digital audio's high quality, you lose very little fidelity by premixing to other tracks. With analog, there is always a build-up of noise and distortion when you premix.

Also note that not all analog machines allow you to bounce to adjacent tracks; you may be limited to bouncing tracks 1 and 2 to track 4, or tracks 3 and 4 to 1. For more information on your individual recorder's limitations with respect to premixing, refer to the owner's manual.

When bouncing with analog decks, equalization can help compensate for deficiencies in the recorder. Since bouncing will tend to build up noise, record your tracks a little brighter than normal so you can cut the treble somewhat on playback. This will restore the signal to its normal brightness, but also, make any hiss less apparent.

Another use of EQ is to compensate for "head bumps." Ever notice with some analog decks that the more you bounce, the boomier the sound? This is because older tape heads add a one or two dB peak in the bass range, called a head bump. As you bounce, these one or two dB peaks can add up until you end up with a pretty serious bass boost. Using EQ to cut the response at the bump's frequency can eliminate the cumulative bass boost and obtain a flatter response.

### Example: Premixing for Four-Track Cassette Decks

Assume you're recording a guitar-bass-drums-piano group, with two vocalists. The keyboard player also plays a synthesizer solo. Here's a step-by-step description of how you'd get all these tracks into a four-track:

1. Record the drums, through microphones and a mixer, into track 1. To avoid leakage problems, you could take the guitar and bass directly into the board and send them to tracks 2 and 3 of the machine.

2. Mix the first three tracks together through your mixer and record the results in track 4. Now track 4 has the composite rhythm section.

3. When you're satisfied with the mix, erase the first three tracks. There's more to the art of mixing than just saying "mix it," but we'll cover that in Chapter 20.

4. Record the piano into track 1 (because it's an overdub, you've also eliminated any leakage problems).

5. Record the synthesizer solo into track 2.

6. Record the two vocal parts, mixed together, into track 3. You now have six tracks.

The only problem is that you had to generate the premixed track from signals already present on the tape, so the premixed track is a second-generation signal. Thus, not only do you have the hiss and distortion that accumulated during the original recording of the basic tracks, but you generate more hiss by re-recording those tracks into another track. Also, if you have any distortion on the original tracks, and you pick up more of it re-recording into track 4, the effect is multiplied. If you record track 4 along with some other tracks into yet another open track, then it would be a third-generation signal with even less fidelity.

Now suppose that after everything was recorded, Megabux Records wants it but the Executive Producer says that the vocals were a little off, you need a lead guitar solo, and the chorus needs a couple of horn parts (fortunately—ahem—the Executive Producer's cousin just happens to play horns). Here's what you would do to satisfy Megabux Records:

1. Wipe the vocals from track 3.
2. Premix track 4 (the rhythm track) and tracks 1 and 2 (piano and synthesizer lead) into track 3.
3. You now have the guitar, bass, and drums present on track 3, along with two second-generation signals (the piano and synthesizer). Notice also that the premix is once again critical, as it's far too late to go back and alter the balance of the bass or drums. However, we have achieved the objective of opening up a few more tracks.
4. Recut the vocals into track 1.
5. Record the lead guitar solo into track 2.
6. Record the horn parts into track 4.
7. Wait for the recording to go platinum.

Unfortunately, though, you don't get something for nothing. The quality of second-generation analog material is inferior to first generation material, and third-generation signals (without benefit of noise reduction) are all but useless except under the most favorable conditions. As a result, it's best to minimize the number of times you have to bounce, something we can do with intelligent track management.

Perhaps a better way to handle the session just described would have been to record the drums into track 1, the bass into track 2, and the guitar and synthesizer parts—mixed together—into track 3. Then, while mixing these into track 4 through a mixer, add the piano part in real time. This does require someone to play the piano and someone to mix, though, so it isn't all that applicable to a single artist doing demo work. Now you have drums, bass, guitar, synthesizer, and piano all in track 4. Then, record the vocals into track 1, the lead guitar line into track 2, and the horns into track 3. There you have it—the same number of tracks as in the first example exist on the finished product, except that we've bypassed having to do any third-generation overdubs, and have thus managed to maintain a higher level of quality.

## The Two-to-Two Bounce for Four-Track Cassette Decks

What sounds like a dance step is actually a variation on the two-machine bounce described earlier. Again, the best way to illustrate this is with an example: a rock group with guitar, bass, drums, keyboard, and lead singer (all other band members sing backup) wants to make a stereo demo that's as impressive as possible. Here's the play-by-play (Fig. 18-6):

1. Mic the various instruments through a good mixer and set stereo locations for all the instrumental tracks. At this point, we don't include any vocals.
2. After getting this mix, send the mixer's left channel output into track 1 and the right channel output into track 2. So, we now have the full instrumental section residing in tracks 1 and 2.
3. Feed the outputs from tracks 1 and 2 into a mixer; also, feed the four backup-vocal mics into this mixer and give them an appropriate stereo spread.
4. Bounce tracks 1 and 2, along with the vocals, into tracks 3 and 4. Now we have instrumental plus vocal backups, in stereo, in tracks 3 and 4, and we haven't gone beyond the second generation.
5. There are still two tracks left: put the lead vocalist in one, and lead guitar (with maybe a couple of other sounds) in the second track.

Mix these four tracks down into a good machine, and you have a stereo mix of the band. You can even add effects such as limiting or EQ when you mix down into the other machine, or mix in another instrument part.

## Recording Along with a Premix

Any time you premix, there's the option to mix in another instrument along with the tracks you're premixing. This gets you another part without using up another track. Even if you're a solo artist and you can't mix and play at the same time, you can still probably add some drones, fills, percussion, harmonies, and other parts during lulls in the mixing; if you keep the

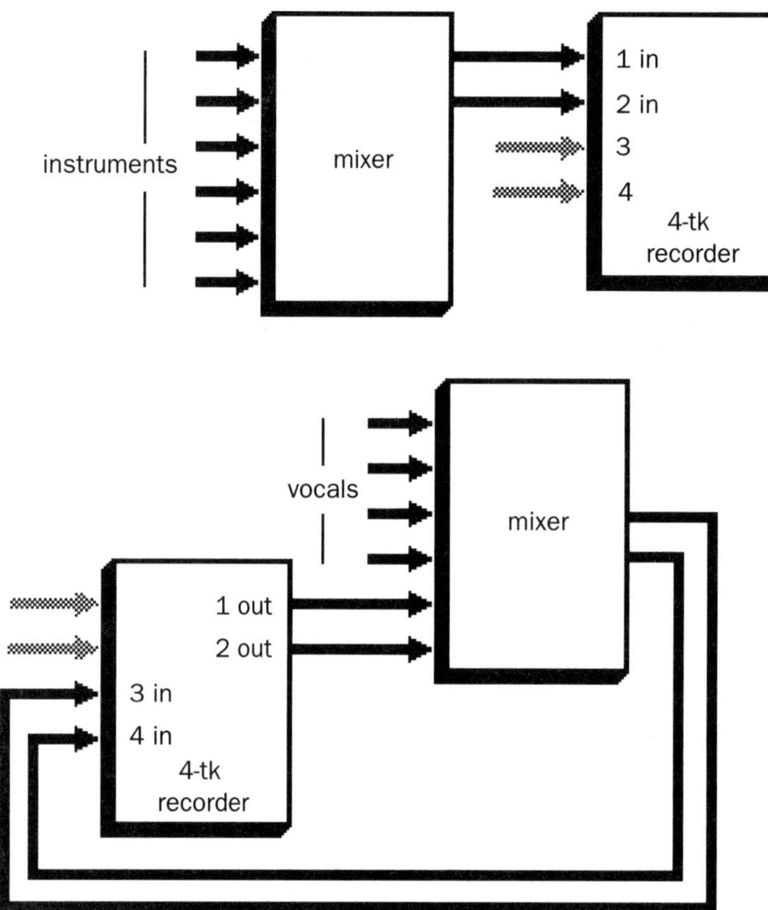


**Fig. 18-6:** *The instrumental track gets recorded into tracks 1 and 2. These are then mixed with vocals into tracks 3 and 4. Next, tracks 1 and 2 could be erased to make room for additional parts.*

mixing requirements simplified, you may even be able to add a fairly complex part. Probably the best example would be playing a right-hand keyboard part on a synthesizer while doing the mixing with your left hand. Doesn't sound easy? Well, it isn't, but practice does make perfect (or at least a little bit more proficient).

## Using an Additional Machine for Stereo

This tip that applies only to four-track cassette decks. If you have a standard cassette recorder, and your four-track cassette machine can play back standard cassettes, here's an easy way to get good stereo.

1. Record your rhythm section on all four tracks on the multitrack machine.

2. Mix these down in stereo to a standard cassette deck.

3. Take the cassette containing the mixed rhythm section and insert it into the multitrack machine. The stereo premix will appear on tracks 1 and 3 of the multitrack recorder, and you still have tracks 2 and 4 left over for overdubs (typically vocals or lead parts).

4. After completing the overdubs, you can mix down all the tracks—stereo premix plus the two overdubs—to a mastering machine to create the final stereo product.

## More Life for Analog

Another one of DAT's many talents is to extend the usefulness of your analog machine. Record into as many tracks as are available on the analog deck, then premix down to stereo DAT. Bounce the DAT back into two tracks of the eight-track, which frees up six tracks on your multitrack for further recording.

## MDM Bouncing

Although modular digital multitracks can do digital bouncing with various accessories (*e.g.*, remote controls or some signal processors with digital inputs), standard bouncing using the analog outputs results in very little loss of fidelity. Tracks can be bounced within the MDM, as well as to other machines.

For example, to turn your MDM into a twelve-track recorder, record on tracks 1 through 6, then mix down to tracks 7 and 8. Now record new parts on tracks 1 through 6 for a total of twelve tracks.

If you also have a DAT, you can easily get fourteen tracks from an MDM. Record on all eight tracks of the MDM, then premix to DAT in stereo. Bounce the DAT tracks back to two MDM tracks (preferably digitally), then record over the six remaining tracks.

## Using Multitrack Recorders with MIDI Sequencers

There is a trend for hard disk recording and playback to occur within a software MIDI sequencer environment, however combining a multitrack recorder with a MIDI sequencer can offer much of the same flexibility without the added expense of a hard disk recording system.

Stripe one multitrack tape track with SMPTE (some MDMs can generate SMPTE without having to give up a track), and sync your sequencer to this SMPTE signal (for more on synchronization, see Chapter 14). As you control the multitrack's motion with the transport controls, the sequencer will automatically follow along, letting you mix digital recording with any sequencer.

Hard disk recording systems can often import MIDI files to accomplish the same kind of integration without having to give up a track. At the very least, they will usually sync to SMPTE, so you can use a common SMPTE clock source for both the hard disk recording system and MIDI sequencer.

## Using Multitrack Tape Recorders with Hard Disk Recorders

Multitrack hard disk recording systems offer exceptional editing capabilities, but require high-capacity hard disks for storage. One way around this is to use an MDM in conjunction with a two-track hard disk recording system. Stripe the MDM with SMPTE (assuming it doesn't generate SMPTE by itself) and sync a hard disk recorder (and possibly MIDI sequencer) to the MDM. Record into the hard disk while synched to tape, and do all your editing and digital signal processing within the hard disk system.

Once the part is perfected, back up the hard disk to something like DAT then bounce the part over to an MDM track, either through analog connections or a digital interface. You can continue recording and editing on the hard disk, then bouncing over to the MDM, until you fill all seven tracks with hard-disk edited material.

## "Infinite" Layering

If you need lots and lots of tracks for something like a choir effect, you can bounce back and forth between tracks, adding a new "live" part each time, until you achieve the desired density. Example: Record a voice in track 1. Then, play back that track, while mixing in a live vocal, into track 2. Now play back track 2, mix in a live vocal, and send the combined sound back into track 1. You can keep bouncing between tracks 1 and 2, adding a new "live" vocal each time, until matters get truly out of hand.

Here's a step-by-step example of how to do infinite layering with a four-track cassette machine. Suppose you want a massive guitar sound and massive keyboard sound on a basic track—like seven tracks of guitars and four tracks of keyboards. Sound impossible? It isn't—just observe the following steps. We'll assume that your particular machine won't allow you to bounce to adjacent tracks.

1. Record your drum track or other metronome reference in track 3.

2. While monitoring track 3, record your first guitar part in track 1 and your second guitar part in track 2.

3. Bounce tracks 1 and 2 (along with a third guitar part played "live") into track 4. We now have three guitar parts in track 4.

4. Listen to track 4, play the fourth guitar part along with it, and mix both of these into track 1.

5. Record the fifth guitar part in track 2 while monitoring track 1, then bounce tracks 1 and 2 (mixed with the sixth guitar part played "live") over to track 4.

6. Mix track 4 with part number 7, and bounce the combination over to track 1. We now have seven guitar tracks in track 1. If that's not a massive enough guitar sound, you can continue this process of bouncing until you run out of patience, lose your sanity, or the quality of sound turns to mud.

7. For the four keyboard parts, record part 1 in track 2, mix track 2 along with part 2 (done "live") into track 4, mix track 4 with part 3 (again done live) into track 2, and finally, mix track 2 with part 4 played live into track 4.

8. The net result: you now have four keyboard parts in track 4, the drums in track 3, and seven guitar parts in track 1. Sing your vocals while playing bass, record the results into track 2, and the tune is done.

I'm not saying that having all these parts is musically desirable, by the way; the main point is to show how you can get lots of tracks out of even a modest four-track setup.

## Track Strategies

The producer and engineer should sit down with the musicians before a session to determine just how many parts need to go down on the tape, whether any premixing will be involved, and so on. This prevents any embarrassing problems that could happen later, such as needing four tracks to record a bunch of instruments and having only one track available.

While each situation is different, there are certain commonalities.

- Put on sweetening first when you're bouncing within a machine. I know, this is the reverse of what we've been taught, but there's a very good reason for this: Parts that don't have to be premixed will have better fidelity than premixed parts. For example, suppose you have a tune with a four-part horn section, rhythm guitar, keyboard, bass, vocals, and drums, and you need to fit all these on a four-track cassette deck . . . and to make life even more complicated, you happen to be playing all the parts yourself so you can't lay down more than one instrument at a time.

  A suitable strategy would be as follows. Record a click track on track 3, and three of the horn parts on tracks 1, 2, and 4. Premix all three horns, plus a live part to complete the four-part section, into track 3. This leaves three tracks to work with. Next, record guitar in track 1, keyboard in track 2, and premix these (in the sync mode) along with bass into track 4. We now have tracks 1 and 2 open, into which the voice and drums will fit nicely.

  Note that we've put the rhythm instruments on closer to the end of the recording process than the beginning—the opposite of the usual process. However, we've also managed to cram a lot of tracks on to our four-track, so there are some compensations.

- Plan to record those instruments requiring highest fidelity last. Repeated bouncing, whether within one machine or by recording back and forth between two machines, affects the sonic quality of a signal to the point where the build-up in noise and distortion can be quite noticeable. However, as you get towards the end of recording a particular piece you will have fewer and fewer free tracks available, which means that there will be fewer possibilities for bouncing, which means that the last few instruments you record will have no bouncing whatsoever. These instruments will have the highest fidelity of anything on the tape.

- Composition versus improvisation. Unfortunately, these kinds of layering techniques really work only if you have a definite idea of where the song is heading—in other words, the song has to be composed down to the very last bar. There may be room for improvisation on an individual track or two, but overall, the song will generally not be able to deviate from a very specific structure.

  This can cause problems with bands that write in the studio rather than working out their material "live." As a producer, you need to be sympathetic to the needs of the musicians, but still get across the fact that when budgets and track space are tight, a song must be well rehearsed. If it is not, premixing becomes much more difficult because you can't alter the levels or equalization of premixed parts, except within very narrow limits.

- Effects: Add during recording, or add during mixdown? In most studios, tracks are recorded as dry as possible, with effects being added later. While there are some engineers who disagree with this approach, it seems that they are in the minority. However, having a limited number of tracks tends to bend the rules a bit: adding effects is no exception.

  For example, most people don't like to put reverb on a drum set's bass drum. This is fine if you have a twenty-four-track machine where the bass drum has its own track, but what if the drums have been premixed along with guitar and bass on to a single track? In a case like that, you're better off adding reverb as you record the drums in the first place, and avoid putting any on the bass drum. So, if any part of the premix needs its own processing, that should be done as the part is being recorded.

## Typical Eight-Track Hookups

An eight-track's input jacks typically hook up in one of three ways:

- To the console's direct tape outs (these patch input signals directly to tape, bypassing most mixer circuitry). This is preferred when the signals going to tape require none of the mixer's features (effects, grouping, routing, *etc.*). *Example:* Consider a live gig using a sixteen-channel mixer for the house mix where you also want to record the parts for possible use in a live album. Assume four mics go into inputs 1 through 4, and various instrument outputs go into inputs 5 through 8. The direct outs feed the multitrack, which receives the unmixed signals. Meanwhile, the person doing the house mix can adjust levels, fade signals in and out, apply effects, and so on, without affecting the recorder's ability to capture the raw signals for later use.

- To eight mixer bus outputs. You can use the mixer for grouping, premixing, effects, *etc.*—in fact, you can put any signal on any track, any time. This puts more circuitry between the input signals and multitrack, although since most routing can be done at the mixer, you'll seldom need to do any repatching.
- To a combination of direct outputs and bus outputs. Some situations require a combination of the two approaches. *Example:* Consider a live gig you want to record with two vocal mics, four mics on drums, two direct feeds from guitar and bass amps, and one direct feed from keyboards. The vocals, bass, guitar, and keyboards could be taken direct and go to five tracks. The four drum mics can be mixed to stereo within the mixer, sent to the submix outs, then go to two tracks. The remaining track could record audience sounds or capture one of the instruments in stereo, if applicable.

## A Real World Example: Mixing in the Solo Studio

When you're trying to be creative, it's best not to have to repatch too much, think too hard, or waste time. In addition to enhancing creativity, eliminating time-wasters makes the working process a lot more fun. This is particularly important when working solo, because you don't have someone else to push the buttons and do the "left brain" work for you.

Anyway, here's a fast, easy, and convenient way to use a mixer in a solo studio environment where you're doing the engineering as well as the playing. Fig. 18-7 shows the basic setup, based on an eight-track multitrack and "generic" mixer (with sixteen or more inputs and two sets of stereo outputs, such as main and submaster, or main and aux). Let's look at the details.

### Inputs

Most of the time, any "special channels" in the mixer (*e.g.*, channels that include features not in other channels, such as XLR inputs) are the lower-numbered ones. Therefore, use the first eight channels for acoustic and MIDI instruments, virtual tracks, microphones, outputs from submixers, and the like.

The eight tape track outputs feed into mixer inputs 9 through 16. So, tape track 1 appears at mixer input 9, track 2 at input 10, track 3 at input 11, *etc.* (If you use track 8 to provide sync, you can leave input 16 open as a spare input.) Reverb and other effects returns feed dedicated return inputs. If these aren't available, you'll need to route effects returns somewhere within channels 1 through 8.

### Outputs

The master outs go to a two-track mixdown deck such as a DAT and also drive the monitor system. The stereo submaster outputs go to the tape track(s) on which you want to record. Rather than repatching these outputs into different tracks all the time, you can build a simple little box that rips off—err, I mean, emulates—a cool feature built into the ADAT eight-track digital recorder.

With ADAT, you only need to plug into inputs 1 and 2 since input 1 is hard-wired to inputs 3, 5, and 7 and input 2 is hard-wired to inputs 4, 6, and 8. So, in a hookup like the one shown, *all* tracks are *always* hearing the submixed output; to record on a track, you simply set the submaster levels as desired, then record enable the track(s) into which you want to record the submix.

With the multiple box (Fig. 18-8), the submaster right output goes simultaneously to tape inputs 1, 3, 5, and 7, while the submaster left out goes to tape inputs 2, 4, 6, and 8. (Most mixers have low enough output impedances so that they can drive multiple tape recorder inputs with no loss of sound quality.) As with ADAT, simply record enable the track(s) you want to record into.

### Recording Basic Tracks

Here's a practical example to demonstrate a typical recording session. The key idea is to use the submaster bus for sending signals to tape, and the master bus for monitoring.

Suppose you're feeding a stereo keyboard's output into mixer inputs 1 and 2. To record that on tape:

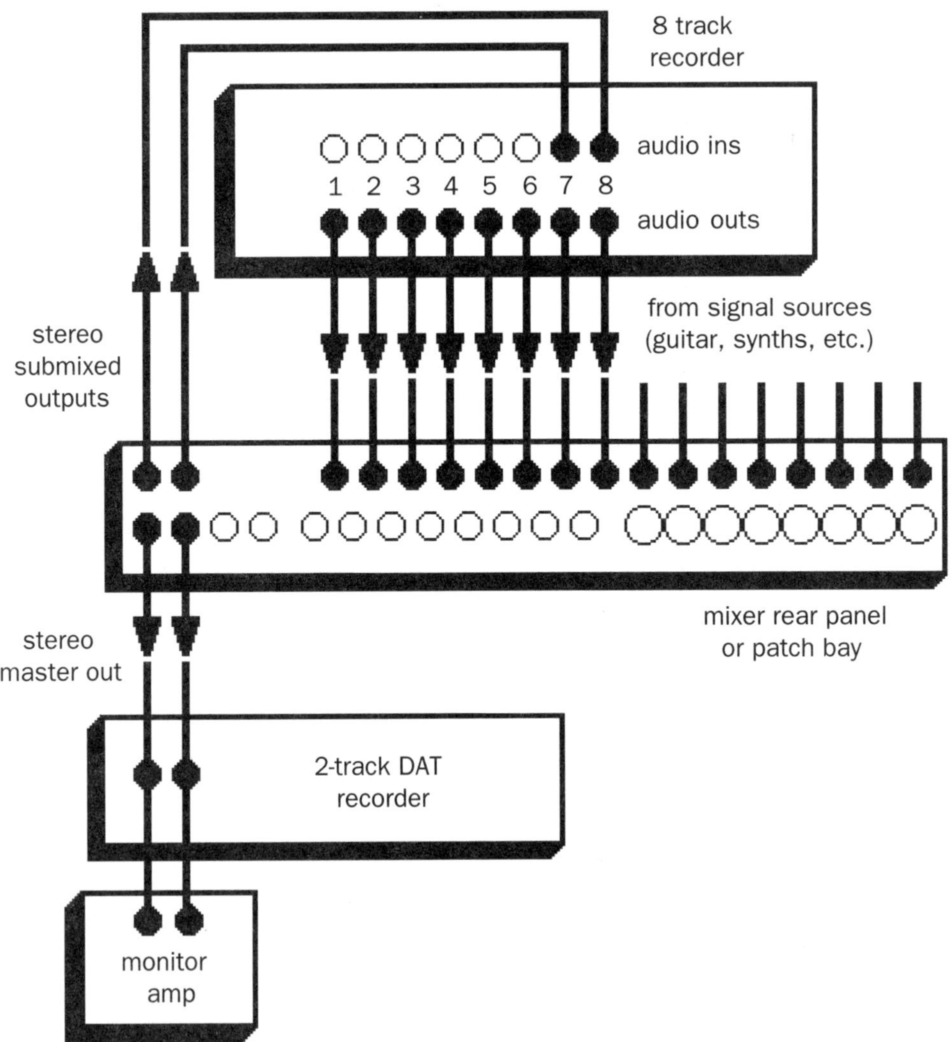


Fig. 18-7: *Typical patching scheme for single-operator studio with eight-track recorder, mixer, and mastering deck.*

1. Configure mixer channels 1 and 2 so that the keyboard does not feed the master bus but feeds the submaster bus. (The procedure for doing this varies for different mixers; refer to your manual.)

2. Record-enable the two tape tracks into which the keyboard output will be recorded (let's say tracks 4 and 5), then set the submaster faders for the appropriate recording levels.

3. To monitor the signal being recorded, you'll need to listen to the tape outputs (all monitoring should be done in sync mode, if applicable). Configure mixer channels 12 and 13 (which are receiving the outputs from tape tracks 4 and 5) to feed the master bus for monitoring. To prevent earsplitting feedback, make sure none of the signal from channels 12 and 13 gets into the submaster bus.

4. Start recording.

## Recording Overdubs

This is similar to recording basic tracks. Monitor the already recorded tracks by feeding them to the master bus, and use the submaster bus to send signals to the tape recorder.

Many mixers now include headphone jacks for monitoring. If so, when doing vocals you can simply use phones and turn down the monitor amp.

## Premixing and Bouncing

Doing premixes and bounces of recorded tape tracks is pretty simple: just switch the group of tracks to be bounced into the submaster bus, adjust the submaster bus faders for the right blend, record enable the tracks where you want the premix recorded, then go into record. Monitor these tracks from the master bus.

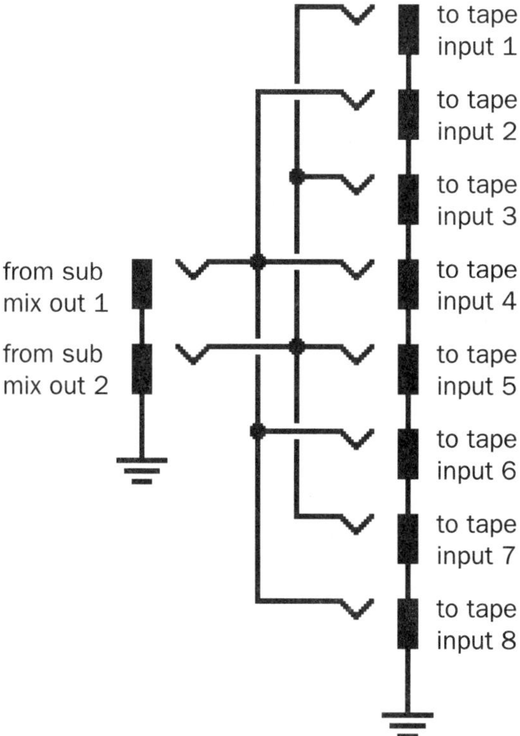


Fig. 18-8: *A multiple box.*

### The Big Caution

The only real caution with using these techniques is you must pay close attention to when something should be switched to the submaster bus (which feeds the tape recorder) and when it should feed the master bus (which you monitor). For example, if you're using the master bus to monitor a tape channel into which you're recording signals and also have this feeding the sub bus, a massive amount of feedback (and maybe a blown speaker!) will probably be your reward. If you do transgress in this respect, just hope you're not wearing headphones. . . .

Another note is that by always going through the submix bus to get to the tape deck rather than just patching directly, you may end up with a bit more noise. However, today's mixers are usually quiet enough that any extra noise will probably not be audible.

One final thought: remember that most mixers have effects returns for reverbs and such, and these can be used in a pinch as inputs. This can be a real lifesaver when doing sessions with lots of virtual MIDI tracks.

## Multiple Modular Digital Multitrack (MDM) Applications

The more MDMs, the merrier. These devices are designed so you can keep adding MDMs until you run out of the need for tracks (or disposable income, whichever comes first). Here are just some of the cool tricks you can do with multiple MDMs.

### Synchronizing Multiple MDMs

MDMs have made synchronization easy. Synchronization usually requires nothing more than a particular cable (consult with your manufacturer) for each pair of MDMs to be synchronized.

1. Connect one end of the cable to the master MDM's sync out jack.
2. Connect the other end of the cable to the slave MDM's sync in jack.
3. If there are additional slaves, connect one end of an additional cable to the first slave's sync out jack, and the other end to the second slave's sync in jack. Its sync out jack then connects to the third slave's sync in jack, and so on. See Fig. 14-2 in Chapter 14.

### Simplified Backup

Hook the master MDM's digital output (with the material to be backed up) into the slave's digital input. Record-enable the slave, press Play on the master, and you can make a digital "clone" of your master tape.

### "Megatracking"

Megatracking is a means of getting far more tracks out of a multiple MDM system than the physical number of tracks would indicate.

*Example:* Suppose your rhythm section is in four tracks of a master MDM, and you want to cut a fabulous guitar solo. You can record eight tracks' worth of solos in the slave MDM, then mix the best parts of these tracks down to one track on your master tape. (You can even keep the original eight tracks of solos, just in case you think you might want to change your mind about remixing the solo.)

Now it's time to cut vocals; you can use the same technique and bounce several tracks of vocals from the slave MDM into one coherent vocal part on the master MDM.

### Easy Collaboration

If you're working with someone who uses the same MDM format, it's easy to exchange cassettes (the two most common formats are S-VHS and Hi-8). Example: Suppose you know a great vocalist who lives a couple of thousand miles away and has a single MDM, and you have two MDMs. Here's the step-by-step procedure for getting some great vocals:

1. Leave one or two tracks open on your master (if you need more tracks, they can go in your slave machine).

2. Insert a blank cassette in the slave MDM, then mix your master down to two tracks on the slave MDM. This leaves six tracks open.

3. Send the slave cassette to your vocalist, who then records six tracks of killer vocals.

4. Insert the cassette with vocals into the slave deck.

5. Mix the vocals down into the empty track(s) on your master tape. Mission accomplished!

## Other MDM Applications

### Combined Multitrack/Mastering Deck + Pseudo-Automated Mixdown!

An eight-track MDM can serve as a combination six-track multitrack recorder and two-track mastering deck. Record your audio into tracks 1 through 6, then run them through a mixer into tracks 7 and 8. Tracks 7 and 8 then contain the stereo master recording.

One great thing about using this technique is that you can also do a kind of primitive automated mixing. Suppose you're mixing and you notice that the lead guitar comes in too soft for the solo. Leave all the other faders as they are, and rewind the tape to before the guitar starts playing the solo. Increase the guitar track fader, then press play. Punch in just before the guitar solo; the other tracks will be at the same level, but the guitar will now be louder. Keep working your way through the song—rewinding, changing levels, and punching as necessary—until you have the perfect mix. Cool!

### Digital Audio Archiving

MDMs are superb for archiving applications. When you add up the number of tracks and multiply it by the amount of time for each track, you have some serious storage (*e.g.*, an eight-track MDM can record over five hours of mono material or two and one-half hours of stereo material by recording forty minutes on each track). This is excellent for archiving speeches and broadcasts, safeties of stereo mixes, or libraries of stereo samples. For example, I have all my samples stored on one ADAT tape, and backed up to a second one.

### Live Recording

MDMs are excellent for live recording because of their compact size and easy operation. Eight tracks allow for recording audience sounds and individual soloists as well as a stereo mix off the PA.

## Special Effects

Although many people think of special effects as something that involves external processing, that's not the only way to manipulate sounds in the studio. Multitrack recorders often include several ways to process sounds within the machines themselves. We'll start off with universally applicable tips, and move on to techniques that apply only to analog recorders.

### Punching In

With recorders that allow punching, at any time during the recording process you can hit the record button to throw any record-enabled tracks into record mode. Example: Suppose you have a vocal, and the first verse is excellent but the chorus is a bit off. Run the tape; when the chorus comes in, punch the record button, have the singer do the part, and then stop the recorder by punching out before you erase the rest of the track.

Punching works differently with different technologies.

- Analog tape. With analog recorders, after punching out there will be a small gap equal to the time it takes for tape to make it from the record head to the playback head. If you have a really tight punch out point, be careful not to erase the beginning of the next section.

  Some analog recorders let you correlate punch points to readings on the footage counter for automated punch-in and punch-out, but be careful. The counter can slip over time, thus shifting the punch point. If you're doing a very tight punch, watch for this.

- Digital tape and hard disk recording. These offer gapless, seamless punching with no delays. Most of the time you can even set up the punch to fade in or out over a short period of time (*e.g.*, 20 to 50 ms), and preprogram punch points so that the punch in and punch out operations occur automatically.

- MIDI sequencing. As with digital audio technology, you can specify punch points with extreme accuracy and automate the punch in and out process. There is no gap.

Punching in can be used in other ways. For example, suppose you have a song with two vocal parts—the singers sing a verse, go away to make room for an instrumental solo, then come back again into the verse. In a case like this you may be able to punch in another part while the vocals are out (sort of like a time-sharing arrangement). When a vocally oriented song ends on an instrumental fadeout, you can always use the vocal track to add another part and deepen the texture.

Here's another use for punching in. If you use effect boxes, unless you have the dandy, computerized kind, it probably takes you a bit of time to change sounds. But with punching in, you can record the first part of a solo, change your settings, go back to the beginning of the solo, play it, and finally punch in where the second half begins.

## Crossfading

Crossfading usually applies to a situation where one cut segues into another cut; in other words, as one fades out, the other fades in. In professional studios, this effect is usually implemented with multiple recorders or with hard disk recording systems (where crossfading is almost always built into the program). In a simple four-track setup, you could have a stereo song recorded in two tracks, and another song on two other tracks. If the beginnings and endings overlap, then with proper mixing you can accomplish a crossfading effect. For more information on using multitrack decks for crossfading, see Chapter 21 on Mastering and Assembling.

## Backwards Effects

This can be done easily only with analog tape or hard disk recording, but still, it's a fun effect. The early pioneers of electronic music were very much into using tape modification to create new sounds, and backwards tape is one example. Early tape recorders recorded over the full width of the tape, which could only record in one direction. If you turned the reels over (Fig. 18-9) and played the tape, the sounds came out "backwards"—for example, a decaying note when played backwards, sounded like it was coming up from nowhere to full volume. Jimi Hendrix probably used a lot of backwards tape effects, especially on *Axis: Bold as Love.*

Pianos, guitars, voices, cymbals, and drums all sound quite unlike their normal selves when played backwards. Once you get your head adjusted to thinking of a melodic line, or rhythm, backwards, you can start playing with this technique.

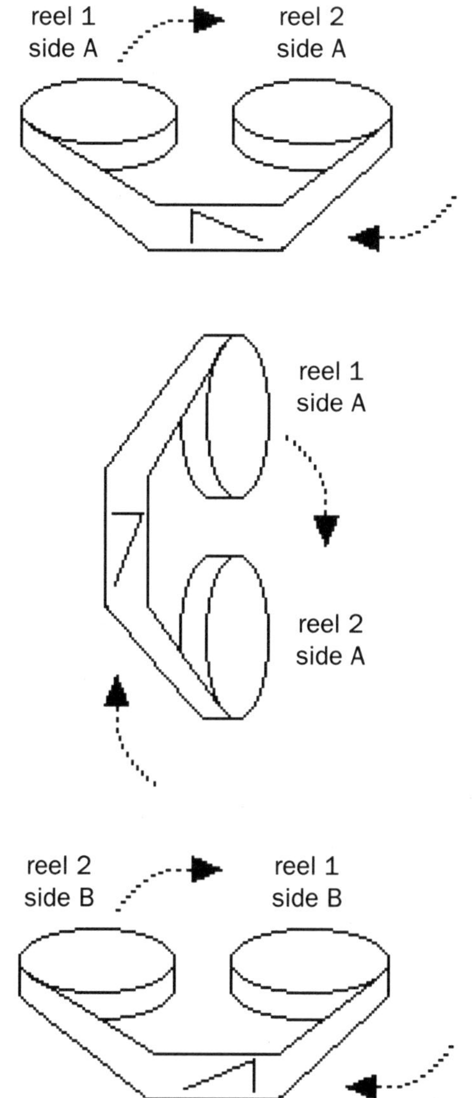


**Fig. 18-9:** *Reversing the reels with reel-to-reel tape gives "backwards" sounds.*

It's easy to do backwards parts with hard disk recording systems that have a "reverse" function. Reverse all the existing audio tracks so that what used to be the end of the file is now at the beginning. Start recording; since the song is going by from end to beginning, when you lay down your part, you start with the climax and end with the introduction. Although it may be hard to catch the exact meter of a song, the tempo will probably be pretty obvious, even when played backwards. Play along with the music as best you can; it's difficult, but luckily, upon playback, the backwards effect is so startling that it usually sounds like it's in time with the music anyway.

After the solo, reverse all the tracks again. The original tracks will play back normally, and the new track you just recorded will play backwards.

It's only a little more complicated to do backwards techniques with analog tape, although you must be careful not to erase tracks accidentally when attempting backwards tape parts, as the positions of the tracks change when the tape is flipped over.

Referring to Fig. 18-10, suppose there's an eight-track tape with guitar on track 1, bass on track 2, and stereo drums on tracks 3 and 4; we want to add a backwards guitar solo on track 5. Let the tape run through to the end of the song (start thinking backwards!), then flip the reels over so that this ending now becomes the beginning of the tape going in the backwards direction.

Note that what we had recorded on track 1 is now being picked up as track 8 as far as the head is concerned, due to flipping the tape. Also, track 2 is now being picked up as track 7, and track 3 is being picked up as track 6. Therefore, we want to record our solo into what the machine sees as track 4, so that it turns into track 5 when the tape is flipped back over to its normal position.

Still with me? Next, set up to record into track 4. Start the recorder and play along with the backwards song. When you flip the tapes back again, the solo will be reversed.

Here's a trick for cueing when a backwards part should begin: before flipping over the tape, if you have an extra track handy, record some type of sound to cue where the backwards part should begin and where it should end. You will like having those markers when you begin the actual solo itself. Make the sound percussive—like clicking drumsticks—so that the beat is easily recognizable when played backwards.

## Preverb

This is reverb that builds up to a sound rather than decays away from it, and again takes advantage of backwards tape techniques. Essentially, what you do is flip the tape (or apply a hard disk system's reverse function) and play a track (or tracks) backwards through reverb, while recording the reverb track. When you reverse the tracks again, the music comes out as expected, but the reverb is backwards—instead of decaying when there's a percussive sound, the reverb fades in until the percussive sound occurs, at which point the reverb goes away.

For hard disk systems, simply reverse the tracks you want to have "preverbed," play them back through a reverb unit, and record into an empty track.

Analog tape requires a bit more work, so here's a step-by-step example.

1. Assume you have a drum track in channel 1 of an eight-track machine, and want to add preverb.

2. Go to the end of the tune, flip the tape, and start playing. You should hear the drums playing backward over channel 8.

3. Feed channel 8's output into a reverb unit and record that into an empty track (*e.g.*, track 7).

4. Flip the tape over again. Track 2 (which we recorded as track 7) contains the reverse reverb sound, giving the preverb effect.

## Echo

Echo is easy to do with MIDI and hard disk systems. Hard disk recording allows for the most flexible recording options because you can simply define a section of audio, copy it, paste it to an empty track, offset the start point by the

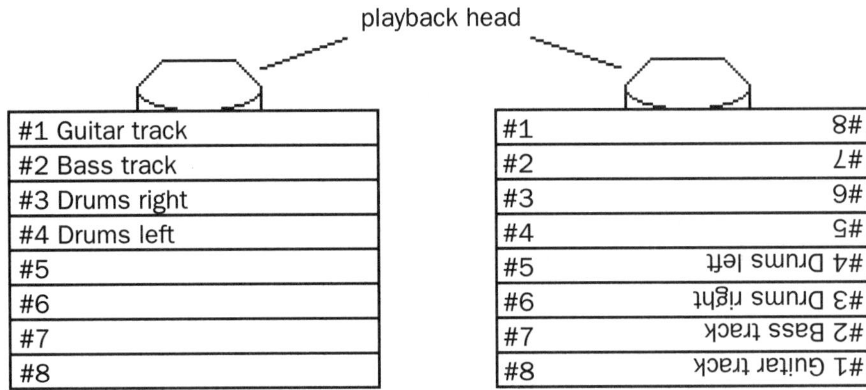


**Fig. 18-10:** *How flipping a tape to create backwards tape effects changes the channels through which sounds play back.*

amount of delay you want, and lower the volume so that the echo is softer than the main signal. If you need more echoes, do more copies to more tracks, and adjust the levels and start points. To reclaim some space, you can then compact all the echo tracks down into one track.

Note that there are no restrictions on echo time—it can be as long or short as you want.

MIDI sequencing also allows for echo effects. As with hard disk recording, define a region of MIDI data, copy it, paste it to an empty track with the desired amount of offset, and lower the volume. However, with MIDI, if you use controller messages to affect the overall level, then it will affect *any* of the tracks containing notes from the synthesizer. For MIDI echo, you'll need to regulate the level by lowering the velocity of the notes. For example, copy a part, reduce the velocities by fifty percent, then paste with the desired offset; then copy that part, reduce the velocities by another fifty percent, paste with the desired offset, and so on.

One disadvantage of using MIDI to generate echo is that all those echoed notes use up synth voices very rapidly. MIDI echo works best if you want something simple, like slapback echo, or if you have a synthesizer with lots of polyphony (at least sixteen voices, and preferably more like twenty-four or thirty-two).

Although an analog tape recorder is limited in its abilities as a tape echo unit, a three-head model can provide that legendary "vintage" tape echo sound used back in the days of Sun Records, Elvis Presley, and Buddy Holly.

Here's the setup (Fig. 18-11):

1. Plug your signal into the mixer (in this example, it's channel 15).

2. Patch the mixer aux bus out into the tape recorder input.

3. Plug the tape recorder output into another mixer input (in this example, channel 16).

4. Thread the tape, put it into record, and monitor off the playback head.

5. Turn up the level on channel 16 to hear a slapback echo effect.

6. For multiple echoes, turn up channel 16's aux send to recirculate some of the tape echo output back to the input. Caution! Turn this up too high, and you'll get major feedback. The only disadvantage to this process is that by feeding the signal back onto itself, you also feed back some of the noise, resulting in a net increase in noise.

7. Try different tape speeds to change the amount of delay. Since the echo's delay time depends on how long it takes a signal recorded at the record head to hit the playback head and get into the loop again, faster tape speed means faster echo. Often echo is done at either 7.5 or 15 ips.

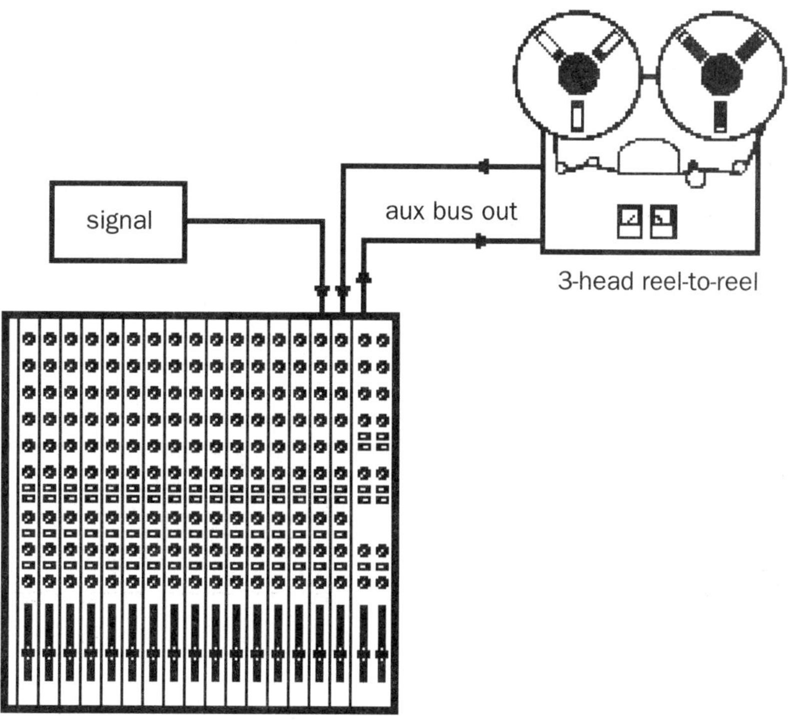


**Fig. 18-11:** *A three-head reel-to-reel recorder can provide echo effects.*

## Variable Speed Effects

If your machine has variable speed, you're in luck. Even slight speed alterations create some stunning effects: if you add a drum part to a track that's sped up about three percent, then on playback, the drums will be slowed down by three percent. This means a lower tuning and a slightly longer decay, which can make drums sound huge (particularly snare drums). Vocals, on the other hand, respond well to speeding up, if the difference is slight. For this, sing along with a track going at a slightly lower than normal speed. When you bring the track back up to speed, the voice will go up too.

Using instruments with a variable-speed recorder is a little more difficult, since the tuning changes as the tape speed changes. This requires either transposition of the piece, or retuning, both of which are messy. Also, you have to "tune" the track to the instrument. But this can have its advantages: if you are laying a piano track onto a piece of tape and the piano is flat by a quarter-tone, then slow the tape down to match the piano, and record along with that.

## Double-Tracking

Double-tracking thickens recorded sounds, such as lead instruments or voices; this can only be accomplished in a multitrack environment (you can use delay lines to get similar effects, but it's just not the same). Listen to the track you want to double, and play along with it as closely as possible while recording the new part into a separate track. Playing these two back in unison (assuming the parts are very close together with respect to timing) appears to give one big, full voice instead of two little ones. This technique has been used for years to help give voices a push and thicken up power chords.

Note that many of the special effects we have dealt with so far involve the idea of making the sound bigger, fatter, richer, and larger than life. This is one of the main reasons why professional tapes shine over amateur ones: the amateur doesn't give too much thought to this kind of enlarging process. But for music to come across the somewhat flat medium of a loudspeaker, then it has to really sparkle or it will get lost. For this reason and others, now is a good time to re-emphasize that playing in the studio is completely different from playing live.

# True Stories of an Encouraging Nature

Back in the eighties, a musician named David Arkenstone (who has since gone on to sell hundreds of thousands of CDs) worked out a demo at home using a Commodore-64 computer and a couple of inexpensive sound generators (primarily a Casio CZ-101 and Yamaha TX7). He then submitted these demos to a record company, who liked what they heard. At the time he was an untested artist, and as expected, the record company wanted the budget as low as possible yet retain high sonic standards.

So David worked out his sequences at home, and his future CD ended up as two disks of data. Up to this point, he still hadn't spent any money on studio time.

The disks were then taken to a studio with a heavy complement of MIDI equipment, and the producer acted more or less as the "voice selector"—in other words, the disks contained the *notes,* but the exact *sounds* to go with those notes still needed to be chosen (that's where I came in). Given that the studio had more gear than most individuals, this approach made a lot of sense. David worked out a complete, tested arrangement, then took advantage of some big-bucks sound generators for the final production.

Most of the parts were dumped to tape to allow for using the same sound generator for more than one part and to simplify mixing, but a lot of the instruments could have gone directly to the two-track master. The only studio time required was for laying some of the tracks to tape, then mixing down; this slashed the budget to a fraction of normal, and allowed the record company to recoup its investment—and the artist to make some money—soon after the recording was released. (Incidentally, the resulting CD, *Valley of the Clouds,* stayed in the instrumental Top 20 chart for months.)

This points up one of the paradoxes of the MIDI studio: projects cost less to do, yet the quality is often higher than a traditional studio. Most of the time-consuming preproduction and arranging can be done in a small studio or even the composer's home, thus saving on studio bills. Essentially, the studio becomes a mixdown and instrument selection suite, with many of these tracks going directly into the master to maintain high quality sound.

For another example, I did a CD called *Forward Motion* in the mid eighties with pianist Spencer Brewer. Back then my studio wasn't "CD-quality" when it came to recording acoustic and electric instruments, so all the compositions were sequenced in a Mac Plus and drove MIDI sound generators in real time, which went directly to DAT. This achieved CD-quality sound with a minuscule studio setup. (Because my primary instrument is guitar, I used a lot of guitar-to-MIDI converters to compensate for the fact that I couldn't use "real" guitar.) Like Arkenstone's CD, this story had a happy ending too: *Forward Motion* sold reasonably well, got *lots* of airplay (and continued to years after its release), and it was selected four times for United Airlines' in-flight entertainment service . . . all this from a studio that cost under $15,000 for everything, including the instruments. At that time a typical budget for that type of recording would have been in the $50,000 to $100,000 range (and you didn't get to keep the gear afterward).

Now here's a story for the rocket scientists in the crowd. At a trade show in New York, Steely Dan engineer Roger Nichols mentioned a very clever technique used by Timbuk 3 to save considerable bucks on a recording project. Although this isn't exactly low-budget (synchronizable DATs aren't cheap), it nonetheless gives some insight on yet another way to use new technology to cut recording costs.

To avoid the expense of laying down basic tracks in a studio, Timbuk 3 used two synchronizable DATs. One had an audio reference track (*e.g.*, drums and chord progression). Overdubs were recorded on the second machine, one or two tracks at a time, resulting in several DAT tapes filled with overdubs. The group then went into the studio, synched up the DATs to a digital multitrack, and bounced the parts over to the multitrack. These tracks were then mixed to produce the master tape.

For a more recent example, the rock group Queensryche decided to put together a small studio based on modular digital multitracks and project studio mixers to cut demos. The results turned out so well they never did recut the tunes, preferring instead to use the originals (although they did rent time at a major studio to do the mixdown). The CD that came out of those sessions, *Promised Land,* went platinum. Not bad for a home studio production!

# Chapter 19 Automation

In the home or project studio, where one person is often responsible for playing, producing, and engineering, automation provides a helpful set of additional hands.

A more subtle benefit is that engineering is more of a left brain, analytical/logical activity; being a musician exercises the right (intuitive, artistic) side of the brain. If you're constantly switching back and forth between the two modes, it's hard to get into a "groove." Automation, by tending to details for you, lets you maintain a more music-oriented frame of mind.

There are many ways to automate gear, so let's start with the basics.

## Automated Transport Functions

These automate common multitrack functions, such as rewinding to a consistent location, programming punch points, and the like. Sometimes these are built into the machine itself; other times an external remote box provides the transport automation features.

### Rewind to Cue

With *rewind-to-cue* (also called *return-to-zero* or *RTZ*), when you tell a machine to rewind, it will automatically stop at a particular cue point (usually where the index counter says 000). Hard disk recording systems typically include a similar feature that instantly puts you at the beginning or end of a file.

This feature shines when doing repeated takes of an overdub, as you can set the index counter to 000 just before where you want to start recording or listening. If you make a mistake and need to try the overdub again, you can easily return to the beginning of the section to be overdubbed.

Some machines offer *block repeat* functions, where you can mark the beginning and end of a section of music. The tape recorder will play to the "end" marker, return to the "begin" marker, play to the "end" marker, and so on until stopped. This is very useful when coming up with words for songs, as well as for repeated listening of a particular part (*e.g.*, to adjust equalization or some other special effect).

However, with analog gear, the index counter readings will often "creep" over time. In other words, every time you initiate the rewind-to-cue function, the tape parks a little farther away from the desired location point than it did the previous time. Therefore, it's a good idea to check the setting on the index counter occasionally, and reset it if necessary.

Digital tape machines do not have this problem since a hidden "control track" recorded on the tape keeps track of timing. When you tell a digital recorder to return to zero, it goes to the zero point *on the tape itself*, not just the zero point on a counter. Hard disk systems also have accurate internal timing.

### Autolocation

You can often specify several different locate points, not just return to zero. In the simplest form, you just hit a button while the tape is playing to set a locate point; more sophisticated devices might allow for a complete list of editable cue points, which you can even name (verse, chorus, *etc.*) instead of just referring to them by number.

Hard disk systems will usually let you drop as many "markers" as desired into the file, which can be used as autolocation points.

### Autoplay

With autoplay enabled, the machine goes into play after completing an autolocation function.

### Automated Punching

This feature automates the punch-in and punch-out process. It's great for when you need to do an extremely precise punch (such as getting rid of one bad note), because automated punching usually has a "rehearse" function that lets you "audition" the punch by muting the region where the punch will occur without going into record. One caution: analog gear often ties this function to the tape counter, which as noted above, may change over time. If you're punching repeatedly on the same points with an analog deck, check the punch-in and punch-out locations periodically to ensure they haven't moved.

### Punch-In/Punch-Out Remote

Rather than having to reach over and press the record button when doing an overdub, you can use your foot (or whatever other appendage happens to be handy) to press the remote record footswitch button instead.

### MIDI Machine Control

MIDI Machine Control (MMC) is a part of the MIDI specification that allows devices such as tape recorders (both analog and digital), video recorders, hard disk recorders, and more to respond to MIDI commands similar to those used to control sequencers (start, stop, *etc.*).

Essentially, MMC transforms these devices into peripherals for MIDI sequencers, with the sequencer serving as a "master control center" (although usually, the multitrack still provides the timing signal to which the sequencer synchronizes). Example: Assume an MMC-compatible digital tape recorder being driven by a sequencer that can issue MMC commands. When you press play at the sequencer, the recorder goes into play as well. If you move to a different point in the sequence, the tape rewinds or fast forwards, as appropriate, to get to the same place. You can also specify punch points within a sequence (accurate to the sequencer's resolution) and the recorder will punch in and out at those points.

An MMC controller needn't be a computer-based sequencer. Mixing consoles could have remote control functions built-in; as MMC commands are standardized, there's no ambiguity about what type of commands would be needed to control different machines. Even keyboards and keyboard sequencers could send out MMC commands to control recorders, making the keyboard a master controller for all devices in the studio.

## Automated Mixing

Automated mixing used to be something that only million dollar facilities could afford, but cheap computing power and MIDI have changed all that. Automation's biggest advantage is that you only have to get a mixing move done right once, because from there on it's stored in the computer's memory.

Almost all automation relies on some form of sequencing, whether it's discreetly hidden away in a console and locked to SMPTE Time Code, or an outboard box that attaches to a personal computer and retrofits an existing mixer.

### Automated Mixing with Moving Faders

Until MIDI became established in the studio world, automated mixing meant a large, expensive console with (primarily) *moving fader* automation. Many high-end consoles continue to use this form of automation, although recent price reductions for moving faders have made them more common.

As you move the faders, the sequencer's memory stores any level changes that occur. On playback, because the faders are motorized, level information drives the fader motors so the fader positions change according to the levels. Although it always looks cool to see faders moving along with the mix, there's also a very practical consideration: if you want to program a level change, you can just press "record," grab a fader, and move it.

### Traditional Automated Mixing without Moving Faders

Because of the expense of motorized faders, less expensive automation systems are often based around traditional faders. As before, moving the faders stores mixing moves in memory. However, on playback, the faders do not move, so you cannot know the level by looking at the fader position.

This complicates matters if you want to overdub some new fader moves, because you first need to set the level to the same value as the existing, recorded level. Otherwise, there could be an undesirable level jump when you start the overdub. Automation systems without moving faders usually include some sort of "nulling" LEDs that indicate if the fader is above, below, or right at the programmed level. Once you move the fader to the current level, you can "punch in" and record new fader moves.

### Automated Mixing with Software Faders

What's even cheaper than real faders are *software faders* that appear on a computer's screen, and are usually driven by MIDI messages (as explained later in the chapter). Because these faders are not physical, you obviously don't need motors to move them. The main problem is that if you use a mouse to change the fader position (*i.e.*, grab the fader with the mouse and move it), you're limited to moving one fader at a time.

There are MIDI-controlled fader boxes that consist of eight to sixteen faders feeding a MIDI output. The faders let you manipulate several software faders simultaneously, but this again brings up the nulling problem unless the fader box has motorized faders. Manufacturers have come up with a variety of ways to deal with this problem, but one of the simplest is to edit mixing data within a MIDI sequencer to get exactly the level changes you want.

## Automated Mixing Limitations

Unfortunately, you can't just pop a disk with automation data into a computer and replicate your mix. Usually there are too many nonprogrammable variables (instrument level controls, signal processing settings, patch bay connections, *etc.*) that are involved in a mix. If you take plenty of written notes and save all the synthesizer/sampler and processing settings in some kind of storage medium (such as a MIDI sys ex storage device), you can approach total repeatability.

The more functions a mixer automates, the closer you can come to a truly repeatable mix. This is why retrofits often aren't as comprehensive as built-in automation—it's extremely difficult to deal with automating EQ settings and the like.

Also, as with life itself, automated mixing involves tradeoffs. It takes a lot of time to program everything so that you can just push a button and hear the perfect mix, but at least you don't have to remember a zillion different mixing moves. I'd also like to add a personal observation. Sometimes automated mixes turn out to be very static-sounding, because the engineer simply gets the levels right and leaves them there. Perhaps it's better to consider a mix as a performance in its own right, with rhythmic level changes that may or may not turn out the same way each time. There's no law against automating some tracks, but riding the more important instruments as you respond to the song. Automation makes it very easy to accept a mix that is technically correct, but that lacks some of the life of a real-time, performance-oriented mix.

So much for the speech, back to reality. There are two main families of automation. One relates exclusively to MIDI instruments, and the other to acoustic sounds recorded on tape or hard disk.

## Mixing with MIDI

Keyboards and signal processors were the first devices to include MIDI, but before long, so did mixers. The same types of MIDI messages that tell a keyboard how much vibrato to add can also tell a mixer how much to change a fader's level. Because so many parameters in MIDI gear can be altered in real time with MIDI messages, MIDI provides a variety of inexpensive automation functions. MIDI-controlled automation is by far the dominant form of automation in the home and project studio.

In general, a sequencer plays back the automation data. You can sync a sequencer to tape or hard disk, record automation data into the sequencer, and automate the gear on playback. Targets for automation messages include:

- Keyboards. Most modern keyboards have their master level respond to MIDI messages (controller 7, if you're curious). Including these messages in a sequence can change levels dynamically, just like using a fader. Other parameters (filter cutoff, modulation, *etc.*) can also be MIDI-controlled if you want to alter some aspect of the sound while it's playing. You can also use MIDI to recall entirely different sounds (patches).
- Signal processors. MIDI can call up different effects, or change parameter values (echo feedback, EQ amount, chorus modulation, *etc.*) within those effects.
- MIDI-controlled mixers. These are self-contained mixers whose controls—faders, EQ settings, send and return controls, and more—can be automated with MIDI commands.
- MIDI controlled attenuators. These consist of (usually) eight or sixteen attenuators that patch into a nonprogrammable mixer's insert points. MIDI messages can control the level of each attenuator independently, which provides automated mixing for tracks entering the mixer.

## MIDI Automation Messages

Although the MIDI spec has many different commands, the ones you'll use the most for automation are *program changes* (which call up different "snapshots" of the parameter values in MIDI devices) and *continuous controller* messages (which alter parameters dynamically, in real time). These were touched on in Chapter 4, but we need to give them a closer look to understand how automation works.

Like other MIDI data, continuous controller and program change messages belong to one of sixteen independent channels over which data can be sent and/or received. However, multicable interfaces (see Chapters 4 and 15) can provide more MIDI channels if needed.

## About Program Changes

MIDI devices usually contain multiple *parameters* (*i.e.,* variable elements that influence the sound) which you can adjust (edit). A "snapshot" of these settings is called a *program.* This could be a particular sound on a synthesizer, a combination of fader and other settings on a mixer, a certain effect in a signal processor, *etc.* You can recall a specific program by pressing some buttons on the front panel, or by sending a MIDI program change message, typically generated by a device such as a sequencer or MIDI footswitch.

MIDI originally allowed for 128 MIDI program change messages; each one calls up an individual program (this is why many MIDI devices incorporate 128 programs). Some equipment now responds to MIDI Bank Select messages (a more recent extension to the MIDI spec), which address up to 16,384 banks of 128 programs.

## Automated Program Changes

Suppose you want to automate a series of program changes to recall mixer "snapshots." The basic process goes like this:

1. Synchronize a MIDI sequencer to your multitrack.

2. Record program changes in the sequencer either by recording in real time and pressing a button that corresponds to the appropriate program change, or in step time using a mouse or keyboard.

3. When you play back the sequence, every time the sequencer plays back a program change command, the mixer calls up the control settings associated with the program change number.

## Program Change Problems

When a device switches from one sound to another, it has to "flush" its memory and load in new parameters, which can take several milliseconds. Different units handle this in different ways—some mute the signal, some bypass the processed sound temporarily, some make nasty noises (called *glitches,* which manifest themselves as unintended clicking or popping noises), while other devices (especially mixers) transition quietly from one setting to another. Glitching is hard to get rid of, but fortunately, with proper engineering volume settings are the least susceptible to glitching.

If you're automating signal processor program changes with a sequencer and experience really nasty glitching, try connecting a MIDI-controlled mixer or attenuator after the effect's audio output, and program a mute while the program changes.

## Continuous Controllers

These messages let you change one or more individual program parameters (synthesizer output level, mixer channel level, multieffects delay feedback, filter frequency, distortion drive, *etc.*). Unlike a program change, which is a single event, continuous controllers generate a series of events, such as a volume fadein (each event raises the volume a bit more than the previous event).

Continuous controller messages came about because synthesizers have pedals, knobs, levers, and other physical "controllers" that alter some aspect of a synth's sound over a continuous range of values (this is why they're called *continuous controllers,* as opposed to a controller such as an on-off switch, which only selects between two possible values). Recording these gestures recreates them on playback.

As with program changes, you need a source of continuous controller messages (*e.g.,* sequencer "software" fader, hardware fader box, footpedal, *etc.;* see sidebar). The transmitter usually digitizes the physical controller motion into 128 discrete values (0 to 127). For example, a hardware fader that's all the way down might generate a value of 0. As you move it up, the values increase until at midpoint, the fader transmits a value of 64. When up all the way, it generates a value of 127. Note that continuous controller transmitters only send messages reflecting a change; for example, leaving a fader in one position doesn't transmit any messages until you change the fader's physical position.

At the receiving end, the parameter being controlled (mixer channel level, synthesizer level, delay amount, or whatever) changes in response to the fader position. Example: Most modern synthesizers allow for master volume control by MIDI continuous controller 7 messages (check the synth's MIDI implementation chart to determine whether it responds to controller 7). When you record master volume controller messages into a sequencer, on playback your sequencer varies the level automatically.

Even if your gear doesn't respond to controller 7 data (some older devices don't) there is a

## MIDI Data Generators

Many devices can generate MIDI data; patching the MIDI out from one of these devices to the sequencer's MIDI in lets you record MIDI data. Here are the most common data generators:

- **MIDI keyboard.** A typical MIDI keyboard can generate program changes and a variety of other control signals such as pitch bend, pressure, mod wheel (controller 01), footpedal (controller 04), *etc.* Not all keyboards can generate all MIDI commands. However, some advanced keyboards and master controllers have dedicated "data sliders" that can be set to any controller number.
- **Footswitch/footpedal combination.** Guitarists who use MIDI footswitches and pedals can generate control data directly from these. The footpedal may or may not be assignable to different controller numbers; if not, the sequencer can often convert data recorded as one controller number into a different controller number.
- **MIDI fader box.** This is a compact box that consists of a number of slide faders, each of which can be assigned to generate a particular type of MIDI data, such as different controllers over one or more MIDI channels. This type of device is well suited to generating MIDI data since you can move several faders at once, or grab a particular fader to generate a particular controller.
- **Software MIDI faders.** Several sequencers include on-screen "virtual faders" that you can assign to various controllers (Fig. 19-1). In this example faders F1 through F5 are assigned to controllers 20 through 24, which all transmit over channel 1. To help remember which fader controls which function, each has been named in the "MIDI Instruments" window.

These "fader" motions can be recorded as part of the sequence or sent in real time to the MIDI output. On playback, with most programs the faders usually move to give a visual indication of the data value (this also looks great, and will surely impress your friends or clients).

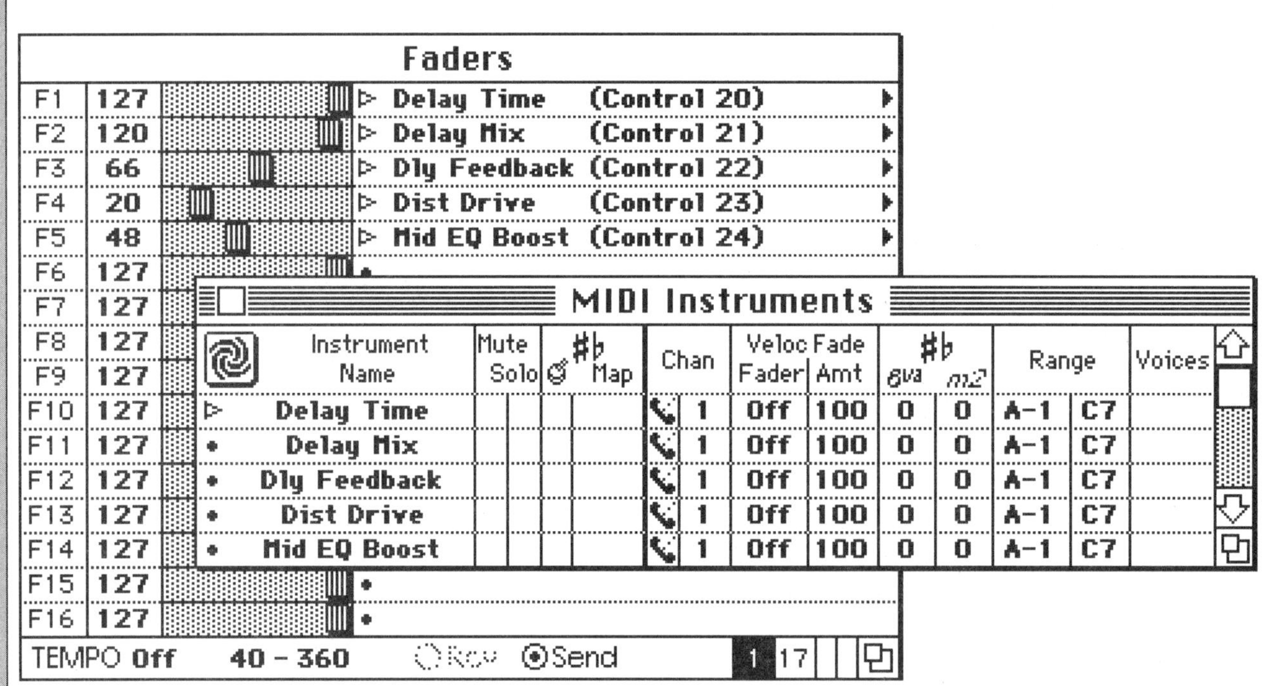


Fig. 19-1: *The faders in the original version of Opcode's* Vision *program. The front window assigns the fader to various channels, ports, and ranges; the rear window shows the faders themselves and their controller assignments. With* Vision, *clicking on the rightmost triangle in a fader strip calls up a popup menu that contains a list of all available controllers.*

way to imitate automated mixdown. You can copy a synth program into several different memory locations, and set each one for a different volume (typically there will be some kind of overall level setting parameter for each patch). Use Program Change commands to call up the program with the appropriate volume level.

Different signal processors may react somewhat differently when receiving a full range of controller values because these devices often let you *scale* and/or *invert* the values. With scaling, you can attenuate the control signal—for example, have the maximum fader position set the parameter value to a third or half way up instead of all the way, thus allowing for more precise control. Inversion reverses the "sense" of the fader so that increasing the fader position *decreases* the parameter value. Often scaling and inversion are combined into one number, such as +50 (which represents fifty percent scaling of full value in a positive direction), –37 (thirty-seven percent scaling of full value in a negative direction), *etc.*

## The Numbers Game

MIDI allows for 128 continuous controller messages, each of which can produce a value from 0 to 127. So, if a signal processor has 128 (or fewer) different parameters, each can be assigned a unique number—say, 1 for EQ frequency, 2 for EQ boost/cut, 3 for delay feedback, and so on. For synthesizers, some controller numbers have been standardized, but this is not the case with mixers or signal processors. Some units have fixed assignments; with others, you can assign particular controller numbers to particular parameters.

There are two main ways to assign controller numbers to parameters.

- With the *per-program* method, you assign one or more parameters in a particular program to your choice of continuous controller numbers. These assignments can be different for different programs.
- With *global* controller assignments, each parameter has a particular continuous controller assignment that is either fixed or which you assign. Example: If delay time is controller 24, then every patch that uses delay will have controller 24 messages alter the delay time.

With many effects, you can assign several parameters to the *same* controller number so that, for example, a single fader motion could increase the level *and* reverberation time *and* boost the upper midrange.

## Other Control Messages

In addition to responding to continuous controllers, some devices respond to other MIDI control messages such as pitch bend, velocity, and pressure (as defined in Chapter 4). However, an increasing number of signal processors can also sync to MIDI timing messages. Some synthesizers can synchronize rhythmic effects (such as vibrato) to these messages, and newer signal processors can tie parameters such as delay time to MIDI clock messages. For example, MIDI clock messages occur twenty-four times per quarter note, so if you want a quarter note delay the processor will set its delay time to equal twenty-four MIDI clock pulses. For a half-note delay, it would count forty-eight clock pulses.

## MIDI Controller Limitations

Some parameters glitch when altered with controller messages, and some don't. Parameters that control time (pitch transposition amount, delay time, and the like) tend to glitch the most. Parameters that control amplitude glitch the least, with the overall amount depending mostly on the number of steps into which a parameter is quantized. An analog control has an essentially infinite number of steps; to replicate that digitally costs a fortune, so most parameters will be quantized into anywhere from 2 to 256 (or sometimes more) steps.

The more steps, the more continuous the control, and the smoother the feel. If you sweep through a control that's quantized into few steps, you'll hear a change with each step—a phenomenon referred to as "zipper noise," since the resulting sound gives a slight glitching as you go through the steps.

There are two main solutions for dealing with continuous controller glitching:

- Avoid playing when changing the value of a glitch-prone parameter
- Use a snapshot approach (instead of doing continuous sweeps) when a parameter needs to jump from one value to another. This doesn't solve all types of controller glitching, but it's worth a try.

Another problem is that controller messages use up much more memory than note data, which reduces the MIDI "bandwidth" (*i.e.,* the maximum number of messages the MIDI line can handle). Having lots of varying controller messages on several MIDI channels could stress your sequencer (or the device receiving the MIDI data) enough that it misses data or otherwise "clogs."

Fortunately, many times you can use a "snapshot" approach and just insert a single controller value at strategic points in a tune. The parameter will remain at this value until changed. Figs. 19-2A through 19-2C show a continuous controller doing a fade in for the master volume parameter. Fig. 19-2A shows the fade entered with a pedal; Fig. 19-2B shows an edited "snapshot" version of the fade. There is little audible difference between the two, but Fig. 19-2B uses much less data.

Some sequencers include data thinning algorithms that reduce the amount of MIDI data automatically, which saves editing time. Fig. 19-2C shows the same signal, but thinned using a sequencer's data thinning algorithm that removes data falling within a specified number of clock pulses, or within certain values compared to a neighboring piece of data. Clearly, 19-2B and 19-2C save a lot more memory compared to 19-2A.

Although in most cases you won't have to resort to editing data, remember that sequencers do have limitations. If you're trying to use lots of controller data and experience timing problems, dig into the data stream and do some editing.

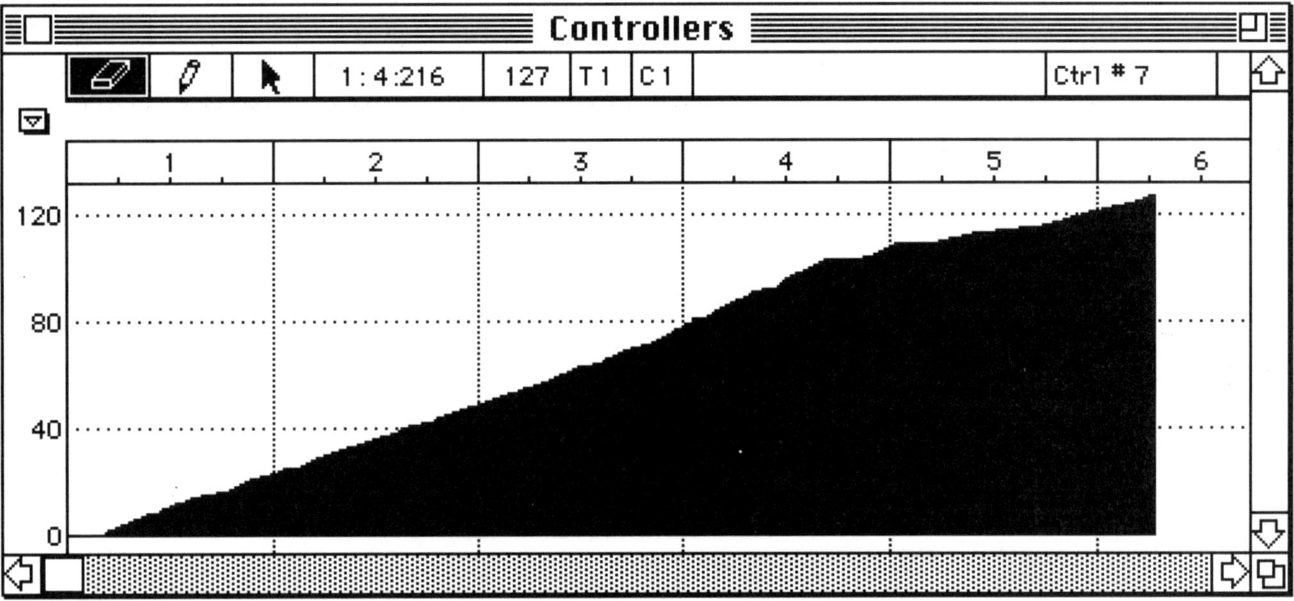


**Fig. 19-2A:** *Controller events for a fadein, recorded from a* MIDI *pedal assigned to volume.*

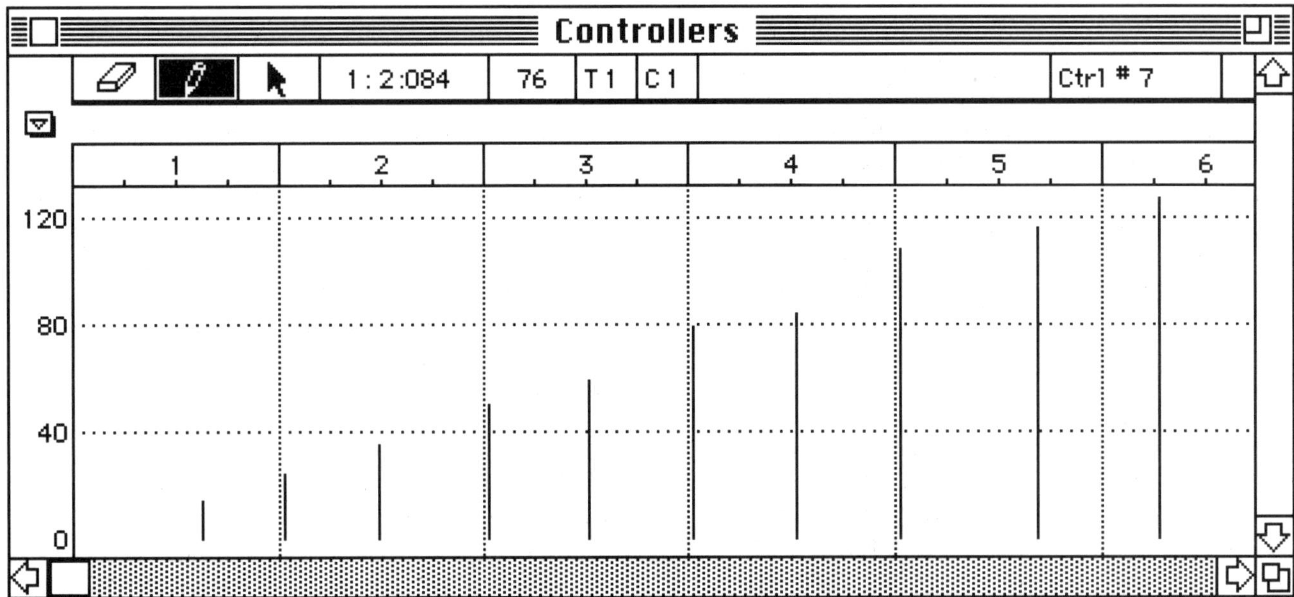


**Fig. 19-2B:** *The controller events from Fig. 19-2A converted to "snapshots."*

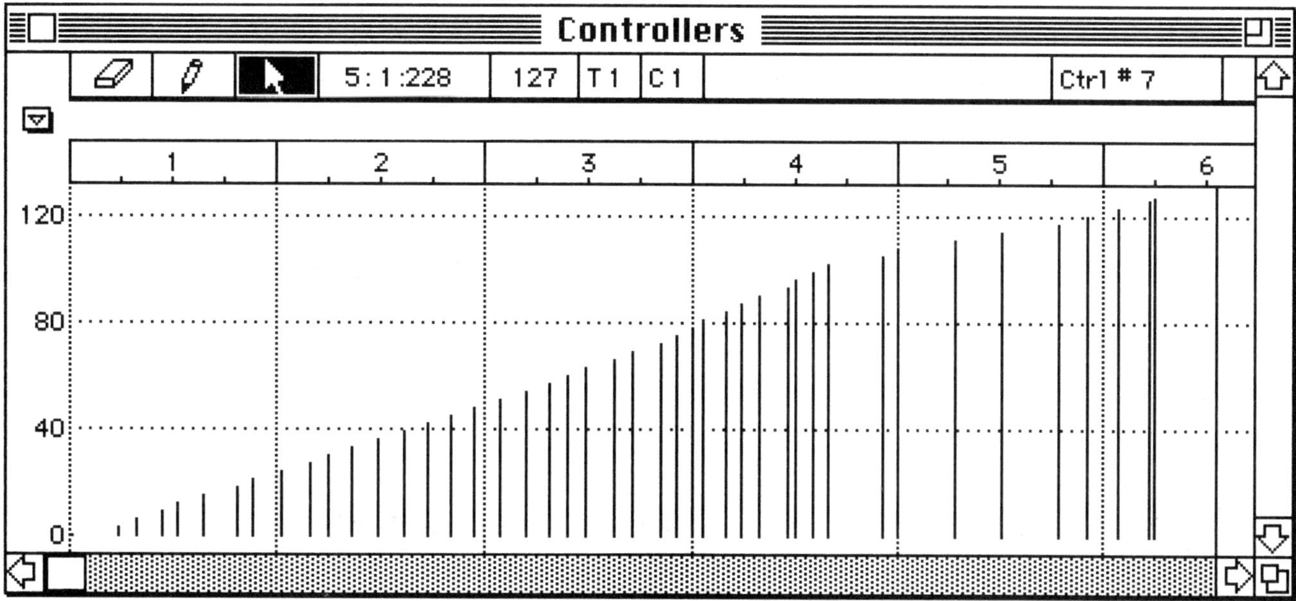


**Fig. 19-2C:** *The controller events from Fig. 19-2A after thinning by a sequencer's thinning algorithm.*

## Automating Prerecorded Tracks with MIDI

In addition to controlling MIDI devices and synthesizer/sampler master levels, MIDI data can also automate acoustic or prerecorded tracks that go through a MIDI-controllable fader module or mixer. Generally, these devices consist of multiple gain control elements, each with an input and output, that insert in series with the audio signal path to be controlled; MIDI messages determine the amount of gain for each channel.

A common misconception is that even in the studio, to automate your effects or mixing moves you'll have to play to a rigid click track or drum machine, not a human drummer. Fortunately, when controlling MIDI devices for mixing or signal processing rather than note generation, synchronization *to any particular tempo* is not an issue as long as the sequencer is synched to the multitrack. This is because a sequencer can serve simply as a way to trigger program changes and other MIDI controller data on cue.

To understand why this is so, we need to distinguish between *absolute* time and *musical* time. Musical time is relative; a quarter note has a different duration at 60 BPM compared to that same note at 140 BPM. Absolute time is a constant. In other words, if you're one minute and twelve seconds into a song, it doesn't matter what the tempo of the tune may be, or even if there is a tempo. You're simply marking a point that's one minute and twelve seconds into the tune, which will always correspond to a particular place in the music if the sequencer plays back at a consistent tempo.

Most of the time, sequencers are used in the context of musical time. For example, you might consider a program change or other MIDI command as occurring at the beginning of the forty-third measure of a tune. However, *by keeping a constant tempo* the sequencer becomes an absolute time device that simply identifies elapsed time since the beginning of the tune. So, as long as the sequencer is synched to tape, if we record a piece of MIDI data into the sequencer at a particular time, it will always play back at that particular time.

One reason it's not necessary to follow a particular tempo is that sequencers identify time with a great deal of precision. A typical computer-based sequencer running at 180 BPM can divide time into approximately 1,000 discrete events *per second*. Think of this as 1,000 "memory slots" into which the sequencer can record data, which means the sequencer can record a piece of MIDI data about every 1/1000th of a second (1 ms).

Suppose you want to record a program change command at the beginning of measure 43. The odds are excellent that there will be a corresponding "memory slot" that falls almost, or maybe even exactly, on that beat. Worst case, though, is that the command will be issued within ±0.5 ms of wherever the musical beat falls—definitely close enough.

## A Practical Example: MIDI-Automated Vocal Mixdown

A typical multieffects processor has EQ, time delay, compression, and the ability to control overall volume with MIDI controller 7. If that sounds like an ideal combination for automated mixing of vocal tracks without having to spend megabucks on a completely automated console or several hundred dollars on a retrofit . . . well, it is. Since mixer automation is fairly straightforward—you move the faders while in record, and on playback, the level changes—let's look at using MIDI automation messages, recorded in a sequencer, to automate several changes to a vocal part going through a multieffects.

Begin by gathering your tools:

- MIDI sequencer
- Sync-to-tape box or interface (if needed to synchronize the sequencer to tape)
- Some way to record program changes and continuous controllers into the sequencer (such as a MIDI fader box, MIDI footswitch/ pedal combination, or a keyboard that can generate the desired types of MIDI data; see the sidebar on MIDI data generators)

Here's the general procedure on how to use them. We'll assume you want to automate program changes and continuous controller messages, and that the song doesn't necessarily follow a consistent tempo (perhaps because you used a real drummer instead of a drum machine). Fig. 19-3 shows the patching diagram.

1. Patch the vocal track output (whether from hard disk, tape, or whatever) into the multieffects. If you don't need to use a mixer's bells and whistles, the multieffects can patch into an effects return rather than a regular channel input, thus freeing up an additional channel as part of the deal.

2. Connect the MIDI data generator's MIDI out to the multieffects' MIDI in so that you can hear the results of the continuous controller and program changes.

3. Patch the MIDI generator's MIDI thru (which transmits a copy of the data appearing at the multieffects' MIDI in) to the sequencer's MIDI in.

4. If needed, record a sync track to which the sequencer can synchronize. Some hard disk devices and sync boxes for digital tape recorders already provide a suitable signal (such as SMPTE) so you don't have to give up a track.

5. Set the sequencer to some arbitrarily fast tempo, such as 120 beats per minute. At this tempo, each half-note marks one second. As the tempo probably won't be following the track, turn off any click or metronome option.

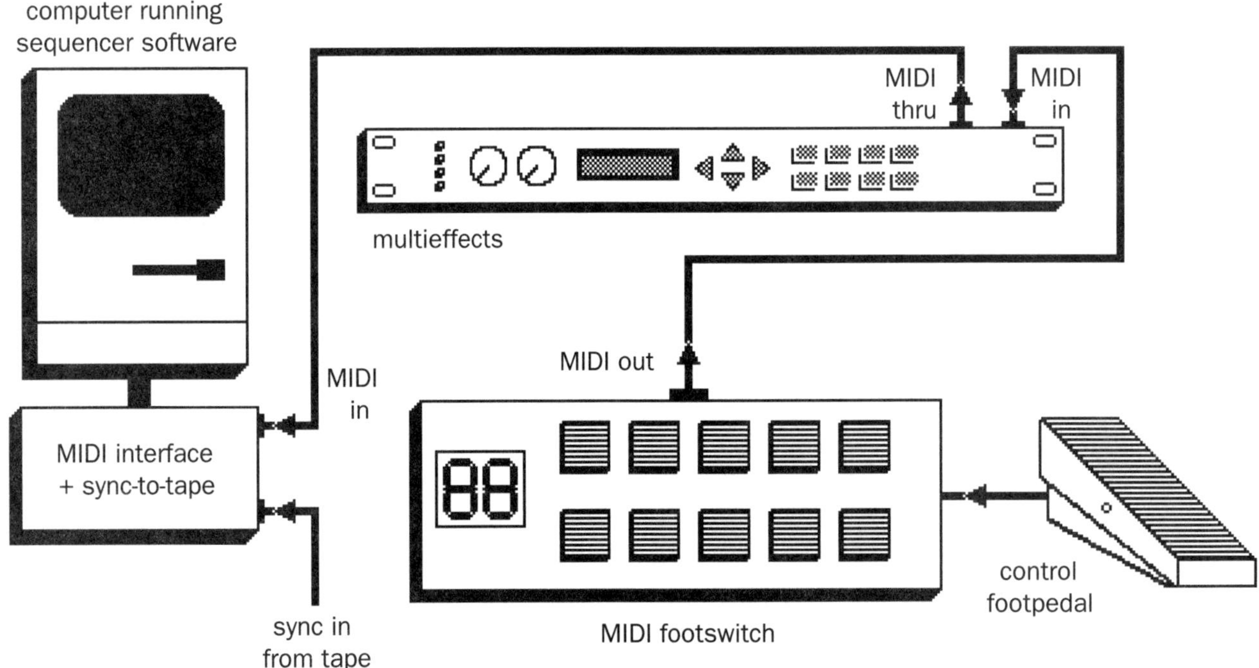


Fig. 19-3: *Hookup for recording MIDI data into a sequencer. The MIDI data generator is a footswitch and footpedal, as typically used by guitarists. Alternatively, you could use one of the other types of generators mentioned in the sidebar.*

6. Start the tape. Record your controller and program changes into the sequencer (which should be synched to tape) while listening to the track.

7. Prior to playback, disconnect the MIDI generator's MIDI out from the multieffects' MIDI in; patch in the sequencer's MIDI out instead (Fig. 19-4).

Start playback anywhere; after a second or two, the sequencer will autolocate to the correct place in the tune and play back any MIDI messages exactly as you recorded them.

That's all there is to it. Also remember that one of the advantages of using a sequencer is that you can edit the data. For example, if a signal processor is slow to respond to program changes, use the sequencer's "track shift" (or equivalent) command to shift the program changes slightly ahead of the beat.

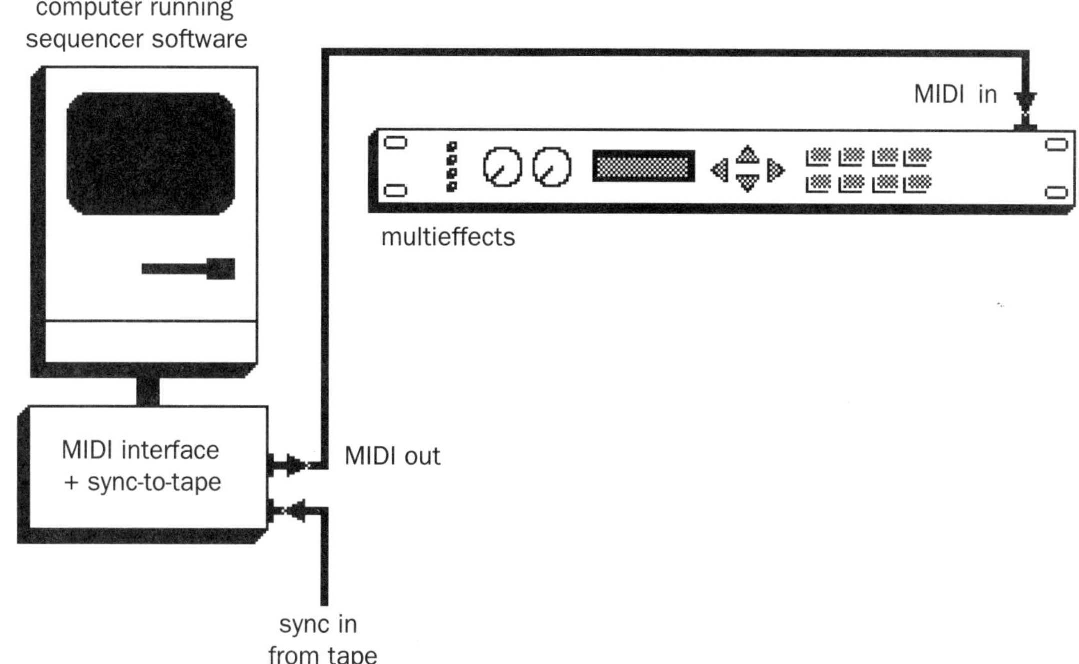


**Fig. 19-4:** *Hooking up a multieffects and sequencer for sequence playback.*

# Chapter 20
# The Art of Mixing

Mixing is not only an art, it's the ultimate arbiter of how your music sounds. A good mix can bring out the best in your music, while a bad mix can obscure it.

An effective mix spotlights a composition's most important elements, adds a few surprises to excite the listener, and sounds good on any system—from a transistor radio to an audiophile's dream system. Translating a collection of tracks into a cohesive song isn't easy; mixing requires the same level of creativity and experience as any part of the musical process.

Start by analyzing well-mixed recordings by engineers such as Bruce Swedien, Roger Nichols, Shelly Yakus, Bob Clearmountain, and other respected engineers. Don't focus on the music, just the mix. Notice how—even with a "wall of sound"—you can pick out every instrument because each element of the music has its own space.

To understand why mixing is so tricky, we need to examine some of the problems involved in trying to make a good mix. But first, let's decide what we're going to mix down to.

## Mixdown Machine Options

It used to be that you mixed down to analog, 15 ips, half-track tape. Like everything else, though, your choices have become more complex. Here are the most popular mixdown machine options.

- 15 ips, half-track, 1/4" analog tape: Although the standard for many years, the poorer sound quality compared to analog tapes run at higher speeds or digital audio devices has made this option less relevant. Anything less—7.5 ips reel-to-reel or cassette—isn't even in the running.
- 30 ips, half-track, 1/2" analog tape: This is still very popular, because it maintains the "analog" sound yet is often superior to 15 ips tapes. Many engineers swear that a good 30 ips tape will beat DAT for sound quality, but whether they're right or wrong doesn't really matter: the bottom line is that 30 ips tapes can sound great. Add Dolby SR noise reduction, and you have sound quality that theoretically is better than digital.
- Sony PCM-F1: This was the original "DAT"—it converted audio into high-bandwidth signals suitable for recording onto a VCR. Although once the format of choice for many duplicators, it's long gone except for a few isolated stragglers. The same goes for using the hi-fi tracks on Beta (remember those?) or VHS decks.
- DAT: This is pretty much the medium of choice as of this writing. Most mastering and duplication houses prefer to receive DAT. Advantages include not only sound quality, but the ability to do transfers in the digital domain to other pieces of gear, including hard disk recorders and signal processors with digital I/O.
- 3/4" U-Matic video deck: Once you submit a DAT to a mastering house, it is usually transferred to a 3/4" U-Matic video deck through a Sony 1630 digital audio processor. However, the cost of a 1630/U-Matic combination makes it an unlikely addition to your home studio.
- CD-R (Recordable CD): More and more people are transferring mixes recorded on tape over to a recordable CD, then submitting that to the duplicators. A CD-R offers the advantage of robustness and also makes a good reference—play it before you send it off, and you'll know the tune is okay.

The bottom line: mix down to a DAT or 30 ips 1/2" tape, and submit either one of those or a CD-R to the mastering house.

## The Slippery Nature of Sound

Hearing is a very intricate process, considering that air waves impinge on little hairs inside your head, and your brain processes these impulses. It's no wonder that some bugs creep into the system; here are the most problematic ones.

- Sound takes time to travel from one place to another. Because how you perceive a sound depends upon your distance from the source, your ears face quite a set of difficulties. Sound waves bounce off hard surfaces, but are absorbed by soft surfaces. As a result, if you sit in the middle of a room, you'll hear several sound waves: the sound source itself, some reflections that result in reinforced frequencies, some reflections that cancel other frequencies, time delays, uneven frequency response, and so on. No matter what your listening environment, it will color your perception of the sound.
- The human ear is a marvelous and amazing transducer, but has some limitations. For example, sounds have slightly different perceived pitches at different volume levels. This isn't too serious a problem with mixing, as levels tend to be within the same general range. A far more serious problem is the ear's loss of bass response at lower listening levels.
- Virtually every person has a different hearing response. At very high listening levels, response to bass and treble will be more or less equal but as the volume gets progressively lower, the loss of bass response becomes more severe. As a result, when you mix you can never be sure of the actual bass content because it changes depending on the room, the level, your age, whether you just took a long flight, and many other factors. The best compromise is to take an average reading of the sound: see how a mix sounds at low volume levels, high volume levels, from another room—does the bass boom through and shake the walls, or is it still balanced compared to other instruments? Also listen through other speakers on other people's systems (but make sure the tone controls and loudness button are set for flat response).
- The ear hears less treble as it ages, or if it is abused. Prolonged exposure to loud volume levels can cause problems not only with high frequencies, but with the midrange too. Engineers who mix at very high volume levels develop an uneven hearing response, which certainly seems to be detrimental to the cause of good music. Also, after a person reaches the age of about twenty-five, the ear's treble response diminishes, whether it is abused or not. *If you remember nothing else from reading this book, remember this:* if you care about music, take good care of your hearing.
- Playback systems do not all have the same response. Musicians spend thousands of dollars of studio time on a product that is frequently played over a two-dollar speaker and listened to by someone who cannot differentiate between a synthesized instrument and the real thing. Therefore, in addition to all the minute sonic details you must attend to while mixing, you must pay particular attention to the overall effect that you are creating—the mood and character of the piece. Even if a playback system is inferior, the *mood* can come through. If your music must be played on only the finest equipment in order to sound good, it's probably not mixed or recorded well enough.

## Proper Monitoring Levels

Loud, extended mixing sessions are very tough on the ears. Mixing at low levels keeps your ears "fresher" and minimizes ear fatigue; you'll also be able to discriminate better between subtle level variations. Loud mixes may get your juices flowing, but they'll also trip your ear's built-in "limiting" (ears don't hear in a linear fashion). And don't forget to play back over a variety of speaker systems and headphones to insure as "translatable" a mix as possible.

## The Gear: Keep It Clean

Preparation for the mix begins the moment you start recording, and part of that involves recording the cleanest possible signal. Eliminate as many active stages as possible between source and recorder; many times, devices set to "bypass" may not be adding any effect but are still in line, which can add some slight noise or signal degradation. How many times do line level signals go through preamps due to lazy engineering? Send sounds directly into the recorder—bypass the mixer altogether. For mic signals, use an ultra-high quality outboard preamp and patch that directly into the recorder rather than use a mixer with its onboard preamps.

If you record with the highest possible fidelity, you can always play with the signal on mixdown if you want to mess with it. Although you may not hear much of a difference when monitoring a single instrument, with multiple tracks the cumulative effect of stripping the signal path to its essentials can make a significant difference in the sound's clarity.

## The Arrangement

Before you even think about turning any knobs, scrutinize the arrangement. Solo project arrangements are particularly prone to "clutter" because as you lay down the early tracks, there's a tendency to overplay to fill up all that empty space. As the arrangement progresses, there's not a lot of space for overdubs.

Here are a couple of suggestions when tracking that will make it much easier to create a good mix:

- Once the arrangement is fleshed out, go back and recut tracks that you cut earlier on. Try to play these tracks as sparsely as possible to leave room for the overdubs you've added. Sometimes I've found it very helpful to recut a song from scratch as soon as I've finished mixing it. Like many others, I write in the studio, and often the song will have a slightly tentative feel because of that. Recutting always seem to both simplify and improve the song; it's the project studio equivalent of road-testing a song, then going into the studio to cut the "real" version.
- Try building a song around the vocalist or other lead instrument instead of completing the rhythm section and then laying down the vocals. I often find it better to record simple "placemarkers" for the drums, bass, and rhythm guitar (or piano, or whatever), then immediately get to work cutting the best possible vocal. Then I go back and rerecord the rhythm section. When you recut the rhythm section for real, you'll be a lot more sensitive to the vocal nuances.
- The former tip is also a real good justification to use sequencers that include digital audio capabilities (Studio Vision, Digital Performer, Cubase Audio, Logic Audio, *etc.*). Lay down the vocal before you get too heavily into sequencing, and your sequenced parts will be more sensitive to the vocals.
- As Sun Ra once said, "Space is the place." The less music you play, the more weight each note has.

## Mixing: The Twelve-Step Program

You "build" a mix over time by making a variety of adjustments. There are (at least!) twelve major steps involved in creating a mix, but what makes mixing so difficult is that these steps interact. Change the equalization, and you also change the level because you're boosting or cutting some element of the sound. Alter a sound's stereo location, and you may need to shift the ambiance or equalization. In fact, you can think of a mix as an "audio combination lock" since when all the elements hit the right combination, you end up with a good mix.

Let's look at these twelve steps, but remember, this is just one person's way of mixing—you might invent a totally different approach that works much better for you.

### Step 1: Mental Preparation

Mixing requires a tremendous amount of concentration and can be extremely tedious, so set up your workspace as efficiently as possible. Have paper and a log book around for taking notes, dim the lighting a little bit so that your ears become more sensitive than your eyes, and in general, psych yourself up for what will be an interesting journey.

For best results, take a break periodically (every hour or so is a good interval) to "rest" your ears and gain a fresher outlook on your return. This may seem like a luxury if you're paying for studio time, but do it anyway! Even a couple of minutes of off time can restore your objectivity and, paradoxically, complete a mix much faster.

### Step 2: Review the Tracks

Listen at low volume to find out what's on the tape; write down track information, and use stick-on labels or erasable markers to indicate which sounds correspond to which mixer channels. Group sounds logically, such as having all the drum sounds on consecutive channels.

### Step 3: Put On Headphones and Listen for Glitches

Fixing glitches is a "left brain" activity, as opposed to the "right brain" creativity involved in doing a mix. Switching back and forth between these two modes can hamper creativity, so do as much cleaning up as possible—erase glitches, bad notes, scratch tracks, and the like—before you get involved in the mix. With sequencers, thin out excessive controller information, check for duplicate notes, and avoid overlapping notes on single-note lines (such as bass and horn parts). You'll often catch problems you wouldn't hear in an ensemble situation; for example, a subtle distortion might get lost in the mix, but stand out in isolation.

To clean up tracks recorded on tape (digital or analog), consider bouncing them over to a hard disk recorder and doing some digital editing (see the end of Chapter 3). It's particularly amazing how many little noises you'll hear on vocal tracks. These low-level glitches may not seem that audible, but multiply them by a couple of dozen tracks and they can muddy things up.

## Step 4: Optimize Any MIDI Sound Generators Being Sequenced

If you're sequencing tracks via MIDI, check the various sound generators and optimize them. For example, if you want more brightness, try increasing the lowpass filter cutoff instead of adding equalization at the console. One tip: with digital synths, keep the volume control at maximum as this usually allows for the maximum dynamic range. Adjust levels at the console if needed (or by sending controller 7 messages to the synth, which is a whole other story—see Chapter 19 on Automation).

## Step 5: Set Up a Relative Level Balance Between the Tracks

Do not add any processing for now; concentrate on the overall effect of the tracks by themselves and work on the overall sound—don't get distracted by left-brain-oriented detail work. With a good mix the tracks sound good by themselves, but sound even better when interacting with the other tracks.

I suggest setting levels in mono at first, because if the instruments sound distinct and separate in mono, they'll only open up more in stereo. Also, you may not notice parts "fighting" with each other if you start off in stereo.

## Step 6: Adjust Equalization (EQ)

This can help dramatize differences between instruments and create a more balanced overall sound. Work on the most important song elements first (vocals, drums, and bass) and once these all "lock" together, deal with the more supportive parts.

The audio spectrum has only so much space, and you need to make sure that each sound occupies its own corner without fighting with other parts. Processing added to one track may affect other tracks; for example, if you boost a guitar part's midrange, it may interfere with vocals, piano, or other midrange instruments. If you add more treble to a bass part so that it cuts better on little speakers, make sure it doesn't start fighting with the low end of a rhythm guitar part. Sometimes boosting a frequency for one instrument implies cutting the same region in another instrument. For example, if you want vocals to stand out more, try notching the vocal frequencies on other instruments instead of just boosting EQ on the voice.

One common mistake I hear with tapes done by singer/songwriters is that they (naturally) feature themselves in the mix, and worry about "details" like the drums later. However, since drums cover so much of the audio spectrum (from the low frequency thud of the kick to the high frequency sheen of the cymbals), and as drums tend to be so up-front in today's mixes, it's usually best to mix the drums first, then find "holes" in which you can place the other instruments. For example, if the kick drum is very prominent, it may not leave enough room for the bass. So, boost the bass around 800 to 1,000 Hz to bring up some of the pick noise and brightness. This is mostly out of the range of the kick drum, so the two don't interfere as much.

Try to think of the song as a spectrum, and decide where you want the various parts to sit, and their prominence (see Fig. 20-1). I often use a spectrum analyzer when mixing, not because your ears don't work well enough for the task, but because it provides invaluable ear training and shows exactly which instruments take up which parts of the audio spectrum. This can often alert you to a buildup of level in a particular region.

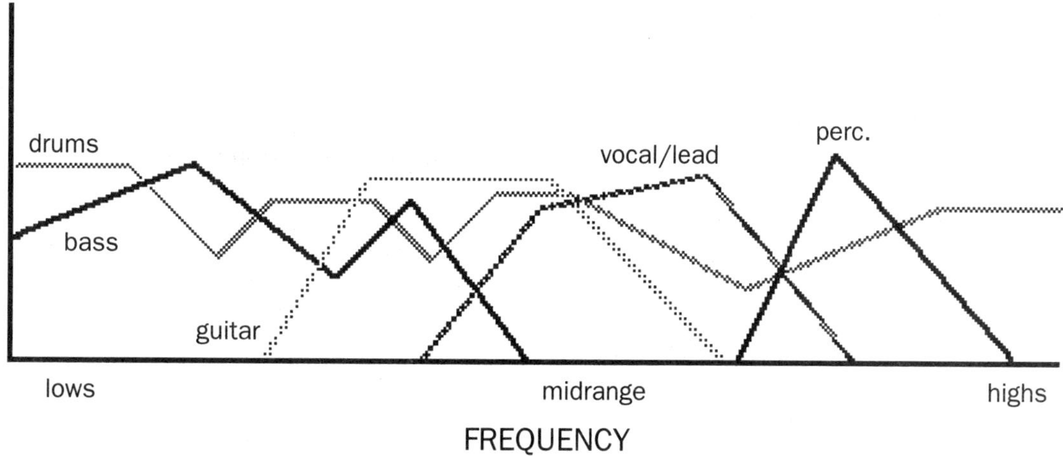


**Fig. 20-1:** *Different instruments take up different parts of the frequency spectrum.*

If you really need a sound to "break through" a mix, try a slight boost in the 1 to 3 kHz region. Just don't do this with all the instruments; the idea is to use boosts (or cuts) to differentiate one instrument from another.

To place a sound farther back in the mix, sometimes engaging the high cut filter will do the job by "dulling" the sound somewhat—you may not even need to use the main EQ. Also, using the low cut filter on instruments that veer toward the bass range, like guitar and piano, can help trim their low end to open up more space for the all-important bass and kick drum.

## Step 7: Add Any Essential Signal Processing

By essential, we don't mean "sweetening," but processing that is an integral part of the sound (such an echo that falls on the beat and therefore changes the rhythmic characteristics of a part, distortion that alters the timbre in a radical way, vocoding, *etc.*).

## Step 8: Create a Stereo Soundstage

Now place your instruments within the stereo field. Your approach might be traditional (*i.e.,* the goal is to re-create the feel of a live performance) or imaginary. Pan mono instruments to a particular location, but avoid panning signals to the *extreme* left or right; they just don't sound quite as substantial as signals that are a little bit off from the extremes.

Since bass frequencies are less directional than highs, place the kick drum and bass toward the center. Consider balance; for example, if you've panned the hi-hat (which has a lot of high frequencies) to the right, pan a tambourine, shaker, or other high-frequency sound somewhat to the left. The same technique applies to midrange instruments as well.

Another spreading technique involves EQ. Send a signal to two channels, but equalize them differently (for example, use a stereo graphic equalizer and cut the even-numbered bands with one channel, and the odd-numbered bands with the other channel).

Stereo placement can significantly alter how we perceive a sound. Consider a doubled vocal line, where a singer sings a part and then doubles it as closely as possible. Try putting both voices in opposite channels; then put both voices together in the center. The center position gives a somewhat smoother sound, which is good for weaker vocalists. The opposite-channel vocals give a more defined, sharp sound, that can really help accent a good singer.

## Step 9: Make Any Final Changes in the Arrangement

Remember that, as with so many things in life, less is more—minimize the number of competing parts to keep the listener focused on the tune, and avoid "clutter." You may be extremely proud of some clever effect you added, but if it doesn't serve the song, get rid of it. Conversely, if you find that a song needs some extra element, this is your final opportunity to add an overdub or two.

You can also use mixing creatively by selectively dropping out and adding specific tracks. This type of mixing is the foundation for a lot of dance music, where you have looped tracks that play continuously, and the mixer sculpts the arrangement by muting parts and doing radical level changes.

## Step 10: The Audio Architect

Start building your space by adding reverberation and delay to give the normally flat soundstage some acoustic depth. This is also the time for more signal processing—sort of the equivalent of adding spices during the cooking process.

Generally, you'll want an overall reverb to create a particular type of space (club, concert hall, auditorium, *etc.*) but you may also want to use a second reverb to add effects, such as a particular "splash" on a snare drum hit or gated reverb on toms.

In the early days of recording, the general procedure was to add just enough reverb to be noticeable and simulate the effect of playing in an acoustical environment. Nowadays, reverb devices have become so sophisticated they can create effects in their own right that become as much a part of a tune as any instrumental line. However, don't drown a part in reverb. If a part is of questionable enough quality that it needs a lot of reverb, redo the part. A bad part is a bad part, no matter how much reverb you put on it.

## Step 11: Tweak, Tweak, and Retweak

Now that the mix is on its way, it's time for fine tuning. If you use automated mixing, start programming your mixing moves. Remember that all of the above steps interact, so go back and forth between EQ, levels, stereo placement, and effects until you get the sound you want. Listen as critically as possible; if you don't fix something that bothers you, it will forever bug you every time you hear the mix.

### Step 12: Check Your Mix Over Different Systems

Before you sign off on a mix, play it back over a variety of speakers and headphones, in stereo and mono. Run off some cassettes and see what they sound like in your car. Listen at high levels and low levels, and maybe even book some time at another studio to hear if there are any radical differences. If the mix sounds good under all these situations, your mission is accomplished.

With a home studio, you have the luxury of leaving a mix and then coming back to it the next day when you're fresh, and even after you've had a chance to listen over several different systems and decide what tweaks you want to make.

I can't emphasize enough that you should mix until you're satisfied. There's nothing worse than hearing one of your tunes six months later and kicking yourself because of some flaw you didn't take the time to correct, or didn't notice because you were in too much of a hurry to complete the mix.

However, you must be equally careful not to beat a mix to death. Once I interviewed Quincy Jones and he offered the opinion that recording with synthesizers and sequencing was like "painting a 747 with Q-Tips." A mix is a performance, and if you overdo it, you'll lose the spontaneity that can add excitement. A mix that isn't perfect but conveys passion will always be more fun to listen to than one that's perfect to the point of sterility. As insurance, don't always rerecord over your mixes—when you listen back to them the next day, you might find that an earlier mix was the "keeper."

In fact, you may not even be able to tell too much difference between the mixes. A record producer once told me about mixing literally dozens of takes of the same song, because he kept hearing small changes that seemed really important at the time. Then, a couple of weeks afterwards he went over the mixes, and he couldn't tell any difference between most of the versions. Be careful not to waste time making changes that no one, even you, will care about a few days later.

One important tip is that once you've captured your ultimate mix, you should also run a couple of extra mixes, such as an instrumental-only mix or a mix without the solo instrument. These additional mixes can really come in handy at a later time, if you have a chance to reuse your music for a film or video score, or need to create extended dance mixes. There are all sorts of future possibilities, so be prepared!

## And Now, for Those Who Don't Like Automation . . .

Chapter 19 talks about automation, which offers many advantages for mixing. Yet despite these advantages, some engineers prefer not to use automation because they feel it destroys spontaneity and soul. And there's no law that says mixing *should* be a static process. One engineer I worked with (and he had a few hits, too) used to work really hard getting his levels and EQ and reverb set just right; then, when it came time for the final mix, he closed his eyes and rode the faders in time with the music. He was mixing eight-track, and had each finger independently riding a fader to move it slightly in time with the beat. The difference was not obvious, but overall, it made songs come alive.

Another trick is something I call "complementary motion." This works best with bass and drums, or bass and guitar; the object is to vary them in opposing ways, but in time with the beat. For example, mix the drums slightly louder for one measure with bass slightly back, and on the next measure, kick the bass up a bit and drop the drums a tiny bit. With mono, this is the closest you can get to simulating the placement of stereo; you can place a sound either more up-front, or farther back in the track. The rhythmic variations build interest and gave a somewhat hypnotic effect (which some people think is the reason we like music anyway).

But you don't just have to restrict your playing to the level controls. Changing equalization during a piece can be great; or add a little treble or midrange "bite" to an instrument during a solo. On fadeouts, sometimes you can make an instrument appear to fade out faster than other instruments, by adding progressively more reverberation to its channel by way of the reverb send.

Whatever you do, keep the mix lively and interesting, but keep it subtle, too. Even minute control changes can make a big change on playback. Don't just add gimmicks for the sake of effect, but add them for the sake of making a more varied and musically interesting piece of music. Keep the levels dancing, and don't be afraid to experiment.

## Fadeouts

The secret of a good fadeout is to key it to the beat of the song. Let's suppose that you end a song with a long instrumental. One option would be to keep it at the existing volume for four measures, then fade out over eight measures. Also, a fadeout doesn't have to be continuous. You can turn a fader down a tiny notch, say, every two beats.

A linear fadeout is not necessarily the best option (see the top drawing in Fig. 20-2). A concave fadeout, especially on a somewhat long, instrumentally oriented piece, can leave listeners hanging on for more. The initial rapid decay tells them to listen closely; once they're hooked, you stretch out the ending. Convex fadeouts, on the other hand, usually don't sound very good, as the music feels like it's slipping away whether you want it to or not.

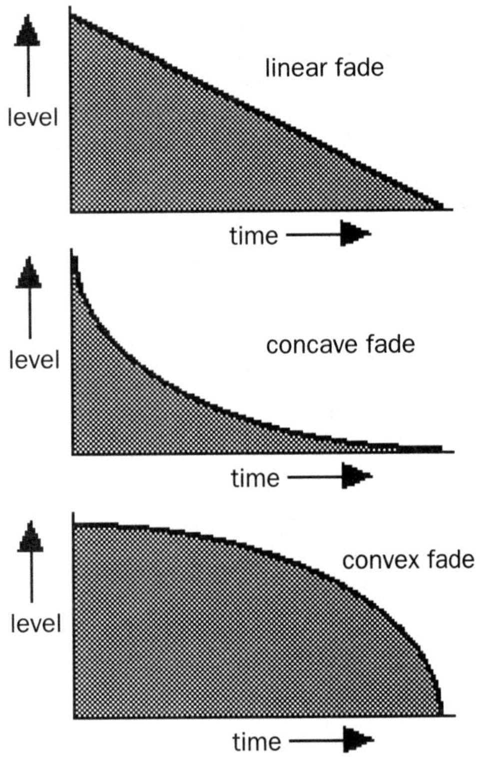


Fig. 20-2: *Different fadeout curves.*

A return fadeout is when you fade something out, only to have it fade back in quickly before fading out again for good. This is the kind of trick you can use once every two CDs or so, and it does add variety. But probably the best implementation I've heard was when a song modulated up a full key during the brief instant that the first fadeout had gone to zero volume. Thus, when the song came back, it had moved up a notch in terms of overall energy.

## Mixing to a Variable-Speed Tape Recorder

Mixing to a variable-speed tape recorder presents some extra options. If the track isn't lively enough or seems a little plodding, set the variable-speed control so that the second machine runs just a little slow as you mix. When you speed the tape back up to normal, the piece will speed up along with it. You can also carefully and slowly speed up a piece as it progresses; this can be very useful in adding "momentum," especially when sessions have been synchronized to a metronome or click track to gave a constant tempo during overdubbing. However, if you change the speed too fast it will sound obvious and out of tune.

Conversely, you can slow a song down by mixing onto a machine that runs slightly fast. Incidentally, you don't need much of a speed change to produce a drastic change in sound.

## Role-Playing: Producer, Engineer, Musician

In professional situations, the musician is part of a team of (hopefully) experienced and musically intelligent people. Two of the people who play an important role on this team are the producer and engineer. In a home environment, the musician doesn't necessarily have access to these high-powered talents, and has to perform those roles from within. Although this may seem difficult at first, this experience is probably one of the greatest teachers you can have in learning how to be objective about your parts, your style, and your sounds.

It helps to be precisely conscious of the ideal role of each of the three participants (musician, producer, engineer) so that you can assume those roles at will—alternately planning the course and arrangement of a piece (producer), playing it (musician), and recording it properly (engineer). By becoming familiar with these roles, you can apply their differing outlooks to your music and obtain a more balanced perspective.

### Producer

This is the person who has the Big Ideas and is responsible for putting together the pieces of a successful piece of music. The producer's role depends a lot on the musician being produced; some producers go in and read a newspaper during the recording process, concerning themselves solely with the mixing. Other producers pick the songs, the musicians, arrange string and horn parts, and in general take charge of most aspects of the music. What you want to acquire is the ability to see each piece as part of a whole, and each track as part of a final composition. If you know where you are going, it's a lot easier to get there; the job of the producer is to figure out just where you are going.

However, sometimes a producer must spend much time and effort dealing with artists. Acting as a liaison between a possibly temperamental star and a record company is sometimes not the best job in the world. In your case, you don't have a producer around to keep you working; that responsibility is up to you. If you blow a recording, don't get discouraged, just start over. If someone else blows a recording, realize that it's not the end of the world and proceed.

If a session is disorganized and confused, then you'll have a harder time recording good music. In your little studio, you can't have too many people hanging around, making noise, having a good time, and laughing; it's hard to get a good sound while competing with partygoers. So, try not to have people waiting around to play parts. If you need vocals after the basic tracks are done, don't have the vocalists hang around getting nervous; ask them to arrive at the studio a few hours after the session begins.

Don't forget that many towns and cities have ordinances that prohibit noise after a certain time. I know it's music to your ears, but it may not be to neighbors. Unless you have neighbors who understand, you'd better schedule your sessions with these ordinances in mind, unless you want to be liable for complaints. Or maybe you can work something out: maybe all the neighbors will like your music, or will let you make noise, if you let them make noise.

When you schedule a session, allot time for getting levels, setting up mics, and breaking down. If a group expects to record seventeen songs in an hour, gently inform them it doesn't work that way, especially in budget studios.

So, don't just record music, produce it. Tie everything together cleanly, vary the instrumentation, and put a little thought into the extra touches that help make a tape sound professional.

A word of caution about producing seems appropriate here: a common mistake among beginning producers is to overproduce. Open tracks do not necessarily need to be used; past a certain point, adding sounds causes more confusion than music. Keep your sense of good taste activated, and before adding a track ask yourself whether it should be edited, or whether it even needs to be there at all.

### Engineer

The engineer is the one at the session who doesn't drink, smoke, snort, talk much, complain, or (other than setting up the mics) even move out of the engineer's chair. While the producer is figuring out the concepts, and the musicians are out in the studio playing, the engineer is making sure that everything is set, organized, and ready to record. Whatever happens, the machines are cued up and the record button is ready to push. Of course, the above is a stereotype and no stereotype is accurate, but every engineer I ever worked with respected the job and took it seriously.

It's always nice to have an enthusiastic engineer who gets off on your music, but believe it or not, you can get some great sessions out of an engineer who doesn't care for your music at all. They are professionals whose job is to capture the sound in the best way possible.

It is very helpful to adopt an engineer's attitude when mixing, balancing, performing critical operations, and running the equipment. Put the music, your concern about whether that last run was really so hot, and all of those worries out of your mind; when you are playing engineer, work with what you have.

### Musician

After the levels are set and you know you aren't going to overload the meter, you again have to switch gears. Forget about the board, and try not to stare at the VU meters. Just dig in and cook. Unfortunately, this is kind of hard, especially when you need to punch in to a track while overdubbing and simultaneously pay careful attention to where you are on the tape so that you don't erase anything you want to keep. Nonetheless, try your best. Musicians are traditionally the dreamers, the visionaries, the artists, the children; engineers arc the computerlike scientists engaged in the noble quest for the Ultimate Sound; and the producer is the conductor, arranger, parent figure, politician, and sometimes mad genius. I tend to think that there is a part of each in all of us; you can get in touch with these parts by studying and getting absorbed in the roles of these characters. It will help your objectivity, and give you better tapes. Ultimately, the tape recorder is a mirror that lets you see a lot about yourself.

## Feel versus Perfection

There is no doubt that some older albums, recorded under technically primitive conditions, still conveyed a joyousness and enthusiasm—a "feel"—that made for great music. And some newer albums are so perfect, so automated and equalized, that the sound is sterile and somehow mechanical. There are some producers who believe that the feel is all important; if a musician does a great part but blows a couple of phrases, that's all right if the feel was good. Other producers insist on doing a part over and over and over until it's technically perfect. Both approaches have their advantages and pitfalls, so try to strike a balance. Don't fall into the trap of being so self-critical that you never get anything down on tape, and end up expending all your energies laying down the first track; but also don't get so loose that everything sounds "great" and you lose the ability to evaluate.

Some musicians try to create a feel in the studio by smoking grass or drinking. Sometimes this is to cover their own insecurities, and the fears that they have of hearing themselves on tape. I think most people would agree that a musician is at a technical peak, in terms of physical reflexes and thought processes, while straight. I'm staying neutral on this, but give the matter some thought.

Music is not all that well defined, but it surely hasn't been taken to its limits yet. Make the music that comes naturally to you: you are unique, and you have your own contribution to make. Remember that no matter who you are or how well you play, there will always be people who like your music, and people who won't like your music. Because you can't please everybody, then please yourself. If you are not a flash lead guitarist, that doesn't make you any less of a musician (less of a guitarist, perhaps, though that is certainly arguable!). Play within your limits, guided by your taste; listen critically to what you do.

Follow your own path and don't get discouraged. You will never get to go as far as you would like musically. I don't think anyone has ever gotten as far as they would like, but that's not the point. The point is the getting there.

Your studio makes you independent of record companies, rules, engineers, clocks, hourly rates, and all the rest. Finally, you are getting to be able to just play your music, without anyone telling you what to do, without time pressure, and without commercial pressures.

## The Performer as Listener

You may find that you have produced, played on, and engineered a piece, and never once did you really get to listen to it for pleasure. Well, now that the mix is over, give yourself a treat. Put on your final mixed tape, and forget you had anything to do with it. Don't listen for those mistakes you were trying to catch during mixdown, don't listen to whether the tracks are mixed right (you can always analyze later); just listen to the music. Pretend you walked in someplace and heard that music playing. What would you think of it?

Of course, maybe you'll decide you don't really like it after all. I've cut a couple of tunes where I would listen back and wish I hadn't wasted my time, but that hasn't happened very often. Most likely when you listen to your stuff, you'll think it's pretty good, or you wouldn't have made it the way you did in the first place.

Now that you're listening, relax, let yourself go, and just enjoy your creation. You've worked for it, you've earned it, and you probably loved every minute of making it. And now you are a little closer to that funny world of dense vibrations we call music.

# Chapter 21
# Assembly and Mastering

Now it's time to assemble our mixes into a final tape, which becomes the *two-track* (or *stereo*) *master.* We'll also cover a few tips that will make life easier for duplication houses when you decide to turn your masterpiece into a CD or cassette.

## Mastering Basics

Mixing all our pieces down onto a second machine (DAT or analog) creates a collection of several different mixes of several different songs, possibly with two or three takes for some songs. Doubtless there are large gaps between the mixes, and the songs are probably in no special order. During the mastering process, we take this collection of music and do some (or all) of the following:

- Select the takes to go on the final CD or cassette.
- Put them in the proper order, either by splicing (with analog gear) or digital editing (with digital gear).
- Balance levels between different cuts, or within different sections of the same cut if needed.
- Apply overall EQ to add "spice," or to compensate for problems (*e.g.,* reduce excessive bass, add brightness, *etc.*).
- Make a tune more "radio-ready" by adding compression or limiting to allow a higher average signal level.
- Crossfade between cuts.
- Add processing, such as a hint of reverb to tunes that seem too dry.
- Create fade outs and fade ins.

Good mastering can make a marginal recording acceptable, or a good recording superb. Often the difference between what comes out of a modest project studio and a multimillion dollar facility is not in the recording, but in the mastering. Good mastering engineers are rare, because they need to make flawless decisions about sound as well as have total command over signal processing technology.

Mastering has typically been the weak link in the project studio. Even though you can now do many of the above steps in your home or project studio, there is much to be said for going to a professional mastering facility as a final "reality check." Someone experienced in mastering may catch small problems that could come back to haunt you during the duplication process.

Remember that duplicators exist to *duplicate,* not make value judgments about your music. They will faithfully reproduce whatever it is you give them, even if it has some glaring error. There's nothing worse than having to pay for a thousand CDs or cassettes that are unusable, so it's definitely worth taking the time to make sure your master tape is the highest possible quality.

### At the Mastering House

The current industry standard is to transfer the master tape to a 3/4" U-Matic video recorder through a Sony PCM-1630 digital processor. This is done either at an independent mastering house, or at the duplicators. Once the U-Matic tape is at the duplicators, they insert the PQ subcodes required for CD production (this step is called *premastering*). These codes provide the timings, index markings for tracks, and all those other computerized kinda goodies that are a part of today's CD. However, it is likely that transferring to U-Matic will become less common now that recordable CDs are inexpensive enough to become the standard way to give your music to duplicators.

## Digital Mastering

Hard disk and digital tape technology are part of what make decent mastering possible for the home or project studio. If you mix to DAT and have a modular digital multitrack, you already have a great premastering machine and may not know it. If you also have a hard disk recording/processing system, you're even further ahead.

## Mastering the Hard (Disk) Way

Two-track hard disk digital audio systems are often used for mastering. You bounce your tracks over to the hard disk system (digitally, if you have a DAT with digital I/O), then apply digital EQ, limiting, gain changes, *etc.* You can then assemble a *playlist* to try out different song orders, and when everything is as desired, transfer the results back to DAT for your final master tape. However, there are some limitations when using only hard disk systems.

- You sacrifice real-time control, which can be important with mastering. For example, to process a piece of music with a hard disk system, you usually have to set up the parameters, then wait while the computer does the processing. It's cumbersome with budget hard disk systems to do something like increase the treble a few dB over several measures, then pull it back a bit later.
- There are device-specific limitations. For example, if crossfades are done in RAM, you need a lot of memory.
- The world is not yet totally digital. Some analog processors are ideal for mastering and have no equivalent function (yet) in any hard disk system.

## The Digital Tape or Multitrack HDR Connection

Adding a digital multitrack (whether tape or hard disk) to the process can overcome these limitations; the only tradeoff is a theoretical loss of quality if you bounce using the analog inputs and outputs (if you can bounce digitally, this isn't an issue). In practice, the difference in quality may not be noticeable; there could even be a subjective improvement. To find out if your system is up to the task, try this experiment:

1. Mix some tracks to DAT.

2. Bounce the DAT over to two tracks of your digital multitrack.

3. Bounce the digital multitrack tracks back to DAT.

4. Compare the original DAT sound with the one that was bounced to the digital multitrack and back. If the bounced version sounds acceptable, you're ready to begin mastering.

## Mastering, Step-by-Step

The following summarizes one way to do mastering with a DAT, two-track hard disk (HDR) system, and one eight-track modular digital multitrack (MDM). You can also substitute a multitrack hard disk recorder for the HDR/MDM combination.

1. Record mixes of all your tunes to DAT.

2. Bounce a DAT mix digitally to the HDR, then do any desired processing: normalization (if needed) to make sure you're using the maximum available headroom, peak limiting to let you get a bit higher average level, and overall EQ changes.

3. Bounce the processed tune digitally back to DAT (but don't go over your original mix so you have the original as backup).

4. Repeat steps 1 through 3 until all the tunes are complete.

5. Figure out the optimum running order. Do this by bouncing them all into the HDR system, and trying out several playlists until you get the right order.

6. Now it's time to assemble. Patch your DAT outs to MDM tracks 1 and 2 (include any analog processing, if appropriate), and record the first tune into the MDM.

7. Record the next tune on tracks 3 and 4. Notice how easy it is to do crossfades with this technique; just start recording the second tune sometime before the first tune ends, and fade in with the level controls.

8. Record the third tune into tracks 1 and 2, and keep alternating tunes between tracks 1 and 2 and tracks 3 and 4 until all the tunes are on the MDM tape.

9. Note that you still have four tracks left over. You can use these to insert additional effects or transitions (great for dance mixes), or add time code for reasons we'll get into next.

10. Now mix the MDM tracks back down to DAT to end up with a final two-track DAT master. If you need to make any volume tweaks, you can do so manually or by synching automation to time code recorded on an MDM track.

11. If needed, you can now bounce the completed DAT back to the HDR system to create additional masters for different purposes. For example, if the piece is going to be duplicated on cassette as well as CD, I often add a bit more compression and "exciter" treble enhancement to compensate for losses in the cassette duplication process.

## Assembling a Master Analog Tape

With digital assembling, we don't have to worry about bouncing because the signal tends to stay in the digital domain (although as in the example above, you may need to do some work in the analog world too). With analog tape, to prevent making too many copies (since there's a loss of fidelity with each transfer), you assemble a complete recording by splicing up the master two-track and physically putting the songs in the correct order. If you then need to change levels or add processing, you do so by playing the final tape into a DAT or other recorder, and running through the desired processing.

Assembling a master tape requires the following:

- The tape containing all final mixes
- Leader tape (paper preferred) for the beginning and end of the reel
- Splicing tape made specifically for audio applications (never use regular adhesive tape!)
- A felt tip marker with a sharp point
- Tape splicing block and demagnetized single-edge razor blade
- Several empty plastic or metal reels to hold bits of tape (both scrap and completed pieces)

Like everything else, assembling takes time and care. Also, this is where you really get into splicing, so let's discuss that before going any further.

### Making a Good Splice

A *splice* joins two pieces of tape or leader tape together. Here's the step-by-step procedure for splicing:

1. Push the tape into the groove in the splicing block (the side of the tape that goes against the record head faces down into the block). Run your finger along the back of the tape to make sure it's seated firmly in the block. Fig. 21-1 shows a splicing block. As you don't want to get skin oils on the tape, wash and dry your hands before splicing; you may even want to wear rubber gloves to insure the tape's cleanliness.

2. While the splicing block holds the tape to be spliced, make an angled cut in the tape with a sharp, demagnetized razor blade (Fig. 21-2).

3. Remove the half of the tape that won't be spliced, and insert the end of the other tape to be spliced into the splicing block. Move the two tapes so that the ends almost touch—any gap should be less than 1/32 of an inch (Fig. 21-3).

4. Apply splicing tape to the outside of the pieces of tape at the splice point (Fig. 21-4).

5. Gently lift the tape out of the groove, and place it face down on a hard surface (the back of the splicing block works well). Use a razor blade to trim off any excess splicing tape (Fig. 21-5). Then, run the flat side of your fingernail over the splice, pressing firmly so that the splicing tape will continue to adhere throughout recording, fast forwarding, *etc.*

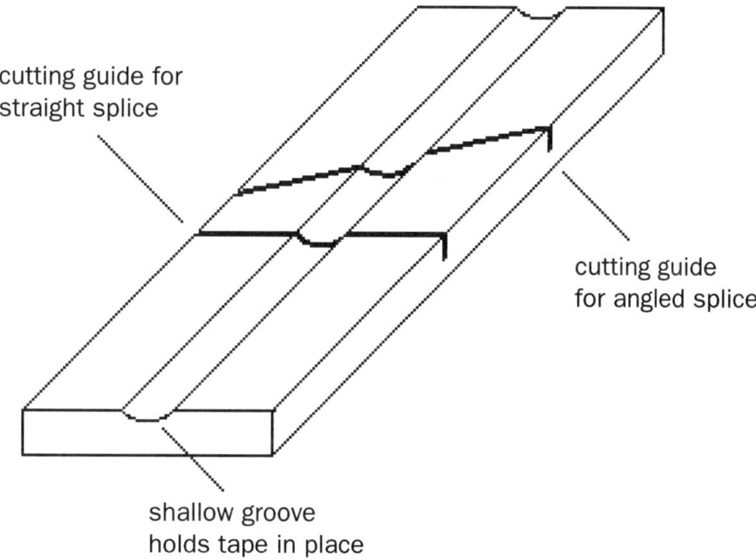


**Fig. 21-1:** *Typical splicing block for 1/4" tape. Blocks for wider tapes have correspondingly wider grooves.*

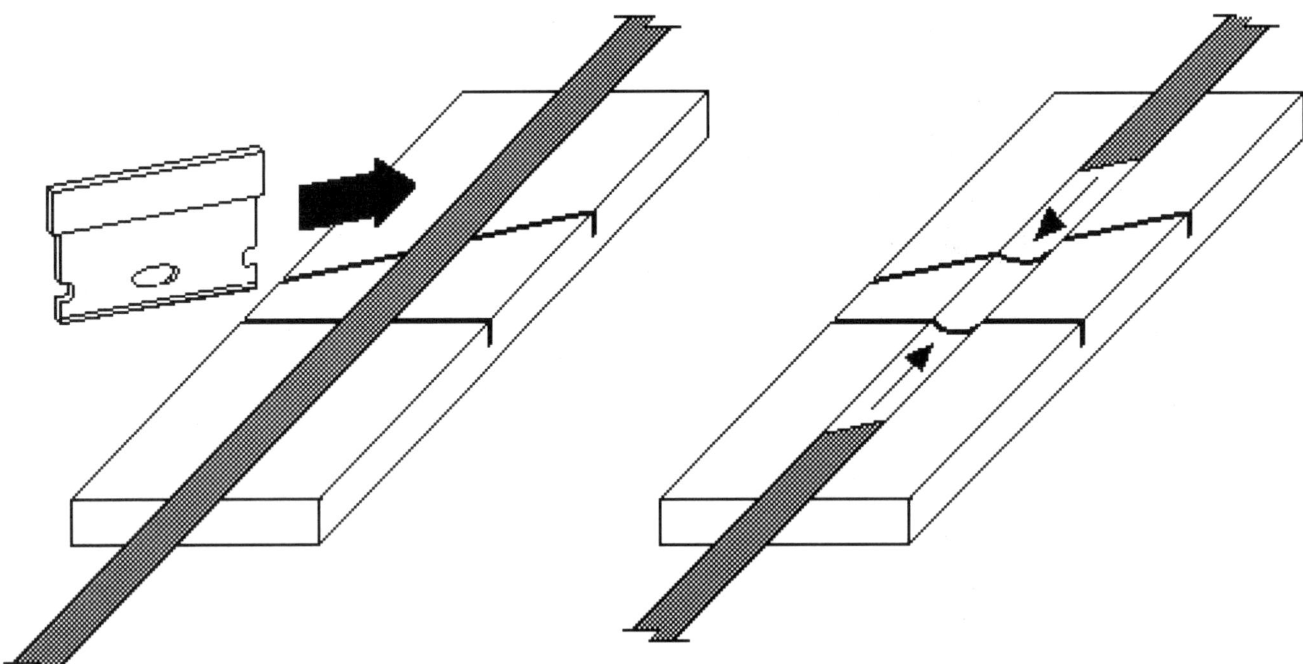

**Fig. 21-2:** *Using a razor to cut the tape.*

**Fig. 21-3:** *Slide the pieces to be spliced so that the two ends meet.*

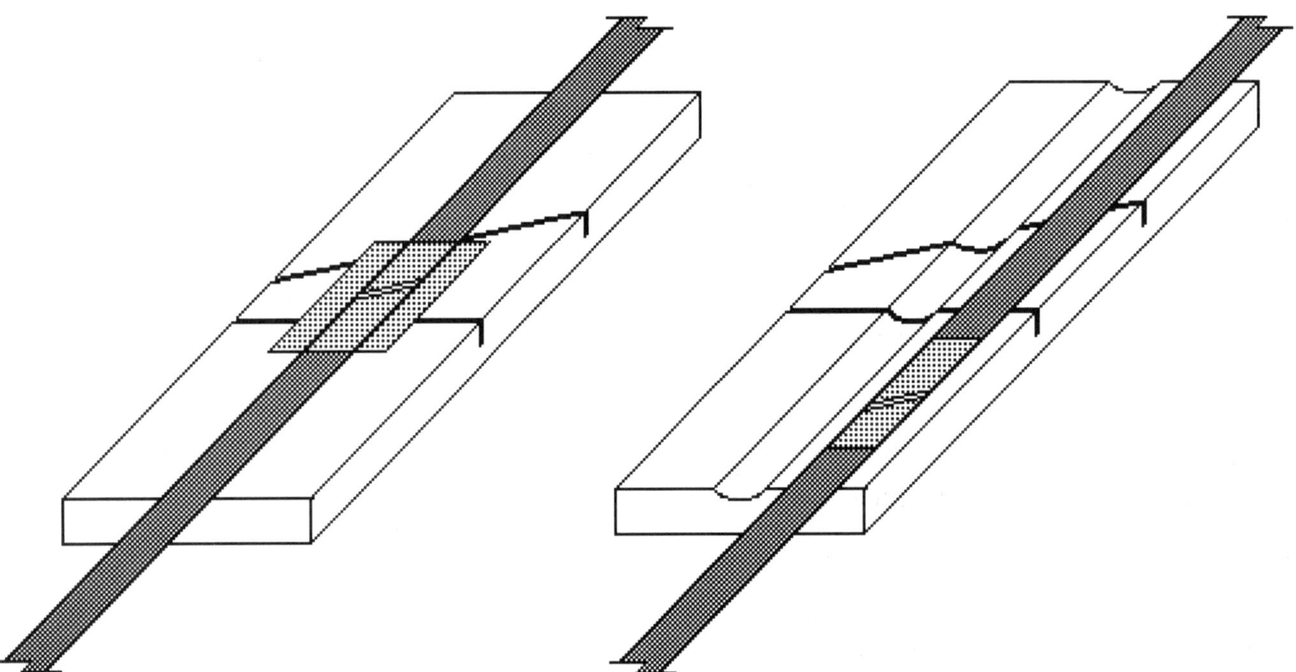

**Fig. 21-4:** *Adding splicing tape to the splice.*

**Fig. 21-5:** *The final splicing step. Make sure you run the flat part of your fingernail along the back of the tape to increase adhesion.*

Although splicing is fairly straightforward, if you ever have to splice a tape running at a very slow speed (such as cassettes), the sounds are packed so closely together on the tape that you may have to resort to a straight splice rather than an angled splice.

Some recorders are better suited to splicing than others. The biggest problem with splicing is to pinpoint the actual location where you want the cut to occur; the usual procedure is to slowly move the tape back and forth past the playback head until you have determined the right spot (Fig. 21-6).

However, when out of play mode many recorders engage lifters that push the tape away from the heads. This is mostly to prevent tape and head wear during fast forward and rewind (why scrape the tape across the head at a high rate of speed if you're not listening?). Fortunately, pro machines can engage either a pause

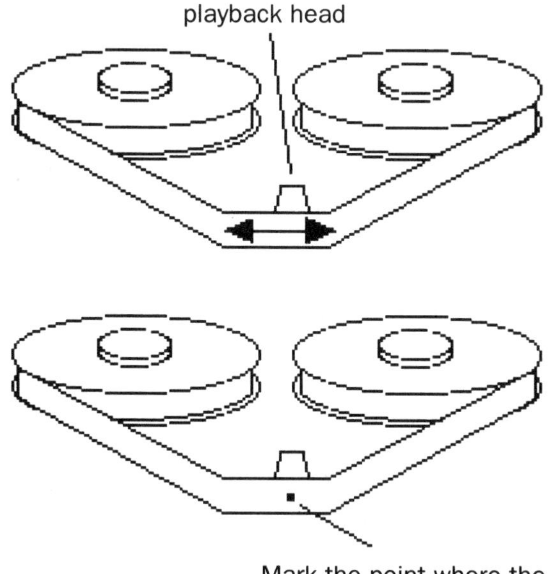


**Fig. 21-6:** *Rock the reels back and forth while listening to the tape to find the exact spot to be spliced (upper drawing), then mark the spot with a sharp point, felt-tip pen.*

or edit feature, which disconnects the mechanism pulling the tape, but leaves it in contact with the playback head, thus allowing "reel-rocking."

As a practical step-by-step example, let's suppose you want to make a splice at the beginning of a song, and connect it to some leader tape. Here's the procedure:

1. Find the beginning of the song by playing the tape until you hear the very first few notes.

2. Immediately hit the pause or edit button. On some machines, pause or edit modes still don't let the tape contact the head, so you may need to move an adjustable cueing arm to do this; check your machine's manual for specific instructions.

3. While in the edit mode, grasp the take-up and supply reels and use them to move the tape back and forth across the playback head (the last head the tape passes, in case you forgot). The sound will be slowed down and unrealistic, but that's not the point; as you move the tape back and forth, you will hear a distinct starting point at the song's beginning.

4. Once you have determined the exact starting point, make a mark with a felt tip marker (a Sanford Sharpie® is recommended) on the outside of the tape over the center of the playback head. This is where you want to cut to make your splice.

## Making Splices within a Tune

Making a splice within a piece is more difficult because you don't have a nice, obvious starting point. The best rule is to splice during silences, or just before a loud sound; again, you will have to move the tape slowly and surely across the head to pinpoint the exact spot. But also remember that if you move the tape too slowly, you won't hear much of anything because the signal will dive into the subsonic range. Practice makes perfect. . . .

Sometimes while splicing, after making several passes back and forth across the playback head you'll lose track of the point you were going to splice. This happens to professional engineers, too; don't feel bad, just start over. If you really blow a splice and cut off a note's beginning, you can usually resplice if you're careful. But try to avoid layering one splice on top of another; when this monster goes past the playback head, there will probably be a dropout.

Also note that it takes some time for a splice to "work in." If you hear a discontinuity, run the tape a few more times and it might settle in.

## Splicing Between Tunes

When splicing in spaces between tunes, you can use paper leader tape or blank recording tape. With paper tape in between selections, all tape hiss drops out completely during the time the paper leader tape passes over the playback head and this sounds weird. By using blank recording tape, the noise level stays consistent when transitioning from song to song, which is psychologically less offensive. For this reason, it's best to use paper tape only at the beginning or end of a tape.

## Assembling Disparate Tunes into a Master Tape

Now let's apply our splicing knowledge to assembling a finished tape. Fig. 21-7 shows in endlessly repetitive detail how to assemble a tape. We are assuming here that there is a tape with three songs on it; as the tape goes by, first you hear song A, then song B, then a bad mix of song B that you don't want to use, then song C. And, to make the example interesting, we will also assume that song C is the one you want to have first on your final tape, followed by song A, and then the proper version of song B.

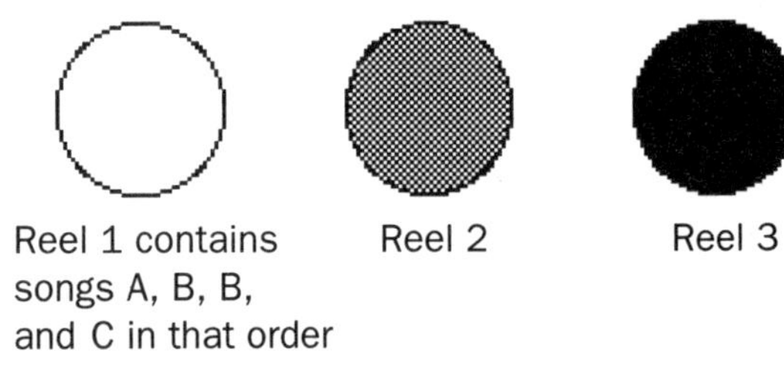


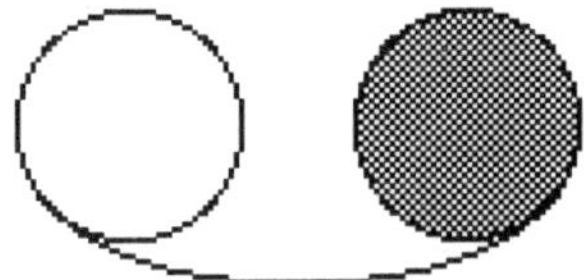

**Step 1:** Play tape until song C hits playback head. Cut tape at beginning of song C. Place reel 2 aside temporarily, which now holds songs A, B and false version of B.

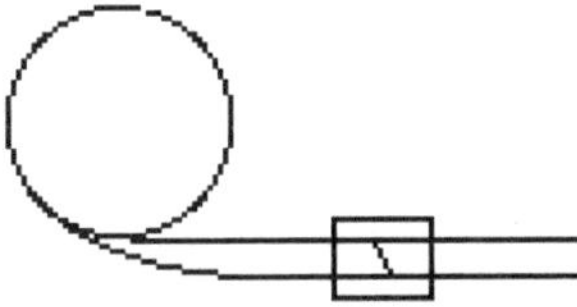

**Step 2:** Splice several feet of paper leader to beginning of song C.

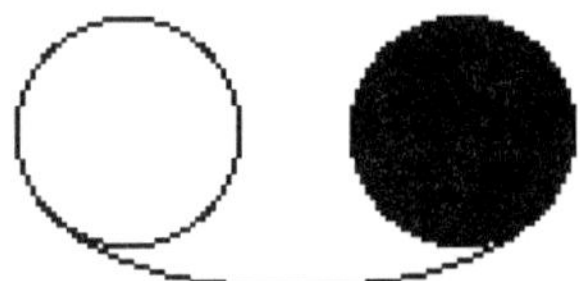

**Step 3:** Wind leader around reel 3; play through to end of song C. Splice a couple of feet of blank tape to the end of song C, then lay reel 3 aside temporarily. Reel 1 now has nothing left on it of use, and it may be used as an extra take-up reel.

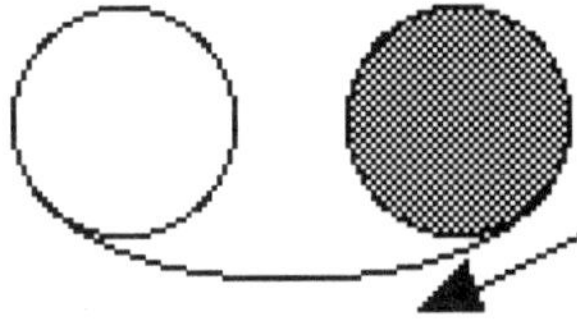

**Step 4:** Rewind onto the take-up reel until you locate the beginning of song A, then make a cut and lay reel 2 aside.

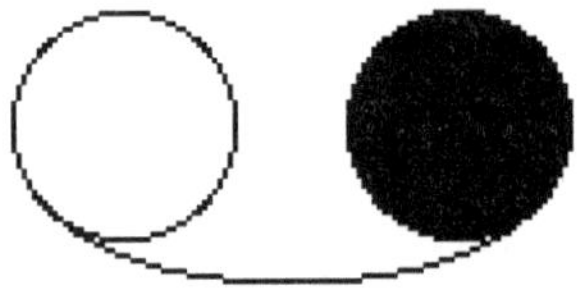

**Step 5:** Splice beginning of song A to the blank tape following song C. Now, we finally have paper leader, song C, a little bit of space, then song A on reel 3.

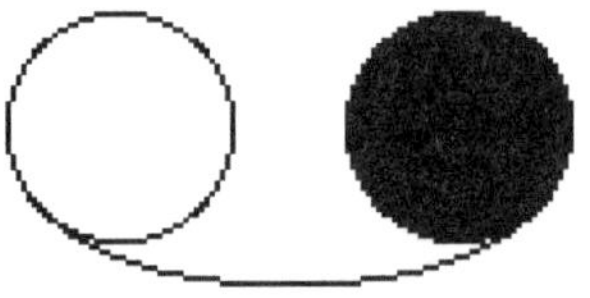

**Step 6:** Make cut at end of song A; add a few feet of blank tape, then lay reel 3 aside.

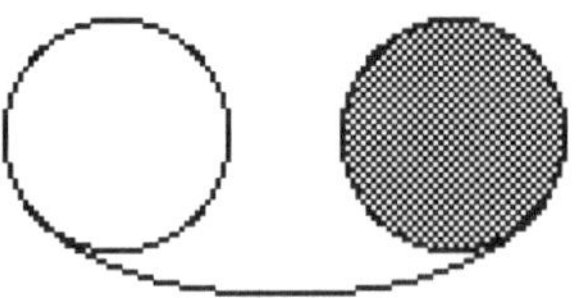

**Step 7:** Using reel 1 as a take-up reel, locate proper mix of song B on reel 2 and cut at beginning of song.

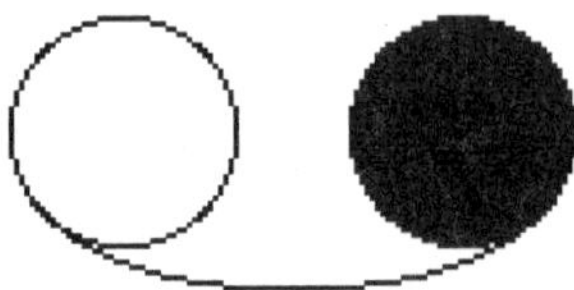

**Step 8:** Splice beginning of song B to the blank tape following song A. Now, we have songs C, A, and B on reel 3, and we are almost finished.

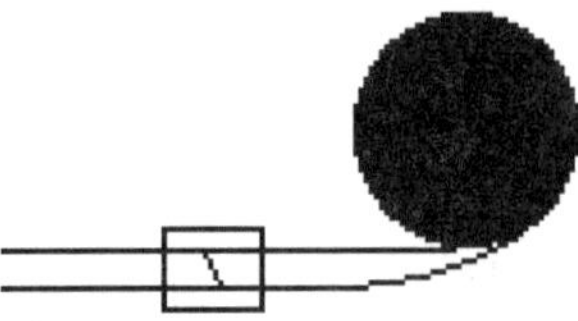

**Step 9:** Make cut at end of song B, then splice several feet of paper leader to end of tape.

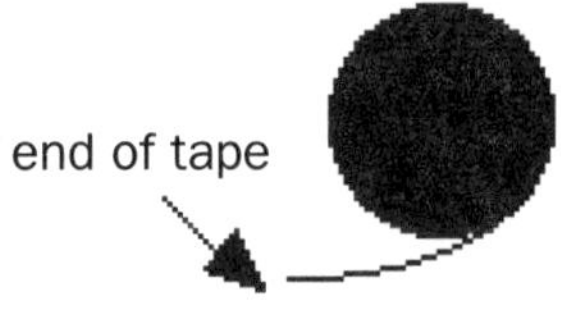


**Step 10:** Reel 3 now contains our final assembled tape. Because the end of the tape is sticking out, this reel is called "tails out" and must be rewound before it can be played.

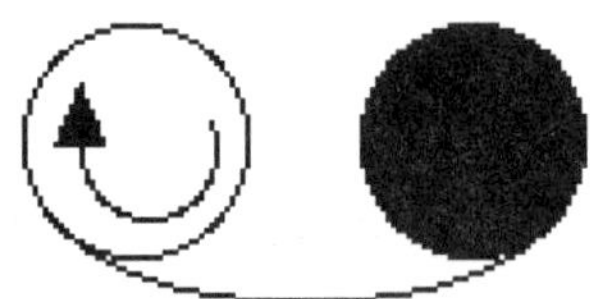

**Step 11:** Rewinding tape onto another reel makes tape ready for play.

Reel 1 is now "heads out."

**Fig. 21-7:** *How to assemble a master tape by rearranging the order of songs and adding leadering.*

### Level-Balancing, Fades, and Other Processing

You may still have some problems with the assembled tape, such as level changes between songs, or differences between pieces recorded on one day compared to pieces recorded on other days. Or you might want to make some changes, such as adding signal processing or doing fades. This situation usually calls for a *two-to-two mix*, where you copy the master to another two-track machine (such as DAT, 30 ips 1/2" analog tape, recordable CD, *etc.*). To avoid degrading the fidelity, you can often avoid going through the board (you can still patch any required signal processing into the signal path). Use the second machine's record level controls to compensate for level changes in the source material.

You can add processing in real time as you transfer the tape to a second machine, or play the analog tape into a DAT and do the digital domain tricks mentioned earlier in the chapter.

## Mastering to Recordable CDs (CD-R)

Although DAT and 30 ips reel-to-reel master tapes have traditionally gone to duplicating facilities, as pointed out earlier they still have to be transferred to some interim medium, usually the Sony 1630/U-Matic recorder combination, before being turned into a CD. If you transfer your DAT over to a recordable CD in your studio, you eliminate the interim steps and also can rest assured that the duplicated CD will sound *exactly* like what you submitted to the duplicator.

Recordable CD machines write Orange Book CDs, a particular specification that defines where and how the data will be written to recordable CDs (the standard, playback-only CD conforms to the Red Book specification). Some also write computer-oriented CD-ROMs that follow the Yellow Book standard.

### Single Session versus Multisession

Older, single session CD-Rs could write only one file on a recordable CD, whether six seconds or sixty minutes. Multisession CD-Rs let you record as many consecutive files as desired on a CD, and these do not have to be recorded at the same session. This is particularly important if you're creating a CD-ROM to back up computer data, since you can keep adding files as you go along. Considering the cost of blank CDs, multisession recorders are much better than single session types; fortunately, the latter are becoming less common.

### Stand Alone versus Computer Peripheral

Because many computer owners want to be able to archive files on CD-ROM, there are several CD-Rs sold as computer peripherals. Most of the time they also let you record audio CDs. If you have a computer in your studio, this is an ideal addition: not only can you make one-off CDs, you can back up your computer data inexpensively on a very stable medium. Computer-oriented CD-Rs can also write faster than standalone types (this saves time when making CDs, which would otherwise occur in real time). However, you'll need to load your files into the computer before making the CD, and will probably require premastering software to add the required P and Q codes that define track start and end points, timing data, *etc.*

In time, the CD-R will probably become the accepted way to submit music to a duplicator. In any event, it's really wonderful to be able to make your own CDs (albeit in small quantities), and for that reason alone the world of home studios eagerly awaits the day when CD-Rs drop in price to the point where anyone can afford them.

## The Aesthetics of Assembling

Assembling a final tape should take as much thought as any other part of the recording process. Pacing in particular is very important when listening to music. Recordings are traditionally paced in several different ways: one common approach is to have a strong, mostly uptempo opener, followed by something softer. The final song is the equivalent of a closer when playing live; it has to be just as strong, if not stronger, than the opener. Then again, CDs offer such long playing times (seventy-four minutes and sometimes even more) that the "grand finale" might occur a tune or two before the end, with the last selections providing the audio equivalent of a play's "falling action." (You know, like in a sci-fi movie where they never end with the big space battle scene, but instead with the post-battle coffee break at the space station as the characters wax philosophical about their recent adventure.) The weakest cut often goes just before the closer since if anybody has listened that far, you've already hooked them (and the closer will compensate anyway).

The first cut on a recording is super-important, due to the tremendous competition for the listening ear, whether DJ, record company A&R VP, or music buyer. As a result, the first song is usually as universally palatable and as uptempo as possible to get people listening. Remember that many DJs audition recordings by playing the first few seconds of each cut—if they don't like what they hear, they move on to the next cut.

Of course, a lot of music does not lend itself to the formulas used with pop music. For example, much "ambient" music starts out fairly simply and quietly, building in intensity and then fading out again. This is directly the opposite of starting and ending strongly. Then again, some music is more poetry-set-to-music than music itself, and the words become a focal point. In a case like this, the main reason to pace is for variety. Follow your own taste, but do give the matter some thought.

Also remember that many people do not have the same passion for music as someone running a budget studio, and their ears are far less trained; people's attention spans can also be very short. If you want to pursue music as a pure art form for your own enlightenment and the enjoyment of whomever else is interested, then satisfy yourself and that's it. But if you are making a demo for commercial acceptance, or one that is aimed to people with a variety of ages, tastes, and outlooks, then you may feel the need to make some concessions to all these different tastes.

However, be careful. Usually what sells the best is when someone is sincere and doing something they truly love, and it just so happens that millions of other people love it too. Attempts to be calculating and create hits sometimes work, but more often than not, they fail. The artists who make it truly big have a distinctive and unique vision. If enough other people like it, then success will result. Sometimes, though, it's necessary to realize that you simply may not make music that will appeal to a large number of people. At that point you'll have to decide between being true to yourself or trying to bend to fit commercial expectations. It's not an easy decision, but in the long run, I think you're better off if you're true to yourself and just let the chips fall where they may.

In addition to pacing by mood, also consider pacing by key. For example, if one piece is in G and another in B, all things being equal, try following the G with the B. Sometimes a recording can almost go up the scale; the effect is subtle but is does excite people more as the tunes progress. With material that is less tonal in character, I frequently pace by rhythm, alternating between slower and faster pieces.

## How to Make Duplicators Love You

As we said earlier, duplicators will produce whatever you give them. However, there are some things you should do before submitting anything for duplication that will make everyone's life easier.

No matter what medium you're submitting, include complete documentation on all aspects of the recording: song titles, running times, total time, sampling rate (for DATs), analog tape speed and type of noise reduction used, calibration tones, *etc.* And of course, all songs should be in the correct order, and be "ready to go." Any extra work the duplicators have to do will cost you money. It's also a good idea to call up the duplicator and ask for specific guidelines on how to submit your recording for duplication, as these vary slightly from duplicator to duplicator. And don't insult your music by submitting your master on anything other than the finest tape you can buy!

### Tips for DAT

Include fifteen to sixty seconds of blank tape before the actual material begins and at the very end. This should be recorded with no inputs connected to the deck so that the tape is recorded at the lowest possible level. In your documentation of timings and such, make sure you identify how much silence there is at the beginning and end of the tape. Some people prefer to record a tone rather than silence so that the engineer knows something is happening.

Don't worry about including precise calibration tones, as is required with analog tapes. Level-matching is not an issue with digital recording.

Many DATs have a choice of 48 kHz or 44.1 kHz sampling rates. Although 48 kHz theoretically gives better response, the difference is extremely slight; besides, CDs are fixed at 44.1 kHz, so that throws away any advantage there might be. Record your DAT at 44.1 kHz if you plan to use it to make a CD; otherwise, you'll need to do a 48-to-44.1 kHz format conversion, which costs money and can degrade sound quality somewhat.

Include a start ID at the precise beginning of each tune. You can give the blank space at the beginning an ID of 0. It's good practice to erase all start IDs and insert them manually before submitting the tape. You'd be surprised how many false start IDs can show up on a tape if you're not careful.

## Tips for Analog Tape

- Include three thirty-second sine wave test tones: 1 kHz, 10 kHz, and 100 Hz. Any noise reduction should be off when recording these tones. If the tape is encoded with Dolby A or Dolby SR (preferred), it also requires the Dolby calibration tone for proper decoding. Adjust the mixer so the 1 kHz tone reads 0 VU, adjust the recorder's input level so that the tone reads 0 VU on the recorder's meters, then start recording. When recording the 10 kHz and 100 Hz tones, adjust the console levels if necessary so that the console meters read 0 VU, but *do not* readjust the tape recorder input control.

  The reason for including tones is that the mastering house or duplicator can compensate for any misalignment. For example, if the 10 kHz tone you recorded plays back on the duplicator's machine at –3 dB, then the mastering facility can boost +3 dB at 10 kHz to compensate.

  Tones can come from a signal generator or reference CDs with test tones (the official ways) or from a synthesizer set to produce a steady sine wave. Key B5 gives a 987.77 Hz note (which is probably more accurate than the average 1 kHz test tone oscillator anyway). For 100 Hz, play G2 (97.999 Hz). High frequencies are harder to get, but C8 gives you 4186 Hz. D#8 is almost exactly 5 kHz, and if you can transpose that up an octave, you'll get 10 kHz. However, you might want to verify the high frequency waveforms with an oscilloscope—they may look more like a square wave than a sine.
- Add several feet of paper leader tape at the beginning and end of the tape to make threading easier.
- If you're going to add noise reduction to the master tape, make sure your duplicator can decode it. Popular choices are Dolby SR and Dolby A.

## Media Requirements

Consider whether you're going to be producing CDs, analog cassettes, or both, as each has different requirements (and we'll even touch on vinyl).

I firmly believe it is necessary to make a separate master for CDs and cassettes, and most pros in the industry agree. Because cassettes have a much narrower dynamic range than CDs, soft sounds that come through fine on the CD could get buried in the noise with tape.

Cassettes also have a harder time handling high frequencies than CDs. Therefore, it's often a good idea to add a little more compression and high end (typically through the user of "exciter" and "enhancer" signal processors) to a master tape intended for cassettes.

Timings are also different. A CD can reliably play back a little over 70 minutes of sound; a cassette can easily do up to 90 or 100 minutes. Generally with cassettes, you want to sequence the material so that the A side is slightly longer than the B side. Otherwise, you'll end up with "dead air" at the end of the A side.

We should also mention vinyl for the few hardcore folks who still use this medium. Vinyl has a very hard time with ultra low frequencies, especially if they're out of phase and in opposite channels—this can be enough to drive a disc cutting lathe insane. Vinyl also has a hard time with high frequencies, so unlike a cassette master, adding a little extra "sheen" can be risky.

There are other compromises: vinyl trades off level, amount of bass, and total time. In other words, you can have a real loud record if you're willing to have it run short and not use a lot of bass; if you want lots of bass and a long playing time (over twenty minutes), you'll have to bring the volume down. There's more distortion in the inner grooves, so it's a good idea to have your softest song be just before the end of the side.

It takes real skill to do a good mastering job on vinyl, but with the ascendancy of digital audio, odds are this is one skill you won't need to learn.

# Chapter 22
# Maintenance and Troubleshooting

A wonderful studio doesn't seem so wonderful when there's an equipment breakdown—it's frustrating, costly, and can stomp on inspiration faster than just about anything else. But there's a lot you can do to keep everything in proper running order.

## Preventive Maintenance: General Tips

This may sound simplistic, but the best way to avoid having to repair equipment is not to have anything break down in the first place. Although people seem to feel that equipment breakdowns are like the weather—namely, you can't do anything about it—this is not always true. Although random failures will crop up, there are many steps you can take to insure that down time is the exception, not the rule. Such as:

### Treat Your Machines Kindly

This is the key to trouble-free operation. Remember that devices such as recorders are precision devices that are calibrated in thousandths of an inch. Don't subject gear to unnecessary transportation or movement; buy it, bring it home, set it up gently and carefully, and move it as little as possible thereafter. Don't drop anything on your machine, bump against it with a guitar neck, or use the top of it as a shelf: treat your recording equipment as the delicate and expensive system that it is.

For field recording, invest in a machine designed for that job—it's worth the extra cost. Consumer-oriented machines operate well in the environment for which they are intended, which is a nice, peaceful, home recording studio. Throw a budget MDM in your car to take to a gig and you're asking for trouble, unless you add considerable padding and protection.

### Burn In Your Gear

Many electronic component failures occur within the first seventy-two hours of operation. This problem, called infant mortality, can be minimized by "burning in" electronic devices for at least seventy-two hours. However, burning in is a time-consuming process, and not many companies burn in gear prior to it leaving the factory; instead, they offer a ninety-day warranty so that *you* can do the quality control. Therefore, when you first get a new piece of equipment, run it continuously for a few days to weed out any failures before the warranty period is up.

### Use Dust Covers

Covers for your gear should be made out of a nonporous material, such as plastic.

### Follow All Alignment/ Maintenance Procedures

Using test tapes on analog decks and generally keeping tabs on a piece of gear can alert you to possible problems. Example: If you note that one tape recorder channel doesn't seem to put out quite as much high frequency energy as it used to, you can possibly catch a serious head wear problem in time to re-lap the head, thus restoring it to proper condition before it deteriorates so far that a replacement head is required.

### Reduce Static Electricity

Once after walking across a carpet, I touched my computer keyboard and—oops, instant file delete! Apparently, the static electricity charge had been sufficient to alter the data in the computer (luckily, no chips were blown in the process).

Fortunately, there are a number of accessories that prevent static build-up, including antistatic floor mats on which you can place your chair as you mix, and spray-on antistatic chemicals such as Static Guard. For your computer, there are antistatic wrist rests (touch them before you touch the keyboard, and you're discharged).

### Work Switches and Controls Periodically

Some controls and switches don't get used much; dust and oxide accumulating in the contacts can result in intermittent operation. Many switches are designed to be self-wiping, where working the switch cleans the contact. I've found it's good practice to periodically toggle the switches and twist the controls.

### Avoid Dust

Unless you're in a "clean room," your gear will accumulate dust. Dust has two main nasty qualities: it interferes with proper contact between moving parts, and forms a layer of insulation on parts, which prevents heat from dissipating. When it's time for spring cleaning, take the cover off of the piece of gear to be cleaned, go outside, and carefully blow out the dust with a can of compressed air. (You can use a regular vacuum cleaner with the hose plugged into the blower, if you run it for a while to clean any dust out of the tube; but compressed air is preferable.) Don't forget to clean out any computer monitors as well; dust and cobwebs can really wreak havoc with high-voltage circuits.

### Read the Manual!

Most manuals include tips on how to prolong the life of a piece of equipment. For example, floppy disk and hard disk drives don't like to be moved around—sudden G-forces can bang the read/write heads together, or at the very least cause misalignment problems. When transporting a device with a disk drive, *unless you're instructed to do otherwise,* insert the cardboard or plastic shipping material that may have been inserted in the disk drive when the unit was first unpacked. A good manual will be filled with advice on preventive maintenance, so read it carefully.

### Check Your Wiring

Make sure that all electrical outlets are properly wired and grounded; I know one composer who had a couple of amplifiers break down due to inadequate wiring. The gauge of wire apparently wasn't thick enough, which caused a voltage drop that simulated "brown-out" conditions and overstressed the amp. And while we're on the subject of AC power, keep all cords routed away from foot traffic areas. More than one device has been destroyed because someone tripped over a cord and took down a piece of equipment with it.

### Temperature Extremes Are the Enemy

Equipment should never be set up where it can receive the full impact of the sun's rays (even when filtered through window glass), nor should it sit in a car overnight. Also, vent holes should never be obstructed. If there are vents in the bottom of a piece of equipment, make sure the device sits on a hard surface where air can flow freely into the unit. Blocked vents can create a safety hazard due to possible overheating of components, and shorten component life if heat sensitive components are constantly forced to run hot. For example, if power resistors build up excessive heat, resistance values can change and, at worst, the resistors can self-destruct and take some other parts with them when they go.

If equipment is built in a rack cabinet or recessed into a wall, adequate ventilation is a must. Adding a small fan (the ones designed for use with computers are generally quiet) can minimize heat build-up. Another consideration with rack mount equipment is to stagger heat-producing equipment. If there's a hot-running power amp at the bottom of the rack cabinet, leave one rack space above it for air to circulate. Assuming that other heat-producing rack units are sufficiently light, mount them toward the top of the rack so that as the heat rises upwards, it doesn't "cook" other units in the rack.

If noise is a problem, sometimes you don't need a fan. I had one piece of gear that wouldn't work above 85°F. So, I did some thermal engineering the company didn't do. First, I felt around for heat build-up; the whole rear panel of the device would get very warm, so I simply removed it. This allowed plenty of air to circulate around the back.

I then took off the cover and touched the outside of each IC and power transistor package; some of them felt excessively hot, so it seemed like a good idea to beef up the heat sinks that help the semiconductors dissipate heat. For the transistors, I added an aluminum plate that carried heat away from the top of the package. (Incidentally, while doing this I found that one of the power transistors had not been screwed down sufficiently to make good contact with its existing heat sink.)

For the ICs, I used thermally conductive epoxy to attach small finned heat sinks (available from electronics supply houses) to the tops of the IC packages. Lo and behold, all thermal problems went away—even when the ambient temperature hit 105°F during a heat wave. (Yes, I know you shouldn't run computer-based gear in that kind of heat; but I don't have air conditioning, and a deadline was looming larger than fear of breakdown.) Since the capacitors sitting next to these semiconductors were no longer being baked by the heat, I expect they'll last longer too.

There are other thermal considerations: try to maintain a reasonably consistent room temperature. Excessive cold can crack rubber parts, or at least age them and make them brittle. Too much heat is bad for the various lubricants in a tape machine; in the presence of heat, oil tends to thin out and loses both its lubricating and heat-dissipating properties.

### Fan and Filter

If the cooling fan has a filter, check it periodically and clean or replace if necessary. Filters can get so clogged with dust that they prevent proper air flow, which increases the machine's internal temperature. Also, the fan itself is often a dust magnet because it's pulling lots of air over those blades. Wipe them off periodically to keep dust from getting into the machine.

### Surge Protection and Uninterruptible Power Supplies (UPS)

If there's a really bad spike on the line, a surge protector will hopefully take care of it. Using a UPS is an almost fail-safe way to prevent problems caused by AC line garbage (spikes, noise, surges, brownouts, *etc.*). For more information on these and other power-conditioning devices, see Chapter 7.

### No Smoking!

Smoke particles look like boulders to the surface of a floppy disk, but any gear—especially tape—can have its performance affected by being in a smoky environment. Smoke usually doesn't cause an immediate, total failure, but does increase the odds of intermittency and other problems.

### Never Touch Cable Pins

Always handle a cable by the casing. Some pins might connect to sensitive parts of a device that could be damaged by static electricity charges (such as what you accumulate walking across a rug on a low-humidity day). Also, it's generally good practice to turn off power before connecting cables (although MIDI ones are okay).

### Avoid Turning Gear On and Off in Quick Succession

Turn-on transients put a strain on components. If you're going to take an hour break, leave the gear on (if you're using a computer monitor, turn the brightness down). Some people insist you're better off just leaving machines on all the time, but that wastes electricity.

### What to Do When Good Gear Goes Bad

Preventive maintenance can only take you so far, and someday you'll be the victim of equipment failure. The best strategy is to prepare yourself for this occasion. Write the address, phone, and fax number of your nearest authorized service center for a given piece of equipment in the unit's manual, and retain all packing material to prevent further damage should you need to ship your gear off for servicing.

Also, keep a log of any previous repairs or modifications that may have been made to a unit; knowing a unit's history can help expedite the repair process. I also keep a list of noncatastrophic problems (sticking control, burnt-out light, bad switch, rattle, *etc.*) so that if something major does go wrong, everything can be taken care of at once.

## Maintaining Digital Recorders

Maintaining and aligning digital recorders, whether multitrack or DAT, requires specialized knowledge and equipment. Even cleaning the heads is not something for beginners. Digital decks use rotating heads that are extremely fragile; traditional analog head-cleaning techniques (*i.e.,* cotton swabs and isopropyl alcohol) are strictly taboo. Small fibers from the swabs can get stuck in the head, and applying a little too much force in the wrong place could permanently destroy the head (and possibly increase the odds of "eating" a tape as well).

For any extensive cleaning, take the machine to an authorized service center or to a repair facility that specializes in video gear. For the adventurous, we'll include general instructions for head cleaning at the end of this section. Meanwhile, here are preventive maintenance steps that can help prevent thoses trips.

### Head Cleaning Cassette

If you experience any problem (*e.g.,* increased error count) with a rotating head-based machine, first run a cleaning cassette and see if the problem fixes itself. This will provide a solution in most cases; if not, you'll need to see a professional.

For multitracks, use a *dry* cleaning cassette intended for VHS or Hi-8 tape, depending on your transport's format (*never* use the kind that requires wetting). For DAT, use the dry cleaning cassettes sold specifically for DAT. Although this type of cleaner is not as effective as actually opening up the deck and cleaning the head manually, it's good preventive maintenance.

If you use good quality tape and operate the machine in a clean environment, you don't have to clean the heads of digital decks all that often. Opinions vary on how often cleaning is necessary; I'd suggest every twenty-five hours or so.

### Minimizing Head Wear

"Cue" and "review" modes offer a quick way to shuttle to a nearby section of the tape, and you can even hear the audio somewhat as the tape whizzes by. But the down side of these modes is they cause more head and tape wear than simply rewinding. Unless you need to monitor the sound as it goes by or are in a real hurry, press stop before selecting rewind or fast forward to disengage the tape from the heads. This is true for both digital multitracks and DAT decks.

Leaving a digital deck in pause mode can also cause wear. Like VCRs, digital recorders will usually kick out of pause mode after a few minutes to minimize wear.

### Removing Tapes before Power-Down

Remove the tape from any digital recorder before turning off the power. Should there be any problem (*e.g.*, blown fuse) when you turn the machine on again, you may have to disassemble the unit to get the tape out. Don't just leave it sticking halfway out, as this lets in dust. Remove the tape completely, and put it in an appropriate sealed container.

### Backing Up Digital Tapes

It's as important to make copies of multitrack and digital tapes as it is to make safety copies of analog tapes. It's best to do digital transfers, but if this isn't possible, at least make analog copies. If at all possible, keep an additional set of tapes off-site in case of fire, flood, earthquake, volcanoes, or UFO visitations. Since DATs are compatible with many hard disk recording systems, if you don't have two DATs to make digital copies, you can copy the data from the DAT to the hard disk recorder, then load in a second DAT tape and bounce the hard disk data to it. Similarly, some multichannel hard disk systems allow for direct digital communication to and from modular digital multitracks. You can bounce the data from the multitrack over to the hard disk system, then save back to another tape to create a copy.

One major caution about making digital copies with DAT: "consumer" grade DAT recorders, and even some pro models, include SCMS (Serial Copy Management System), which is designed to thwart unauthorized digital dubbing and piracy. SCMS inserts "flags" in the digital data stream that let you make only one digital copy of a tape; can't make a digital copy of that copy. (SCMS does not affect the analog inputs and outputs.)

This a problem because if you mix down several tunes to a DAT, then "assemble" these tunes in the proper order by copying them to a second DAT, SCMS will prevent you from making a backup copy of this master. Pro decks either dispense with SCMS entirely, or provide some means to defeat it. If your deck is afflicted with SCMS, you may be able to defeat it; check with a local service center. Also, you can always copy an SCMS tape using the AES/EBU digital outputs, which do not carry the SCMS code.

Finally, date when your digital tapes go into service. After a tape has been around more than five years or so, it's prudent to make a digital copy of it to a new tape, and keep the older tape as a backup.

### The Dual Backup System

Many pros keep two backups. Only one is updated at a time; that way if a problem happens during the backup process, the older version is still available. On the next backup, the older backup is updated. It's good practice to use the write protect tab to differentiate between a "current" and "old" backup. Protect the current backup and unprotect the older backup so that the next time you back up, there won't be any mistaking of which tape to use (the same principle applies to using the write-protect switch on floppy disks).

## Cleaning Digital Deck Heads

I'd like to thank New York repair guru Eddie Ciletti, who knows more about making digital recorders happy than just about anybody, for contributing the following section on digital recorder head cleaning.

But remember, I warned you: this is a very delicate procedure, so do the following at your own risk. Because of machine-to-machine variations, this description is as generic as possible.

### Manual Head Cleaning

While manual DAT maintenance is not recommended, VHS and 8 mm transports are accessible. To clean the heads:

1. Disconnect the power cable.

2. Follow the manufacturer's instructions for removing the cover.

3. Locate the head drum, which is round and has a mirror finish.

4. Dampen a piece of lint-free cloth (*e.g.*, "Twillwipes," made by Chemtronics—chamois sticks are not recommended), with anhydrous isopropyl alcohol (use the kind that's ninety-nine percent pure).

5. Locate the heads (which are black) on each side of the drum. You can find them along the slit that separates the lower, stationary part of the drum from the "upper cylinder" (*i.e.*, the part that spins).

6. Press the cloth gently against the drum's face; rotate the drum clockwise, then counterclockwise. You may feel the heads as they pass under your fingertips. *Big Time Caution:* Do *not* rub the cloth in *any* direction, especially vertically (up or down). This will cause serious, expensive damage.

7. Remove the cloth and check if any dirt has been removed. If there is dirt, repeat if necessary on a clean piece of cloth.

Check the tape guides as well, but be careful. At the top of most adjustable guides is a slot similar to the head of a screw. This part is used for calibration and *should not turn,* even though the guides themselves may be designed to spin. Special tools, test tapes and test equipment (all costing more than your machine) are required for calibration. *Do not touch or attempt to adjust!*

### Checking the Capstan and Pinch Roller

The capstan may be covered with a black substance that is hard to remove. Use ninety-nine percent isopropyl alcohol and a damp, but not soaked, cloth. (Excessive cleaner will drip into the bearing and dissolve the lubricants, causing premature motor failure.) To turn the capstan, you may need to remove the unit's bottom cover to gain access to the flywheel. Turn the flywheel while pressing the cloth against the capstan.

Clean the pinch roller with a cloth soaked in Windex or Fantastic. (Freon was a popular cleaning chemical because it evaporated quickly. However, it is not an environmental pal. Athan Corp. of South San Francisco sells an excellent, environmentally friendly, "rubber" cleaner. Do not use alcohol; it will dry the pinch roller.) If the pinch roller is glazed, order a new one.

Finally, make sure everything is dry before running tape.

## Maintaining Hard Disk Recorders

Fortunately, hard disk recorders require very little specialized maintenance other than the usual preventive maintenance for computer-based gear (keep it cool and keep it clean). However, there are two important aspects that we should address.

### Hard Disk Optimization Software

Over time, as you record and erase files, the disk fragments. Example: Suppose you record two 100 Meg files on a 250 Meg hard drive. So far so good (Fig. 22-1). Now suppose you erase the first 100 Meg file, and record a 120 Meg file (file 3). The file fills up the first 100 Megs, then 20 Megs spill over into the remaining 50 Meg block of memory. This file is considered *fragmented* because it has been split into two parts. The more you record, erase, and rerecord (especially on a disk that's nearly full), the greater the tendency for files to fragment.

This is a problem because the hard drive has

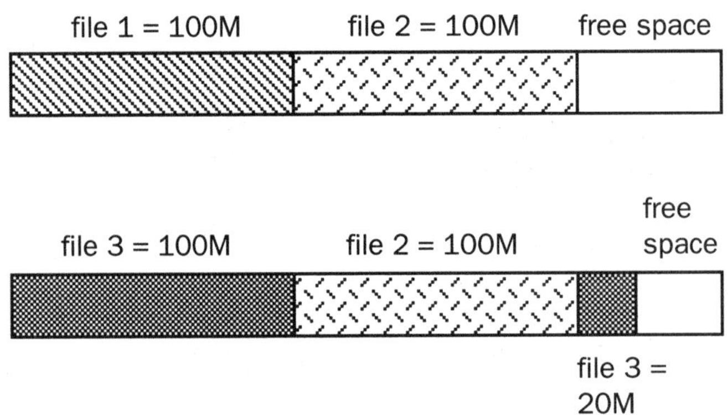


Fig. 22-1: *How a file becomes fragmented on a hard drive.*

to jump all over the place to read the file. Considering that hard disk recording pushes hard drives to the limit, this delay can be enough to cause problems. In fact, some hard disk recording software virtually requires that it write to a contiguous (nonfragmented) block of memory.

Optimization (or defragmentation) programs find sections of the same file that are spread all over a disk, then rearrange these fragments into one contiguous file that the disk drive can read in one fell swoop. There is a noticeable speed-up in operation, and also, the hard drive doesn't have to work as hard. I don't know whether this affects the life of the hard drive, but it certainly can't hurt.

Most of the time, optimization means running your optimization program of choice, then waiting while it shuffles data from the hard disk into the computer's RAM, joins files together, then shoots the joined file back to the hard disk. This can take a long time.

There are two major cautions:

- Back up your disk before optimizing in case a glitch occurs during the process. This could wipe out *all* your data.
- De-install any copy-protected software. Copy-protected software usually comes with a hard disk installation routine that allows you to make one or two copies of the software to a hard disk. This prevents having to insert a "key disk" floppy that indicates your ownership. Hard disk installation routines usually write "invisible" files to the disk that the program recognizes when you boot it up. Optimizing a disk may change the location of these files, so when the program looks for them, it can't find them. This means you have lost an install.

De-installation is usually fairly simple: insert the original disk containing the program, and tell it you want to install the program on the hard disk. Since it's already installed, the software will ask if you want to de-install. Say Yes, and the hard disk install will return to the floppy so you can reinstall again some time in the future.

Newer forms of copy protection let you optimize a hard disk without de-installing the software. This is because the software "authorizes" the drive itself, so even if it's optimized, you're still using the same drive and all is well. If you don't need to de-install software, the manual should mention this. Otherwise, assume that any copy-protected software should be de-installed before optimization. If you have any questions about whether this is necessary or not, consult with the manufacturer.

## Hard Disk Backup

This is the single most important part of maintenance with hard disk recording. Hard drives are very reliable, but eventually, they will fail and take all your data along with it. Following are some popular backup options; these are often computer-oriented peripheral devices that connect via a SCSI port, but some computers and dedicated hard disk systems have mass storage built in.

- Removable hard drive. These are extremely convenient and as of this writing, range in capacity from 44 Megs to 1 Gigabyte. If you need to back up a lot, though, the cost of cartridges can really add up.
- Removable optical drive. These offer high capacities and are more tolerant of abuse than regular hard drives. They aren't subject to deterioration from magnetic fields, however, the cost for 1 Gigabyte cartridges is still fairly expensive compared to other means of backup.
- Digital tape backup. Digital tape backup uses DAT-like cassettes (in fact, they often are DAT cassettes that have been tested for data storage applications). This method is inexpensive—a small cassette can hold Gigabytes of data—but slower than backing up to removable drives.
- MDM backup. You may be able to back up analog files to an MDM. This usually requires a special hardware interface that hooks up between the MDM and hard disk recording system, as well as software that supports the interface. Although backup is slow (it occurs in real time), not only can you back up to a device that you may already have in your studio, but being able to transfer files between hard disk recording systems and digital tape gives you the best of both worlds: you can send MDM tracks over to the hard drive for editing, and/or send edited hard disk files to the MDM for storage.
- Recordable CD. This can be a very cost-effective way to save data, because even though the recorders are costly, the storage media is not. The only drawback is that you can't rerecord over recordable CDs, so if you make a mistake or the CD becomes obsolete, you're stuck with a piece of environmentally unfriendly plastic.

## Maintaining Analog Recorders

Properly maintaining an analog tape recorder is a challenge. You need the recorder's service manual, expensive test tapes, and some costly test equipment just to get off the ground. Then it's time to match levels, move the heads around, dig inside and custom bias the machine for your favorite tape, adjust tension on the reels, *etc.*

Overall, it's a lot easier to practice preventive maintenance and stop problems before they occur. If something really major does go wrong, even if you're knowledgeable about electronics, go to a factory-authorized repair center. Someone who sits at a bench for eight hours a day working on a certain family of tape recorder knows exactly what to look for and can probably fix a problem in an hour or two; it would take me an hour just to locate all the screws that remove the enclosure. Leave the fancy stuff to the people who spend their lives at it. The cost isn't that bad, and they usually have all the replacement parts on hand.

For our purposes, maintenance consists of cleaning/demagnetizing the heads and lubrication.

## Cleaning the Tape Heads

Since miles of tape get dragged by the heads, little pieces of the tape wear off as the tape goes past them. You should also clean any other parts that the tape contacts on its travels. This is a simple operation that requires Q-tips and head-cleaning fluid. Although alcohol is frequently mentioned as a suitable cleaning agent, it really is not that good at dissolving the various binders that hold the oxide layer to the base material of the tape itself. If you scrub enough with alcohol and a Q-tip, you can get a head fairly clean; but a "real" head cleaner does a better job and leaves no residue on the heads.

If you do need to use alcohol in an emergency situation, use ninety-nine percent pure isopropyl alcohol. Rubbing alcohol, or types with lower purity values, can leave a residue on the heads.

To clean, remove any tapes on the machine, then locate the heads. Usually this requires removing a head cover, but often it will just flip up and out of the way. Dip a Q-tip in the fluid, swab it around on the head a few times (neither lightly nor with great force; an insistent, small pressure is fine), and look at the Q-tip—is it brownish red and dirty? Then use the other end of the Q-tip and swab again. When it comes out clean, proceed to the next head. Don't glop lots of fluid over the heads; use just enough to do the job. Contrary to societal programming, more is not always better.

Also clean the capstan. This seems to get dirtier faster, so you might need to use two or three Q-tips on it every ten hours or so. In fact, you really should clean your machine after every ten hours or so of tape travel; the dirt buildup is quite noticeable even after that short a period of time.

The rubber pinch roller is a special case and should *not* be cleaned with head cleaner, as this can crack the rubber. Instead, use Q-tips dipped in warm, not hot, water. Sort of drag/scrape the Q-tip along the roller until all the dirt is off.

Cleaning the capstan and pinch roller is something you should do fairly frequently—it's better to spend one minute a day on cleaning for ten days than to do ten minutes of cleaning in one day. Another suggestion: clean at the end of a session, not the beginning. After all this cleaning the tape recorder should dry off; if you clean at the beginning of a session, you'll have to wait a few minutes before you get started, and maybe during those moments the creative impulse will take a vacation. If you start a session with everything ready to go, you start off right.

## Demagnetizing the Heads

The magnetic coating on a piece of tape is very thin and highly sensitive to extraneous magnetism. Also, iron or steel (which makes up much of a tape transport) is subject to magnetization by stray magnetic fields, such as those generated by loudspeakers and similar equipment. Exposure to stray magnetism degrades the recorded signal by erasing high frequencies and adding hiss; to complicate matters further, each time the tape passes over a magnetized head, tape quality deteriorates until the head is demagnetized. This is why demagnetization is important.

In addition to a good demagnetizer, I'd recommend getting a magnetometer for measuring the actual residual magnetism at the head. As it so happens, the R. B. Annis Company (Indianapolis, IN 46202; tel. 317/637 9282) makes both products and is specifically into pro-level demagnetization. Consumer-style demagetizers are okay for cassette decks but not much else.

Magnetism is an unusual phenomenon, and, before I had a magnetometer, I kind of waved a demagnetizer at the recorder's heads on a regular basis, according to any instructions, and figured I had done the right thing. Reading the magnetism has shown me that tape recorders don't have to be demagnetized on a schedule; they have to be *checked* on a schedule, and if magnetism shows up, then something should be done about it. You might as well do the checking when you clean the heads; it takes only a few seconds.

Even an inexpensive magnetometer can be pretty sensitive. Moving it relative to the earth's magnetic field can change the reading, so take that into account when you take measurements. Also, some magnetometers have a clip-on extension probe for getting at recessed heads and the like, but this reduces the instrument's sensitivity. My general rule is that if the needle just barely moves off its little post, I leave things alone. If the movement is more noticeable, I demagnetize. I know that it sounds unscientific, but you can't totally eliminate stray magnetism; you can only minimize it to the point where it doesn't cause a problem.

While you're at it, check the other parts of the transport that your tape contacts as it travels from one reel to the other. Keep in mind that demagnetizers draw a fair amount of electricity, and should be limited to a fifty percent duty cycle (*e.g.*, if it's on for thirty seconds, leave it off for thirty seconds before continuing use; if it's on for a minute, let it rest for a minute).

The procedure for demagnetization is:

1. Make sure that the recorder is off, and that no tapes are near it (another reason to do your maintenance at the end of a session).

2. While holding the demagnetizer at least two feet away from the tape heads or any tapes, plug it in.

3. Move the demagnetizer's tip toward the head to be demagnetized, coming as close as possible without actually touching the head.

4. Wave the tip slightly from side to side across the face of the head, then slowly withdraw the tip from the head (no faster than three or four inches per second).

5. Turn off or unplug the demagnetizer while it is at least two feet away from the tape heads or any tapes. Make sure that you don't turn the demagnetizer either on or off while it's in the vicinity of the heads, as the resulting surge of current can magnetize the heads and leave you worse off than when you started.

6. Use a similar procedure for the other heads, if required.

It does no good just to hold the probe in front of a head and let it sit there and "cook"; it is the slow withdrawal of the probe that accomplishes the actual process of inducing ever-smaller, opposing AC fields into the head, thus leaving it with (hopefully) no residual magnetism. If you still get strong residual readings, you may have to run the demagnetizing procedure a couple of times until you get an acceptably small reading.

For cassette decks, it's worth the $20 to get one of those nifty demagnetizing cassettes. Pop it in, push a button, and your heads are demagnetized. If only all of life was that simple. . . .

## Lubrication

Your machine has specific instructions for lubricating motors or other points—follow them. Again, more is not necessarily better; if they say a drop of fine oil, put in one and only one drop of fine oil. Don't to use too much oil, and *never use common household or sewing machine oil.* You want the finest quality oil money can buy. Always use oil specifically recommended for lubricating high-tech, sensitive machinery.

## Replacing Heads

Frankly, I wouldn't try replacing a head; I'd rather spend the time making music. I'll gladly do routine maintenance, but this kind of operation requires patience and equipment. Besides, it takes a lot to wear out today's heads.

To know when your heads need replacing, look at them carefully when new, and inspect them whenever cleaning time comes around. As the months go by, you'll notice the tape will wear a flat groove across the heads; you may also hear a corresponding change in high frequency response. As the heads become worn, they may need to be repositioned (realigned) to insure optimum tape contact and positioning. If the head is severely worn, the groove created by the tape may be so deep that the edges of the groove tear at the edges of the tape. The only choice here is replacing the head.

If you have questions about whether your head is up to par, or if it needs realignment or replacement, chances are the store that sold you your machine also has the facilities to keep it in shape. If not, most major metropolitan areas have specialty tape recorder or professional audio shops that can do the job for you.

## Aligning Heads

The physical positioning of a tape head with respect to the tape is very important; improper positioning can cause dropouts or uneven frequency response. Unfortunately, it is not easy to check alignment unless you are conversant with test tapes and test equipment. Therefore, I feel it's a good idea to have a competent service person check the alignment of your heads, *even if the machine is brand new.* Thanks to the long trip from the manufacturer, it is very likely that the heads will be somewhat out of alignment when the machine reaches you.

Also note that alignment can change as the head becomes worn, so have the alignment checked every year or so whether you think you need it or not.

## Maintaining Magnetic Media

We've already mentioned that the magnetic imprint on a piece of tape (analog or digital) or disk is quite weak, and as a result, it can be upset by residual magnetism in the heads—but that's not all. *Any* electrical device that generates a strong alternating current or magnetic field, if close to magnetic media, can cause partial or complete erasure, destroying hours of work in a few seconds (optical media doesn't have this problem, which is one reason why it's so well suited for backup). Keep all magnetic media away from speakers, AC power cords, soldering irons, transformers, headphones, TV sets, or anything that generates a field; if you carry a tape in your car, place it away from the engine and ignition circuits.

The material used for tape has some needs too. Tape should be kept in a cool, dry place. Studios are often climate-controlled but you probably can't go to these lengths. The important point is to keep moisture away from tapes, as dampness fosters a mold growth on the tape which renders it useless. A high humidity environment is very detrimental; if you live in a rain forest, install a small dehumidifier in a storage area to store valuable tapes. And of course, keep tapes out of direct sunlight, as this can warp plastic reels. Handle all magnetic media gently; finger oils stick to tape, and any creases or folds introduced into the tape will show up as dropouts or errors in the final product.

### Preparing a Tape for Storage

The best way to prepare a tape for extended storage is to rewind it back to the beginning (the "head") of the reel. Then, play the tape all the way through to the end (with analog recorders, use as slow a speed as is available). While playing, the tape wraps very evenly around the hub of the takeup reel, which protects the tape for long-term storage. Rewinding or fast forwarding onto a reel just before storage is not recommended, since irregularities in the winding can damage your tape over time.

If you're storing an analog reel-to-reel tape, mark the reel "tails out," so you know that the tail of the tape is facing out and the reel must be rewound before being played. Return the tape to its box, and if you really want to keep out dust or contaminants, wrap the box in a plastic bag.

## Rules of Successful Troubleshooting

It's great having the infinite possibilities today's gear gives, except that when a piece of equipment goes down, you then have to figure out in which corner of infinity the problem lies. No matter how careful you are with your gear, eventually something will fail. Microprocessors add another overlay of complexity, since they introduce software malfunctions to go along with the usual hardware ones.

Remember as you do any troubleshooting that the goal is always to isolate the problem. For example, if a computer drives a synth through a patch bay and the synth doesn't play back, is the problem with the synth, the patch bay, or the sequencer? The more you can narrow down the problem, the easier it is to fix—which piece of gear, which circuit board in the piece of gear, which component on the circuit board, *etc.* And don't forget that the most common reason for nonworking equipment is operator error; sometimes reading the manual will do a lot more good than calling the manufacturer.

Although any kind of down time is bad, there are ways to minimize the damage. One solution is to fix the problem yourself, and get back on the air in minutes instead of days or weeks. However, you don't want the cure to be worse than the disease so it's important to make sure you stay within the limits of your abilities. Here are some general troubleshooting tips.

- Begin by taking no action at all: *think* about the problem. Gather as much data as possible, since collecting this data will often isolate the problem. For example, if a mixer worked at your house yesterday but doesn't work at a friend's house today, odds are the mixer is not the problem, but something that changed—such as a cable, mixer, or amp.
- Maintain a positive attitude about being able to fix the box, since you will think more clearly if you're not agitated. Don't get angry or panic; often the problem is nothing more complex than a miss-set control or incorrectly adjusted parameter.
- Don't be afraid to take a box apart to see what's going on inside—but also observe commonsense precautions, such as not working on AC powered equipment while it's plugged in. You can access the innards of

many rack mount devices by simply removing a few screws that hold the top and bottom panels in place. Be careful, though; if it's not easy to open up the box, don't.

- Visually inspect the effect. See if any jacks are loose or don't feel "tight" when you plug into them, if the AC power cord looks damaged, if one switch doesn't feel as solid as the others, and the like.
- Don't get in over your head. If you see something that's obviously wrong, by all means fix it. But it's always a drag to create a new problem while trying to solve an old one, so recognize that in some cases you'll need a qualified technician to help you out.
- Many so-called "broken" units are often the victims of a miss-set parameter. For example, an effect with no output signal may simply have the output level parameter set to zero. Other "obvious" problems include reversing the audio input and outputs connections, not plugging plugs all the way into their jacks (a very common problem), forgetting to plug in the AC power cord, and so on. Always look for simple problems such as these before taking the box apart and proceeding to the next level of troubleshooting. Remember that most problems are minor problems or due to human error so be on the lookout for the obvious, not the obscure.

## Troubleshooting Techniques That Don't Void the Warranty

### Isolating Problems in MIDI Systems

For isolating MIDI system problems, a MIDI data tester can be invaluable. These range from a single LED that simply indicates the presence or absence of data to elaborate hand-held hardware boxes and even computer programs. The latter are often available on bulletin board services. Furthermore, many newer, high-end signal processors and keyboards include MIDI data monitoring options as a "value added" feature.

### The First Line of Defense: the On-Off Switch

Just about all digital gear includes a microprocessor, and when its little brains get scrambled, sometimes it just needs a break. Turn off power, wait twenty seconds or so, then turn power back on again. During power-up the machine usually goes through various self-tests and startup routines that will restart the machine to an uncorrupted, "ground zero" condition.

The reason for waiting is to make sure that any internal capacitors are completely discharged. Simply turning off and turning right back on again may not provide enough interruption, especially with beefy power supplies.

When you do turn on power again, observe if any error messages flash in the display during startup. This can indicate the possible source of the problem, as well as provide useful information for a company's tech support personnel.

### The Importance of Resetting

If turning power on and off doesn't help, reinitialize (also called reset) the device. This will usually wipe out anything you have edited or programmed and return all parameters to the default factory settings, so hopefully you will have saved everything just prior to the breakdown (another reason for backup procedures).

Reinitialization can solve a variety of baffling problems, including bizarre intermittent MIDI burps. As long as you have everything saved, reinitializing is usually worth trying early on to see if it makes the problem go away.

### Exterminating Bugs

If you experience a consistent problem, check the number of your gear's software version and call the manufacturer's customer service. You may be experiencing a known bug for which an upgrade exists.

## Troubleshooting Techniques for the Adventurous

The following tips are for those who aren't afraid of taking off the cover, voiding their warranty, and facing the prospect of electrocution (don't say you weren't warned).

### Shake, Rattle, and Roll

Before taking off the cover, shake the unit gently and listen for any rattles. An errant nut can cause intermittent (or sometimes serious) problems by shorting out components or circuit board traces. Search it out and eliminate it.

### Checking Internal Batteries

When the internal batteries that keep memory alive get low, operation can become unpredictable. Although today's batteries are very long-lived (one in a drum machine I have that was estimated to last for five years is now starting its second decade), they can still age prematurely and should be checked with a voltmeter. Replacing it may require a trip to the repair shop, as the battery will often be soldered in place; overheating a battery during the soldering process could cause it to explode. Careful!

## Dealing with Fuses

AC powered equipment includes a fuse. Fuses are a musician's security guard, as they protect circuits from damage under an overload condition by interrupting the flow of electricity into it. When a fuse blows, nothing happens—no lights, no transformer hum, nothing.

Fuses don't have to blow for scary reasons; they can also die of natural causes (which includes mechanical vibration). A blown internal fuse should be easy to fix, as long as you always remember to replace the fuse with one of the same rating. However, if a fuse blows consistently, you may have a real problem that requires a trip to the shop.

If the fuse is easily accessible, hold it up to the light and see if the fuse element is blown (*i.e.*, there's a gap in the element—see Fig. 22-2). However, the fuse may be mounted internally to the unit, in which case you'll need to do some disassembly before you can fix the problem. *Never* replace a fuse with one of a higher rating, and if there are any indications of suspicious behavior (smoke, burning smells, sparking, hot parts), shut the power off immediately—odds are you have a serious problem that requires professional attention.

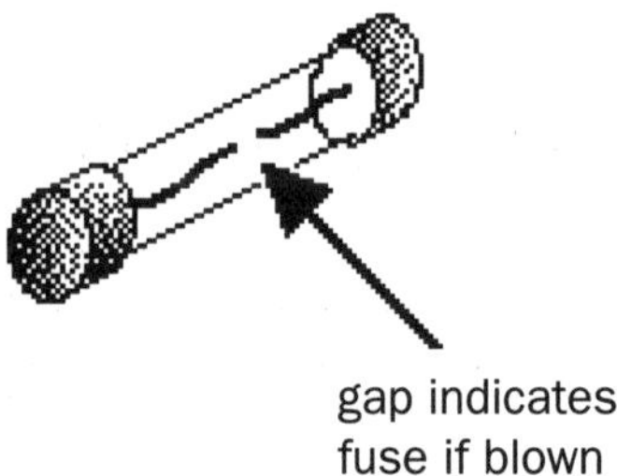


**Fig. 22-2:** *Checking to see whether a fuse is blown.*

## Checking IC Socket Seating

Although sockets have many advantages, one disadvantage is that components such as chips can come loose from their sockets over time. The parts may not fall out, but instead cause intermittent problems that are difficult to pin down. The solution is to push down *very* gently on the top of any socketed ICs to make sure they're firmly seated in their sockets (I've fixed many a computer with this technique). Don't push hard if the board holding the chip is unsupported, as bending a circuit board can cause traces to break (and that's a *major* repair bill).

## Socket Cleaning

Here's an extreme case, but it makes an interesting point. I was having problems with one voice on an analog synthesizer and suspected the filter chip. As I went to replace it, though, there seemed to be a sort of crystalline growth between the IC pins and socket holes, apparently due to the dissimilarity of the metals used for the IC and socket. Removing the IC, brushing away the growth, and applying a contact cleaner (*e.g.*, Caig's DeOxit) solved the problem.

## Checking for Loose or Bent Jacks

A loose jack can cause problems ranging from snaps, crackles, and pops to complete nonfunctionality. Jiggle the input and output jacks to see if they move; if they do, tighten the mounting nut. However, be careful not to overtighten. Sometimes the jacks mount directly to the unit's circuit board; overtightening may stress the board and lead to a *very* expensive repair job.

## Fixing Intermittent Controls

If a volume control or data-setting control acts intermittently, dirt or dust may be caught in the control. Go to your local electronics store and purchase a spray can of contact cleaner that is specifically indicated as being safe for plastics. Unless the control is sealed (in which case dirt probably didn't get into it anyway), there will be some kind of opening into which you can spray the contact cleaner. Typically, this will be a space near the control terminals that solder to the circuit board or wires (Fig. 22-3). Spray some contact cleaner into this space (direct it toward the control's center), and turn the control's knob back and forth vigorously. This wiping action distributes the contact cleaner evenly. Should a second application fail to solve the problem, the control needs to be replaced with one of the same value.

**Fig. 22-3:** *Spraying contact cleaner into a control or switch can sometimes prevent intermittent operation.*

## Connector Jiggling and Contact Cleaning

Computerized devices seem to have a lot of connectors (ribbon cables, various pins, *etc.*) and these are traditionally a weak link in any system. One keyboard that arrived to my studio with nonworking aftertouch was fixed by replugging a connector that ran between the main circuit board and keyboard; one synth that was DOA simply had a battery connector come loose from the battery.

Even if all the connectors do connect, wiggle them gently in case any oxidation has built up along the points of contact. For instruments that have been sitting unused for a while, remove the connector, spray *a small amount* of contact cleaner on any connector pins, replace the connector, and jiggle it gently. For some reason this seems particularly important with digital instruments.

Switches, potentiometers, switching elements of jacks, plug tips, relays, and other devices can also benefit from contact cleaner. Dirty contacts generally cause intermittent problems, but can also cause what appear to be major failures. For example, it once seemed a mixer channel had gone out, but it was just a case of the channel insert jack not being used for a while and building up oxidation so that it was "switched" into an open position. When something was inserted into the channel, it worked fine until the plug was removed, whereupon the switching jack contact landed on a part of the jack that had been oxidized. A little contact cleaner and working the plug back and forth a few times took care of things.

# Updating Digital Devices

Because many devices containing computers are software-based, they can often be updated (either for bug fixes or new features) by replacing the chip (integrated circuit) that contains the software. Although a chip update is an easy way to gain new features, if not done right you could end up with anything from temporary frustration to a massive repair bill. While there's no need to be intimidated, you can't be casual about the process. If you want a successful chip transplant, it's good practice to follow these ten steps.

## 1. Be Prepared

If pertinent, save all memory contents of the unit being updated since after updating, it's often necessary to reinitialize. Then unplug the device, find a well-lit work space, and gather your tools:

- Screwdrivers (for disassembling the case to get to the chip)
- IC inserter/extractor (Radio Shack #276-1581; see Fig. 22-4)
- Needlenose pliers or IC pin aligner (Radio Shack #276-1594)
- Conductive ground strap (Radio Shack #276-2397)
- Small piece of aluminum foil
- Paper and pencil

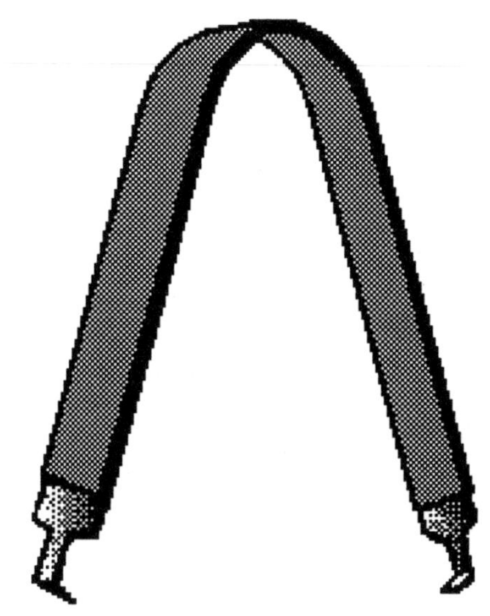

**Fig. 22-4:** *Inexpensive IC extractor. Squeezing on the spring forces the clips together, which inserts between the chip and socket at the top and bottom of the chip. Rocking and pulling gently upward lifts the IC out of its socket.*

## 2. Locate the Chip to Be Replaced

This may or may not be easy. Some units have a "trap door" that escorts you right to the machine's innards, where you can easily replace the chip. With other devices, you may have to disassemble the case, remove circuit boards, and/or unbundle cables to get at the chip. Double-check that the chip designation is the same as the replacement IC.

Remember that you are dealing with a fragile piece of gear where one mistake can cause serious problems. If the chip's location is not obvious, you're probably better off having an authorized service center do the update for you.

## 3. Write Down the Chip Orientation

A chip will have a notch or dot at one end (see Fig. 22-5), and it is vital that the replacement chip be oriented in the same way.

Failure to do so will probably fry the chip, and may damage the power supply too. Also,

## Computer-Specific Preventive Maintenance

Many of the general maintenance tips apply to computers as well (particular the part about ventilation), but here are a few important computer-specific tips.

- **Quickie keyboard maintenance.** Disconnect the keyboard, take it outside, hold it upside down, and shake gently. Blow into the spaces between the keys and shake gently again. This will get rid of some of the dust.
- **Battery problems.** Some computers use batteries to back up functions such as date and time settings. While today's batteries are pretty good about not leaking, leakage can still happen and when it does, corrosive chemicals are let loose inside your computer. Check the battery periodically for leakage or lower-than-normal voltage.
- **Disk drive head cleaning.** Disk drive head cleaners strike me as more hype than substance; even if you exercise your disk drives pretty hard, it takes a long while for heads to get dirty. However, a piece of gunk or loose oxide can stick to the drive head, and that's when head cleaning is definitely recommended. The procedure is quite similar to cleaning the heads on inexpensive consumer VCRs: You put a few drops of cleaner on a fabric "disk," insert it in the disk drive, let the disk spin around for about twenty seconds, and then finally eject it.
- **Don't move the computer while it's on.** This can cause problems with the hard disk (excessive bouncing of the head might cause it to crash into the platter, which corrupts the surface) as well as the floppy drive if it's in action.
- **Don't write on diskettes with pencil.** Pencil leads shed graphite, which can get into your disk drive and cause problems. It's better to use a felt-tip pin for marking diskettes (by the way, these can often write on the disk plastic itself).

Fig. 22-5: *A typical integrated circuit. The dot or notch indicates the "top" of the IC (i.e., pin 1 is in the upper left-hand corner).*

sometimes two or more chips will need to be replaced. Write down their locations and any distinctive markings or part numbers. Do not trust your memory! If the phone rings in the middle of a chip change or you have to run off to a session, you may not remember which chip went where when you return.

## 4. Discharge Yourself of Static Electricity

Touching circuitry after you've accumulated a static charge could destroy sensitive silicon parts. Worse yet, sometimes static damage weakens the chip instead of outright killing it, causing intermittent problems (a repair person's nightmare) or a complete failure when you least expect it.

To discharge yourself, place one end of the conductive ground strap around your wrist, and attach the other end to the unit's chassis ground. If you don't use a ground strap, at least touch a metal ground to discharge any static electricity from yourself before handling any chips, and don't do anything that could accumulate a charge while you're replacing the chip.

Having said all that, modern chips are remarkably resistant to static damage—but there's no need to tempt fate.

## 5. Remove the Old Chip(s)

If the chip is soldered in, forget it. Close the unit back up and go to a service center. Otherwise, use the IC puller to remove the chip. Pull straight up and out of the socket; you may need to rock back and forth *very* slightly to loosen the grip of the socket on the chip, but avoid bending the chip's pins as you pull the chip out. Place the chip on the piece of aluminum foil so that the pins are contacting metal.

As you're replacing the old chip(s), why worry about treating it with care? Simple: The new chip may be defective, or there may be bugs in the new software that make you want to go back to the original chip.

### 6. Insert the New Chip(s)

While you're still connected to the ground strap, remove the new chips from their protective foam, foil, or plastic IC carrier. If the IC pins aren't straight, use an IC pin aligner or needlenose pliers; unstraightened pins can bend under the chip when inserted, or worse yet, break off. Insert the chip in the IC insertion tool, then plug the chip into its accompanying socket. Remember to double-check the orientation of the notch or dot.

Incidentally, you don't absolutely *need* an IC insertion tool; you can always line up one row of pins in the socket, then push gently against the opposite side of the chip until the other row of pins lines up with the other side of the socket. But the proper tool can cost a lot less than a botched IC insertion.

### 7. Push Down Gently on the Chip

Apply even pressure at both ends of the chip to make sure it's well seated. Usually there will be a little resistance as the chip seats firmly in the socket, but *be careful* not to push too hard—bending the board could break a trace or solder connection.

### 8. Double-Check the Chip Orientation against Your Original Drawing

Once you're sure it's okay, close up the unit.

### 9. Reinitialize the Device

This may not be required, but is good practice anyway. If you do reinitialize, then you'll probably want to reload the memory contents you saved back in step 1.

Congratulations! You're updated.

### 10. Return the Old Chip

This is the *coup de grâce:* after you're sure that everything checks out okay and you're satisfied with the new software, return the old chip to the manufacturer (sometimes these can be reused internally for prototyping). Who knows, the service people may be so impressed by your level of consideration that they'll give you special treatment if you ever need a quick repair job.

## A Final Note about Maintenance

Maintenance means more than just keeping the equipment in minimal running condition. If a light bulb goes out, change it. If a fader in your mixing board gets scratchy, replace it if contact cleaner won't bring it back to life. If a battery in a tuning standard goes dead, you should have a couple of spares (or an AC adapter) hanging around.

In the world of professional studios, maintenance technicians and service representatives from various companies stay on top of things so that when the paying client/musician comes in, engineers don't have to hassle with the equipment. You don't have that luxury, but you still must keep things in shape; it's a drag working in an environment where something is always breaking down.

Proper maintenance is a state of mind: when you get behind the eight ball, it's hard to catch up. Take care of your studio so that, no matter what, at a moment's notice you could go in and everything would proceed smoothly. You'll have a happier and more productive studio.

# Appendix
# Relating the dB to Voltage and Power Ratios

Here is the formula for relating the dB to ratios of voltage and power. It is stashed way in the back of the book so it wouldn't scare people off. If you want to know more, check out a good library.

For AC voltage ratios: $dB = 20 \left(\log \frac{V1}{V2}\right)$ V = volts

For power ratios: $dB = 10 \left(\log \frac{P1}{P2}\right)$ P = watts

(Power ratios are independent of source and load impedance values, but voltage ratios hold only when the source and load impedances are equal.)

Example 1: By measuring the peak-to-peak voltage at the output of an amplifier, you determine that, at minimum gain, the output is 0.25V peak-to-peak, and at maximum gain, the output is 5V peak-to-peak. To determine the ratio in dB between minimum and maximum gain,

$dB = 20 \left(\log \frac{5.00V}{0.25V}\right) = 20 (\log 20) = 20 (1.30) = 26\ dB$

Example 2: A microphone needs 60 dB of gain in order to hit 0 VU on the tape recorder meter. Will a preamp with a gain of 1000 suffice?

$dB = 20 (\log 1000) = 20 (3) = 60\ dB$

## About the Author

On his tenth birthday, Craig Anderton received a guitar from his parents and a transistor radio kit from his grandmother. Since then he has split his life between the technical and artistic. He recorded three albums with the sixties group Mandrake, produced three albums by classical guitarist Linda Cohen, did session work in New York, played on/mixed recordings by David Arkenstone and Spencer Brewer, and released a solo instrumental album (*Forward Motion,* distributed by MCA) in 1989.

A prolific author who is seldom seen without a notebook computer, Craig has authored articles for *Guitar Player, Keyboard, EQ, Rolling Stone, Byte,* and many other magazines, including numerous overseas publications. He coined the term "electronic musician" and edited the magazine bearing that name for the first five years of its existence. He has written several "classic" books on musical electronics, including *Electronic Projects for Musicians, The Electronic Musician's Dictionary,* and *Multieffects for Musicians.* He is also a co-author of *Digital Projects for Musicians.*

In addition to serving as Consulting Editor to *Guitar Player* magazine and Technology Editor for *EQ,* lately Craig is much in demand as a lecturer—work that has taken him to twenty-two states and six countries. He also consults to manufacturers in the music business, and is responsible for some of the sounds you hear coming out of various instruments, as well as some of their design features.

## About the Technical Editor

George Petersen is the editor of *Mix* magazine and has written over 500 articles on every aspect of audio and music production. He has also authored several audio books, including *Modular Digital Multitracks: The Power User's Guide.* When not engineering and producing music, George operates a record label and twenty-four-track studio on an island in San Francisco Bay.

# INDEX

## N

## T